Network Basics
Companion Guide

Cisco Networking Academy

Cisco Press

800 East 96th Street

Indianapolis, Indiana 46240 USA

Network Basics Companion Guide

Copyright© 2014 Cisco Systems, Inc.

Published by:
Cisco Press
800 East 96th Street
Indianapolis, IN 46240 USA

Printed in the United States of America

First Printing November 2013

Library of Congress Cataloging-in-Publication data is on file.

ISBN-13: 978-1-58713-317-6

ISBN-10: 1-58713-317-2

Warning and Disclaimer

This book is designed to provide information about the Cisco Networking Academy Network Basics course. Every effort has been made to make this book as complete and as accurate as possible, but no warranty or fitness is implied.

The information is provided on an "as is" basis. The authors, Cisco Press, and Cisco Systems, Inc. shall have neither liability nor responsibility to any person or entity with respect to any loss or damages arising from the information contained in this book or from the use of the discs or programs that may accompany it.

The opinions expressed in this book belong to the author and are not necessarily those of Cisco Systems, Inc.

Publisher
Paul Boger

Associate Publisher
Dave Dusthimer

Business Operation Manager, Cisco Press
Jan Cornelssen

Executive Editor
Mary Beth Ray

Managing Editor
Sandra Schroeder

Development Editor
Ellie C. Bru

Project Editor
Mandie Frank

Copy Editor
Bill McManus

Technical Editor
Tony Chen

Editorial Assistant
Vanessa Evans

Designer
Mark Shirar

Composition
Trina Wurst

Indexer
Ken Johnson

Proofreader
Charlotte Kughen

Trademark Acknowledgments

All terms mentioned in this book that are known to be trademarks or service marks have been appropriately capitalized. Cisco Press or Cisco Systems, Inc., cannot attest to the accuracy of this information. Use of a term in this book should not be regarded as affecting the validity of any trademark or service mark.

Corporate and Government Sales

The publisher offers excellent discounts on this book when ordered in quantity for bulk purchases or special sales, which may include electronic versions and/or custom covers and content particular to your business, training goals, marketing focus, and branding interests.

For more information, please contact:
U.S. Corporate and Government Sales
1-800-382-3419
corpsales@pearsontechgroup.com

For sales outside the United States, please contact:
International Sales
international@pearsoned.com

Feedback Information

At Cisco Press, our goal is to create in-depth technical books of the highest quality and value. Each book is crafted with care and precision, undergoing rigorous development that involves the unique expertise of members from the professional technical community.

Readers' feedback is a natural continuation of this process. If you have any comments regarding how we could improve the quality of this book, or otherwise alter it to better suit your needs, you can contact us through email at feedback@ciscopress.com. Please make sure to include the book title and ISBN in your message.

We greatly appreciate your assistance.

Americas Headquarters	Asia Pacific Headquarters	Europe Headquarters
Cisco Systems, Inc.	Cisco Systems, Inc.	Cisco Systems International BV
170 West Tasman Drive	168 Robinson Road	Haarlerbergpark
San Jose, CA 95134-1706	#28-01 Capital Tower	Haarlerbergweg 13-19
USA	Singapore 068912	1101 CH Amsterdam
www.cisco.com	www.cisco.com	The Netherlands
Tel: 408 526-4000	Tel: +65 6317 7777	www-europe.cisco.com
800 553-NETS (6387)	Fax: +65 6317 7799	Tel: +31 0 800 020 0791
Fax: 408 527-0883		Fax: +31 0 20 357 1100

Cisco has more than 200 offices worldwide. Addresses, phone numbers, and fax numbers are listed on the Cisco Website at **www.cisco.com/go/offices.**

©2007 Cisco Systems, Inc. All rights reserved. CCVP, the Cisco logo, and the Cisco Square Bridge logo are trademarks of Cisco Systems, Inc.; Changing the Way We Work, Live, Play, and Learn is a service mark of Cisco Systems, Inc.; and Access Registrar, Aironet, BPX, Catalyst, CCDA, CCDP, CCIE, CCIP, CCNA, CCNP, CCSP, Cisco, the Cisco Certified Internetwork Expert logo, Cisco IOS, Cisco Press, Cisco Systems, Cisco Systems Capital, the Cisco Systems logo, Cisco Unity, Enterprise/Solver, EtherChannel, EtherFast, EtherSwitch, Fast Step, Follow Me Browsing, FormShare, GigaDrive, GigaStack, HomeLink, Internet Quotient, IOS, IP/TV, iQ Expertise, the iQ logo, iQ Net Readiness Scorecard, iQuick Study, LightStream, Linksys, MeetingPlace, MGX, Networking Academy, Network Registrar, Packet, PIX, ProConnect, RateMUX, ScriptShare, SlideCast, SMARTnet, StackWise, The Fastest Way to Increase Your Internet Quotient, and TransPath are registered trademarks of Cisco Systems, Inc. and/or its affiliates in the United States and certain other countries.

All other trademarks mentioned in this document or Website are the property of their respective owners. The use of the word partner does not imply a partnership relationship between Cisco and any other company. (0609R)

About the Contributing Authors

Antoon (Tony) W. Rufi is Campus Director of Academic Affairs, ECPI University, Newport News, Virginia. Tony is a networking professional who retired from the U.S. Air Force in June 2000 after 29 years. He worked on communication systems. Since retirement, Tony has worked for ECPI University teaching a variety of networking courses. The courses he has led include CCNA, CCNP, and Fundamentals of Network Security in the Cisco Academy at ECPI University, as well as numerous courses in the university's Cloud Computing program. Tony is a PhD candidate, Applied Management and Decision Science, with an Information Systems Management specialty at Walden University.

Rick McDonald is an Associate Professor in the Information Systems department at the University of Alaska Southeast, in Ketchikan, Alaska, where he teaches computer and networking courses. He specializes in developing and delivering networking courses via e-learning. Rick worked in the airline industry for several years before returning to full-time teaching. He taught CCNA and CCNP courses in North Carolina before moving to Alaska in 2003.

Contents at a Glance

Contents

Command Syntax Conventions

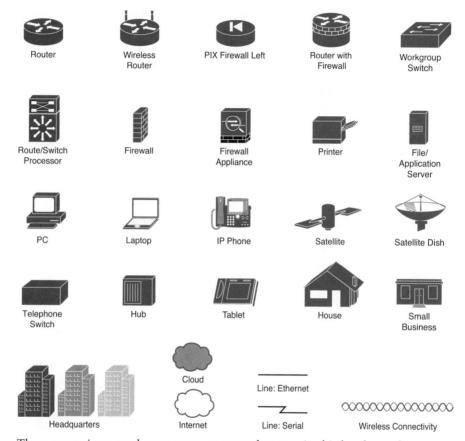

The conventions used to present command syntax in this book are the same conventions used in the IOS Command Reference. The Command Reference describes these conventions as follows:

- **Boldface** indicates commands and keywords that are entered literally as shown. In actual configuration examples and output (not general command syntax), boldface indicates commands that are manually input by the user (such as a **show** command).

- *Italic* indicates arguments for which you supply actual values.

- Vertical bars (|) separate alternative, mutually exclusive elements.

- Square brackets ([ ]) indicate an optional element.

- Braces ({ }) indicate a required choice.

- Braces within brackets ([{ }]) indicate a required choice within an optional element.

Introduction

Network Basics Companion Guide is the official supplemental textbook for the CCNA Routing and Switching Network Basics course in the Cisco Networking Academy Program.

As a textbook, this book provides a ready reference to explain the same networking concepts, technologies, protocols, and devices that are covered in the online course. This book emphasizes key topics, terms, and activities and provides some alternate explanations and examples as compared with the online course. You can use the online curriculum as directed by your instructor and then use this *Companion Guide*'s study tools to help solidify your understanding of all the topics.

Who Should Read This Book

This book is intended for students in the Cisco Networking Academy CCNA Routing and Switching Network Basics course. The goal of this book is to introduce you to fundamental networking concepts and technologies. In conjunction with the online course materials, this book will assist you in developing the skills necessary to plan and implement small networks across a range of applications. The specific skills covered in each chapter are described at the start of each chapter.

Book Features

The educational features of this book focus on supporting topic coverage, readability, and practice of the course material to facilitate your full understanding of the course material.

Topic Coverage

The following features give you a thorough overview of the topics covered in each chapter so that you can make constructive use of your study time:

- **Objectives:** Listed at the beginning of each chapter, the objectives reference the core concepts covered in the chapter. The objectives match the objectives stated in the corresponding chapters of the online curriculum; however, the question format in the *Companion Guide* encourages you to think about finding the answers as you read the chapter.

- **"How-to" feature:** When this book covers a set of steps that you need to perform for certain tasks, the text lists the steps as a how-to list. When you are studying, the icon helps you easily refer to this feature as you skim through the book.

- **Chapter summaries:** Each chapter includes a summary of the chapter's key concepts. It provides a synopsis of the chapter and serves as a study aid.

- **"Practice" section:** The end of each chapter includes a full list of all the Labs, Class Activities, and Packet Tracer Activities covered in that chapter.

Readability

The following features have been updated to assist your understanding of the networking vocabulary:

- **Key terms:** Each chapter begins with a list of key terms, along with a page-number reference for each key term. The key terms are listed in the order in which they are explained in the chapter. This handy reference allows you to find a term, flip to the page where the term appears, and see the term used in context. The Glossary defines all the key terms.

- **Glossary:** This book contains an all-new Glossary with more than 250 terms.

Practice

Practice makes perfect. This new *Companion Guide* offers you ample opportunities to put what you learn to practice. You will find the following features valuable and effective in reinforcing the instruction that you receive:

- **Check Your Understanding questions and answer key:** Updated review questions are presented at the end of each chapter as a self-assessment tool. These questions match the style of questions that you see in the online course. Appendix A, "Check Your Understanding Answer Key," provides an answer key to all the questions and includes an explanation of each answer.

Packet Tracer
☐ Activity

Video

- **Labs and Activities:** Throughout each chapter you will be directed to the online course to take advantage of the activities created to reinforce concepts. In addition, the end of each chapter includes a "Practice" section that collects a list of all the labs and activities to provide practice with the topics introduced in the chapter. The Labs and Class Activities are available in the companion *Network Basics Lab Manual* (978-158713-313-8). The Packet Tracer Activities PKA files are found in the online course.

- **Page references to online course:** After each heading you will see, for example, (1.1.2.3). This number refers to the page number in the online course so that you can easily jump to that spot online to view a video, practice an activity, perform a lab, or review a topic.

Lab Manual

The supplementary book *Network Basics Lab Manual* (978-158713-313-8), contains all the Labs and Class Activities from the course.

Practice and Study Guide

Additional study exercises, activities, and scenarios are available in the new *CCENT Practice and Study Guide* (978-158713-345-9) and *CCNA Routing and Switching Practice and Study Guide* (978-158713-344-2) books by Allan Johnson. Each Practice and Study Guide coordinates with the recommended curriculum sequence—one focusing on courses 1 and 2 (ICND1/CCENT topics) and the second focusing on courses 3 and 4 (ICND2/CCNA topics).

About Packet Tracer Software and Activities

Packet Tracer
☐ Activity

Interspersed throughout the chapters you'll find many activities to work with the Cisco Packet Tracer tool. Packet Tracer enables you to create networks, visualize how packets flow in the network, and use basic testing tools to determine whether the network would work. When you see the Packet Tracer Activity icon, you can use Packet Tracer with the listed file to perform a task suggested in this book. The activity files are available in the course. Packet Tracer software is available only through the Cisco Networking Academy website. Ask your instructor for access to Packet Tracer.

How This Book Is Organized

This book corresponds closely to the Cisco Networking Academy Network Basics course and is divided into 11 chapters, one appendix, and a glossary of key terms:

- **Chapter 1, "Exploring the Network":** This chapter introduces the platform of data networks upon which our social and business relationships increasingly depend. The material lays the groundwork for exploring the services, technologies, and issues encountered by network professionals as they design, build, and maintain the modern network.

- **Chapter 2, "Configuring a Network Operating System":** This chapter references a basic network topology, consisting of two switches and two PCs, to demonstrate the use of Cisco IOS.

- **Chapter 3, "Network Protocols and Communications":** In this chapter you will learn about two layered models that describe network rules and functions. These models, as well as the standards that make the networks work, are discussed here to give context to detailed study of the model layers in the following chapters.

- **Chapter 4, "Application Layer":** This chapter explores the role of the application layer and how the applications, services, and protocols within the application layer make robust communication across data networks possible.

- **Chapter 5, "Transport Layer":** This chapter examines the role of the transport layer in encapsulating application data for use by the network layer. The concepts of reliable data delivery and multiple application conversations are also introduced.

- **Chapter 6, "Network Layer":** This chapter focuses on the role of the network layer. It examines how it divides networks into groups of hosts to manage the flow of data packets within a network. It also covers how communication between networks is facilitated through routing processes.

- **Chapter 7, "IP Addressing":** This chapter describes the structure of IP addresses and their application to the construction and testing of IP networks and subnetworks.

- **Chapter 8, "Subnetting IP Networks":** This chapter examines the creation and assignment of IP network and subnetwork addresses through the use of the subnet mask.

- **Chapter 9, "Network Access":** This chapter introduces the general functions of the data link layer and the protocols associated with it. It also covers the general functions of the physical layer and the standards and protocols that manage the transmission of data across local media.

- **Chapter 10, "Ethernet":** This chapter examines the characteristics and operation of Ethernet as it has evolved from a shared-media, contention-based data communications technology to today's high-bandwidth, full-duplex technology.

- **Chapter 11, "It's A Network":** Having considered the services that a data network can provide to the human network, examined the features of each layer of the OSI model and the operations of TCP/IP protocols, and looked in detail at Ethernet, a universal LAN technology, this chapter discusses how to assemble these elements together in a functioning network that can be maintained

- **Appendix A, "Check Your Understanding Answer Key":** This appendix lists the answers to the "Check Your Understanding" review questions included at the end of each chapter.

- **Glossary:** The Glossary provides you with definitions for all the key terms identified in each chapter.

CHAPTER 1

Exploring the Network

Objectives

Upon completion of this chapter, you will be able to answer the following questions:

- How do networks affect the way we interact when we learn, work, and play?

- How do networks support communication?

- What is a converged network?

- What are the four requirements for a reliable network?

- How are network devices used?

- How do local-area network (LAN) devices compare to wide-area network (WAN) devices?

- What is the basic structure of the Internet?

- How do LANs and WANs interconnect the Internet?

- What is the effect of Bring Your Own Device (BYOD) use, online collaboration, video, and cloud computing on a business network?

- How do expanding networking trends affect security considerations?

- What are the three Cisco enterprise architectures and how do they meet the needs of an evolving network environment?

Key Terms

This chapter uses the following key terms. You can find the definitions in the Glossary.

Internet   page 4

instant messaging (IM)   page 7

social media   page 8

collaboration tools   page 8

weblogs (blogs)   page 8

wikis   page 8

podcasting   page 8

peer-to-peer (P2P) file sharing   page 8

quality of service (QoS)   page 12

converged network   page 13

fault tolerant   page 15

packets   page 17

scalable   page 19

security   page 21

network service   page 24

end devices   page 24

host device   page 24

intermediary devices   page 25

medium (media)   page 25

local-area network (LAN)   page 29

Introduction (1.0.1.1)

We now stand at a critical turning point in the use of technology to extend and empower our ability to communicate. The globalization of the Internet has succeeded faster than anyone could have imagined. The manner in which social, commercial, political, and personal interactions occur is rapidly changing to keep up with the evolution of this global network. In the next stage of our development, innovators will use the Internet as a starting point for their efforts as they create new products and services specifically designed to take advantage of the network capabilities. As developers push the limits of what is possible, the capabilities of the interconnected networks that form the Internet will play an increasing role in the success of these projects.

This chapter introduces the platform of data networks upon which our social and business relationships increasingly depend. The material lays the groundwork for exploring the services, technologies, and issues encountered by network professionals as they design, build, and maintain the modern network.

Class Activity 1.0.1.2: Draw Your Concept of the Internet

The Networking Academy curriculum has a new component called Modeling Activities. You will find them at the beginning and end of each chapter. Some activities can be completed individually (at home or in class), and some will require group or learning-community interaction. Your instructor will be facilitating so that you can obtain the most from these introductory activities. These activities will help you enhance your understanding by providing an opportunity to visualize some of the abstract concepts that you will be learning in this course. Be creative and enjoy these activities!

The Network Basics Lab Manual (ISBN 978-1-58713-313-8) contains all the Labs and Class Activities from the course. You can access the full instructions in the course itself or in this printed Lab Manual.

Here is your first modeling activity:

Draw Your Concept of the Internet

In this activity you will draw and label a map of the Internet as you interpret it now. Include your home or school/university location and its respective cabling, equipment, devices, etc. The following are some items you may want to include:

> Devices/Equipment
>
> Media (cabling)
>
> Link Addresses or Names
>
> Sources & Destinations
>
> Internet Service Providers

Upon completion, be sure to save your work in a hard-copy format, as it will be used for future reference at the end of this chapter. If it is an electronic document, save it to a server location provided by your instructor. Be prepared to share and explain your work in class.

For an example to get you started, please visit http://www.kk.org/internet-mapping/.

Communicating in a Network-Centric World (1.1)

Communication methods are constantly evolving, and the changes affect the way we interact with family, friends, and society. This chapter explores how we came to communicate over computer networks.

Interconnecting Our Lives (1.1.1)

In this section we will look at how people use networked computers to learn, work, and play.

Networks in Our Daily Lives (1.1.1.1)

Among all of the essentials for human existence, the need to interact with others ranks just below our need to sustain life. Communication is almost as important to us as our reliance on air, water, food, and shelter.

The methods that we use to communicate are constantly changing and evolving. Whereas we were once limited to face-to-face interactions, breakthroughs in technology have significantly extended the reach of our communications. From cave paintings to the printing press to radio and television, each new development has improved and enhanced our ability to connect and communicate with others.

The creation and interconnection of robust data networks has had a profound effect on communication, and has become the new platform on which modern communications occur.

Networks connect people and promote unregulated communication. Networks are the platforms on which to run businesses, to address emergencies, to inform individuals, and to support education, science, and government. The Internet is the largest network in existence. In fact, the term *Internet* means a network of networks. It is actually a collection of interconnected private and public networks. It is incredible how quickly the Internet has become an integral part of our daily routines.

Technology Then and Now (1.1.1.2)

Imagine a world without the Internet. No more Google, YouTube, instant messaging, Facebook, Wikipedia, online gaming, Netflix, iTunes, and easy access to current information. No more price comparison websites, avoiding lines by shopping online, or quickly looking up phone numbers and map directions to various locations at the click of a finger. How different would our lives be without all of this? That was the world we lived in just 15 to 20 years ago. But over the years, data networks have slowly expanded and been repurposed to improve the quality of life for people everywhere.

In the course of a day, resources that are available through the Internet can help you

- Post and share your photographs, home videos, and experiences with friends or with the world

- Access and submit school work

- Communicate with friends, family, and peers using email, instant messaging, or video applications

- Watch videos, movies, or television episodes on demand

- Play online games with friends

- Decide what to wear using online current weather conditions

- Find the least congested route to your destination by displaying weather and traffic video from webcams

- Check your bank balance and pay bills electronically

Innovators are figuring out new ways to use the Internet more every day. As developers push the limits of what is possible, the capabilities of the Internet and the role the Internet plays in our lives will expand broader and broader. Consider the changes that have happened within the last couple of decades, as depicted in Figure 1-1. Now consider what changes will happen within the next decade. What else do you think we will be able to do using the network as the platform?

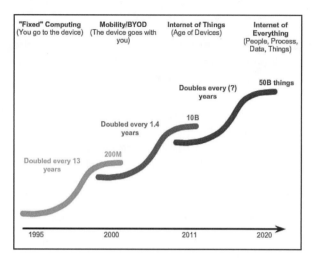

Figure 1-1 Computing Timeline

The Global Community (1.1.1.3)

Advancements in networking technologies are perhaps the most significant change agent in the world today. They are helping to create a world in which national borders, geographic distances, and physical limitations become less relevant, and present ever-diminishing obstacles.

The Internet has changed the manner in which social, commercial, political, and personal interactions occur. The immediate nature of communications over the Internet encourages the creation of global communities. Global communities allow for social interaction that is independent of location or time zone. The creation of online communities for the exchange of ideas and information has the potential to increase productivity opportunities across the globe.

Cisco refers to this as the *human network*. The human network centers on the impact of the Internet and networks on people and businesses.

How has the human network affected you?

Networks Support the Way We Learn (1.1.1.4)

Networks and the Internet have changed everything we do—the way we learn, the way we communicate, how we work, and even how we play.

Changing the Way We Learn

Communication, collaboration, and engagement are fundamental building blocks of education. Institutions are continually striving to enhance these processes to maximize the dissemination of knowledge. Traditional learning methods provide primarily two sources of expertise from which the student can obtain information: the textbook and the instructor. These two sources are limited, both in the format and the timing of the presentation.

Networks have changed the way we learn. Robust and reliable networks support and enrich student learning experiences. They deliver learning material in a wide range of formats, including interactive activities, assessments, and feedback. Networks now

- Support the creation of virtual classrooms
- Provide on-demand video
- Enable collaborative learning spaces
- Enable mobile learning

Access to high-quality instruction is no longer restricted to students living in proximity to where that instruction is being delivered. Online distance learning has removed geographic barriers and improved student opportunity. Online (e-learning) courses can now be delivered over a network. These courses can contain data (text, links), voice, and video available to the students at any time from any place. Online discussion groups and message boards enable a student to collaborate with the instructor, with other students in the class, or even with students across the world. Blended courses can combine instructor-led classes with online courseware to provide the best of both delivery methods.

In addition to the benefits for the student, networks have improved the management and administration of courses as well. Some of these online functions include student enrollment, assessment delivery, and progress tracking.

Networks Support the Way We Communicate (1.1.1.5)

Changes in network communications have enabled friends, families, and businesses to communicate in ways that could only be imagined by previous generations.

Changing the Way We Communicate

The globalization of the Internet has ushered in new forms of communication that empower individuals to create information that can be accessed by a global audience.

Some forms of communications include

- *Instant messaging (IM)* **and texting:** IM and texting both enable instant, real-time communication between two or more people. Many IM and texting applications incorporate features such as file transfer. IM applications can offer additional features such as voice and video communication.

- *Social media*: Social media consists of interactive websites where people and communities create and share user-generated content with friends, family, peers, and the world.

- *Collaboration tools*: Collaboration tools give people the opportunity to work together on shared documents. Without the constraints of location or time zone, individuals connected to a shared system can speak to each other, often across real-time, interactive video. Across the network, they can share text and graphics, and edit documents together. With collaboration tools always available, organizations can move quickly to share information and pursue goals. The broad distribution of data networks means that people in remote locations can contribute on an equal basis with people at the heart of large population centers.

- *Weblogs (blogs)*: Weblogs are web pages that are easy to update and edit. Unlike commercial websites, which are created by professional communications experts, blogs give anyone, including those without technical knowledge of web design, a means to communicate their thoughts to a global audience. There are blogs on nearly every topic one can think of, and communities of people often form around popular blog authors.

- *Wikis*: Wikis are web pages that groups of people can edit and view together. Whereas a blog is more of an individual, personal journal, a wiki is a group creation. As such, it may be subject to more extensive review and editing. Like blogs, wikis can be created in stages, and by anyone, without the sponsorship of a major commercial enterprise. Wikipedia has become a comprehensive resource—an online encyclopedia—of publicly contributed topics. Private organizations and individuals can also build their own wikis to capture collected knowledge on a particular subject. Many businesses use wikis as their internal collaboration tool. With the global Internet, people of all walks of life can participate in wikis and add their own perspectives and knowledge to a shared resource.

- *Podcasting*: Podcasting is an audio-based medium that originally enabled people to record audio and convert it for use. Podcasting allows people to deliver their recordings to a wide audience. The audio file is placed on a website (or blog or wiki) where others can download it and play the recording on their computers, laptops, and other mobile devices.

- *Peer-to-peer (P2P) file sharing*: Peer-to-peer file sharing enables people to share files with each other without having to store the files on and download them from a central server. The user joins the P2P network by simply installing the P2P software. This lets them locate and share files with others in the P2P network. The widespread digitization of media files, such as music and video files, has increased the interest in P2P file sharing. P2P file sharing has not been embraced by everyone. Many people are concerned that widespread use of P2P has enabled many to violate the laws of copyrighted materials.

What other sites or tools do you use to share your thoughts?

Networks Support the Way We Work (1.1.1.6)

Businesses, whether a small family business or a multinational corporation, have changed the way they operate to reap the benefits of network communications.

Changing the Way We Work

In the business world, data networks were initially used by businesses to internally record and manage financial information, customer information, and employee payroll systems. These business networks evolved to enable the transmission of many different types of information services, including email, video, messaging, and telephony.

The use of networks to provide efficient and cost-effective employee training is increasing in acceptance. Online learning opportunities can decrease time-consuming and costly travel yet still ensure that all employees are adequately trained to perform their jobs in a safe and productive manner.

There are many success stories illustrating innovative ways networks are being used to make us more successful in the workplace. Some of these scenarios are available through the Cisco website at http://www.cisco.com.

Networks Support the Way We Play (1.1.1.7)

Games, music, and TV are all enjoyed in significantly different ways than a decade ago due to changes in network communications.

Changing the Way We Play

The widespread adoption of the Internet by the entertainment and travel industries enhances the ability to enjoy and share many forms of recreation, regardless of location. It is possible to explore places interactively that previously we could only dream of visiting, as well as preview the actual destinations before making a trip. Travelers can post the details and photographs from their adventures online for others to view.

In addition, the Internet is used for traditional forms of entertainment. We listen to recording artists, preview or view motion pictures, read entire books, and download material for future offline access. Live sporting events and concerts can be experienced as they are happening, or recorded and viewed on demand.

Networks enable the creation of new forms of entertainment, such as online games. Players participate in any kind of online competition that game designers can imagine. We compete with friends and foes around the world in the same manner as if they were in the same room.

Even offline activities are enhanced using network collaboration services. Global communities of interest have grown rapidly. We share common experiences and hobbies well beyond our local neighborhood, city, or region. Sports fans share opinions and facts about their favorite teams. Collectors display prized collections and get expert feedback about them.

Online markets and auction sites provide the opportunity to buy, sell, and trade all types of merchandise.

Whatever form of recreation we enjoy in the human network, networks are improving our experience.

How do you play on the Internet?

Lab 1.1.1.8: Researching Network Collaboration Tools

In this lab you will use collaboration tools, share documents with Google Drive, explore conferencing and web meetings, and create wiki pages.

Supporting Communication (1.1.2)

This section discusses the various forms of communication, expected communication behaviors, and communication styles.

What Is Communication? (1.1.2.1)

Communication in our daily lives takes many forms and occurs in many environments. We have different expectations depending on whether we are chatting via the Internet or participating in a job interview. Each situation has its corresponding expected behaviors and styles.

Establishing the Rules

Before beginning to communicate with each other, we establish rules or agreements to govern the conversation. These rules, or protocols, must be followed in order for the message to be successfully delivered and understood. Figures 1-2, 1-3, and 1-4 depict a few of these rules. Among the protocols that govern successful human communication are the following:

- Identified sender and receiver

- Agreed-upon method of communicating (face-to-face, telephone, letter, photograph; see Figure 1-2)

- Common language and grammar (see Figure 1-3)

- Speed and timing of delivery
- Confirmation or acknowledgement requirements (see Figure 1-4)

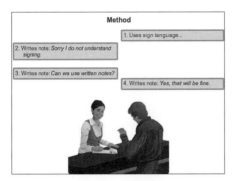

Figure 1-2 Agreeing on a Communication Method

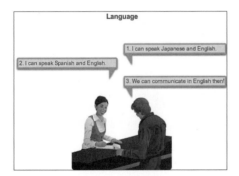

Figure 1-3 Agreeing on a Common Language

Figure 1-4 Confirming a Message

Communication rules may vary according to the context. If a message conveys an important fact or concept, a confirmation that the message has been received and understood is necessary. Less important messages may not require an acknowledgement from the recipient.

The techniques that are used in network communications share these fundamentals with human conversations.

Quality of Communication (1.1.2.2)

Communication between individuals is determined to be successful when the meaning of the message understood by the recipient matches the meaning intended by the sender. For data networks, we use the same basic criteria to judge success. However, as a message moves through the network, many factors can prevent the message from reaching the recipient or distort its intended meaning. These factors can be either external or internal.

External QoS Factors

The external *quality of service (QoS)* factors affecting data communications are related to the complexity of the network and the number of devices a message must pass through on its route to its final destination.

External QoS factors affecting the success of communication include

- The quality of the pathway between the sender and the recipient
- The number of times the message has to change form
- The number of times the message has to be redirected or readdressed
- The number of other messages being transmitted simultaneously on the communication network
- The amount of time allotted for successful communication

QoS will be discussed in greater detail throughout the course.

Internal QoS Factors

Internal QoS factors that interfere with network communications are related to the nature of the message itself. Different types of messages may vary in complexity and importance. Clear and concise messages are usually easier to understand than complex messages. Important communications require more care to ensure that they are delivered and understood by the recipient.

Internal factors affecting successful communications across the network include

- The size of the message
- The complexity of the message
- The importance of the message

Large messages may be interrupted or delayed at different points within the network. A message with a low importance or priority could be dropped if the network becomes overloaded.

Both the internal and external factors that affect the receipt of a message must be anticipated and controlled for network communications to be successful. New innovations in network hardware and software are being implemented to ensure the quality and reliability of network communications.

The Network as a Platform (1.2)

In the past, traditional networks such as television, telephone, and computer networks worked in very different ways. This chapter explores how those differences are rapidly shrinking.

Converged Networks (1.2.1)

In this section you will learn how different types of networks are becoming increasingly alike as network technologies change.

Traditional Service Networks (1.2.1.1)

Modern networks are constantly evolving to meet user demands. Early data networks were limited to exchanging character-based information between connected computer systems. Traditional telephone and television networks were maintained separately from data networks. In the past, every one of these services required a dedicated network, with different communications channels and different technologies to carry a particular communication signal. Each service had its own set of rules and standards to ensure successful communication.

Consider a hospital built 40 years ago. Back then, hospital rooms were cabled for the data network, telephone network, and video network for televisions. These separate networks were disparate, meaning that they could not communicate with each other, as shown on the left in Figure 1-5.

Advances in technology are enabling us to consolidate these different kinds of networks onto one platform, referred to as the *converged network*. Unlike dedicated networks, converged networks are capable of delivering voice, video streams, text, and graphics between many different types of devices over the same communications channel and network structure, as shown on the right in Figure 1-5. Previously separate and distinct communication forms have converged onto a common platform. This platform provides access to a wide range of alternative and new communication methods that enable people to interact directly with each other almost instantaneously.

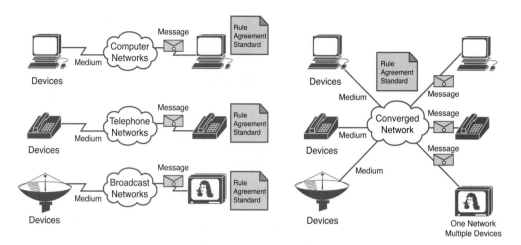

Figure 1-5 Traditional Networks (Left) and Converged Network (Right)

On a converged network, there are still many points of contact and many specialized devices, such as personal computers, phones, TVs, and tablet computers, but there is one common network infrastructure. This network infrastructure uses the same set of rules, agreements, and implementation standards.

Planning for the Future (1.2.1.2)

The convergence of the different types of communications networks onto one platform represents the first phase in building the intelligent information network. We are currently in this phase of network evolution. The next phase will be to not only consolidate the different types of messages onto a single network, but also consolidate the applications that generate, transmit, and secure the messages onto integrated network devices.

Not only will voice and video be transmitted over the same network, the devices that perform the telephone switching and video broadcasting will be the same devices that route the messages through the network. The resulting communications platform will provide high-quality application functionality at a reduced cost.

The pace at which the development of exciting new converged network applications is occurring can be attributed to the rapid growth and expansion of the Internet. This expansion has created a wider audience for whatever message, product, or service can be delivered. The underlying mechanics and processes that drive this explosive growth have resulted in a network architecture that is both capable of supporting changes and able to grow. As the supporting technology platform for living, learning, working, and playing in the human network, the network architecture of the Internet must adapt to constantly changing requirements for a high quality of service and security.

Lab 1.2.1.3: Researching Converged Network Services

In this lab you will explore converged services offered by local ISPs and research how converged networks are in use by institutions.

Reliable Network (1.2.2)

In this section you will learn about characteristics of a reliable network.

The Supporting Network Architecture (1.2.2.1)

Networks must support a wide range of applications and services, as well as operate over many different types of cables and devices that make up the physical infrastructure. The term *network architecture*, in this context, refers to the technologies that support the infrastructure and the programmed services and rules, or protocols, that move messages across the network.

As networks evolve, we are discovering that there are four basic characteristics that the underlying architectures need to address in order to meet user expectations:

- Fault tolerance
- Scalability
- QoS
- Security

Fault Tolerance in Circuit-Switched Networks (1.2.2.2)

Designing for unforeseen problems is an essential element of network design. This section explains how networks can manage unexpected equipment failure.

Fault Tolerance

The expectation is that the Internet is always available to the millions of users who rely on it. This requires a network architecture that is built to be *fault tolerant*. A fault-tolerant network is one that limits the effect of a failure, so that the fewest number of devices are affected by it. It is also built in a way that enables quick recovery when such a failure occurs. Fault-tolerant networks depend on multiple paths between the source and destination of a message. If one path fails, the messages can be instantly sent over a different link. Having multiple paths to a destination is known as redundancy, as shown in Figure 1-6.

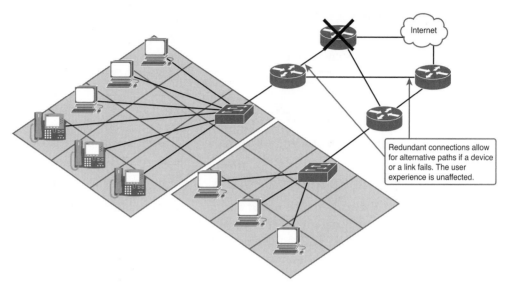

Figure 1-6 Fault Tolerance

Circuit-Switched, Connection-Oriented Networks

To understand the need for redundancy, we can look at how early telephone systems worked. When a person made a call using a traditional telephone set, the call first went through a setup process. This process identified the telephone switching locations between the person making the call (the source) and the phone set receiving the call (the destination). A temporary path, or *circuit*, was created for the duration of the telephone call. If any link or device in the circuit failed, the call was dropped. To reconnect, a new call had to be made, with a new circuit. This connection process is referred to as a circuit-switched process and is illustrated in Figure 1-7.

Many circuit-switched networks give priority to existing circuit connections at the expense of new circuit requests. After a circuit is established, even if no communication is occurring between the persons on either end of the call, the circuit remains connected and resources are used until one of the parties disconnects the call. Because there are only so many circuits that can be created, it is possible to get a message that all circuits are busy and a call cannot be placed. The cost to create many alternative paths with enough capacity to support a large number of simultaneous circuits, and the technologies necessary to dynamically re-create dropped circuits in the event of a failure, are why circuit-switched technology was not optimal for the Internet.

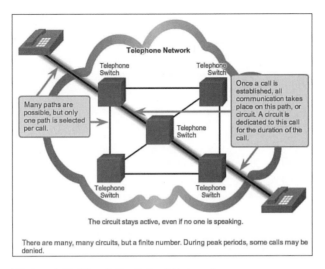

Figure 1-7 Circuit-Switched Network

Packet-Switched Networks (1.2.2.3)

In the search for a network that was more fault tolerant, the early Internet designers researched packet-switched networks. The premise for this type of network is that a single message can be broken into multiple message blocks, with each message block containing addressing information to indicate the origination point and final destination. Using this embedded information, these message blocks, called *packets*, can be sent through the network along various paths, and can be reassembled into the original message when they reach their destination. Figure 1-8 demonstrates how packets can travel different paths and arrive at the correct destination for sorting.

The devices within the network itself are typically unaware of the content of the individual packets. The only packet information used by intermediate devices is the original source address and the final destination address. These addresses are often referred to as *IP addresses*, represented in a dotted decimal format such as 10.10.10.10. Each packet is sent independently from one location to another. At each location, a routing decision is made as to which path to use to forward the packet toward its final destination. If a previously used path is no longer available, the routing function can dynamically choose the next best available path. Because the messages are sent in pieces, rather than as a single complete message, the few packets that may be lost can be retransmitted to the destination along a different path. In many cases, the destination device is unaware that any failure or rerouting occurred.

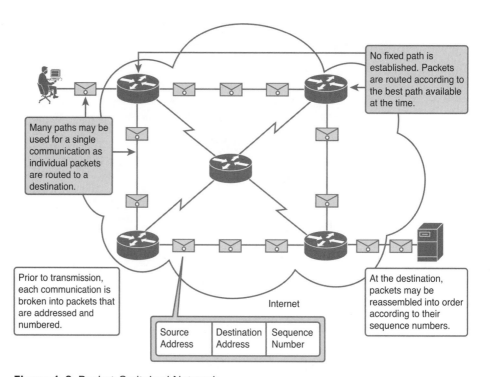

No fixed path is established. Packets are routed according to the best path available at the time.

Many paths may be used for a single communication as individual packets are routed to a destination.

Prior to transmission, each communication is broken into packets that are addressed and numbered.

At the destination, packets may be reassembled into order according to their sequence numbers.

Internet

Source Address	Destination Address	Sequence Number

Figure 1-8 Packet-Switched Network

The need for a single, reserved circuit from end to end does not exist in a packet-switched network. Any piece of a message can be sent through the network using any available path. Additionally, packets containing pieces of messages from different sources can travel the network at the same time. By providing a method to dynamically use redundant paths, without intervention by the user, the Internet has become a fault-tolerant method of communication.

Although packet-switched, connectionless networks are the primary infrastructure for today's Internet, there are some benefits to a connection-oriented system like the circuit-switched telephone system. Because resources at the various switching locations are dedicated to providing a finite number of circuits, the quality and consistency of messages transmitted across a connection-oriented network can be guaranteed. Another benefit is that the provider of the service can charge the users of the network for the period of time that the connection is active. The ability to charge users for active connections through the network is a fundamental premise of the telecommunication service industry.

Scalable Networks (1.2.2.4)

Designing a network that will be able to efficiently expand is an important network design consideration.

Scalability

Thousands of new users and service providers connect to the Internet each week. In order for the Internet to support this rapid amount of growth, it must be scalable. A *scalable* network can expand quickly to support new users and applications without affecting the performance of the service being delivered to existing users. Figure 1-9 depicts a scalable network accepting additional users.

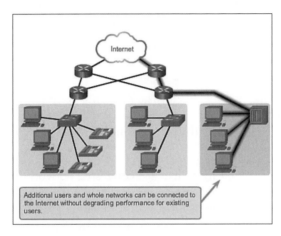

Figure 1-9 Scalability

The fact that the Internet is able to expand at the rate that it is, without seriously impacting the performance experienced by individual users, is a function of the design of the protocols and underlying technologies on which it is built. The Internet has a hierarchical, layered structure for addressing, for naming, and for connectivity services. As a result, network traffic that is destined for local or regional services does not need to traverse to a central point for distribution. Common services can be duplicated in different regions, thereby keeping traffic off the higher-level backbone networks.

Scalability also refers to the ability to accept new products and applications. Although there is no single organization that regulates the Internet, the many individual networks that provide Internet connectivity cooperate to follow accepted standards and protocols. The adherence to standards enables the manufacturers of hardware and software to concentrate on product development and improvements in the areas of performance and capacity, knowing that the new products can integrate with and enhance the existing infrastructure.

The current Internet architecture, while highly scalable, may not always be able to keep up with the pace of user demand. New protocols and addressing structures are under development to meet the increasing rate at which Internet applications and services are being added.

Providing QoS (1.2.2.5)

A well-designed network can prioritize network traffic to provide users with reliable quality of service, or QoS.

Quality of Service

Quality of service is also an ever-increasing requirement of networks today. New applications available to users over internetworks, such as voice and live video transmissions, as shown in Figure 1-10, create higher expectations for the quality of the delivered services. Have you ever tried to watch a video with constant breaks and pauses?

Networks must provide predictable, measurable, and, at times, guaranteed services. The packet-switched network architecture does not guarantee that all packets that comprise a particular message will arrive on time and in their correct order, or even that they will arrive at all.

Networks also need mechanisms to manage congested network traffic. Network bandwidth is the measure of the data-carrying capacity of the network. In other words, how much information can be transmitted within a specific amount of time? Network bandwidth is measured in the number of bits that can be transmitted in a single second, or bits per second (bps). When simultaneous communications are attempted across the network, the demand for network bandwidth can exceed its availability, creating network congestion. The network simply has more bits to transmit than what the bandwidth of the communications channel can deliver.

In most cases, when the volume of packets is greater than what can be transported across the network, devices *queue*, or hold, the packets in memory until resources become available to transmit them, as shown in Figure 1-10. Queuing packets causes delay because new packets cannot be transmitted until previous packets have been processed. If the number of packets to be queued continues to increase, the memory queues fill up and packets are dropped.

Achieving the required QoS by managing the delay and packet loss parameters on a network becomes the secret to providing a successful solution for end-to-end application quality. One way this can be accomplished is through classification. To create QoS classifications of data, we use a combination of communication characteristics and the relative importance assigned to the application. We then treat all data within the same classification according to the same rules. For example, communication that is time-sensitive, such as voice transmissions, would be classified differently from communication that can tolerate delay, such as file transfers.

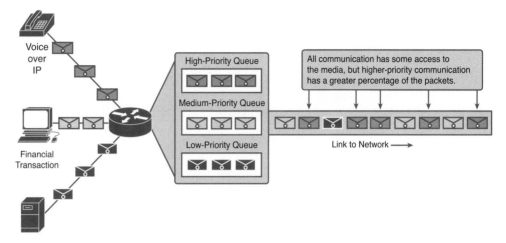

Figure 1-10 Priority Queuing

Examples of priority decisions for an organization might include

- **Time-sensitive communication:** Increase priority for services like telephony or video distribution

- **Non-time-sensitive communication:** Decrease priority for web page retrieval or email

- **High importance to organization:** Increase priority for production control or business transaction data

- **Undesirable communication:** Decrease priority or block unwanted activity, like peer-to-peer file sharing or live entertainment

Providing Network Security (1.2.2.6)

Security is one of the most important design elements in a computer network.

Security

The Internet has evolved from a tightly controlled internetwork of educational and government organizations to a widely accessible means for transmission of business and personal communications. As a result, the security requirements of the network have changed. The network infrastructure, the network services, and the data contained on network-attached devices are crucial personal and business assets. Compromising the integrity of these assets could have serious consequences, such as

- Network outages that prevent communications and transactions from occurring, with consequent loss of business

- Intellectual property (research ideas, patents, or designs) that is stolen and used by a competitor

- Personal or private information that is compromised or made public without the user's consent

- Misdirection and loss of personal or business funds

- Loss of important data that takes a significant labor to replace, or is irreplaceable

There are two types of network security concerns that must be addressed: network infrastructure security and information security.

Securing a network infrastructure includes physically securing devices that provide network connectivity, and preventing unauthorized access to the management software that resides on those devices.

Information security refers to protecting the information contained within the packets being transmitted over the network and the information stored on network-attached devices. Security measures taken in a network should prevent the following:

- Unauthorized disclosure

- Theft of information (see Figure 1-11)

- Unauthorized modification of information

- Denial of service (DoS)

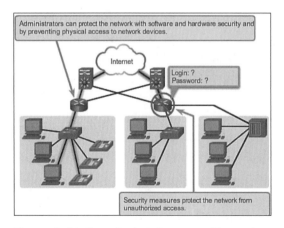

Figure 1-11 Security in a Computer Network.

In order to achieve the goals of network security, there are three primary requirements:

- **Ensuring confidentiality:** Data confidentiality means that only the intended and authorized recipients—individuals, processes, or devices—can access and read data. This is accomplished by having a strong system for user authentication, enforcing passwords that are difficult to guess, and requiring users to change their passwords frequently. Encrypting data, so that only the intended recipient can read it, is also part of confidentiality.

- **Maintaining communication integrity:** Data integrity means having the assurance that the information has not been altered in transmission, from origin to destination. Data integrity can be compromised when information has been corrupted—willfully or accidentally. Data integrity is made possible by requiring validation of the sender and by using mechanisms to validate that the packet has not changed during transmission.

- **Ensuring availability:** *Availability* means having the assurance of timely and reliable access to data services for authorized users. Network firewall devices, along with desktop and server antivirus software, can ensure system reliability and the robustness to detect, repel, and cope with such attacks. Building fully redundant network infrastructures, with few single points of failure, can reduce the impact of these threats.

<table>
<tr><td>Interactive
Graphic</td><td>

Activity 1.2.2.7: Reliable Networks

Go to the online course to perform this practice activity.
</td></tr>
</table>

LANs, WANs, and the Internet (1.3)

Most web users never consider how the Internet works. In this section you will begin to explore the pieces that come together to enable network communications.

Components of a Network (1.3.1)

In this section you will begin to learn about the devices and equipment that work together in networks.

Components of the Network (1.3.1.1)

The path that a message takes from source to destination can be as simple as a single cable connecting one computer to another or as complex as a network that literally spans the globe. This network infrastructure is the platform that supports the network. It provides the stable and reliable channel over which our communications can occur.

The network infrastructure contains three categories of network components:

- End devices
- Intermediary devices
- Network media

Devices and media are the physical elements, or *hardware*, of the network. Hardware comprises the components of the network platform that typically are visible, such as a laptop, PC, switch, router, wireless access point, or the cabling used to connect the devices. Occasionally, some network components may not be visible. In the case of wireless media, for example, messages are transmitted through the air using invisible radio frequency or infrared waves.

Network components are used to provide services and processes. These services and processes are the communication programs, called *software*, that run on the networked devices. A *network service* provides information in response to a request. Services include many of the common network applications people use every day, like email hosting services and web hosting services. Processes provide the functionality that directs and moves the messages through the network. Processes are less obvious to us but are critical to the operation of networks.

End Devices (1.3.1.2)

The network devices that people are most familiar with are called *end devices*, or hosts. These devices form the interface between users and the underlying communication network.

Some examples of end devices are

- Computers (work stations, laptops, file servers, web servers)
- Network printers
- VoIP phones
- TelePresence endpoints
- Security cameras
- Mobile handheld devices (such as smartphones, tablets, PDAs, and wireless debit/credit card readers and barcode scanners)

A *host device* is either the source or destination of a message transmitted over the network. In order to distinguish one host from another, each host on a network is identified by an address. When a host initiates communication, it uses the address of the destination host to specify where the message should be sent.

In modern networks, a host can act as a client, a server, or both. Software installed on the host determines which role it plays on the network. *Servers* are hosts that have software installed that enables them to provide information and services, like email or web pages, to other hosts on the network. *Clients* are hosts that have software installed that enables them to request and display the information obtained from the server.

Intermediary Devices (1.3.1.3)

Intermediary devices interconnect end devices. These devices provide connectivity and work behind the scenes to ensure that data flows across the network. Intermediary devices connect the individual hosts to the network and can connect multiple individual networks to form an internetwork.

Interactive Graphic

Activity 1.3.1.3: Internetworks

Go to the online course and view the animation.

Examples of intermediary network devices are

- Network access devices (switches and wireless access points)
- Internetworking devices (routers)
- Security devices (firewalls)

The management of data as it flows through the network is also a role of the intermediary devices. These devices use the destination host address, in conjunction with information about the network interconnections, to determine the path that messages should take through the network.

Processes running on the intermediary network devices perform these functions:

- Regenerate and retransmit data signals
- Maintain information about which pathways exist through the network and internetwork
- Notify other devices of errors and communication failures
- Direct data along alternate pathways when there is a link failure
- Classify and direct messages according to QoS priorities
- Permit or deny the flow of data, based on security settings

Network Media (1.3.1.4)

Communication across a network is carried on a *medium*. The medium provides the channel over which the message travels from source to destination.

Modern networks primarily use the following three types of media to interconnect devices and to provide the pathway over which data can be transmitted:

- Metallic wires within cables

- Glass or plastic fibers (fiber-optic cable)

- Wireless transmission

Figure 1-12 shows examples of the three types of physical media.

Figure 1-12 Network Media

The signal encoding that must occur for the message to be transmitted is different for each media type. On metallic wires, the data is encoded into electrical impulses that match specific patterns. Fiber-optic transmissions rely on pulses of light, within either infrared or visible light ranges. In wireless transmission, patterns of electromagnetic waves depict the various bit values.

Different types of network media have different features and benefits. Not all network media types have the same characteristics or are appropriate for the same purpose. The criteria for choosing network media are

- The distance the media can successfully carry a signal

- The environment in which the media is to be installed

- The amount of data and the speed at which it must be transmitted

- The cost of the media and installation

Network Representations (1.3.1.5)

When conveying complex information, such as displaying all the devices and media in a large internetwork, it is helpful to use visual representations. A diagram provides an easy way to understand the way the devices in a large network are connected. Such a diagram uses symbols to represent the different devices and connections that make up a network. This type of "picture" of a network is known as a *topology diagram*.

Like any other language, the language of networking uses a common set of symbols to represent the different end devices, network devices, and media, as shown in Figure 1-13. The ability to recognize the logical representations of the physical networking components is critical to being able to visualize the organization and operation of a network. Throughout this course and its accompanying labs, you will learn both how these devices operate and how to perform basic configuration tasks on these devices.

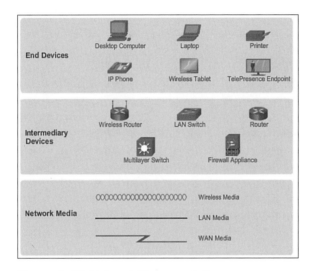

Figure 1-13 Network Representations

In addition to being able to recognize these representations, you need to understand the specialized terminology that is used when discussing how each of these devices and media connect to each other. Important terms to remember are

- **Network interface card (NIC):** Provides the physical connection to the network at the PC or other host device. The media connecting the PC to the networking device plugs directly into the NIC (also known as a LAN adapter).

- **Physical port:** A connector or outlet on a networking device where the media is connected to a host or other networking device.

- **Interface:** Specialized ports on an internetworking device that connect to individual networks. Because routers are used to interconnect networks, the ports on a router are referred to as network interfaces.

Topology Diagrams (1.3.1.6)

Topology diagrams are mandatory for anyone working with a network. A topology diagram provides a visual map of how the network is connected.

There are two types of topology diagrams:

- **Physical topology diagram:** Identifies the physical location of intermediary devices, configured ports, and cable installation, as shown on the left in Figure 1-14.

- **Logical topology diagram:** Identifies devices, ports, and the IP addressing scheme, as shown on the right in Figure 1-14.

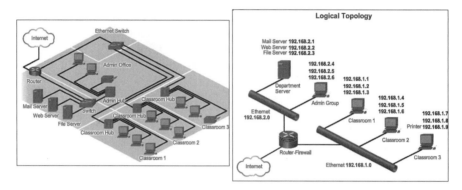

Figure 1-14 Physical Topology (Left) and Logical Topology (Right)

Interactive Graphic

Activity 1.3.1.7: Network Component Representations and Functions

Go to the online course to perform this practice activity.

LANs and WANs (1.3.2)

This section explains how LANs and WANs form computer networks.

Types of Networks (1.3.2.1)

Network infrastructures can vary greatly in terms of

- Size of the area covered
- Number of users connected
- Number and types of services available

Figure 1-15 illustrates the two most common types of network infrastructures:

- *Local-area network (LAN)*: A network infrastructure that provides access to users and end devices in a small geographical area.

- *Wide-area network (WAN)*: A network infrastructure that provides access to other networks over a wide geographical area.

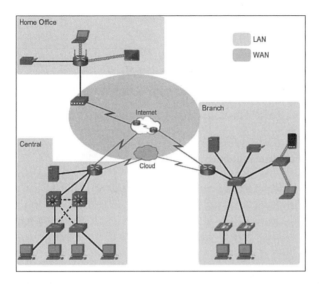

Figure 1-15 LANs Separated by Geographic Distance Connected by a WAN

Other types of networks include

- **Metropolitan-area network (MAN):** A network infrastructure that spans a physical area larger than a LAN but smaller than a WAN (e.g., a city). MANs are typically operated by a single entity, such as a large organization.

- *Wireless LAN (WLAN)*: Similar to a LAN but wirelessly interconnects users and endpoints in a small geographical area.

- *Storage-area network (SAN)*: A network infrastructure designed to support file servers and provide data storage, retrieval, and replication. It involves high-end servers, multiple disk arrays (called *blocks*), and Fibre Channel interconnection technology.

Local-Area Networks (1.3.2.2)

LANs are a network infrastructure that spans a small geographical area. Specific features of LANs include

- LANs interconnect end devices in a limited area such as a home, school, office building, or campus.

- A LAN is usually administered by a single organization or individual. The administrative control that governs the security and access control policies is enforced on the network level.

- LANs provide high-speed bandwidth to internal end devices and intermediary devices.

Wide-Area Networks (1.3.2.3)

WANs are a network infrastructure that spans a wide geographical area. WANs are typically managed by service providers (SPs) or Internet service providers (ISPs).

Specific features of WANs include

- WANs interconnect LANs over wide geographical areas such as between cities, states, provinces, countries, or continents.

- WANs are usually administered by multiple service providers.

- WANs typically provide slower-speed links between LANs.

The Internet (1.3.3)

This section explains how the Internet consists of many connected LANs and WANs.

The Internet (1.3.3.1)

Although there are benefits to using a LAN or WAN, most individuals need to communicate with a resource on another network, outside of the local network within the home, campus, or organization. This is done using the Internet.

As shown in Figure 1-16, the Internet is a worldwide collection of interconnected networks (internetworks or the Internet for short), cooperating with each other to exchange information using common standards. Through telephone wires, fiber-optic cables, wireless transmissions, and satellite links, Internet users can exchange information in a variety of forms.

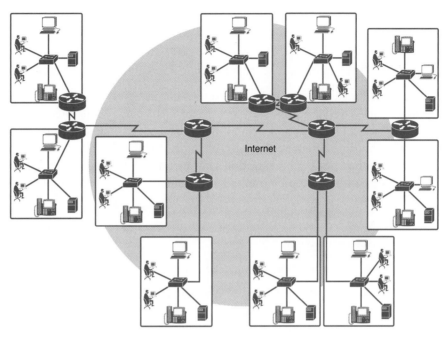

Figure 1-16 Internetworks Made Up of LANs and WANs

The Internet is a conglomerate of networks and is not actually owned by any individual or group. Ensuring effective communication across this diverse infrastructure requires the application of consistent and commonly recognized technologies and standards as well as the cooperation of many network administration agencies. There are organizations that have been developed for the purpose of helping to maintain structure and standardization of Internet protocols and processes. These organizations include the Internet Engineering Task Force (IETF), Internet Corporation for Assigned Names and Numbers (ICANN), and the Internet Architecture Board (IAB), plus many others.

Note

The term internet (with a lower case "i") is used to describe multiple networks interconnected. When referring to the global system of interconnected computer networks or the World Wide Web, the term Internet (with a capital "I") is used.

Intranet and Extranet (1.3.3.2)

Two other terms are similar to the term Internet:

- Intranet

- Extranet

Intranet is a term often used to refer to a private connection of LANs and WANs that belongs to an organization, and is designed to be accessible only by the organization's members, employees, or others who have authorization. An intranet is basically an internet that is usually only accessible from within the organization.

An organization may publish on its intranet web pages about internal events, health and safety policies, staff newsletters, and staff phone directories. For example, a school may have an intranet that includes class schedule information, online curriculum, and discussion forums. Intranets usually help eliminate paperwork and speed up workflows. An organization's intranet may be accessible to staff working outside of the organization by using secure connections to the internal network.

An organization may use an *extranet* to provide secure and safe access to individuals who work for different organizations but require company data. Examples of extranets include

- A company providing access to outside suppliers/contractors

- A hospital providing a booking system to doctors so they can make appointments for their patients

- A local office of education providing budget and personnel information to the schools in its district

Lab 1.3.3.3: Mapping the Internet

In this lab you will test network connectivity, trace network routes using different tools, and compare the results provided by those tools.

Connecting to the Internet (1.3.4)

This section explores the different ways to access the Internet.

Internet Access Technologies (1.3.4.1)

There are many different ways to connect users and organizations to the Internet.

Home users, teleworkers (remote workers), and small offices typically require a connection to an Internet service provider (ISP) to access the Internet. Connection options vary greatly depending on the ISP and the geographical location. However, popular choices include broadband cable, broadband digital subscriber line (DSL), wireless WANs, and mobile services.

Organizations typically require access to other corporate sites and the Internet. Fast connections are required to support business services, including IP phones, video conferencing, and data center storage.

Business-class interconnections are usually provided by service providers (SPs). Popular business-class services include business DSL, leased lines, and Metro Ethernet.

Connecting Remote Users to the Internet (1.3.4.2)

Figure 1-17 illustrates common Internet connection options for small office and home office users, which include

- *Cable*: Typically offered by cable television service providers, the Internet data signal is carried on the same coaxial cable that delivers cable television. It provides a high-bandwidth, always-on connection to the Internet. A special cable modem separates the Internet data signal from the other signals carried on the cable and provides an Ethernet connection to a host computer or LAN.

- *DSL*: Provides a high-bandwidth, always-on connection to the Internet. It requires a special high-speed modem that separates the DSL signal from the telephone signal and provides an Ethernet connection to a host computer or LAN. DSL runs over a telephone line, with the line split into three channels. One channel is used for voice telephone calls. This channel allows an individual to receive phone calls without disconnecting from the Internet. A second channel is a faster download channel, used to receive information from the Internet. The third channel is used for sending or uploading information. This channel is usually slightly slower than the download channel. The quality and speed of the DSL connection depends mainly on the quality of the phone line and the distance from your phone company's central office. The farther you are from the central office, the slower the connection.

- *Cellular*: Cellular Internet access uses a cell phone network to connect. Wherever you can get a cellular signal, you can get cellular Internet access. Performance will be limited by the capabilities of the phone and the cell tower to which it is connected. The availability of cellular Internet access is a real benefit in those areas that would otherwise have no Internet connectivity at all, and for people who are constantly on the go.

- *Satellite*: Satellite service is a good option for homes or offices that do not have access to DSL or cable. Satellite dishes require a clear line of sight to the satellite, so satellite service might not be an option in heavily wooded areas or places with other overhead obstructions. Speeds will vary depending on the contract, though they are generally good. Equipment and installation costs can be high (although check the provider for special deals), with a moderate monthly fee thereafter. The availability of satellite Internet access is a real benefit in those areas that would otherwise have no Internet connectivity at all.

- *Dial-up* **telephone:** An inexpensive option that uses any phone line and a modem. To connect to the ISP, a user calls the ISP access phone number. The low bandwidth provided by a dial-up modem connection is usually not sufficient for large data transfer, although it is useful for mobile access while traveling. A modem dial-up connection should only be considered when higher-speed connection options are not available.

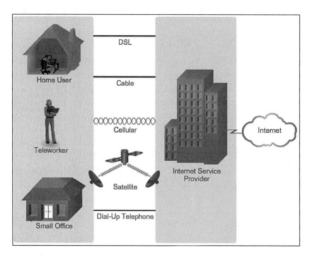

Figure 1-17 Internet Connection Options

Many homes and small offices are more commonly being connected directly with fiber-optic cables. This enables an ISP to provide higher bandwidth speeds and support more services such as Internet, phone, and TV.

The choice of connection varies depending on geographical location and service provider availability.

What are your options for connecting to the Internet?

Connecting Businesses to the Internet (1.3.4.3)

Corporate connection options differ from home-user options. Businesses may require higher bandwidth, dedicated bandwidth, and managed services. Connection options available differ depending on the number of service providers located nearby.

Common connection options for organizations include

- *Dedicated leased line:* This is a dedicated connection from the service provider to the customer premises. Leased lines are actually reserved circuits that connect geographically separated offices for private voice and/or data networking. The circuits are typically rented at a monthly or yearly rate, which tends to make it expensive. In North America, common leased-line circuits include T1 (1.54

Mbps) and T3 (44.7 Mbps), whereas in other parts of the world they are available in E1 (2 Mbps) and E3 (34 Mbps).

■ *Metro Ethernet*: Metro Ethernet is typically available from a provider to the customer premises over a dedicated copper or fiber connection providing bandwidth speeds of 10 Mbps to 10 Gbps. Ethernet over Copper (EoC) is more economical than fiber-optic Ethernet service in many cases, is quite widely available, and reaches speeds of up to 40 Mbps. However, EoC is limited by distance. Fiber-optic Ethernet service delivers the fastest connections available at an economical price per megabit. Unfortunately, there are still many areas where this service is unavailable.

■ **DSL:** Business DSL is available in various formats. A popular choice is symmetric DSL (SDSL), which is similar to asymmetric DSL (ADSL) but provides the same upload and download speeds. ADSL is designed to deliver bandwidth at different rates downstream than upstream. For example, a customer getting Internet access may have downstream rates that range from 1.5 to 9 Mbps, whereas upstream bandwidth ranges are from 16 to 640 kbps. ADSL transmissions work at distances up to 18,000 feet (5,488 meters) over a single copper twisted pair.

■ **Satellite:** Satellite service can provide a connection when a wired solution is not available. Satellite dishes require a clear line of sight to the satellite. Equipment and installation costs can be high, with a moderate monthly fee thereafter. Connections tend to be slower and less reliable than terrestrial competition, which makes satellite less attractive than other alternatives.

The choice of connection varies depending on geographical location and service provider availability.

Packet Tracer Activity 1.3.4.4: Network Representation

In this activity you will learn the essentials of using Packet Tracer. Packet Tracer is a downloadable software program that will help you with your Cisco Certified Network Associate (CCNA) studies. You will explore a relatively complex network that highlights a few of Packet Tracer's features. While doing so, you will learn how to access Help and the tutorials. Finally, you will explore how Packet Tracer serves as a modeling tool for network representations.

The Expanding Network (1.4)

The Internet has continuously expanded in the last two decades, and there is no indication that the expansion is slowing.

Network Trends (1.4.1)

In this section you will learn about emerging Internet trends.

New Trends (1.4.1.1)

When you look at how the Internet has changed so many of the things people do daily, it is hard to believe that it has only been around for most people for about 20 years. It has truly transformed the way individuals and organizations communicate. For example, before the Internet became so widely available, organizations and small businesses largely relied on print marketing to make consumers aware of their products. It was difficult for businesses to determine which households were potential customers, so businesses relied on mass print marketing programs. These programs were expensive and varied in effectiveness. Compare that to how consumers are reached today. Most businesses have an Internet presence where consumers can learn about their products, read reviews from other customers, and order products directly from the website. Social networking sites partner with businesses to promote products and services. Bloggers partner with businesses to highlight and endorse products and services. Most of this product placement is targeted to the potential consumer, rather than to the masses.

As new technologies and end-user devices come to market, businesses and consumers must continue to adjust to this ever-changing environment. The role of the network is transforming to enable the connections of people, devices, and information. There are several new networking trends that will affect organizations and consumers. Some of the top trends include

- Bring Your Own Device (BYOD)

- Online collaboration

- Video communication

- Cloud computing

These trends are interconnected and will continue to build off of one another in the coming years. The next couple of topics will cover these trends in more detail.

But keep in mind, new trends are being dreamed up and engineered every day. How do you think the Internet will change in the next 10 years? 20 years?

Bring Your Own Device (BYOD) (1.4.1.2)

The concept of any device, to any content, in any way is a major global trend occurring in business IT environments that requires significant changes to the way devices are used. This trend is known as *Bring Your Own Device (BYOD)*.

In the past, an employee who needed access to the corporate network would be issued a company-provided device, such as a laptop or PC. These devices were typically expensive and were seen as tools for work. With the growth of consumer devices, and the related drop in cost, employees can be expected to have some of the most advanced tools for personal use. These personal tools include laptops, netbooks, tablets, smartphones, and e-readers. BYOD is about end users having the freedom to use these personal tools to access information and communicate across the corporate network. These can be devices purchased by the employer, devices purchased by the employee, or both. BYOD means any device, with any ownership, used anywhere. Extended connectivity through mobile and remote access to the corporate network gives employees tremendous flexibility and increased productivity.

BYOD is an influential trend that has or will touch every IT organization. There are many effects and considerations when providing for a BYOD environment.

BYOD Considerations (1.4.1.3)

In a BYOD environment, individuals are likely to have multiple devices connected to the network, possibly simultaneously. This leads to a large increase in the overall number of connected devices. The network must be designed in a way to support these additional devices and their traffic.

Additionally, a complete BYOD solution must consider how to extend the full services of the organization seamlessly, providing the same types of services to a user on a BYOD as are available to a user on a corporate PC. This includes collaboration tools such as integrated voice, video, IM, conferencing, and application sharing.

Finally, the network and applications must be able to offer quality of service regardless of whether the connectivity to those applications or collaboration tools occurs in the main campus, branch office, home office, or mobile teleworker location. Any solution must consider not only the employee using their own device, but also the individuals and applications that they are connecting and communicating with.

Security is a major consideration in a BYOD environment; therefore, any solution must be a highly secure mobile solution. Mobile and remote-access devices are typically not under the same strict control and scrutiny as employer-provided desktop and laptop computers. Therefore, appropriate security and user policies need to be applied to protect corporate data when employees connect with these devices. The range of those policies may vary depending on the spectrum of BYOD access that an organization wants.

Depending on the needs of the organization, a range of BYOD policies may be in place, from limited access to advanced BYOD implementation. Each of these implementations must include end-user agreements that outline the use of personal devices on corporate networks, policies for how and what those devices can access, and guidelines for how lost or stolen devices will be handled. Organizations may also need an agreement about when and if data can be accessed from the personal device of an employee. There have been several legal challenges recently for cases involving an employer who remotely "wiped" an employee-owned device, including both the corporate and personal data it contained. Imagine your surprise as an employee when you discover that by using your new tablet to access the corporate network, you unknowingly agreed to let IT delete your favorite family photos remotely.

Online Collaboration (1.4.1.4)

Employees want to connect to the network not only for access to data applications, but also to collaborate with one another. Collaboration is defined as "the act of working with another or others on a joint project."

For businesses, collaboration is a critical and strategic priority. To remain competitive, organizations must answer three primary collaboration questions:

- How can they get everyone on the same page?

- With decreased budgets and personnel, how can they balance resources to be in more places at once?

- How can they maintain face-to-face relationships with a growing network of colleagues, customers, partners, and peers in an environment that is more dependent on 24-hour connectivity?

One way to answer these questions in today's environment is through online collaboration tools. In traditional workspaces, and with BYOD environments alike, employees are taking advantage of voice, video, and conferencing services in collaboration efforts.

The ability to collaborate online is changing business processes. New and expanding collaboration tools allow individuals to quickly and easily collaborate, regardless of physical location. Organizations have much more flexibility in the way they are organized. Employees are no longer restricted to physical locations. Expert knowledge is easier to access than ever before. Expansions in collaboration allow organizations to improve their information gathering, innovation, and productivity

Collaboration tools give employees, customers, and partners a way to instantly connect, interact, and conduct business, through whatever communications channels they prefer, and achieve business objectives.

Collaboration Considerations (1.4.1.5)

The ability to work together to solve a common problem has proven to be one of mankind's greatest accomplishments. Great things can happen when we all work together. However, implementing a collaboration strategy is not always easy and there can be many challenges to overcome.

End users have high expectations that application performance will be maintained, regardless of time, location, and end device. Users also want to be able to have collaboration capabilities regardless of service provider, meaning they want those capabilities to be available whether they are connecting with collaboration tools across a corporate-maintained network or connecting via their home or hotel Internet connection.

For an organization to be successful in its collaboration strategy, it must determine its collaboration needs and establish which tools effectively meet those needs. Additionally, an organization must be able to prioritize traffic and effectively monitor and manage the performance of those collaboration tools. Finally, an organization must consider security requirements for collaboration and establish proper-use policies to ensure corporate data remains secure.

There's a wide range of collaboration tools available on the market today, including mobile applications, telePresence, and online web-conferencing tools, just to name a few.

Video Communication (1.4.1.6)

Another trend in networking that is critical in the communication and collaboration effort is the use of video. Video conferencing and person-to-person video calling are already proving particularly powerful for sales processes and for doing business at a distance, both locally and globally. Today, businesses are using video to transform key business processes to create competitive advantage, lower costs, and reduce environmental impact, particularly by avoiding the need for travel. Figure 1-18 shows the trend of video in communication.

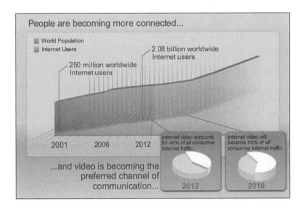

Figure 1-18 Use of Video on the Internet Is Growing.

Both consumers and businesses are driving this change. Video is becoming a key requirement for effective collaboration as organizations extend across geographical and cultural boundaries. Video users now demand the ability to view any content, on any device, anywhere.

Businesses are also recognizing the role of video to enhance the human network. The growth of media, and the new uses to which it is being put, is driving the need to integrate audio and video into many forms of communication. The audio conference will coexist with the video conference. Collaboration tools designed to link distributed employees will integrate desktop video to bring teams closer together.

There are many drivers and benefits for including a strategy for using video. Each organization is unique. The exact mix, and the nature of the drivers for adopting video, will vary from organization to organization, and by business function. Marketing, for example, may focus on globalization and fast-changing consumer tastes, while the focus of the Chief Information Officer (CIO) may be on cost savings by reducing travel costs of employees who need to meet face-to-face.

Cloud Computing (1.4.1.7)

Cloud computing is the use of computing resources (hardware and software) that are delivered as a service over a network. A company uses the hardware and software in the cloud and pays a service fee to the cloud provider.

Local computers no longer have to do all the "heavy lifting" when it comes to running network applications. The network of computers that make up the cloud handles them instead. The hardware and software requirements of the user are decreased. The user's computer must interface with the cloud using software, which may be a web browser, and the cloud's network takes care of the rest.

Cloud computing is another global trend changing the way organizations access and store data. Cloud computing uses cloud-based services to reduce costs and improve business processes. Cloud computing encompasses any subscription-based or pay-per-use service, in real time over the Internet, that extends the capabilities of IT without requiring investment in new infrastructure, training new personnel, or licensing new software. These services are available on demand and delivered economically to any device anywhere in the world without compromising security or function.

Cloud computing helps enterprise IT shift spending from large, one-time capital expenditures to ongoing operating expenses. It also allows enterprise IT to share cloud solution assets and provide dynamic, on-demand delivery of services to the enterprise as a whole.

Cloud computing offers the following potential benefits:

- **Organizational flexibility:** Users can access the information anytime and any-place using a web browser.

- **Agility and rapid deployment:** The IT department can focus on delivering the tools to mine, analyze, and share the information and knowledge from databases, files, and people.

- **Reduced cost of infrastructure:** Technology is moved from on site to a cloud provider, eliminating the cost of hardware and applications.

- **Refocus of IT resources:** Cost savings of hardware and applications can be applied elsewhere.

- **Creation of new business models:** Applications and resources are easily accessible, so companies can react quickly to customer needs. This helps them set strategies to promote innovation while potentially entering new markets.

Types of Clouds (1.4.1.8)

There are four primary types of clouds:

- **Public clouds:** Cloud-based applications and services offered in a public cloud are made available to the general population. Services may be free or may be offered on a pay-per-use model, such as paying for online storage. A public cloud uses the Internet to provide services.

- **Private clouds:** Cloud-based applications and services offered in a private cloud are intended for a specific organization or entity, such as the government. A private cloud can be set up using the organization's private network, though this can be expensive to build and maintain. A private cloud can also be managed by an outside organization with strict access security.

- **Custom clouds:** These are clouds built to meet the needs of a specific industry, such as healthcare or media. Custom clouds can be private or public.

- **Hybrid clouds:** A hybrid cloud is made up of two or more clouds (for example, part custom and part public), where each part remains a distinctive object but both parts are connected using a single architecture. Individuals on a hybrid cloud would be able to have degrees of access to various services based on user access rights.

Data Centers (1.4.1.9)

Cloud computing is possible because of data centers. A *data center* is a facility used to house computer systems and associated components, including

- Redundant data communications connections

- High-speed virtual servers (sometimes referred to as server farms or server clusters)

- Redundant storage systems (typically use SAN technology)

- Redundant or backup power supplies

- Environmental controls (e.g., air conditioning, fire suppression)

- Security devices

A data center can occupy one room of a building, one or more floors, or an entire building. Modern data centers make use of cloud computing and virtualization to efficiently handle large data transactions. Virtualization is the creation of a virtual version of something, such as a hardware platform, operating system (OS), storage device, or network resources. Whereas a physical computer is an actual discrete device, a virtual machine consists of a set of files and programs running on an actual physical system. Unlike multitasking, which involves running several programs on the same OS, virtualization runs several different OSs in parallel on a single CPU. This drastically reduces administrative and cost overheads.

Data centers are typically very expensive to build and maintain. For this reason, only large organizations use privately built data centers to house their data and provide services to users. For example, a large hospital may own a separate data center where patient records are maintained electronically. Smaller organizations that cannot afford to maintain their own private data center can reduce the overall cost of ownership by leasing server and storage services from a larger data center organization in the cloud.

Network Security (1.4.2)

This section explores how securing a network is becoming an increasingly complex task.

Security Threats (1.4.2.1)

Network security is an integral part of computer networking. As new technologies and trends emerge, so too must the protections that organizations use. Network security requirements must take into account the BYOD environment, the collaboration applications, video requirements, and cloud computing needs. Network security must be able to secure the corporate data while still allowing for the quality of service that is expected of each technology.

Securing a network involves protocols, technologies, devices, tools, and techniques to secure data and mitigate threats. Many external network security threats today are spread over the Internet. The most common external threats to networks include

- **Viruses, worms, and Trojan horses:** Malicious software and arbitrary code running on a user device

- **Spyware and adware:** Software installed on a user device that secretly collects information about the user

- **Zero-day attack, also called zero-hour attack:** An attack that occurs on the first day that a vulnerability becomes known

- **Hacker attack:** An attack by a knowledgeable person using software or network vulnerabilities to exploit devices or network resources

- **Denial of service attack:** An attack designed to slow or crash applications and processes on a network device

- **Data interception and theft:** An attack to capture private information from an organization's network

- **Identity theft:** An attack to steal the login credentials of a user in order to access private data

It is equally important to consider internal threats. There have been many studies that show that the most common data breaches happen because of employees. This can be attributed to lost or stolen devices, accidental misuse by employees, and even malicious insiders. With the evolving BYOD strategies, corporate data is much more vulnerable. Therefore, when developing a security policy, it is important to address both external and internal security threats. Figure 1-19 depicts threats from internal and external sources.

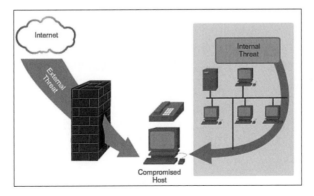

Figure 1-19 Network Threats

Security Solutions (1.4.2.2)

No single solution can protect the network from the variety of threats that exist. For this reason, security should be implemented in multiple layers, using more than one security solution. If one security component fails to identify and protect the network, others still stand.

The network security implementation for a corporate network usually consists of many components built into the network to monitor and filter traffic. Ideally, all components work together, which minimizes maintenance and improves security.

Network security components for a home or small office network should include, at a minimum, the following:

- **Antivirus and antispyware:** To protect user devices from malicious software.

- **Firewall filtering:** To block unauthorized access to the network. This may include a host-based firewall system that is implemented to prevent unauthorized access to the host device, or a basic filtering service on the home router to prevent unauthorized access from the outside world into the network.

Larger networks and corporate networks often have additional security requirements:

- **Dedicated firewall system:** To provide more advanced firewall capability that can filter large amounts of traffic with more granularity

- **Access control lists (ACL):** To further filter access and traffic forwarding

- **Intrusion prevention system (IPS):** To identify fast-spreading threats, such as zero-day or zero-hour attacks

- **Virtual private network (VPN):** To provide secure access to remote workers

Network security requirements must take into account the network environment, as well as the various applications and the computing requirements. Both home environments and businesses must be able to secure their data, while still allowing for the quality of service that is expected of each technology. Additionally, the security solution implemented must be adaptable to the growing and changing trends of the network.

The study of network security threats and mitigation techniques starts with a clear understanding of the underlying switching and routing infrastructure used to organize network services.

Interactive Graphic

Activity 1.4.2.3: Network Security Terminology

Go to the online course to perform this practice activity.

Network Architectures (1.4.3)

This section explores network architectures and how they evolve to handle new technologies.

Cisco Network Architectures (1.4.3.1)

The role of the network has changed from a data-only network to a system that enables the connections of people, devices, and information in a media-rich, converged network environment.

In order for networks to function efficiently and grow, the network must be built upon a standard architecture. The *network architecture* refers to the devices, connections, and products that are integrated to support the necessary technologies and applications. A well-planned network technology architecture helps to ensure that any device can be connected across any combination of network, increases cost efficiency by integrating network security and management, and improves business processes.

With the constant evolution of networks, Cisco has updated its enterprise architectures and frameworks and has created the following three enterprise architectures to address the new network trends, as shown in Figure 1-20:

- Borderless networks architecture

- Collaboration architecture

- Data center and virtualization architecture

These three enterprise technology architectures can be implemented separately, or combined.

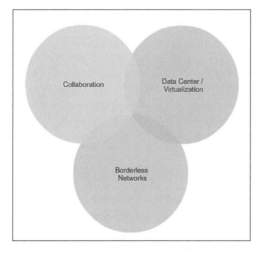

Figure 1-20 Three Cisco Network Architectures

Cisco Borderless Network (1.4.3.2)

The Cisco Borderless Network Architecture is a network solution that enables organizations and individuals to connect securely, reliably, and seamlessly to the corporate network in a BYOD environment.

This architecture separates the network functions into four areas of responsibility:

- **Cisco Borderless End Point/User Services:** Connects the various devices to provide access to network services. Devices that can connect to the borderless network can range from PCs to tablets and smartphones.

- **Cisco Borderless Network Services:** Optimizes the network connection and includes wireless access, secure access to corporate assets, and video performance optimization.

- **Cisco Borderless Network Systems:** Spans an organization from initial device network access to connecting devices to the cloud.

- **Cisco Borderless Infrastructure:** Supports services and systems with an infrastructure of scalable and resilient hardware and software.

The borderless network architecture supports a highly secure, high-performing network that is accessible to a wide range of devices. It needs to be flexible enough to scale in its support for future growth in terms of business expansion, including BYOD, mobility, and cloud computing, and must be able to support the growing requirements for online voice and video.

Collaboration Architecture (1.4.3.3)

To help organizations meet expanding collaboration needs, Cisco provides a collaboration architecture consisting of four categories of collaboration products:

- **TelePresence:** Provides next-generation video conferencing, where everyone, everywhere can be face-to-face and more effective through the most natural and lifelike communications experience available.

- **Collaboration Applications:** Stay connected and productive with voice, video, and web conferencing; messaging; mobile applications; and enterprise social software. For example, Cisco WebEx Meetings enables users to create and attend web conference calls. Users can meet to present ideas, share desktops, work on files together, and collaborate with others. Callers can see one another using webcams, and meetings can be recorded for people who are unable to attend.

- **Customer Collaboration:** Creates the foundation for positive customer service, a primary factor in building a stronger business. An example of this is the Cisco SocialMiner social media customer care solution. It can help companies proactively respond to customers and prospects communicating through public social media networks such as Twitter, Facebook, and other public forums or blogging sites.

- **Unified Communications:** View, optimize, and manage the entire communications system from one screen. With Cisco Unified Communications, organizations can seamlessly manage voice, video, mobility, and presence services between IP endpoints, media-processing devices, Voice over IP (VoIP) gateways, mobile devices, and multimedia applications.

Data Center Architecture (1.4.3.4)

The Cisco Unified Data Center is a complete data center infrastructure architecture that combines computing, networking, security, virtualization, and management solutions in a framework that delivers outstanding performance for physical and virtualized business applications. It is uniquely capable of providing the kind of simplicity, performance, and security that IT departments demand as they transition from physical to virtual to cloud environments.

The Cisco Unified Data Center incorporates three main data center technologies:

- **Cisco Unified Computing:** Integrates computing, networking, and storage resources to provide a unique, open, managed system that can scale to hundreds of server blades and thousands of desktops on virtual machines. Cisco Unified Computing reduces infrastructure costs, and can be deployed nearly 90 percent more quickly than traditional server platforms.

- **Cisco Unified Fabric:** Flexible network solutions deliver network services to servers, storage, and applications, providing transparent convergence, scalability, and sophisticated intelligence using Cisco Nexus and Catalyst switches.

- **Cisco Unified Management:** Provides the framework for IT service-creation and self-service capabilities, enabling IT to operate more efficiently and to more quickly offer new services to the business.

CCNA (1.4.3.5)

The three Cisco architectures previously discussed are built on an infrastructure of scalable and resilient hardware and software. Components of the architectures come together to build network systems that span your organization from network access to the cloud, and provide organizations with the services they need.

At the foundation of all three of these architectures, and in fact, at the foundation of the Internet itself, are routers and switches. Routers and switches transport data, voice, and video communications, allow for wireless access, and provide for security. After a basic network infrastructure with routing and switching is built, organizations can grow their network over time, adding features and functionality in an integrated solution.

As the use of these integrated, expanding networks increases, so does the need for training for individuals who implement and manage network solutions. This training must begin with the routing and switching foundation. Achieving Cisco Certified Network Associate (CCNA) certification is the first step in helping an individual prepare for a career in networking.

CCNA certification validates an individual's ability to install, configure, operate, and troubleshoot medium-size routed and switched networks, including implementation and verification of connections to remote sites in a WAN. This CCNA curriculum includes lessons that address the basic mitigation of security threats, introduction to wireless networking concepts and terminology, and performance-based skills. This CCNA curriculum also includes the use of various protocols, such as Internet Protocol (IP), Open Shortest Path First (OSPF), Serial Line Interface Protocol (SLIP), Frame Relay, VLANs, Ethernet, access control lists (ACLs), and others.

This course helps set the stage for networking concepts and basic routing and switching configurations and is a start on your path for CCNA certification.

Lab 1.4.3.6: Researching IT and Networking Job Opportunities

In this lab you will research job opportunities and reflect on that research.

Summary (1.5)

This section reviews the key networking concepts explained in this chapter.

Class Activity 1.5.1.1: Draw Your Concept of the Internet Now

In this activity you will use the knowledge you have acquired throughout Chapter 1, and the modeling activity document that you prepared at the beginning of this chapter.

Networks and the Internet have changed the way we communicate, learn, work, and even play.

Networks come in all sizes. They can range from simple networks consisting of two computers, to networks connecting millions of devices.

The Internet is the largest network in existence. In fact, the term *Internet* means a network of networks. The Internet provides the services that enable us to connect and communicate with our families, friends, and coworkers.

The network infrastructure is the platform that supports the network. It provides the stable and reliable channel over which communication can occur. It is made up of network components, including end devices, intermediate devices, and network media.

Networks must be reliable. This means the network must be fault tolerant and scalable, provide quality of service, and ensure security of the information and resources on the network. Network security is an integral part of computer networking, regardless of whether the network is limited to a home environment with a single connection to the Internet or is as large as a corporation with thousands of users. No single solution can protect the network from the variety of threats that exist. For this reason, security should be implemented in multiple layers, using more than one security solution.

The network infrastructure can vary greatly in terms of size, number of users, and number and types of services that are supported on it. The network infrastructure must grow and adjust to support the way the network is used. The routing and switching platform is the foundation of any network infrastructure.

This chapter focused on networking as a primary platform for supporting communication. The next chapter will introduce you to the Cisco Internetwork Operating System (IOS) used to enable routing and switching in a Cisco network environment.

Practice

The following activities provide practice with the topics introduced in this chapter. The Labs and Class Activities are available in the companion *Network Basics Lab Manual* (978-1-58713-313-8). The Packet Tracer Activities PKA files are found in the online course.

Class Activities

Class Activity 1.0.1.2: Draw Your Concept of the Internet

Class Activity 1.5.1.1: Draw Your Concept of the Internet Now

Labs

Lab 1.2.1.3: Researching Converged Network Services

Lab 1.1.1.8: Researching Network Collaboration Tools

Lab 1.3.3.3: Mapping the Internet

Lab 1.4.3.6: Researching IT and Networking Job Opportunities

Packet Tracer
☐ Activity

Packet Tracer Activity

Packet Tracer Activity 1.3.4.4: Network Representation

Check Your Understanding

Complete all the review questions listed here to test your understanding of the topics and concepts in this chapter. The appendix, "Answers to the 'Check Your Understanding' Questions," lists the answers.

1. Which of the following is an example of QoS?

    A. Data arrives via different physical media.

    B. Intermediate devices deliver all packets along the same physical route.

    C. Different types of traffic are delivered according to planned priority.

    D. An intermediate device fails and traffic is rerouted and delivered reliably.

2. Fill in the blanks of the sentence with the best terms from the following list (not all of which will be used): *fault tolerance, security, QoS, data integrity, and scalability.*

   The network designer for the small bank needed to plan for the network to double in size over 5 years, requiring her to allow for ____. Of course, all information needed to be kept confidential and safe, so she incorporated __ into the design. She accounted for ___ when she ensured packets arrived with minimal loss or delay, and accounted for ___ by making sure the network would recover quickly if there was a hardware failure.

3. Which type of communications allows for dynamic routing over multiple paths and adaptation to failures in a network?

   A. Circuit switching

   B. QoS

   C. Leased fiber lines for packet delivery

   D. Packet-switched, connectionless data communications

4. Employees of an insurance company accessing company data on restricted local-area and wide-area networks is an example of using a(n)

   A. Internet

   B. Extranet

   C. Intranet

   D. BYOD nets

5. An organization that allows employees to use their own tablets and notebook computers in a secure environment has implemented which type of network?

   A. WAN

   B. BYOD

   C. QoS

   D. Intranet

6. A group of movie critics posting a recording of their weekly radio show about movies is an example of

   A. Podcasting

   B. Webhosting

   C. Blogging

   D. A wiki

7. When instructors provide common space on a computer to create and share documents they can access on their mobile devices or desktops, they are using:

   A. Podcasts

   B. Instant messaging

   C. Social media

   D. Collaboration tools

8. The complexity of a message can affect successful communication across a network. The level of complexity in a message is considered a(n):

   A. Switching factor

   B. External factor

   C. Internal factor

   D. Routing factor

9. Which of the following describes a converged network?

   A. A network that enables people in different countries to work together in the cloud

   B. A network that allows songs and videos to be shared peer to peer

   C. A network that carries voice, video, and data traffic at the same time

   D. A network that allows secure access to the Internet from inside a firewall

10. A system that allows communications between local networks around the world is a/the

   A. BYOD

   B. Internet

   C. LANs

   D. SAN

11. Which of the following is an intermediary device?

   A. Router

   B. Hand-held device

   C. Security camera

   D. Laptop

12. A group of computers connected to store data is which type of network?

    A. LAN

    B. SAN

    C. BYOD

    D. WAN

13. What is the function of a WLAN?

    A. Wireless connection in a small geographical area

    B. Wired connections in a local-area network

    C. Worldwide communications between local-area networks

    D. Wireless communications across the Internet

14. If there are two DSL customers with consistent line quality, which will have the faster connection speed?

    A. The one closest to the cable company

    B. They will have the same connection speed

    C. The one closest to the central office

    D. The one whose cable modem is on the last mile

15. Which items can be associated with network availability? (Choose three.)

    A. Firewall devices

    B. Antivirus software

    C. Collaboration software

    D. Redundant devices

CHAPTER 2

Configuring a Network Operating System

Objectives

Upon completion of this chapter, you will be able to answer the following questions:

- What is the purpose of Cisco IOS software?

- How is Cisco IOS software used to access and configure network devices?

- What is the command structure of Cisco IOS software?

- How are hostnames configured on a Cisco IOS device using the CLI?

- Which commands are used to save the running configuration?

- How do devices communicate across network media?

- How is an IP address applied to a network device?

- How is connectivity verified between two end devices on a network?

Key Terms

This chapter uses the following key terms. You can find the definitions in the Glossary.

Introduction (2.0.1.1)

Networks are made up of many devices. End-user devices, such as PCs and laptops, are connected to computer networks through network switches, creating the local network. To send packets beyond the local network, network switches connect to network routers. Other devices on a network include wireless access points and security devices, such as firewalls. Each device is very different in hardware, use, and capability. But in all cases, it is the operating system that enables the hardware to function.

Operating systems are used on virtually all end-user and network devices connected to the Internet. End-user devices include devices such as smart phones, tablets, PCs, and laptops. Network devices, or *intermediary devices*, are devices used to transport data across the network. Network devices include switches, routers, wireless access points, and firewalls. The operating system on a network device is known as a network operating system.

The Cisco *Internetwork Operating System (IOS)* is a generic term for the collection of network operating systems used on Cisco networking devices. Cisco IOS is used for most Cisco devices regardless of the type or size of the device.

This chapter will reference a basic network topology, consisting of two switches and two PCs, to demonstrate the use of Cisco IOS.

Class Activity 2.0.1.2: It Is Just an Operating System!

In this activity you will learn about the relationship between text commands in the IOS and the spoken language. To do this you will design a set of commands for specific tasks.

IOS Bootcamp (2.1)

In this section you will learn the essentials of the Cisco IOS.

Cisco IOS (2.1.1)

The Cisco Internetwork Operating System (IOS) is the operating system that runs routers and switches.

Purpose of OS (2.1.1.1)

Network operating systems are in many ways similar to the operating systems of PCs. An operating system performs a number of technical functions "behind the scenes" that enable a user to

- Use a mouse

- View output on a monitor

- Enter text commands

- Select options within a dialog box window

The "behind the scenes" functions for switches and routers are very similar. The IOS on a switch or router provides the network technician with an interface. The technician can enter commands to configure, or program, the device to perform various networking functions. The IOS operational details vary on internetworking devices, depending on the purpose of the device and the features supported.

Cisco IOS is a term that encompasses a number of different operating systems that run on various networking devices. There are many distinct variations of Cisco IOS:

- IOS for switches, routers, and other Cisco networking devices

- IOS numbered versions for a given Cisco networking device

- IOS feature sets providing distinct packages of features and services

Just as a PC may be running Microsoft Windows 8 and a MacBook may be running OS X, a Cisco networking device runs a particular version of the Cisco IOS. The version of IOS is dependent on the type of device being used and the required features. Although all devices come with a default IOS and feature set, it is possible to upgrade the IOS version or feature set in order to obtain additional capabilities.

In this course, you will focus primarily on Cisco IOS Release 15.x.

Location of the Cisco IOS (2.1.1.2)

The IOS file itself is several megabytes in size and is stored in a semi-permanent memory area called flash. Flash memory provides non-volatile storage. This means that the contents of the memory are not lost when the device loses power. Although the contents of flash are not lost during a loss of power, they can be changed or overwritten if needed. This allows the IOS to be upgraded to a newer version or to have new features added without replacing hardware. Additionally, flash can be used to store multiple versions of IOS software at the same time.

In many Cisco devices, the IOS is copied from flash into random-access memory (RAM) when the device is powered on. The IOS then runs from RAM when the device is operating. RAM has many functions, including storing data that is used by the device to support network operations. Running the IOS in RAM increases performance of the device; however, RAM is considered volatile memory because data is lost during a power cycle. A *power cycle* is when a device is purposely or accidently powered off and then powered back on, as shown in Figure 2-1.

The quantity of flash memory and RAM memory required for a given IOS varies dramatically. For the purposes of network maintenance and planning, it is important to determine the flash and RAM requirements for each device, including the maximum flash and RAM configurations. It is possible that the requirements of the newest versions of IOS could demand more RAM and flash than can be installed on some devices.

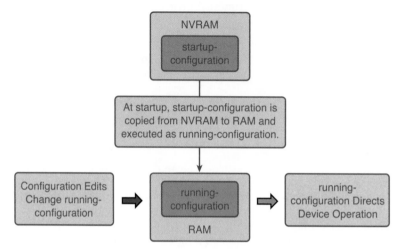

Figure 2-1 NVRAM and RAM Work Together in an IOS Device.

IOS Functions (2.1.1.3)

Cisco IOS routers and switches perform functions that network professionals depend upon to make their networks operate as expected. Major functions performed or enabled by Cisco routers and switches include

- Providing network security
- IP addressing of virtual and physical interfaces
- Enabling interface-specific configurations to optimize connectivity of the respective media
- Routing
- Enabling quality of service (QoS) technologies
- Supporting network management technologies

Each feature or service has an associated collection of configuration commands that allow a network technician to implement it.

The services provided by the Cisco IOS are generally accessed using a command-line interface (CLI).

Video 2.1.1.4:

Video

View the video in the online course for a demonstration of accessing Cisco IOS images.

Accessing a Cisco IOS Device (2.1.2)

In this section you will learn how to access the command-line interface (CLI).

Console Access Method (2.1.2.1)

There are several ways to access the CLI environment, as shown in Figure 2-2. The most common methods are

- Console
- Telnet or SSH
- AUX port

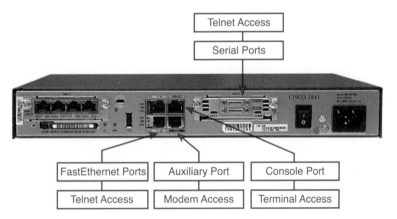

Figure 2-2 Accessing the Cisco IOS on a Device

Console

The console port is a management port that provides *out-of-band access* to a Cisco device. Out-of-band access refers to access via a dedicated management channel that is used for device maintenance purposes only. The advantage of using a console port is that the device is accessible even if no networking services have been configured, such as when performing an initial configuration of the networking device. When performing an initial configuration, a computer running terminal emulation software is connected to the console port of the device using a special cable. Configuration commands for setting up the switch or router can be entered on the connected computer.

The console port can also be used when the networking services have failed and remote access of the Cisco IOS device is not possible. If this occurs, a connection to the console can enable a computer to determine the status of the device. By default, the console conveys the device startup, debugging, and error messages. After the network technician is connected to the device, the network technician can perform any configuration commands necessary using the console session.

For many IOS devices, console access does not require any form of security, by default. However, the console should be configured with passwords to prevent unauthorized device access. In the event that a password is lost, there is a special set of procedures for bypassing the password and accessing the device. The device should also be located in a locked room or equipment rack to prevent unauthorized physical access.

Telnet, SSH, and AUX Access Methods (2.1.2.2)

A console connection requires physical access to a device. In this section you will learn how to remotely access devices.

Telnet

Telnet is a method for remotely establishing a CLI session of a device, through a virtual interface, over a network. Unlike the console connection, Telnet sessions require active networking services on the device. The network device must have at least one active interface configured with an Internet address, such as an IPv4 address. Cisco IOS devices include a Telnet server process that enables users to enter configuration commands from a Telnet client. In addition to supporting the Telnet server process, the Cisco IOS device also contains a Telnet client. This allows a network administrator to telnet from the Cisco device CLI to any other device that supports a Telnet server process.

SSH

The *Secure Shell (SSH)* protocol provides a remote login similar to Telnet, except that it uses more secure network services. SSH provides stronger password authentication than Telnet and uses encryption when transporting session data. This keeps the user ID, password, and the details of the management session private. As a best practice, use SSH instead of Telnet whenever possible.

Most versions of Cisco IOS include an SSH server. In some devices, this service is enabled by default. Other devices require the SSH server to be enabled manually. IOS devices also include an SSH client that can be used to establish SSH sessions with other devices.

AUX

An older way to establish a CLI session remotely is via a telephone dialup connection using a modem connected to the *auxiliary (AUX) port* of a router. Similar to the console connection, the AUX method is also an out-of-band connection and does not require any networking services to be configured or available on the device. In the event that network services have failed, it may be possible for a remote administrator to access the switch or router over a telephone line.

The AUX port can also be used locally, like the console port, with a direct connection to a computer running a terminal emulation program. However, the console port is preferred over the AUX port for troubleshooting because it displays startup, debugging, and error messages by default.

Note

Cisco Catalyst switches do not support an auxiliary connection.

Terminal Emulation Programs (2.1.2.3)

There are a number of excellent terminal emulation programs available for connecting to a networking device either by a serial connection over a console port or by a Telnet/SSH connection. Some of these include

- PuTTY
- Tera Term
- SecureCRT
- HyperTerminal
- OS X Terminal

These programs enable you to enhance your productivity by adjusting window sizes, changing font sizes, and changing color schemes.

Interactive Graphic

Activity 2.1.2.4: Accessing Devices

Go to the online course to perform this access method practice activity.

Navigating the IOS (2.1.3)

This section will introduce the different modes of operation in the Cisco IOS.

Cisco IOS Modes of Operation (2.1.3.1)

After a network technician is connected to a device, it is possible to configure it. The network technician must navigate through various modes of the IOS. The Cisco IOS modes are quite similar for switches and routers. The CLI uses a hierarchical structure for the modes.

In hierarchical order from most basic to most specialized, as shown in Figure 2-3, the major modes are

- User executive (user EXEC) mode

- Privileged executive (privileged EXEC) mode

- Global configuration mode

- Other specific configuration modes, such as interface configuration mode

Each mode has a distinctive prompt and is used to accomplish particular tasks with a specific set of commands that are available only to that mode. For example, global configuration mode allows a technician to configure settings on the device that affect the device as a whole, such as configuring a name for the device. However, a different mode is required if the network technician wants to configure security settings on a specific port on a switch, for example. In this case, the network technician must enter interface configuration mode for that specific port. All configurations that are entered in interface configuration mode apply only to that port.

The hierarchical structure can be configured to provide security. Different authentication can be required for each hierarchical mode. This controls the level of access that network personnel can be granted.

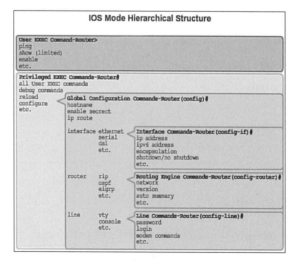

Figure 2-3 IOS Mode Hierarchical Structure with Typical Prompts and Features

Primary Modes (2.1.3.2)

The two primary modes of operation are user EXEC mode and privileged EXEC mode. As a security feature, the Cisco IOS software separates the EXEC sessions into two levels of access. As shown in Figure 2-3, the privileged EXEC mode has a higher level of authority in what it allows the user to do with the device. Refer to this figure as you read about modes in this section and section 2.1.3.3, "Global Configuration Mode and Submodes."

User EXEC Mode

The *user EXEC mode* has limited capabilities but is useful for some basic operations. The user EXEC mode is at the most basic level of the modal hierarchical structure. This mode is the first mode encountered upon entrance into the CLI of an IOS device.

The user EXEC mode allows only a limited number of basic monitoring commands. This is often referred to as view-only mode. The user EXEC level does not allow the execution of any commands that might change the configuration of the device.

By default, there is no authentication required to access the user EXEC mode from the console. However, it is a good practice to ensure that authentication is configured during the initial configuration.

The user EXEC mode is identified by the *CLI prompt* that ends with the > symbol. This is an example that shows the > symbol in the prompt:

```
Switch>
```

Privileged EXEC Mode

The execution of configuration and management commands requires that the network administrator use the *privileged EXEC mode* or a more specific mode in the hierarchy. This means that a user must enter user EXEC mode first, and from there, access privileged EXEC mode.

The privileged EXEC mode can be identified by the prompt ending with the # symbol:

```
Switch#
```

By default, privileged EXEC mode does not require authentication. It is a good practice to ensure that authentication is configured.

Global configuration mode and all other more specific configuration modes can only be reached from the privileged EXEC mode. In the "Getting Basic (2.2)" section of this chapter, we will examine device configuration and some of the configuration modes.

Global Configuration Mode and Submodes (2.1.3.3)

Global configuration mode and interface configuration modes can only be reached from the privileged EXEC mode.

Global Configuration Mode

The primary configuration mode is called *global configuration mode*, or simply global config mode. From global configuration mode, CLI configuration changes are made that affect the operation of the device as a whole. The global configuration mode is accessed before accessing specific configuration modes.

The following CLI command is used to take the device from privileged EXEC mode to the global configuration mode and to allow entry of configuration commands from a terminal:

```
Switch# configure terminal
```

After the command is executed, the prompt changes to show that the switch is in global configuration mode:

```
Switch(config)#
```

Specific Configuration Modes

From the global configuration mode, the user can enter different subconfiguration modes. Each of these modes allows the configuration of a particular part or function of the IOS device. The following list shows a few of them:

- **Interface mode:** To configure one of the network interfaces (Fa0/0, S0/0/0)
- **Line mode:** To configure one of the physical or virtual lines (console, AUX, VTY)

To exit a specific configuration mode and return to global configuration mode, enter **exit** at a prompt. To leave configuration mode completely and return to privileged EXEC mode, enter **end** or use the key sequence **Ctrl-Z**.

Command Prompts

When using the CLI, the mode is identified by the command-line prompt that is unique to that mode. By default, every prompt begins with the device name. Following the name, the remainder of the prompt indicates the mode. For example, the default prompt for the global configuration mode on a switch would be

```
Switch(config)#
```

As commands are used and modes are changed, the prompt changes to reflect the current context, as shown in Figure 2-4.

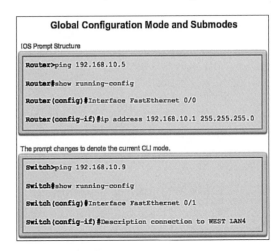

Global Configuration Mode and Submodes

IOS Prompt Structure

```
Router>ping 192.168.10.5

Router#show running-config

Router(config)#Interface FastEthernet 0/0

Router(config-if)#ip address 192.168.10.1 255.255.255.0
```

The prompt changes to denote the current CLI mode.

```
Switch>ping 192.168.10.9

Switch#show running-config

Switch(config)#Interface FastEthernet 0/1

Switch(config-if)#Description connection to WEST LAN4
```

Figure 2-4 Global Configuration Mode and Submodes

Navigating Between IOS Modes (2.1.3.4, 2.1.3.5)

Navigating between modes provides access to different command menus.

Moving Between the User EXEC and Privileged EXEC Modes

The **enable** and **disable** commands are used to change the CLI between the user EXEC mode and the privileged EXEC mode, respectively.

In order to access the privileged EXEC mode, use the **enable** command. The privileged EXEC mode is sometimes called the enable mode.

The syntax for entering the **enable** command is

```
Switch> enable
```

This command is executed without the need for an argument or keyword. After the Enter key is pressed, the prompt changes to

```
Switch#
```

The # at the end of the prompt indicates that the switch is now in privileged EXEC mode.

If password authentication is configured for the privileged EXEC mode, the IOS prompts for the password. For example:

```
Switch> enable
Password: (enter appropriate password)
Switch#
```

The **disable** command is used to return from the privileged EXEC to the user EXEC mode. For example:

```
Switch# disable
Switch>
```

As Figure 2-4 shows, the commands for accessing the privileged EXEC mode and for returning to the user EXEC mode on a Cisco router are identical to those used on a Cisco switch.

Moving from and to Global Configuration Mode and Submodes

To quit from the global configuration mode and return to the privileged EXEC mode, enter the **exit** command.

Note that entering the **exit** command in privileged EXEC mode causes the console session to be ended. That is, upon entering **exit** in privileged EXEC mode, you will be presented with the screen that you see when you first initiate a console session. At this screen you have to press the Enter key to enter user EXEC mode.

To move from any submode of the global configuration mode to the mode one step above it in the hierarchy of modes, enter the **exit** command.

To move from any submode of the privileged EXEC mode to the privileged EXEC mode, enter the **end** command or enter the key combination **Ctrl-Z**.

To move from any submode of the global configuration mode to another "immediate" submode of the global configuration mode, simply enter the corresponding command that is normally entered from global configuration mode. The video demonstration in Activity 2.1.3.6 shows these commands and the resulting prompts.

Video

Video 2.1.3.6:

View the video in the online course for a demonstration of navigation through the different CLI command modes of both a router and a switch using Cisco IOS.

The Command Structure (2.1.4)

Configuring a routing or switching device using the CLI requires specific command syntax.

IOS Command Structure (2.1.4.1)

This section covers the basics of configuring commands in the IOS.

Basic IOS Command Structure

A Cisco IOS device supports many commands. Each IOS command has a specific format or syntax and can only be executed at the appropriate mode. The general syntax for a command is the command followed by any appropriate keywords and arguments. Some commands include a subset of keywords and arguments that provide additional functionality. Commands are used to execute an action, and the keywords are used to identify where or how to execute the command.

As shown in Figure 2-5, the *command* is the initial word or words entered in the command line following the prompt. The commands are not case-sensitive. Following the command are one or more keywords and arguments. After entering each complete command, including any keywords and arguments, press the **Enter** key to submit the command to the command interpreter.

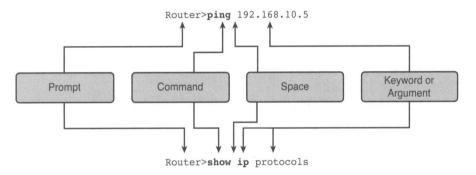

Figure 2-5 Basic IOS Command Structure

The keywords describe specific parameters to the command interpreter. For example, the **show** command is used to display information about the device. This command has various keywords that must be used to define what particular output should be displayed. For example:

```
Switch# show running-config
```

The command **show** is followed by the keyword **running-config**. The keyword specifies that the running configuration is to be displayed as the output.

IOS Command Conventions

A command might require one or more arguments. Unlike a keyword, an *argument* is generally not a predefined word. An argument is a value or variable defined by the user. To determine the keywords and arguments required for a command, refer to the command syntax. The syntax provides the pattern or format that must be used when entering a command.

For instance, the syntax for using the **description** command is

```
Switch(config-if)# description string
```

As shown in the syntax, boldface text indicates commands and keywords that are typed as shown, and italic text indicates an argument for which you supply the value. For the **description** command, the argument is a string value. The string value can be any text string of up to 80 characters.

Therefore, when applying a description to an interface with the **description** command, enter a line such as this:

```
Switch(config-if)# description MainHQ Office Switch
```

The command is **description** and the user-defined argument is **MainHQ Office Switch**.

The following examples demonstrate some conventions used to document and use IOS commands.

For the **ping** command, the syntax is

```
Switch> ping IP address
```

Following is an example with values:

```
Switch> ping 10.10.10.5
```

The command is **ping** and the user-defined argument is **10.10.10.5**.

Similarly, the syntax for entering the **traceroute** command is

```
Switch> traceroute IP address
```

Following is an example with values:

```
Switch> traceroute 192.168.254.254
```

The command is **traceroute** and the user-defined argument is **192.168.254.254**.

Cisco IOS Command Reference (2.1.4.2)

The Cisco IOS *Command Reference* is a collection of online documentation that describes in detail the IOS commands used on Cisco devices. The Command Reference is the ultimate source of information for a particular IOS command, similar to how a dictionary is the ultimate source for information about a particular word.

The Command Reference is a fundamental resource that network engineers use to check various characteristics of a given IOS command. Some of the more common characteristics are

- **Syntax:** The most detailed version of the syntax for a command that can be found

- **Default:** The manner in which the command is implemented on a device with a default configuration

- **Mode:** The configuration mode on the device where the command is entered

- **History:** Descriptions of how the command is implemented relative to the IOS version

- **Usage Guidelines:** Guidelines describing specifically how to implement the command

- **Examples:** Useful examples that illustrate common scenarios that use the command

How To

To navigate to the Command Reference and find a particular command, follow these steps:

Step 1.   Go to www.cisco.com.

Step 2.   Click Support.

Step 3.   Click Networking Software (IOS & NX-OS).

Step 4.   Click 15.2M&T (for example).

Step 5.   Click Reference Guides.

Step 6.   Click Command References.

Step 7.   Click the particular technology that encompasses the command you are referencing.

Step 8.   Click the link on the left that alphabetically matches the command you are referencing.

Step 9.   Click the link for the command.

For example, the **description** command is found under the *Cisco IOS Interface and Component Command Reference*, under the link for the alphabetic range *D through E.*

download complete PDF versions of the command references for a particular technom links on the page that you reach after completing Step 7.

Context-Sensitive Help (2.1.4.3)

The IOS has several forms of help available:

- Context-sensitive help

- Command syntax check

- Hot keys and shortcuts

This section discusses context-sensitive help. The following two sections discuss the other forms of help, in turn.

The *context-sensitive help* provides a list of commands and the arguments associated with those commands within the context of the current mode. To access context-sensitive help, enter a question mark, **?**, at any prompt. There is an immediate response without the need to use the Enter key.

One use of context-sensitive help is to get a list of available commands. You can use the list when you are unsure of the name for a command or you want to see if the IOS supports a particular command in a particular mode.

For example, to list the commands available at the user EXEC level, enter a question mark, **?**, at the Switch> prompt.

Another use of context-sensitive help is to display a list of commands or keywords that start with a specific character or characters. After entering a character sequence, if a question mark is immediately entered, without a space, the IOS will display a list of commands or keywords for this context that start with the characters that were entered.

For example, enter **sh?** to get a list of commands that begins with the character sequence **sh**.

A final type of context-sensitive help is used to determine which options, keywords, or arguments are matched with a specific command. When entering a command, enter a space followed by a **?** to determine what can or should be entered next.

As shown in Figure 2-6, after typing the command **clock set 19:50:00**, you can enter the **?** to determine the additional options or keywords available for this command.

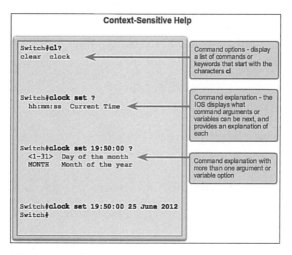

Figure 2-6 Context-Sensitive Help

Command Syntax Check (2.1.4.4)

When a command is submitted by pressing the Enter key, the command-line interpreter parses the command from left to right to determine what action is being requested. The IOS generally only provides negative feedback, as shown in Figure 2-7. If the interpreter understands the command, the requested action is executed and the CLI returns to the appropriate prompt. However, if the interpreter cannot understand the command being entered, it will provide feedback describing what is wrong with the command:

- Ambiguous command
- Incomplete command
- Incorrect command

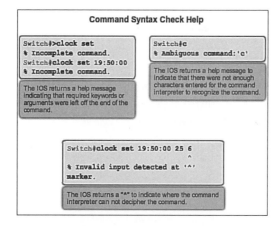

Figure 2-7 Syntax Error Messages

Hot Keys and Shortcuts (2.1.4.5)

The IOS CLI provides hot keys and shortcuts that make configuring, monitoring, and troubleshooting easier.

The following shortcuts are worthy of special note:

- **Tab:** Completes a partially typed command or keyword
- **Ctrl-Z:** Exits the configuration mode and returns to user EXEC mode
- **Ctrl-R:** Redisplays a line
- **Down Arrow:** Allows the user to scroll forward through former commands
- **Up Arrow:** Allows the user to scroll backward through former commands
- **Ctrl-Shift-6:** Interrupts an IOS process such as **ping** or **traceroute**
- **Ctrl-C:** Exits the configuration mode or aborts the current command
- **Ctrl-A:** Moves to the beginning of the line
- **Ctrl-E:** Moves to the end of the line

Some of these shortcuts are examined in more detail next, followed by a quick overview of abbreviating commands and keywords.

Tab

It is possible to use the **Tab** key to complete the remainder of abbreviated commands and parameters if the abbreviation contains enough letters to be different from any other currently available commands or parameters. When enough of the command or keyword has been entered to appear unique, press the **Tab** key and the CLI will display the rest of the command or keyword.

This is a good technique to use when you are learning because it enables you to see the full word used for the command or keyword.

Ctrl-R

Use **Ctrl-R** to redisplay the previous line typed. For example, you may find that the IOS is returning a message to the CLI just as you are typing a line. You can use **Ctrl-R** to refresh the line and avoid having to retype it.

In this example, a message regarding a failed interface is returned in the middle of a command:

```
Switch# show mac-
16w4d: %LINK-5-CHANGED: Interface FastEthernet0/10, changed state to down
16w4d: %LINEPROTO-5-UPDOWN: Line protocol on Interface FastEthernet0/10, changed
  state to down
```

To redisplay to the line that you were typing, use **Ctrl-R**:

```
Switch# show mac
```

Ctrl-Z

Use **Ctrl-Z** to leave any configuration mode and return to privileged EXEC mode. Because the IOS has a hierarchical mode structure, you may find yourself several levels down. Rather than exit each mode individually, use **Ctrl-Z** to return directly to the privileged EXEC prompt at the top level.

Up Arrow and Down Arrow

The Cisco IOS software buffers several past commands and characters so that entries can be recalled. The buffer is useful for re-entering commands without retyping.

Key sequences are available to scroll through these buffered commands. Use the **Up Arrow** key (**Ctrl-P**) to display the previously entered commands. Each time you press this key, the next successively older command will be displayed. Use the **Down Arrow** key (**Ctrl-N**) to scroll forward through the history to display the more recent commands.

Ctrl-Shift-6

The escape sequence **Ctrl-Shift-6** interrupts any running process. When an IOS process is initiated from the CLI, such as a ping or traceroute, the command runs until it is complete or is interrupted. While the process is running, the CLI is unresponsive. To interrupt the output and interact with the CLI, press **Ctrl-Shift-6**.

Ctrl-C

Press **Ctrl-C** to interrupt the entry of a command and exit the configuration mode. This is useful after entering a command that needs to be cancelled.

Abbreviated Commands or Keywords

Commands and keywords can be abbreviated to the minimum number of characters that identify a unique selection. For example, the **configure** command can be abbreviated to **conf** because **configure** is the only command that begins with **conf**. An abbreviation of **con** will not work because more than one command begins with **con**.

Keywords can also be abbreviated.

As another example, **show interfaces** can be abbreviated like this:

```
Switch# show interfaces
Switch# show int
```

You can abbreviate both the command and the keywords; for example:

```
Switch# sh int
```

IOS Examination Commands (2.1.4.6)

In order to verify and troubleshoot network operation, you must examine the operation of the devices. The basic examination command is the **show** command.

There are many different variations of this command. As you develop more skill with the IOS, you will learn to use and interpret the output of the **show** commands. Use the **show ?** command to get a list of available commands in a given context, or mode.

A typical *show command* can provide information about the configuration, operation, and status of parts of a Cisco switch or router. Figure 2-8 highlights some of the common IOS commands.

In this course, we focus mostly on basic **show** commands.

A very commonly used **show** command is **show interfaces**. This command displays statistics for all interfaces on the device. To view the statistics for a specific interface, enter the **show interfaces** command followed by the specific interface type and slot/port number. For example:

```
Switch# show interfaces fastethernet 0/1
```

Some other **show** commands frequently used by network technicians include

- **show startup-config**: Displays the saved configuration located in NVRAM

- **show running-config**: Displays the contents of the currently running configuration file

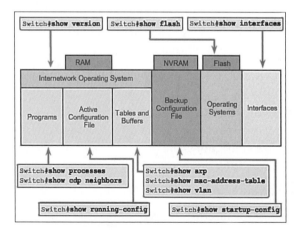

Figure 2-8 *show* Commands Can Provide Information About the Operation and Status of Parts of a Cisco Router or Switch.

The More Prompt

When a command returns more output than can be displayed on a single screen, the **--More--** prompt appears at the bottom of the screen. When a **--More--** prompt appears, press the **Spacebar** to view the next portion of output. To display only the next line, press the **Enter** key. If any other key is pressed, the output is cancelled and you are returned to the prompt.

The show version Command (2.1.4.7)

One of the most commonly used commands on a switch or router is

```
Switch# show version
```

This command displays information about the currently loaded IOS version, along with hardware and device information. If you are logged into a router or switch remotely, the **show version** command is an excellent means of quickly finding useful summary information about the particular device to which you are connected. Some of the information points shown from this command are

- **Software version:** IOS software version (stored in flash)

- **Bootstrap version:** Bootstrap version (stored in Boot ROM)

- **System up-time:** Time since last reboot

- **System restart info:** Method of restart (e.g., power cycle, crash)

- **Software image name:** IOS filename stored in flash

- **Router type and processor type:** Model number and processor type

- **Memory type and allocation (shared/main):** Main Processor RAM and Shared Packet I/O buffering

- **Software features:** Supported protocols/feature sets

- **Hardware interfaces:** Interfaces available on the device

- **Configuration register:** Sets bootup specifications, console speed setting, and related parameters

Packet Tracer Activity 2.1.4.8: Navigating the IOS

In this activity you will practice skills necessary for navigating the Cisco IOS, including different user access modes, various configuration modes, and common commands you use on a regular basis. You will also practice accessing the context-sensitive help by configuring the **clock** command.

Lab 2.1.4.9: Establishing a Console Session with Tera Term

In this lab you will access a Cisco switch through the console port. Then you will display and configure basic device settings.

Getting Basic (2.2)

In this section you will learn the basic commands for configuring routers and switches.

Hostnames (2.2.1)

Devices need to be identifiable to network administrators. This section covers assigning names to switches and routers.

Why the Switch (2.2.1.1)

As discussed, Cisco switches and Cisco routers have many similarities. They support similar operating systems, similar command structures, and many of the same commands. In addition, both devices have identical initial configuration steps.

However, a Cisco IOS switch is one of the simplest devices that can be configured on a network. This is because there are no configurations that are required prior to the device functioning. At its most basic, a switch can be plugged in with no configuration and will still switch data between connected devices.

A switch is also one of the fundamental devices used in the creation of a small network. By connecting two PCs to a switch, those PCs will instantly have connectivity with one another.

For these reasons, the remainder of this chapter will focus on the creation of a small, two-PC network connected via a switch configured with initial settings. Initial settings include setting a name for the switch, limiting access to the device configuration, configuring banner messages, and saving the configuration.

Device Names (2.2.1.2)

When configuring a networking device, one of the first steps is to configure a unique device name, or hostname. Hostnames appear in CLI prompts, can be used in various authentication processes between devices, and should be used on topology diagrams.

If a device name is not explicitly configured, a factory-assigned default device name is used by Cisco IOS. The default name for a Cisco IOS switch is "Switch."

Imagine if an internetwork had several switches that were all named with the default name Switch. This could create considerable confusion during network configuration and maintenance. When accessing a remote device using SSH, it is important to have confirmation that you are connected to the proper device, as shown in Figure 2-9. If all devices were left with their default names, it would be difficult to identify that the proper device is connected.

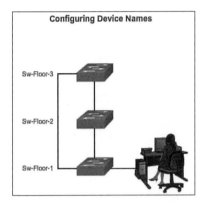

Figure 2-9 Names Make Network Devices Easy to Identify for Configuration and Maintenance Purposes.

By choosing names wisely, it is easier to remember, discuss, document, and identify network devices. To name devices in a consistent and useful way requires the establishment of a naming convention that spans the company or, at least, the location. It is a good practice to create the naming convention at the same time as the addressing scheme to allow for continuity within an organization.

Some guidelines for naming conventions are that names should

- Start with a letter
- Contain no spaces
- End with a letter or digit
- Use only letters, digits, and dashes
- Be less than 64 characters in length

The hostnames used in the device IOS preserve capitalization and lowercase characters. Therefore, you can capitalize a name as you ordinarily would. This contrasts with most Internet naming schemes, where uppercase and lowercase characters are treated identically.

Hostnames (2.2.1.3)

A *hostname* allows a device to be identified by network administrators over a network or the Internet.

Applying Names Example

Let's use the example previously shown in Figure 2-9 of three switches connected together in a network, spanning three different floors. To create a naming convention for switches, take into consideration the location and the purpose of the devices. In Figure 2-9 we have named the three switches as Sw-Floor-1, Sw-Floor-2, and Sw-Floor-3. In the network documentation, we would include these names, and the reasons for choosing them, to ensure continuity in our naming convention as devices are added.

After the naming convention has been identified, the next step is to apply the names to the devices using the CLI.

Configuring Hostnames (2.2.1.4)

From the privileged EXEC mode, access the global configuration mode by entering the **configure terminal** command:

```
Switch# configure terminal
```

After the command is executed, the prompt will change to

```
Switch(config)#
```

In the global configuration mode, enter the hostname (again using the example shown in Figure 2-9):

```
Switch(config)# hostname Sw-Floor-1
```

After the command is executed, the prompt will change to

```
Sw-Floor-1 (config)#
```

Notice that the hostname appears in the prompt. To exit global configuration mode, use the **exit** command.

Always make sure that your documentation is updated each time a device is added or modified. Identify devices in the documentation by their location, purpose, and address.

Note

To undo the effects of a command, preface the command with the **no** keyword.

For example, to remove the name of a device, use

```
Sw-Floor-1 (config)# no hostname
Switch(config)#
```

Notice that the **no hostname** command caused the switch to revert to the default hostname of Switch.

Interactive
Graphic

Activity 2.2.1.4: Entering the Hostname

Go to the online course to practice entering a hostname on a switch.

Limiting Access to Device Configurations (2.2.2)

This section describes methods for securing a network device.

Securing Device Access (2.2.2.1)

Physically limiting access to network devices by placing them in closets and locked racks is good practice; however, passwords are the primary defense against unauthorized access to network devices. Every device, even home routers, should have locally configured passwords to limit access. Later, we will introduce how to strengthen security by requiring a username along with a password. For now, we will present basic security precautions using only passwords.

As discussed previously, the IOS uses hierarchical modes to help with device security. As part of this security enforcement, the IOS can accept several passwords to allow different access privileges to the device.

The passwords introduced here are

- *Enable password*: Limits access to the privileged EXEC mode
- *Enable secret*: Encrypted, limits access to the privileged EXEC mode
- *Console password*: Limits device access using the console connection
- *VTY password*: Limits device access over Telnet

As good practice, use different authentication passwords for each of these levels of access. Although logging in with multiple and different passwords is inconvenient, it is a necessary precaution to properly protect the network infrastructure from unauthorized access.

Additionally, use strong passwords that are not easily guessed. The use of weak or easily guessed passwords continues to be a security issue in many facets of the business world.

Consider these key points when choosing passwords:

- Use passwords that are more than 8 characters in length

- Use a combination of upper- and lowercase letters, numbers, special characters, and/or numeric sequences in passwords

- Avoid using the same password for all devices

- Avoid using common words, such as "password" or "administrator," because these are easily guessed

Note

In most of the labs in this course, we will be using simple passwords such as **cisco** or **class**. These passwords are considered weak and easily guessable and should be avoided in a work environment. We only use these passwords for convenience in a classroom setting or to illustrate configuration examples.

Securing Privileged EXEC Access (2.2.2.2)

To secure privileged EXEC access, use the **enable secret** password command. An older, less secure variation of this command is the **enable password** password command. Although either of these commands can be used to establish authentication before access to privileged EXEC (enable) mode is permitted, it is recommended to use the **enable secret** command. The *enable secret* command provides greater security because the password is encrypted.

Following is an example command to set passwords:

```
Switch(config)# enable secret class
```

The example in Figure 2-10 illustrates how a password is not requested when the **enable** command is first used. Next, the **enable secret class** command is configured, which secures privileged EXEC access. Notice that, for security reasons, the password is not displayed when it is being entered.

```
Sw-Floor-1>enable
Sw-Floor-1#
Sw-Floor-1#conf terminal
Sw-Floor-1(config)#enable secret class
Sw-Floor-1(config)#exit
Sw-Floor-1#
Sw-Floor-1#disable
Sw-Floor-1>enable
Password:
Sw-Floor-1#
```

Figure 2-10 Limiting Device Access with an Encrypted Password

Securing User EXEC Access (2.2.2.3)

The console port of network devices must be secured, at a bare minimum, by requiring the user to supply a strong password. This reduces the chance of unauthorized personnel physically plugging a cable into the device and gaining device access.

The following commands are used in global configuration mode to set a password for the console line:

```
Switch(config)# line console 0
Switch(config-line)# password cisco
Switch(config-line)# login
```

From global configuration mode, the command **line console 0** is used to enter line configuration mode for the console. The **0** is used to represent the first (and in most cases only) console interface.

The second command, **password cisco**, specifies a password for the console line.

The **login** command configures the switch to require authentication upon login. When login is enabled and a password is set, the console user will be prompted to enter a password before gaining access to the CLI.

VTY Password

The vty lines allow access to a Cisco device via Telnet. By default, many Cisco switches support up to 16 vty lines, numbered 0 to 15. The number of vty lines supported on a Cisco router varies with the type of router and the IOS version. However, five is the most common number of vty lines configured. These lines are numbered 0 to 4 by default, though additional lines can be configured. A password needs to be set for all available vty lines. The same password can be set for all connections. However, it is often desirable that a unique password be set for one line to provide a fall-back for administrative entry to the device if the other connections are in use.

Following are some example commands used to set a password on vty lines:

```
Switch(config)# line vty 0 15
Switch(config-line)# password cisco
Switch(config-line)# login
```

By default, the IOS includes the **login** command on the vty lines. This prevents Telnet access to the device without authentication. If, by mistake, the **no login** command is set, which removes the requirement for authentication, unauthorized persons could connect across the network to the line using Telnet. This would be a major security risk.

Figure 2-11 illustrates securing the user EXEC access on the console and Telnet lines.

```
Sw-Floor-1(config)#line console 0
Sw-Floor-1(config-line)#password cisco
Sw-Floor-1(config-line)#login
Sw-Floor-1(config-line)#exit
Sw-Floor-1(config)#
Sw-Floor-1(config)#line vty 0 15
Sw-Floor-1(config-line)#password cisco
Sw-Floor-1(config-line)#login
Sw-Floor-1(config-line)#
```

Figure 2-11 Limiting Device Console and Telnet Access

Encrypting Password Display (2.2.2.4)

Another useful command prevents passwords from showing up as plain text when viewing the configuration files. This is the **service password-encryption** command.

This command causes the encryption of passwords to occur when a password is configured. The **service password-encryption** command applies weak encryption to all unencrypted passwords. This encryption applies only to passwords in the configuration file, not to passwords as they are sent over media. The purpose of this command is to keep unauthorized individuals from viewing passwords in the configuration file.

If you execute the **show running-config** or **show startup-config** command prior to the **service password-encryption** command being executed, the unencrypted passwords are visible in the configuration output. The **service password-encryption** command can then be executed and the encryption will be applied to the passwords. After the encryption has been applied, removing the encryption service does not reverse the encryption.

Interactive Graphic

Activity 2.2.2.4: Entering Password Encryption

Go to the online course to practice password encryption on a switch.

Banner Messages (2.2.2.5)

Although requiring passwords is one way to keep unauthorized personnel out of a network, it is vital to provide a method for declaring that only authorized personnel should attempt to gain entry into the device. To do this, add a banner to the device output.

Banners can be an important part of the legal process in the event that someone is prosecuted for breaking into a device. Some legal systems do not allow prosecution, or even the monitoring of users, unless a notification is visible.

The exact content or wording of a banner depends on the local laws and corporate policies. Here are some examples of information to include in a banner:

- "Use of the device is specifically for authorized personnel."

- "Activity may be monitored."

- "Legal action will be pursued for any unauthorized use."

Because banners can be seen by anyone who attempts to log in, the message must be worded very carefully. Any wording that implies that a login is "welcome" or "invited" is not appropriate. If a person disrupts the network after gaining unauthorized entry, proving liability will be difficult if there is the appearance of an invitation.

The creation of banners is a simple process; however, banners should be used appropriately. When a banner is utilized, it should never welcome someone to the device. It should detail that only authorized personnel are allowed to access the device. Further, the banner can include scheduled system shutdowns and other information that affects all network users.

The IOS provides multiple types of banners. One common banner is the message of the day (MOTD). It is often used for legal notification because it is displayed to all connected terminals.

Configure MOTD using the **banner motd** command from global configuration mode.

The *banner motd* command requires the use of delimiters to identify the content of the banner message. The **banner motd** command is followed by a space and a delimiting character. Then, one or more lines of text are entered to represent the banner message. A second occurrence of the delimiting character denotes the end of the message. The delimiting character can be any character as long as it does not occur in the message. For this reason, symbols such as **#** are often used.

The syntax to configure a MOTD from global configuration mode is

```
Switch(config)# banner motd # message #
```

After the command is executed, the banner will be displayed on all subsequent attempts to access the device until the banner is removed.

The example in Figure 2-12 illustrates a banner configured with the delimiting "#" symbol. Notice how the banner is now displayed when accessing the switch.

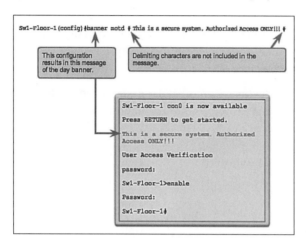

Figure 2-12 Configuring the Banner MOTD

Saving Configurations (2.2.3)

This section describes how to manage configuration files.

Configuration Files (2.2.3.1)

The running configuration file reflects the current configuration applied to a Cisco IOS device. It contains the commands used to determine how the device operates on the network, as shown in Figure 2-13. Modifying a running configuration affects the operation of a Cisco device immediately.

The running configuration file is stored in the working memory of the device, or RAM. This means that the running configuration file is temporarily active while the Cisco device is running (powered on). However, if power to the device is lost or if the device is restarted, all configuration changes will be lost unless they have been saved.

After making changes to a running configuration file, consider these distinct options:

- Return the device to its original configuration

- Remove all configurations from the device

- Make the changed configuration the new startup configuration

The startup configuration file reflects the configuration that will be used by the device upon reboot. The startup configuration file is stored in NVRAM. When a network device has been configured and the running configuration has been modified, it is important to save those changes to the startup configuration file. Doing so prevents changes from being lost due to power failure or a deliberate restart.

Before committing to the changes, use the appropriate **show** commands to verify the device's operation. As shown in Figure 2-13, the **show running-config** command can be used to see a running configuration file. When the changes are verified to be correct, use the **copy running-config startup-config** command at the privileged EXEC mode prompt. The command to save the running configuration to the startup configuration file is

```
Switch# copy running-config startup-config
```

After being executed, the running configuration file updates the startup configuration file.

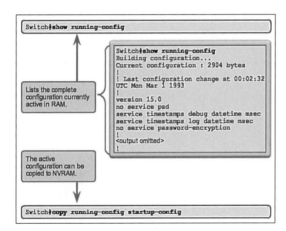

Figure 2-13 Saving the Running Configuration

If the changes made to the running configuration do not have the desired effect, it may become necessary to restore the device to its previous configuration. Assuming that we have not overwritten the startup configuration with the changes, we can replace the running configuration with the startup configuration. This is best done by restarting the device using the **reload** command at the privileged EXEC mode prompt.

When initiating a reload, the IOS will detect that the running configuration has changes that were not saved to the startup configuration. A prompt will appear, asking you whether to save the changes made. To discard the changes, enter **n** or **no**.

An additional prompt will appear to confirm the reload. To confirm, press **Enter**. Pressing any other key will abort the process.

For example:

```
Switch# reload
System configuration has been modified. Save? [yes/no]: n
Proceed with reload? [confirm]
*Apr 13 01:34:15.758: %SYS-5-RELOAD: Reload requested by console. Reload Reason:
Reload Command.
System Bootstrap, Version 12.3(8r)T8, RELEASE SOFTWARE (fc1)
Technical Support: http://www.cisco.com/techsupport
Copyright (c) 2004 by cisco Systems, Inc.
PLD version 0x10
GIO ASIC version 0x127
c1841 processor with 131072 Kbytes of main memory
Main memory is configured to 64 bit mode with parity disabled
```

If undesired changes are saved to the startup configuration, it may be necessary to clear all the configurations. This requires erasing the startup configuration and restarting the device.

The startup configuration is removed by using the **erase startup-config** command.

To erase the startup configuration file, use **erase NVRAM:startup-config** or **erase startup-config** at the privileged EXEC mode prompt:

```
Switch# erase startup-config
```

After the command is issued, the switch will prompt you for confirmation:

```
Erasing the nvram filesystem will remove all configuration files!
Continue? [confirm]
```

Confirm is the default response. To confirm and erase the startup configuration file, press **Enter**. Pressing any other key will abort the process.

Caution

Exercise caution when using the **erase** command. This command can be used to erase any file in the device. Improper use of the command can erase the IOS itself or another critical file.

On a switch, you must also issue the **delete vlan.dat** command in addition to the **erase startup-config** command in order to return the device to its default "out-of-the-box" configuration (comparable to a factory reset):

```
Switch# delete vlan.dat
Delete filename [vlan.dat]?
Delete flash:vlan.dat? [confirm]
Switch# erase startup-config
```

```
Erasing the nvram filesystem will remove all configuration files! Continue? [con-
    firm]
[OK]
Erase of nvram: complete
Switch#
```

After removing the startup configuration from NVRAM (and deleting the vlan.dat file in the case of a switch), reload the device to remove the current running configuration file from RAM. The device will then load the default startup configuration that was originally shipped with the device into the running configuration.

Activity 2.2.3.1: Saving the Running Configuration to RAM

Go to the online course to practice the configuration activity. The activity is located on the second graphic on the page.

Capturing Text (2.2.3.2)

Capturing text means to create a copy of output to analyze or save a backup copy.

Backup Configurations with Text Capture

In addition to saving running configurations to the startup configuration, configuration files can also be saved and archived to a text document. This sequence of steps ensures that a working copy of the configuration files is available for editing or reuse later.

Configuration files can be saved and archived to a text document using Tera Term. The steps are as follows:

Step 1. On the File menu, click **Log.**

Step 2. Choose the location. Tera Term will begin capturing text.

Step 3. After capture has been started, execute the **show running-config** or **show startup-config** command at the privileged EXEC prompt. Text displayed in the terminal window will be placed into the chosen file.

Step 4. When the capture is complete, click **Close** in the Tera Term: Log window.

Step 5. View the output to verify that it was not corrupted.

Restoring Text Configurations

A configuration file can be copied from storage to a device. When copied into the terminal, the IOS executes each line of the configuration text as a command. The file will probably require editing before copying. It is advisable to change the encrypted passwords to plain text and remove the parameter, either the number 5 or 7, which specifies that the password is encrypted. Non-command text such as "--More--" and IOS messages must be removed.

Further, at the CLI, the device must be set at the global configuration mode to receive the commands from the text file being copied.

When using Tera Term, the steps are

Step 1.   Edit text to remove non-commands and save.

Step 2.   On the File menu, click **Send File.**

Step 3.   Locate the file to be copied into the device and click **Open.**

Step 4.   Tera Term will paste the file into the device.

The text in the file will be applied as commands in the CLI and become the running configuration on the device. This is a convenient method for manually configuring a device.

Packet Tracer Activity 2.2.3.3: Configuring Initial Switch Settings

In this activity you will perform basic switch configurations. You will secure access to the CLI and console ports using encrypted and plain text passwords. You will also learn how to configure messages for users logging into the switch.

Address Schemes (2.3)

Network administrators need to plan their networks so that devices have IP addresses that are in the correct networks and subnets.

Ports and Addresses (2.3.1)

In this section you will learn about assigning IP addresses to devices on the network.

IP Addressing of Devices (2.3.1.1)

The use of *IP addresses*, whether IPv4 or IPv6, is the primary means of enabling devices to locate one another and establish end-to-end communication on the Internet. In fact, in any internetwork, IP addresses are essential for devices to communicate from source to destination and back.

Each end device on a network must be configured with IP addresses. Some examples of end devices are

- Computers (work stations, laptops, file servers, web servers)

- Network printers

- VoIP phones

- Security cameras

- Smart phones

- Mobile handheld devices (such as wireless barcode scanners)

The structure of an IPv4 address is called dotted decimal notation and is represented with four decimal numbers between 0 and 255. IPv4 addresses are numbers assigned to individual devices connected to a network. They are logical in nature, in that they provide information about the location of the device.

With the IP address, a *subnet mask* is also necessary. A subnet mask is a special type of IPv4 address that, coupled with the IP address, determines which particular subnet of a larger network the device is a member of.

IP addresses can be assigned to both physical ports and virtual interfaces on devices. A *virtual* interface means that there is no physical hardware on the device associated with it.

Interfaces and Ports (2.3.1.2)

Network communications depend on end-user device interfaces, networking device interfaces, and the cables that connect them.

Each physical interface has specifications, or standards, that define it; a cable connecting to the interface must be designed to match the physical standards of the interface. Types of *network media* include twisted-pair copper cables, fiber-optic cables, coaxial cables, and wireless. Different types of network media have different features and benefits. Not all network media has the same characteristics and is appropriate for the same purpose. Some of the differences between various types of media include

- Distance the media can successfully carry a signal

- Environment in which the media is to be installed

- Amount of data the media can transmit and the speed at which it can transmit it

- Cost of the media and installation

Not only does each link on the Internet require a specific network media type, but each link also requires a particular network technology. *Ethernet* is the most common local-area network (LAN) technology used today. Ethernet ports are found on end-user devices, switch devices, and other networking devices that can physically connect to the network using a cable. For a cable to connect devices using an Ethernet port, the cable must have the correct connector, an RJ-45.

Cisco IOS switches have physical ports for devices to connect to, but also have one or more switch virtual interfaces (SVIs). These are *virtual interfaces* because there is no physical hardware on the device associated with it; an SVI is created in software. The virtual interface provides a means to remotely manage a switch over a network using IPv4. Each switch comes with one SVI appearing in the default configuration "out-of-the-box." The default SVI is interface VLAN1.

Addressing Devices (2.3.2)

Network devices can be configured with IP addresses on both physical and virtual interfaces.

Configuring a Switch Virtual Interface (2.3.2.1)

To access the switch remotely, an IP address and a subnet mask must be configured on the SVI:

- **IP address:** Together with the subnet mask, uniquely identifies the end device on the internetwork

- **Subnet mask:** Determines which part of a larger network is used by an IP address

For now the focus is IPv4; later you will explore IPv6.

You will learn the meaning behind all of these IP addresses soon, but for now the point is to quickly configure the switch to support remote access. The following command enables IP connectivity to S1, using IP address 192.168.10.2:

- **Switch(config)#interface vlan 1:**
  This command navigates to the interface configuration mode from the global configuration mode

- **Switch(config-if)#ip address 192.168.10.2 255.255.255.0:**
  This command configures the IP address and subnet mask for the switch (this is just one of many possible combinations for an IP address and subnet mask)

- **Switch(config-if)#no shutdown:**
  This command administratively enables the interface to an active state

After these commands are configured, the switch has all the IP elements ready for communication over the network.

Note

The switch will still need to have one or more physical ports configured, as well as the vty lines, to complete the configuration that enables remote management of the switch.

**Interactive
Graphic**

Activity 2.3.2.1: Configuring a Switch Virtual Interface

Go to the online course to perform this practice activity.

Manual IP Address Configuration for End Devices (2.3.2.2)

In order for an end device to communicate over the network, it must be configured with the correct IP address information. Much like an SVI, the end device must be configured with an IP address and subnet mask. This information is configured on the PC settings.

All of these settings must be configured on an end device in order for it to properly connect to the network. This information is configured under the PC network settings. In addition to IP address and subnet mask information, it is also possible to configure default gateway and DNS server information.

The *default gateway* address is the IP address of the router interface used for network traffic to exit the local network. The default gateway is an IP address that is often assigned by the network administrator and is used when traffic must be routed to another network.

The *DNS server* address is the IP address of the Domain Name System (DNS) server, which is used to translate IP addresses to web addresses, such as www.cisco.com. All devices on the Internet are assigned and reached via an IP address. However, it is easier for people to remember names over numbers. Therefore, websites are given names for simplicity. The DNS server is used to maintain the mapping between the IP addresses and names of various devices.

Automatic IP Address Configuration for End Devices (2.3.2.3)

IP address information can be entered into the PC manually, or using *Dynamic Host Configuration Protocol (DHCP)*. DHCP allows end devices to have IP information automatically configured.

DHCP is a technology that is used in almost every business network. The best way to understand why DHCP is so popular is by considering all the extra work that would have to take place without it.

DHCP enables automatic IPv4 address configuration for every end device in a network with DHCP enabled. Imagine the amount of time that would be consumed if every time you connected to the network you had to manually enter the IP address, the subnet mask, the default gateway, and the DNS server. Multiply that by every user and every one of their devices on the network and you see the problem.

DHCP is an example of technology at its best. One of the primary purposes of any technology is to make it easier for users to perform the tasks they want to do or need to do. With DHCP, the end user walks into the area served by a given network, plugs in an Ethernet cable or enables a wireless connection, and they are immediately allocated the necessary IPv4 information required to fully communicate over the network.

To configure DHCP on a Windows PC, you only need to select Obtain an IP Address Automatically and Obtain DNS Server Address Automatically under the Internet Protocol (TCP/IP Properties window). Your PC will be assigned information from an IP address pool and associated IP information set up on the DHCP server.

It is possible to display the IP configuration settings on a Windows PC by using the **ipconfig** command at the command prompt. The output will show the IP address, subnet mask, and gateway that the PC received from the DHCP server.

Interactive Graphic	**Activity 2.3.2.3: Verifying Windows IP Configuration** Go to the online course to perform this practice activity.

IP Address Conflicts (2.3.2.4)

If a static (manual) IP address is defined for a network device (for example, a printer), and then a DHCP server is installed, duplicate IP address conflicts may occur between the network device and a PC obtaining automatic IP addressing information from the DHCP server. The conflict also may occur if you manually define a static IP address to a network device during a network failure involving the DHCP server; after the network failure resolves and the DHCP server becomes accessible over the network, the conflict arises.

To resolve such an IP addressing conflict, convert the network device with the static IP address to a DHCP client; or on the DHCP server, exclude the static IP address of the end device from the DHCP scope.

The second solution requires that you have administrative privileges on the DHCP server and that you are familiar with configuring DHCP on a server.

You may also encounter IP addressing conflicts when manually configuring IP on an end device in a network that only uses static IP addresses. In this case you must determine which IP addresses are available on the particular IP subnet and configure accordingly. This case illustrates why it is so important for a network administrator to maintain detailed documentation, including IP address assignments, for end devices.

> **Note**
>
> Usually, static IP addresses are used with servers and printers in a small- to medium-sized business network, whereas employee devices use DHCP-allocated IP address information.

Packet Tracer Activity 2.3.2.5: Implementing Basic Connectivity

In this activity you will first perform basic switch configurations. Then you will implement basic connectivity by configuring IP addressing on switches and PCs. When the IP addressing configuration is complete, you will use various **show** commands to verify configurations and use the **ping** command to verify basic connectivity between devices.

Verifying Connectivity (2.3.3)

After the addressing scheme is applied to devices, it is important to test all network connections.

Test the Loopback Address on an End Device (2.3.3.1)

The **ping** command is used to verify the internal IP configuration on a local host. This test is accomplished by using the **ping** command on a reserved address called the *loopback* (127.0.0.1). The loopback address is defined by the TCP/IP protocol as a reserved address that routes packets back to the host.

You enter **ping** commands into a command line on the local host using the following syntax:

```
C:\> ping 127.0.0.1
```

The reply from this command would look something like this:

```
Reply from 127.0.0.1: bytes=32 time<1ms TTL=128
Reply from 127.0.0.1: bytes=32 time<1ms TTL=128
Reply from 127.0.0.1: bytes=32 time<1ms TTL=128
Reply from 127.0.0.1: bytes=32 time<1ms TTL=128
Ping statistics for 127.0.0.1:
Packets: Sent = 4, Received = 4, Lost = 0 (0% loss),
Approximate round trip times in milli-seconds:
Minimum = 0ms, Maximum = 0ms, Average = 0ms
```

The result indicates that four test packets of 32 bytes each were sent and returned from host 127.0.0.1 in a time of less than 1 ms. This successful ping request verifies that the network interface card, drivers, and the TCP/IP implementation are all functioning correctly.

Activity 2.3.3.1: Testing the Loopback Address

Go to the online course to perform this practice activity. The activity is located on the second graphic on the page.

Testing the Interface Assignment (2.3.3.2)

In the same way that you use commands and utilities to verify a host configuration, you use commands to verify the interfaces of intermediary devices. The IOS provides commands to verify the operation of router and switch interfaces.

Verifying the Switch Interfaces

Examining S1 and S2, in Activity 2.3.3.2, you use the **show ip interface brief** command to verify the condition of the switch interfaces. The IP address assigned to the VLAN 1 interface on S1 is 192.168.10.2. The IP address assigned to the VLAN 1 interface on S2 is 192.168.10.3. The physical interfaces F0/1 and F0/2 on S1 are operational, as are the physical interfaces F0/1 and F0/2 on S2.

Activity 2.3.3.2: Verifying VLAN Interface Assignment

Go to the online course to practice verification of a VLAN interface.

Testing End-to-End Connectivity (2.3.3.3)

After device interfaces are up on a network, the next step is to test connectivity to other network devices.

Testing PC-to-Switch Connectivity

The **ping** command can be used on a PC, just as on a Cisco IOS device. Activity 2.3.3.3 shows that a ping from PC1 to the IP address of the S1 VLAN 1 interface, 192.168.10.2, should be successful.

Testing End-to-End Connectivity

In Activity 2.3.3.3 you will also test connectivity between two PCs.

The IP address of PC1 is 192.168.10.10, with subnet mask 255.255.255.0, and default gateway 192.168.10.1.

The IP address of PC2 is 192.168.10.11, with subnet mask 255.255.255.0, and default gateway 192.168.10.1.

A ping from PC1 to PC2 should also be successful. A successful ping from PC1 to PC2 verifies end-to-end connectivity in the network!

Activity 2.3.3.3: Testing PC-to-Switch Connectivity

Go to the online course to perform the connectivity tests.

Lab 2.3.3.4: Building a Simple Network

In this lab you will set up an Ethernet network topology, configure the hosts on the network, and then configure and verify basic switch settings.

Lab 2.3.3.5: Configuring a Switch Management Address

In this lab you will configure a basic network device, then verify and test network connectivity.

Summary (2.4)

Class Activity 2.4.4.1: Tutor Me

You and a partner will role play, and you will explain the concepts in this chapter to your partner, who you should assume has never worked with Cisco devices before.

Packet Tracer Activity 2.4.1.2: Skills Integration Challenge

In this scenario you are a recently hired LAN technician and your network manager has asked you to demonstrate your ability to configure a small LAN. Your tasks include configuring initial settings on two switches using the Cisco IOS and configuring IP address parameters on host devices to provide end-to-end connectivity.

Cisco IOS is a term that encompasses a number of different operating systems that run on various networking devices. The technician can enter commands to configure, or program, the device to perform various networking functions. Cisco IOS routers and switches perform functions that network professionals depend upon to make their networks operate as expected.

The services provided by the Cisco IOS are generally accessed using a command-line interface (CLI), which is accessed by either the console port, the AUX port, or through Telnet or SSH. When connected to the CLI, network technicians can make configuration changes to Cisco IOS devices. The Cisco IOS is designed as a modal operating system, which means a network technician must navigate through various hierarchical modes of the IOS. Each mode supports different IOS commands.

The Cisco IOS Command Reference is a collection of online documents that describe in detail the IOS commands used on Cisco devices, such as Cisco IOS routers and switches.

Cisco IOS routers and switches support a similar modal operating system, support similar command structures, and support many of the same commands. In addition, both devices have identical initial configuration steps when implementing them in a network.

This chapter introduced the Cisco IOS. It detailed the various modes of the Cisco IOS and examined the basic command structure that is used to configure it. It also walked through the initial settings of a Cisco IOS switch device, include setting a name, limiting access to the device configuration, configuring banner messages, and saving the configuration.

The next chapter explores how packets are moved across the network infrastructure and introduces you to the rules of packet communication.

Practice

The following activities provide practice with the topics introduced in this chapter. The Labs and Class Activities are available in the companion *Network Basics Lab Manual* (978-1-58713-313-8). The Packet Tracer Activities PKA files are found in the online course.

Class Activities

Class Activity 2.0.1.2: It Is Just an Operating System!

Class Activity 2.4.4.1: Tutor Me

Labs

Lab 2.1.4.9: Establishing a Console Session with Tera Term

Lab 2.3.3.4: Building a Simple Network

Lab 2.3.3.5: Configuring a Switch Management Address

Packet Tracer Activities

Packet Tracer Activity 2.1.4.8: Navigating the IOS

Packet Tracer Activity 2.2.3.3: Configuring Initial Switch Settings

Packet Tracer Activity 2.3.2.5: Implementing Basic Connectivity

Packet Tracer Activity 2.4.1.2: Packet Tracer - Skills Integration Challenge

Check Your Understanding

Complete all the review questions listed here to test your understanding of the topics and concepts in this chapter. The appendix, "Answers to the 'Check Your Understanding' Questions," lists the answers.

1. Which of the following do not meet standard hostname conventions for the Cisco CLI? (Choose three.)

   A. Michelles Router

   B. Router-A-Tom

   C. Hiros1stRouter

   D. greta'srouter

   E. MariasReallyFantasticRouter

   F. 1st Routerlogin

2. When a device using the default Cisco IOS configuration boots, which of the following sequences occurs?

   A. The IOS is copied from RAM to flash.

   B. The IOS is copied from NVRAM to flash.

   C. The IOS is copied from flash to RAM.

   D. The IOS is copied from RAM to NVRAM.

3. Which method is used to access a router or switch that has no network configuration?

   A. Use an Ethernet cable to connect the PC to the Ethernet port

   B. Use a console cable to connect to the console port

   C. Use a serial cable to establish an SSH connection

   D. Use a serial cable to connect to the auxiliary (AUX) port

4. When a device using the Cisco IOS boots (in this example, a running configuration file is present), which of the following sequences will usually occur?

   A. The running configuration is copied from NVRAM to flash.

   B. The startup configuration is copied from flash to RAM.

   C. The running configuration is copied from RAM to NVRAM.

   D. The startup configuration is copied from NVRAM to RAM.

5. Which is true about the user executive mode in the CLI?

   A. It has the most restricted list of available commands.

   B. It can only be accessed from the privileged executive mode.

   C. Debugging and other details on network use are available.

   D. By default it requires authentication for access.

6. Which prompt is used in global configuration mode?

   A. Router1(config-line)#

   B. Router1#

   C. Router1(config)#

   D. Router1(config-if)#

7. Entering the **enable** command

   A. Will put the router or switch into global configuration mode.

   B. Always requires a password.

C. Will take the router or switch out of interface configuration mode and into enable configuration mode.

D. Will put the router or switch into user EXEC mode.

8. Entering the **exit** command at the Router1(config-router)# prompt will result in which prompt?

A. Router1>

B. Router1#

C. Router1(config)#

D. Router1(config-if)#

9. Which best describes the *argument* element of a command?

A. The appropriate mode for a command.

B. A predefined command in the CLI.

C. A command variable determined by the user.

D. It precedes a keyword in the command structure.

10. When a command is followed by a space and a question mark, such as **show ?**, what should be the output from the switch or router?

A. A list of the previous ten commands.

B. A list of valid subcommands appropriate to the current user level.

C. Information about who is logged into the current session.

D. The command is invalid; there should be no space between the command and the question mark (**show?**).

11. When an IOS process is running, which hot keys will allow for it to be interrupted?

A. **Up Arrow**

B. **Ctrl-X**

C. **Ctrl-Shift-6**

D. **Ctrl-C**

12. Which is true about scrolling through output with keyboard shortcuts? (Choose two.)

A. The Down Arrow key moves the screen down ten lines.

B. The Enter key scrolls down one line.

C. The Right Arrow key scrolls one page.

D. The Spacebar scrolls down one page.

13. Which command line will provide information about the IOS currently in use?

    A. Router1(config)# **show version**

    B. Router1# **show version**

    C. Router1(config)# **show ios**

    D. Router1# **show running config**

14. When two computers are plugged into a switch on which no configuration changes have been made, which conditions will be true? (Choose two.)

    A. The switch will be ready to use in a LAN.

    B. The switch must first be given a name and an IP address using either the AUX port or the console port.

    C. The hostname of the switch will be "Switch."

    D. The default password must be entered before the computers can communicate.

15. An administrator configured a switch with the hostname "Server_Room Switch_1" and appropriate passwords. When he took the switch to the server room to put into service, the switch booted, but the new configuration could not be found. The default configuration was present. What is a likely reason for this?

    A. The IOS in flash was lost when power was removed.

    B. The administrator did not enter the **copy running-config startup-config** command.

    C. The administrator incorrectly typed the new password and was locked out of the switch.

    D. The startup configuration was not saved to the flash memory.

16. What is the purpose of DHCP?

    A. To resolve Internet names into IP addresses

    B. To test connectivity from a PC to the Internet

    C. To assign IP addresses to devices when they connect to a network

    D. To secure devices against unauthorized access

CHAPTER 3

Network Protocols and Communications

Objectives

Upon completion of this chapter, you will be able to answer the following questions:

- Why are protocols necessary in communication?

- What is the purpose of adhering to a protocol suite?

- What is the role of standards organizations in establishing protocols for network interoperability?

- How are the TCP/IP model and the OSI model used to facilitate standardization in the communication process?

- Why have RFCs become the process for establishing standards?

- What is the RFC process?

- How does data encapsulation allow data to be transported across the network?

- How do local hosts access local resources on a network?

- How do local hosts access remote resources on a network?

Key Terms

This chapter uses the following key terms. You can find the definitions in the Glossary.

protocols   page 103

protocol suite   page 104

Internet Protocol   page 106

Network Access Protocols   page 106

Transmission Control Protocol/IP (TCP/IP)   page 106

standards organizations   page 110

Internet Society (ISOC)   page 110

Internet Architecture Board (IAB)   page 110

Internet Engineering Task Force (IETF)   page 110

Internet Research Task Force (IRTF)   page 110

Institute of Electrical and Electronics Engineers (IEEE)   page 111

International Organization for Standardization (ISO)   page 112

Open Systems Interconnection (OSI) reference model   page 112

Internet Corporation for Assigned Names and Numbers (ICANN)   page 113

Internet Assigned Numbers Authority (IANA)   page 113

OSI model   page 115

TCP/IP protocol model   page 116

Request for Comments (RFC)   page 118

segmentation   page 124

Introduction (3.0.1.1)

More and more, it is networks that connect us. People communicate online from everywhere. Conversations in boardrooms spill into instant message chat sessions, and online debates continue at school. New services are being developed daily to take advantage of the network.

Rather than developing unique and separate systems for the delivery of each new service, the network industry as a whole has adopted a developmental framework that allows designers to understand current network platforms, and maintain them. At the same time, this framework is used to facilitate the development of new technologies to support future communications needs and technology enhancements.

Central to this developmental framework is the use of generally accepted models that describe network rules and functions.

Within this chapter you will learn about these models, as well as the standards that make networks work, and how communication occurs over a network.

Class Activity 3.0.1.2: Designing a Communications System

In this activity you will design a communications model in a customer service scenario.

Network Protocols and Standards (3.1)

In this section you will learn about some of the protocols that work together in computer networks.

Protocols (3.1.1)

Protocols for computer communications over networks were agreed upon by groups of computer professionals. The best way to understand how these protocols work is to compare them to communications protocols you use every day.

Protocols: Rules that Govern Communications (3.1.1.1)

All communication, whether it is face-to-face or over a network, is governed by rules called *protocols*. These protocols vary depending on the type of conversation. In our day-to-day personal communication, the rules we use to communicate over one medium, such as a telephone call, are not necessarily the same as the rules for using another medium, such as sending a letter.

Think of how many different rules or protocols govern all the different methods of communication that exist in the world today. For example, consider two people communicating face-to-face. First, they must agree on how they will communicate. If they agree to communicate using voice, they must agree on the language. Then, they must actually have a message to share, and format that message in a way that is understandable. Each of these tasks describes a protocol put in place to accomplish communication. Similarly, successful communication between hosts on a network requires the interaction of many different protocols. A group of interrelated protocols necessary to perform a communication function is called a *protocol suite*. Protocol suites are implemented by hosts and networking devices in software, hardware, or both. ·

One of the best ways to visualize how the protocols within a suite interact is to view the interaction as a stack. A protocol stack shows how the individual protocols within a suite are implemented. The protocols are viewed in terms of layers, with each higher-layer service depending on the functionality defined by the protocols shown in the lower layers. The lower layers of the stack are concerned with moving data over the network and providing services to the upper layers, which are focused on the content of the message being sent. As Figure 3-1 shows, we can use layers to describe the activity occurring in our face-to-face communication example. At the bottom layer, the physical layer, there are two people, each with a voice that can say words out loud. At the second layer, the rules layer, there is an agreement to speak in a common language. At the top layer, the content layer, there are words that are actually spoken. This is the content of the communication.

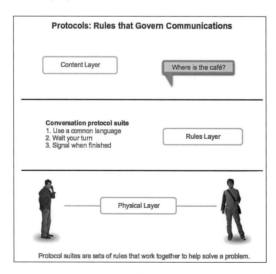

Figure 3-1 Protocol Suites

Were we to witness this conversation, we would not actually see layers floating in space, of course. The use of layers is a model that provides a way to conveniently break a complex task into parts and describe how they work.

Network Protocols (3.1.1.2)

At the human level, some communication rules are formal and others are simply understood based on custom and practice. For devices to successfully communicate, a network protocol suite must describe precise requirements and interactions. Networking protocols define a common format and set of rules for exchanging messages between devices. Some common networking protocols are Internet Protocol (IP), Hypertext Transfer Protocol (HTTP), and Dynamic Host Configuration Protocol (DHCP).

Networking protocols describe the following processes:

- How the message is formatted or structured

- The process by which networking devices share information about pathways with other networks

- How and when error and system messages are passed between devices

- The setup and termination of data transfer sessions

For example, IP defines how a packet of data is delivered within a network or to a remote network. The information in the IPv4 protocol is transmitted in a specific format so that the receiver can interpret it correctly. This protocol is not much different from the protocol used to address an envelope when mailing a letter. The information must adhere to a certain format or else the letter cannot be delivered to the destination by the post office.

Interaction of Protocols (3.1.1.3)

An example of using the protocol suite in network communications is the interaction between a web server and a web client. This interaction uses a number of protocols and standards in the process of exchanging information between the web server and web client. The different protocols work together to ensure that the messages are received and understood by both parties. These protocols can usually be defined by the layer function they perform. Some examples of these protocols are

- **Application layer protocol:** Hypertext Transfer Protocol (HTTP) is a protocol that governs the way a web server and a web client interact. HTTP defines the content and formatting of the requests and responses that are exchanged between the client and server. Both the client and the web server software implement HTTP as part of the application. HTTP relies on other protocols to govern how the messages are transported between the client and server.

- **Transport layer protocol:** Transmission Control Protocol (TCP) is the transport protocol that manages the individual conversations between web servers and web clients. TCP divides the HTTP messages into smaller pieces, called *segments*. These segments are sent between the web server and client processes running at the destination host. TCP is also responsible for controlling the size and rate at which messages are exchanged between the server and the client.

- *Internet Protocol* (**IP**): IP is responsible for taking the formatted segments from TCP, encapsulating them into packets, assigning them the appropriate addresses, and delivering them across the best path to the destination host.

- *Network access protocols*: Network access protocols describe two primary functions: communication over a data link, and the physical transmission of data on the network media. Data-link management protocols take the packets from IP and format them to be transmitted over the media. The standards and protocols for the physical media govern how the signals are sent and how they are interpreted by the receiving clients. An example of a network access protocol is Ethernet.

Protocol Suites (3.1.2)

In the previous section you learned that protocols are designed to perform very specific tasks efficiently, and that groups of protocols that work together to successfully complete the communication process are referred to as protocol suites. This section explores how protocol suites were developed and how they operate.

Protocol Suites and Industry Standards (3.1.2.1)

As stated previously, a protocol suite is a set of protocols that work together to provide comprehensive network communication services. A protocol suite may be specified by a standards organization or developed by a vendor.

The protocols IP, HTTP, and DHCP are all part of the Internet protocol suite known as *Transmission Control Protocol/Internet Protocol (TCP/IP)*. The TCP/IP protocol suite is an open standard, meaning these protocols are freely available to the public, and any vendor is able to implement these protocols on their hardware or in their software.

A standards-based protocol is a process or protocol that has been endorsed by the networking industry and ratified, or approved, by a standards organization. The use of standards in developing and implementing protocols ensures that products from different manufacturers can interoperate successfully. If a protocol is not rigidly observed by a particular manufacturer, their equipment or software may not be able to successfully communicate with products made by other manufacturers.

In data communications, for example, if one end of a conversation is using a protocol to govern one-way communication and the other end is assuming a protocol describing two-way communication, in all probability, no data will be exchanged.

Some protocols are proprietary. Proprietary, in this context, means that one company or vendor controls the definition of the protocol and how it functions. Some proprietary protocols can be used by different organizations with permission from the owner. Others can only be implemented on equipment manufactured by the proprietary vendor. Examples of proprietary protocols are AppleTalk and Novell NetWare.

Several companies may even work together to create a proprietary protocol. It is not uncommon for a vendor (or group of vendors) to develop a proprietary protocol to meet the needs of its customers and later assist in making that proprietary protocol an open standard. For example, Ethernet was a protocol originally developed by Bob Metcalfe at the Xerox Palo Alto Research Center (PARC) in the 1970s. In 1979, Metcalfe formed his own company, 3COM, and worked with Digital Equipment Corporation (DEC), Intel, and Xerox to promote the "DIX" (Digital, Intel, Xerox) standard for Ethernet. In 1985, the Institute of Electrical and Electronics Engineers (IEEE) published the IEEE 802.3 standard that was almost identical to Ethernet. Today, 802.3 is the common standard used on local-area networks (LANs). As another, more recent example, Cisco opened its Enhanced Interior Gateway Routing Protocol (EIGRP) as an informational Request for Comments (RFC) to meet the needs of customers who desire to use the protocol in a multivendor network.

Creation of the Internet and Development of TCP/IP (3.1.2.2)

The IP suite is a suite of protocols required for transmitting and receiving information using the Internet. It is commonly known as TCP/IP because the first two networking protocols defined for this standard were TCP and IP. The open standards–based TCP/IP has replaced other vendor proprietary protocol suites, such as Apple's AppleTalk and Novell's Internetwork Packet Exchange/Sequenced Packet Exchange (IPX/SPX).

The first packet-switched network and the predecessor to today's Internet was the Advanced Research Projects Agency Network (ARPANET), which came to life in 1969 by connecting mainframe computers at four locations. ARPANET was funded by the U.S. Department of Defense for use by universities and research laboratories. Bolt, Beranek and Newman (BBN) was the contractor that did much of the initial development of the ARPANET, including creating the first router, known as an Interface Message Processor (IMP).

In 1973, Robert Kahn and Vinton Cerf began work on TCP to develop the next generation of the ARPANET. TCP was designed to replace ARPANET's current Network Control Program (NCP). In 1978, TCP was divided into two protocols: TCP and IP. Later, other protocols were added to the TCP/IP suite of protocols, including Telnet, FTP, DNS, and many others.

Activity 3.1.2.2: Internet Timeline

Go to the online course and click the blue points on the timeline to see details about the development of other network protocols and applications.

TCP/IP Protocol Suite and Communication Process (3.1.2.3)

Today, the TCP/IP suite includes dozens of protocols.

Activity 3.1.2.3: Protocol Suites.

Go to the online course page 3.1.2.3 and view the first graphic. Click each protocol to view its description. The protocols are organized in layers using the TCP/IP protocol model.

TCP/IP protocols are included in the internet, transport, and application layers to the application layer when referencing the TCP/IP model. The lower-layer protocols in the data link or network access layer are responsible for delivering the IP packet over the physical medium. These lower-layer protocols are developed by standards organizations, such as IEEE.

The TCP/IP protocol suite is implemented as a TCP/IP stack on both the sending and receiving hosts to provide end-to-end delivery of applications over a network. The 802.3 or Ethernet protocols are used to transmit the IP packet over the physical medium used by the LAN.

Video 3.1.2.3:

Click the second and third graphics to access the animations depicting the steps in the communication process.

The following are the steps in the communication process, using an example of a web server transmitting data to a client:

1. The web server's Hypertext Markup Language (HTML) page is the data to be sent.

2. The application protocol HTTP header is added to the front of the HTML data. The header contains various information, including the HTTP version the server is using and a status code indicating it has information for the web client.

3. The HTTP application layer protocol delivers the HTML-formatted web page data to the transport layer. The TCP transport layer protocol is used to manage the individual conversation between the web server and web client.

4. The IP information is added to the front of the TCP information. IP assigns the appropriate source and destination IP addresses. This information is known as an *IP packet*.

5. The Ethernet protocol adds information to both ends of the IP packet, known as a *data link frame*. This frame is delivered to the nearest router along the path toward the web client. This router removes the Ethernet information, analyzes the IP packet, determines the best path for the packet, inserts the packet into a new frame, and sends it to the next neighboring router toward the destination. Each router removes and adds new data link information before forwarding the packet.

6. This data is transported through the internetwork, which consists of media and intermediary devices.

7. The client receives the data link frames that contain the data, and each protocol header is processed and then removed in the opposite order in which it was added. The Ethernet information is processed and removed, followed by the IP protocol information, then the TCP information, and finally the HTTP information.

8. The web page information is passed on to the client's web browser software.

Interactive Graphic

Activity 3.1.2.4: Mapping the Protocols of the TCP/IP Suite

Go to the online course to perform this practice activity.

Standards Organizations (3.1.3)

In this section you will learn about the organizations that define protocol standards.

Open Standards (3.1.3.1)

Open standards encourage competition and innovation. They also guarantee that no single company's product can monopolize the market, or have an unfair advantage over its competition. A good example of this is when purchasing a wireless router for the home. There are many different choices available from a variety of vendors, all of which incorporate standard protocols such as IPv4, DHCP, IEEE 802.3 (Ethernet), and IEEE 802.11 (Wireless LAN). These open standards also allow a client running Apple's OS X operating system to download a web page from a web server running the Linux operating system. This is because both operating systems implement the open standard protocols, such as those in the TCP/IP suite.

Standards organizations are important in maintaining an open Internet with freely accessible specifications and protocols that can be implemented by any vendor. A standards organization may draft a set of rules entirely on its own or, in other cases, select a proprietary protocol as the basis for the standard. If a proprietary protocol is used, the drafting process usually involves the vendor who created the protocol.

Standards organizations are usually vendor-neutral, nonprofit organizations established to develop and promote the concept of open standards.

Standards organizations include

- Internet Society (ISOC)
- Internet Architecture Board (IAB)
- Internet Engineering Task Force (IETF)
- Institute of Electrical and Electronics Engineers (IEEE)
- International Organization for Standardization (ISO)

Each of these organizations is discussed in more detail in the following sections.

ISOC, IAB, and IETF (3.1.3.2)

The *Internet Society (ISOC)* is responsible for promoting open development, evolution, and Internet use throughout the world. ISOC facilitates the open development of standards and protocols for the technical infrastructure of the Internet, including the oversight of the Internet Architecture Board (IAB).

The *Internet Architecture Board (IAB)* is responsible for the overall management and development of Internet standards. The IAB provides oversight of the architecture for protocols and procedures used by the Internet. The IAB consists of 13 members, including the chair of the Internet Engineering Task Force (IETF). IAB members serve as individuals, not as representatives of any company, agency, or other organization.

The mission of the *Internet Engineering Task Force (IETF)* is to develop, update, and maintain Internet and TCP/IP technologies. One of the key responsibilities of the IETF is to produce Request for Comments (RFC) documents, which are a memorandum describing protocols, processes, and technologies for the Internet. The IETF consists of working groups (WGs), the primary mechanism for developing IETF specifications and guidelines. WGs are short term, and after the objectives of the group are met, the WG is terminated. The Internet Engineering Steering Group (IESG) is responsible for the technical management of the IETF and the Internet standards process.

The *Internet Research Task Force (IRTF)* is focused on long-term research related to Internet and TCP/IP protocols, applications, architecture, and technologies. Whereas the IETF focuses on shorter-term issues of creating standards, the IRTF consists of research groups for long-term development efforts. The Internet

Research Steering Group (IRSG) oversees some of the current research groups, which include the Anti-Spam Research Group (ASRG), Crypto Forum Research Group (CFRG), Peer-to-Peer Research Group (P2PRG), and Router Research Group (RRG). Figure 3-2 depicts the organization and responsibilities of Internet engineering and research groups.

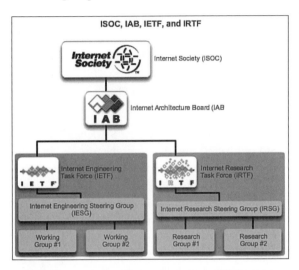

Figure 3-2 ISOC, IAB, IETF, and IRTF Organizations

IEEE (3.1.3.3)

The *Institute of Electrical and Electronics Engineers (IEEE*, pronounced "I-triple-E") is a professional organization for those in the electrical engineering and electronics fields who are dedicated to advancing technological innovation and creating standards. As of 2012, IEEE consists of 38 societies, publishes 130 journals, and sponsors more than 1,300 conferences each year worldwide. The IEEE has over 1,300 standards and projects currently under development.

IEEE has more than 400,000 members in more than 160 countries. More than 107,000 of those members are student members. IEEE provides educational and career enhancement opportunities to promote the skills and knowledge within the electronics industry.

IEEE is one of the leading standard-producing organizations in the world. It creates and maintains standards affecting a range of industries, including power and energy, healthcare, telecommunications, and networking. The IEEE 802 family of standards deals with local-area networks and metropolitan-area networks, including both wired and wireless.

The IEEE 802.3 and IEEE 802.11 standards are significant IEEE standards in computer networking. The IEEE 802.3 standard defines Media Access Control (MAC) for wired Ethernet. This technology is usually for LANs, but also has wide-area network (WAN) applications. The 802.11 standard defines a set of standards for implementing wireless local-area networks (WLANs). This standard defines the Open Systems Interconnection (OSI) physical and data link MAC for wireless communications.

ISO (3.1.3.4)

ISO, the *International Organization for Standardization*, is the world's largest developer of international standards for a variety of products and services. ISO is not an acronym for the organization's name; rather, the ISO term is based on the Greek word "isos," meaning equal. The International Organization for Standardization chose the ISO term to affirm its position as being equal to all countries.

In networking, ISO is best known for its *Open Systems Interconnection (OSI) reference model*. ISO published the OSI reference model in 1984 to develop a layered framework for networking protocols. The original objective of this project was not only to create a reference model but also to serve as a foundation for a suite of protocols to be used for the Internet. This was known as the OSI protocol suite. However, due to the rising popularity of the TCP/IP suite, developed by Robert Kahn, Vinton Cerf, and others, the OSI protocol suite was not chosen as the protocol suite for the Internet. Instead, the TCP/IP protocol suite was selected. The OSI protocol suite was implemented on telecommunications equipment and can still be found in legacy telecommunications networks.

You may be familiar with some of the products that use ISO standards. The ISO file extension is used on many CD images to signify that they use the ISO 9660 standard for their file system. ISO is also responsible for creating standards for routing protocols.

Other Standards Organizations (3.1.3.5)

Networking standards involve several other standards organizations. Some of the more common ones are

- **Electronic Industries Alliance (EIA):** Previously known as the Electronics Industries Association, the EIA is an international standards and trade organization for electronics organizations. The EIA is best known for its standards related to electrical wiring, connectors, and the 19-inch racks used to mount networking equipment.

- **Telecommunications Industry Association (TIA):** The TIA is responsible for developing communications standards in a variety of areas, including radio equipment, cellular towers, Voice over IP (VoIP) devices, satellite communications, and more. Many of its standards are produced in collaboration with the EIA.

- **International Telecommunications Union-Telecommunication Standardization Sector (ITU-T):** The ITU-T is one of the largest and oldest communications standards organizations. The ITU-T defines standards for video compression, Internet Protocol Television (IPTV), and broadband communications, such as a digital subscriber line (DSL). For example, when dialing another country, ITU country codes are used to make the connection.

- *Internet Corporation for Assigned Names and Numbers (ICANN):* ICANN is a nonprofit organization based in the United States that coordinates IP address allocation, the management of domain names used by DNS, and the protocol identifiers or port numbers used by TCP and UDP protocols. ICANN creates policies and has overall responsibility for these assignments.

- *Internet Assigned Numbers Authority (IANA):* IANA is a department of ICANN that is responsible for overseeing and managing IP address allocation, domain name management, and protocol identifiers for ICANN.

Familiarization with the organizations that develop standards used in networking will help you have a better understanding of how these standards create an open, vendor-neutral Internet, and allow you to learn about new standards as they develop.

Lab 3.1.3.6: Researching Networking Standards

In this lab you will research networking standards organizations and note how those organizations formed the Internet we use today.

Interactive Graphic

Activity 3.1.3.7: Standards Body Scavenger Hunt

Go to the online course to perform this practice activity.

Reference Models (3.1.4)

Reference models are a way to clarify the networking process and enable networking professionals to communicate clearly on issues and developments that arise in the field. It is essential that networking professionals understand reference models and be able to use them in professional interactions.

The Benefits of Using a Layered Model (3.1.4.1)

A layered model, such as the TCP/IP model, is often used to help visualize the interaction between various protocols. A layered model depicts the operation of the protocols occurring within each layer, as well as the interaction of protocols with the layers above and below each layer.

There are benefits to using a layered model to describe network protocols and operations. Using a layered model

- Assists in protocol design, because protocols that operate at a specific layer have defined information that they act upon and a defined interface to the layers above and below.

- Fosters competition because products from different vendors can work together.

- Prevents technology or capability changes in one layer from affecting other layers above and below.

- Provides a common language to describe networking functions and capabilities.

There are two basic types of networking models:

- **Protocol model:** This model closely matches the structure of a particular protocol suite. The hierarchical set of related protocols in a suite typically represents all the functionality required to interface the human network with the data network. The TCP/IP model is a protocol model, because it describes the functions that occur at each layer of protocols within the TCP/IP suite.

- **Reference model:** This model provides consistency within all types of network protocols and services by describing what has to be done at a particular layer, but not prescribing how it should be accomplished. A reference model is not intended to be an implementation specification or to provide a sufficient level of detail to define precisely the services of the network architecture. The primary purpose of a reference model is to aid in clearer understanding of the functions and processes involved.

The OSI model is the most widely known internetwork reference model. It is used for data network design, operation specifications, and troubleshooting.

As shown in Figure 3-3, the TCP/IP and OSI models are the primary models used when discussing network functionality. Designers of network protocols, services, or devices can create their own models to represent their products. Ultimately, designers are required to communicate to the industry by relating their product or service to either the OSI model or the TCP/IP model, or to both.

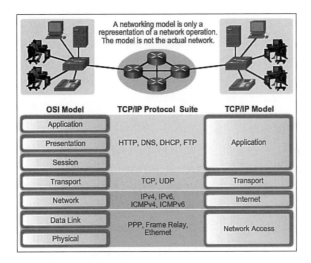

Figure 3-3 OSI and TCP/IP Models

The OSI Reference Model (3.1.4.2)

Initially the *OSI model* was designed by the ISO to provide a framework on which to build a suite of open systems protocols. The vision was that this set of protocols would be used to develop an international network that would not be dependent on proprietary systems.

Ultimately, the speed at which the TCP/IP-based Internet was adopted, and the rate at which it expanded, caused the development and acceptance of the OSI protocol suite to lag behind. Although a few of the developed protocols using the OSI specifications are widely used today, the seven-layer OSI model has made major contributions to the development of other protocols and products for all types of new networks.

The OSI model provides an extensive list of functions and services that can occur at each layer. It also describes the interaction of each layer with the layers directly above and below it. Although the content of this course is structured around the OSI reference model, the focus of discussion is the protocols identified in the TCP/IP protocol model.

Activity 3.1.4.2: The OSI Reference Model

Interactive Graphic

Go to the online course to perform this practice activity.

Note

Whereas the TCP/IP model layers are referred to only by name, the seven OSI model layers are more often referred to by number rather than by name. For instance, the physical layer is referred to as Layer 1 of the OSI model.

The TCP/IP Protocol Model (3.1.4.3)

The *TCP/IP protocol model* for internetwork communications was created in the early 1970s and is sometimes referred to as the Internet model. As shown in Figure 3-4, it defines four categories of functions that must occur for communications to be successful. The architecture of the TCP/IP protocol suite follows the structure of this model. Because of this, the Internet model is commonly referred to as the TCP/IP model.

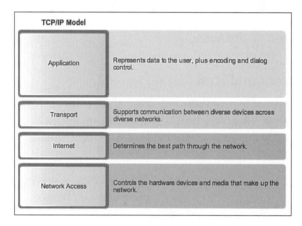

Figure 3-4 TCP/IP Protocol Model

Most protocol models describe a vendor-specific protocol stack. However, because the TCP/IP model is an open standard, one company does not control the definition of the model. The definitions of the standard and the TCP/IP protocols are discussed in a public forum and defined in a publicly available set of RFCs. The RFCs contain both the formal specification of data communications protocols and resources that describe the use of the protocols.

The RFCs also contain technical and organizational documents about the Internet, including the technical specifications and policy documents produced by the IETF.

Comparing the OSI Model with the TCP/IP Model (3.1.4.4)

The protocols that make up the TCP/IP protocol suite can be described in terms of the OSI reference model. In the OSI model, the network access layer and the application layer of the TCP/IP model are further divided to describe discrete functions that must occur at these layers.

At the network access layer, the TCP/IP protocol suite does not specify which protocols to use when transmitting over a physical medium; it only describes the handoff from the Internet layer to the physical network protocols. OSI Layers 1 and 2 discuss the necessary procedures to access the media and the physical means to send data over a network.

As shown in Figure 3-5, the critical parallels between the two network models occur at OSI Layers 3 and 4. OSI Layer 3, the network layer, is almost universally used to describe the range of processes that occur in all data networks to address and route messages through an internetwork. IP is the TCP/IP suite protocol that includes the functionality described at OSI Layer 3.

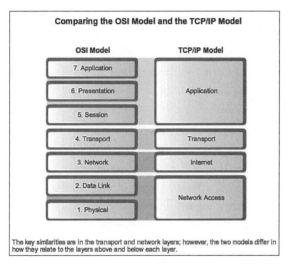

Figure 3-5 Comparing the OSI Model and the TCP/IP Model

Layer 4, the transport layer of the OSI model, describes general services and functions that provide ordered and reliable delivery of data between source and destination hosts. These functions include acknowledgement, error recovery, and sequencing. At this layer, the TCP/IP protocols TCP and User Datagram Protocol (UDP) provide the necessary functionality.

The TCP/IP application layer includes a number of protocols that provide specific functionality to a variety of end-user applications. The OSI model Layers 5, 6, and 7 are used as references for application software developers and vendors to produce products that operate on networks.

Interactive Graphic

Activity 3.1.4.5: Identify Layers and Functions

Go to the online course to perform this practice activity.

<table>
<tr><td>Packet Tracer
☐ Activity</td></tr>
</table>

Packet Tracer Activity 3.1.4.6: Investigating the TCP/IP and OSI Models in Action

This simulation activity is intended to provide a foundation for understanding the TCP/IP protocol suite and the relationship to the OSI model. Go to the online course for more information and to perform this practice activity.

Using Requests for Comments (3.2)

In this section you will learn about RFC documents and their processes.

Why RFCs (3.2.1)

Designing standards to be used in network communications is and always has been very much a collaborative effort. Early developers of these standards recognized that in order to keep track of the many ideas and comments being shared, a system for tracking and publishing them needed to be put in place. The RFC process is the answer to that need.

Request for Comments (RFC) (3.2.1.1)

Request for Comments (RFC) is an official document that specifies standards and protocols related to the Internet and TCP/IP. RFCs are usually published by the IETF, but can also come from the IAB, IRTF, or independent submitters.

> **Note**
>
> Not all RFCs define standards, but the standards are referenced most often in networking. Each protocol in the TCP/IP suite is documented and updated using the RFC process.

Some protocols have multiple RFCs to describe different aspects of the protocol. The following is a list of some of the current RFCs for common TCP/IP protocols:

- **HTTP:** RFC 2616, Hypertext Transfer Protocol - HTTP/1.1
- **DHCP:** RFC 2131, Dynamic Host Configuration Protocol
- **IPv4:** RFC 791, Internet Protocol
- **IPv6:** RFC 2460, Internet Protocol, Version 6 (IPv6) Specification

Some RFCs were created with a sense of humor and were never intended to be used as a standard. RFC 1149 describes an experimental method for delivering IPv4 packets using carrier pigeons. This standard was extended in RFC 6214 to include delivery of IPv6 packets using the same carrier pigeons. Of course this is all meant in fun, but nonetheless these are official IETF informational RFCs. The humorous RFCs are usually published on April 1 (April Fools' Day in the United States) and are meant as pranks.

Individual RFCs are publicly and freely accessible at http://www.rfc-editor.org/index.html.

History of RFCs (3.2.1.2)

On October 29, 1969, the ARPANET came to life with the first message being sent from a mainframe computer at UCLA to a mainframe computer at Stanford Research Institute.

BBN won the contract to build and operate the Interface Message Processors (IMPs), the forerunners to today's modern routers. IMPs were computers with specialized interfaces and software the size of a refrigerator and cost about $100,000 in 1969 U.S. dollars.

Steve Crocker at UCLA had been working on the IMP software and wanted to solicit opinions from others working on the project. In a memorandum entitled "Host Software," he asked others in the development of the ARPANET for their opinions and ideas concerning the IMP software. Needing to track documents of this type, he chose the modest phrase "Request for Comments," along with the number "1" indicating the first number in the sequence. This type of memorandum, more commonly known by its acronym RFC, became the method the early developers of the ARPANET chose to discuss and document standards. At the time there were a very limited number of people working on the development of the ARPANET, so the process was much more informal than it is today.

Today, the Internet is a much different place and a formal structure is used to propose, develop, and implement Internet and TCP/IP standards. RFCs are still the official document used, following a process managed by the IETF.

Sample RFC (3.2.1.3)

A well-known RFC used to reserve a portion of IPv4 address space for private networks is RFC 1918, Address Allocation for Private Internets. Private IPv4 addresses are addresses that are not routed by Internet routers.

The developers of the ARPANET and TCP/IP never envisioned a world where an average person would have multiple computing devices (desktop computer, laptop, smartphone, tablet computer, etc.) all interconnected to a global Internet. Even in the late 1970s personal computers were only of interest to a small minority of computer hobbyists and the idea of networking them was still years away. In 1981, when the current IPv4 RFC was published (RFC 791, Internet Protocol), a 32-bit IPv4 address with a theoretical possibility of just over four billion addresses seemed more than adequate.

However, by the early 1990s, with innovations in personal computing, email, and the World Wide Web, the number of devices accessing the Internet was growing rapidly. By the mid-1990s it was obvious that networks would soon be running out of IPv4 addresses. Additional address space was needed that any organization could use to address devices, with the caveat that these addresses could not be used for accessing the Internet. These addresses became known as "private IPv4 addresses" and were standardized in 1996 with RFC 1918. If you have a home router, you are more than likely using one or more of these private IPv4 addresses. Combined with another technology known as network address translation (NAT), devices using private IP addresses are able to access the Internet through a process where the private IPv4 address is converted to a public IPv4 address.

Private addresses are also known as RFC 1918 addresses. RFC 1918 discusses the motivation behind private addressing and specifies the three ranges of addresses reserved as private IPv4 addresses. As indicated in RFC 1918, the IANA has reserved the following three blocks of IPv4 address space for private networks:

- 10.0.0.0 to 10.255.255.255

- 172.16.0.0 to 172.31.255.255

- 192.168.0.0 to 192.168.255.255

RFC Processes (3.2.2)

This section will describe the process for creating and validating an RFC.

RFC Process (3.2.2.1)

The RFC process is used by ISOC, the IAB, and the IETF for the standardization of protocols and procedures. It is defined in RFC 2026, The Internet Standards Process - Revision 3. This process is used to create a standards track document. Not all RFCs are standards track documents, and not all standards track documents become Internet standards. There are three steps for a proposal to become an Internet standard:

Step 1.   **Internet-Draft (I-D):** The first step for the proposal is to be published as an Internet-Draft (I-D). I-Ds have no formal status and are subject to change or removal at any time. Any paper, report, RFC, or vendor claiming any sort of compliance should never reference I-Ds. I-Ds are subject to review by any member of the public.

Step 2.   **Proposed Standard:** After the I-D has received significant community review and is considered useful, stable, and well understood with community support, the I-D becomes a proposed standard. Proposed standards should be technically complete, but are considered immature specifications until properly tested and validated. Proposed standards receive an RFC number, but are not yet considered an Internet standard. At least two independent implementations are required to demonstrate and verify its functionality. At this point the IETF community considers the proposed standard as mature and useful. (There is another step known as the draft standard. In October 2011, the IETF merged the requirements of the draft standard with the proposed standard.)

Step 3.   **Internet Standard:** The draft standard only becomes an Internet standard after significant implementation and successful operational experience has been obtained. At this point, the Internet standard, or simply "standard," receives a standard (STD) series number.

The RFC development and approval process can take months, or even years, depending upon the complexity of the technology. After an RFC is published as an Internet standard and assigned a number, it cannot be changed. Any change to a published RFC can only be performed through issuing a new RFC that updates or obsoletes the existing RFC. This process allows observation of how individual protocols and services evolve over time. This is in contrast to how documents are issued by different standardization bodies such as the IEEE or ITU-T, which publish newer versions of their standards reusing their original names and numbers.

RFC Types (3.2.2.2)

There are several categories of RFCs, identified by their status. The category is listed in the RFC heading, along with the RFC number, RFC authors, the date, and whether this RFC obsoletes or updates another RFC, as shown in Figure 3-6. The categories of RFCs are as follows:

- **Internet Standard:** Internet standard RFCs are documents defining a mature, useful, and validated protocol or technology. These are also known as normative documents. Internet standards have undergone a thorough process from an I-D, to a proposed standard, and, if approved, to an Internet standard. An example of an Internet standard RFC is RFC 2460, Internet Protocol, Version 6 (IPv6) Specification.

- **Best Current Practice (BCP):** Best current practice RFCs describe official rules or methodologies. The difference between an Internet standard and a BCP is sometimes unclear. Like an Internet standard RFC, a BCP usually goes through the same process as Internet standards. RFC 1918, which defines the use of private IPv4 addresses, is an example of a BCP RFC.

- **Informational:** Information RFCs can be almost anything from describing a DNS Structure and Delegation, RFC 1591, to jokes, such as Hypertext Coffee Pot

Control Protocol (HTCPCP/1.0), described in RFC 2324. Another example of an informational RFC is RFC 1983, Internet Users Glossary, which provides definitions for basic Internet terms and acronyms.

- **Experimental:** Experimental RFCs are documents that are not on the Internet standards approval track. This includes documents that have been submitted by an individual and have not yet been approved as an I-D. It may be that it is not certain that the proposal works as stated, or it is unclear if the proposal can gain wide acceptance. An experimental RFC may be promoted to the Internet standards track if it eventually meets those requirements.

- **Historic:** Historic status is given to an RFC when it has been made obsolete by a newer RFC. RFC numbers are never reused. Any RFC that updates an existing RFC receives a unique number, and the RFC it updates is moved to Historic status. For example, RFC 1883, IPv6, became a standard in 1995. Several changes were made to IPv6, and in 1998, RFC 2460, with the same name, made RFC 1883 obsolete. The header of RFC 2460 includes "Obsoletes: 1883."

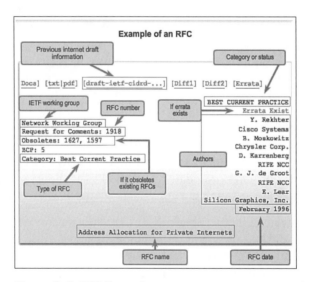

Figure 3-6 RFC Example

Some RFCs are not entirely new technologies or protocols, but instead are an update or extension of an existing RFC. In these cases, the RFC indicates in the header that it is an update and which RFC it is updating.

After an RFC has become an Internet standard, occasionally mistakes or errors are found. In these cases, an errata is created and the RFC includes "Errata Exist" in its header. Errata can be found in the RFC Editor site, http://www.rfc-editor.org/errata.php.

Lab 3.2.2.3: Researching RFCs

In this lab you will research RFCs and how they are published. You will also identify known RFCs used in your network.

Moving Data in the Network (3.3)

Communication across a network may require several steps and many different protocols to be successful. This section covers different elements of the communication process.

Data Encapsulation (3.3.1)

Information is added to data to enable network communication. The following sections explain how the added information assists in the communication process.

Elements of Communication (3.3.1.1)

Communication begins with a message, or information, that must be sent from one individual or device to another. People exchange ideas using many different communication methods. All of these methods have three elements in common:

- **Message source (or sender):** Message sources are people, or electronic devices, that need to send a message to other individuals or devices.

- **Channel:** A channel consists of the media that provides the pathway over which the message can travel from source to destination.

- **Message destination (or receiver):** The message destination receives the message and interprets it.

Consider, for example, the desire to communicate using words, pictures, and sounds. Each of these messages can be sent across a data or information network by first converting them into binary digits, or bits. These bits are then encoded into a signal that can be transmitted over the appropriate medium. In computer networks, the medium is usually a type of cable, or the atmosphere for a wireless transmission.

Video

Video 3.3.1.1:

View the video in the online course for a demonstration of a communication process between two people. Click the second graphic to see the process between two devices over a network.

> **Note**
>
> The term *network* in this course refers to data or information networks capable of carrying many different types of communications, including traditional computer data, interactive voice, video, and entertainment products.

Communicating the Messages (3.3.1.2)

In theory, a single communication, such as a music video or an email message, could be sent across a network from a source to a destination as one massive, uninterrupted stream of bits. If messages were actually transmitted in this manner, it would mean that no other device would be able to send or receive messages on the same network while this data transfer was in progress. These large streams of data would result in significant delays. Further, if a link in the interconnected network infrastructure failed during the transmission, the complete message would be lost and would have to be retransmitted in full.

A better approach is to divide the data into smaller, more manageable pieces to send over the network. This division of the data stream into smaller pieces is called *segmentation*. Segmenting messages has two primary benefits:

- By sending smaller individual pieces from source to destination, many different conversations can be interleaved on the network. The process used to interleave the pieces of separate conversations together on the network is called *multiplexing*.

- Segmentation can increase the reliability of network communications. The separate pieces of each message need not travel the same pathway across the network from source to destination. If a particular path becomes congested with data traffic or fails, individual pieces of the message can still be directed to the destination using alternate pathways. If part of the message fails to make it to the destination, only the missing parts need to be retransmitted. Figure 3-7 depicts segments being multiplexed on a network.

Video

Video 3.3.1.2:

View the video in the online course for a demonstration of segmentation and multiplexing.

The downside to using segmentation and multiplexing to transmit messages across a network is the level of complexity that is added to the process. Imagine if you had to send a 100-page letter, but each envelope would only hold one page. The process of addressing, labeling, sending, receiving, and opening the entire 100 envelopes would be time-consuming for both the sender and the recipient.

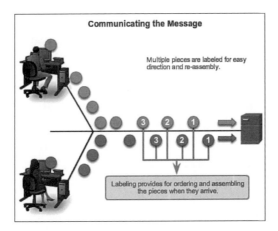

Figure 3-7 Multiplexing Messages on a Network

In network communications, each segment of the message must go through a similar process to ensure that it gets to the correct destination and can be reassembled into the content of the original message.

Various types of devices throughout the network participate in ensuring that the pieces of the message arrive reliably at their destination.

Protocol Data Units (PDUs) (3.3.1.3)

As application data is passed down the protocol stack on its way to be transmitted across the network media, various protocols add information to it at each level. This is commonly known as the *encapsulation process*.

The form that a piece of data takes at any layer is called a *protocol data unit (PDU)*. During encapsulation, each succeeding layer encapsulates the PDU that it receives from the layer above in accordance with the protocol being used. At each stage of the process, a PDU has a different name to reflect its new functions. Although there is no universal naming convention for PDUs, in this course, the PDUs are named according to the protocols of the TCP/IP suite, as shown in Figure 3-8 (in the next section):

- *Data:* The general term for the PDU used at the application layer

- *Segment:* Transport layer PDU

- *Packet:* Internet layer PDU

- *Frame:* Network access layer PDU

- *Bits:* A PDU used when physically transmitting data over the medium

Encapsulation (3.3.1.4)

Data encapsulation is the process that adds additional protocol header information to the data before transmission. In most forms of data communications, the original data is encapsulated, or wrapped, in several protocols before being transmitted.

When sending messages on a network, the protocol stack on a host operates from top to bottom. In the web server example, we can use the TCP/IP model to illustrate the process of sending an HTML web page to a client.

The application layer protocol, HTTP, begins the process by delivering the HTML formatted web page data to the transport layer. There the application data is broken into TCP segments. Each TCP segment is given a label, called a header, containing information about which process running on the destination computer should receive the message. It also contains the information that enables the destination process to reassemble the data back to its original format.

The transport layer encapsulates the web page HTML data within the segment and sends it to the Internet layer, where the IP protocol is implemented. Here the entire TCP segment is encapsulated within an IP packet, which adds another label, called the IP header. The IP header contains source and destination host IP addresses, as well as information necessary to deliver the packet to its corresponding destination process.

Next, the IP packet is sent to the network access layer, where it is encapsulated within a frame header and trailer. Each frame header contains a source and destination physical address. The physical address uniquely identifies the devices on the local network. The trailer contains error checking information. Finally, the bits are encoded onto the media by the server network interface card (NIC). Figure 3-8 depicts the encapsulation process and how information is added to PDUs.

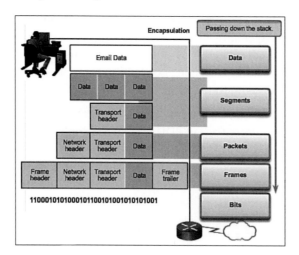

Figure 3-8 The Encapsulation Process

De-encapsulation (3.3.1.5)

The encapsulation process is reversed at the receiving host, and is known as de-encapsulation. De-encapsulation is the process used by a receiving device to remove one or more of the protocol headers. The data is de-encapsulated as it moves up the stack toward the end-user application.

Video

Videos 3.3.1.4 and 3.3.1.5:

View the videos in the online course for a demonstration of encapsulation and de-encapsulation.

Interactive Graphic

Activity 3.3.1.6: Identify the PDU Layer

Go to the online course and perform the PDU exercise.

Accessing Local Resources (3.3.2)

In this section you will learn about addressing data for delivery on the same network.

Network Addresses and Data Link Addresses (3.3.2.1)

The OSI model describes the processes of encoding, formatting, segmenting, and encapsulating data for transmission over the network. The network layer and data link layer are responsible for delivering the data from the source device or sender to the destination device or receiver. Protocols at both layers contain source and destination addresses, but their addresses have different purposes.

Network Address

The network layer, or Layer 3, logical address contains information required to deliver the IP packet from the source device to the destination device. A Layer 3 IP address has two parts, the network prefix and the host part. The network prefix is used by routers to forward the packet to the proper network. The host part is used by the last router in the path to deliver the packet to the destination device.

An IP packet contains two IP addresses:

- *Source IP address:* The IP address of the sending device.
- *Destination IP address:* The IP address of the receiving device. The destination IP address is used by routers to forward a packet to its destination.

Data Link Address

The data link, or Layer 2, physical address has a different role. The purpose of the *data link address* is to deliver the data link frame from one network interface to another network interface on the same network. Before an IP packet can be sent over a wired or wireless network, it must be encapsulated in a data link frame so it can be transmitted over the physical medium, the actual network. Ethernet LANs and wireless LANs are two examples of networks that have different physical media each with its own type of data link protocol.

The IP packet is encapsulated into a data link frame to be delivered to the destination network. The source and destination data link addresses are added (as shown a bit later in Figure 3-9.

- **Source data link address:** The physical address of the device that is sending the packet. Initially this is the NIC that is the source of the IP packet.

- **Destination data link address:** The physical address of the network interface of either the next hop router or the network interface of the destination device.

Communicating with a Device on the Same Network (3.3.2.2)

To understand how communication is successful in the network, it is important to understand the roles of both the network layer addresses and the data link addresses when a device is communicating with another device on the same network.

Network Addresses

The network layer addresses, or IP addresses, indicate the network and host address of the source and destination. The network portion of the address will be the same; only the host or device portion of the address will be different.

- **Source IP address:** The IP address of the sending device, the client computer PC1: 192.168.1.110.

- **Destination IP address:** The IP address of the receiving device, FTP server: 192.168.1.9.

Data Link Addresses

When the sender and receiver of the IP packet are on the same network, the data link frame is sent directly to the receiving device. On an Ethernet network, the data link addresses are known as Ethernet MAC addresses. MAC addresses are 48-bit addresses that are physically embedded on the Ethernet NIC. A *MAC address* is also known as the physical address or burned-in address (BIA). Refer to Figure 3-9 for the following example.

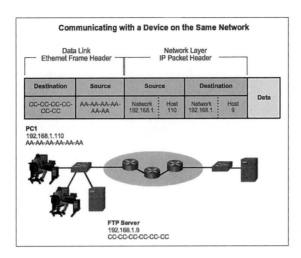

Figure 3-9 Communicating within a Network.

- **Source MAC address:** This is the data link address, or the Ethernet MAC address, of the device that sends the IP packet, PC1. MAC addresses are expressed in hexadecimal notation. The MAC address of the Ethernet NIC of PC1 is AA-AA-AA-AA-AA-AA.

- **Destination MAC address:** When the receiving device is on the same network as the sending device, this is the data link address of the receiving device. In this example, the destination MAC address is the MAC address of the FTP server: CC-CC-CC-CC-CC-CC.

The source and destination addresses are added to the Ethernet frame. The frame with the encapsulated IP packet can now be transmitted from PC1 directly to the FTP server.

MAC and IP Addresses (3.3.2.3)

It should now be clear that to send data to another host on the same LAN, the source host must know both the physical and logical addresses of the destination host. When those are known, the source host can create a frame and send it out on the network media. The source host can learn the destination IP address in a number of ways. For example, it may learn the IP address through the use of the Domain Name System (DNS), or it may know the destination IP address because the address is entered in the application manually, such as when a user specifies the IP address of a destination FTP server. But how does a host determine the Ethernet MAC address of another device?

Most network applications rely on the logical IP address of the destination to identify the location of the communicating hosts. The data link MAC address is required to deliver the encapsulated IP packet inside the Ethernet frame across the network to the destination.

The sending host uses a protocol called *Address Resolution Protocol (ARP)* to discover the MAC address of any host on the same local network. The sending host sends an ARP Request message to the entire LAN. The ARP Request is a broadcast message. The ARP Request contains the IP address of the destination device. Every device on the LAN examines the ARP Request to see if it contains its own IP address. Only the device with the IP address contained in the ARP Request responds with an ARP Reply. The ARP Reply includes the MAC address associated with the IP address in the ARP Request.

Video

Video 3.3.2.3:

View the video in the online course for a demonstration of the Address Resolution Protocol (ARP).

Accessing Remote Resources (3.3.3)

In this section you will learn about addressing data for delivery to remote networks.

Default Gateway (3.3.3.1)

The method that a host uses to send messages to a destination on a remote network differs from the way a host sends messages to a destination on the same local network. When a host needs to send a message to another host located on the same network, it will forward the message directly. A host will use ARP to discover the MAC address of the destination host. It includes the destination IP address within the packet header and encapsulates the packet into a frame containing the MAC address of the destination and forwards it.

When a host needs to send a message to a remote network, it must use the router, also known as the *default gateway*. The default gateway is the IP address of an interface on a router on the same network as the sending host.

It is important that the address of the default gateway be configured on each host on the local network. If no default gateway address is configured in the host TCP/IP settings, or if the wrong default gateway is specified, messages addressed to hosts on remote networks cannot be delivered.

In Figure 3-10, the hosts on the LAN are using R1 as the default gateway with its 192.168.1.1 address configured in their TCP/IP settings. If the destination of a PDU is on a different IP network, the hosts send the PDUs to the default gateway on the router for further transmission.

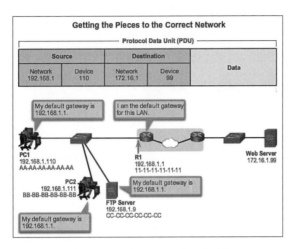

Figure 3-10 Default Gateway Sends Messages out of the Local Network

Communicating with a Device on a Remote Network (3.3.3.2)

But what are the roles of the network layer addresses and the data link layer addresses when a device is communicating with a device on a remote network? Figure 3-11 is an example in which we have a client computer, PC1, communicating with a server, named Web Server, on a different IP network.

Network Addresses

IP addresses indicate the network and device addresses of the source and destination. When the sender of the packet is on a different network from the receiver, the source and destination IP addresses will represent hosts on different networks. This will be indicated by the network portion of the IP address of the destination host.

- **Source IP address:** The IP address of the sending device, the client computer PC1: 192.168.1.110.

- **Destination IP address:** The IP address of the receiving device, the server, Web Server: 172.16.1.99.

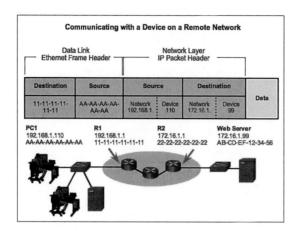

Figure 3-11 Communicating with a Device on a Remote Network

Data Link Addresses

When the sender and receiver of the IP packet are on different networks, the Ethernet data link frame cannot be sent directly to the destination host because the host is not directly reachable in the network of the sender. The Ethernet frame must be sent to another device, known as the router or default gateway. In our example in Figure 3-11, the default gateway is R1. R1 has an interface and an IP address that is on the same network as PC1. This allows PC1 to reach the router directly.

- **Source MAC address:** The Ethernet MAC address of the sending device, PC1. The MAC address of the Ethernet interface of PC1 is AA-AA-AA-AA-AA-AA.

- **Destination MAC address:** When the receiving device is on a different network from the sending device, this is the Ethernet MAC address of the default gateway or router. In this example, the destination MAC address is the MAC address of the R1 Ethernet interface that is attached to the PC1 network, which is 11-11-11-11-11-11.

The Ethernet frame with the encapsulated IP packet can now be transmitted to R1. R1 forwards the packet to the destination, Web Server. This may mean that R1 forwards the packet to another router or directly to Web Server if the destination is on a network connected to R1.

How does the sending device determine the MAC address of the router?

Each device knows the IP address of the router through the default gateway address configured in its TCP/IP settings. The default gateway address is the address of the router interface connected to the same local network as the source device. All devices on the local network use the default gateway address to send messages to the router. After the host knows the default gateway IP address, it can use ARP to determine the MAC address of that default gateway. The MAC address of the default gateway is then placed in the frame.

Packet Tracer Activity 3.3.3.3: Explore a Network

This simulation activity is intended to help you understand the flow of traffic and the contents of data packets as they traverse a complex network. Communications will be examined at three different locations simulating typical business and home networks.

Lab 3.3.3.4: Using Wireshark to View Network Traffic

In this lab you will download and install Wireshark, then use the application to capture and analyze local and remote data.

Summary (3.4)

Class Activity 3.4.1.1: Guaranteed to Work!

Go to the online course to perform the communication activity in which you compare results from the modeling activity at the beginning of this chapter to the networking models used for communications.

Data networks are systems of end devices, intermediary devices, and the media connecting the devices. For communication to occur, these devices must know how to communicate.

These devices must comply with communication rules and protocols. TCP/IP is an example of a protocol suite. Most protocols are created by a standards organization such as the IETF or IEEE. IEEE is a professional organization for those in the electrical engineering and electronics fields. ISO, the International Organization for Standardization, is the world's largest developer of international standards for a variety of products and services.

The most widely used networking models are the OSI and TCP/IP models. Associating the protocols that set the rules of data communications with the different layers of these models is useful in determining which devices and services are applied at specific points as data passes across LANs and WANs.

Data that passes down the stack of the OSI model is segmented into pieces and encapsulated with addresses and other labels. The process is reversed as the pieces are de-encapsulated and passed up the destination protocol stack. The OSI model describes the processes of encoding, formatting, segmenting, and encapsulating data for transmission over the network.

The TCP/IP protocol suite is an open standard protocol that has been endorsed by the networking industry and ratified, or approved, by a standards organization. The IP suite is a suite of protocols required for transmitting and receiving information using the Internet.

PDUs are named according to the protocols of the TCP/IP suite: data, segment, packet, frame, and bits.

Applying models allows individuals, companies, and trade associations to analyze current networks and plan the networks of the future.

Practice

The following activities provide practice with the topics introduced in this chapter. The Labs and Class Activities are available in the companion *Network Basics Lab Manual* (978-1-58713-313-8). The Packet Tracer Activities PKA files are found in the online course.

Class Activities

Class Activity 3.0.1.2: Designing a Communications System

Class Activity 3.4.1.1: Guaranteed to Work!

Labs

Lab 3.1.3.6: Researching Networking Standards

Lab 3.2.2.3: Researching RFCs

Lab 3.3.3.4: Using Wireshark to View Network Traffic

Packet Tracer
☐ Activity

Packet Tracer Activities

Packet Tracer Activity 3.1.4.6: Investigating the TCP/IP and OSI Models in Action

Packet Tracer Activity 3.3.3.3: Explore a Network

Check Your Understanding

Complete all the review questions listed here to test your understanding of the topics and concepts in this chapter. The appendix, "Answers to the 'Check Your Understanding' Questions," lists the answers.

1. Which is *not* a common networking protocol?

   A. DHCP

   B. IP

   C. IPHD

   D. HTTP

2. When multiple protocols interact to perform functions, it is considered to be which of the following?

   A. A protocol suite (also known as a protocol stack)

   B. A proprietary protocol

   C. An open standard protocol

   D. A routing protocol

3. Which of the following groups develop protocol standards? (Choose three.)

   A. IEEE

   B. EAEIO

   C. IETF

   D. AITU

   E. ITU-T

   F. SIOIT

4. What of the following provides descriptions of tasks that need to be accomplished by protocols in layers?

   A. A protocol suite

   B. A protocol model

   C. A reference model

   D. A protocol stack

5. The TCP/IP application layer consists of which three OSI layers?

   A. Application, session, transport

   B. Application, presentation, network access

   C. Application, presentation, session

   D. Application, transport, data link

6. Choose two reasons networking standards are used.

   A. Standards provide a way for consistent development of technologies at each level.

   B. Standards have eliminated the use of proprietary protocols.

   C. Standards allow equipment from different companies a common format for communication.

   D. Standards reduce competition so that fewer vendors can control the development of protocols.

7. The application layer is _____ of the OSI model.

    A. Layer 1

    B. Layer 3

    C. Layer 4

    D. Layer 7

8. A technician responds to a complaint that a computer will not connect to the Internet. He soon realizes the IP address is on a different network. Which layer of the OSI model describes this problem?

    A. Layer 2

    B. Layer 3

    C. Layer 4

    D. Layer 7

9. Which OSI layer is responsible for exchanging frames between network devices?

    A. Layer 1

    B. Layer 2

    C. Layer 3

    D. Layer 4

10. A technician responds to a complaint that a computer will not connect to the Internet. She soon realizes the computer's Ethernet cable has accidently been cut during a move. Which layer of the OSI model describes this problem?

    A. Layer 1

    B. Layer 2

    C. Layer 3

    D. Layer 4

11. Which layers of the OSI model combine to make the network access layer of the TCP/IP model?

    A. Data link and network

    B. Layers 5 and 6

    C. Layers 3 and 4

    D. Data link and physical

12. The numbered documents that specify networking standards and protocols are known as

    A. RFCs

    B. IPXs

    C. IETFs

    D. IMP Statements

13. Which protocol data unit is not correctly matched to its TCP/IP layer? (Choose two.)

    A. Bits: Application layer PDU

    B. Segment: Transport layer PDU

    C. Packet: Network access layer PDU

    D. Frame: Network access layer PDU

14. When an Ethernet frame arrives at its destination, the computer must _____ the frame.

    A. Encapsulate

    B. Un-frame

    C. Segment

    D. De-encapsulate

15. Which of the following is true of packet PDUs? (Choose two.)

    A. They contain destination IP addresses.

    B. They contain source MAC addresses.

    C. They contain timing bits.

    D. They contain source IP addresses.

    E. They contain destination MAC addresses.

16. Which of the following is true of Ethernet frame PDUs? (Choose two.)

    A. They contain destination IP addresses.

    B. They contain source MAC addresses.

    C. They contain timing bits.

    D. They contain source IP addresses.

    E. They contain destination MAC addresses.

CHAPTER 4

Application Layer

Objectives

Upon completion of this chapter, you will be able to answer the following questions:

- How do the functions of the application layer, session layer, and presentation layer work together to provide network services to end-user applications?

- How do common application layer protocols interact with end-user applications?

- Which common application layer protocols provide Internet services to end users, including World Wide Web services and email?

- Which application layer protocols provide IP addressing services, including DNS and DHCP?

- How do well-known application layer protocols allow for sharing services, including FTP, file sharing services, and SMB protocol?

Key Terms

This chapter uses the following key terms. You can find the definitions in the Glossary.

Introduction (4.0.1.1)

We experience the Internet through the World Wide Web, email services, and file sharing programs. These applications, and many others, provide the human interface to the underlying network, enabling us to send and receive data with relative ease. Typically the applications that we use are intuitive and transparent, meaning we can access and use them without knowing how they work. However, for network professionals, it is important to know how an application is able to format, transmit, and interpret messages that are sent and received across the network.

Visualizing the mechanisms that enable communication across the network is made easier if we use the layered framework of the OSI model.

In this chapter, we will explore the role of the application layer and how the applications, services, and protocols within the application layer make robust communication across data networks possible.

Class Activity 4.0.1.2: Application Investigation

In this activity, you will envision what it would be like not to have network applications available to use in the workplace.

Application Layer Protocols (4.1)

Data that is sent across networks is generated by a person or device using some type of computer application. Which protocols an application uses depends on the purpose of the application.

Application, Session, and Presentation (4.1.1)

In this section you will learn about the services of the three top layers of the OSI model and the application layer of the TCP/IP model.

OSI and TCP/IP Models Revisited (4.1.1.1)

Networking professionals use the OSI and TCP/IP models to communicate both verbally and in written technical documentation. As such, networking professionals can use these models to describe the behavior of protocols and applications.

In the OSI model, data is passed from one layer to the next, starting at the application layer on the transmitting host, and proceeding down the hierarchy to the physical layer, and then passing over the communications channel to the destination host, where the data proceeds back up the hierarchy, ending at the application layer.

The application layer is the top layer of both the OSI and TCP/IP models. The TCP/IP application layer includes a number of protocols that provide specific functionality to a variety of end-user applications. The functionality of the TCP/IP application layer protocols fits roughly into the framework of the top three layers of the OSI model: application, presentation, and session layers. The OSI model Layers 5, 6, and 7 are used as references for application software developers and vendors to produce products, such as web browsers that need to access networks.

Application Layer (4.1.1.2)

The process of network communication starts with a device running an application at the application layer, to form a message. The application layer formats that message in preparation for its journey.

The *application layer* is closest to the end user. As shown in Figure 4-1, it is the layer that provides the interface between the applications we use to communicate and the underlying network over which our messages are transmitted. Application layer protocols are used to exchange data between programs running on the source and destination hosts. There are many application layer protocols, and new protocols are always being developed. Some of the most widely known application layer protocols include Hypertext Transfer Protocol (HTTP), File Transfer Protocol (FTP), Trivial File Transfer Protocol (TFTP), Internet Message Access Protocol (IMAP), and Domain Name System (DNS) protocol.

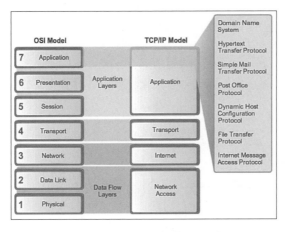

Figure 4-1 Application Layer Protocols

Presentation and Session Layers (4.1.1.3)

The presentation and session layers from the OSI model are folded into the application layer in the TCP/IP model.

The Presentation Layer

The *presentation layer* has three primary functions:

- Formats, or presents, data from the source device into a compatible form for receipt by the destination device

- Compression of the data in a way that can be decompressed by the destination device

- Encryption of the data for transmission and the decryption of data upon receipt by the destination

As shown in Figure 4-2, the presentation layer formats data for the application layer and it sets standards for file formats. Some well-known standards for video include QuickTime and Motion Picture Experts Group (MPEG). QuickTime is an Apple computer specification for video and audio, and MPEG is a standard for video and audio compression and coding.

Among the well-known graphic image formats that are used on networks are Graphics Interchange Format (GIF), Joint Photographic Experts Group (JPEG), and Portable Network Graphics (PNG) format. GIF and JPEG are compression and coding standards for graphic images. PNG was designed to address some of the limitations of the GIF format and to eventually replace it.

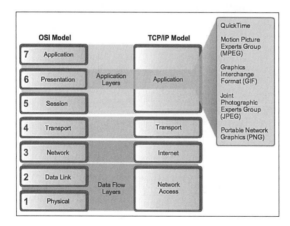

Figure 4-2 Presentation Layer Functions

The Session Layer

As the name implies, functions at the *session layer* create and maintain dialogs between source and destination applications. The session layer handles the exchange of information to initiate dialogs, keep them active, and restart sessions that are disrupted or idle for a long period of time.

TCP/IP Application Layer Protocols (4.1.1.4)

Whereas the OSI model separates the individual application, presentation, and session functions, most widely known and implemented TCP/IP applications incorporate the functionality of all three layers.

The *TCP/IP application layer* protocols specify the format and control information necessary for many common Internet communication functions. Among these TCP/IP protocols are

- **Domain Name System (DNS):** This protocol resolves Internet names to IP addresses.

- **Telnet:** This protocol is used to provide remote access to servers and networking devices.

- **Simple Mail Transfer Protocol (SMTP):** This protocol transfers mail messages and attachments.

- **Dynamic Host Configuration Protocol (DHCP):** This protocol is used to assign an IP address, subnet mask, default gateway, and DNS server addresses to a host.

- **Hypertext Transfer Protocol (HTTP):** This protocol transfers files that make up the web pages of the World Wide Web.

- **File Transfer Protocol (FTP):** This protocol is used for interactive file transfer between systems.

- **Trivial File Transfer Protocol (TFTP):** This protocol is used for connectionless active file transfer.

- **Bootstrap Protocol (BOOTP):** This protocol is a precursor to the DHCP protocol. BOOTP is a network protocol used to obtain IP address information during bootup.

- **Post Office Protocol (POP):** This protocol is used by email clients to retrieve email from a remote server.

- **Internet Message Access Protocol (IMAP):** This is another protocol for email retrieval.

Application layer protocols are used by both the source and destination devices during a communication session. For the communications to be successful, the application layer protocols implemented on the source and destination host must be compatible.

Interactive Graphic

Activity 4.1.1.4: Application Layer Protocols

Go to the online course and perform the application layer protocol exercise.

Services at the Application Layer (4.1.1.5, 4.1.1.6)

Application layer protocols enable humans to interface with the underlying data network. When we open a web browser or an instant message window, an application is started, and the program is put into the device's memory, where it is executed. Each executing program that is loaded on a device is referred to as a *process*.

Within the application layer, there are two forms of software programs or processes that provide access to the network: network-aware applications and application layer services.

Network-Aware Applications

End-user applications are the software programs used by people to communicate over the network. Some end-user applications are *network-aware applications*, meaning that they implement the application layer protocols and are able to communicate directly with the lower layers of the protocol stack. Email clients and web browsers are examples of these types of applications.

Application Layer Services

Other programs may need the assistance of application layer services to use network resources, like file transfer or network print spooling. Though transparent to the user, *application layer services* are programs that interface with the network and prepare the data for transfer. Different types of data—whether it is text, graphics, or video—require different network services to ensure that the data is properly prepared for processing by the functions occurring at the lower layers of the OSI model.

Each application or service uses protocols that define the standards and data formats to be used. Without protocols, the data network would not have a common way to format and direct data. To understand the function of various network services, familiarize yourself with the underlying protocols that govern their operation.

Many different types of applications communicate across data networks. Therefore, application layer services must implement multiple protocols to provide the desired range of communication experiences. Each protocol has a specific purpose and contains the characteristics required to meet that purpose. The right protocol details in each layer must be followed so that the functions at one layer interface properly with the services in the lower layer.

Interactive Graphic

Activity 4.1.1.5: Software Processes

Go to the online course and perform the interactive exercise.

Applications and services may also use multiple protocols in the course of a single conversation. One protocol may specify how to establish the network connection, and another protocol may describe the process for the data transfer when the message is passed to the next-lower layer.

Whereas applications provide people with a way to create messages, and application layer services establish an interface to the network, protocols provide the rules and formats that govern how data is treated. All three components may be used by a single executable program and can even use the same name. For example, when discussing Telnet, we could be referring to the application, the service, or the protocol.

Video

Video 4.1.1.6:

View the video in the online course for a demonstration of services in the OSI model.

Applications Interface with People and Other Applications (4.1.1.7)

In the OSI model, applications that interact directly with people are considered to be above the OSI layers, as are the users themselves. User applications, such as a web browser or email program, are not a part of the OSI or TCP/IP application layer. It is the application layer protocols that enable the function of the user applications.

Interactive Graphic

Activity 4.1.1.8: Application Protocols and Standards

Go to the online course and perform the interactive exercise.

How Application Protocols Interact with End-User Applications (4.1.2)

In this section you will learn about protocols used in peer-to-peer networks and client/server networks.

Peer-to-Peer Networks (4.1.2.1)

When accessing information on a networking device, whether it is a PC, laptop, tablet, smartphone, or some other device connected to a network, the data may not be physically stored on the device. In this case, a request to access that information must be made to the device where the data resides. In the *peer-to-peer (P2P) networking* model, the data is accessed from a peer device without the use of a dedicated server.

The P2P network model involves two parts: P2P networks and P2P applications. Both parts have similar features, but in practice work quite differently.

In a P2P network, two or more computers are connected via a network and can share resources (such as printers and files) without having a dedicated server. Every connected end device (known as a *peer*) can function as both a server and a client. One computer might assume the role of server for one transaction while simultaneously serving as a client for another. The roles of client and server are set on a per-request basis.

An example is a simple home network with two computers, as shown in Figure 4-3. In this example, Peer2 has a printer attached to it directly by USB and is set up to share the printer on the network so that Peer1 can print to it. Peer1 is set up to share a drive or folder on the network. This allows Peer2 to access and save files to the shared folder. In addition to sharing files, a network such as this one would allow users to enable networked games, or share an Internet connection.

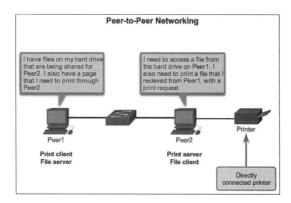

Figure 4-3   Peer-to-Peer Networking

P2P networks decentralize the resources on a network. Instead of locating data to be shared on dedicated servers, data can be located anywhere and on any connected device. Most of the current operating systems support file and print sharing without requiring additional server software. However, P2P networks do not use centralized user accounts or access servers to maintain permissions. Therefore, it is difficult to enforce security and access policies in networks containing more than just a few computers. User accounts and access rights must be set individually on each peer device.

Peer-to-Peer Applications (4.1.2.2)

A peer-to-peer (P2P) application allows a device to act as both a client and a server within the same communication. In this model, every client is a server and every server is a client. Both can initiate a communication and are considered equal in the communication process. However, P2P applications require that each end device provide a user interface and run a background service. When you launch a specific P2P application, it loads the required user interface and background services; afterward, the devices can communicate directly.

Some P2P applications use a hybrid system where resource sharing is decentralized but the indexes that point to resource locations are stored in a centralized directory. In a hybrid system, each peer accesses an index server to get the location of a resource stored on another peer. The index server can also help connect two peers, but after they are connected, the communication takes place between the two peers without additional communication to the index server.

P2P applications can be used on P2P networks, client/server networks, and across the Internet. Figure 4-4 depicts a remote P2P network topology.

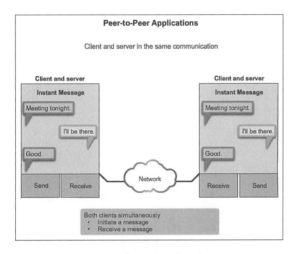

Figure 4-4 Peer-to-Peer Applications

Common P2P Applications (4.1.2.3)

With P2P applications, each computer in the network running the application can act as a client or a server for the other computers in the network running the application. Common P2P applications include

- eDonkey
- eMule
- Shareaza
- BitTorrent
- Bitcoin
- LionShare

Some P2P applications are based on the Gnutella protocol. They enable people to share files on their hard disks with others. Gnutella-compatible client software allows users to connect to Gnutella services over the Internet and to locate and access resources shared by other Gnutella peers. Many client applications are available for accessing the Gnutella network, including BearShare, Gnucleus, LimeWire, Morpheus, WinMX, and XoloX.

While the Gnutella Developer Forum maintains the basic protocol, application vendors often develop extensions to make the protocol work better with their application.

Many P2P applications do not use a central database to record all the files available on the peers. Instead, the devices on the network each tell the others what files are available when queried, and use the file sharing protocol and services to support locating resources.

Lab 4.1.2.4: Researching Peer-to-Peer File Sharing

In this lab you will research P2P networks, protocols, and applications. You will also research P2P file sharing issues and legal issues.

Client-Server Model (4.1.2.5)

In the client/server model, the device requesting the information is called a *client* and the device responding to the request is called a *server*. Client and server processes are considered to be in the application layer. The client begins the exchange by requesting data from the server, which responds by sending one or more streams of data to the client. Application layer protocols describe the format of the requests and responses between clients and servers. In addition to the actual data transfer, this exchange may also require user authentication and the identification of a data file to be transferred.

One example of a client/server network is a corporate environment where employees use a company email server to send, receive, and store email. The email client on an employee computer issues a request to the email server for any unread mail. The server responds by sending the requested email to the client.

Although data is typically described as flowing from the server to the client, some data always flows from the client to the server. Data flow may be equal in both directions, or may even be greater in the direction going from the client to the server. For example, a client may transfer a file to the server for storage purposes. As shown in Figure 4-5, which depicts the client/server model and functions, data transfer from a client to a server is referred to as an *upload* and data transfer from a server to a client is referred to as a *download*.

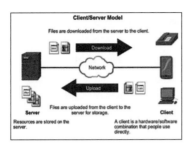

Figure 4-5   Client/Server Model

Well-Known Application Layer Protocols and Services (4.2)

There are hundreds of protocols used in computer networking, but this course will focus on a few well-known protocols.

Everyday Application Layer Protocols (4.2.1)

In this section, you will learn about common application protocols you commonly use.

Application Layer Protocols Revisited (4.2.1.1)

There are dozens of application layer protocols, but on a typical day you probably use only five or six. Three application layer protocols that are involved in everyday work or play are

- Hypertext Transfer Protocol (HTTP)
- Simple Mail Transfer Protocol (SMTP)
- Post Office Protocol (POP)

These application layer protocols make it possible to browse the Web and send and receive email. HTTP is used to enable users to connect to websites across the Internet. SMTP is used to enable users to send email. And POP is used to enable users to receive email.

The next few pages focus on these three application layer protocols.

Hypertext Transfer Protocol and Hypertext Markup Language (4.2.1.2)

When a web address or uniform resource locator (URL) is typed into a web browser, the web browser establishes a connection to the web service running on the server using the HTTP protocol. URLs and Uniform Resource Identifier (URIs) are the names most people associate with web addresses.

The http://www.cisco.com/index.html URL is an example of a URL that refers to a specific resource; a web page named **index.html** on a server identified as **cisco.com**.

Web browsers are the type of client application a computer uses to connect to the World Wide Web and access resources stored on a web server. As with most server processes, the web server runs as a background service and makes different types of files available.

To access the content, web clients make connections to the server and request the desired resources. The server replies with the resources and, upon receipt, the browser interprets the data and presents it to the user.

Browsers can interpret and present many data types (such as plain text or Hypertext Markup Language, the language in which web pages are constructed). Other types of data, however, may require another service or program, typically referred to as *plug-ins* or *add-ons*. To help the browser determine what type of file it is receiving, the server specifies what kind of data the file contains.

Interactive Graphic

Activity 4.2.1.2: HTTP Protocol Process

Go to the online course and click the four graphics demonstrating how HTTP loads a web page in a browser.

To better understand how the web browser and web client interact, we can examine how a web page is opened in a browser. For this example, use the http://www.cisco.com/index.html URL.

First the browser interprets the three parts of the URL:

1. **http** (the protocol or scheme)

2. **www.cisco.com** (the server name)

3. **index.html** (the specific filename requested)

The browser then checks with a name server to convert www.cisco.com into a numeric address, which it uses to connect to the server (this is a DNS process and will be explained later in the chapter). Using HTTP requirements, the browser sends a GET request to the server and asks for the **index.html** file. The server sends the

HTML code for this web page to the browser. Finally, the browser deciphers the HTML code and formats the page for the browser window.

HTTP and HTTPS (4.2.1.3)

HTTP is used across the network for data transfer and is one of the most used application protocols today. It was originally developed to simply publish and retrieve HTML pages; however, the flexibility of HTTP has made it a vital application within distributed, collaborative information systems.

HTTP is a request/response protocol. When a client, typically a web browser, sends a request to a web server, HTTP specifies the message types used for that communication. The three common message types are GET, POST, and PUT.

GET is a client request for data. A client (web browser) sends the GET message to the web server to request HTML pages. When the server receives the GET request, it responds with a status line, such as HTTP/1.1 200 OK, and a message of its own. The message from the server may include the requested HTML file, if available, or it may contain an error or information message, such as "The location of the requested file has changed."

POST and *PUT* are used to upload data files to the web server. For example, when the user enters data into a form that is embedded within a web page (such as when completing an order request), the POST message is sent to the web server. Included within the POST message is the data that the user submitted in the form.

PUT uploads resources or content to the web server. For example, if a user attempts to upload a file or image to a website, a PUT message is sent from the client to the server with the attached file or image.

Although HTTP is remarkably flexible, it is not a secure protocol. The request messages send information to the server in plain text that can be intercepted and read. Similarly, the server responses, typically HTML pages, are also unencrypted.

For secure communication across the Internet, the *HTTP Secure (HTTPS) protocol* is used for accessing or posting web server information. HTTPS can use authentication and encryption to secure data as it travels between the client and server. HTTPS specifies additional rules for passing data between the application layer and the transport layer. HTTPS uses the same client request–server response process as HTTP, but the data stream is encrypted with Secure Sockets Layer (SSL) before being transported across the network. HTTPS creates additional load and processing time on the server due to the encryption and decryption of traffic.

SMTP and POP (4.2.1.4–4.2.1.7)

Email, the most popular network service, has revolutionized how people communicate through its simplicity and speed. Yet to run on a computer or other end device, email requires several applications and services. Two example application layer protocols are *Post Office Protocol (POP)* and *Simple Mail Transfer Protocol (SMTP)*, shown in Figure 4-6. As with HTTP, these protocols define client/server processes.

When people compose email messages, they typically use an email client, otherwise known as a Mail User Agent (MUA). The email client allows messages to be sent and places received messages into the client's mailbox, both of which are distinct processes.

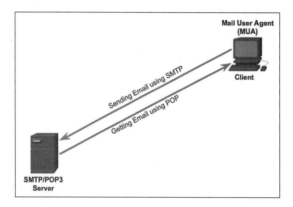

Figure 4-6 Email with SMTP and POP3

To receive email messages from an email server, the email client can use POP. Sending email from either a client or a server uses message formats and command strings defined by SMTP. Usually an email client provides the functionality of both protocols within one application.

The email server operates two separate processes:

- *Mail Transfer Agent (MTA)*
- *Mail Delivery Agent (MDA)*

The MTA process is used to forward email. As shown in Figure 4-7, the MTA receives messages from the email client or from another MTA on another email server. Based on the message header, it determines how a message must be forwarded to reach its destination. If the mail is addressed to a user whose mailbox is on the local server, the mail is passed to the MDA. If the mail is for a user that is not on the local server, the MTA routes the email to the MTA on the appropriate server.

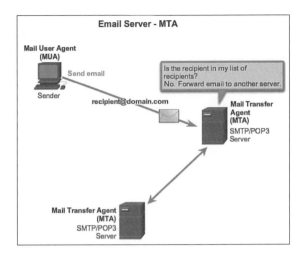

Figure 4-7 Email Server - MTA

In Figure 4-8, the MDA accepts a piece of email from an MTA and performs the actual delivery. The MDA receives all the inbound mail from the MTA and places it into the appropriate users' mailboxes. The MDA can also resolve final delivery issues, such as virus scanning, spam filtering, and return-receipt handling. Most email communications use the MUA, MTA, and MDA applications; however, there are other alternatives for email delivery.

A client may be connected to a corporate email system, such as IBM's Lotus Notes, Novell's GroupWise, or Microsoft's Exchange. These systems often have their own internal email format, and their clients typically communicate with the email server using a proprietary protocol. The server sends or receives email via the Internet through the product's Internet mail gateway, which performs any necessary reformatting.

As another alternative, computers that do not have an email client can still connect to a mail service on a web browser to retrieve and send messages. Some computers may run their own MTA and manage interdomain email. If, for example, two people who work for the same company exchange email with each other using a proprietary protocol, their messages may stay completely within the company's corporate email system.

Email can use the application layer protocols POP and SMTP, as shown in Figure 4-8. POP and POP3 are inbound mail delivery protocols and are typical client/server protocols. They deliver email from the email server to the client (MUA). The MDA listens for a client to connect to a server. After a connection is established, the server can deliver the email to the client.

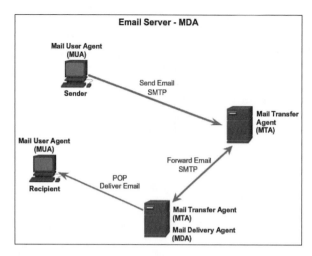

Figure 4-8 Email server - MDA.

The SMTP, on the other hand, governs the transfer of outbound email from the sending client to the email server (MDA), as well as the transport of email between email servers (MTA). SMTP enables email to be transported across data networks between different types of server and client software, and makes email exchange over the Internet possible.

The SMTP message format uses a rigid set of commands and replies. These commands support the procedures used in SMTP, such as session initiation, mail transaction, forwarding mail, verifying mailbox names, expanding mailing lists, and the opening and closing exchanges.

Packet Tracer Activity 4.2.1.8: Web and Email

In this activity you will configure HTTP and email services using the simulated server in Packet Tracer. You will then configure clients to access the HTTP and email services.

Providing IP Addressing Services (4.2.2)

In this section you will learn about DNS and DHCP protocols and services.

Domain Name Service (4.2.2.1)

In data networks, devices are labeled with numeric IP addresses to send and receive data over networks. Most people cannot remember this numeric address. Domain names were created to convert the numeric address into a simple, recognizable name.

On the Internet, these *domain names*, such as http://www.cisco.com, are much easier for people to remember than 198.133.219.25, which is the actual numeric address for this server. If Cisco decides to change the numeric address of www.cisco.com, it is transparent to the user, because the domain name remains the same. The new address is simply linked to the existing domain name and connectivity is maintained. When networks were small, it was a simple task to maintain the mapping between domain names and the addresses they represented. As networks grew and the number of devices increased, this manual system became unworkable.

The *Domain Name System (DNS)* was created for domain name to address resolution for these networks. DNS uses a distributed set of servers to resolve the names associated with these numbered addresses.

Interactive Graphic

Activity 4.2.2.1: Resolving DNS

Go to the online course to observe the steps involved in DNS resolution. Click the buttons in the figure to see the steps.

The DNS protocol defines an automated service that matches resource names with the required numeric network address. It includes the format for queries, responses, and data. The DNS protocol communications use a single format called a *message format*. This message format is used for all types of client queries and server responses, error messages, and the transfer of resource record information between servers.

DNS Message Format (4.2.2.2)

A DNS server provides the name resolution using the *Berkeley Internet Name Domain* (BIND), or the name daemon, which is often called "named" (pronounced name-dee). BIND was originally developed by four students at the University of California Berkley in the early 1980s. The DNS message format used by BIND is the most widely used DNS format on the Internet.

The DNS server stores different types of resource records used to resolve names. These records contain the name, address, and type of record.

Some of these record types are

- **A:** An end device address

- **NS:** An authoritative name server

- **CNAME:** The canonical name (or Fully Qualified Domain Name) for an alias; used when multiple services have the single network address but each service has its own entry in DNS

- **MX:** Mail exchange record; maps a domain name to a list of mail exchange servers for that domain

When a client makes a query, the server's BIND process first looks at its own records to resolve the name. If it is unable to resolve the name using its stored records, it contacts other servers to resolve the name.

The request may be passed along to a number of servers, which can take extra time and consume bandwidth. After a match is found and returned to the original requesting server, the server temporarily stores the numbered address that matches the name in cache memory.

If that same name is requested again, the first server can return the address by using the value stored in its name cache. Caching reduces both the DNS query data network traffic and the workloads of servers higher up the hierarchy. The DNS Client service on Windows PCs optimizes the performance of DNS name resolution by also storing previously resolved names in memory. The **ipconfig /displaydns** command displays all of the cached DNS entries on a Windows computer system.

DNS Hierarchy (4.2.2.3)

The DNS protocol uses a hierarchical system to create a database to provide name resolution. As shown in Figure 4-9, the hierarchy looks like an inverted tree, with the root DNS server at the top and branches below. DNS uses domain names to form the hierarchy.

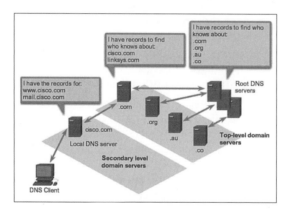

Figure 4-9 Hierarchy of DNS Servers

The naming structure is broken down into small, manageable zones. Each DNS server maintains a specific database file and is only responsible for managing name-to-IP mappings for that small portion of the entire DNS structure. When a DNS server receives a request for a name translation that is not within its DNS zone, the DNS server forwards the request to another DNS server within the proper zone for translation.

Note

DNS is scalable because hostname resolution is spread across multiple servers.

The different top-level domains represent either the type of organization or the country of origin. Examples of top-level domains are

- **.au:** Australia
- **.co:** Colombia
- **.com:** a business or industry
- **.jp:** Japan
- **.org:** A nonprofit organization

After top-level domains are second-level domain names, and below them are other lower-level domains. Each domain name is a path down this inverted tree, starting from the root. For example, as shown in Figure 4-9, the root DNS server may not know exactly where the record for the email server, mail.cisco.com, is located, but it maintains a record for the .com domain within the top-level domain. Likewise, the servers within the .com domain may not have a record for mail.cisco.com, but they do have a record for the domain. The servers within the cisco.com domain have a record (an MX record to be precise) for mail.cisco.com.

DNS relies on this hierarchy of decentralized servers to store and maintain these resource records. The resource records list domain names that the server can resolve and alternative servers that can also process requests. If a given server has resource records that correspond to its level in the domain hierarchy, it is said to be *authoritative* for those records. For example, a name server in the cisco.netacad.net domain would not be authoritative for the mail.cisco.com record, because that record is held at a higher domain level server; specifically the name server in the cisco.com domain.

nslookup (4.2.2.4)

DNS is a client/server service; however, it differs from the other client/server services. Whereas other services use a client that is an application (such as web browser, email client), the DNS client runs as a service itself. The DNS client, sometimes called the DNS resolver, supports name resolution for other network applications and other services that need it.

When configuring a network device, we generally provide one or more DNS server addresses that the DNS client can use for name resolution. Usually the Internet service provider (ISP) provides the addresses to use for the DNS servers. When a user's application requests to connect to a remote device by name, the requesting DNS client queries one of these name servers to resolve the name to a numeric address.

Computer operating systems also have a utility called *nslookup* that allows the user to manually query the name servers to resolve a given hostname. This utility can also be used to troubleshoot name resolution issues and to verify the current status of the name servers.

In Figure 4-10, when the **nslookup** command is issued, the default DNS server configured for your host is displayed. In this example, the DNS server is dns-sj.cisco. com, which has an address of 171.70.168.183.

Figure 4-10 *nslookup* Command

The name of a host or domain can be entered at the **nslookup** prompt. In the first query in Figure 4-10, a query is made for www.cisco.com. The responding name server provides the address 198.133.219.25.

The queries shown in Figure 4-10 are only simple tests. The nslookup utility has many options available for extensive testing and verification of the DNS process. When finished, type **exit** to leave the nslookup utility.

Interactive Graphic	**Activity 4.2.2.5: Syntax Checker - DNS CLI Commands in Windows and UNIX** Go to the online course and practice nslookup in the simulation.

Dynamic Host Configuration Protocol (4.2.2.6)

The Dynamic Host Configuration Protocol (DHCP) service enables devices on a network to obtain IP addresses and other information from a DHCP server. This service automates the assignment of IP addresses, subnet masks, gateway, and other IP networking parameters. This is referred to as *dynamic addressing*. The alternative to dynamic addressing is *static addressing*. When using static addressing, the network administrator manually enters IP address information on network hosts.

DHCP allows a host to obtain an IP address dynamically when it connects to the network. The DHCP server is contacted and an address is requested. The DHCP server chooses an address from a configured range of addresses called a *pool* and assigns (leases) that address to the host for a set period.

On larger local networks, or where the user population changes frequently, DHCP is preferred for address assignment. New users may arrive with laptops and need a connection; others may have new workstations that must be connected. Rather than have the network administrator assign IP addresses for each workstation, it is more efficient to have IP addresses assigned automatically using DHCP.

DHCP-distributed addresses are not permanently assigned to hosts, but rather are only leased for a period of time. If the host is powered down or taken off the network, the address is returned to the pool for reuse. This is especially helpful with mobile users that come and go on a network. Users can freely move from location to location and re-establish network connections. The host can obtain an IP address after the hardware connection is made, via either a wired or wireless LAN.

DHCP makes it possible to access the Internet using wireless hotspots at airports or coffee shops. When a wireless device enters a hotspot, the device DHCP client contacts the local DHCP server via a wireless connection, and the DHCP server assigns an IP address to the device.

Various types of devices can be DHCP servers when running DHCP service software. The DHCP server in most medium-to-large networks is usually a local, dedicated, PC-based server. With home networks, the DHCP server is usually located on the local router that connects the home network to the ISP. Local hosts receive IP address information directly from the local router. The local router receives an IP address from the DHCP server at the ISP.

DHCP can pose a security risk because any device connected to the network can receive an address. This risk makes physical security a determining factor of whether to use dynamic or manual addressing. Both dynamic and static addressing have a place in network design. Many networks use both DHCP and static addressing. DHCP is used for general-purpose hosts, such as end-user devices; static addressing is used for network devices, such as gateways, switches, servers, and printers.

DHCP Operation (4.2.2.7)

Without DHCP, users have to manually input the IP address, subnet mask, and other network settings to join the network. The DHCP server maintains a pool of IP addresses and leases an address to any DHCP-enabled client when the client is powered on. Because the IP addresses are dynamic (leased), rather than static (permanently assigned), addresses no longer in use are automatically returned to the pool for reallocation. As shown in Figure 4-11, when a DHCP-configured device boots up or connects to the network, the client broadcasts a DHCP discover (DHCPDISCOVER) message to identify any available DHCP servers on the network.

A DHCP server replies with a DHCP offer (DHCPOFFER) message, which offers a lease to the client. The offer message contains the IP address and subnet mask to be assigned, the IP address of the DNS server, and the IP address of the default gateway. The lease offer also includes the duration of the lease.

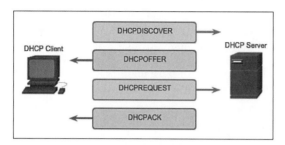

Figure 4-11 DHCP Messages Exchanged

The client may receive multiple DHCPOFFER messages if there is more than one DHCP server on the local network; therefore, it must choose between them, and send a DHCP request (DHCPREQUEST) message that identifies the explicit server and lease offer that the client is accepting. A client may also choose to request an address that it had previously been allocated by the server.

Assuming that the IP address requested by the client, or offered by the server, is still available, the server returns a DHCP acknowledgement (DHCPACK) message that acknowledges to the client that the lease is finalized. If the offer is no longer valid, perhaps due to a timeout or another client taking the lease, then the selected server responds with a DHCP negative acknowledgement (DHCPNAK) message. If a DHCPNAK message is returned, then the selection process must begin again with a new DHCPDISCOVER message being transmitted. After the client has the lease, it must be renewed prior to the lease expiration through another DHCPREQUEST message.

The DHCP server ensures that all IP addresses are unique (the same IP address cannot be assigned to two different network devices simultaneously). Using DHCP enables network administrators to easily reconfigure client IP addresses without having to manually make changes to the clients. Most Internet providers use DHCP to allocate addresses to their customers that do not require a static address.

Packet Tracer Activity 4.2.2.8: DNS and DHCP

In this activity you will configure and verify static IP addressing and DHCP addressing. You will then configure a DNS server to map IP addresses to the website names.

Lab 4.2.2.9: Observing DNS Resolution

In this lab you will observe the DNS conversion of a URL to an IP address and observe DNS lookup using **nslookup** on a website and a mail server.

Providing File Sharing Services (4.2.3)

File Transfer Protocol and Server Message Block are two important file sharing protocols explored in this section.

File Transfer Protocol (4.2.3.1)

The *File Transfer Protocol (FTP)* is another commonly used application layer protocol. FTP was developed to allow for data transfers between a client and a server. An FTP client is an application that runs on a computer that is used to push and pull data from a server running an FTP daemon (FTPd).

As Figure 4-12 illustrates, to successfully transfer data, FTP requires two connections between the client and the server, one for commands and replies, the other for the actual file transfer:

- The client establishes the first connection to the server for control traffic, consisting of client commands and server replies.

- The client establishes the second connection to the server for the actual data transfer. This connection is created every time there is data to be transferred.

The data transfer can happen in either direction. The client can download (pull) data from the server, or the client can upload (push) data to the server.

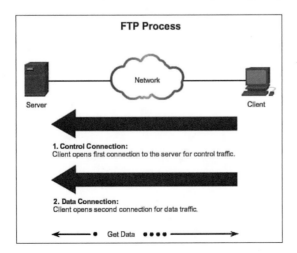

Figure 4-12 FTP Processes

Packet Tracer Activity 4.2.3.2: FTP

In this activity you will configure FTP services. You will then use the FTP services to transfer files between clients and the server.

Lab 4.2.3.3: Exploring FTP

In this lab you will use FTP both from a command prompt and from a browser to download a file.

Server Message Block (4.2.3.4)

The *Server Message Block (SMB)* is a client/server file sharing protocol, developed by IBM in the late 1980s, to describe the structure of shared network resources, such as directories, files, printers, and serial ports. It is a request-response protocol.

The SMB protocol describes file system access and how clients can make requests for files. It also describes the SMB protocol interprocess communication. All SMB messages share a common format. This format uses a fixed-sized header, followed by a variable-sized parameter and data component.

SMB messages can

- Start, authenticate, and terminate sessions
- Control file and printer access
- Allow an application to send or receive messages to or from another device

SMB file-sharing and print services have become the mainstay of Microsoft networking. With the introduction of the Windows 2000 software series, Microsoft changed the underlying structure for using SMB. In previous versions of Microsoft products, the SMB services used a non-TCP/IP protocol to implement name resolution. Beginning with Windows 2000, all subsequent Microsoft products use DNS naming, which allows TCP/IP protocols to directly support SMB resource sharing, as shown in Figure 4-13.

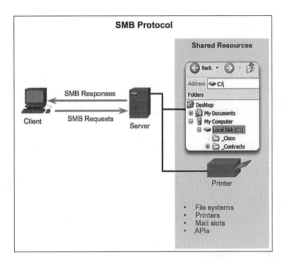

Figure 4-13 SMB Protocol

Unlike the file sharing supported by FTP, clients establish a long-term connection to servers. After the connection is established, the user of the client can access the resources on the server as if the resources are local to the client host.

The Linux and UNIX operating systems also provide a method of sharing resources with Microsoft networks using a version of SMB called SAMBA. The Apple OS X operating systems also support resource sharing using the SMB protocol.

Summary (4.3)

Class Activity 4.3.1.1: Make It Happen!

Use the same scenario you completed in the introduction modeling activity (Class Activity 4.0.1.2) to answer questions about your solutions.

Packet Tracer Activity 4.3.1.2: Packet Tracer Multiuser - Tutorial

The multiuser feature in Packet Tracer allows multiple point-to-point connections between multiple instances of Packet Tracer. This first Packet Tracer Multiuser (PTMU) activity is a quick tutorial demonstrating the steps to establish and verify a multiuser connection to another instance of Packet Tracer within the same LAN. Ideally, this activity is meant for two students. However, it can also be completed as a solo activity simply by opening the two separate files to create two separate instances of Packet Tracer on your local machine.

Packet Tracer Activity 4.3.1.3: Packet Tracer Multiuser - Implement Services

In this multiuser activity, two students (players) cooperate to implement and verify services including DHCP, HTTP, Email, DNS, and FTP. The server-side player will implement and verify services on one server. The client-side player will configure two clients and verify access to services.

The application layer is responsible for directly accessing the underlying processes that manage and deliver communication to the human network. This layer serves as the source and destination of communications across data networks. The application layer applications, services, and protocols enable users to interact with the data network in a way that is meaningful and effective.

- Applications are computer programs with which the user interacts and which initiate the data transfer process at the user's request.

- Services are background programs that provide the connection between the application layer and the lower layers of the networking model.

- Protocols provide a structure of agreed-upon rules and processes that ensure services running on one particular device can send and receive data from a range of different network devices.

Delivery of data over the network can be requested from a server by a client, or between devices that operate in a P2P arrangement, where the client/server relationship is established according to which device is the source and destination at that time.

Messages are exchanged between the application layer services at each end device in accordance with the protocol specifications to establish and use these relationships.

Protocols like HTTP, for example, support the delivery of web pages to end devices. SMTP and POP support sending and receiving email. SMB and FTP enable users to share files. P2P applications make it easier for consumers to seamlessly share media in a distributed fashion. DNS resolves the human-legible names used to refer to network resources into numeric addresses usable by the network.

All of these elements work together, at the application layer. The application layer enables users to work and play over the Internet.

Practice

The following activities provide practice with the topics introduced in this chapter. The Labs and Class Activities are available in the companion *Network Basics Lab Manual* (978-1-58713-313-8). The Packet Tracer Activities PKA files are found in the online course.

Class Activities

Class Activity 4.0.1.2: Application Investigation

Class Activity 4.3.1.1: Make It Happen!

Labs

Lab 4.1.2.4: Researching Peer-to-Peer File Sharing

Lab 4.2.2.9: Observing DNS Resolution

Lab 4.2.3.3: Exploring FTP

Packet Tracer Activities

Packet Tracer Activity 4.2.1.8: Web and Email

Packet Tracer Activity 4.2.2.8: DNS and DHCP

Packet Tracer Activity 4.2.3.2: FTP

Packet Tracer Activity 4.3.1.2: Packet Tracer Multiuser - Tutorial

Packet Tracer Activity 4.3.1.3: Packet Tracer Multiuser - Implement Services

Check Your Understanding

Complete all the review questions listed here to test your understanding of the topics and concepts in this chapter. The appendix, "Answers to the 'Check Your Understanding' Questions," lists the answers.

1. Which three layers of the OSI model make up the application layer in the TCP/IP model?

   A. Application, presentation, and transport

   B. Session, presentation, and application

   C. Application, session, and transport

   D. Application, transport, and Internet

2. HTTP, DHCP, Telnet, and TFTP are examples of

   A. Layer 4 protocols

   B. Layer 5 protocols

   C. Layer 6 protocols

   D. Layer 7 protocols

3. Which layer is responsible for maintenance of dialogs between source and destination applications?

   A. Layer 7

   B. Layer 6

   C. Layer 5

   D. Layer 4

4. *Choose the correct order of protocols to complete the sentences*: Application layer protocols make it possible to browse the Web and send and receive email. _____ is used to enable users to connect to websites across the Internet. _____ is used to enable users to send email. And _____ is used to enable users to receive email.

   A. HTTP, SMTP, POP

   B. DNS, POP, HTTP

   C. HTTP, P2P, SMTP

   D. P2P, HTTP, POP

5. Which is not a component of the web address http://cisco.com/index.htm?

   A. The server name

   B. The DNS tag

   C. The protocol

   D. The desired filename

6. Which is true about the HTTP protocol?

   A. It uses a POST message to request data from a client.

   B. It authenticates the sources that send requests.

   C. It uses less processing power than HTTPS.

   D. It uses SSL.

7. What is true of both HTTP and HTTPS? (Choose two.)

   A. They use SSL encryption.

   B. They use GET messages to request pages.

   C. They use the same computing resources.

   D. POST and PUT messages are used to upload files.

   E. HTTPS was developed prior to HTTP.

8. Which protocol is used to transport email over the Internet?

   A. POP

   B. POP3

   C. SMTP

   D. SNMP

9. Which protocol is responsible for converting text Internet addresses (for example, www.cisco.com) into numeric Internet addresses?

   A. POP

   B. DNS

   C. UDP

   D. NDS

10. Which servers are at the top of the DNS hierarchy?

   A. Primary servers

   B. Top-level servers

   C. Secondary servers

   D. Root servers

11. Entering nslookup at the command prompt will provide which of the following?

    A. An IP address from a domain name

    B. The default name server for your host

    C. The domain name for a given IP address

    D. The name of the root server for the connected network

12. When a student enters a Wi-Fi hotspot on campus, she can log on to the Internet. Which protocol contributes to making this possible by assigning her device an IP address?

    A. DHCP

    B. nslookup

    C. IPHD

    D. SMB

13. Which DHCP requests are made by the client requesting an address? (Choose two.)

    A. DHCP DISCOVER

    B. DHCP OFFER

    C. DHCP REQUEST

    D. DHCP ACK

    E. DHCP SETUP

14. FTP requires ____ connection(s) between client and server to successfully transfer files.

    A. 1

    B. 2

    C. 3

    D. 4

15. Which is not a function of the SMB protocol?

    A. Resolving IP addresses

    B. Controlling access to files and printers

    C. Initiating, authenticating, and terminating sessions

    D. Permitting applications to exchange information with other devices

CHAPTER 5

Transport Layer

Objectives

Upon completion of this chapter, you will be able to answer the following questions:

- What is the purpose of the transport layer in managing the transportation of data in end-to-end communication?

- What are the characteristics of the TCP and UDP protocols, including port numbers and their uses?

- How do the TCP session establishment and termination processes facilitate reliable communication?

- How are TCP protocol data units (PDUs) transmitted and acknowledged to guarantee delivery?

- What is the UDP client process to establish communication with a server?

- How can you determine whether high-reliability TCP transmissions or non-guaranteed UDP transmissions are best suited for common applications?

Key Terms

This chapter uses the following key terms. You can find the definitions in the Glossary.

Introduction (5.0.1.1)

Data networks and the Internet support the human network by supplying seamless, reliable communication between people—both locally and around the globe. On a single device, people can use multiple applications and services, such as email, the Web, and instant messaging, to send messages or retrieve information.

Data from each of these applications is packaged, transported, and delivered to the appropriate server daemon or application on the destination device. The processes described in the Open Systems Interconnection (OSI) transport layer accept data from the application layer and prepare it for addressing at the network layer. The transport layer is responsible for the overall end-to-end transfer of application data.

In this chapter we will examine the role of the transport layer in encapsulating application data for use by the network layer. The transport layer also encompasses these functions:

- Enables multiple applications to communicate over the network at the same time on a single device

- Ensures that, if required, all the data is received reliably and in order by the correct application

- Employs error handling mechanisms

Class Activity 5.0.1.2: We Need To Talk

In this activity you will determine whether high or low data communication delivery methods should be utilized in a situational context.

Transport Layer Protocols (5.1)

In this section you will learn how transport layer protocols work to move data across the Internet

Transportation of Data (5.1.1)

To understand how transport protocols work, you must first understand the role of the transport layer.

Role of the Transport Layer (5.1.1.1, 5.1.1.2)

The transport layer is responsible for establishing a temporary communication session between two applications and delivering data between them. Users access the network through network applications that run independently of the operational details of the network in use. An application generates data that is sent from an application on a source host to an application on a destination host, without regard to the destination host type, the type of media over which the data must travel, the path taken by the data, the congestion on a link, or the size of the network. As shown in Figure 5-1, the transport layer is the link between the application layer and the lower layers that are responsible for network transmission.

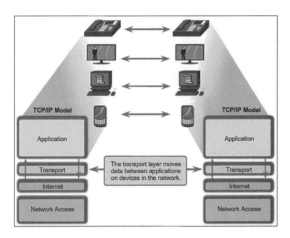

Figure 5-1 Transport Layer

The transport layer accepts data from different applications and passes that data down to the lower layers as manageable pieces that can be multiplexed, or inserted with other data packets, over the media. The transport layer provides for the segmentation of data and the controls necessary to reassemble these segments into the various communication streams. In TCP/IP, these segmentation and reassembly processes can be achieved using two very different transport layer protocols: Transmission Control Protocol (TCP) and User Datagram Protocol (UDP).

The primary responsibilities of transport layer protocols are

- Tracking the individual communication between applications on the source and destination hosts

- Segmenting data for manageability and reassembling segmented data into streams of application data at the destination

- Identifying the proper application for each communication stream

Tracking Individual Conversations

At the transport layer, each particular set of data flowing between a source application and a destination application is known as a conversation, as depicted in Figure 5-2. A host may have multiple applications that are communicating across the network simultaneously. Each of these applications communicates with one or more applications on one or more remote hosts. It is the responsibility of the transport layer to maintain and track these multiple conversations.

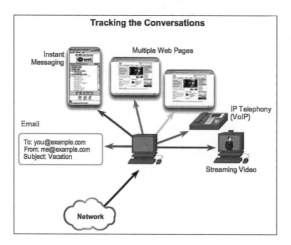

Figure 5-2 Transport Layer Tracking Conversations

Segmenting Data and Reassembling Segments

Data must be prepared to be sent across the media in manageable pieces. Most networks have a limitation on the amount of data that can be included in a single packet. As shown in Figure 5-3, transport layer protocols have services that segment the application data into blocks of data that are an appropriate size. This service includes the encapsulation required on each piece of data. A header, used for reassembly, is added to each block of data. This header is used to track the data stream.

At the destination, the transport layer must be able to reconstruct the pieces of data into a complete data stream that is useful to the application layer. The protocols at the transport layer describe how the transport layer header information is used to reassemble the data pieces into streams to be passed to the application layer.

Identifying the Applications

Figure 5-4 depicts how there may be many applications or services running on each host in the network. To pass data streams to the proper applications, the transport layer must identify the target application. To accomplish this, the transport layer assigns each application an identifier. This identifier is called a *port number*. Each software process that needs to access the network is assigned a port number unique in that host. The transport layer uses ports to identify the application or service.

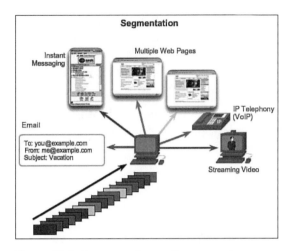

Figure 5-3 Transport Layer Segmentation

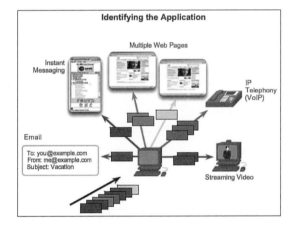

Figure 5-4 Transport Layer Identifying Applications

Conversation Multiplexing (5.1.1.3)

Sending some types of data (for example, a streaming video) across a network as one complete communication stream could use all of the available bandwidth and prevent other communications from occurring at the same time. It also makes error recovery and retransmission of damaged data difficult.

Figure 5-5 shows that segmenting the data into smaller chunks enables many different communications, from many different users, to be interleaved (multiplexed) on the same network. Segmentation of the data by transport layer protocols also provides the means to both send and receive data when running multiple applications concurrently on a computer.

Without segmentation, only one application would be able to receive data. For example, with a streaming video, the media would be completely consumed by the one communication stream instead of shared. You could not receive emails, chat on instant messenger, or view web pages while also viewing the video.

To identify each segment of data, the transport layer adds to the segment a header containing binary data. This header contains fields of bits. It is the values in these fields that enable different transport layer protocols to perform different functions in managing data communication.

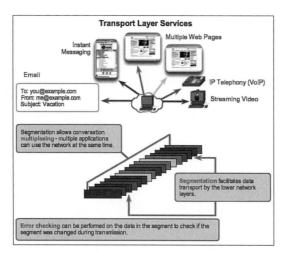

Figure 5-5 Transport Layer Multiplexing Conversations

Transport Layer Reliability (5.1.1.4)

The transport layer is also responsible for managing reliability requirements of a conversation. Different applications have different transport reliability requirements.

IP is concerned only with the structure, addressing, and routing of packets. IP does not specify how the delivery or transportation of the packets takes place. Transport protocols specify how to transfer messages between hosts. TCP/IP provides two transport layer protocols, Transmission Control Protocol (TCP) and *User Datagram Protocol (UDP)*, as shown in Figure 5-6. IP uses these transport protocols to enable hosts to communicate and transfer data.

TCP is considered a reliable, full-featured transport layer protocol, which ensures that all of the data arrives at the destination. In contrast, UDP is a very simple transport layer protocol that does not provide for any reliability.

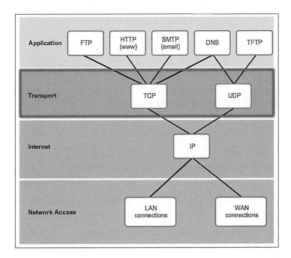

Figure 5-6 TCP and UDP Work at the Transport Layer.

TCP (5.1.1.5)

As previously stated, TCP is considered a reliable transport protocol, which means that TCP includes processes to ensure reliable delivery between applications through the use of acknowledged delivery. TCP is analogous to sending packages that are tracked from source to destination. If a FedEx order is broken up into several shipments, a customer can check online to see the order of the delivery.

With TCP, the three basic operations of reliability are

- Tracking transmitted data segments
- Acknowledging received data
- Retransmitting any unacknowledged data

TCP breaks up a message into small pieces known as *segments*. The segments are numbered in sequence and passed to the IP process for assembly into packets. TCP keeps track of the number of segments that have been sent to a specific host from a specific application. If the sender does not receive an acknowledgement within a certain period of time, it assumes that the segments were lost and retransmits them. Only the portion of the message that is lost is re-sent, not the entire message. On the receiving host, TCP is responsible for reassembling the message segments and passing them to the application. FTP and HTTP are examples of applications that use TCP to ensure data delivery.

These reliability processes place additional overhead on network resources due to the processes of acknowledgement, tracking, and retransmission. To support these reliability processes, more control data is exchanged between the sending and receiving hosts. This control information is contained in a TCP header.

Video

Video 5.1.1.5:

Go to the online course and play the animation of TCP segments being transmitted from sender to receiver.

UDP (5.1.1.6)

Although the TCP reliability functions provide robust communication between applications, they also incur additional overhead and possible delays in transmission. There is a trade-off between the value of reliability and the burden it places on network resources. Imposing overhead to ensure reliability for some applications could reduce the usefulness of the application and can even be detrimental to the application. In such cases, UDP is a better transport protocol.

UDP provides just the basic functions for delivering data segments between the appropriate applications, with very little overhead and data checking. UDP is known as a best-effort delivery protocol. In the context of networking, best-effort delivery is referred to as unreliable because there is no acknowledgement that the data is received at the destination. With UDP, there are no transport layer processes that inform the sender if successful delivery has occurred.

UDP is similar to placing a regular, non-registered letter in the mail. The sender of the letter is not aware of whether a receiver is available to receive the letter, nor is the post office responsible for tracking the letter or informing the sender if the letter does not arrive at the final destination.

Video

Video 5.1.1.6:

Go to the online course and play the animation of UDP segments being transmitted from sender to receiver.

The Right Transport Layer Protocol for the Right Application (5.1.1.7)

Both TCP and UDP are valid transport protocols. Depending upon the application requirements, either one, or sometimes both, of these transport protocols can be used. Application developers must choose which transport protocol type is appropriate based on the requirements of the applications, as shown in Figure 5-7.

For some applications, segments must arrive in a very specific sequence to be processed successfully. With other applications, all data must be fully received before any of it is considered useful. In both of these instances, TCP is used as the transport protocol. For example, applications such as databases, web browsers, and email clients require that all data that is sent arrives at the destination in its original condition. Any missing data could cause a corrupt communication that is either incomplete or unreadable. Therefore, these applications are designed to use TCP. The additional network overhead is considered to be required for these applications.

In other cases, an application can tolerate some data loss during transmission over the network, but delays in transmission are unacceptable. UDP is the better choice for these applications because less network overhead is required. UDP is preferable with applications such as streaming audio, video, and Voice over IP (VoIP). Acknowledgements would slow down delivery, and retransmissions are undesirable.

For example, if one or two segments of a video stream fail to arrive, it creates a momentary disruption in the stream. This may appear as distortion in the image, but may not even be noticeable to the user. On the other hand, the image in a streaming video would be greatly degraded if the destination device had to account for lost data and delay the stream while waiting for retransmissions. In this case, it is better to render the best video possible with the segments received, and forego reliability.

Internet radio is another example of an application that uses UDP. If some of the message is lost during its journey over the network, it is not retransmitted. If a few packets are missed, the listener might hear a slight break in the sound. If TCP were used and the lost packets were re-sent, the transmission would pause to receive them and the disruption would be more noticeable.

Figure 5-7 depicts key differences between the TCP and UDP protocols in the transport layer.

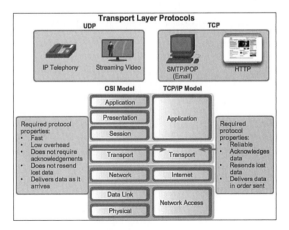

Figure 5-7   Application Developers Choose the Appropriate Transport Layer Protocol Based on the Nature of the Application

**Interactive
Graphic**

Activity 5.1.1.8: TCP, UDP, or Both?

Go to the online course and perform the activity matching applications to the appropriate protocol.

Introducing TCP and UDP (5.1.2)

To really understand the differences between TCP and UDP, it is important to understand how each protocol implements specific reliability functions and how they track communications.

Introducing TCP (5.1.2.1)

TCP was initially described in RFC 793. In addition to supporting the basic functions of data segmentation and reassembly, TCP also provides

- Connection-oriented conversations by establishing sessions
- Reliable delivery
- Ordered data reconstruction
- Flow control

Establishing a Session

TCP is a connection-oriented protocol. A *connection-oriented protocol* is one that negotiates and establishes a permanent connection (or session) between source and destination devices prior to forwarding any traffic. Session establishment prepares the devices to communicate with one another. Through session establishment, the devices negotiate the amount of traffic that can be forwarded at a given time, and the communication data between the two can be closely managed. The session is terminated only after all communication is completed.

Reliable Delivery

TCP can implement a method to ensure reliable delivery of the data. In networking terms, *reliability* means ensuring that each piece of data that the source sends arrives at the destination. For many reasons, it is possible for a piece of data to become corrupted, or lost completely, as it is transmitted over the network. TCP can ensure that all pieces reach their destination by having the source device retransmit lost or corrupted data.

Same-Order Delivery

Because networks may provide multiple routes that can have different transmission rates, data can arrive in the wrong order. By numbering and sequencing the segments, TCP can ensure that these segments are reassembled into the proper order.

Flow Control

Network hosts have limited resources, such as memory or bandwidth. When TCP is aware that these resources are overtaxed, it can request that the sending application reduce the rate of data flow. This is done by TCP regulating the amount of data the source transmits. *Flow control* can prevent the loss of segments on the network and avoid the need for retransmission.

Role of TCP (5.1.2.2)

After TCP establishes a session, it is then able to keep track of the conversation within that session. Because of the ability of TCP to track actual conversations, it is considered a stateful protocol. A *stateful protocol* is a protocol that keeps track of the state of the communication session. For example, when data is transmitted using TCP, the sender expects the destination to acknowledge that it has received the data. TCP tracks which information it has sent and which information has been acknowledged. If the data is not acknowledged, the sender assumes the data did not arrive and resends it. The stateful session begins with the session establishment and ends when the session is closed with session termination.

Note

Maintaining the state of information in TCP requires resources that are not necessary for a stateless protocol, such as UDP.

TCP incurs additional overhead to gain these functions. As shown in Figure 5-8, each TCP segment has 20 bytes of overhead in the header encapsulating the application layer data. This is considerably more than a UDP segment, which only has 8 bytes of overhead. Extra overhead in TCP includes

- **Sequence number (32 bits):** Used for data reassembly purposes.

- **Acknowledgement number (32 bits):** Indicates the data that has been received.

- **Header length (4 bits):** Known as "data offset." Indicates the length of the TCP segment header.

- **Reserved (6 bits):** This field is reserved for the future.

- **Control bits (6 bits):** Includes bit codes, or *flags*, that indicate the purpose and function of the TCP segment.

- **Window size (16 bits):** Indicates the number of segments that can be accepted at one time.

- **Checksum (16 bits):** Used for error checking of the segment header and data.

- **Urgent (16 bits):** Indicates if data is urgent.

Examples of applications that use TCP are web browsers, email, and file transfers.

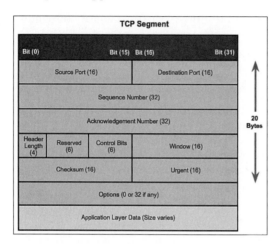

Figure 5-8 TCP Segment

Introducing UDP (5.1.2.3)

UDP is considered a best-effort transport protocol, described in RFC 768. UDP is a lightweight transport protocol that offers the same data segmentation and reassembly as TCP, but without TCP reliability and flow control. UDP is such a simple protocol that it is usually described in terms of what it does not do compared to TCP.

The following features describe UDP:

- **Connectionless:** UDP does not establish a connection between the hosts before data can be sent and received.

- **Unreliable delivery:** UDP does not provide services to ensure that the data will be delivered reliably. There are no processes within UDP to have the sender retransmit any data that is lost or is corrupted.

- **No ordered data reconstruction:** Occasionally data is received in a different order than it was sent. UDP does not provide any mechanism for reassembling the data in its original sequence. The data is simply delivered to the application in the order that it arrives.

- **No flow control:** There are no mechanisms within UDP to control the amount of data transmitted by the source to avoid overwhelming the destination device.

The source sends the data. If resources on the destination host become over-taxed, the destination host mostly likely drops data sent until resources become available. Unlike TCP, with UDP there is no mechanism for automatic retransmission of dropped data.

Figure 5-9 depicts the UDP datagram. Because it has less overhead than the TCP datagram, it is only 8 bytes in length.

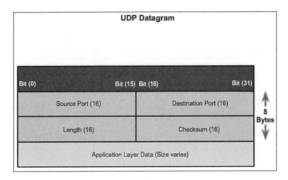

Figure 5-9 UDP Segment

Role of UDP (5.1.2.4)

Although UDP does not include the reliability and flow-control mechanisms of TCP, UDP's low-overhead data delivery makes it an ideal transport protocol for applications that can tolerate some data loss. The pieces of communication in UDP are called *datagrams*. These datagrams are sent as best effort by the transport layer protocol. A few applications that use UDP are DNS, video streaming, and VoIP.

One of the most important requirements for delivering live video and voice over the network is that the data continues to flow quickly. Video and voice applications can tolerate some data loss with minimal or no noticeable effect, and are perfectly suited to UDP.

UDP is a *stateless protocol*, meaning neither the client nor the server is obligated to keep track of the state of the communication session. UDP is not concerned with reliability or flow control. Data may be lost or received out of sequence without any UDP mechanisms to recover or reorder the data. If reliability is required when using UDP as the transport protocol, it must be handled by the application.

Separating Multiple Communications (5.1.2.5)

The transport layer must be able to separate and manage multiple communications with different transport requirement needs. For example, consider a user connected to a network on an end device. The user is simultaneously receiving and sending email and instant messages, viewing websites, and conducting a VoIP phone call. Each of these applications is sending and receiving data over the network at the same time, despite different reliability requirements. Additionally, data from the phone call is not directed to the web browser, and text from an instant message does not appear in an email.

For reliability, users require that an email or web page be completely received and presented in full, for the information to be considered useful. Slight delays in loading the email or web page are generally acceptable as long as the final product is shown in its entirety and correctly. In this example, the network manages the resending or replacement of missing information, and does not display the final product until everything is received and correctly assembled.

In contrast, occasionally missing small parts of a telephone conversation might be considered acceptable. Even if some small parts of a few words are dropped, one can either infer the missing audio from the context of the conversation or ask the other person to repeat what was said. This is considered preferable to the incurred delays if the network were to manage and resend missing segments. In this example, the user, not the network, manages the resending or replacement of missing information.

As shown in Figure 5-10, for TCP and UDP to manage these simultaneous conversations with varying requirements, the TCP- and UDP-based services must keep track of the various applications that are communicating. To differentiate the segments and datagrams for each application, both TCP and UDP have header fields that can uniquely identify these applications. These unique identifiers are the port numbers.

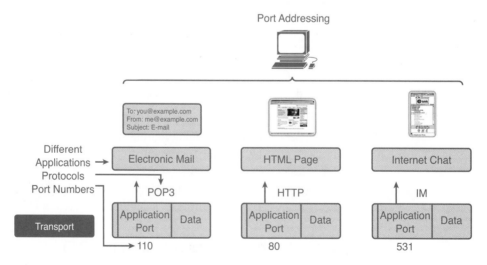

Figure 5-10 Port Addressing

TCP and UDP Port Addressing (5.1.2.6–5.1.2.9)

In the header of each segment or datagram, there is a source and destination port. The source port number is the number for this communication associated with the originating application on the local host. As shown in Figure 5-11, the destination port number is the number for this communication associated with the destination application on the remote host.

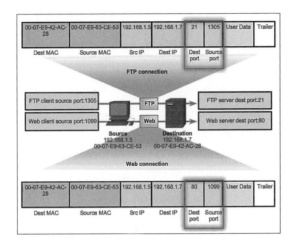

Figure 5-11 Source and Destination Ports in a Segment

When a message is delivered using either TCP or UDP, the protocols and services requested are identified by a port number. A *port* is a numeric identifier within each segment that is used to keep track of specific conversations and destination services requested. Every message that a host sends contains both a source port and a destination port.

- **Destination port:** The client places a destination port number in the segment to tell the destination server which service is being requested. For example, port 80 refers to HTTP or web service. When a client specifies port 80 in the destination port, the server that receives the message knows that web services are being requested. A server can offer more than one service simultaneously. For example, a server can offer web services on port 80 at the same time that it offers FTP connection establishment on port 21.

- **Source port:** The source port number is randomly generated by the sending device to identify a conversation between two devices. This allows multiple conversations to occur simultaneously. In other words, a device can send multiple HTTP service requests to a web server at the same time. The separate conversations are tracked based on the source ports.

The source and destination ports are placed within the segment. The segments are then encapsulated within an IP packet. The IP packet contains the IP address of the source and destination. The combination of the source and destination IP addresses and the source and destination port numbers is known as a *socket*. The socket is used to identify the server and service being requested by the client. Every day thousands of hosts communicate with millions of different servers. Those communications are identified by the sockets.

It is the combination of the transport layer port number and the network layer IP address of the host that uniquely identifies a particular application process running on an individual host device. This combination is called a *socket*. A *socket pair*, consisting of the source and destination IP addresses and port numbers, is also unique and identifies the specific conversation between the two hosts.

A client socket might look like what is shown in Figure 5-11, with 1099 representing the source port number: 192.168.1.5:1099.

The socket on a web server might be 192.168.1.7:80.

Together, these two sockets combine to form a socket pair: 192.168.1.5:1099, 192.168.1.7:80.

With the creation of sockets, communication endpoints are known so that data can move from an application on one host to an application on another. Sockets enable multiple processes running on a client to distinguish themselves from each other, and multiple connections to a server process to be distinguished from each other.

The source port of a client request is randomly generated. This port number acts like a return address for the requesting application. The transport layer keeps track of this port and the application that initiated the request so that when a response is returned, it can be forwarded to the correct application. The requesting application port number is used as the destination port number in the response coming back from the server.

The Internet Assigned Numbers Authority (IANA) assigns port numbers. IANA is a standards body that is responsible for assigning various addressing standards.

There are different types of port numbers:

- **Well-known ports (numbers 0 to 1023):** As shown in Table 5-1, numbers are reserved for services and applications. They are commonly used for applications such as HTTP (web server), IMAP/SMTP (email server), and Telnet. By defining these well-known ports for server applications, client applications can be programmed to request a connection to that specific port, and its associated service.

Table 5-1 Well-Known Ports

Well-Known Port	Application	Protocol
20	File Transfer Protocol (FTP) Data	TCP
21	File Transfer Protocol (FTP) Control	TCP
23	Telnet	TCP
25	Simple Mail Transfer Protocol (SMTP)	TCP
69	Trivial File Transport Protocol (TFTP)	UDP
80	Hypertext Transfer Protocol (HTTP)	TCP
110	Post Office Protocol 3 (POP3)	TCP
194	Instant Relay Chat (IRC)	TCP
443	Secure HTTP (HTTPS)	TCP
520	Routing Information Protocol	UDP

- **Registered ports (numbers 1024 to 49151):** As shown in Table 5-2, these port numbers are assigned to user processes or applications. These processes are primarily individual applications that a user has chosen to install, rather than common applications that would receive a well-known port number. When not used for a server resource, these ports may also be dynamically selected by a client as its source port.

Table 5-2 Registered Ports

Registered Port	Application	Protocol
1812	RADIUS Authentication Protocol	UDP
1863	MSN Messenger	TCP
2000	Cisco Skinny Control Protocol (SCCP, used in VoIP applications)	UDP
5004	Real-Time Transport Protocol (RTP, a voice and video transport protocol)	UDP
5060	Session Initiation Protocol (SIP, used in VoIP applications)	UDP
8008	Alternate HTTP	TCP
8080	Alternate HTTP	TCP

- **Dynamic or private ports (numbers 49152 to 65535):** Also known as *ephemeral ports*, these are usually assigned dynamically to client applications when the client initiates a connection to a service. The dynamic port is most often used to identify the client application during communication, whereas the client uses the well-known port to identify and connect to the service being requested on the server. It is uncommon for a client to connect to a service using a dynamic or private port (although some peer-to-peer file sharing programs do use these ports).

Using Both TCP and UDP

Some applications may use both TCP and UDP, as shown in Table 5-3. For example, the low overhead of UDP enables DNS to serve many client requests very quickly. Sometimes, however, sending the requested information may require the reliability of TCP. In this case, the well-known port number, 53, is used by both TCP and UDP with this service.

Table 5-3 TCP/UDP Common Ports

Common Port	Application	Port Type
53	DNS	Well-known TCP/UDP common port
161	SNMP	Well-known TCP/UDP common port
531	AOL Instant Messenger, IRC	Well-known TCP/UDP common port
1433	MS SQL	Registered TCP/UDP common port
2948	WAP (MMS)	Registered TCP/UDP common port

A current list of port numbers and the associated applications can be found at http://www.iana.org/assignments/port-numbers.

Sometimes it is necessary to know which active TCP connections are open and running on a networked host. Netstat is an important network utility that can be used to verify those connections. Netstat lists the protocol in use, the local address and port number, the foreign address and port number, and the connection state.

Unexplained TCP connections can pose a major security threat because they can indicate that something or someone is connected to the local host. Additionally, unnecessary TCP connections can consume valuable system resources, thus slowing down the host's performance. Netstat should be used to examine the open connections on a host when performance appears to be compromised.

Many useful options are available for the **netstat** command. Example 5-1 shows output information from the **netstat** command.

```
Example 5-1 netstat Command
C:\> netstat

Active Connections
Proto     Local Address     Foreign Address            State
TCP       kenpc:3126        192.168.0.2:netbios-ssn    ESTABLISHED
TCP       kenpc:3158        207.138.126.152:http       ESTABLISHED
TCP       kenpc:3159        207.138.126.169:http       ESTABLISHED
TCP       kenpc:3160        207.138.126.169:http       ESTABLISHED
TCP       kenpc:3161        sc.msn.com:http            ESTABLISHED
TCP       kenpc:3166        www.cisco.com:http         ESTABLISHED
C:\>
```

TCP and UDP Segmentation (5.1.2.10)

PDUs are built by passing data from an application down through the protocol layers. Each layer adds specific information. The PDU is then transmitted on the medium. At the destination host, this process is reversed until the data can be passed up to the application.

Some applications transmit large amounts of data—in some cases, many gigabytes. It would be impractical to send all of this data in one large piece. No other network traffic could be transmitted while this data was being sent. A large piece of data could take minutes or even hours to send. In addition, if there were any errors, the entire data file would be lost or have to be re-sent. Network devices would not have memory buffers large enough to store this much data while it is transmitted or received. The limit varies depending on the networking technology and specific physical medium in use.

Dividing application data into segments ensures both that data is transmitted within the limits of the media and that data from different applications can be multiplexed on to the media.

TCP and UDP Handle Segmentation Differently

As shown earlier in Figure 5-8, each TCP segment header contains a sequence number that allows the transport layer functions on the destination host to reassemble segments in the order in which they were transmitted. This ensures that the destination application has the data in the exact form the sender intended.

Although services using UDP also track the conversations between applications, they are concerned neither with the order in which the information was transmitted nor with maintaining a connection. There is no sequence number in the UDP header. UDP is a simpler design and generates less overhead than TCP, resulting in a faster transfer of data.

Information may arrive in a different order than it was transmitted because different packets may take different paths through the network. An application that uses UDP must tolerate the fact that data may not arrive in the order in which it was sent.

Interactive Graphic

Activity 5.1.2.10: TCP and UDP Segmentation

Go to the online course and click the header boxes for more information.

Interactive Graphic

Activity 5.1.2.11: TCP and UDP Characteristics

Go to the online course and perform the interactive activity comparing TCP and UDP.

TCP and UDP (5.2)

TCP and UDP deliver messages and handle information in different ways. This section takes a closer look at how they function. This section explains how PDUs are used in TCP and UDP messages.

TCP Communication (5.2.1)

First you will learn how TCP uses messages to establish connections and provide reliable data delivery.

TCP Reliable Delivery (5.2.1.1)

The key distinction between TCP and UDP is reliability. The reliability of TCP communication is obtained through the use of connection-oriented sessions. Before a host using TCP sends data to another host, TCP initiates a process to create a connection with the destination. This stateful connection enables the tracking of a session, or communication stream between the hosts. This process ensures that each host is aware of and prepared for the communication stream. A TCP conversation requires the establishment of a session between the hosts in both directions.

Video

Video 5.2.1.1:

View the video in the online course for a demonstration of TCP initiating a stateful connection.

After a session has been established, and data transfer begins, the destination sends acknowledgements to the source for the segments that it receives. These acknowledgements form the basis of reliability within the TCP session. When the source receives an acknowledgement, it knows that the data has been successfully delivered and that it can quit tracking that data. If the source does not receive an acknowledgement within a predetermined amount of time, it retransmits that data to the destination.

Part of the additional overhead of using TCP is the network traffic generated by acknowledgements and retransmissions. The establishment of sessions creates *overhead* in the form of additional segments being exchanged. There is also additional overhead on the individual hosts, created by the necessity to keep track of which segments are awaiting acknowledgement and by the retransmission process.

TCP Server Processes (5.2.1.2)

Application processes run on servers. A single server may run multiple application processes at the same time. These processes wait until a client initiates communication with a request for information or other services.

Each application process running on the server is configured to use a port number, either by default or manually by a system administrator. An individual server cannot have two services assigned to the same port number within the same transport layer services. A host running a web server application and a file transfer application cannot have both configured to use the same port (for example, TCP port 8080). An active server application assigned to a specific port is considered to be open, which means that the transport layer accepts and processes segments addressed to that port. Any incoming client request addressed to the correct socket is accepted and the data is passed to the server application. There can be many simultaneous ports open on a server, one for each active server application. It is common for a server to provide more than one service at the same time, such as a web server and an FTP server.

One way to improve security on a server is to restrict server access to only those ports associated with the services and applications that should be accessible by authorized requestors.

Interactive Graphic

Activity 5.2.1.2: Source and Destination Ports

Go to the online course and click panels 1 through 5 to see the typical allocation of source and destination ports in TCP client/server operations.

TCP Connection Establishment (5.2.1.3)

In some cultures, when two persons meet, they often greet each other by shaking hands. The act of shaking hands is understood by both parties as a signal for a friendly greeting. Connections on the network are similar. The first handshake requests synchronization. The second handshake acknowledges the initial synchronization request and synchronizes the connection parameters in the opposite direction.

The third handshake segment is an acknowledgement used to inform the destination that both sides agree that a connection has been established.

When two hosts communicate using TCP, a connection is established before data can be exchanged. After the communication is completed, the sessions are closed and the connection is terminated. The connection and session mechanisms enable TCP's reliability function. See Figure 5-12 for the steps to establish and terminate a TCP connection.

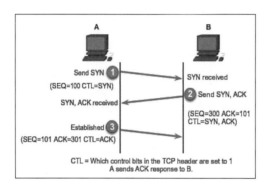

Figure 5-12 TCP Connection Establishment: SYN ACK

Hosts track each data segment within a session and exchange information about what data is received using the information in the TCP header. TCP is a full-duplex protocol, where each connection represents two one-way communication streams, or sessions. To establish the connection, the hosts perform a *three-way handshake*. Control bits in the TCP header indicate the progress and status of the connection. The three-way handshake

- Establishes that the destination device is present on the network

- Verifies that the destination device has an active service and is accepting requests on the destination port number that the initiating client intends to use for the session

- Informs the destination device that the source client intends to establish a communication session on that port number

In TCP connections, the host client establishes the connection with the server. The three steps in TCP connection establishment are

Step 1.   The initiating client requests a client-to-server communication session with the server.

Step 2.   The server acknowledges the client-to-server communication session and requests a server-to-client communication session.

Step 3.   The initiating client acknowledges the server-to-client communication session.

The following sections analyze each of these steps in turn.

Within the TCP segment header, there are six 1-bit fields that contain control information used to manage the TCP processes:

- **URG:** Urgent pointer field significant
- **ACK:** Acknowledgement field significant
- **PSH:** Push function
- **RST:** Reset the connection
- **SYN:** Synchronize sequence numbers
- **FIN:** No more data from sender

The ACK and SYN fields are relevant to our analysis of the three-way handshake.

TCP Three-way Handshake Analysis: Step 1 (5.2.1.4)

Using the output of protocol analysis software, such as Wireshark outputs, you can examine the operation of the TCP three-way handshake.

Step 1. The initiating client requests a client-to-server communication session with the server.

A TCP client begins the three-way handshake by sending a segment with the sequence number (SYN) control flag set, indicating an initial value in the sequence number field in the header. This initial value for the sequence number, known as the *initial sequence number (ISN),* is randomly chosen and is used to begin tracking the flow of data from the client to the server for this session. The ISN in the header of each segment is increased by one for each byte of data sent from the client to the server as the data conversation continues.

As shown in Figure 5-13, output from a protocol analyzer shows the SYN control flag and the relative sequence number. The SYN control flag is set and the relative sequence number is at 0. Although the protocol analyzer in Figure 5-13 indicates the relative values for the sequence and acknowledgement numbers, the true values are 32-bit binary numbers. The figure shows the 4 bytes represented in hexadecimal.

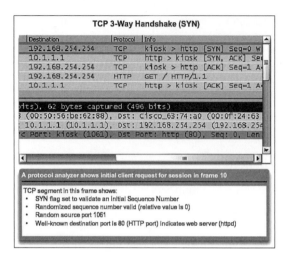

Figure 5-13 Protocol Analyzer Output Depicting Step 1 of Three-Way Handshake

TCP Three-way Handshake Analysis: Step 2 (5.2.1.5)

Step 2: The server acknowledges the client-to-server communication session and requests a server-to-client communication session.

The TCP server must acknowledge the receipt of the *SYN segment* from the client to establish the session from the client to the server. To do so, the server sends a segment back to the client with the *acknowledgement (ACK) flag* set indicating that the acknowledgement number is significant. With this flag set in the segment, the client recognizes this as an acknowledgement that the server received the SYN from the TCP client.

The value of the acknowledgement number field is equal to the ISN plus 1. This establishes a session from the client to the server. The ACK flag remains set for the balance of the session. Recall that the conversation between the client and the server is actually two one-way sessions: one from the client to the server, and the other from the server to the client. In this second step of the three-way handshake, the server must initiate the response to the client. To start this session, the server uses the SYN flag in the same way that the client did. It sets the SYN control flag in the header to establish a session from the server to the client. The *SYN flag* indicates that the initial value of the sequence number field is in the header. This value is used to track the flow of data in this session from the server back to the client.

As shown in Figure 5-14, the protocol analyzer output shows that the ACK and SYN control flags are set and the relative sequence and acknowledgement numbers are displayed.

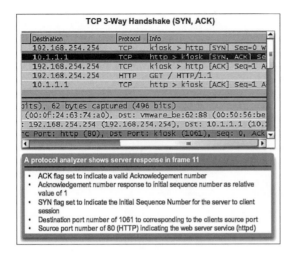

Figure 5-14 Protocol Analyzer Output Depicting Step 2 of Three-Way Handshake

TCP Three-way Handshake Analysis: Step 3 (5.2.1.6)

Step 3: The initiating client acknowledges the server-to-client communication session.

Finally, the TCP client responds with a segment containing an ACK that is the response to the TCP SYN sent by the server. There is no user data in this segment. The value in the acknowledgement number field contains one more than the ISN received from the server. After both sessions are established between client and server, all additional segments exchanged in this communication will have the ACK flag set.

As shown in Figure 5-15, the protocol analyzer output shows the ACK control flag set and the relative sequence and acknowledgement numbers.

Security can be added to the data network by

- Denying the establishment of TCP sessions
- Only allowing sessions to be established for specific services
- Only allowing traffic as a part of already established sessions

These security measures can be implemented for all TCP sessions or only for selected sessions.

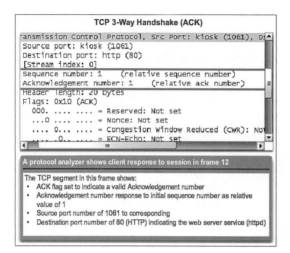

Figure 5-15 Protocol Analyzer Output Depicting Step 3 of Three-Way Handshake

TCP Session Termination Analysis (5.2.1.7)

To close a connection, the *Finish (FIN) control flag* must be set in the segment header. To end each one-way TCP session, a two-way handshake is used, consisting of a FIN segment and an ACK segment. Therefore, to terminate a single conversation supported by TCP, the following four exchanges are needed to end both sessions.

> **Note**
>
> In this explanation, the terms *client* and *server* are used as a reference for simplicity, but the termination process can be initiated by any two hosts that have an open session:

Step 1. When the client has no more data to send in the stream, it sends a segment with the FIN flag set.

Step 2. The server sends an ACK to acknowledge the receipt of the FIN to terminate the session from client to server.

Step 3. The server sends a FIN to the client, to terminate the server-to-client session.

Step 4. The client responds with an ACK to acknowledge the FIN from the server.

When the client has no more data to transfer, it sets the FIN flag in the header of a segment. Next, the server end of the connection sends a normal segment containing data with the ACK flag set using the acknowledgement number, confirming that all the bytes of data have been received. When all segments have been acknowledged, the session is closed.

The session in the other direction is closed using the same process. The receiver indicates that there is no more data to send by setting the FIN flag in the header of a segment sent to the source. A return acknowledgement confirms that all bytes of data have been received, and that session is, in turn, closed.

It is also possible to terminate the connection by a three-way handshake. When the client has no more data to send, it sends a FIN to the server. If the server also has no more data to send, it can reply with both the FIN and ACK flags set, combining two steps into one. The client then replies with an ACK.

Interactive Graphic

Activity 5.2.1.7: TCP Connection Establishment and Termination

Go to the online course and click through buttons 1, 2, and 3 to see the TCP connection establishment and termination. Click the SYN and ACK steps to view the steps in the processes.

Lab 5.2.1.8: Using Wireshark to Observe the TCP 3-way Handshake

This simulation lab is intended to help you understand the steps in the process of the TCP three-way handshake. You will prepare Wireshark to capture packets, and then you will examine the packets for TCP information.

Interactive Graphic

Activity 5.2.1.9: TCP Connection and Termination Process

Go to the online course and click through the interactive activity demonstrating TCP connection and termination processes.

Protocol Data Units (5.2.2)

In this section you will learn how PDUs are handled by TCP.

TCP Reliability—Ordered Delivery (5.2.2.1)

One of the essential tasks of TCP is to sort segments that arrive out of sequence.

Resequencing Segments

When services send data using TCP, segments may arrive at their destination out of order. For the original message to be understood by the recipient, the data in these segments is reassembled into the original order. Sequence numbers are assigned in the header of each packet to achieve this goal.

During session setup, an initial sequence number (ISN) is set. This ISN represents the starting value for the bytes for this session that is transmitted to the receiving application. As data is transmitted during the session, the sequence number is incremented by the number of bytes that have been transmitted. This data byte tracking enables each segment to be uniquely identified and acknowledged. Missing segments can be identified.

Segment sequence numbers enable the reliability by indicating how to reassemble and reorder received segments.

The receiving TCP process places the data from a segment into a receiving buffer. Segments are placed in the proper sequence number order and passed to the application layer when reassembled. Any segments that arrive with non-contiguous sequence numbers are held for later processing. Then, when the segments with the missing bytes arrive, these segments are processed in order.

TCP Reliability—Acknowledgement and Window Size (5.2.2.2)

In this section you will learn how TCP provides reliability with acknowledgement messages. You will also see how TCP reduces overhead by sending data at varying rates.

Confirming Receipt of Segments

One of the functions of TCP is to ensure that each segment reaches its destination. The TCP services on the destination host acknowledge the data that it has received by the source application.

The sequence (SEQ) number and acknowledgement (ACK) number are used together to confirm receipt of the bytes of data contained in the transmitted segments. The *SEQ number* indicates the relative number of bytes that have been transmitted in this session, including the bytes in the current segment. TCP uses the *ACK number* sent back to the source to indicate the next byte that the receiver expects to receive. This is called *expectational acknowledgement.*

The source is informed that the destination has received all bytes in this data stream up to, but not including, the byte indicated by the ACK number. The sending host is expected to send a segment that uses a sequence number that is equal to the ACK number.

Remember, each connection is actually two one-way sessions. SEQ and ACK numbers are being exchanged in both directions.

In the example in Figure 5-16, the host on the left is sending data to the host on the right. It sends a segment containing 10 bytes of data for this session and a sequence number equal to 1 in the header.

The receiving host receives the segment at Layer 4 and determines that the sequence number is 1 and that it has 10 bytes of data. The host then sends a segment back to the host on the left to acknowledge the receipt of this data. In this segment, the host sets the ACK number to 11 to indicate that the next byte of data it expects to receive in this session is byte number 11. When the sending host receives this acknowledgement, it can now send the next segment containing data for this session starting with byte number 11.

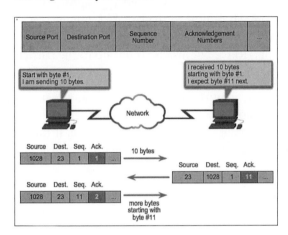

Figure 5-16 Acknowledgement of TCP Segments

Looking at this example, if the sending host had to wait for acknowledgement of receiving each 10 bytes, the network would have a lot of overhead. To reduce the overhead of these acknowledgements, multiple segments of data can be sent and acknowledged with a single TCP message in the opposite direction. This acknowledgement contains an ACK number based on the total number of bytes received in the session. For example, starting with a sequence number of 2000, if 10 segments of 1,000 bytes each were received, an ACK number of 12001 would be returned to the source.

The amount of data that a source can transmit before an acknowledgement must be received is called the *window size*, which is a field in the TCP header that enables the management of lost data and flow control.

TCP Reliability—Data Loss and Retransmission (5.2.2.3)

Another essential task of TCP is to ensure delivery of data. When segments are lost in transit, TCP can help replace the missing data.

Handling Segment Loss

No matter how well designed a network is, data loss occasionally occurs; therefore, TCP provides methods of managing these segment losses. Among these is a mechanism to retransmit segments with unacknowledged data.

A destination host service using TCP usually only acknowledges data for contiguous sequence bytes. If one or more segments are missing, only the data in the first contiguous sequence of bytes is acknowledged. For example, if segments with sequence numbers 1500 to 3000 and 3400 to 3500 were received, the ACK number would be 3001. This is because there are segments with the SEQ numbers 3001 to 3399 that have not been received.

When TCP at the source host has not received an acknowledgement after a predetermined amount of time, it returns to the last ACK number received and retransmits the data from that point forward. The retransmission process is not specified by the Request for Comments (RFC), but instead is left up to the particular implementation of TCP.

For a typical TCP implementation, a host may transmit a segment, put a copy of the segment in a retransmission queue, and start a timer. When the data acknowledgement is received, the segment is deleted from the queue. If the acknowledgement is not received before the timer expires, the segment is retransmitted.

Video

Video 5.2.2.3:

View the video in the online course to see a demonstration of the retransmission of lost segments.

Hosts today may also employ an optional feature called selective acknowledgements (SACKs). If both hosts support SACKs, it is possible for the destination to acknowledge bytes in discontinuous segments and the host would only need to retransmit the missing data.

TCP Flow Control—Window Size and Acknowledgements (5.2.2.4)

As part of ensuring reliability, TCP helps control the flow of data.

Flow Control

TCP also provides mechanisms for flow control. Flow control helps maintain the reliability of TCP transmission by adjusting the rate of data flow between source and destination for a given session. Flow control is accomplished by limiting the amount of data segments forwarded at one time and by requiring acknowledgements of receipt prior to sending more.

To accomplish flow control, the first thing that TCP determines is the amount of data segments that the destination device can accept. As previously indicated, the TCP header includes a 16-bit field called the window size. This indicates the number of bytes that the destination device of a TCP session is able to accept and process at one time. The initial window size is agreed upon during the session startup via the three-way handshake between source and destination. Once agreed upon, the source device must limit the amount of data segments sent to the destination device based on the window size. Only after the source device receives an acknowledgement that the data segments have been received can it continue sending more data for the session.

During the delay in receiving the acknowledgement, the sender does not send any additional segments. In periods when the network is congested or the resources of the receiving host are strained, the delay may increase. As this delay grows longer, the effective transmission rate of the data for this session decreases. The slowdown in data transmission from each session helps reduce resource conflict on the network and destination device when multiple sessions are running.

See Figure 5-17 for a simplified representation of window size and acknowledgements. In this example, the initial window size for a TCP session represented is set to 3,000 bytes. When the sender has transmitted 3,000 bytes, it waits for an acknowledgement of these bytes before transmitting more segments in this session. After the sender has received an acknowledgement from the receiver, the sender can transmit an additional 3,000 bytes.

TCP uses window sizes to attempt to manage the rate of transmission to the maximum flow that the network and destination device can support, while minimizing loss and retransmissions.

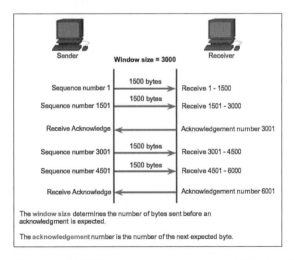

Figure 5-17 TCP Acknowledgement and Window Size

TCP Flow Control—Congestion Avoidance (5.2.2.5)

TCP can aid reliability by adjusting data flow to reliable and efficient levels.

Reducing Window Size

Another way to control the data flow is to use *dynamic window sizes*. When network resources are constrained, TCP can reduce the window size to require that received segments be acknowledged more frequently. This effectively slows down the rate of transmission because the source waits for data to be acknowledged more frequently.

The receiving host sends the window size value to the sending host to indicate the number of bytes that it is prepared to receive. If the destination needs to slow down the rate of communication because of limited buffer memory, for example, it can send a smaller window size value to the source as part of an acknowledgement.

As shown in Figure 5-18, if a receiving host has congestion, it may respond to the sending host with a segment that specifies a reduced window size. In this figure, there was a loss of one of the segments. The receiver changed the window field in the TCP header of the returning segments in this conversation from 3000 down to 1500, which caused the sender to reduce the window size to 1,500 bytes.

After a period of transmission with no data losses or constrained resources, the receiver begins to increase the window field, which reduces the overhead on the network because fewer acknowledgements must be sent. The window size continues to increase until there is data loss, which causes the window size to decrease.

This dynamic increasing and decreasing of window size is a continuous process in TCP. In highly efficient networks, window sizes may become very large because data is not lost. In networks where the underlying infrastructure is under stress, the window size likely remains small.

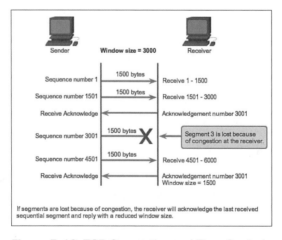

Figure 5-18 TCP Congestion and Flow Control

UDP Communication (5.2.3)

In this section you will learn about the UDP protocol and when its use may be preferred over TCP.

UDP Low Overhead Versus Reliability (5.2.3.1)

UDP is a simple protocol that provides the basic transport layer functions. It has much lower overhead than TCP because it is not connection-oriented and does not offer the sophisticated retransmission, sequencing, and flow-control mechanisms that provide reliability.

This does not mean that applications that use UDP are always unreliable, nor does it mean that UDP is an inferior protocol. It simply means that these functions are not provided by the transport layer protocol and must be implemented elsewhere, if required.

Although the total amount of UDP traffic found on a typical network is often relatively low, key application layer protocols that use UDP include

- Domain Name System (DNS)
- Simple Network Management Protocol (SNMP)
- Dynamic Host Configuration Protocol (DHCP)
- Routing Information Protocol (RIP)
- Trivial File Transfer Protocol (TFTP)
- IP telephony or Voice over IP (VoIP)
- Online games

Some applications, such as online games or VoIP, can tolerate some data loss. If these applications used TCP, they could experience large delays while TCP detects data loss and retransmits data. These delays would be more detrimental to the performance of the application than small data losses. Some applications, such as DNS, simply retry the request if no response is received; therefore, they do not need TCP to guarantee message delivery. The low overhead of UDP makes it very desirable for such applications.

UDP Datagram Reassembly (5.2.3.2)

Because UDP is *connectionless*, sessions are not established before communication takes place as they are with TCP. UDP is said to be transaction-based; that is, when an application has data to send, it simply sends the data.

Many applications that use UDP send small amounts of data that can fit in one segment. However, some applications send larger amounts of data that must be split into multiple segments. The UDP PDU is referred to as a datagram, although the terms *segment* and *datagram* are sometimes used interchangeably to describe a transport layer PDU.

When multiple datagrams are sent to a destination, they may take different paths and arrive in the wrong order. UDP does not track sequence numbers the way TCP does. UDP has no way to reorder the datagrams into their transmission order.

Therefore, UDP simply reassembles the data in the order that it was received and forwards it to the application. If the data sequence is important to the application, the application must identify the proper sequence and determine how the data should be processed.

UDP Server Processes and Requests (5.2.3.3)

Like TCP-based applications, UDP-based server applications are assigned well-known or registered port numbers. When these applications or processes are running on a server, they accept the data matched with the assigned port number. When UDP receives a datagram destined for one of these ports, it forwards the application data to the appropriate application based on its port number.

UDP Client Processes (5.2.3.4)

As with TCP, client/server communication is initiated by a client application that requests data from a server process. The UDP client process randomly selects a port number from the range of dynamic port numbers and uses this as the source port for the conversation. The destination port is usually the well-known or registered port number assigned to the server process.

Randomized source port numbers also help with security. If there is a predictable pattern for destination port selection, an intruder can more easily simulate access to a client by attempting to connect to the port number most likely to be open.

Because there is no session to be created with UDP, as soon as the data is ready to be sent and the ports have been identified, UDP can form the datagrams and pass them to the network layer to be addressed and sent on the network.

After a client has selected the source and destination ports, the same pair of ports is used in the header of all datagrams used in the transaction. For the data returning to the client from the server, the source and destination port numbers in the datagram header are reversed.

Interactive Graphic

Activity 5.2.3.4: UDP Client Processes

Go to the online course and click through the panels on the right to see details of UDP client processes.

Lab 5.2.3.5: Using Wireshark to Examine a UDP DNS Capture

In this lab you will capture and analyze DNS and UDP packets.

TCP or UDP—That Is the Question (5.2.4)

Application developers must consider the benefits and costs of TCP and UDP when designing applications. This section will look at the issues they must consider.

Applications That Use TCP (5.2.4.1)

Many applications require reliability and other services provided by TCP. These are applications that can tolerate some delay or performance loss due to the overhead imposed by TCP.

This makes TCP best suited for applications that need reliable transport and can tolerate some delay. TCP is a great example of how the different layers of the TCP/IP protocol suite have specific roles. Because the transport layer protocol TCP handles all tasks associated with segmenting the data stream into segments, reliability, flow control, and reordering of segments, it frees the application from having to manage any of this. The application can simply send the data stream to the transport layer and use the services of TCP.

Some examples of well-known applications that use TCP include

- HTTP
- FTP
- SMTP
- Telnet

Applications That Use UDP (5.2.4.2)

There are three types of applications that are best suited for UDP:

- Applications that can tolerate some data loss, but require little or no delay
- Applications with simple request and reply transactions
- Unidirectional communications where reliability is not required or can be handled by the application

Many video and multimedia applications, such as VoIP and Internet Protocol Television (IPTV), use UDP. These applications can tolerate some data loss with little or no noticeable effect. The reliability mechanisms of TCP introduce some delay that can be noticeable in the quality of the sound or video being received.

Other types of applications well suited for UDP are those that use simple request and reply transactions. This is where a host sends a request and may or may not receive a reply. These types of applications include

- DHCP

- DNS (may also use TCP)

- SNMP

- TFTP

Some applications handle reliability themselves. These applications do not need the services of TCP, and can better utilize UDP as the transport layer protocol. TFTP is one example of this type of protocol. TFTP has its own mechanisms for flow control, error detection, acknowledgements, and error recovery. It does not need to rely on TCP for those services.

Lab 5.2.4.3: Using Wireshark to Examine FTP and TFTP Captures

In this lab you will identify TCP and UDP header fields and operations.

Summary (5.3)

Class Activity 5.3.1.1: We Need to Talk, Again – Game

In this activity, given a scenario, you will determine whether high-reliability messaging should be used. You will focus on whether the final message is complete, correct, and delivered in a timely manner.

Packet Tracer Activity 5.3.1.2: TCP and UDP Communications

This activity is intended to provide a foundation for understanding TCP and UDP in detail. It also provides an opportunity to explore the functionality of the TCP and UDP protocols, multiplexing, and the function of port numbers in determining which local application requested the data or is sending the data.

The transport layer provides transport-related services by

- Dividing data received from an application into segments

- Adding a header to identify and manage each segment

- Using the header information to reassemble the segments back into application data

- Passing the assembled data to the correct application

UDP and TCP are common transport layer protocols.

UDP datagrams and TCP segments have headers added in front of the data that include a source port number and destination port number. These port numbers enable data to be directed to the correct application running on the destination computer.

TCP does not pass any data to the network until it knows that the destination is ready to receive it. TCP then manages the flow of the data and resends any data segments that are not acknowledged as being received at the destination. TCP uses mechanisms of handshaking, timers, acknowledgement messages, and dynamic windowing to achieve reliability. The reliability process, however, imposes overhead on the network in terms of much larger segment headers and more network traffic between the source and destination.

If the application data needs to be delivered across the network quickly, or if network bandwidth cannot support the overhead of control messages being exchanged between the source and the destination systems, UDP would be the developer's preferred transport layer protocol. UDP does not track or acknowledge the receipt of datagrams at the destination; it just passes received datagrams to the application layer as they arrive. UDP does not resend lost datagrams. However, this does not necessarily mean that the communication itself is unreliable; there may be mechanisms in the application layer protocols and services that process lost or delayed datagrams if the application has these requirements.

The application developer decides which transport layer protocol best meets the requirements for the application. It is important to remember that the other layers all play a part in data network communications and influence its performance.

Practice

The following activities provide practice with the topics introduced in this chapter. The Labs and Class Activities are available in the companion *Networking Basics Lab Manual* (978-1-58713-313-8). The Packet Tracer Activities PKA files are found in the online course.

Class Activities

Class Activity 5.0.1.2: We Need To Talk

Class Activity 5.3.1.1: We Need to Talk, Again – Game

Labs

Lab 5.2.1.8: Using Wireshark to Observe the TCP 3-way Handshake

Lab 5.2.3.5: Using Wireshark to Examine a UDP DNS Capture

Lab 5.2.4.3: Using Wireshark to Examine FTP and TFTP Captures

Packet Tracer
☐ Activity

Packet Tracer Activity

Packet Tracer Activity 5.3.1.2: TCP and UDP Communications

Check Your Understanding

Complete all the review questions listed here to test your understanding of the topics and concepts in this chapter. The appendix, "Answers to the 'Check Your Understanding' Questions," lists the answers.

1. What is the purpose of the transport layer? (Choose two.)

    A. It is responsible for establishing a permanent communication link between two applications and delivering data between them.

    B. It is the link between the application layer and the lower layers that is responsible for network transmission.

    C. It uses IP information to identify the appropriate application for each communication stream.

    D. If necessary, it reassembles segments into the order in which they were sent.

2. How does the transport layer aid in end-to-end communication for applications? (Choose two.)

    A. At the source, data is sorted into frames, or conversations.

    B. It adds a header to the segment to enable data reassembly.

    C. It passes data down to the lower layers as manageable pieces that can be multiplexed, or inserted with other data packets, over the media.

    D. At the destination, it sends segments to the presentation layer for reassembly.

3. In TCP/IP, segmentation and reassembly processes can be achieved using which transport layer protocol?

    A. IP

    B. TCP

    C. UDP

    D. TFTP

4. What does the transport layer use to track application conversations?

    A. Port numbers

    B. MAC addresses

    C. IP addresses

    D. VLAN tags

5. Which statements are true? (Choose two.)

    A. TCP is stateful and connectionless.

    B. UDP is stateful and connection-oriented.

    C. TCP is stateless and connection-oriented.

    D. UDP is connectionless and stateless.

    E. TCP is connection-oriented and stateful.

    F. UDP is stateless and connection-oriented.

6. What is an example of a protocol that uses TCP?

    A. IP

    B. FTP

    C. UDP

    D. IPX

7. Which is *not* true of TCP?

    A. Different applications have different reliability requirements.

    B. It is used by the IP protocol.

    C. It functions at OSI Layer 3.

    D. It ensures that all data arrives at its destination.

8. Which is *not* a function of the transport layer?

    A. Tracking transmitted data segments

    B. Initiating data streams in the application layer

    C. Acknowledging received data

    D. Retransmitting any unacknowledged data

9. When a message fails to deliver the first time, how will TCP respond?

    A. Resend the message when the user requests it

    B. Resend the message when a portion is not acknowledged

    C. Resend only the acknowledged segments

    D. Resend the unacknowledged segments

10. Which is true about UDP?

    A. It lacks the reliability of transport layer processes found in TCP.

    B. It is older and rarely preferred to TCP.

    C. It resends complete unacknowledged data in a conversation.

    D. It resends only unacknowledged segments in a conversation.

11. Which is true about both TCP and UDP?

    A. They are easily interchangeable by application developers.

    B. Application developers must choose one depending on the characteristics of the application.

    C. TCP is better if an application can tolerate data loss.

    D. UDP uses slightly more processing overhead than TCP.

12. Which application would be better suited to TCP?

    A. Streaming video

    B. VoIP

    C. Pandora Music

    D. Email

13. Which is a feature of TCP?

    A. Connectionless

    B. Ordered data reconstruction

    C. Best-effort delivery

    D. Used in music streaming applications

14. Which is a feature of UDP?

    A. Connection-oriented conversations by establishing sessions

    B. Best-effort delivery

    C. Ordered data reconstruction

    D. Flow control

15. How many bytes of overhead data are in the TCP data header?

    A. 64

    B. 32

    C. 20

    D. 16

    E. 8

16. A socket consists of

    A. The combination of the source and destination MAC addresses and port numbers

    B. The combination of SYN flags and ACK flags

    C. The combination of the source and destination IP addresses and port numbers

    D. The combination of only the destination IP addresses and MAC addresses

17. In which scenario will the transport layer at the destination use HTTP to retrieve a web page from a web server?

    A. The header contains the HTTP port of 110.

    B. Port 21 is listed as the source port in the header.

    C. The source port in the header is 23.

    D. The destination port in the header is 80.

18. Which destination IP address indicates an email application must be used?

    A. 172.16.20.10:80

    B. 192.168.15.5:110

    C. 172.16.4.12:23

    D. 192.168.15.78:53

19. What does the flow-control window size indicate?

    A. The expected number of bits in each sequence

    B. The number of the first acknowledgement number

    C. The number of the next expected byte

    D. The number of the last byte received

20. With a window size of 2500, what would be the second acknowledgement number sent by the receiver?

    A. 2500

    B. 2501

    C. 2502

    D. 5001

21. How does a sender know which segments were not received and need to be re-sent?

    A. The three-way handshake

    B. The SEQ and ACK messages

    C. The window size decreases

    D. The window closes for a time

22. Which two statements are likely true when a receiving host adjusts the window size from 2500 to 2000 during transmission? (Choose two.)

    A. Static window sizing is in use.

    B. The transmission will become more efficient.

    C. The transmission time of the complete message will increase.

    D. There will be more SEQ and ACK messages.

    E. There is a reduction in traffic on the network.

    F. The flow of data is stopped while the window size is adjusted.

Objectives

Upon completion of this chapter, you will be able to answer the following questions:

- What is the purpose of the network layer in data communication?

- Why does the IPv4 protocol require other layers to provide reliability?

- What is the role of the major header fields in IPv4 and IPv6 packets?

- How does a host device use routing tables to direct packets to itself, a local destination, or a default gateway?

- How does a host routing table compare to a routing table in a router?

- What are the common components and interfaces of a router?

- What is the boot process of a Cisco IOS router?

- How do you configure the initial settings on a Cisco IOS router?

- How do you configure two active interfaces on a Cisco IOS router?

- How do you configure the default gateway on a network device?

Key Terms

This chapter uses the following key terms. You can find the definitions in the Glossary.

local default route   page 226

router   page 227

metric   page 231

directly connected routes   page 232

remote routes   page 232

route source   page 235

administrative distance   page 235

route timestamp   page 236

outgoing interface   page 236

next hop   page 236

branch   page 241

WAN   page 241

service provider   page 241

RAM   page 241

running configuration file   page 242

ARP cache   page 242

packet buffer   page 242

*dynamic random-access memory
  (DRAM)   page 242*

*dual in-line memory module
  (DIMM)   page 242*

ROM   page 242

NVRAM   page 242

flash memory   page 243

console ports   page 244

LAN interface   page 244

EHWIC slots   page 244

management ports   page 245

inband router interfaces   page 245

Ethernet LAN interfaces   page 246

serial WAN interfaces   page 246

startup configuration file   page 247

Power-On Self Test (POST)   page 248

TFTP server   page 249

description text   page 253

show ip interface brief command   page 253

Introduction (6.0.1.1)

Network applications and services on one end device can communicate with applications and services running on another end device. How is this data communicated across the network in an efficient way?

The protocols of the OSI model network layer specify addressing and processes that enable transport layer data to be packaged and transported. The network layer encapsulation enables data to be passed to a destination within a network (or on another network) with minimum overhead.

This chapter focuses on the role of the network layer. It examines how it divides networks into groups of hosts to manage the flow of data packets within a network. It also covers how communication between networks is facilitated. This communication between networks is called *routing*.

Class Activity 6.0.1.2: The Road Less Traveled...or Is It?

In this activity you will visualize how a hop-by-hop routing paradigm, with correct path selection at each hop, results in a successful delivery of packets. You will recognize that each router on the path must have correct knowledge about the destination network, and the path toward that network, to deliver packets over the shortest path.

Network Layer Protocols (6.1)

In this section you will learn how network layer protocols find a path for data across networks.

Network Layer in Communication (6.1.1)

Network layer protocols add network addressing and route information to data from the upper layers.

The Network Layer (6.1.1.1)

The network layer, or OSI Layer 3, provides services to allow end devices to exchange data across the network. To accomplish this end-to-end transport, the network layer uses four basic processes:

- **Addressing end devices:** In the same way that a phone has a unique telephone number, end devices must be configured with a unique IP address for identification on the network. An end device with a configured IP address is referred to as a *host*.

- **Encapsulation:** The network layer receives a protocol data unit (PDU) from the transport layer. In a process called encapsulation, the network layer adds IP header information such as the IP address of the source (sending) and destination (receiving) hosts. After header information is added to the PDU, the PDU is called a *packet*.

- **Routing:** The network layer provides services to direct packets to a destination host on another network. To travel to other networks, the packet must be processed by a router. The role of the router is to select paths for and direct packets toward the destination host in a process known as routing. A packet may cross many intermediary devices before reaching the destination host. Each route the packet takes to reach the destination host is called a *hop*.

- **De-encapsulation:** When the packet arrives at the destination host, the host checks the IP header of the packet. If the destination IP address within the header matches its own IP address, the IP header is removed from the packet. This process of removing headers from lower layers is known as de-encapsulation. After the packet is de-encapsulated by the network layer, the resulting Layer 4 PDU contained in the packet is passed up to the appropriate service at the transport layer.

Unlike the transport layer (OSI Layer 4), which manages the data transport between the processes running on each host, network layer protocols specify the packet structure and processing used to carry the data from one host to another host. Operating without regard to the data carried in each packet allows the network layer to carry packets for multiple types of communications between multiple hosts.

<table>
<tr><td>Video</td></tr>
</table>

Video 6.1.1.1:

View the video in the online course for a demonstration of the exchange of data.

Network Layer Protocols (6.1.1.2)

There are several network layer protocols in existence; however, only the following two are commonly implemented:

- *Internet Protocol version 4 (IPv4)*

- *Internet Protocol version 6 (IPv6)*

Other legacy network layer protocols that are not widely used include

- Novell Internetwork Packet Exchange (IPX)

- AppleTalk

- Connectionless Network Service (CLNS/DECNet)

Discussion of these legacy protocols will be minimal.

Characteristics of the IP Protocol (6.1.2)

This section explores the Internet Protocol (IP portion of the TCP/IP protocol stack). This is the most common networking protocol in use on the Web.

Characteristics of IP (6.1.2.1)

IP is the network layer service implemented by the TCP/IP protocol suite. IP was designed as a protocol with low overhead. It provides only the functions that are necessary to deliver a packet from a source to a destination over an interconnected system of networks. The protocol was not designed to track and manage the flow of packets. These functions, if required, are performed by other protocols in other layers.

The basic characteristics of IP are

- **Connectionless:** No connection with the destination is established before sending data packets.

- **Best effort (unreliable):** Packet delivery is not guaranteed.

- *Media independent*: Operation is independent of the medium carrying the data.

IP – Connectionless (6.1.2.2)

The role of the network layer is to transport packets between hosts while placing as little burden on the network as possible. The network layer is not concerned with, or even aware of, the type of communication contained inside of a packet. IP is connectionless, meaning that no dedicated end-to-end connection is created before data is sent. Connectionless communication is conceptually similar to sending a letter to someone without notifying the recipient in advance.

The postal service uses the information on a letter to deliver the letter to a recipient. The address on the envelope does not provide information as to whether the receiver is present, whether the letter arrives, or whether the receiver can read the letter. In fact, the postal service is unaware of the information contained within the contents of the packet that it is delivering and, therefore, cannot provide any error correction mechanisms.

Connectionless data communications work on the same principle. IP is connectionless and, therefore, requires no initial exchange of control information to establish an end-to-end connection before packets are forwarded. IP also does not require additional fields in the PDU header to maintain an established connection. This process greatly reduces the overhead of IP. However, with no pre-established end-to-end connection, senders are unaware whether destination devices are present and functional when sending packets, nor are they aware whether destination devices receive the packet or are able to access and read the packet. Figure 6-1 shows an example of connectionless communication.

IP – Best-Effort Delivery (6.1.2.3)

IP is often referred to as an unreliable or best-effort delivery protocol. This does not mean that IP works properly sometimes and does not function well at other times, nor does it mean that it is a poor data communications protocol. "Unreliable" simply means that IP does not have the capability to manage and recover from undelivered or corrupt packets. This is because IP packets are sent with information about the location of delivery, but they contain no information that can be processed to inform the sender whether delivery was successful. There is no synchronization data included in the packet header for tracking the order of packet delivery. There are also no acknowledgments of packet delivery with IP, and there is no error control data to track whether packets were delivered without corruption. Packets may arrive at the destination corrupted, out of sequence, or not at all. Based on the information provided in the IP header, there is no capability for packet retransmissions if errors such as these occur.

If out-of-order or missing packets create problems for the application using the data, then upper-layer services, such as TCP, must resolve these issues. This allows IP to function very efficiently. If reliability overhead were included in IP, then communications that do not require connections or reliability would be burdened with the bandwidth consumption and delay produced by this overhead. In the TCP/IP suite, the transport layer can use either TCP or UDP based on the need for reliability in communication. Leaving the reliability decision to the transport layer makes IP more adaptable and accommodating for different types of communication.

Figure 6-1 shows an example of IP communications. Connection-oriented protocols, such as TCP, require that control data be exchanged to establish the connection. To maintain information about the connection, TCP also requires additional fields in the PDU header.

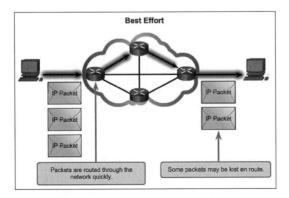

Figure 6-1   IP: a Best Effort Protocol

IP – Media Independent (6.1.2.4)

The network layer is also not burdened with the characteristics of the media on which packets are transported. IP operates independently of the media that carry the data at lower layers of the protocol stack. As shown in Figure 6-2, any individual IP packet can be communicated electrically over cable, as optical signals over fiber, or wirelessly as radio signals.

It is the responsibility of the OSI data link layer to take an IP packet and prepare it for transmission over the communications medium. This means that the transport of IP packets is not limited to any particular medium.

There is, however, one major characteristic of the media that the network layer considers: the maximum size of the PDU that each medium can transport. This characteristic is referred to as the *maximum transmission unit (MTU)*. Part of the control communication between the data link layer and the network layer is the establishment of a maximum size for the packet. The data link layer passes the MTU value up to the network layer. The network layer then determines how large packets should be.

In some cases, an intermediate device, usually a router, must split up a packet when forwarding it from one medium to a medium with a smaller MTU. This process is called fragmenting the packet, or *fragmentation*.

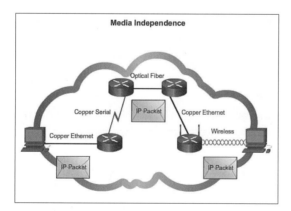

Figure 6-2   Media Independence

Encapsulating IP (6.1.2.5)

IP encapsulates, or packages, the transport layer segment or datagram by adding an IP header. This header is used to deliver the packet to the destination host. The IP header remains in place from the time the packet leaves the network layer of the source host until it arrives at the network layer of the destination host. Figure 6-3 shows the process for creating the network layer PDU.

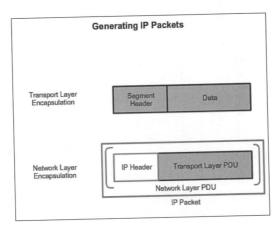

Figure 6-3   Network Layer PDU

The process of encapsulating data layer by layer enables the services at the different layers to develop and scale without affecting other layers. This means that transport layer segments can be readily packaged by IPv4 or IPv6 or by any new protocol that might be developed in the future.

Routers can implement these different network layer protocols to operate concurrently over a network to and from the same or different hosts. The routing performed by the intermediate devices only considers the contents of the packet header that encapsulates the segment. In all cases, the data portion of the packet, that is, the encapsulated transport layer PDU, remains unchanged during the network layer processes.

Interactive Graphic

Activity 6.1.2.6: IP Characteristics

Go to the online course and perform the network layer protocol exercise.

IPv4 Packet (6.1.3)

This section will explain the IPv4 packet header fields and their functions.

IPv4 Packet Header (6.1.3.1)

IPv4 has been in use since 1983 when it was deployed on the Advanced Research Projects Agency Network (ARPANET), which was the precursor to the Internet. The Internet is largely based on IPv4, which is still the most widely used network layer protocol.

An IPv4 packet has two parts:

- *IP header*: Identifies the packet characteristics

- *Payload*: Contains the Layer 4 segment information and the actual data

As shown in Figure 6-4, an IPv4 packet header consists of fields containing important information about the packet. These fields contain binary numbers that are examined by the Layer 3 process. The binary values of each field identify various settings of the IP packet.

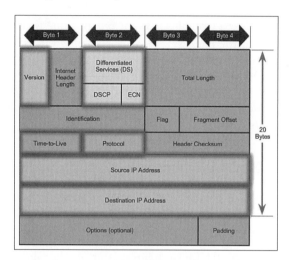

Figure 6-4   IPv4 Packet Header

Significant fields in the IPv4 header include

- *Version*: Contains a 4-bit binary value identifying the IP packet version. For IPv4 packets, this field is always set to 0100.

- *Differentiated Services (DS)*: Formerly called the Type of Service (ToS) field, the DS field is an 8-bit field used to determine the priority of each packet. The first 6 bits identify the Differentiated Services Code Point (DSCP) value that is used by a quality of service (QoS) mechanism. The last 2 bits identify the Explicit Congestion Notification (ECN) value that can be used to prevent dropped packets during times of network congestion.

- *Time-to-Live (TTL)*: Contains an 8-bit binary value that is used to limit the lifetime of a packet. It is specified in seconds but is commonly referred to as *hop count*. The packet sender sets the initial TTL value, which is decreased by one each time the packet is processed by a router, or hop. If the TTL field decrements to 0, the router discards the packet and sends an Internet Control Message Protocol (ICMP) Time Exceeded message to the source IP address. The **traceroute** command uses this field to identify the routers used between the source and destination.

- *Protocol*: This 8-bit binary value indicates the data payload type that the packet is carrying, which enables the network layer to pass the data to the appropriate upper-layer protocol. Common values include ICMP (0x01), TCP (0x06), and UDP (0x11).

- *Source IP Address*: Contains a 32-bit binary value that represents the source IP address of the packet.

- *Destination IP Address*: Contains a 32-bit binary value that represents the destination IP address of the packet.

The two most commonly referenced fields are Source IP Address and Destination IP Address. These fields identify where the packet is from and where it is going. Typically these addresses do not change while the packet is travelling from the source to the destination.

IPv4 Header Fields (6.1.3.2)

The remaining fields are used to identify and validate the packet, or to reorder a fragmented packet.

The fields used to identify and validate the packet include

- **Internet Header Length (IHL):** Contains a 4-bit binary value identifying the number of 32-bit words in the header. The IHL value varies due to the Options and Padding fields. The minimum value for this field is 5 (i.e., 5×32 = 160 bits = 20 bytes) and the maximum value is 15 (i.e., 15×32 = 480 bits = 60 bytes).

- **Total Length:** Sometimes referred to as the Packet Length, this 16-bit field defines the entire packet (fragment) size, including header and data, in bytes. The minimum-length packet is 20 bytes (20-byte header + 0 bytes data) and the maximum is 65,535 bytes.

- **Header Checksum:** This 16-bit field is used for error checking of the IP header. The checksum of the header is recalculated and compared to the value in the header's checksum field. If the values do not match, the packet is discarded.

A router may have to fragment a packet when forwarding it from one medium to another medium that has a smaller MTU. When this happens, fragmentation occurs and the IPv4 packet uses the following fields to keep track of the fragments:

- **Identification:** This 16-bit field uniquely identifies the fragment of an original IP packet.

- **Flag:** This 3-bit field identifies how the packet is fragmented. It is used with the Fragment Offset and Identification fields to help reconstruct the fragment into the original packet.

- **Fragment Offset:** This 13-bit field identifies the order in which to place the packet fragment in the reconstruction of the original unfragmented packet.

> **Note**
>
> The Options and Padding fields are rarely used and are beyond the scope of this chapter.

Sample IPv4 Headers (6.1.3.3)

Wireshark is a useful network monitoring tool for anyone working with networks and can be used with most labs in the Cisco Certified Network Associate (CCNA) courses for data analysis and troubleshooting. It can be used to view sample values contained in IP header fields.

Interactive Graphic

Activity 6.1.3.3: IPv4 Packet Captures

Go to the online course and click through the three Wireshark captures for examples of various IP packets.

Interactive Graphic

Activity 6.1.3.4: IPv4 Header Fields

Go to the online course and click through the activity exploring IPv4 header fields.

IPv6 Packet (6.1.4)

This section will explain the need for IPv6 and then describe the IPv6 header and fields and their functions.

Limitations of IPv4 (6.1.4.1)

Through the years, IPv4 has been updated to address new challenges. However, even with changes, IPv4 still has three major issues:

- **IP address depletion:** IPv4 has a limited number of unique public IP addresses available. Although there are approximately 4 billion IPv4 addresses, the increasing number of new IP-enabled devices, the increasing reliance on always-on connections, and the potential growth of less-developed regions have increased the need for more addresses.

- **Internet routing table expansion:** As the number of servers (nodes) connected to the Internet increases, so too does the number of network routes. These IPv4 routes consume a great deal of memory and processor resources on Internet routers.

- **Lack of end-to-end connectivity:** Network Address Translation (NAT) is a technology commonly implemented within IPv4 networks. NAT provides a way for multiple devices to share a single public IP address. However, because the public IP address is shared, the IP address of an internal network host is hidden. This can be problematic for technologies that require end-to-end connectivity.

Introducing IPv6 (6.1.4.2)

In the early 1990s, the Internet Engineering Task Force (IETF) grew concerned about the issues with IPv4 and began to look for a replacement. This activity led to the development of IPv6. IPv6 overcomes the limitations of IPv4 and is a powerful enhancement with features that better suit current and foreseeable network demands.

Improvements that IPv6 provides include

- **Increased address space:** IPv6 addresses are based on 128-bit hierarchical addressing, as opposed to IPv4 with 32 bits. This dramatically increases the number of available IP addresses.

- **Improved packet handling:** The IPv6 header has been simplified with fewer fields. This improves packet handling by intermediate routers and also provides support for extensions and options for increased scalability/longevity.

- **Eliminates the need for NAT:** With such a large number of public IPv6 addresses, NAT is not needed. Customer sites, from the largest enterprises to single households, can get a public IPv6 network address. This avoids some of the NAT-induced application problems experienced by applications requiring end-to-end connectivity.

- **Integrated security:** IPv6 natively supports authentication and privacy capabilities. With IPv4, additional features had to be implemented to do this.

The 32-bit IPv4 address space provides approximately 4,294,967,296 unique addresses. Of these, only 3.7 billion addresses are assignable, because the IPv4 addressing system separates the addresses into classes, and reserves addresses for multicasting, testing, and other specific uses.

As shown in Figure 6-5, IPv6 address space provides 340,282,366,920,938,463,463, 374,607,431,768,211,456, or 340 undecillion, addresses, which is roughly equivalent to every grain of sand on Earth.

Number Name	Scientific Notation	Number of Zeros
1 Thousand	10^3	1,000
1 Million	10^6	1,000,000
1 Billion	10^9	1,000,000,000
1 Trillion	10^12	1,000,000,000,000
1 Quadrillion	10^15	1,000,000,000,000,000
1 Quintillion	10^18	1,000,000,000,000,000,000
1 Sextillion	10^21	1,000,000,000,000,000,000,000
1 Septillion	10^24	1,000,000,000,000,000,000,000,000
1 Octillion	10^27	1,000,000,000,000,000,000,000,000,000
1 Nonillion	10^30	1,000,000,000,000,000,000,000,000,000,000
1 Decillion	10^33	1,000,000,000,000,000,000,000,000,000,000,000
1 Undecillion	10^36	1,000,000,000,000,000,000,000,000,000,000,000,000

Legend

☐ There are 4 billion IPv4 addresses

▨ There are 340 undecillion IPv6 addresses

Figure 6-5   IPv6 Provides Address Space for the Foreseeable Future.

Encapsulating IPv6 (6.1.4.3)

One of the major design improvements of IPv6 over IPv4 is the simplified IPv6 header.

The IPv4 header consists of 20 octets (up to 60 bytes if the Options field is used) and 12 basic header fields, not including the Options field and Padding field.

The IPv6 header consists of 40 octets (largely due to the length of the source and destination IPv6 addresses) and eight header fields (three IPv4 basic header fields and five additional header fields).

Figures 6-6 and 6-7 demonstrate the differences between an IPv4 header and an IPv6 header. In IPv6, some fields have remained the same, some fields are not used, and some fields have changed names and positions.

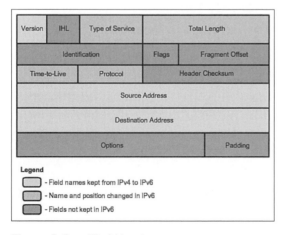

Figure 6-6   IPv4 Headers

In addition, a new field (Flow Label) has been added to IPv6 that is not used in IPv4. The IPv6 simplified header is shown in Figure 6-7.

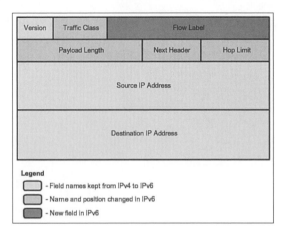

Figure 6-7   IPv6 Header

The IPv6 simplified header offers several advantages over IPv4:

- Better routing efficiency for performance and forwarding-rate scalability

- No requirement for processing checksums

- Simplified and more efficient extension header mechanisms (as opposed to the IPv4 Options field)

- A Flow Label field for per-flow processing with no need to open the transport inner packet to identify the various traffic flows

IPv6 Packet Header (6.1.4.4)

The fields in the IPv6 packet header include

- **Version:** This field contains a 4-bit binary value identifying the IP packet version. For IPv6 packets, this field is always set to 0110.

- *Traffic Class*: This 8-bit field is equivalent to the IPv4 Differentiated Services (DS) field in the IPv4 header. It also contains a 6-bit Differentiated Services Code Point (DSCP) value used to classify packets and a 2-bit Explicit Congestion Notification (ECN) used for traffic congestion control.

- *Flow Label*: This 20-bit field provides a special service for real-time applications. It can be used to inform routers and switches to maintain the same path for the packet flow so that packets are not reordered.

- **Payload Length:** This 16-bit field is equivalent to the Total Length field in the IPv4 header. It defines the entire packet (fragment) size, including header and optional extensions.

- **Next Header:** This 8-bit field is equivalent to the IPv4 Protocol field. It indicates the data payload type that the packet is carrying, enabling the network layer to pass the data to the appropriate upper-layer protocol. This field is also used if there are optional extension headers added to the IPv6 packet.

- *Hop Limit*: This 8-bit field replaces the IPv4 TTL field. This value is decremented by one by each router that forwards the packet. When the counter reaches 0 the packet is discarded and an ICMPv6 message is forwarded to the sending host, indicating that the packet did not reach its destination.

- **Source IP Address:** This 128-bit field identifies the IPv6 address of the sending host.

- **Destination IP Address:** This 128-bit field identifies the IPv6 address of the receiving host.

An IPv6 packet may also contain extension headers (EHs), which provide optional network layer information. EHs are optional and are placed between the IPv6 header and the payload. EHs are used for fragmentation, security, to support mobility, and more.

Sample IPv6 Headers (6.1.4.5)

Wireshark is a useful network monitoring tool for anyone working with networks and can be used with most labs in the Cisco Certified Network Associate (CCNA) courses for data analysis and troubleshooting. It can be used to view sample values contained in IP header fields.

Interactive Graphic

Activity 6.1.4.5: IPv6 Packet Captures

Go to the online course and click through the three Wireshark captures for examples of various IPv6 packets.

Interactive Graphic

Activity 6.1.4.6: IPv6 Header Fields

Go to the online course and click through the activity exploring IPv6 header fields.

Routing (6.2)

Routing is the process of finding an appropriate path for packets across a network. This section explains ways in which network information is stored in order to perform path selection.

Host Routing Tables (6.2.1)

This section explains the local routing tables kept by host devices.

Host Packet Forwarding Decision (6.2.1.1)

Another role of the network layer is to provide routing of packets between hosts. A host could send a packet to

- **Itself:** This is a special IP address of 127.0.0.1, which is referred to as the *loopback interface*. This loopback address is automatically assigned to a host when TCP/IP is running. The ability for a host to send a packet to itself using network functionality is useful for testing purposes. Any IP within the network 127.0.0.0/8 refers to the local host.

- *Local host*: This is a host on the same network as the sending host. The hosts share the same network address.

- *Remote host*: This is a host on a remote network. The hosts do not share the same network address.

Hosts require a local routing table to ensure that network layer packets are directed to the correct destination network. The local table of the host typically contains

- **Direct connection:** This is a route to the loopback interface.

- *Local network route*: The network to which the host is connected is automatically populated in the host routing table.

- *Local default route*: The default gateway is added to the host routing table and represents all other routes. The default gateway is either configured manually or learned dynamically and creates the local default route.

The *default gateway* is the device that routes traffic from the local network to devices on remote networks. It is often used to connect a local network to the Internet. The network is determined by the IP address and subnet mask combination. If a host is sending a packet to a device that is configured with the same IP network as the host device, the packet is simply forwarded out of the host interface to the destination device directly. A default gateway is not needed in this situation.

However, if the host is sending a packet to a device on a different IP network, then the host must forward the packet to the default gateway because a host device cannot communicate directly with devices outside of the local network. The default gateway, which is most often a *router*, maintains routing table entries for all of its directly connected networks, as well as entries for remote networks it may know about. The router is responsible for determining the best path to reach all of those destinations. The default gateway address is the IP address of the router's network interface connected to the local network.

Figure 6-8 highlights areas associated with the entries in the local host routing table. In this example, the default gateway address is 192.168.10.1.

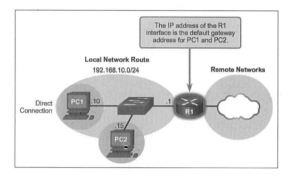

Figure 6-8   Elements of a Local Network Route

IPv4 Host Routing Table (6.2.1.2)

On a Windows host, the **route print** or **netstat -r** command can be used to display the host routing table. Both commands generate the same output. The output may seem overwhelming at first, but is fairly simple to understand.

Entering the **netstat -r** command, or the equivalent **route print** command, displays three sections related to the current TCP/IP network connections:

- **Interface List:** Lists the Media Access Control (MAC) address and assigned interface number of every network-capable interface on the host, including Ethernet, Wi-Fi, and Bluetooth adapters.

- **IPv4 Route Table:** Lists all known IPv4 routes, including direct connections, local networks, and local default routes.

- **IPv6 Route Table:** Lists all known IPv6 routes, including direct connections, local networks, and local default routes.

Note

Command output varies, depending on how the host is configured and the interface types it has.

Figure 6-9 displays the IPv4 Route Table section of the output. Notice the output is divided into five columns:

- **Network Destination:** Lists the reachable networks.

- **Netmask:** Lists a subnet mask that informs the host how to determine the network and the host portions of the IP address.

- **Gateway:** Lists the address used by the local computer to get to a network destination. If a destination is directly reachable, it will show as "On-link" in this column.

- **Interface:** Lists the address of the physical interface used to send the packet to the gateway that is used to reach the network destination.

- **Metric:** Lists the cost of each route and is used to determine the best route to a destination.

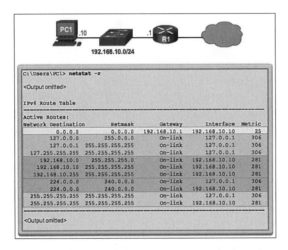

Figure 6-9   Output from the *netstat -r* Command on a Host

IPv4 Host Routing Entries (6.2.1.3)

To help simplify the output, the destination networks can be grouped into five sections, as identified by the highlighted areas in Figure 6-9.

0.0.0.0

The local default route; that is, all packets with destinations that do not match other specified addresses in the routing table are forwarded to the gateway. Therefore, all nonmatching destination routes are sent to the gateway with IP address 192.168.10.1 (R1) exiting from the interface with IP address 192.168.10.10. Note that the final destination address specified in the packet does not change; rather, the host simply knows to forward the packet to the gateway for further processing.

127.0.0.0–127.255.255.255

These loopback addresses all relate to the direct connection and provide services to the local host.

192.168.10.0–192.168.10.255

These addresses all relate to the host and local network. All packets with destination addresses that fall into this category will exit out of the 192.168.10.10 interface.

- **192.168.10.0:** The local network route address; represents all computers on the 192.168.10.x network

- **192.168.10.10:** The address of the local host

- **192.168.10.255:** The network broadcast address; sends messages to all hosts on the local network route

224.0.0.0–239.255.255.255

These are special multicast class D addresses reserved for use through either the loopback interface (127.0.0.1) or the host IP address (192.168.10.10).

255.255.255.255

The last two addresses represent the limited broadcast IP address values for use through either the loopback interface (127.0.0.1) or the host IP address (192.168.10.10). These addresses can be used to find a DHCP server before the local IP is determined.

Sample IPv4 Host Routing Table (6.2.1.4)

For example, as shown in Figure 6-10, if PC1 wanted to send a packet to 192.168.10.20, it would take the following steps:

1. Consult the IPv4 Route Table.

2. Match the destination IP address with the 192.168.10.0 Network Destination entry to reveal that the host is on the same network (On-link).

3. Send the packet toward the final destination using its local interface (192.168.10.10).

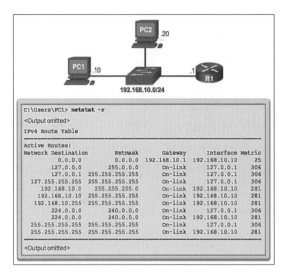

Figure 6-10 Finding a Route on a Local Network

As shown in Figure 6-11, if PC1 wanted to send a packet to a remote host located at 10.10.10.10, it would take these steps:

1. Consult the IPv4 Route Table.

2. Find that there is no exact match for the destination IP address.

3. Choose the local default route (0.0.0.0) to reveal that it should forward the packet to the 192.168.10.1 gateway address.

4. Forward the packet to the gateway to use its local interface (192.168.10.10). The gateway device then determines the next path for the packet to reach the final destination address of 10.10.10.10.

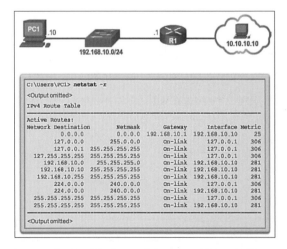

Figure 6-11 Finding a Route on a Remote Network Using the Default Gateway

Sample IPv6 Host Routing Table (6.2.1.5)

The output of the IPv6 Route Table differs in column headings and format due to the longer IPv6 addresses.

The IPv6 Route Table section displays four columns:

- **If:** Lists the interface numbers from the Interface List section of the **netstat –r** command. The interface numbers correspond to the network-capable interfaces on the host, including Ethernet, Wi-Fi, and Bluetooth adapters.

- *Metric*: Lists the cost of each route to a destination. Lower numbers indicate preferred routes.

- **Network Destination:** Lists the reachable networks.

- **Gateway:** Lists the address used by the local host to forward packets to a remote network destination. On-link indicates that the host is currently connected to it.

For example, Figure 6-12 displays the IPv6 Route Table section generated by the **netstat –r** command to reveal the following network destinations:

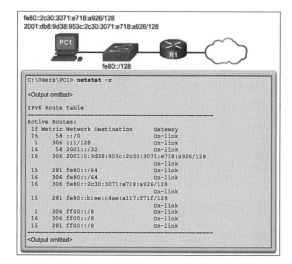

Figure 6-12   IPv6 Host Routing Table

- **::/0:** This is the IPv6 equivalent of the local default route.

- **::1/128:** This is equivalent to the IPv4 loopback address and provides services to the local host.

- **2001::/32:** This is the global unicast network prefix.

- **2001:0:9d38:953c:2c30:3071:e718:a926/128:** This is the global unicast IPv6 address of the local computer.

- **fe80::/64**: This is the link local network route address and represents all computers on the local link in an IPv6 network.

- **fe80::2c30:3071:e718:a926/128**: This is the link local IPv6 address of the local computer.

- **ff00::/8**: These are special reserved multicast class D addresses equivalent to the IPv4 224.x.x.x addresses.

> **Note**
>
> Interfaces in IPv6 commonly have two IPv6 addresses: a link local address and a global unicast address. Also, notice that there are no broadcast addresses in IPv6.

Interactive Graphic

Activity 6.2.1.6: Identify Elements of a Host Routing Table Entry

Go to the online course and perform the host routing table exercise.

Router Routing Tables (6.2.2)

This section explains the elements of routing tables that routers use to choose paths for packets.

Router Packet Forwarding Decision (6.2.2.1)

When a host sends a packet to another host, it uses its routing table to determine where to send the packet. If the destination host is on a remote network, the packet is forwarded to the address of a gateway device.

What happens when a packet arrives on a router interface? The router looks at its routing table to determine where to send the packet.

The routing table of a router stores information about

- *Directly connected routes*: These routes come from the active router interfaces. Routers add a directly connected route when an interface is configured with an IP address and is activated. Each of the router's interfaces is connected to a different network segment. Routers maintain information about the network segments that they are connected to within the routing table.

- *Remote routes*: These routes come from remote networks connected to other routers. Routes to these networks can be either manually configured on the local router by the network administrator or dynamically configured by enabling the local router to exchange routing information with other routers using dynamic routing protocols.

Figure 6-13 identifies the directly connected networks and remote networks of router R1.

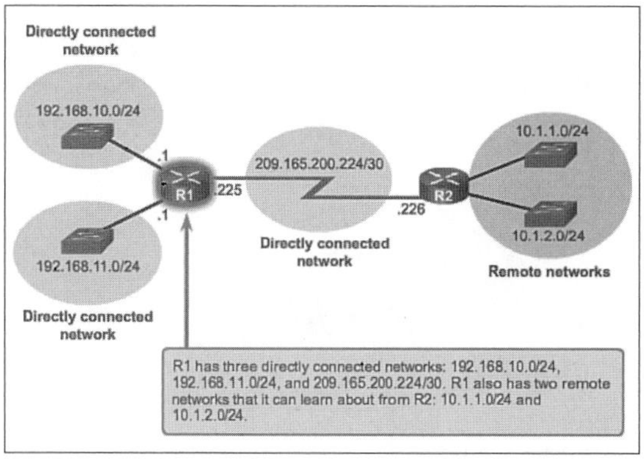

Figure 6-13   Directly Connected and Remotely Connected Networks

IPv4 Router Routing Table (6.2.2.2)

A host routing table includes information about directly connected networks. A host requires a default gateway to send packets to a remote destination. The routing table of a router contains similar information, and it can also identify specific remote networks.

The routing table of a router is similar to the routing table of a host. They both identify

- Destination network

- Metric associated with the destination network

- Gateway to get to the destination network

On a Cisco IOS router, the **show ip route** command can be used to display the routing table of a router. A router also provides additional route information, including how the route was learned, when it was last updated, and which specific interface to use to get to a predefined destination.

When a packet arrives at the router interface, the router examines the packet header to determine the destination network. If the destination network matches a route in the routing table, the router forwards the packet using the information specified in the routing table. If there are two or more possible routes to the same destination, the metric is used to decide which route appears on the routing table.

Unlike the host routing table, there are no column headings identifying the information contained in a routing table entry. Therefore, it is important to learn the meaning of the different types of information included in each entry.

Directly Connected Routing Table Entries (6.2.2.3)

Two routing table entries are automatically created when an active router interface is configured with an IP address and subnet mask. Figure 6-14 displays the routing table entries on R1 for the directly connected network 192.168.10.0. These entries were automatically added to the routing table when the Gigabit Ethernet 0/0 interface was configured and activated. The entries contain the following information:

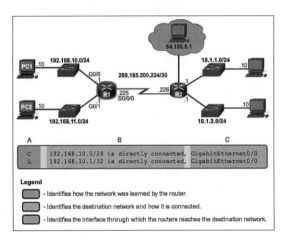

Figure 6-14 Partial Routing Table Output

- **Route source:** Labeled "A" in Figure 6-14, it identifies how the route was learned. Directly connected interfaces have two route source codes:

  - **C:** Identifies a directly connected network. Directly connected networks are automatically created when an interface is configured with an IP address and activated.

  - **L:** Identifies that this is a link local route. Link local routes are automatically created when an interface is configured with an IP address and activated.

- **Destination network:** Labeled "B" in Figure 6-14, it identifies the address of the destination network.

- **Outgoing interface:** Labeled "C" in Figure 6-14, it identifies the exit interface to use when forwarding packets to the destination network.

Note

Link local routing table entries did not appear in routing tables prior to Cisco IOS Release 15.

A router typically has multiple interfaces configured. The routing table stores information about both directly connected routes and remote routes. As with directly connected networks, the route source identifies how the route was learned. For example, common codes for remote networks include

- **S:** Identifies that the route was manually created by an administrator to reach a specific network. This is known as a static route.

- **D:** Identifies that the route was learned dynamically from another router using the Enhanced Interior Gateway Routing Protocol (EIGRP).

- **O:** Identifies that the route was learned dynamically from another router using the Open Shortest Path First (OSPF) routing protocol.

Note

Other codes are beyond the scope of this chapter.

Remote Network Routing Table Entries (6.2.2.4)

Figure 6-15 displays a routing table entry on R1 for the route to remote network 10.1.1.0. The entry identifies the following information:

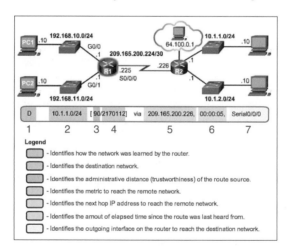

Figure 6-15   A Learned Route in a Routing Table

- *Route source*: Identifies how the route was learned.

- **Destination network:** Identifies the address of the destination network.

- *Administrative distance*: Identifies the trustworthiness of the route source.

- **Metric:** Identifies the value assigned to reach the destination network. Lower values indicate preferred routes.

- **Next-hop:** Identifies the IP address of the next router to forward the packet.

- *Route timestamp*: Identifies when the route was last heard from.

- *Outgoing interface*: Identifies the exit interface to use to forward a packet toward the final destination.

Next-Hop Address (6.2.2.5)

A *next hop* is the address of the device that will process the packet next. For a host on a network, the address of the default gateway (router interface) is the next hop for all packets that must be sent to another network. In the routing table of a router, each route to a remote network lists a next hop.

When a packet destined for a remote network arrives at the router, the router matches the destination network to a route in the routing table. If a match is found, the router forwards the packet to the IP address of the next hop router using the interface identified by the route entry.

A next hop router is the gateway to remote networks.

Referring again to Figure 6-15 for an example, a packet arriving at R1 destined for either the 10.1.1.0 or 10.1.2.0 network is forwarded to the next-hop address 209.165.200.226 using the Serial 0/0/0 interface.

Networks directly connected to a router have no next-hop address, because a router can forward packets directly to hosts on these networks using the designated interface.

Packets cannot be forwarded by the router without a route for the destination network in the routing table. If a route representing the destination network is not in the routing table, the packet is dropped (that is, not forwarded).

However, just as a host can use a default gateway to forward a packet to an unknown destination, a router can also be configured to use a default static route to create a gateway of last resort. The gateway of last resort will be covered in more detail in the CCNA Routing course.

Sample Router IPv4 Routing Table (6.2.2.6)

Assume PC1 with IP address 192.168.10.10 wants to send a packet to another host on the same network. PC1 would check the IPv4 routing table based on the destination IP address. Then, PC1 would discover that the host is on the same network and simply send it out of its interface (On-link).

> **Note**
>
> R1 is not involved in the transfer of the packet if the PC1 and the destination host is on the same local network. If PC1 forwards a packet to any network other than its local network, then it must use the services of router R1, and forward the packet to its local default route (192.168.10.1).

The following examples illustrate how a host and a router make packet routing decisions by consulting their respective routing tables: Some router output is omitted from the examples for clarity.

Example 1: The sending host and receiving host are on the same local network. PC1 wants to verify connectivity to its local default gateway at 192.168.10.1 (the router interface):

1. PC1 consults the IPv4 route table based on the destination IP address.

2. PC1 discovers that the host is on the same network and simply sends a ping packet out of its interface (On-link).

3. R1 receives the packet on its Gigabit Ethernet 0/0 (G0/0) interface and looks at the destination IP address.

4. R1 consults its routing table.

5. R1 matches the destination IP address to the L **192.168.10.1/32** routing table entry and discovers that this route points to its own local interface, as shown in Figure 6-16.

6. R1 opens the remainder of the IP packet and responds accordingly.

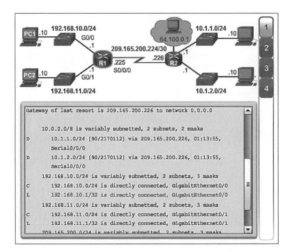

Figure 6-16 Example 1: Sending Host and Receiving Host Are on the Same Local Network.

Example 2: The sending host and receiving host are not on the same local network but are connected to the same router. PC1 wants to send a packet to PC2 (192.168.11.10):

1. PC1 consults the IPv4 route table and discovers that there is no exact match.

2. PC1 therefore uses the all route network (0.0.0.0) and sends the packet using the local default route (192.168.10.1).

3. R1 receives the packet on its Gigabit Ethernet 0/0 (G0/0) interface and looks at the destination IP address (192.168.11.10).

4. R1 consults its routing table and matches the destination IP address to the C **192.168.11.0/24** routing table entry, as shown in Figure 6-17.

5. R1 forwards the packet out of its directly connected Gigabit Ethernet 0/1 interface (G0/1).

6. PC2 receives the packet and consults its host IPv4 routing table.

7. PC2 discovers that the packet is addressed to it, opens the remainder of the packet, and responds accordingly.

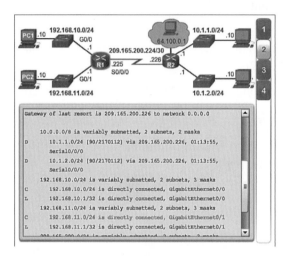

Figure 6-17   Example 2: Sending Host and Receiving Host Are Not on the Same Local Network But Are Connected to the Same Router.

Example 3: The sending host and receiving host are not on the same local network and are not on the same router. PC1 wants to send a packet to 209.165.200.226:

1. PC1 consults the IPv4 route table and discovers that there is no exact match.

2. PC1 therefore uses the default route (0.0.0.0/0) and sends the packet using the default gateway (192.168.10.1).

3. R1 receives the packet on its Gigabit Ethernet 0/0 (G0/0) interface and looks at the destination IP address (209.165.200.226).

4. R1 consults its routing table and matches the destination IP address to the C **209.165.200.224/30** routing table entry, as shown in Figure 6-18.

5. R1 forwards the packet out of its directly connected Serial 0/0/0 interface (S0/0/0).

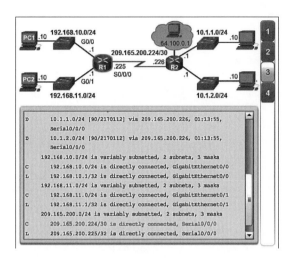

Figure 6-18   Example 3: Sending Host and Receiving Host Are Not on the Same Local Network and Are Not on the Same Router.

Example 4: The sending host and receiving host are not on the same local network and not connected to the same router. PC1 wants to send a packet to the host with IP address 10.1.1.10:

1. PC1 consults the IPv4 route table and discovers that there is no exact match.

2. PC1 therefore uses the all route network (0.0.0.0) and sends it to its local default route (192.168.10.1).

3. R1 receives the packet on its Gigabit Ethernet 0/0 (G0/0) interface and looks at the destination IP address (10.1.1.10).

4. R1 consults its routing table and matches the destination IP address to the **D 10.1.1.0/24** routing table entry, as shown in Figure 6-19.

5. R1 discovers it has to send the packet to the next-hop address 209.165.200.226.

6. R1 again consults its routing table and matches the destination IP address to the **C 209.165.200.224/30** routing table entry, as shown in Figure 6-19.

7. R1 forwards the packet out of its directly connected Serial 0/0/0 interface (S0/0/0).

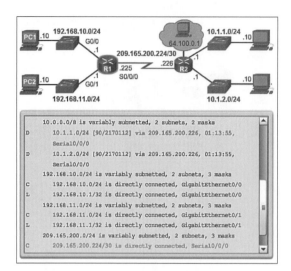

```
        10.0.0.0/8 is variably subnetted, 2 subnets, 2 masks
D          10.1.1.0/24 [90/2170112] via 209.165.200.226, 01:13:55,
           Serial0/0/0
D          10.1.2.0/24 [90/2170112] via 209.165.200.226, 01:13:55,
           Serial0/0/0
        192.168.10.0/24 is variably subnetted, 2 subnets, 3 masks
C          192.168.10.0/24 is directly connected, GigabitEthernet0/0
L          192.168.10.1/32 is directly connected, GigabitEthernet0/0
        192.168.11.0/24 is variably subnetted, 2 subnets, 3 masks
C          192.168.11.0/24 is directly connected, GigabitEthernet0/1
L          192.168.11.1/32 is directly connected, GigabitEthernet0/1
        209.165.200.0/24 is variably subnetted, 2 subnets, 3 masks
C          209.165.200.224/30 is directly connected, Serial0/0/0
```

Figure 6-19 Example 4: Sending Host and Receiving Host Are Not on the Same Local Network and Are Not Connected to the Same Router.

Interactive Graphic

Activity 6.2.2.7: Identify Elements of a Router Routing Table Entry

Go to the online course and perform the routing table elements exercise.

Lab 6.2.2.8: View Host Routing Tables

In this lab you will access a host routing table, an IPv4 routing table, and an IPv6 routing table.

Routers (6.3)

Routers are specialized computers made to perform path selections for communication between networks.

Anatomy of a Router (6.3.1)

In this section you will learn about the physical characteristics of a router.

A Router Is a Computer (6.3.1.1)

There are many types of infrastructure routers available. In fact, Cisco routers are designed to address the needs of

- *Branch*: Teleworkers, small businesses, and medium-size branch sites. Includes Cisco 800, 1900, 2900, and 3900 Integrated Series Routers (ISR) G2 (2nd generation).

- *WAN*: Large businesses, organizations, and enterprises. Includes the Cisco Catalyst 6500 Series Switches and the Cisco Aggregation Service Router (ASR) 1000.

- *Service Provider*: Large service providers. Includes Cisco ASR 1000, Cisco ASR 9000, Cisco XR 12000, Cisco CRS-3 Carrier Routing System, and 7600 Series routers.

The focus of CCNA certification is on the branch family of routers.

Regardless of their function, size, or complexity, all router models are essentially computers. Just like computers, tablets, and smart devices, routers also require

- An operating system (OS)

- A central processing unit (CPU)

- Random-access memory (RAM)

- Read-only memory (ROM)

A router also has special memory that includes flash and non-volatile RAM (NVRAM).

Router CPU and OS (6.3.1.2)

Like all computers, tablets, and smart devices, Cisco devices require a CPU to execute OS instructions, such as system initialization, routing functions, and switching functions.

The CPU requires an OS to provide routing and switching functions. The Cisco Internetwork Operating System (IOS) is the system software used for most Cisco devices, regardless of the size and type of the device. It is used for routers, LAN switches, small wireless access points, large routers with dozens of interfaces, and many other devices.

Router Memory (6.3.1.3)

A router has access to four types of memory: RAM, ROM, NVRAM, and flash.

RAM

RAM is used to store various applications and processes, including

- **Cisco IOS:** The IOS is copied into RAM during bootup.

- *Running configuration file*: This is the configuration file that stores the configuration commands that the router IOS is currently using. It is also known as the *running-config*.

- **IP routing table:** This file stores information about directly connected networks and remote networks. It is used to determine the best path to use to forward packets.

- *ARP cache*: This cache contains the IPv4 address to MAC address mappings, similar to the ARP cache on a PC. The ARP cache is used on routers that have LAN interfaces, such as Ethernet interfaces.

- *Packet buffer*: Packets are temporarily stored in a buffer when received on an interface or before they exit an interface.

Like computers, Cisco routers actually use *dynamic random-access memory (DRAM)*. DRAM is a very common kind of RAM that stores the instructions and data needed to be executed by the CPU. Unlike ROM, RAM is volatile memory and requires continual power to maintain its information. It loses all of its content when the router is powered down or restarted.

By default, Cisco 1941 routers come with 512 MB of DRAM soldered on the main system board (onboard) and one *dual in-line memory module (DIMM)* slot for memory upgrades of up to an additional 2.0 GB. Cisco 2901, 2911, and 2921 models come with 512 MB of onboard DRAM. Note that first-generation ISRs and older Cisco routers do not have onboard RAM.

ROM

ROM is firmware embedded on an integrated circuit inside the router and does not lose its contents when the router loses power or is restarted Cisco routers use ROM to store the following:

- **Bootup instructions:** Provides the startup instructions.

- **Basic diagnostic software:** Performs the Power-On Self Test (POST) of all components.

- **Limited IOS:** Provides a limited backup version of the OS, in case the router cannot load the full-featured IOS.

NVRAM

NVRAM is used by the Cisco IOS as permanent storage for the startup configuration file (startup-config). Like ROM, NVRAM does not lose its contents when power is turned off.

Flash Memory

Flash memory is non-volatile computer memory used as permanent storage for the IOS and other system-related files. The IOS is copied from flash into RAM during the bootup process.

Cisco 1941 routers come with two external CompactFlash slots. Each slot can support high-speed storage densities upgradeable to 4GB in density.

Figure 6-20 summarizes the four types of memory.

Memory	Volatile / Non-Volatile	Stores
RAM	Volatile	• Running IOS • Running configuration file • IP routing and ARP tables • Packet buffer
ROM	Non-Volatile	• Bootup instructions • Basic diagnostic software • Limited IOS
NVRAM	Non-Volatile	• Startup configuration file
Flash	Non-Volatile	• IOS • Other system files

Figure 6-20   Four Types of Memory in a Router

Inside a Router (6.3.1.4)

Although there are several different types and models of routers, every router has the same general hardware components.

Interactive Graphic

Activity 6.3.1.4: Inside a Router

The interactive graphic shows the inside of a Cisco 1841 first-generation ISR. Click the components to see a brief description of each. Note that the graphic also includes highlights of other components found in a router, such as the power supply, cooling fan, heat shields, and an advanced integration module (AIM), which are beyond the scope of this chapter.

Note

A networking professional should be familiar with and understand the function of the main internal components of a router, rather than the exact location of those components inside a specific router. Depending on the model, those components are located in different places inside the router.

Router Backplane (6.3.1.5)

A Cisco 1941 router includes the following connections:

- *Console ports*: Two console ports for the initial configuration and command-line interface (CLI) management access using a regular RJ-45 port and a new USB Type-B (mini-B USB) connector

- **AUX port:** An RJ-45 port for remote management access; similar to the console port

- **Two** *LAN interfaces*: Two Gigabit Ethernet interfaces for LAN access

- **Enhanced high-speed WAN interface card** *(EHWIC) slots*: Two slots that provide modularity and flexibility by enabling the router to support different types of interface modules, including serial, digital subscriber line (DSL), switch port, and wireless

The Cisco 1941 ISR also has storage slots to support expanded capabilities. Dual-CompactFlash memory slots are capable of supporting a 4-GB CompactFlash card each for increased storage space. Two USB host ports are included for additional storage space and secure token capability.

CompactFlash can store the Cisco IOS software image, log files, voice configuration files, HTML files, backup configurations, or any other file needed for the system. By default, only slot 0 is populated with a CompactFlash card from the factory, and it is the default boot location.

Figure 6-21 identifies the location of these connections and slots.

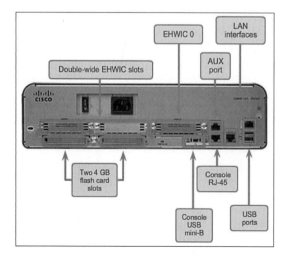

Figure 6-21   Router Ports and Interfaces

Connecting to a Router (6.3.1.6)

Cisco devices, routers, and switches typically interconnect many devices. For this reason, these devices have several types of ports and interfaces. These ports and interfaces are used to connect cables to the device.

The connections on a Cisco router can be grouped into two categories:

- *Management ports*: These are the console and auxiliary ports used to configure, manage, and troubleshoot the router. Unlike LAN and WAN interfaces, management ports are not used for packet forwarding.

- *Inband router interfaces*: These are the LAN and WAN interfaces configured with IP addressing to carry user traffic. Ethernet interfaces are the most common LAN connections, while common WAN connections include serial and DSL interfaces.

Like many networking devices, Cisco devices use light emitting diode (LED) indicators to provide status information. An interface LED indicates the activity of the corresponding interface. If an LED is off when the interface is active and the interface is correctly connected, this may be an indication of a problem with that interface. If an interface is extremely busy, its LED is always on, and may be blinking very fast.

LAN and WAN Interfaces (6.3.1.7)

Similar to a Cisco switch, there are several ways to access the CLI environment on a Cisco router. The most common methods are

- **Console:** Uses a low-speed serial or USB connection to provide direct connect, out-of-band management access to a Cisco device

- **Telnet or SSH:** Two methods for remotely accessing a CLI session across an active network interface

- **AUX port:** Used for remote management of the router using a dial-up telephone line and modem

The console and AUX port are located on the router.

In addition to these ports, routers also have network interfaces to receive and forward IP packets. Routers have multiple interfaces that are used to connect to multiple networks. Typically, the interfaces connect to various types of networks, which means that different types of media and connectors are required.

Every interface on the router is a member or host on a different IP network. Each interface must be configured with an IP address and subnet mask of a different network. The Cisco IOS does not allow two active interfaces on the same router to belong to the same network.

Router interfaces can be grouped into two categories:

- *Ethernet LAN interfaces*: Used for connecting cables that terminate with LAN devices, such as computers and switches. This interface can also be used to connect routers to each other. Several conventions for naming Ethernet interfaces are popular: the older Ethernet, Fast Ethernet, and Gigabit Ethernet. The name used depends on the device type and model.

- *Serial WAN interfaces*: Used for connecting routers to external networks, usually over a larger geographical distance. Similar to LAN interfaces, each serial WAN interface has its own IP address and subnet mask, which identifies it as a member of a specific network.

Figure 6-22 shows the LAN Interfaces and serial interfaces on the router.

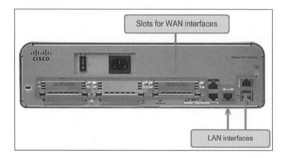

Figure 6-22 WAN and LAN Interfaces on a Router

Activity 6.3.1.8: Identify Router Components

Go to the online course and perform the interactive exercise.

Lab 6.3.1.9: Exploring Router Physical Characteristics

In this lab you will examine a router's internal and external characteristics.

Packet Tracer Activity 6.3.1.10: Exploring Internetworking Devices

In this activity you will explore the different options available on internetworking devices. You will also be required to determine which options provide the necessary connectivity when connecting multiple devices. Finally, you will add the correct modules and connect the devices.

Router Bootup (6.3.2)

This section will explore what happens when a Cisco IOS router boots up.

Cisco IOS (6.3.2.1)

The Cisco IOS operational details vary on different internetworking devices, depending on the device's purpose and feature set. However, Cisco IOS for routers provides the following:

- Addressing
- Interfaces
- Routing
- Security
- QoS
- Resources management

The IOS file itself is several megabytes in size, and similar to the files for Cisco IOS switches, is stored in flash memory. Using flash allows the IOS to be upgraded to newer versions or to have new features added. During bootup, the IOS is copied from flash memory into RAM. DRAM is much faster than flash; therefore, copying the IOS into RAM increases the performance of the device.

Bootset Files (6.3.2.2)

A router loads the following two files into RAM when it is booted:

- **IOS image file:** The IOS facilitates the basic operation of the device's hardware components. The IOS image file is stored in flash memory.

- *Startup configuration file:* The startup configuration file contains commands that are used to initially configure a router and create the running configuration file stored in RAM. The startup configuration file is stored in NVRAM. All configuration changes are stored in the running configuration file and are implemented immediately by the IOS.

The running configuration is modified when the network administrator performs device configuration. When changes are made to the running-config file, it should be saved to NVRAM as the startup configuration file, in case the router is restarted or loses power.

Router Bootup Process (6.3.2.3)

There are three major phases to the bootup process, as shown in Figure 6-23:

1. Perform the POST and load the bootstrap program.

2. Locate and load the Cisco IOS software.

3. Locate and load the startup configuration file or enter setup mode.

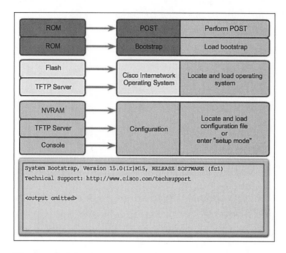

Figure 6-23 Three Phases in the Router Boot Process

Step 1. **Perform POST and Load Bootstrap Program**

The *Power-On Self Test (POST)* is a common process that occurs on almost every computer during bootup. The POST process is used to test the router hardware. When the router is powered on, software on the ROM chip conducts the POST. During this self-test, the router executes diagnostics from ROM on several hardware components, including the CPU, RAM, and NVRAM. After the POST has been completed, the router executes the bootstrap program.

After the POST, the bootstrap program is copied from ROM into RAM. Once in RAM, the CPU executes the instructions in the bootstrap program. The main task of the bootstrap program is to locate the Cisco IOS and load it into RAM.

Note

At this point, if you have a console connection to the router, you begin to see output on the screen.

Step 2.   Locate and Load Cisco IOS

The IOS is typically stored in flash memory and is copied into RAM for execution by the CPU. After the IOS begins to load, a string of pounds signs (#) will be displayed while the image decompresses.

If the IOS image is not located in flash, then the router may look for it using a TFTP server. If a full IOS image cannot be located, a scaled-down version of the IOS is copied from ROM into RAM. This version of IOS is used to help diagnose any problems and can be used to load a complete version of the IOS into RAM.

Step 3.   Locate and Load the Configuration File

The bootstrap program then searches for the startup configuration file (also known as startup-config) in NVRAM. This file has the previously saved configuration commands and parameters. If it exists, then it is copied into RAM as the running configuration file, running-config. The running-config file contains interface addresses, starts routing processes, configures router passwords, and defines other characteristics of the router.

If the startup-config file does not exist in NVRAM, the router may search for a *TFTP server*. If the router detects that it has an active link to another configured router, it sends a broadcast searching for a configuration file across the active link.

If a TFTP server is not found, then the router displays the setup mode prompt. Setup mode is a series of questions prompting the user for basic configuration information. Setup mode is not intended to be used to enter complex router configurations, and it is not commonly used by network administrators.

Note

Setup mode is not used in this course to configure the router. When prompted to enter setup mode, always answer **no**. If you answer yes and enter setup mode, press **Ctrl-C** at any time to terminate the setup process.

Show Version Output (6.3.2.4)

You can use the **show version** command to verify and troubleshoot some of the basic hardware and software components of the router. The command displays information about the version of the Cisco IOS software currently running on the router, the version of the bootstrap program, and information about the hardware configuration, including the amount of system memory.

The output from the **show version** command includes

- **IOS version:** Version of the Cisco IOS software in RAM and that is being used by the router.

- **ROM Bootstrap Program:** Displays the version of the system bootstrap software, stored in ROM, that was initially used to boot up the router.

- **Location of IOS:** Displays the version and location of the bootstrap program and the complete filename of the IOS image.

- **CPU and Amount of RAM:** The first part of this line displays the type of CPU on this router. The last part of this line displays the amount of DRAM. Some series of routers, such as the Cisco 1941 ISR, use a fraction of DRAM as packet memory. Packet memory is used for buffering packets. To determine the total amount of DRAM on the router, add both numbers.

- **Interfaces:** Displays the physical interfaces on the router. In this example, the Cisco 1941 ISR has two Gigabit Ethernet interfaces and two low-speed serial interfaces.

- **Amount of NVRAM and Flash:** This is the amount of NVRAM and the amount of flash memory on the router. NVRAM is used to store the startup-config file, and flash is used to permanently store the Cisco IOS.

The last line of the **show version** command displays the current, configured value of the software configuration register in hexadecimal. If there is a second value displayed in parentheses, it denotes the configuration register value that is used during the next reload.

The configuration register has several uses, including password recovery. The factory default setting for the configuration register is 0x2102. This value indicates that the router attempts to load a Cisco IOS software image from flash memory and load the startup configuration file from NVRAM.

Video

Video 6.3.2.5:

View the video in the online course for a demonstration of the IOS boot process.

Interactive Graphic

Activity 6.3.2.6: The Router Boot Process

Go to the online course and perform the interactive exercise.

Configuring a Cisco Router (6.4)

Networks differ greatly in their design and complexity. Routers can be configured to meet the needs of the network.

Configure Initial Settings (6.4.1)

A router needs to know about the network it will belong to. This essential information must be provided before a router can perform routing tasks.

Router Configuration Steps (6.4.1.1)

Cisco routers and Cisco switches have many similarities. They support a similar modal operating system, support similar command structures, and support many of the same commands. In addition, both devices have identical initial configuration steps when implementing them in a network.

Similar to configuring a switch, the following steps should be completed when configuring initial settings on a router:

1. Assign a device name using the hostname global configuration command.

2. Set passwords:

   - Secure privileged EXEC mode access using the **enable secret** command.

   - Secure EXEC mode access for console using the **login** command on the console port, and the **password** command to set the password.

   - Secure virtual access similar to securing EXEC access mode for console, except on the vty port.

   - Use the **service password-encryption** global configuration command to prevent passwords from displaying as plain text in the configuration file.

3. Provide legal notification using the **banner motd** (message of the day [MOTD]) global configuration command.

4. Save the configuration using the **copy run start** command.

5. Verify the configuration using the **show run** command.

Interactive Graphic

Activity 6.4.1.1: Configuring a Cisco Router

Go to the online course and click through panels 1 through 4 to see examples of the commands in this section. On panel 5, try your hand at entering the commands in the syntax checker.

Packet Tracer Activity 6.4.1.2: Configure Initial Router Settings

In this activity you will perform basic router configurations. You will secure access to the CLI and console port using encrypted and plain text passwords. You will also configure messages for users logging into the router. These banners also warn unauthorized users that access is prohibited. Finally, you will verify and save your running configuration.

Configure Interfaces (6.4.2)

In this section you will practice configuring LAN and serial interfaces.

Configure LAN Interfaces (6.4.2.1)

For routers to be reachable, router interfaces must be configured. Therefore, to enable a specific interface, enter interface configuration mode using the **interface** *type-and-number* global configuration mode command.

There are many different types of interfaces available on Cisco routers. In the example in Figure 6-24, the Cisco 1941 router is equipped with two Gigabit Ethernet interfaces and a serial WAN interface card (WIC) consisting of two interfaces; the interfaces are named as follows:

- Gigabit Ethernet 0/0 (G0/0)

- Gigabit Ethernet 0/1 (G0/1)

- Serial 0/0/0 (S0/0/0)

- Serial 0/0/1 (S0/0/1)

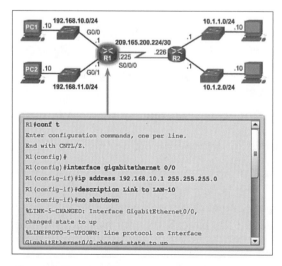

Figure 6-24   Configuring LAN Interfaces

To enable a router interface, configure the following:

- **IPv4 address and subnet mask:** Configures the IP address and subnet mask using the **ip address** *subnet-mask* interface configuration command.

- **Activate the interface:** By default, LAN and WAN interfaces are not activated. The interface must be activated using the **no shutdown** command. This is similar to powering on the interface. The interface must also be connected to another device (a hub, a switch, or another router) for the physical layer to be active.

Although not required, it is good practice to configure a description on each interface to help document the network information. The *description text* is limited to 240 characters. On production networks, a description can be helpful in troubleshooting by providing information about the type of network that the interface is connected to and if there are any other routers on that network. If the interface connects to an ISP or service carrier, it is helpful to enter the third-party connection and contact information.

Interactive Graphic

Activity 6.4.2.1: Configuring a LAN Interface

Go to the online course and click panel 2 to practice entering the commands in the syntax checker. Note that command abbreviations are used for the configuration of Gigabit Ethernet 0/1.

Verify Interface Configuration (6.4.2.2)

There are several commands that can be used to verify interface configuration. The most useful of these is the *show ip interface brief command*. The output generated displays all interfaces, their IP address, and their current status. The configured and connected interfaces should display a Status of "up" and Protocol of "up." Anything else would indicate a problem with either the configuration or the cabling.

You can verify connectivity from the interface using the **ping** command. Cisco routers send five consecutive pings and measure minimal, average, and maximum round-trip times. Exclamation marks verify connectivity.

Interactive Graphic

Activity 6.4.2.2: Commands to Test and Display Active Links and Routes

Go to the online course and click panel 1 to observe output from the **show ip interface brief** command, the **ping** command, and the **show ip route** command.

Note how the **show ip interface brief** command reveals that the LAN interfaces and the WAN link are all active and operational. Notice that the **ping** command generated five exclamation marks verifying connectivity to R2.

Panel 2 displays the output of the **show ip route** command. Notice the three directly connected network entries and the local link interface entries.

Other interface verification commands include

- **show ip route:** Displays the contents of the IPv4 routing table stored in RAM
- **show interfaces:** Displays statistics for all interfaces on the device
- **show ip interface:** Displays the IPv4 statistics for all interfaces on a router

Remember to save the configuration using the **copy running-config startup-config** (or just type copy run start) command.

Configuring the Default Gateway (6.4.3)

For devices that need to communicate beyond the local network, a default gateway must be identified.

Default Gateway on a Host (6.4.3.1)

Most routers have, at a minimum, two interfaces. Each interface is configured with a separate IP address in a separate network.

For an end device to communicate over the network, it must be configured with the correct IP address information, including the default gateway address. The default gateway is only used when the host wants to send a packet to a device on another network. The default gateway address is generally the router interface address attached to the local network of the host. Although it does not matter what address is actually configured on the router interface, the IP address of the host device and the router interface address must be in the same network.

Figure 6-25 displays a topology of a router with two separate interfaces. Each interface is connected to a separate network. G0/0 is connected to network 192.168.10.0, and G0/1 is connected to network 192.168.11.0. Each host device is configured with the appropriate default gateway address.

In Figure 6-25, PC1 sends a packet to PC2. In this example, the default gateway is not used; rather, PC1 addresses the packet with the IP address of PC2 and forwards the packet directly to PC2 through the switch.

In Figure 6-26, PC1 sends a packet to PC3. In this example, PC1 addresses the packet with the IP address of PC3, but then forwards the packet to the router. The router accepts the packet, accesses its route table to determine the appropriate exit interface based on the destination address, and then forwards the packet out of the appropriate interface to reach PC3.

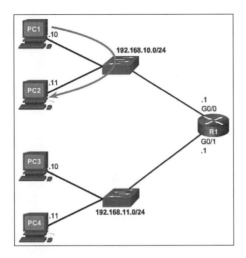

Figure 6-25   Local LANs Do Not Use the Default Gateway to Forward Messages.

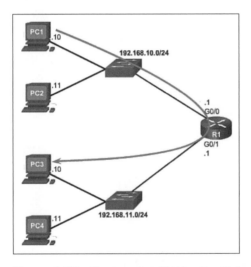

Figure 6-26   Hosts on a LAN Use the Default Gateway to Forward Messages to Remote Networks.

Default Gateway on a Switch (6.4.3.2)

A default gateway is used by all devices that require the use of a router to determine the best path to a remote destination. End devices require default gateway addresses, but so do intermediate devices, such as the Cisco IOS switch.

The IP address information on a switch is only necessary to manage the switch remotely. In other words, to be able to telnet to the switch, the switch must have an IP address to telnet to. If the switch is only accessed from devices within the local network, only an IP address is required.

Configuring the IP address on a switch is done on the switch virtual interface (SVI):

`S1(config)#` **interface vlan1**

`S1(config-vlan)#` **ip address 192.168.10.50 255.255.255.0**

`S1(config-vlan)#` **no shut**

However, if the switch must be accessible by devices in a different network, the switch must be configured with a default gateway address, because packets that originate from the switch are handled just like packets that originate from a host device. Therefore, packets that originate from the switch and are destined for a device on the same network are forwarded directly to the appropriate device. Packets that originate from the switch and are destined for a device on a remote network must be forwarded to the default gateway for path determination.

To configure a default gateway on a switch, use the following global configuration command:

`S1(config)#` **ip default-gateway 192.168.10.1**

Figure 6-27 shows an administrator connecting to a switch on a remote network. For the switch to forward response packets to the administrator, the default gateway must be configured.

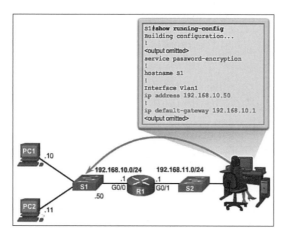

Figure 6-27   Using the Default Gateway for Remote Connections

A common misconception is that the switch uses its configured default gateway address to determine where to forward packets originating from hosts connected to the switch and destined for hosts on a remote network. Actually, the IP address and default gateway information is only used for packets that originate from the switch. Packets originating from hosts connected to the switch must already have default gateway information configured to communicate on remote networks.

Activity 6.4.3.2: Configuring a Default Gateway on a Switch

Go to the online course and practice configuring a default gateway on a switch.

Packet Tracer Activity 6.4.3.3: Connect a Router to a LAN

In this activity you will use various **show** commands to display the current state of the router. You will then use the routing table to configure router Ethernet interfaces. Finally, you will use commands to verify and test your configurations.

Packet Tracer Activity 6.4.3.4: Troubleshooting Default Gateway Issues

In this activity you will finish documenting a network. You will then verify the network documentation by testing end-to-end connectivity and troubleshooting issues.

Lab 6.4.3.5: Initializing and Reloading a Router and Switch

In this lab you will set up a topology and initialize devices. You will then configure the devices and verify connectivity. You will finish by displaying device information.

Summary (6.5)

Class Activity 6.5.1.1: Can You Read This Map?

In this activity you will build a network using information from a **show ip route** command.

Packet Tracer Activity 6.5.1.2: Skills Integration Challenge

In this scenario your network manager is impressed with your performance in your job as a LAN technician. She would like you to now demonstrate your ability to configure a router connecting two LANs. Your tasks include configuring basic settings on a router and a switch using the Cisco IOS. You will then verify your configurations, as well as configurations on existing devices, by testing end-to-end connectivity.

The network layer, or OSI Layer 3, provides services to allow end devices to exchange data across the network. To accomplish this end-to-end transport, the network layer uses four basic processes: IP addressing for end devices, encapsulation, routing, and de-encapsulation.

The Internet is largely based on IPv4, which is still the most widely used network layer protocol. An IPv4 packet contains the IP header and the payload. However, IPv4 has a limited number of unique public IP addresses available. This led to the development of IPv6. The IPv6 simplified header offers several advantages over IPv4, including better routing efficiency, simplified extension headers, and capability for per-flow processing. Plus, IPv6 addresses are based on 128-bit hierarchical addressing as opposed to IPv4 with 32 bits. This dramatically increases the number of available IP addresses.

In addition to hierarchical addressing, the network layer is also responsible for routing. Hosts require a local routing table to ensure that packets are directed to the correct destination network. The local table of a host typically contains the direct connection, the local network route, and the local default route. The local default route is the route to the default gateway.

The default gateway is the IP address of a router interface connected to the local network. When a host needs to forward a packet to a destination address that is not on the same network as the host, the packet is sent to the default gateway for further processing.

When a router, such as the default gateway, receives a packet, it examines the destination IP address to determine the destination network. The routing table of a router stores information about directly connected routes and remote routes to IP networks. If the router has an entry in its routing table for the destination network, the router forwards the packet. If no routing entry exists, the router may forward the packet to its own default route, if one is configured, or it will drop the packet.

Routing table entries can be configured manually on each router to provide static routing, or the routers may communicate route information dynamically between each other using a routing protocol.

In order for routers to be reachable, the router interface must be configured. To enable a specific interface, enter interface configuration mode using the **interface** *type-and-number* global configuration mode command.

Practice

The following activities provide practice with the topics introduced in this chapter. The Labs and Class Activities are available in the companion *Networking Basics Lab Manual* (978-1-58713-313-8). The Packet Tracer Activities PKA files are found in the online course.

Class Activities

Class Activity 6.0.1.2: The Road Less Traveled...or Is It?

Class Activity 6.5.1.1: Can You Read This Map?

Labs

Lab 6.2.2.8: View Host Routing Tables

Lab 6.3.1.9: Exploring Router Physical Characteristics

Lab 6.4.3.5: Initializing and Reloading a Router and Switch

Packet Tracer Activities

Packet Tracer Activity 6.3.1.10: Exploring Internetworking Devices

Packet Tracer Activity 6.4.1.2: Configure Initial Router Settings

Packet Tracer Activity 6.4.4.3: Connect a Router to a LAN

Packet Tracer Activity 6.4.3.4: Troubleshooting Default Gateway Issues

Packet Tracer Activity 6.5.1.2: Skills Integration Challenge

Check Your Understanding

Complete all the review questions listed here to test your understanding of the topics and concepts in this chapter. The appendix, "Answers to the 'Check Your Understanding' Questions," lists the answers.

1. Which device is responsible for determining the path to another network?

   A. Switch

   B. Router

   C. Hub

   D. Modem

2. What is true about OSI Layer 3? (Choose two.)

   A. It uses data encapsulated in the transport layer.

   B. It removes IP information before sending the Layer 3 PDU to the next level.

   C. Layer 3 addresses are permanent.

   D. Layer 3 addresses are 32 bits in length.

3. Which network protocol is not considered legacy?

   A. IPX

   B. IPv6

   C. AppleTalk

   D. DECNet

4. Which protocol provides connectionless network layer services?

   A. IP

   B. TCP

   C. DNS

   D. OSI

5. Which of the following are *not* functions of the network layer? (Choose two.)

   A. Routing

   B. Addressing packets with an IP address

   C. Delivery reliability

   D. Application data analysis

   E. Encapsulation

   F. De-encapsulation

6. Which of the following are true about IP? (Choose three.)

   A. It is connection oriented.

   B. It is the most common network layer protocol.

   C. It analyzes presentation layer data.

   D. It operates at OSI Layer 2.

   E. It encapsulates transport layer segments.

   F. It is media independent.

   G. Packet delivery is assured.

7. Which commands can be used to view a host's routing table? (Choose two.)

   A. **show ip interface brief**

   B. **route print**

   C. **show ip route**

   D. **show run**

   E. **netstat-r**

8. Select three pieces of information about a route that a routing table contains.

   A. Next-hop

   B. Source address

   C. Metric

   D. Destination network address

   E. Last hop

   F. Destination MAC address

9. What kinds of problems are caused by excessive broadcast traffic on a network segment? (Choose three.)

   A. Consumes network bandwidth

   B. Increases overhead on network

   C. Requires complex address schemes

   D. Interrupts other host functions

   E. Divides networks based on ownership

   F. Advanced hardware required

10. Which is a characteristic of the IP protocol?

    A. Media dependent

    B. Reliable

    C. Connectionless

    D. Addresses give segments with IP addresses

11. Which of the following are not functions of the network layer? (Choose two.)

    A. Routing

    B. Addressing packets with an IP address

    C. Delivery reliability

    D. Application data analysis

    E. Encapsulation

    F. De-encapsulation

12. Which of the following are true about IP? (Choose two.)

    A. IP stands for International Protocol.

    B. It is the most common network layer protocol.

    C. It analyzes presentation layer data.

    D. It operates at OSI Layer 2.

    E. It encapsulates transport layer segments.

13. What is the name of the process of removing the OSI Layer 2 information from an IP packet?

    A. Frame fragmenting

    B. Bit dropping

    C. De-encapsulation

    D. De-segmenting

14. Which of the following is true about IP?

    A. It is connection oriented.

    B. It uses application data to determine the best path.

    C. It is used by both routers and hosts.

    D. It is reliable.

15. Which of the following are true about the network layer encapsulation process? (Choose two.)

    A. It adds a header to a segment.

    B. It can happen many times on the path to the destination host.

    C. It is performed by the last router on the path.

    D. Both source and destination IP addresses are added.

    E. It encapsulates transport layer information into a frame.

16. Which of the following are true about TCP and IP? (Choose two.)

    A. TCP is connectionless and IP is connection oriented.

    B. TCP is reliable and IP is unreliable.

    C. IP is connectionless and TCP is connection oriented.

    D. TCP is unreliable and IP is reliable.

    E. IP operates at the transport layer.

17. Why is IP "media independent"?

    A. It encapsulates Layer 1 instructions.

    B. It works the same on all Layer 1 media.

    C. It carries both video and voice data.

    D. It works without Layer 1 media.

18. TCP is an OSI Layer _____ protocol.

    A. 3

    B. 5

    C. 4

    D. 6

    E. 7

19. How many bits are in an IPv4 address?

    A. 20

    B. 8

    C. 32

    D. 64

    E. 128

20. Which statement is true about local default routes?

    A. They forward LAN traffic to the proper local host.

    B. They are configured on the first physical interface of a switch.

    C. They are configured on router interfaces.

    D. They send packets that do not match in the routing table to the default gateway.

Objectives

Upon completion of this chapter, you will be able to answer the following questions:

- What is the structure of an IPv4 address?

- What is the purpose of the subnet mask?

- What are the characteristics and uses of the unicast, broadcast, and multicast IPv4 addresses?

- How do you use public address space and private address space?

- Why transition from IPv4 to IPv6?

- How is an IPv6 address represented?

- What are the different types of IPv6 network addresses?

- How do you configure global unicast addresses?

- What is a multicast address?

- What is the role of ICMP in an IP network (both IPv4 and IPv6)?

- How would you use ping and traceroute utilities to test network connectivity?

Key Terms

This chapter uses the following key terms. You can find the definitions in the Glossary.

classless addressing   page 303

dual stack   page 309

tunneling   page 309

translation   page 310

hexadecimal numbering   page 311

IPv6 link-local address   page 321

IPv6 global unicast addresses   page 322

global routing prefix   page 323

*Stateless Address Autoconfiguration (SLAAC)
  page 327*

*Dynamic Host Configuration Protocol for IPv6
  (DHCPv6)   page 329*

solicited-node multicast address   page 338

Router Solicitation message (RS)   page 342

Router Advertisement message (RA)   page 342

Neighbor Solicitation   page 342

Neighbor Advertisement   page 342

Introduction (7.0.1.1)

Addressing is a key function of network layer protocols that enables data communication between hosts, regardless of whether the hosts are on the same network or on different networks. Both Internet Protocol version 4 (IPv4) and Internet Protocol version 6 (IPv6) provide hierarchical addressing for packets that carry data.

Designing, implementing, and managing an effective IP addressing plan ensures that networks can operate effectively and efficiently.

This chapter examines in detail the structure of IP addresses and their application to the construction and testing of IP networks and subnetworks.

Class Activity 7.0.1.2: The Internet of Everything (IoE)

In this activity you will begin to think about not only what will be identified in the IoE world, but how everything will be addressed in the same world!

IPv4 Network Addresses (7.1)

This section provides an in-depth overview of the IPv4 networking protocol that functions as an address for devices connected to a network.

IPv4 Address Structure (7.1.1)

In this section you will learn the essentials of IPv4 addressing.

Binary Notation (7.1.1.1)

To understand the operation of devices on a network, you need to look at addresses and other data the way devices do: in *binary notation*. Binary notation is a representation of information using only ones (1s) and zeros (0s). Computers communicate using binary data. Binary data can be used to represent many different forms of data. For example, when typing letters on a keyboard, those letters appear on screen in a form that you can read and understand; however, the computer translates each letter to a series of binary digits for storage and transport. To translate those letters, the computer uses *American Standard Code for Information Interchange* (*ASCII*; pronounced ask-ee).

Using ASCII, the letter "A" is represented in bit form as 01000001, whereas the lowercase letter "a" is represented in bit form as 01100001. Use the ASCII translator available in the online course to convert ASCII characters to binary.

Interactive
Graphic

Activity 7.1.1.1: ASCII Digital Translator

Go to the online course to perform this ASCII translation practice activity.

Although it is not generally necessary for people to concern themselves with binary conversion of letters, it is necessary to understand the use of binary for IP addressing. Each device on a network must be uniquely identified using a binary address. In IPv4 networks, this address is represented using a string of 32 bits (1s and 0s). At the network layer, the packets then include this unique identification information for both the source and destination systems. Therefore, in an IPv4 network, each packet includes a 32-bit source address and a 32-bit destination address in the OSI Layer 3 header.

For most individuals, a string of 32 bits is difficult to interpret and even more difficult to remember. Therefore, we represent IPv4 addresses using dotted decimal format instead of binary. This means that we look at each byte (octet) as a decimal number in the range of 0 to 255. For clarification, 1 byte equals 8 bits equal one octet. To understand how this works you need to have some skill in binary to decimal conversion.

Positional Notation

Learning to convert binary to decimal requires an understanding of the mathematical basis of a numbering system called *positional notation*. Positional notation means that a digit represents different values depending on the position the digit occupies. In a positional notation system, the number base is called the *radix*. In the base 10 system (also known as the decimal system), the radix is 10. In the binary system, we use a radix of 2. The terms *radix* and *base* can be used interchangeably. More specifically, the value that a digit represents is that value multiplied by the power of the base, or radix, represented by the position the digit occupies. Some examples will help to clarify how this system works.

For the decimal number 192, the value that the 1 represents is $1 * 10^2$ (1 times 10 to the power of 2). The 1 is in what we commonly refer to as the "100s" position. Positional notation refers to this position as the $base^2$ position because the base, or radix, is 10 and the power is 2. The 9 represents $9 * 10^1$ (9 times 10 to the power of 1). Positional notation for the decimal number 192 is shown in Figure 7-1.

Using positional notation in the base 10 numbering system, 192 represents

$$192 = (1 * 10^2) + (9 * 10^1) + (2 * 10^0)$$

or

$$192 = (1 * 100) + (9 * 10) + (2 * 1)$$

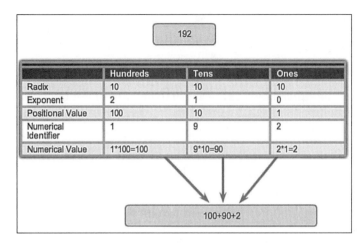

Figure 7-1   Positional Notation

Binary Number System (7.1.1.2)

In IPv4, addresses are 32-bit binary numbers. However, for ease of use by people, binary patterns representing IPv4 addresses are expressed as dotted decimals. This is first accomplished by separating each byte (8 bits) of the 32-bit binary pattern, called an *octet*, with a dot. It is called an octet because each decimal number represents 1 byte or 8 bits.

The binary address

11000000 10101000 00001010 00001010

is expressed in dotted decimal as

192.168.10.10

Interactive Graphic

Activity 7.1.1.2: 32-Bit Binary Represented as Dotted Decimal

Go to the online course to perform this dotted decimal practice activity. In the interactive graphic, select each button to see how the 32-bit binary address is represented in dotted decimal octets.

But how are the actual decimal equivalents determined?

Binary Numbering System

In the binary numbering system, the radix is 2. Therefore, each position represents increasing powers of 2. In 8-bit binary numbers, the positions represent these quantities:

2^7	2^6	2^5	2^4	2^3	2^2	2^1	2^0
128	64	32	16	8	4	2	1

The base 2 numbering system only has two digits: 0 and 1.

When we interpret a byte as a decimal number, we have the quantity that position represents if the digit is a 1, and we do not have that quantity if the digit is a 0, as shown in Activity 7.1.1.2.

Figure 7-2 illustrates the representation of the decimal number 192 in binary. A 1 in a certain position means we add that value to the total. A 0 means we do not add that value. The binary number 11000000 has a 1 in the 2^7 position (decimal value 128) and a 1 in the 2^6 position (decimal value 64). The remaining bits are all 0, so we do not add the corresponding decimal values. The result of adding 128 + 64 is 192, the decimal equivalent of 11000000.

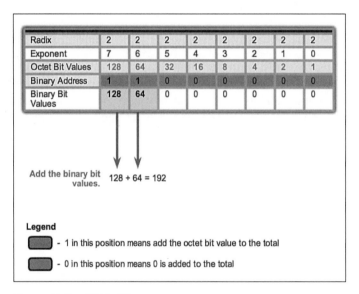

Figure 7-2   192 in Binary

Here are two more examples:

Example 1: An octet containing all 1s: 11111111

A 1 in each position means that we add the value for that position to the total. All 1s means that the values of every position are included in the total; therefore, the value of all 1s in an octet is 255:

128 + 64 + 32 + 16 + 8 + 4 + 2 + 1 = 255

Example 2: An octet containing all 0s: 00000000

A 0 in each position indicates that the value for that position is not included in the total. A 0 in every position yields a total of 0:

0 + 0 + 0 + 0 + 0 + 0 + 0 + 0 = 0

A different combination of 1s and 0s yields a different decimal value.

Converting a Binary Address to Decimal (7.1.1.3)

Each octet is made up of 8 bits and each bit has a value, either 0 or 1. The four groups of 8 bits have the same set of valid values in the range of 0 to 255 inclusive. The value of each bit placement, from right to left, is 1, 2, 4, 8, 16, 32, 64, and 128.

Determine the value of the octet by adding the values of positions wherever there is a binary 1 present:

- If there is a 0 in a position, do not add the value.

- If all 8 bits are 0s, 00000000, the value of the octet is 0.

- If all 8 bits are 1s, 11111111, the value of the octet is 255 (128 + 64 + 32 + 16 + 8 + 4 + 2 + 1).

- If the 8 bits are mixed, the values are added together. For example, the octet 00100111 has a value of 39 (32 + 4 + 2 + 1).

So the value of each of the four octets can range from 0 to a maximum of 255.

Using the 32-bit IPv4 address, 11000000101010000000101000001010, convert the binary representation to dotted decimal using the following steps:

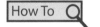

Step 1.   Divide the 32 bits into four octets.

Step 2.   Convert each octet to decimal.

Step 3.   Add a "dot" between each decimal.

Video 7.1.1.3

View this video in the online course for a demonstration on how a binary address is converted to a dotted decimal address.

Activity 7.1.1.4: Binary-to-Decimal Conversion Activity

Go to the online course to perform this binary-to-decimal conversion practice activity. This activity allows you to practice 8-bit binary-to-decimal conversion as much as necessary. You should work with this tool until you are able to do the conversion without error. Convert the binary number shown in the octet to its decimal value.

Converting from Decimal to Binary (7.1.1.5, 7.1.1.6)

In addition to being able to convert binary to decimal, it is also necessary to understand how to convert decimal to binary.

Because we represent IPv4 addresses using dotted decimal format, it is only necessary that we examine the process of converting decimal values of 0 to 255 for each octet in an IPv4 address to the 8-bit binary.

To begin the conversion process, we start by determining if the decimal number is equal to or greater than our largest decimal value represented by the most-significant bit. In the highest position, we determine if the octet number is equal to or greater than 128. If the octet number is smaller than 128, we place a 0 in the bit position for decimal value 128 and move to the bit position for decimal value 64.

If the octet number in the bit position for decimal value 128 is larger than or equal to 128, we place a 1 in the bit position for decimal value 128 and subtract 128 from the octet number being converted. We then compare the remainder of this operation to the next smaller value, 64. We continue this process for all the remaining bit positions. Look at Figures 7-3 through 7-8 to see the process of converting 168 to the binary equivalent of 10101000.

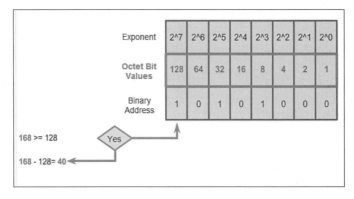

Figure 7-3 Converting 168, Step 1

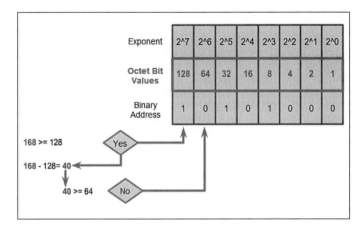

Figure 7-4   Converting 168, Step 2

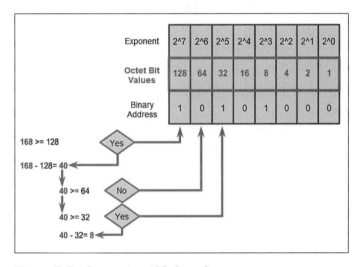

Figure 7-5   Converting 168, Step 3

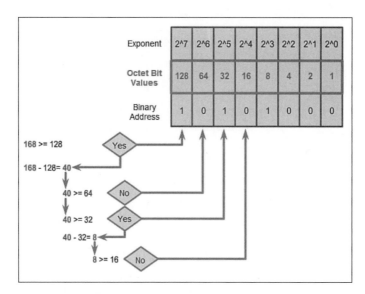

Figure 7-6   Converting 168, Step 4

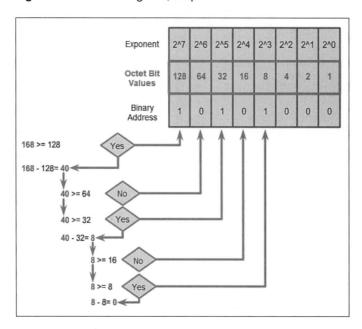

Figure 7-7   Converting 168, Step 5

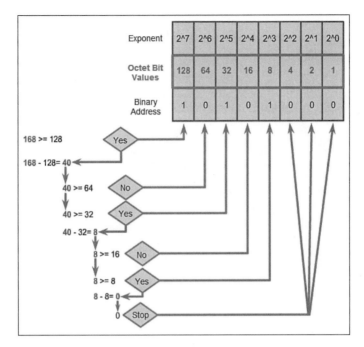

Figure 7-8 Converting 168, Step 6

Follow the conversion steps in Figures 7-9 through 7-13 to see how an IP address is converted to binary.

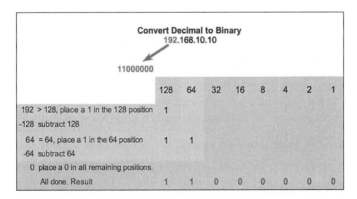

Figure 7-9 Convert 192 to Binary

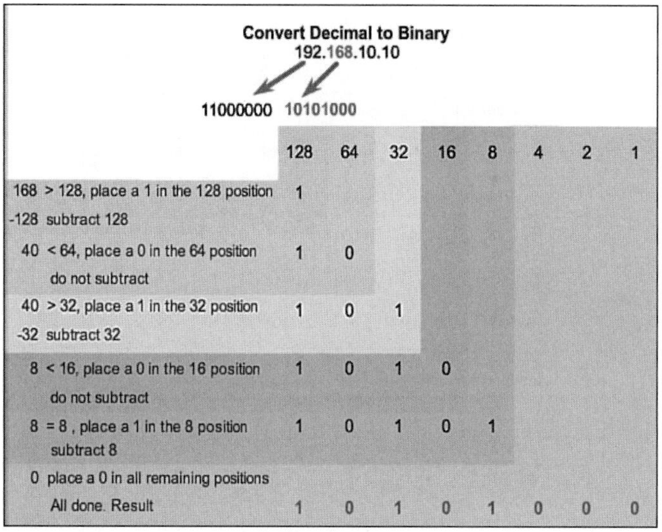

Figure 7-10   Convert 168 to Binary

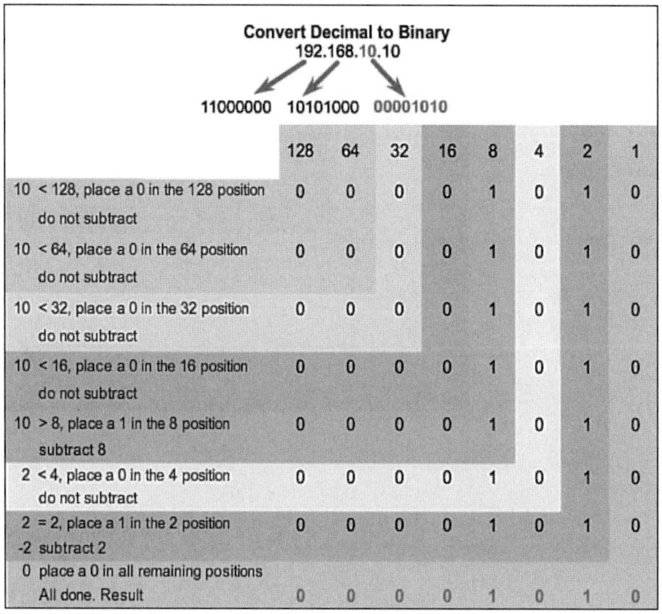

Figure 7-11   Convert 10 to Binary

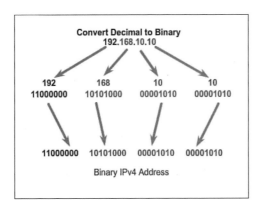

Convert Decimal to Binary
192.168.10.10

11000000 10101000 00001010 00001010

	128	64	32	16	8	4	2	1
10 < 128, place a 0 in the 128 position do not subtract	0	0	0	0	1	0	1	0
10 < 64, place a 0 in the 64 position do not subtract	0	0	0	0	1	0	1	0
10 < 32, place a 0 in the 32 position do not subtract	0	0	0	0	1	0	1	0
10 < 16, place a 0 in the 16 position do not subtract	0	0	0	0	1	0	1	0
10 > 8, place a 1 in the 8 position subtract 8	0	0	0	0	1	0	1	0
2 < 4, place a 0 in the 4 position do not subtract	0	0	0	0	1	0	1	0
2 = 2, place a 1 in the 2 position -2 subtract 2	0	0	0	0	1	0	1	0
0 place a 0 in all remaining positions All done. Result	0	0	0	0	1	0	1	0

Figure 7-12   Convert 10 to Binary

Convert Decimal to Binary
192.168.10.10

192 → 11000000
168 → 10101000
10 → 00001010
10 → 00001010

11000000 10101000 00001010 00001010

Binary IPv4 Address

Figure 7-13   Combine the Converted Octets, Beginning with the First Octet

Interactive Graphic

Activity 7.1.1.7: Decimal-to-Binary Conversion Activity

Go to the online course to perform this decimal-to-binary conversion practice activity. This activity allows you to practice decimal conversion to 8-bit binary values. You should work with this tool until you are able to do the conversions without error. Convert the decimal number shown in the Decimal Value row to its binary bits.

Activity 7.1.1.8: Cisco Binary Game

The Cisco Binary Game provides a fun way to learn binary numbers for networking.

Game link: http://forums.cisco.com/CertCom/game/binary_game_page.htm.

IPv4 Subnet Mask (7.1.2)

An important part of mastering networking is understanding the use of subnet masks. This section provides you with the principles.

Network Portion and Host Portion of an IPv4 Address (7.1.2.1)

Understanding binary notation is important when determining if two hosts are in the same network. Recall that an IP address is a hierarchical address that is made up of two parts: a network portion and a host portion. But when determining the network portion versus the host portion, it is necessary to look not at the decimal value but at the 32-bit stream. Within the 32-bit stream, a portion of the bits makes up the network and a portion of the bits makes up the host.

The bits within the network portion of the address must be identical for all devices that reside in the same network. The bits within the host portion of the address must be unique to identify a specific host within a network. Regardless of whether the decimal numbers between two IPv4 addresses match up, if two hosts have the same bit pattern in the specified network portion of the 32-bit stream, those two hosts will reside in the same network.

But how do hosts know which portion of the 32 bits is network and which is host? That is the job of the subnet mask, as shown in Figure 7-14.

When an IP host is configured, a subnet mask is assigned along with an IP address. Like the IP address, the subnet mask is 32 bits long. The subnet mask signifies which part of the IP address is network and which part is host.

The subnet mask is compared to the IP address from left to right, bit for bit. The 1s in the subnet mask represent the network portion; the 0s represent the host portion. As shown in Figure 7-14, the subnet mask is created by placing a binary 1 in each bit position that represents the network portion and placing a binary 0 in each bit position that represents the host portion. Note that the subnet mask does not actually contain the network or host portion of an IPv4 address, it just tells the computer where to look for these portions in a given IPv4 address.

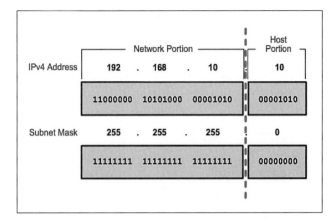

Figure 7-14 IPv4 Address and Subnet Mask

Similar to IPv4 addresses, the subnet mask is represented in dotted decimal format for ease of use. The subnet mask is configured on a host device, in conjunction with the IPv4 address, and is required so the host can determine which network it belongs to. Figure 7-15 displays the valid subnet masks for an IPv4 octet.

Subnet Value	Bit Value							
	128	64	32	16	8	4	2	1
255	1	1	1	1	1	1	1	1
254	1	1	1	1	1	1	1	0
252	1	1	1	1	1	1	0	0
248	1	1	1	1	1	0	0	0
240	1	1	1	1	0	0	0	0
224	1	1	1	0	0	0	0	0
192	1	1	0	0	0	0	0	0
128	1	0	0	0	0	0	0	0
0	0	0	0	0	0	0	0	0

Figure 7-15 Valid Subnet Masks

Examining the Prefix Length (7.1.2.2)

This section looks at the use of the prefix length in IPv4 addressing.

Network Prefixes

The *prefix length* is another way of expressing the subnet mask. The prefix length is the number of bits set to 1 in the subnet mask. It is written in *slash notation*, a "/" followed by the number of bits set to 1. For example, if the subnet mask is 255.255.255.0, there are 24 bits set to 1 in the binary version of the subnet mask, so the prefix length is 24 bits, or /24. The prefix and the subnet mask are different ways of representing the same thing: the network portion of an address.

Networks are not always assigned a /24 prefix. Depending on the number of hosts on the network, the prefix assigned may be different. Having a different prefix number changes the host range and broadcast address for each network.

The following figures illustrate different prefixes using the same 10.1.1.0 address. Figure 7-16 illustrates the /24 to /26 prefixes, and Figure 7-17 illustrates the /27 and /28 prefixes.

	Dotted Decimal	Significant bits shown in binary
Network Address	10.1.1.0/24	10.1.1.00000000
First Host Address	10.1.1.1	10.1.1.00000001
Last Host Address	10.1.1.254	10.1.1.11111110
Broadcast Address	10.1.1.255	10.1.1.11111111
Number of hosts: 2^8 – 2 = 254 hosts		
Network Address	10.1.1.0/25	10.1.1.00000000
First Host Address	10.1.1.1	10.1.1.00000001
Last Host Address	10.1.1.126	10.1.1.01111110
Broadcast Address	10.1.1.127	10.1.1.01111111
Number of hosts: 2^7 – 2 = 126 hosts		
Network Address	10.1.1.0/26	10.1.1.00000000
First Host Address	10.1.1.1	10.1.1.00000001
Last Host Address	10.1.1.62	10.1.1.00111110
Broadcast Address	10.1.1.63	10.1.1.00111111
Number of hosts: 2^6 – 2 = 62 hosts		

Figure 7-16   /24 to /26 Prefixes

Notice that the network address could remain the same, but the host range and the broadcast address are different for the different prefix lengths. In the figures, you can see that the number of hosts that can be addressed on the network also changes.

	Dotted Decimal	Significant bits shown in binary
Network Address	10.1.1.0/27	10.1.1.00000000
First Host Address	10.1.1.1	10.1.1.00000001
Last Host Address	10.1.1.30	10.1.1.00011110
Broadcast Address	10.1.1.31	10.1.1.00011111
Number of hosts: 2^5 – 2 = 30 hosts		
Network Address	10.1.1.0/28	10.1.1.00000000
First Host Address	10.1.1.1	10.1.1.00000001
Last Host Address	10.1.1.14	10.1.1.00001110
Broadcast Address	10.1.1.15	10.1.1.00001111
Number of hosts: 2^4 – 2 = 14 hosts		

Figure 7-17   /27 and /28 Prefixes

IPv4 Network, Host, and Broadcast Addresses (7.1.2.3)

There are three types of addresses within the address range of each IPv4 network:

- Network address
- Host address
- Broadcast address

Network Address

The *network address* is a standard way to refer to a network. The subnet mask or the prefix length might also be used when referring to the network address. For example, the network shown in Figure 7-18 could be referred to as the 10.1.1.0 network, the 10.1.1.0 255.255.255.0 network, or the 10.1.1.0/24 network. All hosts in the 10.1.1.0/24 network will have the same network portion bits.

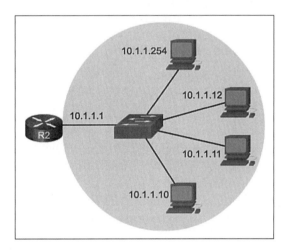

Figure 7-18 10.1.1.0/24 Network

As shown in Figure 7-19, within the IPv4 address range of a network, the first address is reserved for the network address. This address has a 0 for each host bit in the host portion of the address. All hosts within the network share the same network address.

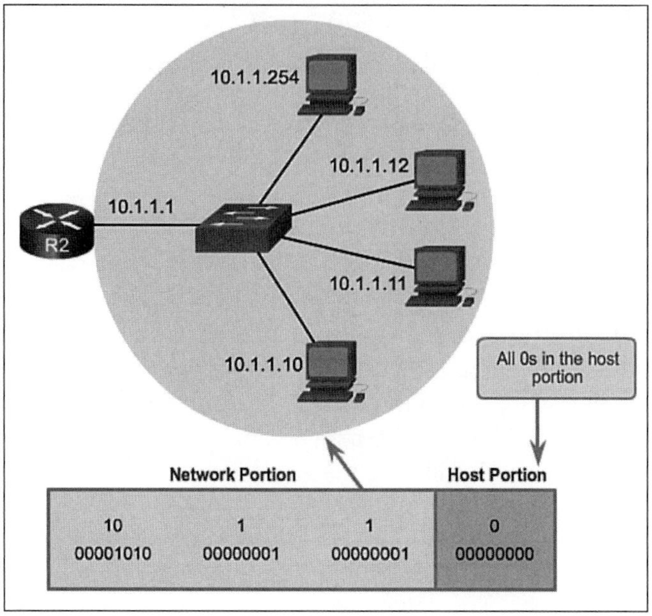

Figure 7-19   Network Portion

Host Address

Every end device requires a unique *host address* to communicate on the network. In IPv4 addresses, the values between the network address and the broadcast address can be assigned to end devices in a network. As shown in Figure 7-20, this address has any combination of 0 and 1 bits in the host portion of the address but cannot contain all 0 bits or all 1 bits.

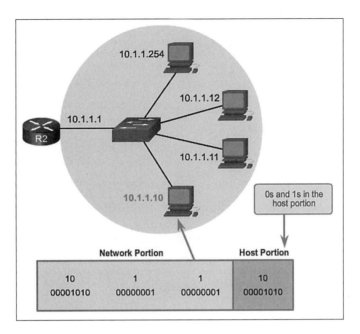

Figure 7-20   Host Address

Broadcast Address

The IPv4 *broadcast address* is a special address for each network that allows communication to all the hosts in that network. To send data to all hosts in a network at once, a host can send a single packet that is addressed to the broadcast address of the network, and each host in the network that receives this packet will process its contents.

The broadcast address uses the highest address in the network range. This is the address in which the bits in the host portion are all 1s. All 1s in an octet in binary form is equal to the number 255 in decimal form. Therefore, as shown in Figure 7-21, for the network 10.1.1.0/24, in which the last octet is used for the host portion, the broadcast address would be 10.1.1.255. This address is also referred to as the *directed broadcast*. Note that the host portion will not always be an entire octet.

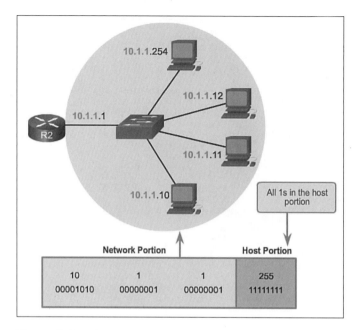

Figure 7-21 Broadcast Address

First Host and Last Host Addresses (7.1.2.4)

To ensure that all hosts within a network are assigned a unique IP address within that network range, it is important to identify the first host address and the last host address. Hosts within a network can be assigned IP addresses within this range.

First Host Address

As shown in Figure 7-22, the host portion of the first host address will contain all 0 bits with a 1 bit for the lowest-order or rightmost bit. This address is always one greater than the network address. In this example the first host address on the 10.1.1.0/24 network is 10.1.1.1. It is common in many addressing schemes to use the first host address for the router or default gateway address.

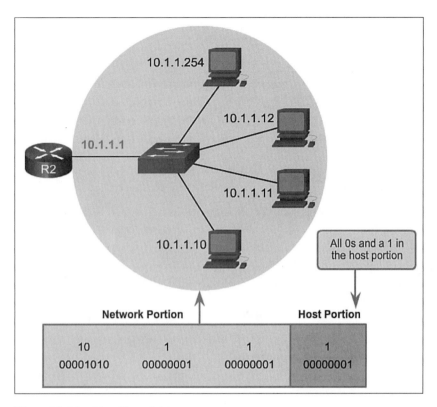

Figure 7-22   First Host Address

Last Host Address

The host portion of the last host address will contain all 1 bits with a 0 bit for the lowest-order or rightmost bit. This address is always one less than the broadcast address. As shown in Figure 7-23, the last host address on the 10.1.1.0/24 network is 10.1.1.254.

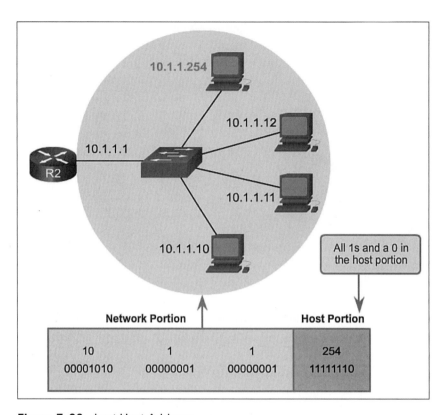

Figure 7-23   Last Host Address

Bitwise AND Operation (7.1.2.5)

When an IPv4 address is assigned to a device, that device uses the subnet mask to determine which network address the device belongs to. As previously mentioned, the network address is the address that represents all the devices on the same network.

When sending network data, the device uses this information to determine whether it can send packets locally or must send the packets to a default gateway for remote delivery. When a host sends a packet, it compares the network portion of its own IP address to the network portion of the destination IP address, based on subnet masks. If the network bits match, both the source and destination host are on the same network and the packet can be delivered locally. If they do not match, the sending host forwards the packet to the default gateway, to be sent on to the other network.

The AND Operation

The AND operation (also referred to as *ANDing*) is one of three basic binary operations used in digital logic. The other two are OR and NOT. Although all three are used in data networks, AND is used in determining the network address. Therefore, our discussion here will be limited to logical AND. Logical AND is the comparison of two bits that yields the following results:

1 AND 1 = 1 (see Figure 7-24)

0 AND 1 = 1 (see Figure 7-25)

0 AND 0 = 1 (see Figure 7-26)

1 AND 0 = 1 (see Figure 7-27)

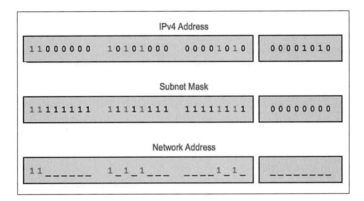

Figure 7-24 1 AND 1 = 1

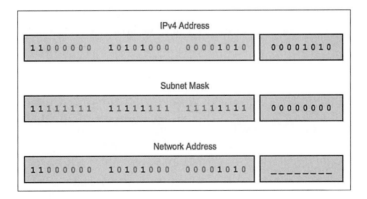

Figure 7-25 0 AND 1 = 0

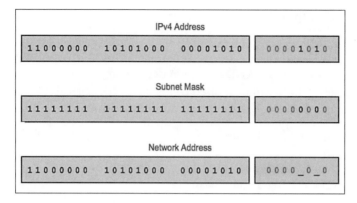

Figure 7-26   0 AND 0 = 0

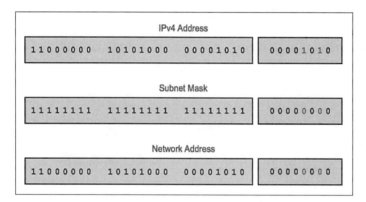

Figure 7-27   1 AND 0 = 0

The IPv4 host address is logically ANDed, bit by bit, with its subnet mask to determine the network address to which the host is associated. When this bitwise ANDing between the address and the subnet mask is performed, the result yields the network address.

Importance of ANDing (7.1.2.6)

Any address bit ANDed with a 1 bit value from the subnet mask will yield the original bit value from the address. So, a 0 (from the IPv4 address) AND 1 (from the subnet mask) is 0. A 1 (from the IPv4 address) AND 1 (from the subnet mask) is 1. Consequently, anything ANDed with a 0 yields a 0. These properties of ANDing are used with the subnet mask to "mask" the host bits of an IPv4 address. Each bit of the address is ANDed with the corresponding bit of the subnet mask.

Because all the bits of the subnet mask that represent host bits are 0s, the host portion of the resulting network address becomes all 0s. Recall that an IPv4 address with all 0s in the host portion represents the network address.

Likewise, all the bits of the subnet mask that indicate the network portion are 1s. When each of these 1s is ANDed with the corresponding bit of the address, the resulting bits are identical to the original address bits.

As shown in Figure 7-28, the 1 bits in the subnet mask will result in the network portion of the network address having the same bits as the network portion of the host. The host portion of the network address will result in all 0s.

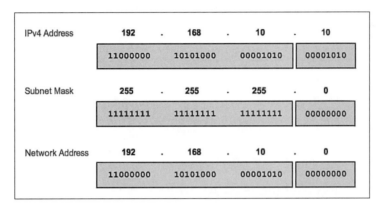

Figure 7-28   IPv4 Address with Subnet Mask and Network Address

For a given IP address and its subnet, ANDing can be used to determine what subnetwork the address belongs to, as well as what other addresses belong to the same subnet. Remember that if two addresses are in the same network or subnetwork, they are considered to be local to each other and can therefore communicate directly with each other. Addresses that are not in the same network or subnetwork are considered to be remote to each other and must therefore have a Layer 3 device (like a router or Layer 3 switch) between them to communicate.

In network verification/troubleshooting, we often need to determine two hosts are on the same local network. We need to make this determination from the perspective of the network devices. Due to improper configuration, a host may see itself on a network that was not the intended one. This can create an operation that seems erratic unless diagnosed by examining the ANDing processes used by the host.

Lab 7.1.2.7: Using the Windows Calculator with Network Addresses

In this lab you will use the Windows Calculator to convert between numbering systems, convert an IPv4 address and subnet mask into binary, determine the number of hosts in a network using powers of 2, and convert a MAC address and an IPv6 address to binary.

Lab 7.1.2.8: Converting IPv4 Addresses to Binary

In this lab, you will convert IPv4 addresses from dotted decimal to binary and use bitwise ANDing operation to determine network address. Applying network address calculations is also covered in this lab.

Interactive
Graphic

Activity 7.1.2.9: ANDing to Determine the Network Address

Go to the online course and use the interactive activity to practice ANDing for network address determination.

IPv4 Unicast, Broadcast, and Multicast (7.1.3)

This section presents the three types of packet transmission. Assigning IP addresses is covered first.

Assigning a Static IPv4 Address to a Host (7.1.3.1)

Let's discuss identifying a host by assigning a static IP address to the host.

Addresses for User Devices

In most data networks, the largest population of hosts includes the end devices, such as PCs, tablets, smartphones, printers, and IP phones. Because this represents the largest number of devices within a network, the largest number of addresses should be allocated to these hosts. These hosts are assigned IP addresses from the range of available addresses in the network. These IP addresses can be assigned either statically or dynamically.

Static Assignment

With a static assignment, the network administrator must manually configure the network information for a host. Figure 7-29 shows the window for the network adapter properties. To configure a static IPv4 address, choose IPv4 on the network adapter screen, then key in the static address, subnet mask, and default gateway. Figure 7-30 shows the minimum static configuration: the host IP address, subnet mask, and default gateway.

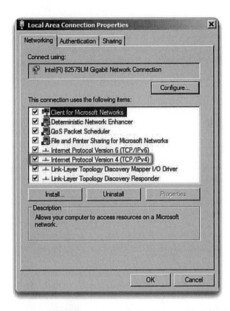

Figure 7-29   Local Area Network (LAN) Interface Properties

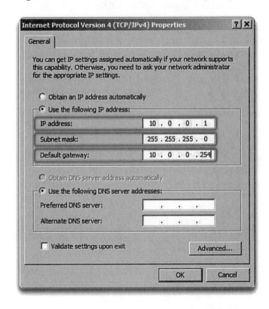

Figure 7-30   Configuring a Static IPv4 Address

There are several advantages to *static addressing*. For instance, static addresses are useful for printers, servers, and other networking devices that do not change location often and need to be accessible to clients on the network based on a fixed IP address. If hosts normally access a server at a particular IP address, it would cause problems if that address changed. Additionally, static assignment of addressing information can provide increased control of network resources. For example, it is possible to create access filters based on traffic to and from a specific IP address. However, static addressing can be time consuming to enter on each host.

When using static IP addressing, it is necessary to maintain an accurate list of the IP address assigned to each device. These are permanent addresses and are not normally reused.

Assigning a Dynamic IPv4 Address to a Host (7.1.3.2)

This section discusses the use of dynamic IP addressing on a host.

Dynamic Assignment

On local networks it is often the case that the user population changes frequently. New users arrive with laptops and need a connection. Others have new workstations or other network devices, such as smartphones, that need to be connected. Rather than have the network administrator assign IP addresses for each workstation, it is easier to have IP addresses assigned automatically. This is done using the Dynamic Host Configuration Protocol (DHCP), which was introduced in Chapter 2, "Configuring a Network Operating System." Figure 7-31 shows the configuration for obtaining a dynamic IPv4 address.

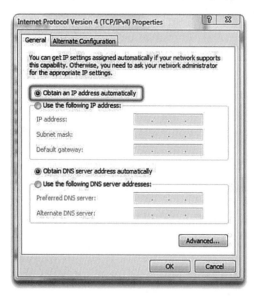

Figure 7-31   Assigning a Dynamic IPv4 Address

DHCP enables the automatic assignment of addressing information such as IP address, subnet mask, default gateway, and other configuration information. The configuration of the DHCP server requires that a block of addresses, called an *address pool*, be used for assigning to the DHCP clients on a network. Addresses assigned to this pool should be planned so that they exclude any static addresses used by other devices.

Using DHCP is generally the preferred method of assigning IPv4 addresses to hosts on large networks because it reduces the burden on network support staff and virtually eliminates entry errors.

Another benefit of DHCP is that an address is not permanently assigned to a host but is only "leased" for a period of time. If the host is powered down or taken off the network, the address is returned to the pool for reuse. This feature is especially helpful for mobile users that come and go on a network.

If DCHP is enabled on a host device, the **ipconfig** command can be used to view the IP address information assigned by the DHCP server, as shown in Figure 7-32.

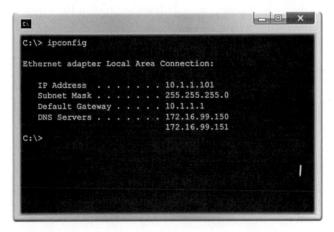

Figure 7-32   Verifying a Dynamic IPv4 Address

Unicast Transmission (7.1.3.3)

In an IPv4 network, the hosts can communicate one of three ways:

- *Unicast*: The process of sending a packet from one host to an individual host

- *Broadcast*: The process of sending a packet from one host to all hosts in the network

- *Multicast*: The process of sending a packet from one host to a selected group of hosts, possibly in different networks

These three types of communication are used for different purposes in data networks. In all three cases, the IPv4 address of the originating host is placed in the packet header as the source address.

Unicast Traffic

Unicast communication is used for normal host-to-host communication in both client/server and peer-to-peer networks. Unicast packets use the addresses of the destination device as the destination address and can be routed through an internetwork.

Video

Video 7.1.3.3

View this video in the online course for an example of a unicast transmission.

In an IPv4 network, the unicast address applied to an end device is referred to as the host address. For unicast communication, the addresses assigned to the two end devices are used as the source and destination IPv4 addresses. During the encapsulation process, the source host places its IPv4 address in the unicast packet header as the source address and places the IPv4 address of the destination host in the packet header as the destination address. Regardless of whether the destination specified in a packet is unicast, broadcast, or multicast, the source address of any packet is always the unicast address of the originating host.

Note

In this course, all communications between devices is unicast communication unless otherwise noted.

IPv4 host addresses are unicast addresses and are in the address range of 0.0.0.0 to 223.255.255.255. However, within this range are many addresses that are reserved for special purposes. These special-purpose addresses will be discussed later in this chapter.

Note

The address range from 0.0.0.0 through 0.255.255.255 should not be considered part of the normal class A range. 0.x.x.x addresses serve no particular function in IP.

Broadcast Transmission (7.1.3.4)

Now that you have an understanding of how a unicast transmission works, this section examines how to reach all hosts through a broadcast transmission.

Broadcast Transmission

Broadcast traffic is used to send packets to all hosts in the network using the broadcast address for the network. With a broadcast, the packet contains a destination IP address with all 1s in the host portion. This means that all hosts on that local network (broadcast domain) will receive and look at the packet. Many network protocols, such as DHCP, use broadcasts. When a host receives a packet sent to the network broadcast address, the host processes the packet as it would a packet addressed to its unicast address.

Some examples for using broadcast transmission are

- Mapping upper-layer addresses to lower-layer addresses, such as ARP

- Requesting an address, such as DHCP

Unlike unicast, where the packets can be routed throughout the internetwork, broadcast packets are usually restricted to the local network. This restriction is dependent on the configuration of the gateway router and the type of broadcast. There are two types of broadcasts: directed broadcast and limited broadcast.

Directed Broadcast

A directed broadcast is sent to all hosts on a specific network. This type of broadcast is useful for sending a broadcast to all hosts on a non-local network. For example, for a host outside of the 172.16.4.0/24 network to communicate with all of the hosts within that network, the destination address of the packet would be 172.16.4.255. Although routers do not forward directed broadcasts by default, they may be configured to do so.

Limited Broadcast

The limited broadcast is used for communication that is limited to the hosts on the local network. These packets always use a destination IPv4 address of 255.255.255.255. Routers do not forward a limited broadcast. For this reason, an IPv4 network is also referred to as a *broadcast domain*. Routers form the boundary for a broadcast domain.

As an example, a host within the 172.16.4.0/24 network would broadcast to all hosts in its network using a packet with a destination address of 255.255.255.255.

Video

Video 7.1.3.4

View this video in the online course for an example of a limited broadcast transmission.

When a packet is broadcast, it uses resources on the network and causes every receiving host on the network to process the packet. Therefore, broadcast traffic should be limited so that it does not adversely affect performance of the network or devices. Because routers separate broadcast domains, subdividing networks with excessive broadcast traffic can improve network performance.

Multicast Transmission (7.1.3.5)

The third type of packet transmission will be discussed in this section. IP multicast is a technique for one-to-many communication over an IP infrastructure in a network.

Multicast Transmission

Multicast transmission is designed to conserve the bandwidth of an IPv4 network. It reduces traffic by allowing a host to send a single packet to a selected set of hosts that are part of a subscribing multicast group. To reach multiple destination hosts using unicast communication, a source host would need to send an individual packet addressed to each host. With multicast, the source host can send a single packet that can reach thousands of destination hosts. The internetwork's responsibility is to replicate the multicast flows in an efficient manner so that they reach only their intended recipients.

Some examples of multicast transmission are

- Video and audio broadcasts
- Routing information exchange by routing protocols
- Distribution of software
- News feeds

Multicast Addresses

IPv4 has a block of addresses reserved for addressing multicast groups. This address range is 224.0.0.0 to 239.255.255.255. The multicast address range is subdivided into different types of addresses: reserved link-local addresses and globally scoped addresses. One additional type of multicast address is the administratively scoped address, also called limited-scope address.

The IPv4 multicast addresses 224.0.0.0 to 224.0.0.255 are reserved link-local addresses. These addresses are to be used for multicast groups on a local network. A router connected to the local network recognizes that these packets are addressed to a link-local multicast group and never forwards them further. A typical use of reserved link-local addresses is in routing protocols using multicast transmission to exchange routing information.

The globally scoped addresses are 224.0.1.0 to 238.255.255.255. They may be used to multicast data across the Internet. For example, 224.0.1.1 has been reserved for the Network Time Protocol (NTP) to synchronize the time-of-day clocks of network devices.

The administratively scoped addresses (or limited-scope addresses) are the 239.0.0.0 to 239.255.255.255 range.

Multicast Clients

Hosts that receive particular multicast data are called *multicast clients*. The multicast clients use services requested by a client program to subscribe to the multicast group.

Each multicast group is represented by a single IPv4 multicast destination address. When an IPv4 host subscribes to a multicast group, the host processes packets addressed to this multicast address and packets addressed to its uniquely allocated unicast address.

Video

Video 7.1.3.5

View this video in the online course for a demonstration of how clients accept multicast packets.

Interactive Graphic

Activity 7.1.3.6: Unicast, Broadcast, or Multicast?

Go to the online course and click Start in this practice activity to view the destination IP address and see which host or hosts receive a packet based on the address.

Interactive Graphic

Activity 7.1.3.7: Calculate the Network, Broadcast, and Host Addresses

Go to the online course and use the practice activity to identify the network, broadcast, and first and last usable host IP addresses.

Packet Tracer ☐ **Activity**

Packet Tracer Activity 7.1.3.8: Investigate Unicast, Broadcast, and Multicast Traffic

In this activity you will examine unicast, broadcast, and multicast behavior. Most traffic in a network is unicast. When a PC sends an ICMP echo request to a remote router, the source address in the IP packet header is the IP address of the sending PC. The destination address in the IP packet header is the IP address of the interface on the remote router. The packet is sent only to the intended destination.

Using the **ping** command or the Add Complex PDU feature of Packet Tracer, you can directly ping broadcast addresses to view broadcast traffic.

For multicast traffic, you will view EIGRP traffic.

Types of IPv4 Addresses (7.1.4)

IPv4 designates several different types of IPv4 addresses, as described in this section.

Public and Private IPv4 Addresses (7.1.4.1)

Although most IPv4 host addresses are public addresses designated for use in networks that are accessible on the Internet, there are blocks of addresses that are used in networks that require limited or no Internet access. These addresses are called *private addresses*.

Private Addresses

The private address blocks are

> 10.0.0.0 to 10.255.255.255 (10.0.0.0/8)
>
> 172.16.0.0 to 172.31.255.255 (172.16.0.0/12)
>
> 192.168.0.0 to 192.168.255.255 (192.168.0.0/16)

Private addresses are defined in RFC 1918, Address Allocation for Private Internets, and are sometimes referred to as RFC 1918 addresses. Private space address blocks, as shown in Figure 7-33, are used in private networks. Hosts that do not require access to the Internet can use private addresses. However, within the private network, hosts still require unique IP addresses within the private space.

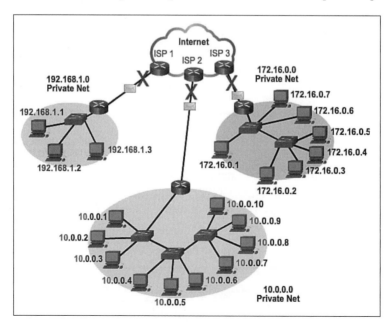

Figure 7-33   Private Addresses Cannot Be Routed over the Internet

Hosts in different networks may use the same private space addresses. Packets using these addresses as the source or destination should not appear on the public Internet. The router or firewall device at the perimeter of these private networks must block or translate these addresses. Even if these packets were to make their way to the Internet, the routers would not have routes to forward them to the appropriate private network.

In RFC 6598, the Internet Assigned Numbers Authority (IANA) reserved another group of addresses known as *shared address space*. Similar to RFC 1918 private address space, shared address space addresses are not globally routable. However, these addresses are intended only for use in service provider networks. The shared address block is 100.64.0.0/10.

Public Addresses

The vast majority of the addresses in the IPv4 unicast host range are *public addresses*, which are designed to be used in the hosts that are publicly accessible from the Internet. Even within these IPv4 address blocks, there are many addresses that are designated for other special purposes.

Interactive Graphic

Activity 7.1.4.2: Pass or Block IPv4 Addresses

Go to the online course and click on start. You will then have to either click the Pass or Block buttons based on whether it is a Public (Pass) or Private address (Block).

Special-Use IPv4 Addresses (7.1.4.3)

There are certain addresses that cannot be assigned to hosts. There are also special-use addresses that can be assigned to hosts, but with restrictions on how those hosts can interact within the network.

Network and Broadcast Addresses

As explained earlier, within each network the first and last addresses cannot be assigned to hosts. These are the network address and the broadcast address, respectively.

Loopback

One such reserved address is the IPv4 loopback address, 127.0.0.1. Often simply called the *loopback*, this is a special address that hosts use to direct traffic to themselves. The loopback address creates a shortcut method for TCP/IP applications and services that run on the same device to communicate with one another. By using the loopback address instead of the assigned IPv4 host address, two services on the same host can bypass the lower layers of the TCP/IP stack. You can also ping the loopback address to test the configuration of TCP/IP on the local host.

Although only the single 127.0.0.1 address is used, addresses 127.0.0.0 to 127.255.255.255 are reserved. Any address within this block will loop back to the local host. No address within this block should ever appear on any network.

Link-Local Addresses

IPv4 addresses in the address block 169.254.0.0 to 169.254.255.255 (169.254.0.0/16) are designated as *link-local addresses*. These addresses can be automatically assigned to the local host by the operating system in environments where no IP configuration is available. These might be used in a small peer-to-peer network or for a host that could not automatically obtain an address from a DHCP server.

Communication using IPv4 link-local addresses is only suitable for communication with other devices connected to the same network, as shown in Figure 7-34. A host must not send a packet with an IPv4 link-local destination address to any router for forwarding and should set the IPv4 Time-to-Live (TTL) field for these packets to 1.

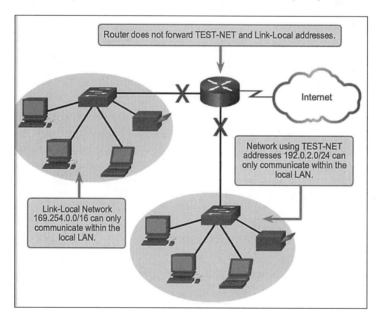

Figure 7-34 Special IPv4 Addresses

Link-local addresses do not provide services outside of the local network. However, many client/server and peer-to-peer applications will work properly with IPv4 link-local addresses.

TEST-NET Addresses

The address block 192.0.2.0 to 192.0.2.255 (192.0.2.0/24) is set aside for teaching and learning purposes. These *TEST-NET addresses* can be used in documentation and network examples. Unlike the experimental addresses, network devices will accept these addresses in their configurations. You may often find these addresses used with the domain names example.com or example.net in RFCs, vendor documentation, and protocol documentation. Addresses within this block should not appear on the Internet.

Experimental Addresses

The addresses in the block 240.0.0.0 to 255.255.255.254 are listed as reserved for future use (RFC 3330). Currently, these addresses can be used only for research or experimentation purposes, and cannot be used in an IPv4 network. Though, according to RFC 3330, they could, technically, be converted to usable addresses in the future.

Legacy Classful Addressing (7.1.4.4)

Historically, RFC 1700, Assigned Numbers, grouped the unicast ranges into specific sizes called class A, class B, and class C addresses. It also defined class D (multicast) and class E (experimental) addresses, as previously presented. The unicast address classes A, B, and C defined specifically sized networks and specific address blocks for these networks. A company or organization was assigned an entire network from a class A, class B, or class C address block. This use of address space is referred to as *classful addressing*.

Class A Blocks

A *class A* address block was designed to support extremely large networks with more than 16 million host addresses. Class A IPv4 addresses used a fixed /8 prefix with the first octet to indicate the network address. The remaining three octets were used for host addresses. All class A addresses required that the most significant bit of the high-order octet (the leftmost bit of the 32 bits) be a 0. This meant that there were only 128 possible class A networks, 0.0.0.0/8 to 127.0.0.0/8. Even though the class A addresses reserved one-half of the address space, because of their limit of 128 networks, they could only be allocated to approximately 120 companies or organizations.

Class B Blocks

Class B address space was designed to support the needs of midsize to large networks with up to approximately 65,000 hosts. A class B IP address used the two high-order octets to indicate the network address. The other two octets specified host addresses. For class B addresses, the most significant two bits of the high-order octet were 10. This restricted the address block for class B to 128.0.0.0/16 to 191.255.0.0/16. Class B had slightly more efficient allocation of addresses than class A because it equally divided 25% of the total IPv4 address space among approximately 16,000 networks.

Class C Blocks

The *class C* address space was the most commonly available of the historic address classes. This address space was intended to provide addresses for small networks with a maximum of 254 hosts. Class C address blocks used a /24 prefix. This meant that a class C network used only the last octet as host addresses, with the three high-order octets used to indicate the network address. Class C address blocks set aside address space by using a fixed value of 110 for the three most significant bits of the high-order octet. This restricted the address block for class C from 192.0.0.0/24 to 223.255.255.0/24. Although it occupied only 12.5% of the total IPv4 address space, it could provide addresses to 2 million networks.

Figure 7-35 illustrates how these address classes are divided.

```
11111111.00000000.00000000.00000000    /8  (255.0.0.0) 16,777,214 host addresses
11111111.10000000.00000000.00000000    /9  (255.128.0.0) 8,388,606 host addresses
11111111.11000000.00000000.00000000    /10 (255.192.0.0) 4,194,302 host addresses
11111111.11100000.00000000.00000000    /11 (255.224.0.0) 2,097,150 host addresses
11111111.11110000.00000000.00000000    /12 (255.240.0.0) 1,048,574 host addresses
11111111.11111000.00000000.00000000    /13 (255.248.0.0) 524,286 host addresses
11111111.11111100.00000000.00000000    /14 (255.252.0.0) 262,142 host addresses
11111111.11111110.00000000.00000000    /15 (255.254.0.0) 131,070 addresses
11111111.11111111.00000000.00000000    /16 (255.255.0.0) 65,534 host addresses
11111111.11111111.10000000.00000000    /17 (255.255.128.0) 32,766 host addresses
11111111.11111111.11000000.00000000    /18 (255.255.192.0) 16,382 host addresses
11111111.11111111.11100000.00000000    /19 (255.255.224.0) 8,190 host addresses
11111111.11111111.11110000.00000000    /20 (255.255.240.0) 4,094 host addresses
11111111.11111111.11111000.00000000    /21 (255.255.248.0) 2,046 host addresses
11111111.11111111.11111100.00000000    /22 (255.255.252.0) 1,022 host addresses
11111111.11111111.11111110.00000000    /23 (255.255.254.0) 510 host addresses
11111111.11111111.11111111.00000000    /24 (255.255.255.0) 254 host addresses
11111111.11111111.11111111.10000000    /25 (255.255.255.128) 126 host addresses
11111111.11111111.11111111.11000000    /26 (255.255.255.192) 62 host addresses
11111111.11111111.11111111.11100000    /27 (255.255.255.224) 30 host addresses
11111111.11111111.11111111.11110000    /28 (255.255.255.240) 14 host addresses
11111111.11111111.11111111.11111000    /29 (255.255.255.248) 6 host addresses
11111111.11111111.11111111.11111100    /30 (255.255.255.252) 2 host addresses
11111111.11111111.11111111.11111110    /31 (255.255.255.254) 0 host addresses
11111111.11111111.11111111.11111111    /32 (255.255.255.255) "Host Route"
```

Figure 7-35   Address Classes

Limits to the Class-Based System

Not all organizations' requirements fit well into one of these three classes. Classful allocation of address space often wasted many addresses, which exhausted the availability of IPv4 addresses. For example, a company that had a network with 260 hosts would need to be given a class B address with more than 65,000 addresses.

Even though this classful system was all but abandoned in the late 1990s, you will see remnants of it in networks today. For example, when you assign an IPv4 address to a computer, the operating system examines the address being assigned to determine if this address is a class A, class B, or class C address. The operating system then assumes the prefix used by that class and makes the default subnet mask assignment.

Figure 7-36 shows the classful address ranges.

IP Address Classes					
Address Class	1st octet range (decimal)	1st octet bits (green bits do not change)	Network (N) and Host (H) parts of address	Default subnet mask (decimal and binary)	Number of possible networks and host per network
A	1-127***	00000000–01111111	N.H.H.H.	255.0.0.0	128 nets (2^7) 16,777,214 hosts per net (2^24-2)
B	128-191	10000000–10111111	N.N.H.H.	255.255.0.0	16,384 nets (2^14) 65,534 hosts per net (2^16-2)
C	192-223	11000000–11011111	N.N.N.H.	255.255.255.0	2,097,150 nets (2^21) 254 hosts per net (2^8-2)
D	224-239	11100000–11101111	NA (multicast)		
E	240-255	11110000–11111111	NA (experimental)		
Note: All zeros (0) and all ones (1) are invalid hosts addresses.					

Figure 7-36   Classful Address Ranges

Classless Addressing

The system in use today is referred to as *classless addressing*. The formal name is Classless Inter-Domain Routing (CIDR, pronounced "cider"). The classful allocation of IPv4 addresses was very inefficient, allowing for only /8, /16, or /24 prefix lengths, each from a separate address space. In 1993, the Internet Engineering Task Force (IETF) created a new set of standards that allowed service providers to allocate IPv4 addresses on any address bit boundary (prefix length) instead of only by a class A, B, or C address.

The IETF knew that CIDR was only a temporary solution and that a new IP protocol would have to be developed to accommodate the rapid growth in the number of Internet users. In 1994, the IETF began its work to find a successor to IPv4, which eventually became IPv6.

Assignment of IP Addresses (7.1.4.5, 7.1.4.6)

For a company or organization to have network hosts, such as web servers, accessible from the Internet, that organization must have a block of public addresses assigned. Remember that public addresses must be unique, and use of these public addresses is regulated and allocated to each organization separately. This is true for IPv4 and IPv6 addresses.

IANA and RIRs

The Internet Assigned Numbers Authority (IANA) (http://www.iana.org) manages the allocation of IPv4 and IPv6 addresses. Until the mid-1990s, all IPv4 address space was managed directly by IANA. At that time, the remaining IPv4 address space was allocated to various other registries to manage for particular purposes or for regional areas. These registration companies are called Regional Internet Registries (RIRs) and their general regions are depicted in Figure 7-37.

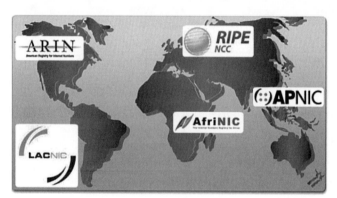

Figure 7-37   Assignment of IP Addresses by Regional Internet Registry (RIR)

The following are the major RIRs, the regions they cover, and their URLs:

- AfriNIC (African Network Information Centre): Africa Region; http://www.afrinic.net

- APNIC (Asia Pacific Network Information Centre): Asia/Pacific Region; http://www.apnic.net

- ARIN (American Registry for Internet Numbers): North America Region; http://www.arin.net

- LACNIC (Regional Latin-American and Caribbean IP Address Registry): Latin America and some Caribbean Islands; http://www.lacnic.net

- RIPE NCC (Reseaux IP Europeans): Europe, the Middle East, and Central Asia; http://www.ripe.net

ISPs

RIRs are responsible for allocating IP addresses to the Internet service providers (ISPs). Most companies or organizations obtain their IPv4 address blocks from an ISP. An ISP will generally supply a small number of usable IPv4 addresses (8 or 16) to their customers as a part of their services. Larger blocks of addresses can be obtained based on justification of needs and for additional service costs.

In a sense, the ISP loans or rents these addresses to the organization. If we choose to move our Internet connectivity to another ISP, the new ISP will provide us with addresses from the address blocks that have been provided to them, and our previous ISP returns the blocks loaned to us to their allocation to be loaned to another customer.

IPv6 addresses can be obtained from the ISP or, in some cases, directly from the RIR. IPv6 addresses and typical address block sizes will be discussed later in this chapter.

ISP Services

To get access to the services of the Internet, we have to connect our data network to the Internet using an ISP. ISPs have their own set of internal data networks to manage Internet connectivity and to provide related services. Among the other services that an ISP generally provides to its customers are DNS services, e-mail services, and a website. Depending on the level of service required and available, customers use different tiers of an ISP.

ISP Tiers

ISPs are designated by a hierarchy based on their level of connectivity to the Internet backbone. Each lower tier obtains connectivity to the backbone via a connection to a higher-tier ISP, as shown in Figure 7-38.

Tier 1

As shown in Figure 7-38, at the top of the ISP hierarchy are Tier 1 ISPs. These ISPs are large national or international ISPs that are directly connected to the Internet backbone. The customers of Tier 1 ISPs are either lower-tiered ISPs or large companies and organizations. Because they are at the top of Internet connectivity, Tier 1 ISPs engineer highly reliable connections and services. Among the technologies used to support this reliability are multiple connections to the Internet backbone.

The primary advantages for customers of Tier 1 ISPs are reliability and speed. Because these customers are only one connection away from the Internet, there are fewer opportunities for failures or traffic bottlenecks. The drawback for Tier 1 ISP customers is its high cost.

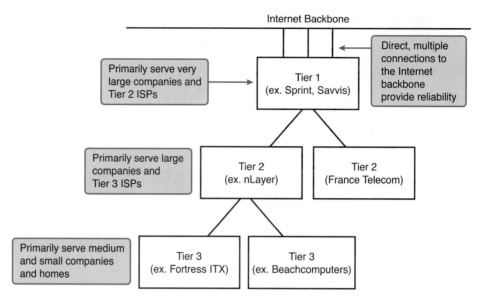

Figure 7-38   Three Tiers of ISP

Tier 2

As shown in Figure 7-38, Tier 2 ISPs acquire their Internet service from Tier 1 ISPs. Tier 2 ISPs generally focus on business customers. Tier 2 ISPs usually offer more services than the other two tiers of ISPs. These Tier 2 ISPs tend to have the information technology (IT) resources to operate their own services such as Domain Name Service (DNS), e-mail servers, and web servers. Other services that Tier 2 ISPs may offer include website development and maintenance, e-commerce/e-business, and Voice over Internet Protocol (VoIP).

The primary disadvantage of Tier 2 ISPs, as compared to Tier 1 ISPs, is slower Internet access. Because Tier 2 ISPs are at least one more connection away from the Internet backbone, they also tend to have lower reliability than Tier 1 ISPs.

Tier 3

As shown in Figure 7-38, Tier 3 ISPs purchase their Internet service from Tier 2 ISPs. The focus of these ISPs is the retail and home markets in a specific locale. Tier 3 customers typically do not need many of the services required by Tier 2 customers. Their primary need is connectivity and support.

These customers often have little or no computer or network expertise. Tier 3 ISPs often bundle Internet connectivity as a part of network and computer service contracts for their customers. Although they may have reduced bandwidth and less reliability than Tier 1 and Tier 2 providers, Tier 3 ISPs are often good choices for small to midsize companies.

Interactive Graphic

Activity 7.1.4.7: Public or Private IPv4 Address

Go to the online course to drag each IP address to the correct category, Public or Private.

Lab 7.1.4.8: Identifying IPv4 Addresses

In this lab you will identify and classify IPv4 addresses.

IPv6 Network Addresses (7.2)

Internet Protocol version 6 (IPv6) is the latest revision of the Internet Protocol. This section introduces the new protocol and explains why it is needed.

IPv4 Issues (7.2.1)

This section discusses some of the reasons why IPv4 needs to be updated to IPv6.

The Need for IPv6 (7.2.1.1)

IPv6 is designed to be the successor to IPv4. IPv6 has a larger, 128-bit address space, providing for 340 undecillion addresses. (That is the number 340, followed by 36 zeros.) However, IPv6 is much more than just larger addresses. When the IETF began its development of a successor to IPv4, it used this opportunity to fix the limitations of IPv4 and include additional enhancements. One example is Internet Control Message Protocol version 6 (ICMPv6), which includes address resolution and address auto-configuration not found in ICMP for IPv4 (ICMPv4). ICMPv4 and ICMPv6 are discussed later in this chapter.

IPv4 Address Depletion

The depletion of IPv4 address space has been the motivating factor for moving to IPv6. As Africa, Asia, and other areas of the world become more connected to the Internet, there are not enough IPv4 addresses to accommodate this growth. On Monday, January 31, 2011, IANA allocated the last two /8 IPv4 address blocks to the RIRs. Various projections show that all five RIRs will have run out of IPv4 addresses between 2015 and 2020. At that point, the remaining IPv4 addresses will have been allocated to ISPs.

IPv4 has a theoretical maximum of 4.3 billion addresses. RFC 1918 private addresses in combination with network address translation (NAT) have been instrumental in slowing the depletion of IPv4 address space. NAT has limitations that severely impede peer-to-peer communications.

Internet of Things

Figure 7-39 shows the changes through the years in the number of things connected by the Internet.

Figure 7-39   Internet of Things

The Internet of today is significantly different than the Internet of past decades. The Internet of today is more than e-mail, web pages, and file transfer between computers. The evolving Internet is becoming an Internet of things. As depicted in Figure 7-39, no longer will the only devices accessing the Internet be computers, tablets, and smartphones. The sensor-equipped, Internet-ready devices of tomorrow will include everything from automobiles and biomedical devices to household appliances and natural ecosystems. Imagine a meeting at a customer site that is automatically scheduled on your calendar application to begin an hour before you normally start work. This could be a significant problem, especially if you forget to check the calendar or adjust the alarm clock accordingly. Now imagine that the calendar application communicates this information directly to your alarm clock and to your automobile. Your alarm clock wakes you up in plenty of time to get ready for your meeting, and your car automatically warms up to melt the ice on the windshield before you enter the car, and then gives you instructions for which route to take to your meeting.

With an increasing Internet population, a limited IPv4 address space, issues with NAT, and an Internet of things, the time has come to begin the transition to IPv6.

IPv4 and IPv6 Coexistence (7.2.1.2)

There is not a single date to move to IPv6. For the foreseeable future, both IPv4 and IPv6 will coexist. The transition is expected to take years. The IETF has created various protocols and tools to help network administrators migrate their networks to IPv6. The migration techniques can be divided into three categories:

- *Dual stack*: As shown in Figure 7-40, a dual stack allows IPv4 and IPv6 to coexist on the same network. Dual-stack devices run both IPv4 and IPv6 protocol stacks simultaneously.

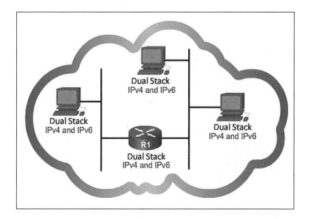

Figure 7-40   Dual Stack

- *Tunneling*: As shown in Figure 7-41, tunneling is a method of transporting an IPv6 packet over an IPv4 network. The IPv6 packet is encapsulated inside an IPv4 packet, similar to other types of data.

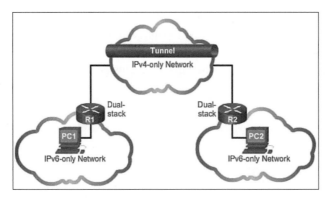

Figure 7-41 Tunneling

■ *Translation*: As shown in Figure 7-42, Network Address Translation 64 (NAT64) allows IPv6-enabled devices to communicate with IPv4-enabled devices using a translation technique similar to NAT for IPv4. An IPv6 packet is translated to an IPv4 packet, and vice versa.

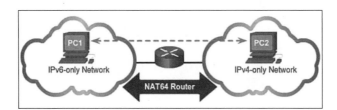

Figure 7-42 Translation

Interactive
Graphic

Activity 7.2.1.3: IPv4 and IPv6 Terms and Descriptions

Go to the online course to complete the activity. This activity is designed to have you drag and drop the provided IPv4 and IPv6 term to the field next to the appropriate description

IPv6 Addressing (7.2.2)

This section looks at the process of IPv6 addressing.

Hexadecimal Number System (7.2.2.1)

Unlike IPv4 addresses that are expressed in dotted decimal notation, IPv6 addresses are represented using hexadecimal values. You have seen hexadecimal used in the Packets Byte pane of Wireshark. In Wireshark, hexadecimal is used to represent the binary values within frames and packets. Hexadecimal is also used to represent Ethernet Media Access Control (MAC) addresses.

Hexadecimal Numbering

Hexadecimal ("Hex") is a convenient way to represent binary values. Just as decimal is a base 10 numbering system and binary is base 2, hexadecimal is a base 16 numbering system.

The base 16 numbering system uses the numbers 0 to 9 and the letters A to F. Figure 7-43 shows the equivalent decimal, binary, and hexadecimal values. There are 16 unique combinations of 4 bits, from 0000 to 1111. The 16-digit hexadecimal numbering system is the perfect numbering system to use, because any 4 bits can be represented with a single hexadecimal value.

Representing Hexadecimal Values

Hexadecimal	Decimal	Binary
0	0	0000
1	1	0001
2	2	0010
3	3	0011
4	4	0100
5	5	0101
6	6	0110
7	7	0111
8	8	1000
9	9	1001
A	10	1010
B	11	1011
C	12	1100
D	13	1101
E	14	1110
F	15	1111

Figure 7-43   Hexadecimal Numbering

Understanding Bytes

Given that 8 bits (1 byte) is a common binary grouping, binary 00000000 to 11111111 can be represented in hexadecimal as the range 00 to FF. Leading zeros can be displayed to complete the 8-bit representation. For example, the binary value 0000 1010 is shown in hexadecimal as 0A.

Representing Hexadecimal Values

Hexadecimal is usually represented in text by the value preceded by 0x (for example, 0x73) or a subscript 16. Less commonly, it may be followed by an H (for example, 73H). However, because subscript text is not recognized in command-line or programming environments, the technical representation of hexadecimal is preceded with "0x" (zero X). Therefore, the earlier examples would be shown as 0x0A and 0x73, respectively.

Note

It is important to distinguish hexadecimal values from decimal values regarding the characters 0 to 9.

Hexadecimal Conversions

Number conversions between decimal and hexadecimal values are straightforward, but quickly dividing or multiplying by 16 is not always convenient.

With practice, it is possible to recognize the binary bit patterns that match the decimal and hexadecimal values. Figure 7-44 shows these patterns for selected 8-bit values.

Hexadecimal Conversions of Binary Octets		
Hexadecimal	**Decimal**	**Binary**
00	0	0000 0000
01	1	0000 0001
02	2	0000 0010
03	3	0000 0011
04	4	0000 0100
05	5	0000 0101
06	6	0000 0110
07	7	0000 0111
08	8	0000 1000
0A	10	0000 1010
0F	15	0000 1111
10	16	0001 0000
20	32	0010 0000
40	64	0100 0000
80	128	1000 0000
C0	192	1100 0000
CA	202	1100 1010
F0	240	1111 0000
FF	255	1111 1111

Figure 7-44   Hexadecimal Conversion Patterns

IPv6 Address Representation (7.2.2.2)

IPv6 addresses are 128 bits in length and written as a string of hexadecimal values. Every 4 bits is represented by a single hexadecimal digit, for a total of 32 hexadecimal values. IPv6 addresses are not case sensitive and can be written in either lowercase or uppercase.

Preferred Format

As shown in Figure 7-45, the preferred format for writing an IPv6 address is x:x:x:x:x:x:x:x, with each "x" consisting of four hexadecimal values. In IPv6, a *hextet* is the unofficial term used to refer to a segment of 16 bits or four hexadecimal values. Each "x" is a single hextet, 16 bits or four hexadecimal digits.

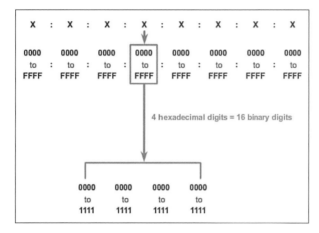

Figure 7-45   Hextets

"Preferred format" means the IPv6 address is written using all 32 hexadecimal digits. It does not necessarily mean it is the ideal method for representing the IPv6 address. In the following pages, we will see two rules to help reduce the number of digits needed to represent an IPv6 address. Figure 7-46 has examples of IPv6 addresses in the preferred format.

2001 :	0DB8 :	0000 :	1111 :	0000 :	0000 :	0000 :	0200
2001 :	0DB8 :	0000 :	00A3 :	ABCD :	0000 :	0000 :	1234
2001 :	0DB8 :	000A :	0001 :	0000 :	0000 :	0000 :	0100
2001 :	0DB8 :	AAAA :	0001 :	0000 :	0000 :	0000 :	0200
FE80 :	0000 :	0000 :	0000 :	0123 :	4567 :	89AB :	CDEF
FE80 :	0000 :	0000 :	0000 :	0000 :	0000 :	0000 :	0001
FF02 :	0000 :	0000 :	0000 :	0000 :	0000 :	0000 :	0001
FF02 :	0000 :	0000 :	0000 :	0000 :	0001 :	FF00 :	0200
0000 :	0000 :	0000 :	0000 :	0000 :	0000 :	0000 :	0001
0000 :	0000 :	0000 :	0000 :	0000 :	0000 :	0000 :	0000

Figure 7-46   Preferred Format Examples

Rule 1: Omitting Leading 0s (7.2.2.3)

The first rule to help reduce the notation of IPv6 addresses is that any leading 0s in any 16-bit section or hextet can be omitted. For example:

- 01AB can be represented as 1AB.

- 09F0 can be represented as 9F0.

- 0A00 can be represented as A00.

- 00AB can be represented as AB.

This rule only applies to leading 0s, *not* to trailing 0s; otherwise the address would be ambiguous. For example, the hextet ABC could be either 0ABC or ABC0.

Figures 7-47 through 7-54 show several examples of how omitting leading 0s can be used to reduce the size of an IPv6 address. For each example the preferred format is shown. Notice how omitting the leading 0s in all examples results in a smaller address representation.

Preferred	2001:0DB8:0000:1111:0000:0000:0000:0200
No leading 0s	2001: DB8: 0:1111: 0: 0: 0: 200

Figure 7-47   Omitting Leading 0s: Example 1

Preferred	2001:0DB8:0000:A300:ABCD:0000:0000:1234
No leading 0s	2001: DB8: 0:A300:ABCD: 0: 0:1234

Figure 7-48   Omitting Leading 0s: Example 2

Preferred	2001:0DB8:000A:1000:0000:0000:0000:0100
No leading 0s	2001: DB8: A:1000: 0: 0: 0: 100

Figure 7-49   Omitting Leading 0s: Example 3

Preferred	FE80:0000:0000:0000:0123:4567:89AB:CDEF
No leading 0s	FE80: 0: 0: 0: 123:4567:89AB:CDEF

Figure 7-50   Omitting Leading 0s: Example 4

Preferred	FF02:0000:0000:0000:0000:0000:0000:0001
No leading 0s	FF02: 0: 0: 0: 0: 0: 0: 1

Figure 7-51   Omitting Leading 0s: Example 5

Preferred	FF02:0000:0000:0000:0000:0001:FF00:0200
No leading 0s	FF02: 0: 0: 0: 0: 1:FF00: 200

Figure 7-52   Omitting Leading 0s: Example 6

Preferred	0000:0000:0000:0000:0000:0000:0000:0001
No leading 0s	0: 0: 0: 0: 0: 0: 0: 1

Figure 7-53   Omitting Leading 0s: Example 7

Preferred	0000:0000:0000:0000:0000:0000:0000:0000
No leading 0s	0: 0: 0: 0: 0: 0: 0: 0

Figure 7-54   Omitting Leading 0s: Example 8

Rule 2: Omitting All 0 Segments (7.2.2.4)

The second rule to help reduce the notation of IPv6 addresses is that a double colon (::) can replace any single, contiguous string of one or more 16-bit segments (hextets) consisting of all 0s.

The double colon (::) can be used only once within an address; otherwise there would be more than one possible resulting address. When used with the omitting leading 0s technique, the notation of IPv6 address can often be greatly reduced. This is commonly known as the compressed format.

The following address is incorrect because it includes two sets of double colons:

- 2001:0DB8::ABCD::1234

Possible expansions for the preceding ambiguous compressed address include the following:

- 2001:0DB8::ABCD:0000:0000:1234
- 2001:0DB8::ABCD:0000:0000:0000:1234
- 2001:0DB8:0000:ABCD::1234
- 2001:0DB8:0000:0000:ABCD::1234

Figures 7-55 through 7-61 show several examples of how using the double colon (::) and omitting leading 0s can reduce the size of an IPv6 address.

Preferred	2001:0DB8:0000:1111:0000:0000:0000:0200
No leading 0s	2001: DB8: 0:1111: 0: 0: 0: 200
Compressed	2001:DB8:0:1111::200

Figure 7-55   Using Double Colons: Example 1

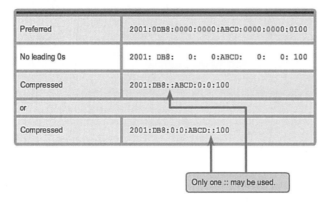

Preferred	2001:0DB8:0000:0000:ABCD:0000:0000:0100
No leading 0s	2001: DB8: 0: 0:ABCD: 0: 0: 100
Compressed	2001:DB8::ABCD:0:0:100
or	
Compressed	2001:DB8:0:0:ABCD::100

Only one :: may be used.

Figure 7-56   Using Double Colons: Example 2

Preferred	FE80:0000:0000:0000:0123:4567:89AB:CDEF
No leading 0s	FE80: 0: 0: 0: 123:4567:89AB:CDEF
Compressed	FE80::123:4567:89AB:CDEF

Figure 7-57   Using Double Colons: Example 3

Preferred	FF02:0000:0000:0000:0000:0000:0000:0001
No leading 0s	FF02: 0: 0: 0: 0: 0: 0: 1
Compressed	FF02::1

Figure 7-58   Using Double Colons: Example 4

Preferred	FF02:0000:0000:0000:0000:0001:FF00:0200
No leading 0s	FF02: 0: 0: 0: 0: 1:FF00: 200
Compressed	FF02::1:FF00:200

Figure 7-59 Using Double Colons: Example 5

Preferred	0000:0000:0000:0000:0000:0000:0000:0001
No leading 0s	0: 0: 0: 0: 0: 0: 0: 1
Compressed	::1

Figure 7-60 Using Double Colons: Example 6

Preferred	0000:0000:0000:0000:0000:0000:0000:0000
No leading 0s	0: 0: 0: 0: 0: 0: 0: 0
Compressed	::

Figure 7-61 Using Double Colons: Example 7

Interactive Graphic

Activity 7.2.2.5: Practicing IPv6 Address Representations

Go to the online course to complete the activity. This activity provides practice in converting IPv6 addresses into short and compressed forms.

Types of IPv6 Addresses (7.2.3)

This section takes a closer look at the different types of IPv6 addresses.

IPv6 Address Types (7.2.3.1)

There are three types of IPv6 addresses:

- **Unicast:** An IPv6 unicast address uniquely identifies an interface on an IPv6-enabled device. As shown in Figure 7-62, a source IPv6 address must be a unicast address.

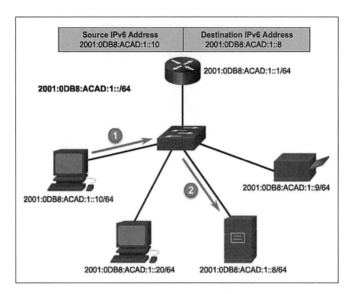

Figure 7-62   IPv6 Unicast Communications

- **Multicast:** An IPv6 multicast address is used to send a single IPv6 packet to multiple destinations.

- **Anycast:** An IPv6 anycast address is any IPv6 unicast address that can be assigned to multiple devices. A packet sent to an anycast address is routed to the nearest device having that address. Anycast addresses are beyond the scope of this course.

Unlike IPv4, IPv6 does not have a broadcast address. However, there is an IPv6 all-nodes multicast address that essentially gives the same result.

IPv6 Prefix Length (7.2.3.2)

Recall that the prefix, or network, portion of an IPv4 address can be identified by a dotted-decimal subnet mask or prefix length (slash notation). For example, an IP address of 192.168.1.10 with dotted-decimal subnet mask 255.255.255.0 is equivalent to 192.168.1.10/24.

IPv6 uses the prefix length to represent the prefix portion of the address. IPv6 does not use the dotted-decimal subnet mask notation. The prefix length is used to indicate the network portion of an IPv6 address using the IPv6 address/prefix length.

The prefix length can range from 0 to 128. A typical IPv6 prefix length for LANs and most other types of networks is /64. This means the prefix or network portion of the address is 64 bits in length, leaving another 64 bits for the Interface ID (host portion) of the address, as shown in Figure 7-63.

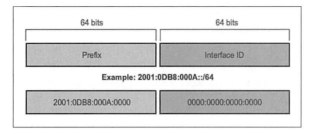

Figure 7-63 /64 Prefix

IPv6 Unicast Addresses (7.2.3.3)

An IPv6 unicast address uniquely identifies an interface on an IPv6-enabled device. A packet sent to a unicast address is received by the interface that is assigned that address. Similar to IPv4, a source IPv6 address must be a unicast address. The destination IPv6 address can be either a unicast address or a multicast address.

There are six types of IPv6 unicast addresses, as shown in Figure 7-64 and described in the following list.

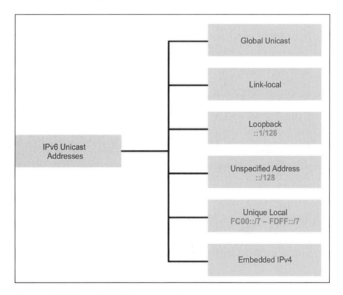

Figure 7-64 IPv6 Unicast Addresses

- **Global unicast:** A global unicast address is similar to a public IPv4 address. These are globally unique, Internet-routable addresses. Global unicast addresses can be configured statically or assigned dynamically. There are some important differences in how a device receives its IPv6 address dynamically compared to DHCP for IPv4.

■ **Link-local:** Link-local addresses are used to communicate with other devices on the same local link. With IPv6, the term *link* refers to a subnet. Link-local addresses are confined to a single link. Their uniqueness must be confirmed on that link only because they are not routable beyond the link. In other words, routers will not forward packets with a link-local source or destination address.

■ **Loopback:** The loopback address is used by a host to send a packet to itself and cannot be assigned to a physical interface. Similar to an IPv4 loopback address, you can ping an IPv6 loopback address to test the configuration of TCP/IP on the local host. The IPv6 loopback address is all 0s except for the last bit, represented as ::1/128 or just ::1 in the compressed format.

■ **Unspecified address:** An unspecified address is an all-0s address represented as ::/128 or just :: in the compressed format. It cannot be assigned to an interface and can only be used as a source address in an IPv6 packet. An unspecified address is used as a source address when the device does not yet have a permanent IPv6 address or when the source of the packet is irrelevant to the destination.

■ **Unique local:** IPv6 unique local addresses have some similarity to RFC 1918 private addresses for IPv4, but there are significant differences as well. Unique local addresses are used for local addressing within a site or between a limited number of sites. These addresses should not be routable in the global IPv6. Unique local addresses are in the range of FC00::/7 to FDFF::/7.

With IPv4, private addresses are combined with NAT/PAT to provide a many-to-one translation of private-to-public addresses. This is done because of the limited availability of IPv4 address space. Many sites also use the private nature of RFC 1918 addresses to help secure or hide their network from potential security risks. However, this was never the intended use of these technologies, and the IETF has always recommended that sites take the proper security precautions on their Internet-facing routers. Although IPv6 does provide for site-specific addressing, it is not intended to be used to help hide internal IPv6-enabled devices from the IPv6 Internet. IETF recommends that limiting access to devices should be accomplished using proper, best-practice security measures.

Note

The original IPv6 specification defined site-local addresses for a similar purpose, using the prefix range FEC0::/10. There were several ambiguities in the specification, and site-local addresses were deprecated by the IETF in favor of unique local addresses.

■ Embedded IPv4: The last type of unicast address is the IPv4 embedded address. These addresses are used to help transition from IPv4 to IPv6. IPv4 embedded addresses are beyond the scope of this course.

IPv6 Link-Local Unicast Addresses (7.2.3.4)

An *IPv6 link-local address* enables a device to communicate with other IPv6-enabled devices on the same link, and only on that link (subnet). Packets with a source or destination link-local address cannot be routed beyond the link from where the packet originated.

Unlike IPv4 link-local addresses, IPv6 link-local addresses have a significant role in various aspects of the network. The global unicast address is not a requirement; however, every IPv6-enabled network interface is required to have a link-local address.

If a link-local address is not configured manually on an interface, the device will automatically create its own without communicating with a DHCP server. IPv6-enabled hosts create an IPv6 link-local address even if the device has not been assigned a global unicast IPv6 address. This allows IPv6-enabled devices to communicate with other IPv6-enabled devices on the same subnet. This includes communication with the default gateway (router).

IPv6 link-local addresses are in the FE80::/10 range. The /10 indicates that the first 10 bits are 1111 1110 10xx xxxx. The first hextet has a range of 1111 1110 **1000 0000** (FE80) to 1111 1110 10**11 1111** (FEBF).

Figure 7-65 shows an example of communication using IPv6 link-local addresses. Figure 7-66 shows the format of an IPv6 link-local address.

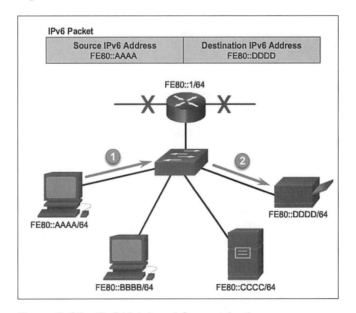

Figure 7-65 IPv6 Link-Local Communications

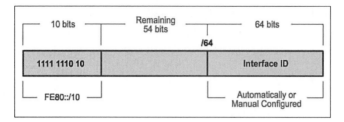

Figure 7-66   IPv6 Link-Local Address

IPv6 link-local addresses are also used by IPv6 routing protocols to exchange messages and as the next-hop address in the IPv6 routing table

> **Note**
>
> Typically, it is the link-local address of the router, not the global unicast address, that is used as the default gateway for other devices on the link.

Interactive Graphic

Activity 7.2.3.5: Identify Types of IPv6 Addresses

Go to the online course to complete the drag-and-drop activity by dragging the IPv6 address type to the most appropriate description.

IPv6 Unicast Addresses (7.2.4)

This section looks at the structure, static and dynamic configuration of IPv6 unicast addresses. The section also discusses the static and dynamic link-local address, as well as how to verify IPv6 configuration.

Structure of an IPv6 Global Unicast Address (7.2.4.1)

IPv6 global unicast addresses are globally unique and routable on the IPv6 Internet. These addresses are equivalent to public IPv4 addresses. The Internet Committee for Assigned Names and Numbers (ICANN), the operator for IANA, allocates IPv6 address blocks to the five RIRs. Currently, only global unicast addresses with the first three bits of 001 or 2000::/3 are being assigned. This is only 1/8th of the total available IPv6 address space, excluding only a very small portion for other types of unicast and multicast addresses. Figure 7-67 shows the structure and range of a global unicast address.

> **Note**
>
> The 2001:0DB8::/32 address has been reserved for documentation purposes, including use in examples.

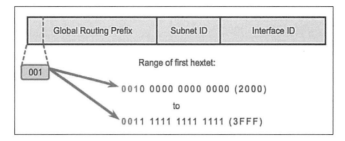

Figure 7-67 IPv6 Global Unicast Address

A global unicast address has three parts:

- *Global routing prefix*: The global routing prefix is the prefix, or network, portion of the address that is assigned by the provider, such as an ISP, to a customer or site. Currently, RIRs assign a /48 global routing prefix to customers. This includes everyone from enterprise business networks to individual households. This is more than enough address space for most customers.

  Figure 7-68 shows the structure of a global unicast address using a /48 global routing prefix. /48 prefixes are the most common global routing prefixes assigned and will be used in most of the examples throughout this course.

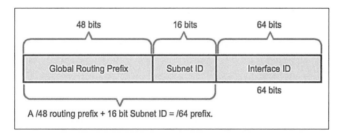

Figure 7-68 IPv6 /48 Global Routing Prefix

  For example, the IPv6 address 2001:0DB8:ACAD::/48 has a prefix that indicates that the first 48 bits (three hextets) (2001:0DB8:ACAD) is the prefix, or network, portion of the address. The double colon (::) prior to the /48 prefix length means the rest of the address contains all 0s.

- **Subnet ID:** The Subnet ID is used by an organization to identify subnets within its site.

- **Interface ID:** The IPv6 Interface ID is equivalent to the host portion of an IPv4 address. The term Interface ID is used because a single host may have multiple interfaces, each having one or more IPv6 addresses.

Note

Unlike IPv4, in IPv6 the all-0s address can be assigned to a device because there are no broadcast addresses in IPv6. However, the all-0s address is reserved as a Subnet-Router anycast address, and should be assigned only to routers.

An easy way to read most IPv6 addresses is to count the number of hextets. As shown in Figure 7-69, in a /64 global unicast address the first four hextets are for the network portion of the address, with the fourth hextet indicating the Subnet ID. The remaining four hextets are for the Interface ID.

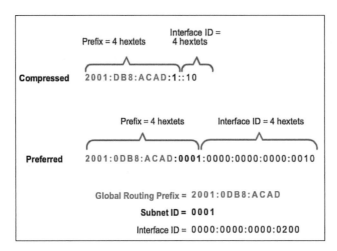

Figure 7-69 IPv6 Reading a Global Unicast Address

Static Configuration of a Global Unicast Address (7.2.4.2)

This section provides procedures for setting up global unicast addresses on devices.

Router Configuration

Most IPv6 configuration and verification commands in the Cisco IOS software are similar to their IPv4 counterparts. In many cases the only difference is the use of **ipv6** in place of **ip** within the commands.

The **interface** command to configure an IPv6 global unicast address on an interface is **ipv6 address** *ipv6-address/prefix-length*.

Notice that there is not a space between *ipv6-address* and *prefix-length*.

The example configuration will use the topology shown in Figure 7-70 and these IPv6 subnets:

- 2001:0DB8:ACAD:0001:/64 (*or* 2001:DB8:ACAD:1::/64)

- 2001:0DB8:ACAD:0002:/64 (*or* 2001:DB8:ACAD:2::/64)

- 2001:0DB8:ACAD:0003:/64 (*or* 2001:DB8:ACAD:3::/64)

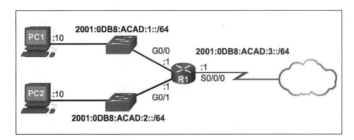

Figure 7-70   Configuring IPv6 on a Router

As shown in Figure 7-71, configuring the IPv6 global unicast address on the Gigabit
Ethernet 0/0 (G0/0) interface of R1 would require the following commands:

```
Router(config)# interface GigabitEthernet 0/0
Router(config-if)# ipv6 address 2001:db8:acad:1::1/64
Router(config-if)# no shutdown
```

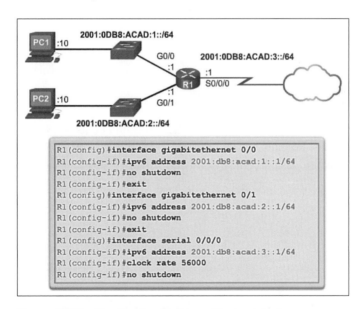

Figure 7-71   Configuring IPv6 on a Router Interface

Host Configuration

Manually configuring the IPv6 address on a host is similar to configuring an IPv4
address.

As shown in Figure 7-72, the default gateway address configured for PC1 is 2001:DB8:ACAD:1::1, the global unicast address of the R1 Gigabit Ethernet interface on the same network.

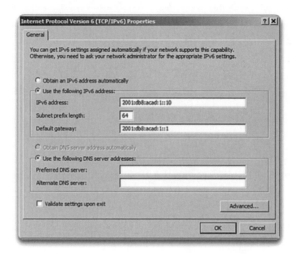

Figure 7-72   Configuring IPv6 on a Host

Activity 7.2.4.2: Syntax Checker

Go to the online course to use the Syntax Checker to configure the IPv6 global unicast address.

Just as with IPv4, configuring static addresses on clients does not scale to larger environments. For this reason, most network administrators in an IPv6 network will enable dynamic assignment of IPv6 addresses.

There are two ways in which a device can obtain an IPv6 global unicast address automatically:

- Stateless Address Autoconfiguration (SLAAC)
- DHCPv6

Dynamic Configuration of a Global Unicast Address Using SLAAC (7.2.4.3)

This section examines how Stateless Address Autoconfiguration (SLAAC) is used in the configuration of a global unicast address.

Stateless Address Autoconfiguration

Stateless Address Autoconfiguration (SLAAC) is a method that allows a device to obtain its prefix, prefix length, and default gateway address information from an *IPv6 router* without the use of a DHCPv6 server. Using SLAAC, devices rely on the local router's ICMPv6 Router Advertisement (RA) messages to obtain the necessary information.

IPv6 routers periodically send out ICMPv6 RA messages to all IPv6-enabled devices on the network. By default, Cisco routers send out RA messages every 200 seconds to the IPv6 all-nodes multicast group address. An IPv6 device on the network does not have to wait for these periodic RA messages. A device can send a Router Solicitation (RS) message to the router, using the IPv6 all-routers multicast group address. When an IPv6 router receives an RS message, it will immediately respond with an RA.

Even though an interface on a Cisco router can be configured with an IPv6 address, this does not make it an "IPv6 router." An IPv6 router is a router that

- Forwards IPv6 packets between networks
- Can be configured with static IPv6 routes or a dynamic IPv6 routing protocol
- Sends ICMPv6 RA messages

IPv6 routing is not enabled by default. To enable a router as an IPv6 router, the **ipv6 unicast-routing** global configuration command must be used.

Note

IPv4 is enabled on Cisco routers by default.

The ICMPv6 RA message contains the prefix, prefix length, and other information for the IPv6 device. The RA message also informs the IPv6 device how to obtain its addressing information. The RA message can contain one of the following three options, as shown in Figure 7-73:

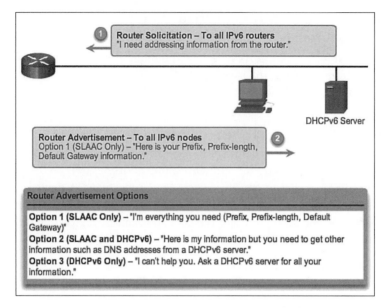

Figure 7-73 Router Solicitation and Router Advertisement Messages

- **Option 1 – SLAAC Only:** The device should use the prefix, prefix-length, and default gateway address information contained in the RA message. No other information is available from a DHCPv6 server.

- **Option 2 – SLAAC and DHCPv6:** The device should use the prefix, prefix-length, and default gateway address information in the RA message. Other information is available from a DHCPv6 server, such as the DNS server address. The device will, through the normal process of discovering and querying a DHCPv6 server, obtain this additional information. This is known as *stateless* DHCPv6 because the DHCPv6 server does not need to allocate or keep track of any IPv6 address assignments; it only needs to provide additional information, such as the DNS server address.

- **Option 3 – DHCPv6 Only:** The device should not use the information in this RA message for its addressing information. Instead, the device should use the normal process of discovering and querying a DHCPv6 server to obtain all of its addressing information. This includes an IPv6 global unicast address, prefix length, a default gateway address, and the addresses of DNS servers. In this case, the DHCPv6 server is acting as a stateful DHCP server similar to DHCP for IPv4. The DHCPv6 server allocates and keeps track of IPv6 addresses so it does not assign the same IPv6 address to multiple devices.

Routers send ICMPv6 RA messages using the link-local address as the source IPv6 address. Devices using SLAAC use the router's link-local address as their default gateway address.

Dynamic Configuration of a Global Unicast Address Using DHCPv6 (7.2.4.4)

The other option for dynamically configuring a global unicast address is to use DHCPv6, as described in this section.

DHCPv6

Dynamic Host Configuration Protocol for IPv6 (DHCPv6) is similar to DHCP for IPv4. A device can automatically receive its addressing information, including a global unicast address, prefix length, default gateway address, and the addresses of DNS servers, by using the services of a DHCPv6 server.

A device may receive all or some of its IPv6 addressing information from a DHCPv6 server, depending upon whether option 2 (SLAAC and DHCPv6) or option 3 (DHCPv6 Only) is specified in the ICMPv6 RA message. Additionally, the host OS may choose to ignore whatever is in the router's RA message and obtain its IPv6 address and other information directly from a DHCPv6 server, as shown in Figure 7-74.

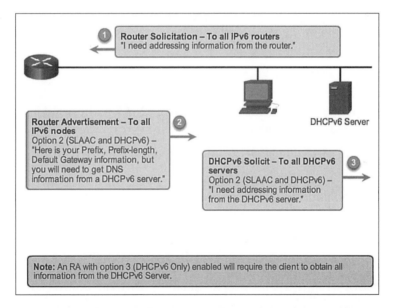

Figure 7-74   Router Solicitation and Router Advertisement Messages (DHCPv6)

Before deploying IPv6 devices in a network, it is a good idea to first verify whether the host observes the options within the router's ICMPv6 RA message.

A device may obtain its IPv6 global unicast address dynamically and also be configured with multiple static IPv6 addresses on the same interface. IPv6 allows for multiple IPv6 addresses, belonging to the same IPv6 network, to be configured on the same interface.

A device may also be configured with more than one default gateway IPv6 address. For further information about how the decision is made regarding which address is used as a source IPv6 address or which default gateway address is used, refer to RFC 6724, Default Address Selection for IPv6.

The Interface ID

If the client does not use the information contained within the RA message and relies solely on DHCPv6, then the DHCPv6 server will provide the entire IPv6 global unicast address, including the prefix and the Interface ID.

EUI-64 Process or Randomly Generated (7.2.4.5)

If we use SLAAC Only or SLAAC with DHCPv6, the client does not obtain the actual Interface ID portion of the address. The client device must determine its own 64-bit Interface ID, either by using the EUI-64 process or by generating a random 64-bit number.

This section looks at the Extended Unique Identifier (EUI-64) process, and the randomly generated identifier that does not use the MAC address.

EUI-64 Process

IEEE defined the Extended Unique Identifier (EUI) or modified EUI-64 process. This process uses a client's 48-bit Ethernet MAC address and inserts another 16 bits in the middle of the 48-bit MAC address to create a 64-bit Interface ID.

Ethernet MAC addresses are usually represented in hexadecimal and are made up of two parts:

- **Organizationally Unique Identifier (OUI):** The OUI is a 24-bit (six hexadecimal digits) vendor code assigned by IEEE.

- **Device identifier:** The device identifier is a unique 24-bit (six hexadecimal digits) value within a common OUI.

An EUI-64 Interface ID is represented in binary and is made up of three parts:

- 24-bit OUI from the client MAC address, but the 7th bit (the Universally/ Locally [U/L] bit) is reversed. This means that if the 7th bit is a 0. it becomes a 1, and vice versa.

- The inserted 16-bit value FFFE (in hexadecimal).

- 24-bit Device Identifier from the client MAC address.

The EUI-64 process is described next and illustrated in Figure 7-75, using R1's Gigabit Ethernet MAC address of FC99:4775:CEE0.

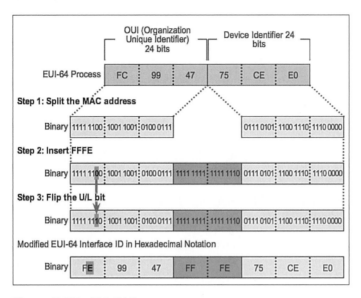

Figure 7-75 EUI-64 Process

Step 1.   Divide the MAC address between the OUI and device identifier.

Step 2.   Insert the hexadecimal value FFFE, which in binary is 1111 1111 1111 1110.

Step 3.   Convert the first two hexadecimal values of the OUI to binary and flip the U/L bit (bit 7). In this example, the 0 in bit 7 is changed to a 1.

The result is an EUI-64-generated Interface ID of FE99:47FF:FE75:CEE0.

Note

The use of the U/L bit and the reasons for reversing its value are discussed in RFC 5342.

The advantage of EUI-64 is that the Ethernet MAC address can be used to determine the Interface ID. It also allows network administrators to easily track an IPv6 address to an end device by using the unique MAC address. However, this has caused privacy concerns among many users. They are concerned that their packets can be traced to the actual physical computer. Due to these concerns, a randomly generated Interface ID may be used instead.

Randomly Generated Interface IDs

Depending upon the operating system, a device may use a randomly generated Interface ID instead of using the MAC address and the EUI-64 process. For example, beginning with Windows Vista, Windows uses a randomly generated Interface

ID instead of one created with EUI-64. Windows XP and previous Windows operating systems used EUI-64.

An easy way to identify that an address was more than likely created using EUI-64 is the FFFE located in the middle of the Interface ID.

Create a Global Unicast or Link-Local Address

After the Interface ID is established, either through the EUI-64 process or through random generation, it can be combined with an IPv6 prefix to create a global unicast address or a link-local address:

- **Global unicast address:** When using SLAAC, the device receives its prefix from the ICMPv6 RA and combines it with the Interface ID.

- **Link-local address:** A link-local prefix begins with FE80::/10. A device typically uses FE80::/64 as the prefix/prefix length, followed by the Interface ID.

Dynamic Link-Local Addresses (7.2.4.6)

When using SLAAC (SLAAC Only or SLAAC with DHCPV6), a device receives its prefix and prefix length from the ICMPv6 RA. Because the prefix of the address has been designated by the RA message, the device must provide only the Interface ID portion of its address, as shown in Figure 7-76. As stated previously, the Interface ID can be automatically generated using the EUI-64 process or, depending on the OS, randomly generated. Using the information from the RA message and the Interface ID, the device can establish its global unicast address.

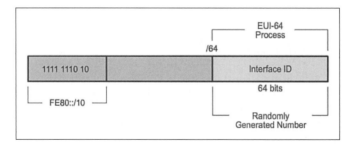

Figure 7-76   IPv6 Link-Local Address

After a global unicast address is assigned to an interface, the IPv6-enabled device will automatically generate its link-local address. IPv6-enabled devices must have, at a minimum, the link-local address. Recall that an IPv6 link-local address enables a device to communicate with other IPv6-enabled devices on the same subnet.

Note

An IPv6 PC will create the link-local address before it enables the IPv6 global address.

IPv6 link-local addresses are used for a variety of purposes, including

- A host uses the link-local address of the local router for its default gateway IPv6 address.

- Routers exchange dynamic routing protocol messages using link-local addresses.

- Routers' routing tables use the link-local address to identify the next-hop router when forwarding IPv6 packets.

A link-local address can be established dynamically or configured manually as a static link-local address.

Dynamically Assigned Link-Local Address

The link-local address is dynamically created using the FE80::/10 prefix and the Interface ID. By default, Cisco IOS routers use EUI-64 to generate the Interface ID for all link-local addresses on IPv6 interfaces. For serial interfaces, the router will use the MAC address of an Ethernet interface. Recall that a link-local address must be unique only on that link or network. However, a drawback to using the dynamically assigned link-local address is its length, which makes identifying and remembering assigned addresses challenging.

Static Link-Local Addresses (7.2.4.7)

This section explains how to manually create a link-local address on a router interface.

Static Link-Local Address

Configuring the link-local address manually provides the ability to create an address that is recognizable and easier to remember. Link-local addresses can be configured manually using the same interface command used to create IPv6 global unicast addresses but with an additional parameter:

```
Router(config-if)# ipv6 address link-local-address link-local
```

Figure 7-77 shows that a link-local address has a prefix within the range FE80 to FEBF. When an address begins with this hextet (16-bit segment), the **link-local** parameter must follow the address.

```
R1(config)#interface gigabitethernet 0/0
R1(config-if)#ipv6 address fe80::1 ?
  link-local  Use link-local address

R1(config-if)#ipv6 address fe80::1 link-local
R1(config-if)#exit
R1(config)#interface gigabitethernet 0/1
R1(config-if)#ipv6 address fe80::1 link-local
R1(config-if)#exit
R1(config)#interface serial 0/0/0
R1(config-if)#ipv6 address fe80::1 link-local
R1(config-if)#
```

Figure 7-77 Configuring Link-Local Addresses on R1

Figure 7-78 shows the configuration of a link-local address using the **ipv6 address interface** command. The link-local address FE80::1 is used to make it easily recognizable as belonging to router R1. The same IPv6 link-local address is configured on all of R1's interfaces. FE80::1 can be configured on each link because it only has to be unique on that link.

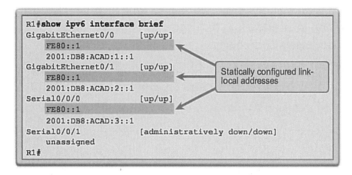

Figure 7-78 Configuring Link-Local Addresses on R1 (**show** Command)

Similar to R1, router R2 would be configured with FE80::2 as the IPv6 link-local address on all of its interfaces.

Verifying IPv6 Address Configuration (7.2.4.8)

As shown in Figure 7-79, the command to verify the IPv6 interface configuration is similar to the command used for IPv4.

The **show interface** command displays the MAC address of the Ethernet interfaces. EUI-64 uses this MAC address to generate the Interface ID for the link-local address. Additionally, the **show ipv6 interface brief** command displays abbreviated output for each of the interfaces. The [up/up] output on the same line as the interface indicates the Layer 1/Layer 2 interface state. This is the same as the Status and Protocol columns in the equivalent IPv4 command.

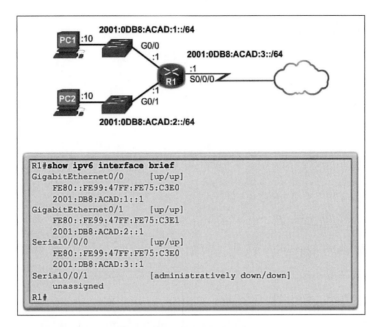

Figure 7-79   show ipv6 interface brief Command

Notice that each interface has two IPv6 addresses. The second address for each interface is the global unicast address that was configured. The first address, the one that begins with FE80, is the link-local unicast address for the interface. Recall that the link-local address is automatically added to the interface when a global unicast address is assigned.

Also, notice that R1's Serial 0/0/0 link-local address is the same as its Gigabit Ethernet 0/0 interface. Serial interfaces do not have an Ethernet MAC address, so Cisco IOS uses the MAC address of the first available Ethernet interface. This is possible because link-local interfaces only have to be unique on that link.

The link-local address of the router interface is typically the default gateway address for devices on that link or network.

As shown in Figure 7-80, the **show ipv6 route** command can be used to verify that IPv6 networks and specific IPv6 interface addresses have been installed in the IPv6 routing table. The **show ipv6 route** command will only display IPv6 networks, not IPv4 networks.

```
R1#show ipv6 route
IPv6 Routing Table - default - 7 entries
Codes: C - Connected, L - Local, S - Static, U - Per-user
Static

<output omitted>

C    2001:DB8:ACAD:1::/64 [0/0]
       via GigabitEthernet0/0, directly connected
L    2001:DB8:ACAD:1::1/128 [0/0]
       via GigabitEthernet0/0, receive
C    2001:DB8:ACAD:2::/64 [0/0]
       via GigabitEthernet0/1, directly connected
L    2001:DB8:ACAD:2::1/128 [0/0]
       via GigabitEthernet0/1, receive
C    2001:DB8:ACAD:3::/64 [0/0]
       via Serial0/0/0, directly connected
L    2001:DB8:ACAD:3::1/128 [0/0]
       via Serial0/0/0, receive
L    FF00::/8 [0/0]
       via Null0, receive
R1#
```

Figure 7-80   show ipv6 route Command

Within the route table, a C next to a route indicates that this is a directly connected network. When the router interface is configured with a global unicast address and is in the "up/up" state, the IPv6 prefix and prefix length is added to the IPv6 routing table as a connected route.

The IPv6 global unicast address configured on the interface is also installed in the routing table as a local route. The local route has a /128 prefix. Local routes are used by the routing table to efficiently process packets with a destination address of the router's interface address.

The **ping** command for IPv6 is identical to the command used with IPv4, except that an IPv6 address is used. In the example shown in Figure 7-81, the command is used to verify Layer 3 connectivity between R1 and PC1. When pinging a link-local address from a router, Cisco IOS will prompt the user for the exit interface. Because the destination link-local address can be on one or more of its links or networks, the router needs to know to which interface to send the ping.

```
R1#ping 2001:db8:acad:1::10
Type escape sequence to abort.
Sending 5, 100-byte ICMP Echos to 2001:DB8:ACAD:1::10, timeout
is 2 seconds:
!!!!!
Success rate is 100 percent (5/5)
R1#
```

Figure 7-81   ping Command

Activity 7.2.4.8: Verifying IPv6 Address Configuration

Go to the online course to use the Syntax Checker to verify IPv6 address configuration

IPv6 Multicast Addresses (7.2.5)

IPv6 multicast addresses are similar to IPv4 multicast addresses. Recall that a multicast address is used to send a single packet to one or more destinations (multicast group). IPv6 multicast addresses have the prefix FF00::/8.

Note

Multicast addresses can be destination addresses only, not source addresses.

There are two types of IPv6 multicast addresses:

- Assigned multicast

- Solicited-node multicast

Assigned Multicast

Assigned multicast addresses are reserved multicast addresses for predefined groups of devices. An assigned multicast address is a single address used to reach a group of devices running a common protocol or service. Assigned multicast addresses are used in context with specific protocols such as DHCPv6.

Two common IPv6 assigned multicast groups are

- **FF02::1 All-nodes multicast group:** This is a multicast group that all IPv6-enabled devices join. A packet sent to this group is received and processed by all IPv6 interfaces on the link or network. This has the same effect as a broadcast address in IPv4. Figure 7-82 shows an example of communication using the all-nodes multicast address. An IPv6 router sends ICMPv6 RA messages to the all-nodes multicast group. The RA message informs all IPv6-enabled devices on the network about addressing information, such as the prefix, prefix length, and default gateway.

- **FF02::2 All-routers multicast group:** This is a multicast group that all IPv6 routers join. A router becomes a member of this group when it is enabled as an IPv6 router with the **ipv6 unicast-routing** global configuration command. A packet sent to this group is received and processed by all IPv6 routers on the link or network.

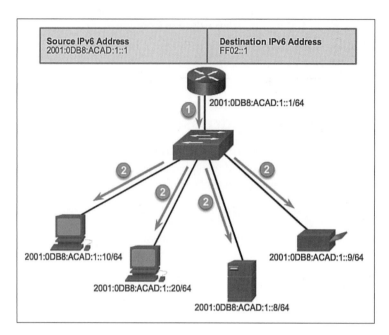

Figure 7-82   IPv6 All-Nodes Multicast Communications

IPv6-enabled devices send ICMPv6 RS messages to the all-routers multicast address. The RS message requests an RA message from the IPv6 router to assist the device in its address configuration.

Solicited-Node IPv6 Multicast Addresses (7.2.5.2)

A *solicited-node multicast address* is similar to the all-nodes multicast address. Recall that the all-nodes multicast address is essentially the same thing as an IPv4 broadcast. All devices on the network must process traffic sent to the all-nodes address. To reduce the number of devices that must process traffic, use a solicited-node multicast address.

A solicited-node multicast address is an address that matches only the last 24 bits of the IPv6 global unicast address of a device. The only devices that need to process these packets are those devices that have these same 24 bits in the least significant, far-right portion of their Interface ID, as shown in Figure 7-83.

An IPv6 solicited-node multicast address is automatically created when the global unicast or link-local unicast addresses are assigned. The IPv6 solicited-node multicast address is created by combining a special FF02:0:0:0:0:FF00::/104 prefix with the rightmost 24 bits of its unicast address.

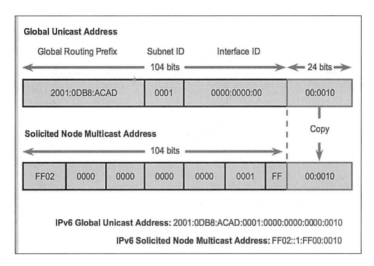

Figure 7-83   IPv6 Solicited-Node Multicast Address

The solicited-node multicast address consists of two parts:

- **FF02:0:0:0:0:1:FF00::/104 multicast prefix:** This is the first 104 bits of the solicited-node multicast address.

- **Least significant 24 bits:** These are the last or rightmost 24 bits of the solicited-node multicast address. These bits are copied from the rightmost 24 bits of the global unicast or link-local unicast address of the device.

It is possible that multiple devices will have the same solicited-node multicast address. Although rare, this can occur when devices have the same rightmost 24 bits in their Interface IDs. This does not create any problems because the device will still process the encapsulated message, which will include the complete IPv6 address of the device in question.

Packet Tracer Activity 7.2.5.3: Configuring IPv6 Addressing

In this activity you will practice configuring IPv6 addresses on a router, servers, and clients. You will also practice verifying your IPv6 addressing implementation.

Lab 7.2.5.4: Identifying IPv6 Addresses

In this lab you will identify different types of IPv6 addresses, examine a host IPv6 Network Interface and address, practice IPv6 address abbreviations, and identify the IPv6 global unicast address network prefix.

Lab 7.2.5.5: Configuring IPv6 Addresses on Network Devices

In this lab you will set up the topology and configure basic router and switch setting applying IPv6 addresses and verifying network connectivity.

Connectivity Verification (7.3)

This section looks at the different tools available to verify connectivity.

ICMP (7.3.1)

One of the tools available to verify connectivity is the Internet Control Message Protocol.

ICMPv4 and ICMPv6 Messages (7.3.1.1)

Although IP is not a reliable protocol, the TCP/IP suite does provide for four messages to be sent in the event of certain errors. These messages are sent using the services of ICMP. The purpose of these messages is to provide feedback about issues related to the processing of IP packets under certain conditions, not to make IP reliable. ICMP messages are not required, and often they are not allowed within a network for security reasons.

ICMP is available for both IPv4 and IPv6. ICMPv4 is the messaging protocol for IPv4. ICMPv6 provides these same services for IPv6 but includes additional functionality. In this course, the term ICMP will be used when referring to both ICMPv4 and ICMPv6.

The types of ICMP messages, and the reasons why they are sent, are extensive. We will discuss some of the more common messages.

ICMP messages common to both ICMPv4 and ICMPv6 include

- Host Confirmation
- Destination or Service Unreachable
- Time Exceeded
- Route Redirection

Host Confirmation

ICMP Echo messages can be used to determine if a host is operational. The local host sends an ICMP Echo Request to a host. If the host is available, the destination host responds with an Echo Reply. This use of the ICMP Echo messages is the basis of the ping utility.

Video 7.3.1.1:

View this video in the online course for a demonstration of the ICMP Echo Request/ Echo Reply message. In the video, click the Play button to see an animation of the ICMP Echo Request/Echo Reply.

Destination or Service Unreachable

When a host or gateway receives a packet that it cannot deliver, it can use an ICMP Destination Unreachable message to notify the source that the destination or service is unreachable. The message will include a code that indicates why the packet could not be delivered.

Some of the Destination Unreachable codes for ICMPv4 are

- **0**: Net Unreachable
- **1**: Host Unreachable
- **2**: Protocol Unreachable
- **3**: Port Unreachable

Note

ICMPv6 has similar but slightly different codes for Destination Unreachable messages.

Time Exceeded

An ICMPv4 Time Exceeded message is used by a router to indicate that a packet cannot be forwarded because the TTL field of the packet was decremented to 0. If a router receives a packet and decrements the TTL field in the IPv4 packet to 0, it discards the packet and sends a Time Exceeded message to the source host.

ICMPv6 also sends a Time Exceeded message if the router cannot forward an IPv6 packet because the packet has expired. IPv6 does not have a TTL field; it uses the Hop Limit field to determine if the packet has expired.

Route Redirection

A router may use the ICMP Route Redirection message to notify the hosts on a network that a better route is available for a particular destination. This message may only be used when the source host is on the same physical network as both gateways.

Both ICMPv4 and ICMPv6 use Route Redirection messages.

ICMPv6 Router Solicitation and Router Advertisement Messages (7.3.1.2)

The informational and error messages found in ICMPv6 are very similar to the control and error messages implemented by ICMPv4. However, ICMPv6 has new features and improved functionality not found in ICMPv4.

ICMPv6 includes four new protocols as part of the Neighbor Discovery Protocol (ND or NDP):

- *Router Solicitation* message (RS)
- *Router Advertisement* message (RA)
- *Neighbor Solicitation* message (NS)
- *Neighbor Advertisement* message (NA)

Router Solicitation and Router Advertisement Messages

IPv6-enabled devices can be divided into two categories: routers and hosts. Router Solicitation and Router Advertisement messages are sent between hosts and routers as shown in Figure 7-84 and described here:

- **RS message:** When a host is configured to obtain its addressing information automatically using SLAAC, the host will send an RS message to the router. The RS message is sent as an IPv6 all-routers multicast message.

- **RA message:** RA messages are sent by routers to provide addressing information to hosts using SLAAC. The RA message can include addressing information for the host, such as the prefix and prefix length. A router will send an RA message periodically or in response to an RS message. By default, Cisco routers send RA messages every 200 seconds. RA messages are sent to the IPv6 all-nodes multicast address. A host using SLAAC will set its default gateway to the link-local address of the router that sent the RA.

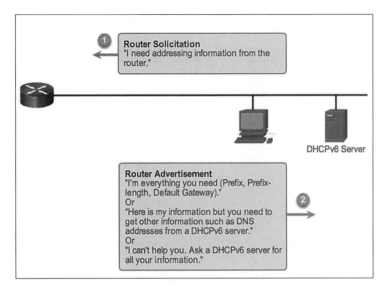

Figure 7-84   Router Solicitation and Router Advertisement Messages

ICMPv6 Neighbor Solicitation and Neighbor Advertisement Messages (7.3.1.3)

ICMPv6 Neighbor Discovery Protocol includes two additional message types, Neighbor Solicitation (NS) and Neighbor Advertisement (NA) messages.

As shown in Figure 7-85, Neighbor Solicitation and Neighbor Advertisement messages are used for

- **Address resolution:** Address resolution is used when a device on the LAN knows the IPv6 unicast address of a destination but does not know its Ethernet MAC address. To determine the MAC address for the destination, the device will send an NS message to the solicited-node multicast address. The message will include the known (targeted) IPv6 address. The device that has the targeted IPv6 address will respond with an NA message containing its Ethernet MAC address. Address resolution in IPv6 works similarly to ARP in IPv4.

- **Duplicate Address Detection (DAD):** When a device is assigned a global unicast or link-local unicast address, performing DAD on the address is recommended to ensure that it is unique. To check the uniqueness of an address, the device sends an NS message with its own IPv6 address as the targeted IPv6 address. If another device on the network has this address, it responds with an NA message. This NA message will notify the sending device that the address is in use. If a corresponding NA message is not returned within a certain period of time, the unicast address is unique and acceptable for use, DAD works similarly to gratuitous ARP in IPv4.

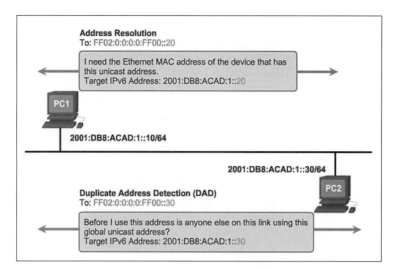

Figure 7-85 ICMPv6 Neighbor Discovery Protocol

Testing and Verification (7.3.2)

Several utilities are available to assist in the testing and verification of network connectivity. This section looks at two of them: **ping** and **traceroute**.

Ping: Testing the Local Stack (7.3.2.1)

Ping is a testing utility that uses ICMP Echo Request and Echo Reply messages to test connectivity between hosts. Ping works with both IPv4 and IPv6 hosts.

To test connectivity to another host on a network, an Echo Request is sent to the host address using the **ping** command. If the host at the specified address receives the Echo Request, it responds with an Echo Reply. As each Echo Reply is received, ping provides feedback on the length of time between when the Echo Request was sent and when the Echo Reply was received. This can be a measure of network performance.

Ping has a timeout value for the reply. If a reply is not received within the timeout, ping provides a message indicating that a response was not received. This usually indicates that there is a problem, but could also indicate that security features blocking ping messages have been enabled on the network.

After all the requests are sent, the ping utility provides a summary that includes the success rate and average round-trip time to the destination.

Pinging the Local Loopback

There are some special testing and verification cases for which we can use ping. One case is for testing the internal configuration of IPv4 or IPv6 on the local host. To perform this test, we ping the local loopback address of 127.0.0.1 for IPv4 or ::1 for IPv6. Testing the IPv4 loopback is shown in Figure 7-86.

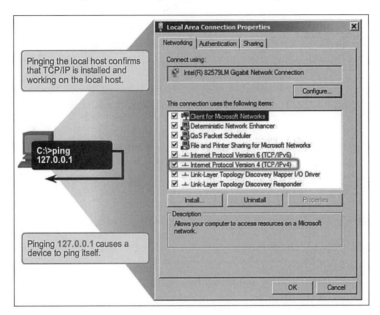

Figure 7-86   ICMPv4 Testing Local TCP/IP Stack

A response from 127.0.0.1 for IPv4, or ::1 for IPv6, indicates that IP is properly installed on the host. This response comes from the network layer. This response is not, however, an indication that the addresses, masks, or gateways are properly configured. Nor does it indicate anything about the status of the lower layer of the network stack. This simply tests IP down through the network layer of IP. If we get an error message, it is an indication that TCP/IP is not operational on the host.

Ping: Testing Connectivity to the Local LAN (7.3.2.2)

You can also use ping to test the ability of a host to communicate on the local network. This is generally done by pinging the IP address of the gateway of the host. A successful ping to the gateway indicates that the host and the router interface serving as the gateway are both operational on the local network, as shown in Figure 7-87.

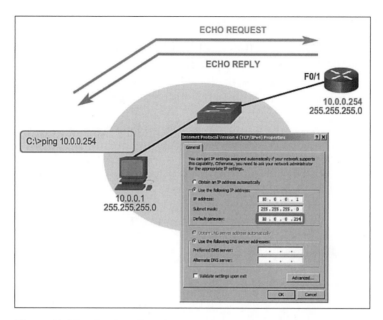

Figure 7-87   Testing IPv4 Connectivity to Local Network

For this test, the gateway address is most often used because the router is normally always operational. If the gateway address does not respond, a ping can be sent to the IP address of another host on the local network that is known to be operational.

If either the gateway or another host responds, then the local host can successfully communicate over the local network. If the gateway does not respond but another host does, this could indicate a problem with the router interface serving as the gateway.

One possibility is that the wrong gateway address has been configured on the host. Another possibility is that the router interface may be fully operational but have security applied to it that prevents it from processing or responding to ping requests.

Ping: Testing Connectivity to Remote Device (7.3.2.3)

Ping can also be used to test the ability of a local host to communicate across an internetwork. The local host can ping an operational IPv4 host of a remote network.

Video

Video 7.3.2.3

View this video in the online course for a demonstration of the use of ping to test the ability of a local host to communicate across an internetwork.

If this ping is successful, the operation of a large piece of the internetwork can be verified. A successful ping across the internetwork confirms communication on the local network, the operation of the router serving as our gateway, and the operation of all other routers that might be in the path between the local network and the network of the remote host.

Additionally, functionality of the remote host can be verified. If the remote host could not communicate outside of its local network, it would not have responded.

> **Note**
>
> Many network administrators limit or prohibit the entry of ICMP messages into the corporate network; therefore, the lack of a ping response could be due to security restrictions.

Traceroute: Testing the Path (7.3.2.4)

Ping is used to test connectivity between two hosts, but it doesn't provide information about the details of devices between the hosts. Traceroute (tracert) is a utility that generates a list of hops that were successfully reached along the path. This list can provide important verification and troubleshooting information. If the data reaches the destination, then the trace lists the interface of every router in the path between the hosts. If the data fails at some hop along the way, the address of the last router that responded to the trace can provide an indication of where the problem or security restrictions are found.

Round-Trip Time (RTT)

Using traceroute provides the round-trip time for each hop along the path and indicates if a hop fails to respond. The round-trip time is the time a packet takes to reach the remote host and for the response from the host to return. An asterisk (*) is used to indicate a lost or unreplied packet.

This information can be used to locate a problematic router in the path. When the display shows high response times or data losses from a particular hop, it is an indication that the resources of the router or its connections may be stressed.

IPv4 TTL and IPv6 Hop Limit

Traceroute makes use of a function of the TTL field in IPv4 and the Hop Limit field in IPv6 in the Layer 3 headers, along with the ICMP Time Exceeded message.

Play the animation in the video to see how traceroute takes advantage of TTL.

Video 7.3.2.4

Video

View this video in the online course for a demonstration on the use of TTL by traceroute.

The first sequence of messages sent from traceroute will have a TTL field value of 1. This causes the TTL to time out the IPv4 packet at the first router. This router then responds with an ICMPv4 message. Traceroute now has the address of the first hop.

Traceroute then progressively increments the TTL field (2, 3, 4...) for each subsequent sequence of messages. This provides the trace with the address of each hop as the packets time out further down the path. The TTL field continues to be increased until the destination is reached or the field is incremented to a predefined maximum.

When the final destination is reached, the host responds with either an ICMP Port Unreachable message or an ICMP Echo Reply message instead of the ICMP Time Exceeded message.

Packet Tracer Activity 7.3.2.5: Verifying IPv4 and IPv6 Addressing

IPv4 and IPv6 can coexist on the same network. From the command prompt of a PC, there are some differences in the way commands are issued and in the way output is displayed. In this activity you will use ifconfig to verify both IPv4 and IPv6 addressing as well as use tracert to discover IPv4 and IPv6 paths.

Packet Tracer Activity 7.3.2.6: Pinging and Tracing to Test the Path

There are connectivity issues in this activity. In addition to gathering and documenting information about the network, you will locate the problems and implement acceptable solutions to restore connectivity.

Lab 7.3.2.7: Testing Network Connectivity with Ping and Traceroute

In this lab, you will complete the following objectives:

- Part 1: Build and Configure the Network
- Part 2: Use Ping Command for Basic Network Testing
- Part 3: Use Tracert and Traceroute Commands for Basic Network Testing
- Part 4: Troubleshoot the Topology

Packet Tracer Activity 7.3.2.8: Troubleshooting IPv4 and IPv6 Addressing

In this scenario you are a network technician working for a company that has decided to migrate from IPv4 to IPv6. In the interim, they must support both protocols (dual stack). Three co-workers have called the help desk with problems and have received limited assistance. The help desk has escalated the matter to you, a Level 2 support technician.

Summary (7.4)

Class Activity 7.4.1.1: The Internet of Everything...Naturally!

In this class activity you will complete the following objectives:

- Part 1: Choose an activity
- Part 2: Devise an IPv6 addressing scheme
- Part 3: Present your addressing scheme to the class

Packet Tracer
☐ Activity

Packet Tracer Activity 7.4.1.2: Skills Integration Challenge

In this scenario your company has won a contract to set up a small network for a restaurant owner. There are two restaurants near each other, and they share one connection. The equipment and cabling is installed and the network administrator has designed the implementation plan. You job is to implement the rest of the addressing scheme according to the abbreviated Addressing Table and verify connectivity.

IP addresses are hierarchical, with network, subnetwork, and host portions. An IP address can represent a complete network, a specific host, or the broadcast address of the network.

Understanding binary notation is important when determining if two hosts are in the same network. The bits within the network portion of the IP address must be identical for all devices that reside in the same network. The subnet mask or prefix length is used to determine the network portion of an IP address. IP addresses can be assigned either statically or dynamically. DHCP enables the automatic assignment of addressing information such as the IP address, subnet mask, default gateway, and other configuration information.

IPv4 hosts can communicate in one of three different ways: unicast, broadcast, or multicast. Blocks of addresses that are used in networks that require limited or no Internet access are called private addresses. The private IPv4 address blocks are 10.0.0.0/8, 172.16.0.0/12, and 192.168.0.0/16.

The depletion of IPv4 address space is the motivating factor for moving to IPv6. Each IPv6 address has 128 bits, versus the 32 bits in an IPv4 address. IPv6 does not use the dotted-decimal subnet mask notation. The prefix length is used to indicate the network portion of an IPv6 address using the following format: IPv6 address/ prefix length.

There are three types of IPv6 addresses: unicast, multicast, and anycast. An IPv6 link-local address enables a device to communicate with other IPv6-enabled devices on the same link, and only on that link (subnet). Packets with a source or destination link-local address cannot be routed beyond the link from where the packet originated. IPv6 link-local addresses are in the FE80::/10 range.

ICMP is available for both IPv4 and IPv6. ICMPv4 is the messaging protocol for IPv4. ICMPv6 provides the same services for IPv6 but includes additional functionality.

After it is implemented, an IP network needs to be tested to verify its connectivity and operational performance. The ping and traceroute utilities are two tools that can be used to test network connectivity.

Practice

The following activities provide practice with the topics introduced in this chapter. The Labs and Class Activities are available in the companion *Network Basics Lab Manual* (978-1-58713-313-8). The Packet Tracer Activities PKA files are found in the online course.

Class Activities

Class Activity 7.0.1.2: The Internet of Everything (IoE)

Class Activity 7.4.1.1: The Internet of Everything...Naturally!

Labs

Lab 7.1.2.7: Using the Windows Calculator with Network Addresses

Lab 7.1.2.8: Converting IPv4 Addresses to Binary

Lab 7.1.4.8: Identifying IPv4 Addresses

Lab 7.2.5.4: Identifying IPv6 Addresses

Lab 7.2.5.5: Configuring IPv6 Addresses on Network Devices

Lab 7.3.2.7: Testing Network Connectivity with Ping and Traceroute

Packet Tracer Activities

Packet Tracer Activity 7.1.3.8: Investigate Unicast, Broadcast, and Multicast Traffic

Packet Tracer Activity 7.2.5.3: Configuring IPv6 Addressing

Packet Tracer Activity 7.3.2.5: Verifying IPv4 and IPv6 Addressing

Packet Tracer Activity 7.3.2.6: Pinging and Tracing to Test the Path

Packet Tracer Activity 7.3.2.8: Troubleshooting IPv4 and IPv6 Addressing

Packet Tracer Activity 7.4.1.2: Skills Integration Challenge

Check Your Understanding

Complete all the review questions listed here to test your understanding of the topics and concepts in this chapter. The appendix, "Answers to the 'Check Your Understanding' Questions," lists the answers.

1. The eight-digit binary value of the last octet of the IPv4 address 172.17.10.7 is
   _____.

2. Which two statements describe broadcast transmissions on a wired network? (Choose two.)

   A. Directed broadcasts use the IP address of 255.255.255.255.

   B. Limited broadcasts are intended for local and remote hosts listening for a multicast packet.

   C. Directed broadcasts are intended for all hosts on a local or remote network.

   D. Limited broadcasts are only intended for all hosts on a local network.

   E. Limited broadcasts are forwarded by routers.

3. What is the prefix length notation for the subnet mask 255.255.255.224?

   A. /25

   B. /26

   C. /27

   D. /28

4. The greatest part of the /8 block IPv4 address bit space consists of what types of addresses?

   A. Private addresses

   B. Public addresses

   C. Multicast addresses

   D. Experimental address

5. The most compact form of the IPv6 address 2001:0DB8:0000:AB00:0000:0000:0 000:00AB is _____.

6. Which type of IPv6 address is not routable and is used only for communication on a single subnet?

   A. Global unicast address

   B. Link-local address

   C. Loopback address

   D. Unique local address

   E. Unspecified address

7. An organization is assigned an IPv6 global prefix of 2001:db8:1234::/48. What is the maximum number of /64 subnets the organization can create with this space?

   A. 4

   B. 16

   C. 1,024

   D. 65,536

8. Match the description to the IPv6 addressing component. (Not all options are used.)

   A. This part of the address is used by an   Subnet mask
      organization to identify subnets.

   B. This network portion of the address is   Global routing prefix
      assigned by the provider.

   C. This part of the address is the equivalent   Interface ID
      to the host portion of an IPv4 address.

                                                       Subnet ID

9. Which two ICMPv6 messages are not present in ICMP for IPv4?

   A. Destination Unreachable

   B. Host Confirmation

   C. Neighbor Solicitation

   D. Route Redirection

   E. Router Advertisement

   F. Time Exceeded

10. Which IP addresses are network addresses? (Choose two.)

    A. 64.104.3.7/28

    B. 192.168.12.64/26

    C. 192.135.12.191/26

    D. 198.18.12.16/28

    E. 209.165.200.254/27

    F. 220.12.12.33/27

11. A network administrator is building a network for a small business that has 22 hosts. The ISP has assigned only one Internet-routable IP address. Which IP address block can the network administrator use to address the network?

    A. 10.11.12.16/28

    B. 172.31.255.128/27

    C. 192.168.1.0/28

    D. 209.165.202.128/27

12. Which subnet mask would be used with the hosts in the 128.107.176.0/22 network?

    A. 255.0.0.0

    B. 255.248.0.0

    C. 255.255.252.0

    D. 255.255.255.0

    E. 255.255.255.252

13. You have been assigned the address block 10.255.255.224/28 to create the network addresses for point-to-point wide area network (WAN) links. How many of these WAN links can you support with this address block?

    A. 1

    B. 4

    C. 7

    D. 14

14. A network administrator needs to create a new network that has 14 computers and two router interfaces. What subnet mask will provide the appropriate[99] number of IPv4 addresses for this network with minimal wasted addresses?

   A. 255.255.255.128

   B. 255.255.255.192

   C. 255.255.255.224

   D. 255.255.255.240

   E. 255.255.255.248

   F. 255.255.255.252

15. A host in the south branch cannot access the server with the address 192.168.254.222/224. While examining the host, you determine that its IPv4 address is 169.254.11.15/16. What is the apparent problem?

   A. The host is using a link-local address.

   B. The server is using an invalid subnet mask.

   C. The host has been assigned a broadcast address.

   D. The server thinks that the host is on the logical network with the server.

Objectives

Upon completion of this chapter, you will be able to answer the following questions:

- Why is routing necessary for hosts on different subnets to be able to communicate?

- How would you calculate the number of host addresses if you were given a network and subnet mask?

- How would you calculate the correct subnet mask to accommodate a given number of hosts?

- What are the benefits of Variable Length Subnet Masking (VLSM)?

- How would you design and implement a hierarchical addressing scheme?

- How are IPv6 address assignments implemented in a business network?

Key Terms

This chapter uses the following key terms. You can find the definitions in the Glossary.

flat network design   page 357

subnet   page 357

Gigabit Ethernet   page 361

Variable Length Subnet Mask (VLSM)   page 385

nibble boundary   page 401

Introduction (8.0.1.1)

Designing, implementing, and managing an effective IP addressing plan ensures that networks can operate effectively and efficiently. This is especially true as the number of host connections to a network increases. Understanding the hierarchical structure of the IP address and how to modify that hierarchy in order to more efficiently meet routing requirements is an important part of planning an IP addressing scheme.

In the original IPv4 address, there are two levels of hierarchy: a network and a host. These two levels of addressing allow for basic network groupings that facilitate in routing packets to a destination network. A router forwards packets based on the network portion of an IP address; after the network is located, the host portion of the address allows for identification of the destination device.

However, as networks grow, with many organizations adding hundreds, and even thousands, of hosts to their network, the two-level hierarchy is insufficient.

Subdividing a network adds a level to the network hierarchy, creating, in essence, three levels: a network, a subnetwork, and a host, as shown in Figure 8-1.

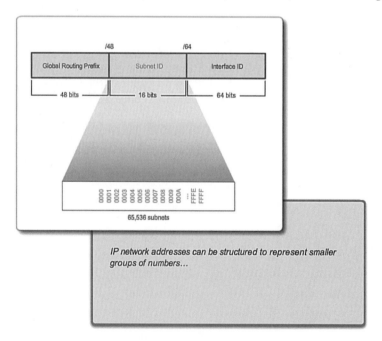

Figure 8-1   IPv6 /48 Address Block

Introducing an additional level to the hierarchy creates additional subgroups within an IP network that facilitates faster packet delivery and added filtration, by helping to minimize "local" traffic.

This chapter examines, in detail, the creation and assignment of IP network and sub-network addresses through the use of the subnet mask.

Class Activity 8.0.1.2: Call Me!

In this modeling activity, you are asked to think about a number you probably use every day: your telephone number. As you complete the activity, think about how your telephone number compares to strategies that network administrators might use to identify hosts for efficient data communication.

Subnetting an IPv4 Network (8.1)

One of the most important tasks that you have as a network administrator is to sub-net the networks that have been assigned to you. This enables you to manage the limited IP addresses that are available to you. This section discusses the process of subnetting an IPv4 network.

Network Segmentation (8.1.1)

This section takes a look at breaking up a network into smaller networks.

Reasons for Subnetting (8.1.1.1)

In early network implementations, it was common for organizations to have all com-puters and other networked devices connected to a single IP network. All devices in the organization were assigned an IP address with a matching network ID. This type of configuration is known as a *flat network design*. In a small network, with a limited number of devices, a flat network design is not problematic. However, as the network grows, this type of configuration can create major issues.

Consider how on an Ethernet local area network (LAN), devices use broadcasts to locate needed services and devices. Recall that a broadcast is sent to all hosts on an IP network, as shown in Figure 8-2.

The Dynamic Host Configuration Protocol (DHCP) is an example of a network service that depends on broadcasts. Devices send broadcasts across the network to locate the DHCP server. On a large network, this could create a significant amount of traffic, slowing network operations. Additionally, because a broadcast is addressed to all devices, all devices must accept and process the traffic, resulting in increased device processing requirements. If a device must process a significant num-ber of broadcasts, it could even slow device operations. For reasons such as these, larger networks must be segmented into smaller subnetworks, keeping them local-ized to smaller groups of devices and services.

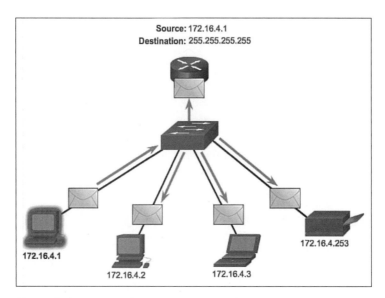

Figure 8-2   Limited Broadcast

The process of segmenting a network, by dividing it into multiple smaller network spaces, is called *subnetting*. These subnetworks are called *subnets*. Network administrators can group devices and services into subnets based on geographic location (perhaps the third floor of a building), organizational unit (perhaps the Sales department), device type (printers, servers, WAN, etc.), or any other division that makes sense for the network. Subnetting can reduce overall network traffic and improve network performance.

Note

A *subnet* is equivalent to a network, and these terms can be used interchangeably. Most networks are a subnet of some larger address block.

Communication Between Subnets (8.1.1.2)

A router is necessary for devices on different networks to communicate. Devices on a network use the router interface attached to their LAN as their default gateway. Traffic that is destined for a device on a remote network will be processed by the router and forwarded toward the destination. To determine if traffic is local or remote, the router uses the subnet mask.

In a subnetted network space, this works exactly the same way. As shown in Figure 8-3, subnetting creates multiple logical networks from a single address block or network address. Each subnet is treated as a separate network space. Devices on the same subnet must use an address, subnet mask, and default gateway that correlate to the subnet that they are a part of.

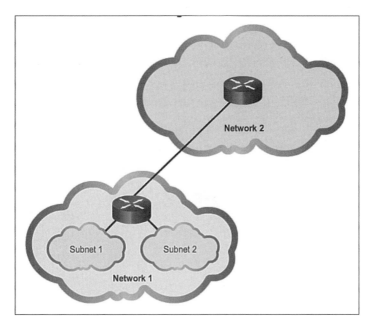

Figure 8-3   Communicating Between Networks

Traffic cannot be forwarded between subnets without the use of a router. Every interface on the router must have an IPv4 host address that belongs to the network or subnet to which the router interface is connected.

Subnetting an IPv4 Network (8.1.2)

This section provides additional information on how to address the segmented networks.

Basic Subnetting (8.1.2.1)

Every network address has a valid range of host addresses. All devices attached to the same network will have an IPv4 host address for that network and a common subnet mask or network prefix. The prefix and the subnet mask are different ways of representing the same thing—the network portion of an address.

IPv4 subnets are created by using one or more of the host bits as network bits. This is done by extending the mask to borrow some of the bits from the host portion of the address to create additional network bits. The more host bits borrowed, the more subnets that can be defined. For each bit borrowed, the number of subnetworks available is doubled. For example, if 1 bit is borrowed, two subnets are created; if 2 bits are borrowed, four subnets are created; if 3 bits are borrowed, eight subnets are created; and so on. However, with each bit borrowed, fewer host addresses are available per subnet.

Bits can only be borrowed from the host portion of the address. The network portion of the address is allocated by the service provider and cannot be changed.

> **Note**
>
> In the examples in the figures, only the last octet is shown in binary; other octets are shown in numerical format because only bits from the host portion can be borrowed.

As shown in Figure 8-4, the 192.168.1.0/24 network has 24 bits in the network portion and 8 bits in the host portion, which is indicated with the subnet mask 255.255.255.0 or /24 notation. With no subnetting, this network supports a single LAN interface. If an additional LAN is needed, the network would need to be subnetted.

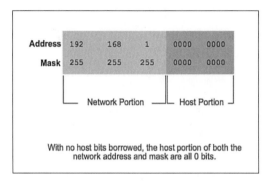

Figure 8-4   192.168.1.0/24 Network

In Figure 8-5, 1 bit is borrowed from the most significant bit (leftmost bit) in the host portion, thus extending the network portion to 25 bits. This creates two subnets, identified by using a 0 in the borrowed bit for the first network and a 1 in the borrowed bit for the second network. The subnet mask for both networks uses a 1 in the borrowed bit position to indicate that this bit is now part of the network portion.

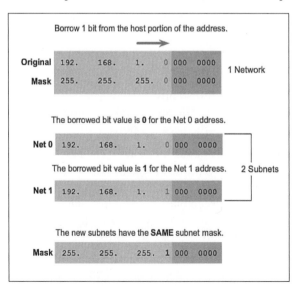

Figure 8-5   Borrow 1 Bit

As shown in Figure 8-6, when we convert the binary octet to decimal we see that the first subnet address is 192.168.1.0 and the second subnet address is 192.168.1.128. Because a bit has been borrowed, the subnet mask for each subnet is 255.255.255.128 or /25.

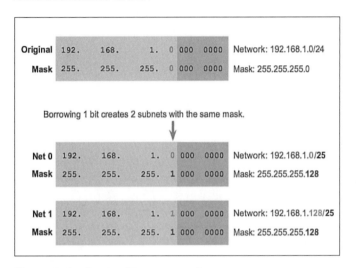

Figure 8-6   Decimal Representation

Subnets in Use (8.1.2.2)

In the previous example, the 192.168.1.0/24 network was subnetted to create two subnets:

192.168.1.0/25

192.168.1.128/25

In Figure 8-7, notice that router R1 has two LAN segments attached to its *GigabitEthernet* interfaces. The subnets will be used for the segments attached to these interfaces. To serve as the gateway for devices on the LAN, each of the router interfaces must be assigned an IP address within the range of valid addresses for the assigned subnet. It is common practice to use the first or last available address in a network range for the router interface address.

The first subnet, 192.168.1.0/25, is used for the network attached to GigabitEthernet 0/0, and the second subnet, 192.168.1.128/25, is used for the network attached to GigabitEthernet 0/1. To assign an IP address for each of these interfaces, it is necessary to determine the range of valid IP addresses for each subnet.

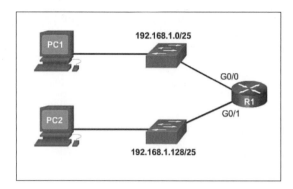

Figure 8-7 Gateway Router

The following are guidelines for each of the subnets:

- **Network address:** All 0 bits in the host portion of the address

- **First host address:** All 0 bits plus a rightmost 1 bit in the host portion of the address

- **Last host address:** All 1 bits plus a rightmost 0 bit in the host portion of the address

- **Broadcast address:** All 1 bits in the host portion of the address

As shown in Figure 8-8, the first host address for the 192.168.1.0/25 network is 192.168.1.1, and the last host address is 192.168.1.126.

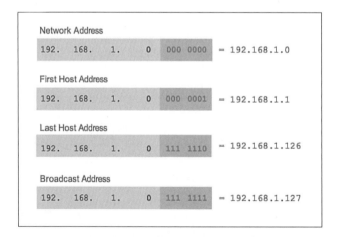

Figure 8-8 Address Range for 192.168.1.0/25 Subnet

Figure 8-9 shows that the first host address for the 192.168.1.128/25 network is 192.168.1.129, and the last host address is 192.168.1.254.

Network Address

| 192. | 168. | 1. | 1 | 000 0000 | = 192.168.1.128 |

First Host Address

| 192. | 168. | 1. | 1 | 000 0001 | = 192.168.1.129 |

Last Host Address

| 192. | 168. | 1. | 1 | 111 1110 | = 192.168.1.254 |

Broadcast Address

| 192. | 168. | 1. | 1 | 111 1111 | = 192.168.1.255 |

Figure 8-9   Address Range for 192.168.1.128/25 Subnet

To assign the first host address in each subnet to the router interface for that subnet, use the **ip address** command in interface configuration mode, as shown in Figure 8-10. Notice that each subnet uses the subnet mask of 255.255.255.128 to indicate that the network portion of the address is 25 bits.

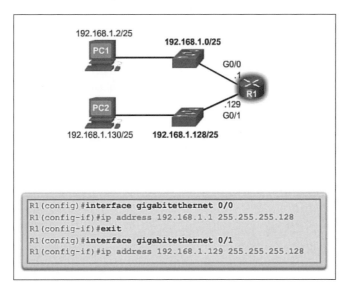

```
R1(config)#interface gigabitethernet 0/0
R1(config-if)#ip address 192.168.1.1 255.255.255.128
R1(config-if)#exit
R1(config)#interface gigabitethernet 0/1
R1(config-if)#ip address 192.168.1.129 255.255.255.128
```

Figure 8-10   Interface Configuration

A host configuration for the 192.168.1.128/25 network is shown in Figure 8-11. Notice that the gateway IP address is the address configured on the G0/1 interface of R1, 192.168.1.129, and the subnet mask is 255.255.255.128.

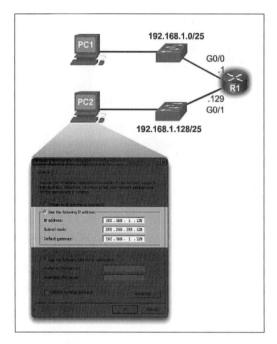

Figure 8-11 Host Configuration

Subnetting Formulas (8.1.2.3)

In this section we take a look at some basic formulas that will assist you in subnetting.

Calculating Subnets

Use this formula to calculate the number of subnets:

2^n (where n = the number of bits borrowed)

As shown in Figure 8-12, for the 192.168.1.0/25 example, the calculation looks like this:

$2^1 = 2$ subnets

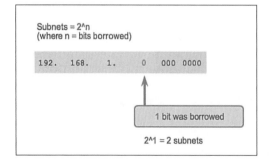

Figure 8-12 Calculate Number of Subnets

Calculating Hosts

Use this formula to calculate the number of hosts per network:

2^n (where n = the number of bits remaining in the host field)

As shown in Figure 8-13, for the 192.168.1.0/25 example, the calculation looks like this:

$2^7 = 128$

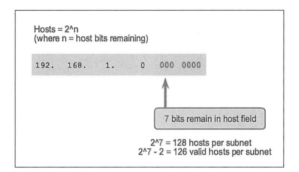

Figure 8-13   Calculate Number of Hosts

Because hosts cannot use the network address or broadcast address from a subnet, two of these addresses are not valid for host assignment. This means that each of the subnets has 126 (128 − 2) valid host addresses.

So in this example, borrowing 1 host bit toward the network results in creating two subnets, and each subnet can have a total of 126 hosts assigned.

Creating 4 Subnets (8.1.2.4)

Consider an internetwork that requires three subnets. Using the same 192.168.1.0/24 address block, host bits must be borrowed to create at least three subnets. Borrowing a single bit would provide only two subnets. To provide more networks, more host bits must be borrowed. Calculate the number of subnets created if 2 bits are borrowed using the formula $2^{number\ of\ bits\ borrowed}$:

$2^2 = 4$ subnets

Borrowing 2 bits creates four subnets, as shown in Figure 8-14.

Recall that the subnet mask must change to reflect the borrowed bits. In this example, when 2 bits are borrowed, the mask is extended 2 bits into the last octet. In decimal, the mask is represented as 255.255.255.192, because the last octet is 1100 0000 in binary.

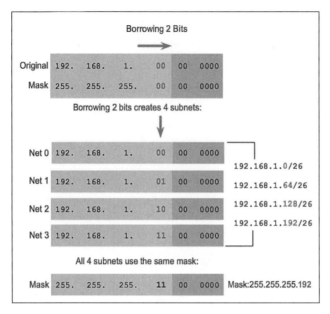

Figure 8-14   Borrowing 2 Bits

Host Calculation

To calculate the number of hosts, examine the last octet. After borrowing 2 bits for the subnet, there are 6 host bits remaining.

Apply the following host calculation formula as shown in Figure 8-15:

$$2^6 = 64$$

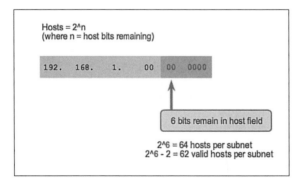

Figure 8-15   Calculate Number of Hosts

But remember that all 0 bits in the host portion of the address is the network address, and all 1s in the host portion is a broadcast address. Therefore, there are only 62 host addresses that are actually available for each subnet.

As shown in Figure 8-16, the first host address for the first subnet is 192.168.1.1 and the last host address is 192.168.1.62.

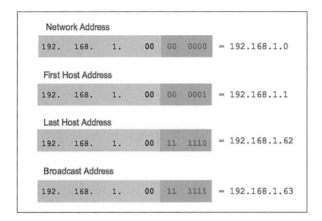

Figure 8-16   Address Range for 192.168.1.0/26 Subnet

Figure 8-17 shows the ranges for subnets 0, 1, and 2. Remember that each host must have a valid IP address within the range defined for that network segment. The subnet assigned to the router interface will determine which segment a host belongs to.

	Network	192.	168.	1.	00	00	0000	192.168.1.0
	First	192.	168.	1.	00	00	0001	192.168.1.1
Net 0								
	Last	192.	168.	1.	00	11	1110	192.168.1.62
	Broadcast	192.	168.	1.	00	11	1111	192.168.1.63
	Network	192.	168.	1.	01	00	0000	192.168.1.64
	First	192.	168.	1.	01	00	0001	192.168.1.65
Net 1								
	Last	192.	168.	1.	01	11	1110	192.168.1.126
	Broadcast	192.	168.	1.	01	11	1111	192.168.1.127
	Network	192.	168.	1.	10	00	0000	192.168.1.128
	First	192.	168.	1.	10	00	0001	192.168.1.129
Net 2								
	Last	192.	168.	1.	10	11	1110	192.168.1.190
	Broadcast	192.	168.	1.	10	11	1111	192.168.1.191

Figure 8-17   Address Ranges for Subnets 0 to 2

Figure 8-18 shows a sample configuration in which the first network is assigned to the GigabitEthernet 0/0 interface, the second network is assigned to the GigabitEthernet 0/1 interface, and the third network is assigned to the Serial 0/0/0 network.

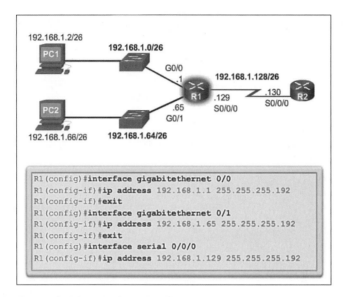

```
R1(config)#interface gigabitethernet 0/0
R1(config-if)#ip address 192.168.1.1 255.255.255.192
R1(config-if)#exit
R1(config)#interface gigabitethernet 0/1
R1(config-if)#ip address 192.168.1.65 255.255.255.192
R1(config-if)#exit
R1(config)#interface serial 0/0/0
R1(config-if)#ip address 192.168.1.129 255.255.255.192
```

Figure 8-18   Interface Configuration

Again, using a common addressing plan, the first host address in the subnet is assigned to the router interface. Hosts on each subnet will use the address of the router interface as the default gateway address:

- PC1 (192.168.1.2/26) will use 192.168.1.1 (G0/0 interface address of R1) as its default gateway address.

- PC2 (192.168.1.66/26) will use 192.168.1.65 (G0/1 interface address of R1) as its default gateway address.

Note

All devices on the same subnet will have a host IPv4 address from the range of host addresses and will use the same subnet mask.

Creating 8 Subnets (8.1.2.5)

Next, consider an internetwork that requires five subnets, as shown in Figure 8-19.

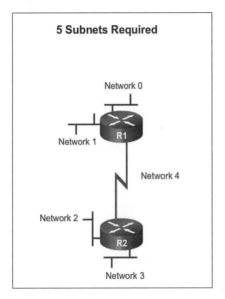

Figure 8-19   Five Subnets Required

Using the same 192.168.1.0/24 address block, host bits must be borrowed to create at least five subnets. Borrowing 2 bits would provide only four subnets, as shown in the previous example. To provide more networks, more host bits must be borrowed. Calculate the number of subnets created if 3 bits are borrowed using the following formula:

$2\char`^3 = 8$ subnets

As shown in Figures 8-20 and 8-21, borrowing 3 bits creates eight subnets. When 3 bits are borrowed, the subnet mask is extended 3 bits into the last octet (/27), resulting in a subnet mask of 255.255.255.224. All devices on these subnets will use the subnet mask 255.255.255.224 (/27).

Net 0	Network	192.	168.	1.	000	0	0000	192.168.1.0
	First	192.	168.	1.	000	0	0001	192.168.1.1
	Last	192.	168.	1.	000	1	1110	192.168.1.30
	Broadcast	192.	168.	1.	000	1	1111	192.168.1.31
Net 1	Network	192.	168.	1.	001	0	0000	192.168.1.32
	First	192.	168.	1.	001	0	0001	192.168.1.33
	Last	192.	168.	1.	001	1	1110	192.168.1.62
	Broadcast	192.	168.	1.	001	1	1111	192.168.1.63
Net 2	Network	192.	168.	1.	010	0	0000	192.168.1.64
	First	192.	168.	1.	010	0	0001	192.168.1.65
	Last	192.	168.	1.	010	1	1110	192.168.1.94
	Broadcast	192.	168.	1.	010	1	1111	192.168.1.95
Net 3	Network	192.	168.	1.	011	0	0000	192.168.1.96
	First	192.	168.	1.	011	0	0001	192.168.1.97
	Last	192.	168.	1.	011	1	1110	192.168.1.126
	Broadcast	192.	168.	1.	011	1	1111	192.168.1.127

Figure 8-20   Networks 0 to 3

Net 4	Network	192.	168.	1.	100	0	0000	192.168.1.128
	First	192.	168.	1.	100	0	0001	192.168.1.129
	Last	192.	168.	1.	100	1	1110	192.168.1.158
	Broadcast	192.	168.	1.	100	1	1111	192.168.1.159
Net 5	Network	192.	168.	1.	101	0	0000	192.168.1.160
	First	192.	168.	1.	101	0	0001	192.168.1.161
	Last	192.	168.	1.	101	1	1110	192.168.1.190
	Broadcast	192.	168.	1.	101	1	1111	192.168.1.191
Net 6	Network	192.	168.	1.	110	0	0000	192.168.1.192
	First	192.	168.	1.	110	0	0001	192.168.1.193
	Last	192.	168.	1.	110	1	1110	192.168.1.222
	Broadcast	192.	168.	1.	110	1	1111	192.168.1.223
Net 7	Network	192.	168.	1.	111	0	0000	192.168.1.224
	First	192.	168.	1.	111	0	0001	192.168.1.225
	Last	192.	168.	1.	111	1	1110	192.168.1.254
	Broadcast	192.	168.	1.	111	1	1111	192.168.1.255

Figure 8-21   Networks 4 to 7

Host Calculation

To calculate the number of hosts, examine the last octet. After borrowing 3 bits for the subnet, there are 5 host bits remaining.

Apply the host calculation formula, $2^5 = 32$, but subtract 2 for the all 0s in the host portion (network address) and all 1s in the host portion (broadcast address).

The subnets are assigned to the network segments required for the topology, as shown in Figure 8-22.

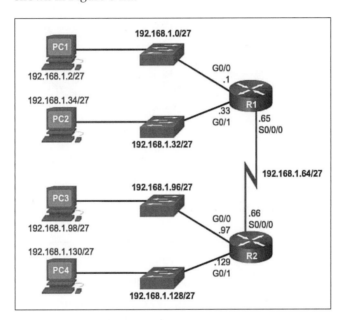

Figure 8-22 Subnet Allocation

Again, using a common addressing plan, the first host address in the subnet is assigned to the router interface, as shown in Figure 8-23.

Hosts on each subnet will use the address of the router interface as the default gateway address:

- PC1 (192.168.1.2/27) will use 192.168.1.1 as its default gateway address.
- PC2 (192.168.1.34/27) will use 192.168.1.33 as its default gateway address.
- PC3 (192.168.1.98/27) will use 192.168.1.97 as its default gateway address.
- PC4 (192.168.1.130/27) will use 192.168.1.129 as its default gateway address.

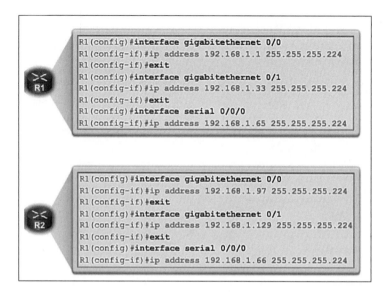

```
R1(config)#interface gigabitethernet 0/0
R1(config-if)#ip address 192.168.1.1 255.255.255.224
R1(config-if)#exit
R1(config)#interface gigabitethernet 0/1
R1(config-if)#ip address 192.168.1.33 255.255.255.224
R1(config-if)#exit
R1(config)#interface serial 0/0/0
R1(config-if)#ip address 192.168.1.65 255.255.255.224
```

```
R1(config)#interface gigabitethernet 0/0
R1(config-if)#ip address 192.168.1.97 255.255.255.224
R1(config-if)#exit
R1(config)#interface gigabitethernet 0/1
R1(config-if)#ip address 192.168.1.129 255.255.255.224
R1(config-if)#exit
R1(config)#interface serial 0/0/0
R1(config-if)#ip address 192.168.1.66 255.255.255.224
```

Figure 8-23 Interface Address Configuration

Interactive Graphic

Activity 8.1.2.6: Determining the Network Address (Basic)

Go to the online course to perform this practice activity of determining the network address.

Interactive Graphic

Activity 8.1.2.7: Calculate the Number of Valid Hosts (Basic)

Go to the online course to perform this practice activity of determining the number of hosts.

Interactive Graphic

Activity 8.1.2.8: Determining the Valid Addresses for Hosts (Basic)

Go to the online course to perform this practice activity.

Interactive Graphic

Activity 8.1.2.9: Calculate the Subnet Mask

Go to the online course to perform this practice activity.

Creating 100 Subnets with a /16 Prefix (8.1.2.10)

In the previous examples, we considered an internetwork that required three subnets and an internetwork that required five subnets. To achieve the goal of creating four subnets, we borrowed 2 bits from the 8 host bits available with an IP address that has a default mask of 255.255.255.0, or a /24 prefix. The resulting subnet mask was 255.255.255.192, and a total of four possible subnets were created. Applying the host calculation formula of $2^6 - 2$, we determined that on each of those four subnets we could have 62 host addresses to assign to nodes.

To acquire five subnets, we borrowed 3 bits from the 8 host bits available with an IP address that has a default mask of 255.255.255.0, or a /24 prefix. In borrowing those 3 bits from the host portion of the address, we left 5 host bits remaining. The resulting subnet mask was 255.255.255.224, with a total of eight subnets created, and 30 host addresses per subnet.

Consider large organizations or campuses with an internetwork that requires 100 subnets. Just as in the previous examples, to achieve the goal of creating 100 subnets, we must borrow bits from the host portion of the IP address of the existing internetwork. As before, to calculate the number of subnets, we must look at the number of available host bits and use the subnet calculation formula $2^{number\ of}$ *bits borrowed*. Using the IP address of the last example, 192.168.10.0/24, we have 8 host bits; to create 100 subnets, we must borrow 7 bits. Calculate the number of subnets if 7 bits are borrowed: $2^7 = 128$ subnets.

However, borrowing 7 bits will leave just 1 remaining host bit, and if we apply the host calculation formula, the result would be no hosts on these subnets. Calculate the number of hosts if 1 bit is remaining, $2^1 = 2$, and then subtract 2 for the network address and the network broadcast; the result is 0 hosts ($2^1 - 2 = 0$).

In a situation requiring a larger number of subnets, an IP network is required that has more host bits to borrow from, such as an IP address with a default subnet mask of /16, or 255.255.0.0. Addresses that have a range of 128–191 in the first octet have a default mask of 255.255.0.0, or /16. Addresses in this range have 16 bits in the network portion and 16 bits in the host portion. The 16 bits that are in the host portion are the bits that are available to be borrowed for creating subnets.

Using a new IP address of 172.16.0.0/16 address block, host bits must be borrowed to create at least 100 subnets. Starting from left to right with the first available host bit, we will borrow a single bit at a time until we reach the number of bits necessary to create 100 subnets. Borrowing 1 bit, we would create two subnets; borrowing 2 bits, we would create four subnets; borrowing 3 bits, we would create eight subnets; and so on. Calculate the number of subnets created if 7 bits are borrowed using the formula $2^{number\ of\ bits\ borrowed}$:

$2^7 = 128$ subnets

Borrowing 7 bits creates 128 subnets, as shown in Figure 8-24.

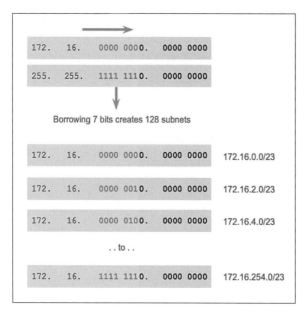

Figure 8-24   Borrowing 7 Bits

Recall that the subnet mask must change to reflect the borrowed bits. In this example, when 7 bits are borrowed, the mask is extended 7 bits into the third octet. In decimal, the mask is represented as 255.255.254.0, or a /23 prefix, because the third octet is 11111110 in binary and the fourth octet is 00000000 in binary. Subnetting will be done in the third octet, with the host bits in the third and fourth octets.

Calculating the Hosts (8.1.2.11)

To calculate the number of hosts, examine the third and fourth octets. After borrowing 7 bits for the subnet, there is 1 host bit remaining in the third octet and 8 host bits remaining in the fourth octet.

Apply the following host calculation formula as shown in Figure 8-25:

$$2^9 = 512$$

But remember that all 0 bits in the host portion of the address is the network address, and all 1s in the host portion is a broadcast address. Therefore, there are only 510 host addresses that are actually available for each subnet.

As shown in Figure 8-26, the first host address for the first subnet is 172.16.0.1 and the last host address is 172.16.1.254. Remember that each host must have a valid IP address within the range defined for that network segment. The subnet assigned to the router interface will determine which segment a host belongs to.

Hosts = 2^n
(where n = host bits remaining)

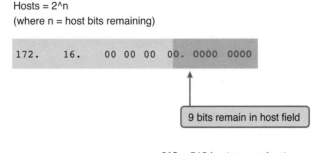

2^9 = 512 hosts per subnet
2^9 - 2 = 510 valid hosts per subnet

Figure 8-25   Calculate Number of Hosts

Network Address

| 172. | 16. | 00 00 00 | 00. 0000 0000 | = 172.16.0.0/23 |

First Host Address

| 172. | 16. | 00 00 00 | 00. 0000 0001 | = 172.16.0.1/23 |

Last Host Address

| 172. | 16. | 00 00 00 | 01. 1111 1110 | = 172.16.0.254/23 |

Broadcast Address

| 172. | 16. | 00 00 00 | 01. 1111 1111 | = 172.16.1.255 |

Figure 8-26   Address Range for 172.16.0.0/23 Subnet

Note

Remember that bits can be borrowed only from the host portion of the address. The network portion of the address is allocated by the service provider and cannot be changed. So, organizations that require a significant number of subnets are required to communicate this need to their ISP so that the ISP can allocate an IP address block with a default mask that has enough bits to create the needed subnets.

Creating 1000 Subnets with a /8 Prefix (8.1.2.12)

Some organizations, such as small service providers, might need more than 100 subnets. Consider, for example, an organization that requires 1000 subnets. As always, to create subnets, we must borrow bits from the host portion of the IP address of the existing internetwork. As before, to calculate the number of subnets, it is necessary to look at the number of available host bits. A situation such as this requires that the IP address assigned by the ISP have enough host bits available to calculate 1000 subnets. IP addresses that have the range of 1–126 in the first octet have a default mask of 255.0.0.0 or /8. This means there are 8 bits in the network portion and 24 host bits available to borrow toward subnetting.

Using the 10.0.0.0/8 address block, host bits must be borrowed to create at least 1000 subnets. Starting from left to the right with the first available host bit, we will borrow a single bit at a time until we reach the number of bits necessary to create 1000 subnets. Calculate the number of subnets created if 10 bits are borrowed using the formula 2^*number of bits borrowed*:

2^10 = 1024 subnets

Borrowing 10 bits creates 1024 subnets, as shown in Figure 8-27.

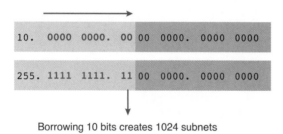

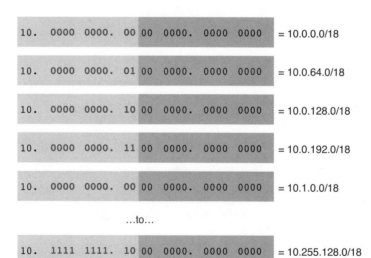

Figure 8-27 Borrowing 10 Bits

Recall that the subnet mask must change to reflect the borrowed bits. In this example, when 10 bits are borrowed, the mask is extended 10 bits into the third octet. In decimal, the mask is represented as 255.255.192.0 or a /18 prefix, because the third octet of the subnet mask is 11000000 in binary and the fourth octet is 00000000 in binary. Subnetting will be done in the third octet, but don't forget about the host bits in the third and fourth octets.

Host Calculation

To calculate the number of hosts, examine the third and fourth octet. After borrowing 10 bits for the subnet, there are 6 host bits remaining in the third octet and 8 host bits remaining in the fourth octet. A total of 14 host bits remain.

Apply the following host calculation formula as shown in Figure 8-28:

$$2^{14} - 2 = 16382$$

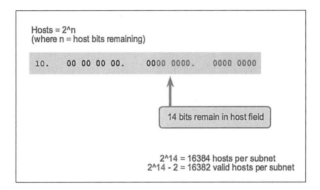

Figure 8-28   Calculate Number of Hosts

The first host address for the first subnet is 10.0.0.1 and the last host address is 10.0.63.254, as shown in Figure 8-29. Remember that each host must have a valid IP address within the range defined for that network segment. The subnet assigned to the router interface will determine which segment a host belongs to.

```
Network Address
10.    00 00 00 00.    0000 0000.    0000 0000    = 10.0.0.0/18

First Host Address
10.    00 00 00 00.    0000 0000.    0000 0001    = 10.0.0.1/18

Last Host Address
10.    00 00 00 00.    0011 1111.    1111 1110    = 10.0.63.254/18

Broadcast Address
10.    00 00 00 00.    0011 1111.    1111 1111    = 10.0.63.255/18
```

Figure 8-29   Address Range for 10.0.0.0/18 Subnet

Note

All devices on the same subnet will have a host IPv4 address from the range of host addresses and will use the same subnet mask.

Interactive Graphic

Activity 8.1.2.13: Determining the Network Address – Advanced

Go to the online course to perform this practice activity.

Interactive Graphic

Activity 8.1.2.14: Calculating the Number of Hosts – Advanced

Go to the online course to perform this practice activity.

Interactive Graphic

Activity 8.1.2.15: Determining the Valid Addresses for Hosts – Advanced

Go to the online course to perform this practice activity.

Determining the Subnet Mask (8.1.3)

This section covers the parameters for determining the subnet mask you require.

Subnetting Based on Host Requirements (8.1.3.1)

The decision about how many host bits to borrow to create subnets is an important planning decision. There are two considerations when planning subnets: the number of host addresses required for each network, and the number of individual subnets needed. The selection of the number of bits for the subnet ID affects both the number of possible subnets and the number of host addresses in each subnet.

Video

Video 8.1.3.1: Subnet Possibilities

This video shows the subnet possibilities for the 192.168.1.0 network. Go to the online course to view this animation.

Notice that there is an inverse relationship between the number of subnets and the number of hosts. The more bits borrowed to create subnets, the fewer host bits available; therefore, fewer hosts per subnet. If more host addresses are needed, more host bits are required, resulting in fewer subnets.

Number of Hosts

When borrowing bits to create multiple subnets, you leave enough host bits for the largest subnet. The number of host addresses required in the largest subnet will determine how many bits must be left in the host portion. The formula 2^n (where n is the number of host bits remaining) is used to calculate how many addresses will be available on each subnet. Recall that two of the addresses cannot be used, so that the usable number of addresses can be calculated as $2^n - 2$.

Subnetting Network-Based Requirements (8.1.3.2)

Sometimes an organization may require a certain number of subnets, with less emphasis on the number of host addresses per subnet. This may be the case if an organization chooses to separate its network traffic based on internal structure or department setup. For example, an organization may choose to put all host devices used by employees in the Engineering department in one network, and all host devices used by management in a separate network, as shown in Figure 8-30. In this case, the number of subnets is most important in determining how many bits to borrow.

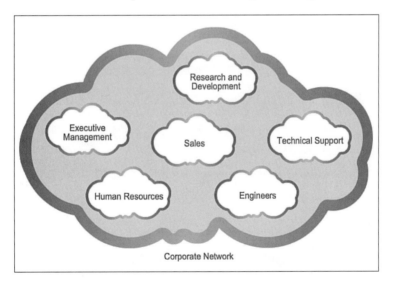

Figure 8-30   Subnets Based on Organizational Structure

Recall that the number of subnets created when bits are borrowed can be calculated using the formula 2^n (where n is the number of bits borrowed). There is no need to subtract any of the resulting subnets, as they are all usable.

The key is to balance the number of subnets needed and the number of hosts required for the largest subnet. More bits borrowed to create additional subnets means fewer hosts available per subnet.

Subnetting to Meet Network Requirements (8.1.3.3, 8.1.3.4)

Every network within an organization is designed to accommodate a finite number of hosts. Basic subnetting requires enough subnets to accommodate the networks while also providing enough host addresses per subnet.

Some networks, such as point-to-point wide area network (WAN) links, require only two hosts. Other networks, such as a user LAN in a large building or department, may need to accommodate hundreds of hosts. Network administrators must devise the internetwork addressing scheme to accommodate the maximum number of hosts for each network. The number of hosts in each division should allow for growth in the number of hosts.

Determine the Total Number of Hosts

First, consider the total number of hosts required by the entire corporate internetwork. A block of addresses large enough to accommodate all devices in all the corporate networks must be used. These devices include end-user devices, servers, intermediate devices, and router interfaces.

Consider the example of a corporate internetwork that must accommodate a total of 800 hosts in its five locations, as depicted in Figure 8-31.

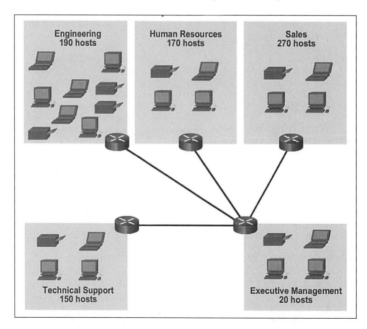

Figure 8-31   Corporate Network

In this example, the service provider has allocated a network address of 172.16.0.0/22 (10 host bits). As shown in Figure 8-32, this will provide 1022 host addresses, which will more than accommodate the addressing needs for this internetwork.

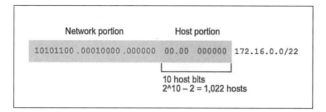

Figure 8-32   Network Address

Determine the Number and Size of the Networks

Next, consider the number of subnets required and the number of host addresses needed on each subnet. Based on the network topology consisting of five LAN segments and four internetwork connections between routers, nine subnets are required. The largest subnet requires 40 hosts. When designing an addressing scheme, you should anticipate growth in both the number of subnets and the number of hosts per subnet.

The 172.16.0.0/22 network address has 10 host bits. Because the largest subnet requires 40 hosts, a minimum of 6 host bits should be borrowed. This is determined by using this formula: $2^6 - 2 = 62$ hosts. The 4 remaining host bits can be used to allocate subnets. Using the formula for determining subnets, this results in 16 subnets: $2^4 = 16$. Because the example internetwork requires nine subnets, this will meet the requirement and allow for some additional growth.

When 4 bits are borrowed, the new prefix length is /26 with a subnet mask of 255.255.255.192.

As shown in Figure 8-33, using the /26 prefix length, the 16 subnet addresses can be determined. Only the subnet portion of the address is incremented. The original 22 bits of the network address cannot change and the host portion will contain all 0 bits.

> **Note**
>
> Because the subnet portion is in both the third and fourth octets, one or both of these values will vary in the subnet addresses.

As shown in Figure 8-34, the original 172.16.0.0/22 network was a single network with 10 host bits, providing 1022 usable addresses to assign to hosts. By borrowing 4 host bits, 16 subnets (0000 through 1111) can be created. Each subnet has 6 host bits or 62 usable host addresses per subnet.

```
10101100.00010000.00000000 00.00 000000  172.16.0.0/22
```

```
0  10101100.00010000.00000000 00.00 000000  172.16.0.0/26
1  10101100.00010000.00000000 00.01 000000  172.16.0.64/26
2  10101100.00010000.00000000 00.10 000000  172.16.0.128/26
3  10101100.00010000.00000000 00.11 000000  172.16.0.192/26
4  10101100.00010000.00000000 01.00 000000  172.16.1.0/26
5  10101100.00010000.00000000 01.01 000000  172.16.1.64/26
6  10101100.00010000.00000000 01.10 000000  172.16.1.128/26
```

Nets 7 – 13 not shown

```
14  10101100.00010000.00000000 11.10 000000  172.16.3.128/26
15  10101100.00010000.00000000 11.11 000000  172.16.3.192/26
```

4 bits borrowed from host portion to create subnets

Figure 8-33   Subnet Scheme

```
10101100.00010000.00000000 00.00 000000  172.16.0.0/22
```

```
0  10101100.00010000.00000000 00.00 000000  172.16.0.0/26
1  10101100.00010000.00000000 00.01 000000  172.16.0.64/26
2  10101100.00010000.00000000 00.10 000000  172.16.0.128/26
3  10101100.00010000.00000000 00.11 000000  172.16.0.192/26
4  10101100.00010000.00000000 01.00 000000  172.16.1.0/26
5  10101100.00010000.00000000 01.01 000000  172.16.1.64/26
6  10101100.00010000.00000000 01.10 000000  172.16.1.128/26
```

Nets 7 – 13 not shown

```
14  10101100.00010000.00000000 11.10 000000  172.16.3.128/26
15  10101100.00010000.00000000 11.11 000000  172.16.3.192/26
```

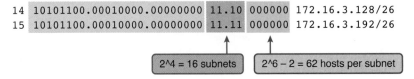

2^4 = 16 subnets   2^6 – 2 = 62 hosts per subnet

Figure 8-34   Subnets and Addresses

As shown in Figure 8-35, the subnets can be assigned to the LAN segments and router-to-router connections.

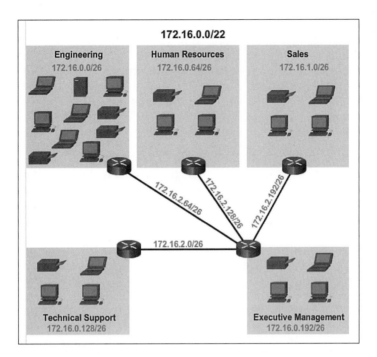

Figure 8-35   LAN Segments and Router-to-Router Connections

Activity 8.1.3.5: Determining the Number of Bits to Borrow

Go to the online course to perform this practice activity.

Packet Tracer Activity 8.1.3.6: Subnetting Scenario 1

In this activity, you are given the network address of 192.168.100.0/24 to subnet and provide the IP addressing for the network shown in the topology. Each LAN in the network requires enough space for, at least, 25 addresses for end-user devices, the switch, and the router. The connection between R1 to R2 will require an IP address for each end of the link.

Packet Tracer Activity 8.1.3.7: Subnetting Scenario 2

In this activity, you are given the network address of 172.31.1.0/24 to subnet and provide the IP addressing for the network shown in the topology. The required host addresses for each WAN and LAN link are labeled in the topology.

Lab 8.1.3.8: Calculating IPv4 Subnets

In this lab, you will complete the following objectives:

- Part 1: Determine IPv4 Address Subnetting
- Part 2: Calculate IPv4 Address Subnetting

Lab 8.1.3.9: Subnetting Network Topologies

In this lab you will have to determine the number of subnets, design an appropriate addressing scheme, assign IP address and subnet mask to the interface, and examine the use of the available network address space and future growth potential.

Lab 8.1.3.10: Researching Subnet Calculators

In this lab, you will complete the following objectives:

- Part 1: Review Available Subnet Calculators
- Part 2: Perform Network Calculations Using a Subnet Calculator

Benefits of Variable Length Subnet Masking (8.1.4)

This section addresses some of the benefits of Variable Length Subnet Masking.

Traditional Subnetting Wastes Addresses (8.1.4.1)

Using traditional subnetting allocates the same number of addresses for each subnet. If all the subnets happened to have the same requirements for the number of hosts, these fixed-size address blocks would be efficient. However, most often that is not the case.

For example, the topology shown in Figure 8-36 requires seven subnets, one for each of the four LANs and one for each of the three WAN connections between routers. Using traditional subnetting with the given address of 192.168.20.0/24, 3 bits can be borrowed from the host portion in the last octet to meet the subnet requirement of seven subnets.

As shown in Figure 8-37, borrowing 3 bits creates eight subnets and leaves 5 host bits with 30 usable hosts per subnet. This scheme creates the needed subnets and meets the host requirement of the largest LAN.

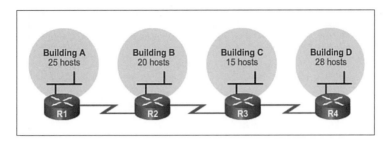

Figure 8-36   Network Topology: Basic Subnets

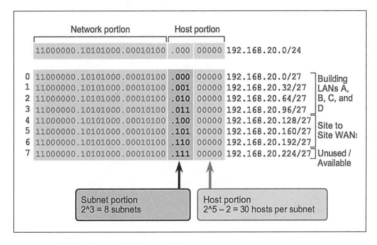

Figure 8-37   Basic Subnet Scheme

Although this traditional subnetting meets the needs of the largest LAN and divides the address space into an adequate number of subnets, it results in significant waste of unused addresses.

For example, only two addresses are needed in each subnet for the three WAN links. Because each subnet has 30 usable addresses, there are 28 unused addresses in each of these subnets. As shown in Figure 8-38, this results in 84 unused addresses (28 × 3).

Further, this limits future growth by reducing the total number of subnets available. This inefficient use of addresses is characteristic of traditional subnetting of classful networks.

Applying a traditional subnetting scheme to this scenario is not very efficient and is wasteful. In fact, this example is a good model for showing how subnetting a subnet can be used to maximize address utilization.

Subnetting a subnet, or using *Variable Length Subnet Mask (VLSM)*, was designed to avoid wasting addresses.

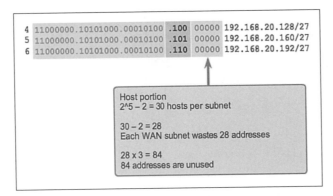

Figure 8-38   Unused Addresses on WAN Subnet

VLSM (8.1.4.2)

In all of the previous examples of subnetting, notice that the same subnet mask was applied for all the subnets. This means that each subnet has the same number of available host addresses.

As illustrated in Figure 8-39, traditional subnetting creates subnets of equal size. Each subnet in a traditional scheme uses the same subnet mask.

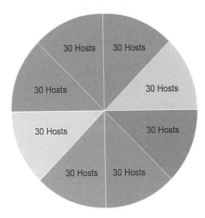

Figure 8-39   Traditional Subnetting Creates Equal-Sized Subnets

As shown in Figure 8-40, VLSM allows a network space to be divided in unequal parts. With VLSM, the subnet mask will vary depending on how many bits have been borrowed for a particular subnet, thus the "variable" part of the term VLSM.

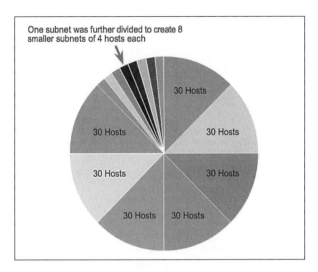

One subnet was further divided to create 8 smaller subnets of 4 hosts each

30 Hosts

30 Hosts

30 Hosts

30 Hosts

30 Hosts

30 Hosts

30 Hosts

Figure 8-40   Subnets of Varying Sizes

VLSM subnetting is similar to traditional subnetting in that bits are borrowed to create subnets. The formulas to calculate the number of hosts per subnet and the number of subnets created still apply. The difference is that subnetting is not a single-pass activity. With VLSM, the network is first subnetted, and then the subnets are subnetted again. This process can be repeated multiple times to create subnets of various sizes.

Basic VLSM (8.1.4.3)

To better understand the VLSM process, consider again the previous example, shown in Figure 8-41, in which the network 192.168.20.0/24 is subnetted into eight equal-sized subnets; seven of the eight subnets are allocated. Four subnets are used for the LANs, and three subnets are used for the WAN connections between the routers. The wasted address space is in the subnets used for the WAN connections, because those subnets require only two usable addresses: one for each router interface. To avoid this waste, VLSM can be used to create smaller subnets for the WAN connections.

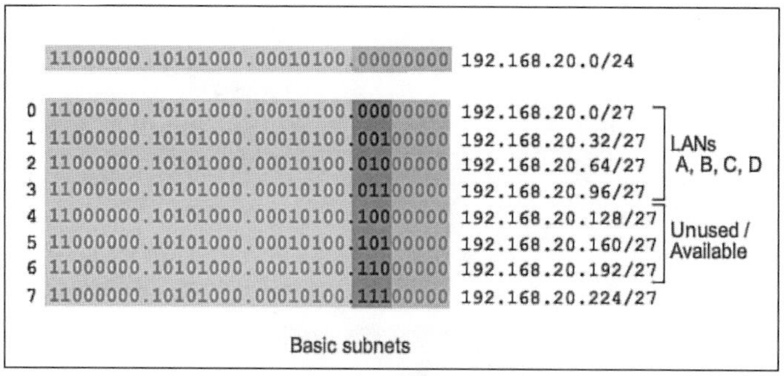

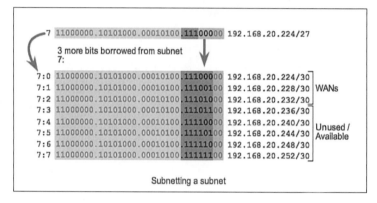

Figure 8-41 Traditional Subnetting Scheme

In Figure 8-42, the last subnet, 192.168.20.224/27, will be further subnetted.

Figure 8-42 VLSM Subnetting Scheme, Last Subnet

Recall that when the number of host addresses needed is known, the formula $2^n - 2$ (where n equals the number of host bits remaining) can be used. To provide two usable addresses, 2 host bits must be left in the host portion:

$$2^2 - 2 = 2$$

Because there are 5 host bits in the 192.168.20.224/27 address space, 3 bits can be borrowed, leaving 2 bits in the host portion.

The calculations at this point are exactly the same as those used for traditional subnetting. The bits are borrowed and the subnet ranges are determined.

As shown in Figure 8-42, this VLSM subnetting scheme reduces the number of addresses per subnet to a size appropriate for the WANs. Subnetting subnet 7 for WANs allows subnets 4, 5, and 6 to be available for future networks and allows several other subnets to be available for WANs.

VLSM in Practice (8.1.4.4)

Using the VLSM subnets, the LAN and WAN segments can be addressed without unnecessary waste. The hosts in each of the LANs will be assigned a valid host address with the range for that subnet and a /27 mask. Each of the four routers will have a LAN interface with a /27 subnet and one or more serial interfaces with a /30 subnet.

Using a common addressing scheme, the first host IPv4 address for each subnet is assigned to the LAN interface of the router. The WAN interfaces of the routers are assigned the IP addresses and mask for the /30 subnets.

Figures 8-43 through 8-46 show the interface configuration for each of the routers. Hosts on each subnet will have a host IPv4 address from the range of host addresses for that subnet and an appropriate mask. Hosts will use the address of the attached router LAN interface as the default gateway address.

- Building A hosts (192.168.20.0/27) will use router interface address 192.168.20.1 as the default gateway address.

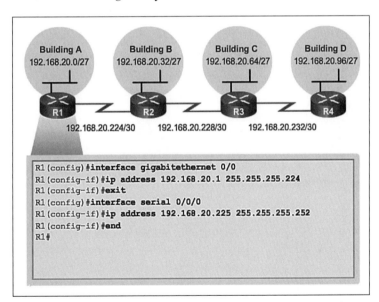

Figure 8-43   Network Topology: VLSM Subnet 192.168.20.0/27

- Building B hosts (192.168.20.32/27) will use router interface address 192.168.20.33 as the default gateway address.

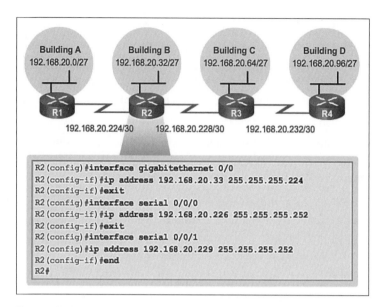

Figure 8-44   Network Topology: VLSM Subnet 192.168.20.32/27

- Building C hosts (192.168.20.64/27) will use router interface address 192.168.20.65 as the default gateway address.

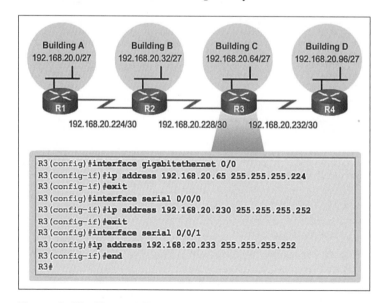

Figure 8-45   Network Topology: VLSM Subnet 192.168.20.64/27

- Building D hosts (192.168.20.96/27) will use router interface address 192.168.20.97 as the default gateway address.

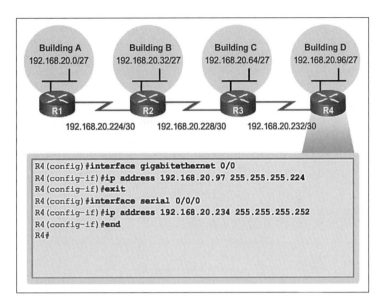

```
R4(config)#interface gigabitethernet 0/0
R4(config-if)#ip address 192.168.20.97 255.255.255.224
R4(config-if)#exit
R4(config)#interface serial 0/0/0
R4(config-if)#ip address 192.168.20.234 255.255.255.252
R4(config-if)#end
R4#
```

Figure 8-46 Network Topology: VLSM Subnet 192.168.20.96/27

VLSM Chart (8.1.4.5)

Address planning can also be accomplished using a variety of tools. One method is to use a VLSM chart to identify which blocks of addresses are available for use and which ones are already assigned. This method helps to prevent assigning addresses that have already been allocated. Using the network from the previous example, the VLSM chart can be used to plan address assignment.

Examining the /27 Subnets

As shown in Figure 8-47, when using traditional subnetting, the first seven address blocks are allocated for LANs and WANs. Recall that this scheme results in eight subnets with 30 usable addresses each (/27). While this scheme works for the LAN segments, there are many wasted addresses in the WAN segments.

	/27 Network	Hosts
Building A	.0	.1 - .30
Building B	.32	.33 - .62
Building C	.64	.65 - .94
Building D	.96	.97 - .126
WAN R1 – R2	.128	.129 - .158
WAN R2 – R3	.160	.161 - .190
WAN R3 – R4	.192	.193 - .222
Unused	.224	.225 - .254

Figure 8-47 Basic Subnetting of 192.168.20.0/24

When designing the addressing scheme on a new network, the address blocks can be assigned in a way that minimizes waste and keeps unused blocks of addresses contiguous.

Assigning VLSM Address Blocks

As shown in Figure 8-48, in order to use the address space more efficiently, the following /30 subnets are created for WAN links. To keep the unused blocks of addresses together, the last /27 subnet is further subnetted to create the /30 subnets. The first three subnets are assigned to WAN links.

	/27 Network	Hosts
Bldg A	.0	.1 - .30
Bldg B	.32	.33 - .62
Bldg C	.64	.65 - .94
Bldg D	.96	.97 - .126
Unused	.128	.129 - .158
Unused	.160	.161 - .190
Unused	.192	.193 - .222
	.224	.225 - .254

	/30 Network	Hosts
WAN R1–R2	.224	.225 - .226
WAN R2–R3	.228	.229 - .230
WAN R3–R4	.232	.233 - .234
Unused	.236	.237 - .238
Unused	.240	.241 - .242
Unused	.244	.245 - .246
Unused	.248	.249 - .250
Unused	.252	.253 - .254

Figure 8-48   VLSM Subnetting of 192.168.20.0/24

- .224 /30 host address range 225 to 226: WAN link between R1 and R2

- .228 /30 host address range 229 to 230: WAN link between R2 and R3

- .232 /30 host address range 233 to 234: WAN link between R3 and R4

- 236 /30 host address range 237 to 238: Available to be used

- 240 /30 host address range 241 to 242: Available to be used

- .244 /30 host address range 245 to 246: Available to be used

- .248 /30 host address range 249 to 250: Available to be used

- .252 /30 host address range 253 to 254: Available to be used

Designing the addressing scheme in this way leaves three unused /27 subnets and five unused /30 subnets.

Interactive Graphic

Activity 8.1.4.6: Practicing VLSM

Go to the online course to perform this practice activity.

Addressing Schemes (8.2)

There are several addressing schemes that can be used; this section looks at some of them.

Structured Design (8.2.1)

The first schemes we will examine are the structure design schemes.

Planning to Address the Network (8.2.1.1)

As shown in Figure 8-49, the allocation of network layer address space within the corporate network needs to be well designed. Address assignment should not be random. There are three primary considerations when planning address allocation:

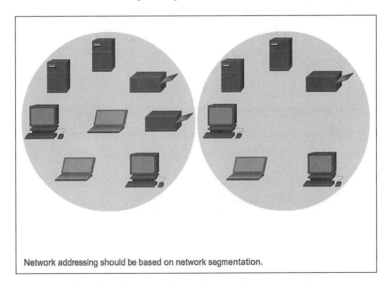

Network addressing should be based on network segmentation.

Figure 8-49   IPv4 Address Planning and Assignment

- **Preventing duplication of addresses:** Each host in an internetwork must have a unique address. Without the proper planning and documentation, an address could be assigned to more than one host, resulting in access issues for both hosts.

394 Network Basics Companion Guide

- **Providing and controlling access:** Some hosts, such as servers, provide resources to internal hosts as well as to external hosts. The Layer 3 address assigned to a server can be used to control access to that server. If, however, the address is randomly assigned and not well documented, controlling access is more difficult.

- **Monitoring security and performance:** Similarly, the security and performance of network hosts and the network as a whole must be monitored. As part of the monitoring process, network traffic is examined for addresses that are generating or receiving excessive packets. With proper planning and documentation of the network addressing, problematic network devices can be easily found.

Assigning Addresses Within a Network

Within a network, there are different types of devices, including

- End-user clients
- Servers and peripherals
- Hosts that are accessible from the Internet
- Intermediary devices
- Gateway

When developing an IP addressing scheme, it is generally recommended to have a set pattern of how addresses are allocated to each type of device. This benefits administrators when adding and removing devices and when filtering traffic based on IP. It also simplifies documentation.

Assigning Addresses to Devices (8.2.1.2)

A network addressing plan might include using a different range of addresses within each subnet, for each type of device, as shown in Figure 8-50.

Network: 192.168.1.0/24

Use	First	Last
Host Devices	.1	.229
Servers	.230	.239
Printers	.240	.249
Intermediary Devices	.250	.253
Gateway (router LAN interface)	.254	

Figure 8-50 IP Address Ranges

Addresses for Clients

Because of the challenges associated with static address management, end-user devices often have addresses dynamically assigned, using DHCP. DHCP is generally the preferred method of assigning IP addresses to hosts on large networks because it reduces the burden on network support staff and virtually eliminates entry errors.

Another benefit of DHCP is that an address is not permanently assigned to a host but rather is only leased for a period of time. If we need to change the subnetting scheme of our network, we do not have to statically reassign individual host addresses. With DHCP, we only need to reconfigure the DHCP server with the new subnet information. After this has been done, the hosts only need to automatically renew their IP addresses.

Addresses for Servers and Peripherals

Any network resource, such as a server or a printer, should have a static IP address. The client hosts access these resources using the IP addresses of these devices. Therefore, predictable addresses for each of these servers and peripherals are necessary.

Servers and peripherals are a concentration point for network traffic. There are many packets sent to and from the IPv4 addresses of these devices. When monitoring network traffic with a tool like Wireshark, a network administrator should be able to rapidly identify these devices. Using a consistent numbering system for these devices makes the identification easier.

Addresses for Hosts That Are Accessible from the Internet

In most internetworks, only a few devices are accessible by hosts outside of the corporation. For the most part, these devices are usually servers of some type. As with all devices in a network that provide network resources, the IP addresses for these devices should be static.

In the case of servers accessible by the Internet, each must have a public space address associated with it. Additionally, variations in the address of one of these devices will make that device inaccessible from the Internet. In many cases, these devices are on a network that is numbered using private addresses. This means that the router or firewall at the perimeter of the network must be configured to translate the internal address of the server into a public address. Because of this additional configuration in the perimeter intermediary device, it is even more important that these devices have a predictable address.

Addresses for Intermediary Devices

Intermediary devices are also a concentration point for network traffic. Almost all traffic within or between networks passes through some form of intermediary device. Therefore, these network devices provide an opportune location for network management, monitoring, and security.

Most intermediary devices are assigned Layer 3 addresses, either for the device management or for their operation. Devices, such as hubs, switches, and wireless access points, do not require IPv4 addresses to operate as intermediary devices. However, if we must access these devices as hosts to configure, monitor, or troubleshoot network operation, they must have addresses assigned.

Because we must know how to communicate with intermediary devices, they should have predictable addresses. Therefore, their addresses are typically assigned manually. Additionally, the addresses of these devices should be in a different range within the network block than user device addresses.

Address for the Gateway (Routers and Firewalls)

Unlike the other intermediary devices mentioned, routers and firewall devices have an IP address assigned to each interface. Each interface is in a different network and serves as the gateway for the hosts in that network. Typically, the router interface uses either the lowest or highest address in the network. This assignment should be uniform across all networks in the corporation so that network personnel will always know the gateway of the network no matter which network they are working on.

Router and firewall interfaces are the concentration point for traffic entering and leaving the network. Because the hosts in each network use a router or firewall device interface as the gateway out of the network, many packets flow through these interfaces. Therefore, these devices can play a major role in network security by filtering packets based on source and/or destination IP addresses. Grouping the different types of devices into logical addressing groups makes the assignment and operation of this packet filtering more efficient.

Lab 8.2.1.3: Designing and Implementing a Subnetted IPv4 Addressing Scheme

In this lab, you will complete the following objectives:

- Part 1: Design a Network Subnetting Scheme

- Part 2: Configure the Devices

- Part 3: Test and Troubleshoot the Network

Lab 8.2.1.4: Designing and Implementing a VLSM Addressing Scheme

In this lab, you will complete the following objectives:

- Part 1: Examine Network Requirements
- Part 2: Design the VLSM Address Scheme
- Part 3: Cable and Configure the IPv4 Network

Packet Tracer Activity 8.2.1.5: Designing and Implementing a VLSM Addressing Scheme

In this activity you are given a network address to develop a VLSM addressing scheme for the network shown in the included topology.

Design Considerations for IPv6 (8.3)

This section looks at how to design an IPv6 network.

Subnetting an IPv6 Network (8.3.1)

As shown in this section, the rules for subnetting an IPv6 network are entirely different from the rules for subnetting an IPv4 network.

Subnetting Using the Subnet ID (8.3.1.1)

IPv6 subnetting requires a different approach from that taken in IPv4 subnetting, primarily because IPv6 has so many addresses that the reason for subnetting is completely different. An IPv6 address space is not subnetted to conserve addresses; rather, it is subnetted to support hierarchical, logical design of the network. Whereas IPv4 subnetting is about managing address scarcity, IPv6 subnetting is about building an addressing hierarchy based on the number of routers and the networks they support.

Recall that an IPv6 address block with a /48 prefix has 16 bits for the Subnet ID, as shown in Figure 8-51. Subnetting using the 16-bit Subnet ID yields a possible 65,536 /64 subnets and does not require borrowing any bits from the Interface ID, or host portion, of the address. Each IPv6 /64 subnet contains roughly 18 quintillion addresses, obviously more than will ever be needed in one IP network segment.

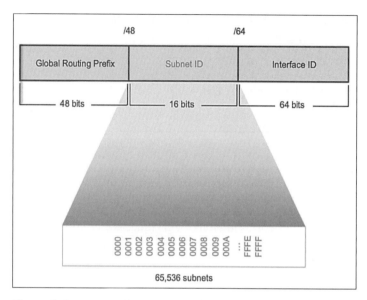

Figure 8-51 IPv6 /48 Address Block

Subnets created from the subnet ID are easy to represent because no conversion to binary is required. To determine the next available subnet, just count up in hexadecimal. As shown in Figure 8-52, this means counting by hexadecimal in the subnet ID portion.

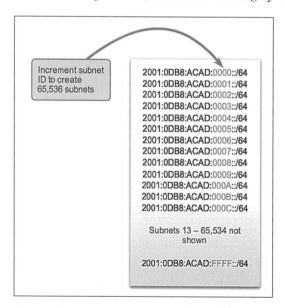

Figure 8-52 Address Block: 2001:0DB8:ACAD::/48

The global routing prefix is the same for all subnets. Only the subnet ID quartet is incremented for each subnet.

IPv6 Subnet Allocation (8.3.1.2)

With more than 65,000 subnets to choose from, the task of the network administrator becomes one of designing a logical scheme to address the network.

As shown in Figure 8-53, the example topology will require subnets for each LAN as well as for the WAN link between R1 and R2. Unlike the example for IPv4, with IPv6 the WAN link subnet will not be subnetted further. Although this may "waste" addresses, that is not a concern when using IPv6.

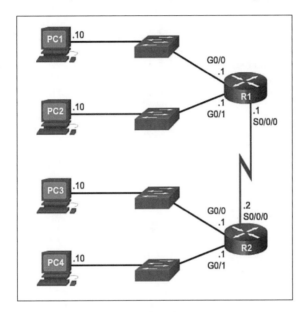

Figure 8-53 Example Topology

As shown in Figure 8-54, the allocation of five IPv6 subnets, with the Subnet ID field 0001 through 0005, will be used for this example. Each /64 subnet will provide more addresses than will ever be needed.

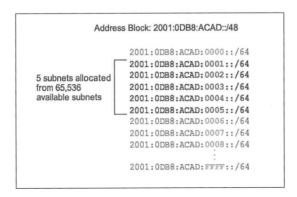

Figure 8-54 IPv6 Subnetting

As shown in Figure 8-55, each LAN segment and the WAN link are assigned a /64 subnet.

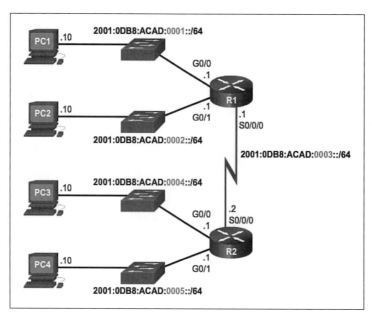

Figure 8-55   IPv6 Subnet Allocation

Similar to configuring IPv4, Figure 8-56 shows that each of the router interfaces has been configured to be on a different IPv6 subnet.

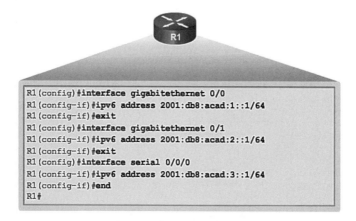

```
R1(config)#interface gigabitethernet 0/0
R1(config-if)#ipv6 address 2001:db8:acad:1::1/64
R1(config-if)#exit
R1(config)#interface gigabitethernet 0/1
R1(config-if)#ipv6 address 2001:db8:acad:2::1/64
R1(config-if)#exit
R1(config)#interface serial 0/0/0
R1(config-if)#ipv6 address 2001:db8:acad:3::1/64
R1(config-if)#end
R1#
```

Figure 8-56   IPv6 Address Configuration

Subnetting into the Interface ID (8.3.1.3)

Similar to borrowing bits from the host portion of an IPv4 address, with IPv6, bits can be borrowed from the interface ID to create additional IPv6 subnets. This is typically done for security reasons, to create fewer hosts per subnet, and not necessarily to create additional subnets.

When extending the subnet ID by borrowing bits from the interface ID, the best practice is to subnet on a *nibble boundary*. A nibble is 4 bits, or one hexadecimal digit. As shown in Figure 8-57, the /64 subnet prefix is extended 4 bits or 1 nibble to /68. Doing this reduces the size of the interface ID by 4 bits, from 64 to 60 bits.

Subnetting on nibble boundaries means only using nibble-aligned subnet masks. Starting at /64, the nibble-aligned subnet masks are /68, /72, /76, /80, etc.

Subnetting on a nibble boundary creates subnets by using the additional hexadecimal value. In Figure 8-57, the new subnet ID consists of the five hexadecimal values ranging from 00000 through FFFFF.

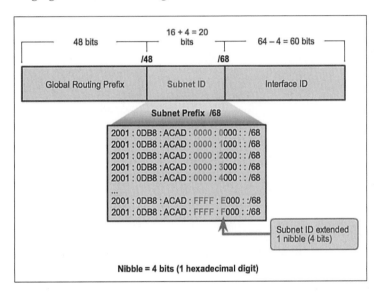

Figure 8-57   Subnetting on a Nibble Boundary

It is possible to subnet within a nibble boundary, within a hexadecimal digit, but it is not recommended or even necessary. Subnetting within a nibble takes away the advantage of easily determining the prefix from the interface ID. For example, if a /66 prefix length is used, the first 2 bits would be part of the subnet ID and the second 2 bits would be part of the interface ID.

Packet Tracer Activity 8.3.1.4: Implementing a Subnetted IPv6 Addressing Scheme

In this activity your network administrator wants you to assign five /64 IPv6 subnets to the network shown in the topology. Your job is to determine the IPv6 subnets, assign IPv6 addresses to the routers, and set the PCs to automatically receive IPv6 addressing. Your final step is to verify connectivity between IPv6 hosts.

Summary (8.4)

Class Activity 8.4.1.1: Can You Call Me Now?

Note

This activity may be completed individually or in small/large groups using Packet Tracer software.

You are setting up a dedicated, computer addressing scheme for patient rooms in a hospital. The switch will be centrally located in the nurses' station, as each of the five rooms will be wired so that patients can just connect to an RJ-45 port built into the wall of their room. Devise a physical and logical topology for only one of the six floors using the following addressing scheme requirements:

- There are six floors, with five patient rooms on each floor, for a total of 30 connections. Each room needs a network connection.

- Subnetting must be incorporated into your scheme.

- Use one router, one switch, and five host stations for addressing purposes.

- Validate that all PCs can connect to the hospital's in-house services.

- Keep a copy of your scheme to share later with the class or learning community. Be prepared to explain how subnetting, unicasts, multicasts, and broadcasts would be incorporated, and where your addressing scheme could be used.

Packet Tracer Activity 8.4.1.2: Skills Integration Challenge

As a network technician familiar with IPv4 and IPv6 addressing implementations, you are now ready to take an existing network infrastructure and apply your knowledge and skills to finalize the configuration. The network administrator has already configured some commands on the routers. **Do not erase or modify those configurations.** Your task is to complete the IPv4 and IPv6 addressing scheme, implement IPv4 and IPv6 addressing, and verify connectivity.

In this chapter you have learned how devices can be grouped into subnets, or smaller network groups, from a large network.

The process of segmenting a network by dividing it into multiple smaller network spaces is called subnetting, and is depicted in Figure 8-58.

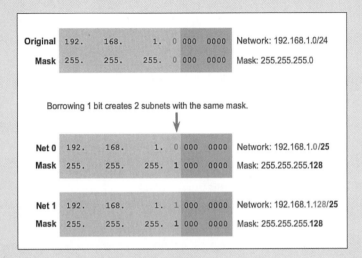

Figure 8-58   Segmenting a Network

Every network address has a valid range of host addresses. All devices attached to the same network will have an IPv4 host address for that network and a common subnet mask or network prefix. Traffic can be forwarded between hosts directly if they are on the same subnet. Traffic cannot be forwarded between subnets without the use of a router. To determine if traffic is local or remote, the router uses the subnet mask. The prefix and the subnet mask are different ways of representing the same thing—the network portion of an address.

IPv4 subnets are created by using one or more of the host bits as network bits. Two very important factors will lead to the determination of the IP address block with the subnet mask: the number of subnets required, and the maximum number of hosts needed per subnet. There is an inverse relationship between the number of subnets and the number of hosts. The more bits borrowed to create subnets, the fewer host bits available; therefore, fewer hosts per subnet.

The formula 2^n (where n is the number of host bits remaining) is used to calculate how many addresses will be available on each subnet. However, the network address and the broadcast address within a range are not useable; therefore, to calculate the useable number of addresses, the calculation $2^n - 2$ is required.

Subnetting a subnet, or using VLSM, was designed to avoid wasting addresses.

IPv6 subnetting requires a different approach from that taken in IPv4 subnetting. An IPv6 address space is not subnetted to conserve addresses; rather, it is subnetted to support hierarchical, logical design of the network. So, while IPv4 subnetting is about managing address scarcity, IPv6 subnetting is about building an addressing hierarchy based on the number of routers and the networks they support.

Careful planning is required to make best use of the available address space. Size, location, use, and access requirements are all considerations in the address planning process.

After it is implemented, an IP network needs to be tested to verify its connectivity and operational performance.

Practice

The following activities provide practice with the topics introduced in this chapter. The Labs and Class Activities are available in the companion *Network Basics Lab Manual* (978-1-58713-313-8). The Packet Tracer Activities PKA files are found in the online course.

Class Activities

Class Activity 8.0.1.2: Call Me!

Class Activity 8.4.1.1: Can You Call Me Now?

Labs

Lab 8.1.3.8: Calculating IPv4 Subnets

Lab 8.1.3.9: Subnetting Network Topologies

Lab 8.1.3.10: Researching Subnet Calculators

Lab 8.2.1.3: Designing and Implementing a Subnetted IPv4 Addressing Scheme

Lab 8.2.1.4: Designing and Implementing a VLSM Addressing Scheme

Packet Tracer
☐ Activity

Packet Tracer Activities

Packet Tracer Activity 8.1.3.6: Subnetting Scenario 1

Packet Tracer Activity 8.1.3.7: Subnetting Scenario 2

Packet Tracer Activity 8.2.1.5: Designing and Implementing a VLSM Addressing Scheme

Packet Tracer Activity 8.3.1.4: Implementing a Subnetted IPv6 Addressing Scheme

Packet Tracer Activity 8.4.1.2: Skills Integration Challenge

Check Your Understanding

Complete all the review questions listed here to test your understanding of the topics and concepts in this chapter. The appendix, "Answers to the 'Check Your Understanding' Questions," lists the answers.

1. How many host bits must be borrowed from an IPv4 address in order to create exactly 32 subnets of equal size?

   A. 3

   B. 4

   C. 5

   D. 6

2. Given the subnet 192.168.1.0/26, what are the first and last valid host addresses of the first subnet?

   A. 192.168.1.0 and 192.168.1.255

   B. 192.168.1.1 and 192.168.1.254

   C. 192.168.1.1 and 192.168.1.126

   D. 192.168.1.0 and 192.168.1.63

   E. 192.168.1.1 and 192.168.1.62

3. A PC has been assigned the IP address 192.168.0.168/29. How many more useable host addresses are left to be assigned on this network?

   A. 1

   B. 5

   C. 6

   D. 7

   E. 13

   F. 28

4. A host has been assigned an IP address and network prefix of 192.168.1.59/28. What is the network address of the subnet on which the host resides?

   A. 192.168.1.0

   B. 192.168.1.16

   C. 192.168.1.32

   D. 192.168.1.48

5. Which pair of hosts will require a router to forward packets between them?

   A. Host A: 192.168.1.32/24 and host B: 192.168.1.64/24

   B. Host A: 192.168.1.34/25 and host B: 192.168.1.55/25

   C. Host A: 192.168.1.59/26 and host B: 192.168.1.71/26

   D. Host A: 192.168.1.3/28 and host B: 192.168.1.12/28

6. What is the prefix notation for the subnet mask 255.255.254.0?

   A. /23

   B. /24

   C. /25

   D. /29

   E. /30

   F. /31

7. When applied to network 192.168.0.0, what subnet mask will yield 126 usable host addresses on two equally sized subnets?

   A. 255.255.255.128

   B. 255.255.255.240

   C. 255.255.255.248

   D. 255.255.255.252

8. A host is assigned the IP address of 192.31.7.200/28. Which two IP addresses could be used for other network devices on the same network? (Choose two.)

   A. 192.31.7.1

   B. 192.31.7.192

   C. 192.31.7.193

   D. 192.31.7.200

   E. 192.31.7.208

   F. 192.31.7.206

   G. 192.31.7.222

9. What is the main reason that a network administrator would use VLSM?

   A. Cost savings

   B. Enhanced security

   C. Efficient use of address space

   D. Shorter delay of data transmissions

10. What is the size of a nibble in binary bits?

   A. 2 bits

   B. 4 bits

   C. 8 bits

   D. 16 bits

11. How many usable host addresses are on the same subnet as host 10.10.30.40/20?

   A. 1022

   B. 1024

   C. 2047

   D. 2048

   E. 4094

   F. 4096

12. What does the acronym VLSM stand for?

   A. Variable length subnet mask

   B. Very long subnet mask

   C. Vociferous longitudinal subnet mask

   D. Vector length subnet mask

   E. Vector loop subnet mask

13. R1 has configured interface Fa0/0 with the **ip address 10.5.48.1 255.255.240.0** command. Which of the following subnets, when configured on another interface on R1, would not be considered an overlapping VLSM subnet?

   A. 10.5.0.0 255.255.240.0

   B. 10.4.0.0 255.254.0.0

   C. 10.5.32.0 255.255.224.0

   D. 10.5.0.0 255.255.128.0

14. R4 has a connected route for 172.16.8.0/22. Which of the following answers lists a subnet that overlaps with this subnet?

   A. 172.16.0.0/21

   B. 172.16.6.0/23

   C. 172.16.16.0/20

   D. 172.16.11.0/25

15. A design already includes subnets 192.168.1.0/26, 192.168.1.128/30, and 192.168.1.160/29. Which of the following subnets is the numerically lowest subnet ID that could be added to the design, if you wanted to add a subnet that uses a /28 mask?

A. 192.168.1.144/28

B. 192.168.1.112/28

C. 192.168.1.64/28

D. 192.168.1.80/28

E. 192.168.1.96/28

CHAPTER 9

Network Access

Objectives

Upon completion of this chapter, you will be able to answer the following questions:

- What is the purpose and function of the data link layer in preparing communication for transmission on specific media?

- What is the structure of the Layer 2 frame and which generic frame field types does it include?

- What are some of the protocols and standards used by the data link layer?

- What are the functions of logical topologies and physical topologies?

- What are the basic characteristics of media access control methods on WAN topologies?

- What are the basic characteristics of media access control methods on LAN topologies?

- What are the characteristics and the functions of the data link layer frame?

- What are the purpose and the function of the physical layer in the network?

- How are standards established for the data link layer and the physical layer?

- What are the basic characteristics of copper cabling?

- How do you build a UTP cable used in Ethernet networks?

- What is fiber-optic cabling and what are its main advantages over other media?

- How do you connect devices using wired and wireless media?

Key Terms

This chapter uses the following key terms. You can find the definitions in the Glossary.

data link layer   page 411

physical layer   page 411

Logical Link Control (LLC)   page 413

Media Access Control (MAC)   page 413

media access control method   page 414

Header   page 416

Data   page 416

Trailer   page 416

International Telecommunication Union (ITU)   page 418

American National Standards Institute (ANSI)   page 418

topology   page 420

media sharing   page 420

physical topology   page 420

logical topology   page 420

point-to-point   page 422

hub and spoke   page 422

mesh   page 422

half-duplex communication   page 424

Introduction (9.0.1.1)

To support our communication, the Open Systems Interconnection (OSI) model divides the functions of a data network into layers. To recap:

- The application layer provides the interface to the user.

- The transport layer is responsible for dividing and managing communications between the processes running in the two end systems.

- The network layer protocols organize our communication data so that it can travel across internetworks from the originating host to a destination host.

For network layer packets to be transported from source host to destination host, they must traverse different physical networks. These physical networks can consist of different types of physical media, such as copper wires, microwaves, optical fibers, and satellite links. Network layer packets do not have a way to directly access these different media.

It is the role of the OSI *data link layer* to prepare network layer packets for transmission and to control access to the physical media.

OSI upper-layer protocols prepare data from the human network for transmission to its destination. The *physical layer* controls how data is transmitted on the communication media by encoding the binary digits that represent data link layer frames into signals. It then transmits and receives these signals across the physical media (e.g., copper wires, optical fiber, and wireless) that connect network devices.

This chapter introduces the general functions of the data link layer and the protocols associated with it. It also covers the general functions of the physical layer and the standards and protocols that manage the transmission of data across local media.

Class Activity 9.0.1.2: Managing the Medium

In this modeling activity, pretend that you and your colleague are attending a networking conference. There are many lectures and presentations held during this event, and because they overlap, each of you can only choose a limited set of sessions to attend.

Therefore, you decide to split, each of you attending a separate set of presentations, and after the event ends, you share the slides and the knowledge each of you gained during the event.

Try to answer the following questions:

- How would you personally organize a conference where multiple sessions are held at the same time? Would you put all of them into a single conference room or would you use multiple rooms? What would be the reason?

- Assume that the conference room is properly fitted with audiovisual equipment to display large-size video and amplify voice. If a person wanted to attend a specific session, does the seating arrangement make a difference, or is it sufficient to visit the proper conference room?

- Would it be considered positive or harmful if the speech from one conference room somehow leaked into another?

- If questions or inquiries arise during a presentation, should attendees simply shout out their questions, or should there be some form of process for handling questions, such as documenting them and handing them over to a facilitator? What would happen without this process?

- If an interesting topic elicits a larger discussion where many attendees have questions or comments, can this result in the session running out of its time without going through the entire intended content? Why is that so?

- Imagine that the session is a panel; that is, a freer discussion of attendees with panelists and, optionally, among themselves. If a person wants to address another person within the same room, can he/she do it directly? What would be necessary to do if a panelist wanted to invite another person to join who is not presently in the room?

- What was accomplished by the isolation of multiple sessions into separate conference rooms if, after the event, people can meet and share the information?

Data Link Layer (9.1)

The data link layer (Layer 2 in the OSI model) prepares network data for the physical network. This section looks at this layer in depth.

The Data Link Layer (9.1.1.1)

The TCP/IP network access layer is the equivalent of the combined OSI data link layer (Layer 2) and physical layer (Layer 1). As shown in Figure 9-1, the data link layer is responsible for the exchange of frames between nodes over a physical network media. It allows the upper layers to access the media and controls how data is placed and received on the media.

Note

Specifically, the data link layer performs these two basic services:

- It accepts Layer 3 packets and packages them into data units called *frames*.
- It controls media access control and performs error detection.

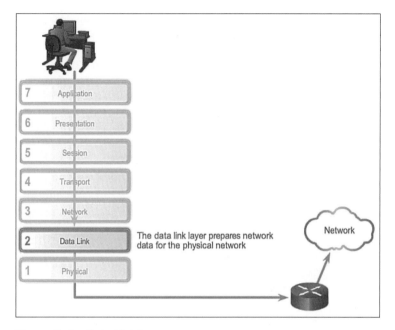

Figure 9-1 Data Link Layer

The data link layer effectively separates the media transitions that occur as the packet is forwarded from the communication processes of the higher layers. The data link layer receives packets from and directs packets to an upper-layer protocol, in this case IPv4 or IPv6. This upper-layer protocol does not need to be aware of which media the communication will use.

Note

In this chapter, *media* and *medium* do not refer to digital content and multimedia such as audio, animation, television, and video. *Media* refers to the material that actually carries the data signals, such as copper cable and optical fiber.

Data Link Sublayers (9.1.1.2)

The data link layer is actually divided into two sublayers:

- *Logical Link Control (LLC)*: This upper sublayer defines the software processes that provide services to the network layer protocols. It places information in the frame that identifies which network layer protocol is being used for the frame. This information allows multiple Layer 3 protocols, such as IPv4 and IPv6, to utilize the same network interface and media.

- *Media Access Control (MAC)*: This lower sublayer defines the media access processes performed by the hardware. It provides data link layer addressing and delimiting of data according to the physical signaling requirements of the medium and the type of data link layer protocol in use.

Separating the data link layer into sublayers allows for one type of frame defined by the upper layer to access different types of media defined by the lower layer. Such is the case in many local area network (LAN) technologies, including Ethernet.

Figure 9-2 illustrates how the data link layer is separated into the LLC and MAC sublayers. The LLC sublayer communicates with the network layer, and the MAC sublayer allows various network access technologies. For instance, the MAC sublayer communicates with Ethernet LAN technology to send and receive frames over copper or fiber-optic cable. The MAC sublayer also communicates with wireless technologies such as Wi-Fi and Bluetooth to send and receive frames wirelessly.

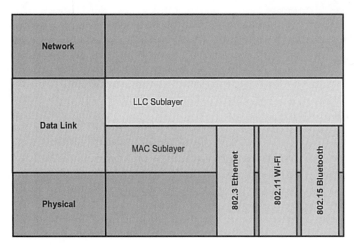

Figure 9-2 Data Link Sublayers

Media Access Control (9.1.1.3)

Layer 2 protocols specify the encapsulation of a packet into a frame and the techniques for getting the encapsulated packet on and off each medium. The technique used for getting the frame on and off media is called the *media access control* method.

As packets travel from source host to destination host, they typically traverse over different physical networks. These physical networks can consist of different types of physical media, such as copper wires, optical fibers, and wireless, which consist of different electromagnetic signals, such as radio and microwave frequencies and satellite links.

The packets do not have a way to directly access these different media. It is the role of the OSI data link layer to prepare network layer packets for transmission and to control access to the physical media. The media access control methods described by the data link layer protocols define the processes by which network devices can access the network media and transmit frames in diverse network environments.

Without the data link layer, network layer protocols such as IP would have to make provisions for connecting to every type of media that could exist along a delivery path. Moreover, IP would have to adapt every time a new network technology or medium was developed. This process would hamper protocol and network media innovation and development. This is a key reason for using a layered approach to networking.

Video

Video 9.1.1.3:

This video provides an example of a PC in Paris connecting to a laptop in Japan. Go to the online course to view this animation.

Providing Access to Media (9.1.1.4)

Different media access control methods may be required during the course of a single communication. Each network environment that packets encounter as they travel from a local host to a remote host can have different characteristics. For example, an Ethernet LAN consists of many hosts contending to access the network medium on an ad hoc basis. Serial links consist of a direct connection between only two devices over which data flows sequentially as bits in an orderly way.

Router interfaces encapsulate the packet into the appropriate frame, and a suitable media access control method is used to access each link. In any given exchange of network layer packets, there may be numerous data link layer and media transitions. At each hop along the path, a router

- Accepts a frame from a medium
- De-encapsulates the frame
- Re-encapsulates the packet into a new frame
- Forwards the new frame appropriate to the medium of that segment of the physical network

Video

Video 9.1.1.4: Transfer of Frames

This video demonstrates how frames are transferred, de-encapsulated, and re-encapsulated. Go to the online course to view this animation.

Layer 2 Frame Structure (9.1.2)

This section takes a look at how the data link layer frames are structured. It covers formatting of data as well as creating a frame.

Formatting Data for Transmission (9.1.2.1)

The data link layer prepares a packet for transport across the local media by encapsulating it with a header and a trailer to create a frame. The description of a frame is a key element of each data link layer protocol.

Data link layer protocols require control information to enable the protocols to function. Control information typically answers the following questions:

- Which nodes are in communication with each other?
- When does communication between individual nodes begin and when does it end?
- Which errors occurred while the nodes communicated?
- Which nodes will communicate next?

Unlike the other protocol data units (PDUs) that have been discussed in this course, the data link layer frame includes the following elements:

- *Header*: Contains control information, such as addressing, and is located at the beginning of the PDU
- *Data*: Contains the IP header, transport layer header, and application data
- *Trailer*: Contains control information for error detection and is added to the end of the PDU

These frame elements are shown in Figure 9-3, and will be discussed in greater detail.

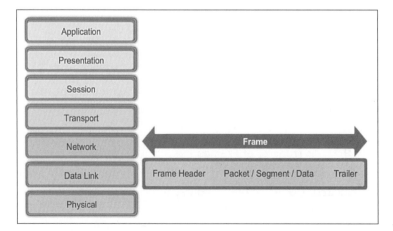

Figure 9-3   Frame Elements

Creating a Frame (9.1.2.2)

When data travels on the media, it is converted into a stream of bits, or 1s and 0s. If a node is receiving long streams of bits, how does it determine where a frame starts and stops or which bits represent the address?

Framing breaks the stream into decipherable groupings, with control information inserted in the header and trailer as values in different fields. This format gives the physical signals a structure that can be received by nodes and decoded into packets at the destination.

As shown in Figure 9-4, generic frame field types include the following:

- **Frame start and Frame stop indicator flags:** Used by the MAC sublayer to identify the beginning and end limits of the frame.

- **Addressing:** Used by the MAC sublayer to identify the source and destination nodes.

- **Type:** Used by the LLC sublayer to identify the Layer 3 protocol.

- **Control:** Identifies special flow control services.

- **Data:** Contains the frame payload (i.e., packet header, segment header, and the data).

- **Error Detection:** Included after the data to form the trailer, these frame fields are used for error detection.

Not all protocols include all of these fields. The standards for a specific data link layer protocol define the actual frame format.

Note

Examples of frame formats are discussed toward the end of this chapter.

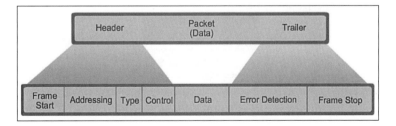

Figure 9-4   Frame Fields

Activity 9.1.2.3: Generic Frame Fields

Go to the online course to perform this practice activity (which has two parts).

Interactive
Graphic

Layer 2 Standards (9.1.3)

Several organizations have developed the Layer 2 standards. This section discusses those organizations.

Data Link Layer Standards (9.1.3.1)

Unlike the protocols of the upper layers of the TCP/IP suite, data link layer protocols generally are not defined by Requests for Comments (RFCs). Although the Internet Engineering Task Force (IETF) maintains the functional protocols and services for the TCP/IP protocol suite in the upper layers, the IETF does not define the functions and operation of that model's network access layer.

Specifically, the data link layer services and specifications are defined by multiple standards based on a variety of technologies and media to which the protocols are applied. Some of these standards integrate both Layer 2 and Layer 1 services.

The functional protocols and services at the data link layer are described by

- Engineering organizations that set public and open standards and protocols
- Communications companies that set and use proprietary protocols to take advantage of new advances in technology or market opportunities

Engineering organizations that define open standards and protocols that apply to the data link layer include

- Institute of Electrical and Electronics Engineers (IEEE)
- *International Telecommunication Union (ITU)*
- International Organization for Standardization (ISO)
- *American National Standards Institute (ANSI)*

Table 9-1 highlights various standards organizations and some of their more important data link layer protocols.

Table 9-1   Standards Organizations and Networking Standards

Standards Organization	Networking Standards
IEEE	802.2: Logical Link Control (LLC)
	802.3: Ethernet
	802.4 Token Bus
	802.5 Token Ring
	802.11: Wireless LAN (WLAN) & Mesh (Wi-Fi certification)
	802.15: Bluetooth
	802.16: WiMAX

Standards Organization	Networking Standards
ITU-T	G.992: ADSL
	G.8100–G.8199: MPLS over Transport Aspects
	Q.921: ISDN
	Q.922: Frame Relay
ISO	HDLC (High-Level Data Link Control)
	ISO 9314: FDDI Media Access Control (MAC)
ANSI	X3T9.5 and X3T12: Fiber Distributed Data Interface (FDDI)

Interactive Graphic

Activity 9.1.3.2: Data Link Layer Standards Organizations

Go to the online course to perform practice activity of matching each data link layer protocol to its corresponding standards organization.

Media Access Control (9.2)

Regulating the placement of data frames onto the media is controlled by the MAC sublayer.

Topologies (9.2.1)

This section first looks at how to control access to the media and then describes the physical and logical topologies of a network.

Controlling Access to the Media (9.2.1.1)

Media access control is the equivalent of traffic rules that regulate the entrance of motor vehicles onto a roadway. The absence of any media access control would be the equivalent of vehicles ignoring all other traffic and entering the road without regard to the other vehicles. However, not all roads and entrances are the same. Traffic can enter the road by merging, by waiting for its turn at a stop sign, or by obeying signal lights. A driver follows a different set of rules for each type of entrance.

In the same way, there are different ways to regulate placing frames onto the media. The protocols at the data link layer define the rules for access to different media. Some media access control methods use highly controlled processes to ensure that frames are safely placed on the media. These methods are defined by sophisticated protocols, which require mechanisms that introduce overhead onto the network.

Among the different implementations of the data link layer protocols, there are different methods of controlling access to the media. These media access control techniques define if and how the nodes share the media.

The actual media access control method used depends on

- *Topology*: How the connection between the nodes appears to the data link layer.

- *Media sharing*: How the nodes share the media. The media sharing can be point-to-point, such as in wide area network (WAN) connections, or shared, such as in LAN networks, as shown in Figure 9-5.

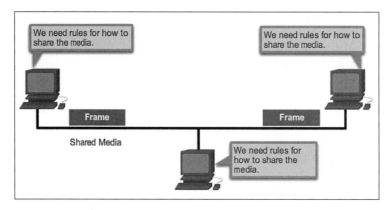

Figure 9-5   Sharing the Media

Physical and Logical Topologies (9.2.1.2)

The *topology* of a network is the arrangement or relationship of the network devices and the interconnections between them. LAN and WAN topologies can be viewed in two ways:

- *Physical topology*: Refers to the physical connections and identifies how end devices and infrastructure devices such as routers, switches, and wireless access points are interconnected. Physical topologies are usually point-to-point or star, as shown in Figure 9-6.

- *Logical topology*: Refers to the way a network transfers frames from one node to the next. This arrangement consists of virtual connections between the nodes of a network. These logical signal paths are defined by data link layer protocols. The logical topology of point-to-point links is relatively simple whereas shared media offers deterministic and non-deterministic media access control methods. Deterministic media access is the protocol used to control access to the physical medium in a token ring or FDDI network. Non-determinicstic media access is the CSMA/CD method used by Ethernet. See Figure 9-7.

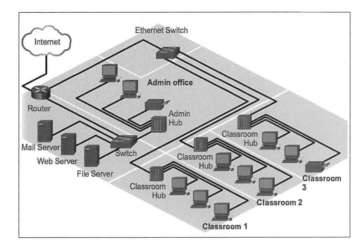

Figure 9-6   Physical Topology

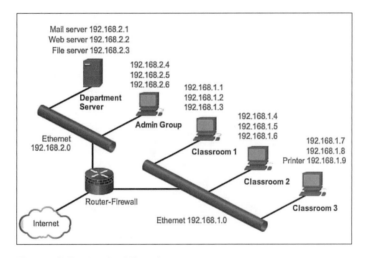

Figure 9-7   Logical Topology

The data link layer "sees" the logical topology of a network when controlling data access to the media. It is the logical topology that influences the type of network framing and media access control used.

WAN Topologies (9.2.2)

Understanding the differences between WAN and LAN topologies is essential to understanding network access in general. This section covers the WAN topologies.

Common Physical WAN Topologies (9.2.2.1)

WANs are commonly interconnected using the following physical topologies:

- *Point-to-point*: This is the simplest topology, consisting of a permanent link between two endpoints. For this reason, this is a very popular WAN topology.

- *Hub and spoke*: This is a WAN version of the star topology in which a central site interconnects branch sites using point-to-point links.

- *Mesh*: This topology provides high availability but requires that every end system be interconnected to every other system. Therefore, the administrative and physical costs can be significant. Each link is essentially a point-to-point link to the other node. Variations of this topology include a partial mesh, where some but not all end devices are interconnected.

The three common physical WAN topologies are illustrated in Figure 9-8.

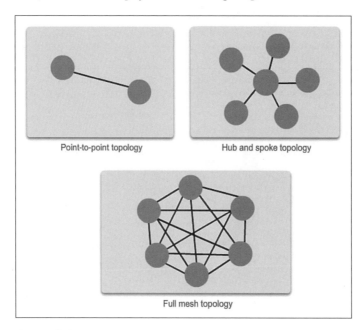

Figure 9-8   WAN Topologies

Physical Point-to-Point Topology (9.2.2.2)

Physical point-to-point topologies directly connect two nodes, as shown in Figure 9-9.

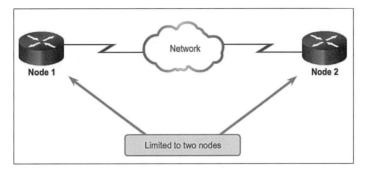

Figure 9-9   Point-to-Point Topology

In this arrangement, two nodes do not have to share the media with other hosts. Additionally, a node does not have to make any determination about whether an incoming frame is destined for it or another node. Therefore, the logical data link protocols can be very simple, as all frames on the media can only travel to or from the two nodes. The frames are placed on the media by the node at one end of the point-to-point circuit and are taken off the media by the node at the other end.

Data link layer protocols could provide more sophisticated media access control processes for logical point-to-point topologies, but this would only add unnecessary protocol overhead.

Logical Point-to-Point Topology (9.2.2.3)

The end nodes communicating in a point-to-point network can be physically connected via a number of intermediate devices. However, the use of physical devices in the network does not affect the logical topology.

As shown in Figure 9-10, the source and destination nodes may be indirectly connected to each other over some geographical distance. In some cases, the logical connection between nodes forms what is called a *virtual circuit*. A virtual circuit is a logical connection created within a network between two network devices. The two nodes on either end of the virtual circuit exchange the frames with each other. This occurs even if the frames are directed through intermediary devices. Virtual circuits are important logical communication constructs used by some Layer 2 technologies.

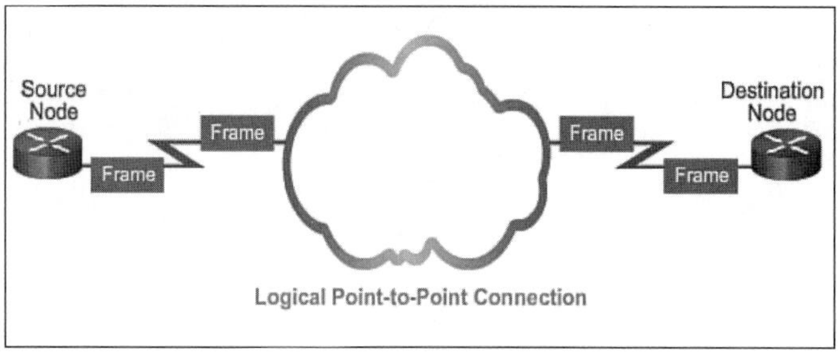

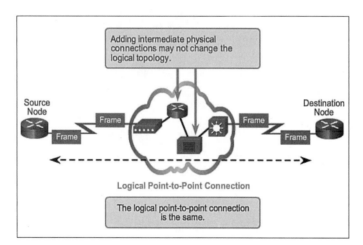

Figure 9-10   Logical Connection

The media access method used by the data link protocol is determined by the logical point-to-point topology, not the physical topology. This means that the logical point-to-point connection between two nodes may not necessarily be between two physical nodes at each end of a single physical link. Figure 9-11 shows the physical devices in-between the two routers.

Figure 9-11   Logical Point-to-Point Topology

Half and Full Duplex (9.2.2.4)

Figure 9-12 shows a point-to-point topology. In point-to-point networks, data can flow in one of two ways:

- *Half-duplex communication*: Both devices can both transmit and receive on the media but cannot do so simultaneously. Ethernet has established arbitration rules for resolving conflicts arising from instances when more than one station attempts to transmit at the same time.

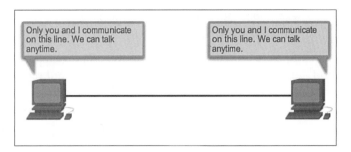

Figure 9-12   Point-to-Point Connection

Video

Video 9.2.2.4 Part 2: Half-Duplex Communications

Go to the online course to view this half-duplex video.

■ *Full-duplex communication*: Both devices can transmit and receive on the media at the same time. The data link layer assumes that the media is available for transmission for both nodes at any time. Therefore, there is no media arbitration necessary in the data link layer.

Video

Video 9.2.2.4 Part 3: Full-Duplex Communications

Go to the online course to view this full-duplex video.

LAN Topologies (9.2.3)

This section takes a look at the physical and logical LAN topologies, as well as the multi-access topology. It also describes the two basic media access control methods for shared media, contention-based access and controlled access. A short discussion on ring topology is also presented.

Physical LAN Topologies (9.2.3.1)

As shown in Figure 9-13, physical topology defines how the end systems are physically interconnected. In shared media LANs, end devices can be interconnected using the following physical topologies:

■ *Star*: End devices are connected to a central intermediate device. Early star topologies interconnected end devices using hubs. However, star topologies now use switches. The star topology is the most common physical LAN topology primarily because it is easy to install, very scalable (easy to add and remove end devices), and easy to troubleshoot.

- *Extended star or hybrid*: This is a combination of the other topologies, such as star networks interconnected to each other using a bus topology.

- *Bus*: All end systems are chained to each other and terminated in some form on each end. Infrastructure devices such as switches are not required to interconnect the end devices. Bus topologies were used in legacy Ethernet networks because they were inexpensive to use and easy to set up.

- *Ring*: All end systems are connected to their respective closest two neighbors, forming a ring. Unlike the bus topology, the ring does not need to be terminated. Ring topologies were used in legacy Token Ring and Fiber Distributed Data Interface (FDDI) networks. Specifically, FDDI networks employ a second ring for fault tolerance or performance enhancements.

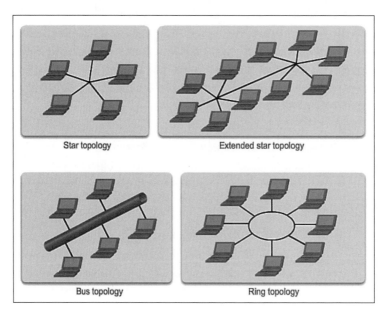

Figure 9-13 Physical Topologies

Logical Topology for Shared Media (9.2.3.2)

Logical topology of a network is closely related to the mechanism used to manage network access. Access methods provide the procedures to manage network access so that all stations have access. When several entities share the same media, some mechanism must be in place to control access. Access methods are applied to networks to regulate this media access.

Some network topologies share a common medium with multiple nodes. At any one time, there may be a number of devices attempting to send and receive data using the network media. There are rules that govern how these devices share the media.

There are two basic media access control methods for shared media:

- *Contention-based access*: All nodes compete for the use of the medium but have a plan if there are collisions. Figure 9-14 shows contention-based access.

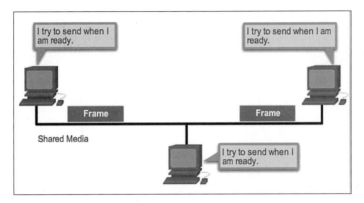

Figure 9-14   Contention-Based Access

- *Controlled access*: Each node has its own time to use the medium. Figure 9-15 shows controlled access.

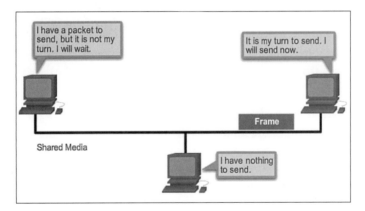

Figure 9-15   Controlled Access

The data link layer protocol specifies the media access control method that will provide the appropriate balance between frame control, frame protection, and network overhead.

Contention-Based Access (9.2.3.3)

When using a non-deterministic contention-based method, a network device can attempt to access the medium whenever it has data to send. To prevent complete chaos on the media, these methods use a carrier sense multiple access (CSMA) process to first detect if the media is carrying a signal.

If a carrier signal on the media from another node is detected, it means that another device is transmitting. When the device attempting to transmit sees that the media is busy, it will wait and try again after a short time period. If no carrier signal is detected, the device transmits its data. Ethernet and wireless networks use contention-based media access control.

It is possible that the CSMA process will fail and two devices will transmit at the same time, creating a data collision. If this occurs, the data sent by both devices will be corrupted and will need to be re-sent.

Contention-based media access control methods do not have the overhead of controlled access methods. A mechanism for tracking whose turn it is to access the media is not required. However, the contention-based systems do not scale well under heavy media use. As use and the number of nodes increase, the probability of successful media access without a collision decreases. Additionally, the recovery mechanisms required to correct errors due to these collisions further diminish the throughput.

CSMA is usually implemented in conjunction with a method for resolving the media contention. The two commonly used methods are

- *Carrier sense multiple access with collision detection (CSMA/CD)*: The end device monitors the media for the presence of a data signal. If a data signal is absent and therefore the media is free, the device transmits the data. If signals are then detected that show another device was transmitting at the same time, all devices stop sending and try again later. Traditional forms of Ethernet use this method.

- *Carrier sense multiple access with collision avoidance (CSMA/CA)*: The end device examines the media for the presence of a data signal. If the media is free, the device sends a notification across the media of its intent to use it (Request to Send frame). After it receives a clearance to transmit (Clear to Send frame), the device then sends the data. This method is used by 802.11 wireless networking technologies.

Figure 9-16 illustrates the following:

- How contention-based access methods operate
- Characteristics of contention-based access methods
- Examples of contention-based access methods

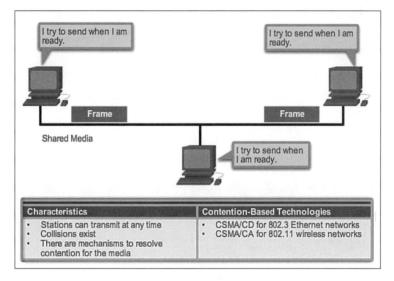

Figure 9-16   Contention-Based Access

Multi-Access Topology (9.2.3.4)

A logical multi-access topology enables a number of nodes to communicate by using the same shared media. Data from only one node can be placed on the medium at any one time. Every node sees all the frames that are on the medium, but only the node to which the frame is addressed processes the contents of the frame.

Having many nodes share access to the medium requires a data link media access control method to regulate the transmission of data and thereby reduce collisions between different signals.

Play Video 9.2.3.4 to see how nodes access the media in a multi-access topology.

Video 9.2.3.4: Logical Multi-Access Topology

This video demonstrates how nodes access the media in a multi-access topology. Go to the online course to view this animation.

Controlled Access (9.2.3.5)

When using the controlled access method, network devices take turns, in sequence, to access the medium. If an end device does not need to access the medium, then the opportunity passes to the next end device. This process is facilitated by use of a token. An end device acquires the token and places a frame on the media, and no other device can do so until the frame has arrived and been processed at the destination, releasing the token.

> **Note**
>
> This method is also known as *scheduled access* or *deterministic*.

Although controlled access is well ordered and provides predictable throughput, deterministic methods can be inefficient because a device has to wait for its turn before it can use the medium.

Controlled access examples include

- Token Ring (IEEE 802.5)

- FDDI, which is based on the IEEE 802.4 token bus protocol

> **Note**
>
> Both of these media access control methods are considered obsolete. Synchronous Optical Network (SONET) is the standard for optical networks now.

Figure 9-17 illustrates the following:

- How controlled access methods operate

- Characteristics of controlled access methods

- Examples of controlled access methods

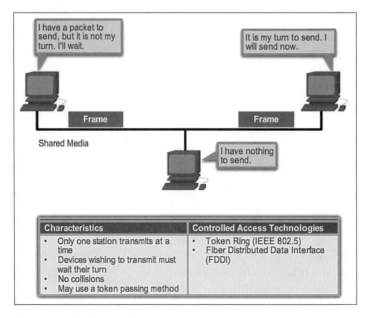

Figure 9-17   Controlled Access

Ring Topology (9.2.3.6)

In a *logical ring topology*, each node in turn receives a frame. If the frame is not addressed to the node, the node passes the frame to the next node. This allows a ring to use a controlled media access control technique called *token passing*.

Nodes in a logical ring topology remove the frame from the ring, examine the address, and send it on if it is not addressed for that node. In a ring, all nodes around the ring (between the source and destination node) examine the frame.

There are multiple media access control techniques that could be used with a logical ring, depending on the level of control required. For example, only one frame at a time is usually carried by the media. If there is no data being transmitted, a signal (known as a token) may be placed on the media, and a node can place a data frame on the media only when it has the token.

Remember that the data link layer "sees" a logical ring topology. The actual physical cabling topology could be another topology.

Play Video 9.2.3.6 to see how nodes access the media in a logical ring topology.

Video

Video 9.2.3.6: Logical Ring Topology

This video demonstrates how nodes access the media in a logical ring topology. Go to the online course view this animation.

Interactive Graphic

Activity 9.2.3.7: Logical and Physical Topologies

Go to the online course to perform this practice activity involving data link layer media access control methods.

Data Link Frame (9.2.4)

This section looks at the different pieces of the data link frame.

The Frame (9.2.4.1)

Although there are many different data link layer protocols that describe data link layer frames, each frame type has three basic parts:

- Header
- Data
- Trailer

All data link layer protocols encapsulate the Layer 3 PDU within the Data field of the frame. However, the structure of the frame and the fields contained in the header and trailer vary according to the protocol.

The data link layer protocol describes the features required for the transport of packets across different media. These features of the protocol are integrated into the encapsulation of the frame. When the frame arrives at its destination and the data link protocol takes the frame off the media, the framing information is read and discarded.

There is no one frame structure that meets the needs of all data transportation across all types of media. Depending on the environment, the amount of control information needed in the frame varies to match the media access control requirements of the media and logical topology.

As shown in Figure 9-18, a fragile environment requires more control. However, a protected environment, as shown in Figure 9-19, requires fewer controls.

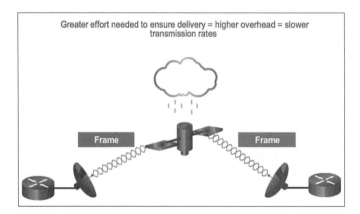

Figure 9-18 Fragile Environment

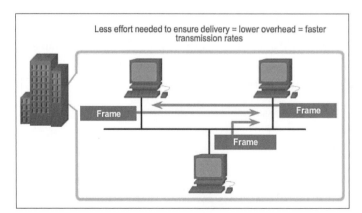

Figure 9-19 Protected Environment

The Header (9.2.4.2)

The frame header contains the control information specified by the data link layer protocol for the specific logical topology and media used.

Frame control information is unique to each type of protocol. It is used by the Layer 2 protocol to provide features demanded by the communication environment.

Figure 9-20 displays the Ethernet frame header fields:

- **Start Frame field:** Indicates the beginning of the frame

- **Source and Destination Address fields:** Indicate the source and destination nodes on the media

- **Type field:** Indicates the upper-layer service contained in the frame

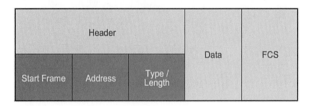

Figure 9-20   Role of the Header

Different data link layer protocols may use different fields from those mentioned. For example, other Layer 2 protocol header frame fields could include

- **Priority/Quality of Service field:** Indicates a particular type of communication service for processing

- **Logical Connection Control field:** Used to establish a logical connection between nodes

- **Physical Link Control field:** Used to establish the media link

- **Flow Control field:** Used to start and stop traffic over the media

- **Congestion Control field:** Indicates congestion in the media

Because the purposes and functions of data link layer protocols are related to the specific topologies and media, each protocol has to be examined to gain a detailed understanding of its frame structure. As protocols are discussed in this course, more information about the frame structure will be explained.

Layer 2 Address (9.2.4.3)

The data link layer provides addressing that is used in transporting a frame across a shared local media. Device addresses at this layer are referred to as physical addresses. Data link layer addressing is contained within the frame header and specifies the frame destination node on the local network. The frame header may also contain the source address of the frame.

Unlike Layer 3 logical addresses, which are hierarchical, physical addresses do not indicate on what network the device is located. Rather, the physical address is a unique, device-specific address. If the device is moved to another network or subnet, it will still function with the same Layer 2 physical address.

An address that is device specific and nonhierarchical cannot be used to locate a device across large networks or the Internet. This would be like trying to find a single house within the entire world, with nothing more than a house number and street name. The physical address, however, can be used to locate a device within a limited area. For this reason, the data link layer address is only used for local delivery. Addresses at this layer have no meaning beyond the local network. Compare this to Layer 3, where addresses in the packet header are carried from source host to destination host regardless of the number of network hops along the route.

If the data must pass onto another network segment, an intermediate device, such as a router, is necessary. The router must accept the frame based on the physical address and de-encapsulate the frame in order to examine the hierarchical Layer 3 address. Using the Layer 3 address, the router is able to determine the network location of the destination device and the best path to reach it. When it knows where to forward the packet, the router then creates a new frame for the packet, and the new frame is sent on to the next segment toward its final destination. Figure 9-21 highlights Layer 2 address requirements in multi-access and point-to-point topologies.

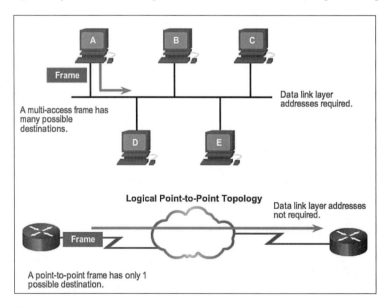

Figure 9-21   Logical Multi-Access Topology

The Trailer (9.2.4.4)

Data link layer protocols add a trailer to the end of each frame. The trailer is used to determine if the frame arrived without error. This process is called error detection and is accomplished by placing a mathematical summary of the bits that comprise the frame in the trailer. Error detection is added at the data link layer because the signals on the media could be subject to interference, distortion, or loss that would substantially change the bit values that those signals represent.

A transmitting node creates a mathematical summary of the contents of the frame. This is known as the cyclic redundancy check (CRC) value. This value is placed in the Frame Check Sequence (FCS) field of the frame to represent the contents of the frame.

Interactive Graphic

Activity 9.2.4.4: Frame Trailer

Go to the online course to perform the FCS and Stop Frame practice activity.

When the frame arrives at the destination node, the receiving node calculates its own logical summary, or CRC, of the frame. The receiving node compares the two CRC values. If the two values are the same, the frame is considered to have arrived as transmitted. If the CRC value in the FCS field differs from the CRC calculated at the receiving node, the frame is discarded.

Therefore, the FCS field is used to determine if errors occurred in the transmission and reception of the frame. The error detection mechanism provided by the use of the FCS field discovers most errors caused on the media.

There is always the small possibility that a frame with a good CRC result is actually corrupt. Errors in bits may cancel each other out when the CRC is calculated. Upper-layer protocols would then be required to detect and correct this data loss.

LAN and WAN Frames (9.2.4.5)

In a TCP/IP network, all OSI Layer 2 protocols work with the IP at OSI Layer 3. However, the actual Layer 2 protocol used depends on the logical topology of the network and the implementation of the physical layer. Given the wide range of physical media used across the range of topologies in networking, there are a correspondingly high number of Layer 2 protocols in use.

Each protocol performs media access control for specified Layer 2 logical topologies. This means that a number of different network devices can act as nodes that operate at the data link layer when implementing these protocols. These devices include the network adapter or network interface cards (NICs) on computers as well as the interfaces on routers and Layer 2 switches.

The Layer 2 protocol used for a particular network topology is determined by the technology used to implement that topology. The technology is, in turn, determined by the size of the network—in terms of the number of hosts and the geographic scope—and the services to be provided over the network.

A LAN typically uses a high-bandwidth technology that is capable of supporting large numbers of hosts. A LAN's relatively small geographic area (a single building or a multi-building campus) and its high density of users make this technology cost effective.

However, using a high-bandwidth technology is usually not cost effective for WANs that cover large geographic areas (cities or multiple cities, for example). The cost of the long-distance physical links and the technology used to carry the signals over those distances typically result in lower bandwidth capacity.

Difference in bandwidth normally results in the use of different protocols for LANs and WANs.

Common data link layer protocols include

- Ethernet

- Point-to-Point Protocol (PPP)

- 802.11 Wireless

Other protocols covered in the CCNA curriculum are High-Level Data Link Control (HDLC) and Frame Relay.

Video

Video 9.2.4.5: Examples of Layer 2 Protocols

This video provides examples of Layer 2 protocols. Go to the online course to view this animation.

Ethernet Frame (9.2.4.6)

Ethernet is the dominant LAN technology. It is a family of networking technologies that are defined in the IEEE 802.2 and 802.3 standards.

Ethernet standards define both the Layer 2 protocols and the Layer 1 technologies. Ethernet is the most widely used LAN technology and supports data bandwidths of 10 Mbps, 100 Mbps, 1 Gbps (1,000 Mbps), or 10 Gbps (10,000 Mbps).

The basic frame format and the IEEE sublayers of OSI Layers 1 and 2 remain consistent across all forms of Ethernet. However, the methods for detecting and placing data on the media vary with different implementations.

Ethernet provides unacknowledged connectionless service over a shared media using CSMA/CD as the media access methods. Shared media requires that the Ethernet frame header use a data link layer address to identify the source and destination nodes. As with most LAN protocols, this address is referred to as the MAC address of the node. An Ethernet MAC address is 48 bits and is generally represented in hexadecimal format.

Figure 9-22 shows the many fields of the Ethernet frame. At the data link layer, the frame structure is nearly identical for all speeds of Ethernet. However, at the physical layer, different versions of Ethernet place the bits onto the media differently. Ethernet is discussed in more detail in the next chapter.

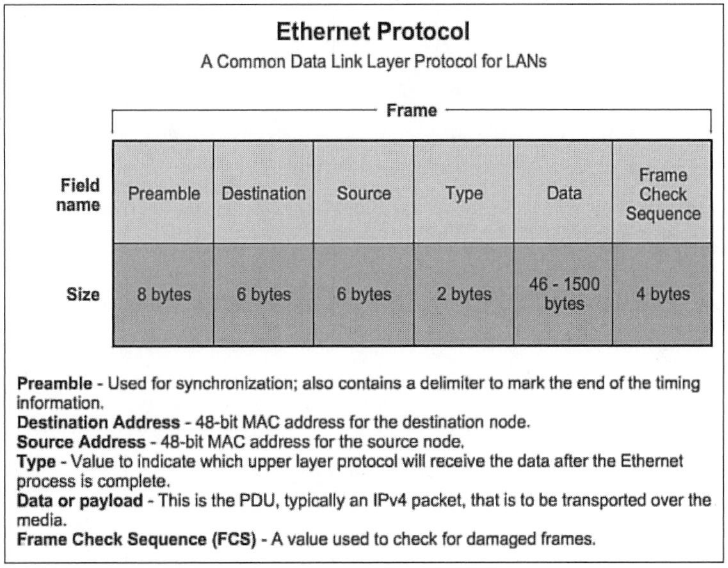

Ethernet Protocol
A Common Data Link Layer Protocol for LANs

				Frame		
Field name	Preamble	Destination	Source	Type	Data	Frame Check Sequence
Size	8 bytes	6 bytes	6 bytes	2 bytes	46 - 1500 bytes	4 bytes

Preamble - Used for synchronization; also contains a delimiter to mark the end of the timing information.
Destination Address - 48-bit MAC address for the destination node.
Source Address - 48-bit MAC address for the source node.
Type - Value to indicate which upper layer protocol will receive the data after the Ethernet process is complete.
Data or payload - This is the PDU, typically an IPv4 packet, that is to be transported over the media.
Frame Check Sequence (FCS) - A value used to check for damaged frames.

Figure 9-22   Ethernet Protocol

Point-to-Point (PPP) Frame (9.2.4.7)

Another data link layer protocol is the *Point-to-Point Protocol (PPP)*, which is used to deliver frames between two nodes. Unlike many data link layer protocols that are defined by electrical engineering organizations, the PPP standard is defined by RFCs. PPP was developed as a WAN protocol and remains the protocol of choice to implement many serial WANs. PPP can be used on various physical media, including twisted pair, fiber-optic lines, and satellite transmission, as well as for virtual connections.

PPP uses a layered architecture. To accommodate the different types of media, PPP establishes logical connections, called *sessions*, between two nodes. The PPP session hides the underlying physical media from the upper PPP protocol. These sessions also provide PPP with a method for encapsulating multiple protocols over a point-to-point link. Each protocol encapsulated over the link establishes its own PPP session.

PPP also allows the two nodes to negotiate options within the PPP session. This includes authentication, compression, and multilink (the use of multiple physical connections). Refer to Figure 9-23 for the basic fields in a PPP frame.

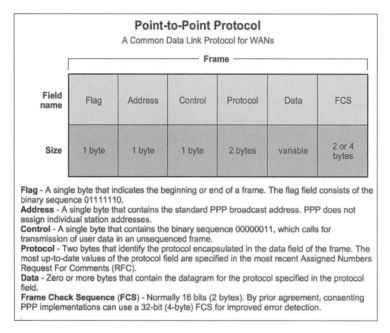

Figure 9-23   Point-to-Point Protocol

802.11 Wireless Frame (9.2.4.8)

The *IEEE 802.11 Wireless* standard uses the same 802.2 LLC and 48-bit addressing scheme as other 802 LANs. However, there are many differences at the MAC sublayer and physical layer. In a wireless environment, the environment requires special considerations. There is no definable physical connectivity; therefore, external factors may interfere with data transfer and it is difficult to control access. To meet these challenges, wireless standards have additional controls.

The IEEE 802.11 standard is commonly referred to as Wi-Fi. It is a contention-based system using a CSMA/CA media access process. CSMA/CA specifies a random backoff procedure for all nodes that are waiting to transmit. The most likely opportunity for medium contention is just after the medium becomes available. Making the nodes back off for a random period greatly reduces the likelihood of a collision.

802.11 networks also use data link acknowledgements to confirm that a frame is received successfully. If the sending station does not detect the acknowledgement frame, either because the original data frame or the acknowledgment was not received intact, the frame is retransmitted. This explicit acknowledgement overcomes interference and other radio-related problems.

Other services supported by 802.11 are authentication, association (connectivity to a wireless device), and privacy (encryption). Figure 9-24 shows the different wireless protocol fields.

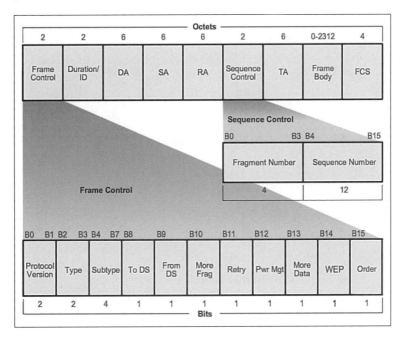

Figure 9-24 802.11 Wireless LAN Protocol

As shown in Figure 9-24, an 802.11 frame contains these fields:

- **Protocol Version field:** Version of 802.11 frame in use

- **Type and Subtype fields:** Identify one of three functions and subfunctions of the frame: control, data, and management

- **To DS field:** Set to 1 in data frames destined for the distribution system (devices in the wireless structure)

- **From DS field:** Set to 1 in data frames exiting the distribution system

- **More Fragments field:** Set to 1 for frames that have another fragment

- **Retry field:** Set to 1 if the frame is a retransmission of an earlier frame

- **Power Management field:** Set to 1 to indicate that a node will be in power-save mode

- **More Data field:** Set to 1 to indicate to a node in power-save mode that more frames are buffered for that node

- **Wired Equivalent Privacy (WEP) field:** Set to 1 if the frame contains WEP encrypted information for security

- **Order field:** Set to 1 in a data type frame that uses Strictly Ordered service class (does not need reordering)

- **Duration/ID field:** Depending on the type of frame, represents either the time, in microseconds, required to transmit the frame or an association identity (AID) for the station that transmitted the frame

- **Destination Address (DA) field:** MAC address of the final destination node in the network

- **Source Address (SA) field:** MAC address of the node that initiated the frame

- **Receiver Address (RA) field:** MAC address that identifies the wireless device that is the immediate recipient of the frame

- **The Sequence control fields are made up of following two fields:**

  - **Fragment Number field:** Indicates the number for each fragment of a frame

  - **Sequence Number field:** Indicates the sequence number assigned to the frame; retransmitted frames are identified by duplicate sequence numbers

- **Transmitter Address (TA) field:** MAC address that identifies the wireless device that transmitted the frame

- **Frame Body field:** Contains the information being transported; for data frames, typically an IP packet

- **FCS field:** Contains a 32-bit cyclic redundancy check (CRC) of the frame

---

Interactive Graphic

Activity 9.2.4.9 Part 1: Ethernet Frame Fields

Go to the online course to perform the Ethernet frame building practice activity.

Interactive Graphic

Activity 9.2.4.9 Part 2: PPP Frame

Go to the online course to perform the PPP frame building practice activity.

Interactive Graphic

Activity 9.2.4.9 Part 3: 802.11 Wireless Frame

Go to the online course to perform the 802.11 Wireless frame building practice activity.

Physical Layer (9.3)

This section discusses the purpose and characteristics of the physical layer.

Purpose of the Physical Layer (9.3.1)

Let's look at the physical layer, the physical layer media, and the physical layer standards.

The Physical Layer (9.3.1.1)

The OSI physical layer provides the means to transport across the network media the bits that make up a data link layer frame. This layer accepts a complete frame from the data link layer and encodes it as a series of signals that is transmitted onto the local media. The encoded bits that comprise a frame are received by either an end device or an intermediate device. Figure 9-25 shows the process of encapsulation and de-encapsulation.

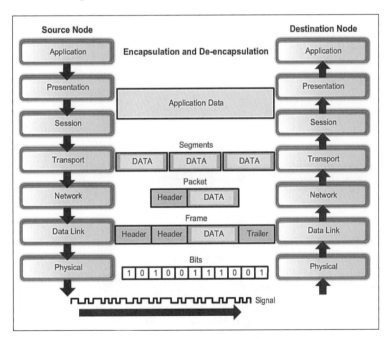

Figure 9-25   Encapsulation and De-encapsulation

The process that data undergoes from a source node to a destination node is as follows:

1. The user data is segmented by the transport layer, placed into packets by the network layer, and further encapsulated as frames by the data link layer.

2. The physical layer encodes the frames and creates the electrical, optical, or radio wave signals that represent the bits in each frame.

3. These signals are then sent on the media one at a time.

4. The destination node physical layer retrieves these individual signals from the media, restores them to their bit representations, and passes the bits up to the data link layer as a complete frame.

Physical Layer Media (9.3.1.2)

There are three basic forms of network media. The physical layer produces the representation and groupings of bits for each type of media as follows:

- *Copper cable*: The signals are patterns of electrical pulses.

- *Fiber-optic cable*: The signals are patterns of light.

- *Wireless*: The signals are patterns of microwave transmissions.

Figure 9-26 displays signaling examples for copper cable, fiber-optic cable, and wireless.

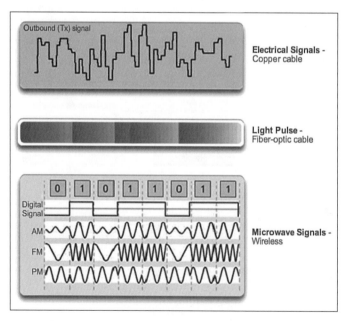

Figure 9-26   Signaling Examples

To enable physical layer interoperability, all aspects of these functions are governed by standards organizations.

Physical Layer Standards (9.3.1.3)

The protocols and operations of the upper OSI layers are performed in software designed by software engineers and computer scientists. For example, the services and protocols in the TCP/IP suite are defined by the IETF in RFCs, as represented in Figure 9-27.

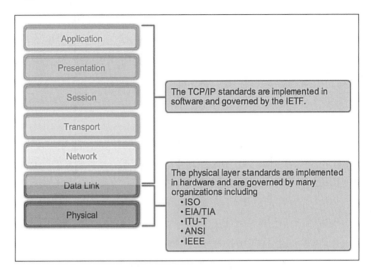

Figure 9-27   OSI Model Standards Organizations

The physical layer consists of electronic circuitry, media, and connectors developed by engineers. Therefore, it is appropriate that the standards governing this hardware are defined by the relevant electrical and communications engineering organizations.

There are many different international and national organizations, regulatory government organizations, and private companies involved in establishing and maintaining physical layer standards. For instance, the physical layer hardware, media, encoding, and signaling standards are defined and governed by the following organizations:

- International Organization for Standardization (ISO)

- Telecommunications Industry Association/Electronic Industries Association (TIA/EIA)

- International Telecommunication Union (ITU)

- American National Standards Institute (ANSI)

- Institute of Electrical and Electronics Engineers (IEEE)

- National telecommunications regulatory authorities, including the Federal Communication Commission (FCC) in the United States and the European Telecommunications Standards Institute (ESTI)

In addition to these organizations, regional cabling standards groups such as Canadian Standards Association (CSA), European Committee for Electrotechnical Standardization (CENELEC), and Japanese Standards Association (JSA/JIS) develop local specifications. Table 9-2 lists the major contributors and some of their relevant physical layer standards.

Table 9-2   Major Contributors to Physical Layer Standards

Standards Organization	Network Standards
ISO	ISO 8877: Officially adopted the RJ connectors (E.G., RJ-11, RJ-45)
	ISO 11801: Network cabling standard similar to TIA/EIA-568
TIA/EIA	TIA-568-C: Telecommunications cabling standards, used by nearly all voice, video, and data networks
	TIA-569-B: Commercial Building Standards for Telecommunications Pathways and Spaces
	TIA-598-C: Optical Fiber Cable Color Coding
	TIA-942: Telecommunications Infrastructure Standard for Data Centers
ANSI	568-C: RJ-45 pinouts; co-developed with EIA/TIA
ITU-T	G.992: ADSL
IEEE	802.3: Ethernet
	802.11: Wireless LAN (WLAN) & Mesh (Wi-Fi certification)
	802.15: Bluetooth

Lab 9.3.1.4: Identifying Network Devices and Cabling

In this lab, you will complete the following objectives:

Part 1: Identify Network Devices

Part 2: Identify Network Media

Characteristics of the Physical Layer (9.3.2)

This section looks at the physical layer functions and components as well as encoding techniques.

Physical Layer Functions (9.3.2.1)

The physical layer standards address three functional areas:

- *Physical components*: Includes electronic hardware devices, media, and connectors that transmit and carry the signals to represent the bits.

- *Frame encoding technique*: Refers to the method of converting a stream of data bits into a predefined code. Codes are groupings of bits used to provide a predictable pattern that can be recognized by both the sender and the receiver. Using predictable patterns helps to distinguish data bits from control bits and provide better media error detection.

- *Signaling method*: Refers to the electrical, optical, or wireless signals that represent the "1" and "0" on the media. The physical layer standards must define what type of signal represents a 1 and a 0. This can be as simple as a change in the level of an electrical signal or optical pulse or a more complex signaling method. Signaling method varies depending on the encoding scheme.

Table 9-3 displays a few examples of physical components, frame encoding techniques, and signaling methods used by copper cable.

Table 9-3   Physical Layer Functions

Media	Physical Components	Frame Encoding Technique	Signaling Method
Copper cable	UTP	Manchester encoding	Changes in the electromagnetic field
	Coaxial	Non-Return to Zero (NRZ) techniques	
	Connectors	4B/5B codes used with Multi-Level Transition Level 3 (MLT-3) signaling	Intensity of the electromagnetic field
	NICs		
	Ports	8B/10B encoding	Phase of the electromagnetic wave
	Interfaces	PAM5	

Physical Components (9.3.2.2)

Various standards organizations have contributed to the definition of the physical, electrical, and mechanical properties of the media available for different data communications. These specifications guarantee that cables and connectors will function as anticipated with different data link layer implementations.

Hardware components such as NICs, interfaces and connectors, cable materials, and cable designs are all specified in standards associated with the physical layer. The various ports and interfaces on a Cisco 1941 router are highlighted in Figure 9-28. Each connector has specific connectors and pinouts resulting from standards.

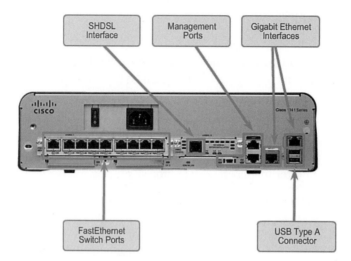

Figure 9-28   Ports on Router

As an example, standards for copper media are defined for the following:

- Type of copper cabling used

- Bandwidth of the communication

- Type of connectors used

- Pinout and color codes of connections to the media

- Maximum distance of the media

Frame Encoding Techniques (9.3.2.3)

Encoding is a method of converting a stream of data bits into a predefined code. Codes are groupings of bits used to provide a predictable pattern that can be recognized by both the sender and the receiver. Using predictable patterns helps to distinguish data bits from control bits and provide better media error detection.

Encoding methods at the physical layer may also provide codes for control purposes such as identifying the beginning and end of a frame. The transmitting host will transmit the specific pattern of bits, or code, to identify (i.e., pattern of bits = code) the beginning and end of the frame.

To illustrate this concept, consider the Morse code system developed more than 100 years ago. Each character (letter or numeral) is represented by a unique sequence of dots and dashes. The duration of a dash is three times the duration of a dot. For efficiency, the most common letters in the English language have the shortest codes assigned to them. For example, the letter "E" is a single dot. Consider the international code for the distress call, SOS. The letter "S" is three dots and the code for the letter "O" is three dashes. Video 9.3.2.3 shows an example of a telegraph operator sending the SOS distress call.

Video 9.3.2.3: Example of Encoding

This video provides an example of a telegraph operator sending an SOS distress call. Go to the online course to view this video.

A telegraph operator would encode messages into Morse code and then transmit that code to another telegraph operator, who would then decode the message to reveal the message. Telegraph operators would follow each dot or dash by a short silence, equal to the dot duration, and separate letters of a word by a space equal to three dots (one dash).

Modern encoding techniques perform the same process except that the telegraph operators are now computerized and capable of encoding and decoding messages at lightning speed. Frame encoding methods are far more complex than Morse code but essentially serve the same purpose.

Examples of network encoding methods include

- *Manchester encoding*: A 0 is represented by a high-to-low voltage transition in the middle of the bit time, and a 1 is represented by a low-to-high voltage transition in the middle of the bit time. Used in older versions of Ethernet, radio-frequency identification (RFID), and Near Field Communication (NFC).

- *Non-Return to Zero (NRZ)*: A common means of encoding data that has two states, "zero" and "one," and no neutral or rest position. A 0 may be represented by one voltage level on the media during the bit time, and a 1 may be represented by a different voltage on the media during the bit time.

Note

Faster data rates require more complex encoding, such as 4B/5B; however, explanation of these methods is beyond the scope of this chapter.

Signaling Method (9.3.2.4)

The physical layer must generate the electrical, optical, or wireless signals that represent the binary numbers of the encoded frame. The method of representing the binary bits is called the *signaling method*.

The physical layer standards must define what type of signal represents a "1" and a "0" and how they will be transmitted. This can be as simple as a change in the level of an electrical signal or optical pulse, or a more complex signaling method. The receiving node must convert the signals back into bits. The bits are then examined for the start-of-frame and end-of-frame bit patterns to determine that a complete frame has been received. The physical layer then delivers all the bits of a frame to the data link layer. As shown in Figure 9-29, signals can be transmitted in one of two ways:

- *Asynchronous*: Data signals are transmitted without an associated clock signal. The time spacing between data characters or blocks may be of arbitrary duration, meaning the spacing is not standardized; therefore, frames require start and stop indicator flags.

- *Synchronous*: Data signals are sent along with a clock signal that occurs at evenly spaced time intervals. This is referred to as the *bit time*.

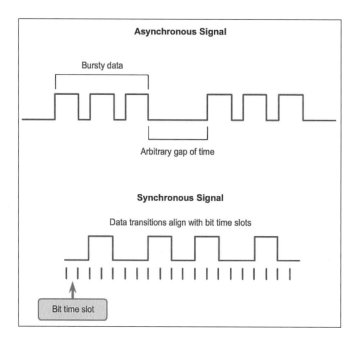

Figure 9-29 Asynchronous Signal and Synchronous Signal

There are many ways to transmit signals. A common method to send data is to use modulation techniques. *Modulation* is the process by which the characteristic of one wave (the signal) modifies another wave (the carrier). The following modulation techniques have been widely used in transmitting data on a medium:

- *Frequency modulation (FM)*: A method of transmission in which the carrier frequency varies in accordance with the signal.

- *Amplitude modulation (AM)*: A transmission technique in which the amplitude of the carrier varies in accordance with the signal.

■ *Pulse-coded modulation (PCM)*: A technique in which an analog signal, such as a voice, is converted into a digital signal by sampling the signal's amplitude and expressing the different amplitudes as a binary number. The sampling rate must be at least twice the highest frequency in the signal.

The nature of the actual signals representing the bits on the media will depend on the signaling method in use. Some methods may use one attribute of a signal to represent a single 0 and use another attribute of a signal to represent a single 1. Figure 9-30 illustrates how AM and FM techniques are used to send a signal.

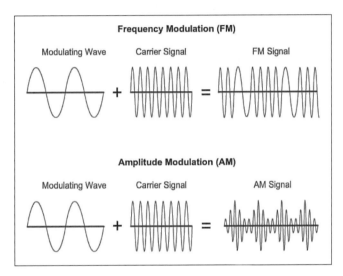

Figure 9-30   Comparing Frequency Modulation and Amplitude Modulation

Video 9.3.2.4 3 shows an example of amplitude modulation displayed on an oscilloscope.

Video

Video 9.3.2.4 3: Example of Amplitude Modulation

This video provides an example of amplitude modulation displayed on an oscilloscope. Go to the online course to view this video.

Bandwidth (9.3.2.5)

Different physical media support the transfer of bits at different speeds. Data transfer is usually discussed in terms of bandwidth and throughput.

Bandwidth is the capacity of a medium to carry data. Digital bandwidth measures the amount of data that can flow from one place to another in a given amount of time. Bandwidth is typically measured in kilobits per second (kbps) or megabits per second (Mbps).

The practical bandwidth of a network is determined by a combination of factors:

- The properties of the physical media

- The technologies chosen for signaling and detecting network signals

Physical media properties, current technologies, and the laws of physics play a role in determining available bandwidth.

Table 9-4 shows the commonly used units of measure for bandwidth.

Table 9-4   Bandwidth (FM)

Unit of Bandwidth	Abbreviation	Equivalence
Bits per second	bps	1 bps = fundamental unit of bandwidth
Kilobits per second	Kbps	1 Kbps = 1,000 bps = 10^3 bps
Megabits per second	Mbps	1 Mbps = 1,000,000 bps = 10^6 bps
Gigabits per second	Gbps	1 Gbps = 1,000,000,000 bps = 10^9 bps
Terabits per second	Tbps	1 Tbps = 1,000,000,000,000 bps = 10^12 bps

Throughput (9.3.2.6)

Throughput is the measure of the transfer of bits across the media over a given period of time.

Due to a number of factors, throughput usually does not match the specified bandwidth in physical layer implementations such as Ethernet. Many factors influence throughput, including

- The amount of traffic

- The type of traffic

- The latency created by the number of network devices encountered between source and destination

Latency refers to the amount of time for data to travel from one given point to another.

In a multi-access topology such as Ethernet, nodes are competing for media access and its use. Therefore, the throughput of each node is degraded as usage of the media increases.

In an internetwork or network with multiple segments, throughput cannot be faster than the slowest link of the path from source to destination. Even if all or most of the segments have high bandwidth, it will only take one segment in the path with low throughput to create a bottleneck to the throughput of the entire network.

There are many online speed tests that can reveal the throughput of an Internet connection. Figure 9-31 provides sample results from a speed test.

Figure 9-31   Speed Test

Note

There is a third measurement to measure the transfer of usable data that is known as *goodput*. Goodput is the measure of usable data transferred over a given period of time. Goodput is throughput minus traffic overhead for establishing sessions, acknowledgements, and encapsulation.

Interactive Graphic

Activity 9.3.2.7: Parts 1 and 2: Physical Layer Terminology

Go to the online course to perform this practice activity of identifying physical layer terminology.

Network Media (9.4)

This section looks at the different media types: copper cabling, UTP cabling, fiber-optic cabling, and wireless.

Copper Cabling (9.4.1)

The most popular type of network media is copper cable; this section takes a look at this media.

Characteristics of Copper Media (9.4.1.1)

Networks use copper media because it is inexpensive, easy to install, and has low resistance to electrical current. However, copper media is limited by distance and signal interference.

Data is transmitted on copper cables as electrical pulses. A detector in the network interface of a destination device must receive a signal that can be successfully decoded to match the signal sent. However, the longer the signal travels, the more it deteriorates in a phenomenon referred to as *signal attenuation*. For this reason, all copper media must follow strict distance limitations as specified by the guiding standards.

The timing and voltage values of the electrical pulses are also susceptible to interference from two sources:

- *Electromagnetic interference (EMI) and radio frequency interference (RFI)*: EMI and RFI signals can distort and corrupt the data signals being carried by copper media. Potential sources of EMI and RFI include radio waves and electromagnetic devices such as fluorescent lights or electric motors.

- *Crosstalk*: Crosstalk is a disturbance caused by the electric or magnetic fields of a signal on one wire affecting the signal in an adjacent wire. In telephone circuits, crosstalk can result in hearing part of another voice conversation from an adjacent circuit. Specifically, when electrical current flows through a wire, it creates a small, circular magnetic field around the wire that can be picked up by an adjacent wire.

Play Video 9.4.1.1 to see how data transmission can be affected by interference.

Video

Video 9.4.1.1: Data Transmission

This video shows how data transmission can be affected by interference. Go to the online course to view this animation.

To counter the negative effects of EMI and RFI, some types of copper cables are wrapped in metallic shielding and require proper grounding connections.

To counter the negative effects of crosstalk, some types of copper cables have opposing circuit wire pairs twisted together, which effectively cancels the crosstalk.

The susceptibility of copper cables to electronic noise can also be limited by

- Selecting the cable type or category most suited to a given networking environment

- Designing a cable infrastructure to avoid known and potential sources of interference in the building structure

- Using cabling techniques that include the proper handling and termination of the cables

Copper Media (9.4.1.2)

There are three main types of copper media used in networking (as shown in Figure 9-32):

- *Unshielded twisted-pair (UTP)* cable

- *Shielded twisted-pair (STP)* cable

- *Coaxial* cable

Unshielded Twisted-Pair (UTP) cable   Shielded Twisted-Pair (STP) cable

Coaxial cable

Figure 9-32 Copper Media

These cables are used to interconnect nodes on a LAN and infrastructure devices such as switches, routers, and wireless access points. Each type of connection and the accompanying devices have cabling requirements stipulated by physical layer standards.

Different physical layer standards specify the use of different connectors. These standards specify the mechanical dimensions of the connectors and the acceptable electrical properties of each type. Networking media use modular jacks and plugs to provide easy connection and disconnection. Also, a single type of physical connector may be used for multiple types of connections. For example, the RJ-45 connector is widely used in LANs with one type of media and in some WANs with another media type.

UTP Cable (9.4.1.3)

UTP cabling is the most common networking media. UTP cable, terminated with RJ-45 connectors, is used for interconnecting network hosts with intermediate networking devices, such as switches and routers.

In LANs, UTP cable consists of four pairs of color-coded wires that have been twisted together and then encased in a flexible plastic sheath that protects the wires from minor physical damage. The twisting of wires helps protect against signal interference from other wires.

As shown in Figure 9-33, the color codes identify the individual pairs and the wires in the pairs and aid in cable termination.

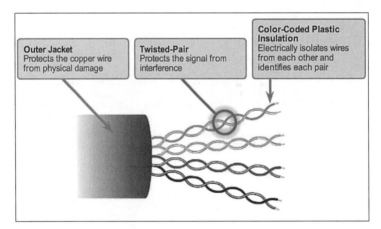

Figure 9-33   Unshielded Twisted-Pair Cable

STP Cable (9.4.1.4)

STP cable provides better noise protection than UTP cable. However, compared to UTP cable, STP cable is significantly more expensive and difficult to install. Like UTP cable, STP cable uses an RJ-45 connector.

STP cable combines the techniques of shielding (to counter EMI and RFI) and wire twisting (to counter crosstalk). To gain the full benefit of the shielding, STP cables are terminated with special shielded STP data connectors. If the cable is improperly grounded, the shield may act like an antenna and pick up unwanted signals.

Different types of STP cables with different characteristics are available. However, there are two common variations of STP:

- STP cable shields the entire bundle of wires with foil, eliminating virtually all interference (more common).

- STP cable shields the entire bundle of wires and the individual wire pairs with foil, eliminating all interference.

The STP cable shown in Figure 9-34 uses four pairs of wires, each wrapped in a foil shield, which are then wrapped in an overall metallic braid or foil.

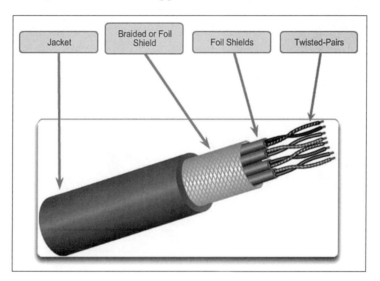

Figure 9-34   Shielded Twisted-Pair Cable

For many years, STP was the cabling structure specified for use in Token Ring network installations. With the decline of Token Ring, the demand for STP cabling also waned. However, the new 10 GB standard for Ethernet has a provision for the use of STP cabling, which is providing a renewed interest in STP cabling.

Coaxial Cable (9.4.1.5)

Coaxial cable, or *coax* for short, gets its name from the fact that there are two conductors that share the same axis. As shown in Figure 9-35, the structure of coaxial cable is as follows:

- A copper conductor is used to transmit the electronic signals.

- The copper conductor is surrounded by a layer of flexible plastic insulation.

- The insulating material is surrounded in a woven copper braid, or metallic foil, that acts as the second wire in the circuit and as a shield for the inner conductor. This second layer, or shield, also reduces the amount of outside electromagnetic interference.

- The entire cable is covered with a cable jacket to protect it from minor physical damage.

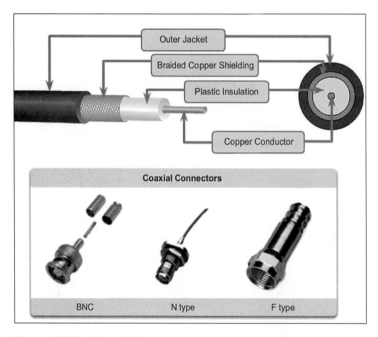

Figure 9-35   Coax Cable

Note

There are different types of connectors used with coax cable.

Coaxial cable was traditionally used in cable television capable of transmitting in one direction. It was also used extensively in early Ethernet installations.

Although UTP cable has essentially replaced coaxial cable in modern Ethernet installations, the coaxial cable design has been adapted for use in

- **Wireless installations:** Coaxial cables attach antennas to wireless devices. The coaxial cable carries radio frequency (RF) energy between the antennas and the radio equipment.

- **Cable Internet installations:** Cable service providers are currently converting their one-way systems to two-way systems to provide Internet connectivity to their customers. To provide these services, portions of the coaxial cable and supporting amplification elements are replaced with fiber-optic cable. However, the final connection to the customer's location and the wiring inside the customer's premises is still coax cable. This combined use of fiber and coax is referred to as hybrid fiber-coax (HFC).

Copper Media Safety (9.4.1.6)

All three types of copper media are susceptible to fire and electrical hazards.

Fire hazards exist because cable insulation and sheaths may be flammable or produce toxic fumes when heated or burned. Building authorities or organizations may stipulate related safety standards for cabling and hardware installations (for example, plenum cable).

Electrical hazards are a potential problem because the copper wires could conduct electricity in undesirable ways. This could subject personnel and equipment to a range of electrical hazards. For example, a defective network device could conduct currents to the chassis of other network devices. Additionally, network cabling could present undesirable voltage levels when used to connect devices that have power sources with different ground potentials. Such situations are possible when copper cabling is used to connect networks in different buildings or on different floors of buildings that use different power facilities. Finally, copper cabling may conduct voltages caused by lightning strikes to network devices.

The result of undesirable voltages and currents can include damage to network devices and connected computers, or injury to personnel. It is important that copper cabling be installed appropriately, and according to the relevant specifications and building codes, in order to avoid potentially dangerous and damaging situations. Figure 9-36 displays proper cabling practices to avoid potential fire and electrical hazards.

Interactive Graphic

Activity 9.4.1.7: Copper Media Characteristics

Go to the online course to perform the practice activity of identifying copper media characteristics.

The separation of data and electrical power cabling must comply with safety codes.

Cables must be connected correctly.

Installations must be inspected for damage.

Equipment must be grounded correctly.

Figure 9-36   Copper Media Safety

UTP Cabling (9.4.2)

Unshielded twisted-pair (UTP) cabling is the most common networking media and thus is discussed in depth in this section.

Properties of UTP Cabling (9.4.2.1)

When used as a networking medium, UTP cabling consists of four pairs of color-coded wires that have been twisted together and then encased in a flexible plastic sheath. Network UTP cable has four pairs of either 22- or 24-gauge copper wire. A UTP cable has an external diameter of approximately 0.43 cm (0.17 inch), and its small size can be advantageous during installation.

UTP cable does not use shielding to counter the effects of EMI and RFI. Instead, cable designers have discovered that they can limit the negative effect of crosstalk by using these techniques:

- **Cancellation:** Designers now pair wires in a circuit. When two wires in an electrical circuit are placed close together, their magnetic fields are the exact opposite of each other. Therefore, the two magnetic fields cancel each other out and also cancel out any outside EMI and RFI signals.

- **Varying the number of twists per wire pair:** To further enhance the cancellation effect of paired circuit wires, designers vary the number of twists of each wire pair in a cable. UTP cable must follow precise specifications governing how many twists or braids are permitted per meter (3.28 feet) of cable. Notice in Figure 9-37 that the orange/orange white pair (shown at the bottom of the figure) is twisted less than the blue/white blue pair (shown as the second pair from the bottom). Each colored pair is twisted a different number of times.

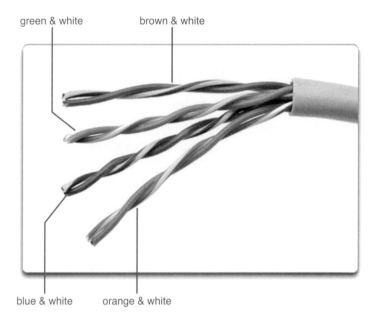

Figure 9-37   Varying the Number of Twists per Wire Pair

UTP cable relies solely on the cancellation effect produced by the twisted wire pairs to limit signal degradation and effectively provide self-shielding for wire pairs within the network media.

UTP Cabling Standards (9.4.2.2)

UTP cabling conforms to the standards established jointly by the TIA and EIA. Specifically, TIA/EIA-568A stipulates the commercial cabling standards for LAN installations and is the standard most commonly used in LAN cabling environments. Some of the elements defined are

- Cable types
- Cable lengths
- Connectors
- Cable termination
- Methods of testing cable

The electrical characteristics of copper cabling are defined by the IEEE. IEEE rates UTP cabling according to its performance. Cables are placed into categories according to their ability to carry bandwidth rates. For example, Category 5 (Cat5) cable is used commonly in 100BASE-TX Fast Ethernet installations. Other categories include Enhanced Category 5 (Cat5e) cable, Category 6 (Cat6), and Category 6a.

Cables in higher categories are designed and constructed to support higher data rates. As new gigabit-speed Ethernet technologies are being developed and adopted, Cat5e is now the minimally acceptable cable type, with Cat6 being the recommended type for new building installations.

Interactive Graphic

Activity 9.4.2.2: Categories of UTP Cabling

Go to the online course to perform the UTP cabling identification practice activity.

Note

Some manufacturers are making cables that exceed the TIA/EIA Category 6a specifications and are referring to these as Category 7.

UTP Connectors (9.4.2.3)

UTP cable is usually terminated with an ISO 8877 specified RJ-45 connector. This connector is used for a range of physical layer specifications, one of which is Ethernet. The TIA/EIA-568 standard describes the wire color codes to pin assignments (pinouts) for Ethernet cables.

Video 9.4.2.3 displays a UTP cable terminated with an RJ-45 connector.

Video

Video 9.4.2.3 Part 1: UTP Cable Termination

This video shows how a UTP cable is terminated with an RJ45 connector. Go to the online course to view this video.

As shown in Figure 9-38, the RJ-45 connector is the male component, crimped at the end of the cable. The socket is the female component in a network device, wall, cubicle partition outlet, or patch panel.

Each time copper cabling is terminated, there is the possibility of signal loss and the introduction of noise to the communication circuit. When terminated improperly, each cable is a potential source of physical layer performance degradation. It is essential that all copper media terminations be of high quality to ensure optimum performance with current and future network technologies.

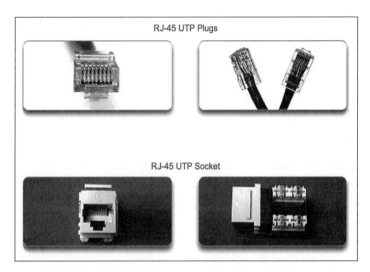

Figure 9-38   RJ-45 UTP Plugs and Socket

Figure 9-39 displays examples of a badly terminated UTP cable and a well-terminated UTP cable.

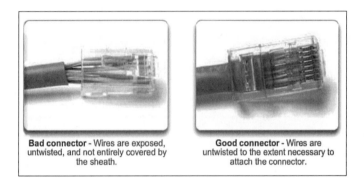

Figure 9-39   Examples of Termination

Types of UTP Cable (9.4.2.4)

Different situations may require UTP cables to be wired according to different wiring conventions. This means that the individual wires in the cable have to be connected in different orders to different sets of pins in the RJ-45 connectors.

The following are main cable types that are obtained by using specific wiring conventions:

- *Ethernet straight-through* **cable:** The most common type of networking cable. It is commonly used to interconnect a host to a switch and a switch to a router.

- *Ethernet crossover* **cable:** An uncommon cable used to interconnect similar devices together (for example, a switch to a switch, a host to a host, or a router to a router).

■ *Rollover* **cable:** A Cisco proprietary cable used to connect to a router or switch console port.

Using a crossover or straight-through cable incorrectly between devices may not damage the devices, but connectivity and communication between the devices will not take place. This is a common error in the lab, and checking that the device connections are correct should be the first troubleshooting action if connectivity is not achieved.

Figure 9-40 shows the UTP cable type, related standards, and typical application of these cables. It also identifies the individual wire pairs for the TIA-568A and TIA-568B standards.

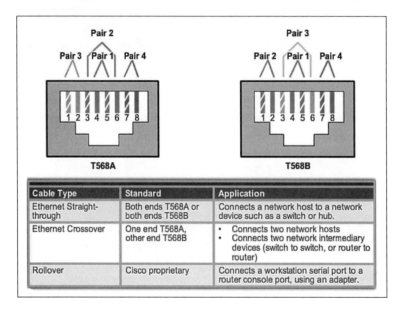

Cable Type	Standard	Application
Ethernet Straight-through	Both ends T568A or both ends T568B	Connects a network host to a network device such as a switch or hub.
Ethernet Crossover	One end T568A, other end T568B	• Connects two network hosts • Connects two network intermediary devices (switch to switch, or router to router)
Rollover	Cisco proprietary	Connects a workstation serial port to a router console port, using an adapter.

Figure 9-40   UTP Cable Standards

LAN Cabling Areas (9.4.2.5)

As shown in Figure 9-41, the TIA/EIA-568 standard divides the LAN cabling distribution system into the following sections:

■ *Work area*: Consists of the communication outlets (wall boxes and faceplates), wiring, and connectors needed to connect network hosts using the horizontal wiring subsystem to the telecommunications room. The standard requires that two outlets be provided at each wall plate: one for voice and one for data.

■ *Horizontal cabling*: The cabling run from each outlet to the equipment room. The maximum horizontal distance is 90 meters (295 feet) independent of media type. An additional 6 meters (20 feet) is allowed for patch cables at the tele-communications room and at the workstation, but the combined length cannot exceed 10 meters (33 feet).

- *Telecommunications room*: Sometimes referred to as the wiring closet, it provides an endpoint for horizontal cabling and backbone cabling. Typically contains patch panels and infrastructure devices such as switches and routers. Multiple telecommunications rooms exist in large organizations and connect to a central equipment room using backbone cabling.

- *Backbone cabling*: The backbone wiring runs up through the floors of the building (risers) or across a campus and provides the interconnection between the equipment room and telecommunications room. The distance limitations of this cabling depend on the type of cable and facilities it connects, but the popu-lar cabling consists of optical fiber cables.

- *Central equipment room:* Sometimes referred to as the network operation cen-ter (NOC), this room provides the endpoint for all backbone cabling and may contain enterprise-class switches, routers, firewall appliances, servers, and access to the provider entrance facility.

- *Entrance facility*: This contains the service provider telecommunications service entrance to the building. This facility may also contain campus-wide backbone connections. This area also defines the network demarcation point, which is the interconnection to the local exchange carrier's telecommunications facilities. The demarcation point forms the boundary between the part of the network that is the responsibility of the organization and the part of the network that is the responsibility of the carrier.

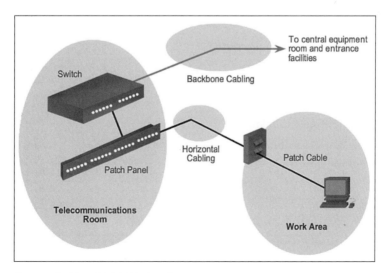

Figure 9-41   UTP LAN Cabling Distribution

Testing UTP Cables (9.4.2.6)

After installation, a UTP cable tester, as shown in Figure 9-42, should be used to test for the following parameters:

- Wire map
- Cable length
- Signal loss due to attenuation
- Crosstalk

It is recommended that you thoroughly check that all UTP installation requirements are met.

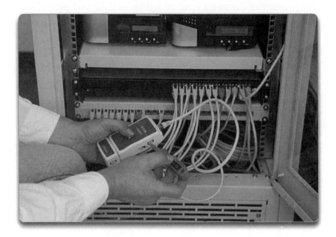

Figure 9-42   Testing Cable

Activity 9.4.2.7: Cable Pinouts

Go to the online course to perform the cable build practice activity.

Lab 9.4.2.8: UTP Cabling

In this lab, you will complete the following objectives:

- Part 1: Analyze Ethernet Cabling Standards and Pinouts
- Part 2: Build an Ethernet Crossover Cable
- Part 3: Test an Ethernet Crossover Cable

Fiber Optic Cabling (9.4.3)

Fiber Optic Cabling is gaining in popularity as a media for network application. There are various reasons for this discussed in this section.

Properties of Fiber Optic Cabling (9.4.3.1)

Optical fiber cable has become very popular for interconnecting infrastructure network devices.

Optical fiber is a flexible but extremely thin transparent strand of very pure glass (silica) not much bigger than a human hair. Bits are encoded on the fiber as light impulses. The fiber-optic cable acts as a waveguide, or "light pipe," to transmit light between the two ends with minimal loss of signal.

As an analogy, consider an empty paper towel roll with the inside coated like a mirror that is a thousand meters in length and a small laser pointer is used to send Morse code signals at the speed of light. The signals bounce from the mirrored surface of the tube, traveling the entire distance of the tube. Essentially that is how a fiber-optic cable operates, except that it is smaller in diameter and uses sophisticated light emitting and receiving technologies.

Unlike copper wires, fiber-optic cable can transmit signals with less attenuation and is completely immune to EMI and RFI.

Fiber-optic cabling is now being used in four types of industry:

- *Enterprise networks*: Fiber is used for backbone cabling applications and interconnecting infrastructure devices.

- *FTTH and access networks*: Fiber to the home (FTTH) is used to provide always-on broadband services to homes and small businesses. FTTH supports affordable high-speed Internet access, as well as telecommuting, telemedicine, and video on demand.

- *Long-Haul networks*: Service providers use long-haul terrestrial optical fiber networks to connect countries and cities. Networks typically range from a few dozen to a few thousand kilometers and use up to 10-Gbps-based systems.

- *Submarine networks*: Special fiber cables are used to provide reliable high-speed, high-capacity solutions capable of surviving in harsh undersea environments up to transoceanic distances.

Our focus is the use of fiber within the enterprise.

Fiber Media Cable Design (9.4.3.2)

Although an optical fiber is very thin, it is composed of two kinds of glass and a protective outer shield. Specifically, these are the

- **Core:** Consists of pure glass and is the part of the fiber where light is carried.

- **Cladding:** The glass that surrounds the core and acts as a mirror. The light pulses propagate down the core while the cladding reflects the light pulses. This keeps the light pulses contained in the fiber core in a phenomenon known as *total internal reflection*.

- **Jacket:** Typically a PVC jacket that protects the core and cladding. It may also include strengthening materials and a buffer (coating) whose purpose is to protect the glass from scratches and moisture.

Although susceptible to sharp bends, the properties of the core and cladding have been altered at the molecular level to make them very strong. Optical fiber is proof tested through a rigorous manufacturing process for strength at a minimum of 100,000 pounds per square inch. Optical fiber is durable enough to withstand handling during installation and deployment in harsh environmental conditions in networks all around the world.

Interactive Graphic

Activity 9.4.3.2: Fiber Cable

Go to the online course to perform the fiber cable identification practice activity.

Types of Fiber Media (9.4.3.3)

Light pulses representing the transmitted data as bits on the media are generated by either lasers or light emitting diodes (LEDs).

Electronic semiconductor devices called photodiodes detect the light pulses and convert them to voltages that can then be reconstructed into data frames.

Note

The laser light transmitted over fiber-optic cabling can damage the human eye. Care must be taken to avoid looking into the end of an active optical fiber.

Fiber-optic cables can be broadly classified into two types:

- *Single-mode fiber (SMF)*: Consists of a very small core and uses expensive laser technology to send a single ray of light. SMF is popular in long-distance situations spanning hundreds of kilometers such as those required in long-haul telephony and cable TV applications.

- *Multimode fiber (MMF)*: Consists of a larger core and uses LED emitters to send light pulses. Specifically, light from an LED enters the multimode fiber at different angles. MMF is popular in LANs because they can be powered by low-cost LEDs. It provides bandwidth up to 10 Gbps over link lengths of up to 550 meters.

Figures 9-43 and 9-44 highlight the characteristics of single-mode fiber and multimode fiber, respectively. One of the highlighted differences between SMF and MMF is the amount of *dispersion*, which refers to the spreading out of a light pulse over time and distance. The more dispersion there is, the greater the loss in signal strength.

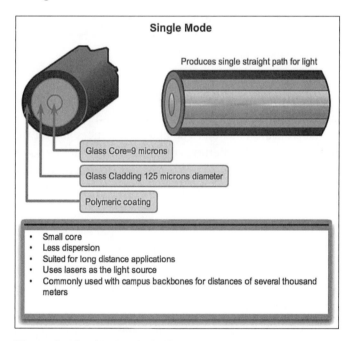

Figure 9-43 Single-Mode Fiber

Multimode

Allows multiple paths for light

Glass Core=50/62.5 microns

Glass Cladding 125 microns diameter

Coating

- Larger core than single mode cable
- Allows greater dispersion and therefore, loss of signal
- Suited for long-distance applications, but shorter than single mode
- Uses LEDs as the light source
- Commonly used with LANs or distances of a couple hundred meters within a campus network

Figure 9-44   Multimode Fiber

Network Fiber Connectors (9.4.3.4)

An optical fiber connector terminates the end of an optical fiber. A variety of optical fiber connectors are available. The main differences among the types of connectors are dimensions and methods of mechanical coupling. Generally, organizations standardize on one kind of connector, depending on the equipment that they commonly use, or they standardize per type of fiber (one for MMF, one for SMF). Taking into account all the generations of connectors, about 70 connector types are in use today.

As shown in Figure 9-45, the three most popular network fiber-optic connectors include

- *Straight-tip (ST) connector*: An older, bayonet-style connector widely used with multimode fiber.

- *Subscriber connector (SC)*: Sometimes referred to as square connector or standard connector, it is a widely adopted LAN and WAN connector that uses a push-pull mechanism to ensure positive insertion. This connector type is used with MMF and SMF.

- *Lucent connector (LC)*: Sometimes called a little connector or local connector, it is quickly growing in popularity due to its smaller size. It is used with SMF and also supports MMF.

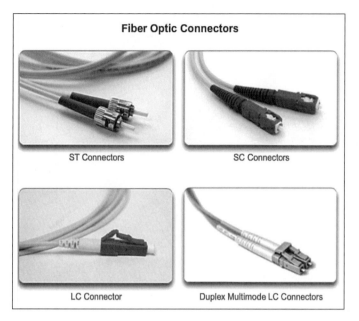

Figure 9-45 Fiber-Optic Connectors

> **Note**
>
> Other fiber connectors such as the ferrule connector (FC) and sub-miniature A (SMA) are not popular in LAN and WAN deployments. Obsolete connectors include biconic and D4 connectors. These connectors are beyond the scope of this chapter.

Because light can only travel in one direction over optical fiber, two fibers are required to support full-duplex operation. Therefore, fiber-optic patch cables bundle together two optical fiber cables and terminate them with a pair of standard single-fiber connectors. Some fiber connectors accept both the transmitting and receiving fibers in a single connector, known as a *duplex connector* (also shown in Figure 9-45).

Fiber patch cords are required for interconnecting infrastructure devices. For example, Figure 9-46 displays the following common patch cords:

- SC-SC multimode patch cord

- LC-LC single-mode patch cord

- ST-LC multimode patch cord

- SC-ST single-mode patch cord

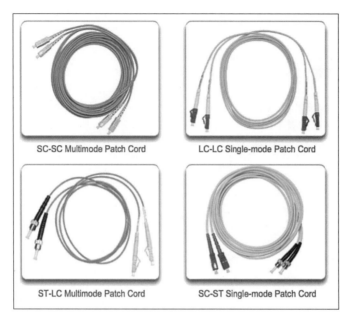

Figure 9-46 Common Fiber Patch Cords

Fiber cables should be protected with a small plastic cap when not in use. Also notice the use of color to distinguish between single-mode and multimode patch cords. The TIA-598 standard recommends the use of a yellow jacket for single-mode fiber cables and an orange (or aqua) jacket for multimode fiber cables.

Testing Fiber Cables (9.4.3.5)

Terminating and splicing fiber-optic cabling requires special training and equipment. Incorrect termination of fiber-optic media will result in diminished signaling distances or complete transmission failure.

Three common types of fiber-optic termination and splicing errors are

- *Misalignment*: The fiber-optic media are not precisely aligned to one another when joined.

- *End gap*: The media does not completely touch at the splice or connection.

- *End finish*: The media ends are not well polished or dirt is present at the termination.

A quick and easy field test can be performed by shining a bright flashlight into one end of the fiber while observing the other end of the fiber. If light is visible, then the fiber is capable of passing light. Although this does not ensure the performance of the fiber, it is a quick and inexpensive way to find a broken fiber.

It is recommended that an optical tester such as what's shown in Figure 9-47 be used to test fiber-optic cables. An optical time-domain reflectometer (OTDR) can be used to test each fiber-optic cable segment. This device injects a test pulse of light into the cable and measures scatter and reflection of light detected as a function of time. The OTDR will calculate the approximate distance at which these faults are detected along the length of the cable.

Figure 9-47   Optical Time-Domain Reflectometer

Fiber Versus Copper (9.4.3.6)

There are many advantages to using fiber-optic cable instead of copper cable. Given that the fibers used in fiber-optic media are not electrical conductors, the media is immune to EMI and will not conduct unwanted electrical currents due to grounding issues. Because optical fibers are thin and have relatively low signal loss, they can be operated at much greater lengths than copper media, without the need for signal regeneration. Some optical fiber physical layer specifications allow lengths that can reach multiple kilometers.

Optical fiber media implementation issues include

- More expensive than copper media over the same distance

- Requires different skills and equipment to terminate and splice the cable infrastructure

- Requires more careful handling than copper media

At present, in most enterprise environments, optical fiber is primarily used as backbone cabling for high-traffic point-to-point connections between data distribution facilities and for the interconnection of buildings in multi-building campuses. Because optical fiber does not conduct electricity and has low signal loss, it is well suited for these uses.

Table 9-5 highlights some of the differences between fiber-optic cabling and copper cabling.

Table 9-5 Fiber Versus Copper

Implementation Issues	UTP Cabling	Fiber-optic Cabling
Bandwidth supported	10 Mbps–100 Gbps	10 Mbps–100 Gbps
Distance	Relatively short (1–100 meters)	Relatively high (1–1000.000 meters)
Immunity to EMI and RFI	Low	High (completely immune)
Immunity to electrical hazards	Low	High (completely immune)
Media and connector costs	Lowest	Highest
Installation skills required	Lowest	Highest
Safety precautions	Lowest	Highest

Interactive Graphic

Activity 9.4.3.7: Fiber-optics Terminology

Go to the online course to perform the fiber-optic media identification practice activity.

Wireless Media (9.4.4)

The use of radio waves (wireless connectivity) is becoming more popular. This section discusses the use of wireless media to access networks.

Properties of Wireless Media (9.4.4.1)

Wireless media carry electromagnetic signals that represent the binary digits of data communications using radio or microwave frequencies.

As a networking medium, wireless is not restricted to conductors or pathways, as are copper and fiber media. Wireless media provides the greatest mobility options of all media. As well, the number of wireless-enabled devices is continuously increasing. For these reasons, wireless has become the medium of choice for home networks. As network bandwidth options increase, wireless is quickly gaining in popularity in enterprise networks.

Figure 9-48 highlights various wireless-related symbols.

Figure 9-48   Wireless Media Symbols

However, wireless does have some areas of concern, including the following:

- **Coverage area:** Wireless data communication technologies work well in open environments. However, certain construction materials used in buildings and structures can limit the effective coverage, as can the local terrain.

- **Interference:** Wireless is susceptible to interference and can be disrupted by such common devices as household cordless phones, some types of fluorescent lights, microwave ovens, and other wireless communications.

- **Security:** Wireless communication coverage requires no access to a physical strand of media. Therefore, devices and users who are not authorized for access to the network can gain access to the transmission. Consequently, network security is a major component of wireless network administration.

Although wireless is increasing in popularity for desktop connectivity, copper and fiber are the most popular physical layer media for enterprise network deployments.

Types of Wireless Media (9.4.4.2)

The IEEE and telecommunications industry standards for wireless data communications cover both the data link and physical layers.

As shown in Figure 9-49, three common data communications standards apply to wireless media:

- *IEEE 802.11*: Wireless LAN (WLAN) technology, commonly referred to as Wi-Fi, uses a contention or non-deterministic system with a CSMA/CA media access process.

- *IEEE 802.15*: Wireless Personal Area Network (WPAN) standard, commonly known as Bluetooth, uses a device-pairing process to communicate over distances from 1 to 100 meters.

- *IEEE 802.16*: Commonly known as Worldwide Interoperability for Microwave Access (WiMAX), uses a point-to-multipoint topology to provide wireless broadband access.

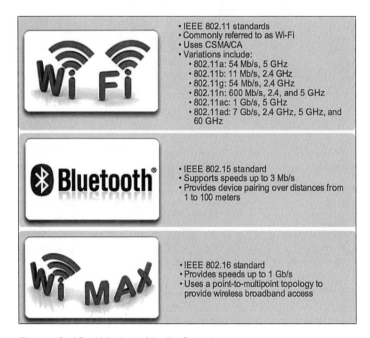

Figure 9-49   Wireless Media Standards

Note

Other wireless technologies such as cellular and satellite communications can also provide data network connectivity. However, these wireless technologies are out of scope for this chapter.

In each of the examples shown in Figure 9-49, physical layer specifications are applied to areas that include

- Data to radio signal encoding

- Frequency and power of transmission

- Signal reception and decoding requirements
- Antenna design and construction

Note

Wi-Fi is a trademark of the Wi-Fi Alliance. Wi-Fi is used with certified products that belong to WLAN devices that are based on the IEEE 802.11 standards.

Wireless LAN (9.4.4.3)

A common wireless data implementation is to enable devices to wirelessly connect via a LAN. In general, a wireless LAN requires the following network devices:

- *Wireless Access Point (AP)*: Concentrates the wireless signals from users and connects, usually through a copper cable, to the existing copper-based network infrastructure, such as Ethernet. Home and small business wireless routers integrate the functions of a router, switch, and access point into one device, as shown in Figure 9-50.

- *Wireless NIC adapters*: Provides wireless communication capability to each network host.

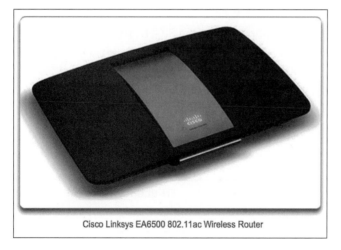

Cisco Linksys EA6500 802.11ac Wireless Router

Figure 9-50   Wireless Access Point

As the technology has developed, a number of WLAN Ethernet-based standards have emerged. Care needs to be taken in purchasing wireless devices to ensure compatibility and interoperability.

The benefits of wireless data communications technologies are evident, especially the savings on costly premises wiring and the convenience of host mobility.

However, network administrators need to develop and apply stringent security policies and processes to protect wireless LANs from unauthorized access and damage.

802.11 Wi-Fi Standards (9.4.4.4)

Various 802.11 standards have evolved over the years. Standards include the following:

- **IEEE 802.11a:** Operates in the 5 GHz frequency band and offers speeds of up to 54 Mbps. Because this standard operates at higher frequencies, it has a smaller coverage area and is less effective at penetrating building structures. Devices operating under this standard are not interoperable with the 802.11b and 802.11g standards described next.

- **IEEE 802.11b:** Operates in the 2.4 GHz frequency band and offers speeds of up to 11 Mbps. Devices implementing this standard have a longer range and are better able to penetrate building structures than devices based on 802.11a.

- **IEEE 802.11g:** Operates in the 2.4 GHz frequency band and offers speeds of up to 54 Mbps. Devices implementing this standard therefore operate at the same radio frequency and range as 802.11b but with the bandwidth of 802.11a.

- **IEEE 802.11n:** Operates in the 2.4 GHz or 5 GHz frequency bands. The typical expected data rates are 100 Mbps to 600 Mbps with a distance range of up to 70 meters. It is backward compatible with 802.11a/b/g devices.

- **IEEE 802.11ac:** Operates in the 5 GHZ frequency band, providing data rates up to 450 Mbps and 1.3 Gbps (1300 Mbps.) It is backward compatible with 802.11a/b/g/n devices.

- **IEEE 802.11ad:** Also known as WiGig, it uses a tri-band Wi-Fi solution using 2.4 GHz, 5 GHz, and 60 GHz and offers theoretical speeds of up to 7 Gbps.

Table 9-6 highlights some of these differences in the 802.11 Wi-Fi standards.

Table 9-6   Differences in 802.11 Wi-Fi Standards

Standard	Maximum Speed	Frequency	Backward Compatible
802.11a	54 Mbps	5 GHZ	No
802.11b	11 Mbps	2.4 GHZ	No
802.11g	54 Mbps	2.4 GHZ	802.11b
802.11n	600 Mbps	2.4 GHz or 5 GHz	802.11a/b/g
802.11ac	1.3 Gbps (1300 Mbps)	5 GHz	802.11a/n
802.11ad	7 Gbps (7000 Mbps)	60 GHz	No

Packet Tracer Activity 9.4.4.5: Connecting a Wired and Wireless LAN

When working in Packet Tracer (a lab environment or a corporate setting), you should know how to select the appropriate cable and how to properly connect devices. This activity will examine device configurations in Packet Tracer, selecting the proper cable based on the configuration, and connecting the devices. This activity will also explore the physical view of the network in Packet Tracer.

Lab 9.4.4.6: Viewing Wired and Wireless NIC Information

In this lab, you will complete the following objectives:

- Part 1: Identify and Work with PC NICs
- Part 2: Identify and Use the System Tray Network Icons

Summary (9.5)

 Class Activity 9.5.1.1: Linked In!

Go to the online course to perform this practice activity of designing a network.

Note

This activity is best completed in groups of two to three students.

Your small business is moving to a new location! Your building is brand new, and you have been tasked to come up with a physical model so that network port installation can begin.

Use the blueprint provided for this activity (your instructor will provide you with a copy from the *Instructor Planning Guide*)—the area indicated by Number 1 is the reception area, and the area labeled RR is the restroom area.

All rooms are within Category 6, UTP specifications (100 meters), so you have no worries about hard-wiring the building to code. Each room in the diagram must have at least one network connection available for users/intermediary devices.

With your teammate(s), indicate the following on the drawing:

- The location of your network main distribution facility, while keeping security in mind

- The number of intermediary devices that you would use and where you would place them

- The type of cabling that would be used (UTP, STP, wireless, fiber optics, etc.) and where the ports would be placed

- The types of end devices that would be used (wired, wireless, laptops, desktops, tablets, etc.).

Do not go "overboard" on your design—just use the content from the chapter to be able to justify your decisions to the class.

The TCP/IP network access layer is the equivalent of the OSI data link layer (Layer 2) and the physical layer (Layer 1).

The data link layer is responsible for the exchange of frames between nodes over a physical network media. It allows the upper layers to access the media and controls how data is placed and received on the media.

Among the different implementations of the data link layer protocols, there are different methods of controlling access to the media. These media access control techniques define if and how the nodes share the media. The actual media access control method used depends on the topology and media sharing. LAN and WAN topologies can be physical or logical. It is the logical topology that influences the type of network framing and media access control used. WANs are commonly interconnected using the point-to-point, hub and spoke, or mesh physical topologies. In shared media LANs, end devices can be interconnected using the star, bus, ring, or extended star (hybrid) physical topologies.

All data link layer protocols encapsulate the Layer 3 PDU within the Data field of the frame. However, the structure of the frame and the fields contained in the header and trailer vary according to the protocol.

The OSI physical layer provides the means to transport across the network media the bits that make up a data link layer frame. The physical components are the electronic hardware devices, media, and other connectors that transmit and carry the signals to represent the bits. Hardware components such as network adapters (NICs), interfaces and connectors, cable materials, and cable designs are all specified in standards associated with the physical layer. The physical layer standards address three functional areas: physical components, frame encoding technique, and signaling method.

Using the proper media is an important part of network communications. Without the proper physical connection, either wired or wireless, communications between any two devices will not occur.

Wired communication consists of copper media and fiber cable:

- Three main types of copper media are used in networking: UTP, STP, and coaxial cable. UTP cabling is the most common copper networking media.

- Optical fiber cable has become very popular for interconnecting infrastructure network devices. It permits the transmission of data over longer distances and at higher bandwidths (data rates) than any other networking media. Unlike copper wires, fiber-optic cable can transmit signals with less attenuation and is completely immune to EMI and RFI.

Wireless media carry electromagnetic signals that represent the binary digits of data communications using radio or microwave frequencies.

The number of wireless-enabled devices continues to increase. For these reasons, wireless has become the medium of choice for home networks and is quickly gaining in popularity in enterprise networks.

Figure 9-51 shows a typical end-to-end communication path.

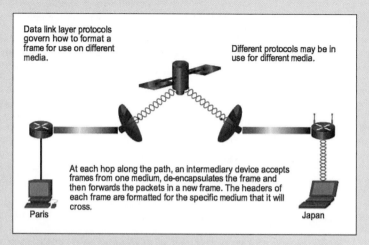

Data link layer protocols govern how to format a frame for use on different media.

Different protocols may be in use for different media.

At each hop along the path, an intermediary device accepts frames from one medium, de-encapsulates the frame and then forwards the packets in a new frame. The headers of each frame are formatted for the specific medium that it will cross.

Paris

Japan

Figure 9-51   End-to-End Communication Path

Practice

The following activities provide practice with the topics introduced in this chapter. The Labs and Class Activities are available in the companion *Network Basics Lab Manual* (978-1-58713-313-8). The Packet Tracer Activities PKA files are found in the online course.

Class Activities

Class Activity 9.0.1.2: Managing the Medium

Class Activity 9.5.1.1: Linked In!

Labs

Lab 9.3.1.4: Identifying Network Devices and Cabling

Lab 9.4.2.8: UTP Cabling

Lab 9.4.4.6: Viewing Wired and Wireless NIC Information

Packet Tracer Activity

Packet Tracer Activity 9.4.4.5: Connecting a Wired and Wireless LAN

Check Your Understanding

Complete all the review questions listed here to test your understanding of the topics and concepts in this chapter. The appendix, "Answers to the 'Check Your Understanding' Questions," lists the answers.

1. Which two statements describe the services provided by the data link layer? (Choose two.)

   A. It defines the end-to-end delivery addressing scheme.

   B. It maintains the path between the source and destination devices during the data transmission.

   C. It manages the access of frames to the network media.

   D. It provides reliable delivery through link establishment and flow control.

   E. It ensures that application data will be transmitted according to the prioritization.

   F. It packages various Layer 3 PDUs into a frame format that is compatible with the network interface.

2. Match each field of a frame to its content. The fields are not in the correct sequence. (Not all options are used.)

A. Addressing	Data reordering
B. Control	Payload
C. Data	Physical addresses
D. Frame Check Sequence	Flow control services
E. Frame Start	Logical addresses
F. Frame Stop	Error detection
G. Type	Beginning of the frame
	End of the frame
	Layer 3 protocol

3. Which two engineering organizations define open standards and protocols that apply to the data link layer? (Choose two.)

   A. International Organization for Standardization (ISO)

   B. Internet Assigned Numbers Authority (IANA)

   C. International Telecommunication Union (ITU)

   D. Electronic Industries Alliance (EIA)

   E. Internet Society (ISOC)

4. An enterprise has four branches. The headquarters needs full connectivity to all branches. The branches do not need to be connected directly to each other. Which WAN topology is most suitable?

   A. Bus

   B. Full mesh

   C. Hub and spoke

   D. Mesh

   E. Point-to-point

5. What is a characteristic of CSMA/CA that differs from CSMA/CD?

   A. CSMA/CA is suitable for networks with Token Ring topology.

   B. An end device sends a notification across the media before it sends a data frame.

   C. No collisions can exist within a local CSMA/CA network.

   D. CSMA/CA is a deterministic access method that controls use of the network.

6. What are three characteristics of valid Ethernet Layer 2 addresses? (Choose three.)

   A. They are 48 binary bits in length.

   B. They are considered physical addresses.

   C. They are generally represented in hexadecimal format.

   D. They consist of four 8-bit octets of binary numbers.

   E. They are used to determine the data path through the network.

   F. They must be changed when an Ethernet device is added or moved within the network.

7. What is the purpose of the OSI physical layer?

   A. Controlling access to media

   B. Transmitting bits across the local media

   C. Performing error detection on received frames

   D. Exchanging frames between nodes over physical network media

8. What is a characteristic of a frame encoding technique related to fiber-optic cable?

    A. Direct-sequence spread spectrum (DSSS)

    B. Non-Return to Zero (NRZ)

    C. Orthogonal frequency-division multiplexing (OFDM)

    D. Wavelength multiplexing

9. With the use of unshielded twisted-pair copper wire in a network, what causes crosstalk within the cable pairs?

    A. The magnetic field around the adjacent pairs of wire

    B. The use of braided wire to shield the adjacent wire pairs

    C. The reflection of the electrical wave back from the far end of the cable

    D. The collision caused by two nodes trying to use the media simultaneously

10. What is Wi-Fi?

    A. A WPAN standard that is used to communicate over distances from 1 to 100 meters

    B. A point-to-multipoint topology that uses a deterministic system to provide access to the media

    C. A technology based on the IEEE 802.16 standards

    D. A WLAN technology that uses a contention system with a CSMA/CA media access process

Objectives

Upon completion of this chapter, you will be able to answer the following questions:

- How would you describe the operation of the Ethernet sublayers?

- What are the major fields of the Ethernet frame?

- What is the purpose and characteristics of the Ethernet MAC address?

- What are the roles of the MAC address and the IP address?

- What is the purpose of ARP?

- How do ARP requests affect network and host performance?

- What are the basic switching concepts?

- What are the differences between fixed configuration switches and modular configuration switches?

- How do you configure a Layer 3 switch?

Key Terms

This chapter uses the following key terms. You can find the definitions in the Glossary.

Introduction (10.0.1.1)

Up to this point in the course, each chapter has focused on the different functions of each layer of the OSI and TCP/IP protocol models as well as how protocols are used to support network communication. TCP, UDP, and IP are repeatedly referenced in these discussions. These protocols provide the foundation for the way that the smallest of networks to the largest, the Internet, work today. They comprise the TCP/IP protocol stack, and because the Internet was built using these protocols, Ethernet is now the predominant LAN technology in the world.

IETF maintains the functional protocols and services for the TCP/IP protocol suite in the upper layers. However, the functional protocols and services at the OSI data link layer and physical layer are described by various engineering organizations (IEEE, ANSI, ITU) or by private companies (proprietary protocols). Because Ethernet is composed of standards at these lower layers, it may best be understood in reference to the OSI model. The OSI model separates the data link layer functionalities of addressing, framing, and accessing the media from the physical layer standards of the media. Ethernet standards define both the Layer 2 protocols and the Layer 1 technologies. Although Ethernet specifications support different media, bandwidths, and other Layer 1 and 2 variations, the basic frame format and address scheme is the same for all varieties of Ethernet.

This chapter examines the characteristics and operation of Ethernet as it has evolved from a shared-media, contention-based data communications technology to today's high-bandwidth, full-duplex technology.

Class Activity 10.0.1.2: Join My Social Circle!

Much of our network communication takes the form of messaging (text or instant), video contact, social media postings, etc.

For this activity, choose one of the communication networks you use most:

- Text (or instant) messaging
- Audio/video conferencing
- Emailing
- Gaming

Now that you have selected a network communication type, record your answers to the following questions:

- Is there a procedure you must follow to register others and yourself so that you form a communications group?
- How do you initiate contact with the person/people with whom you wish to communicate?

- How do you limit your conversations so they are received by only those with whom you wish to communicate?

Be prepared to discuss your recorded answers in class.

Ethernet Protocol (10.1)

This section looks at Ethernet operation, Ethernet frame attributes, and MAC and IP addresses in Ethernet.

Ethernet Operation (10.1.1)

Ethernet is the most widely used LAN technology in use today. This section discusses how Ethernet operates.

Ethernet operates in the data link layer and the physical layer. It is a family of networking technologies defined in the IEEE 802.2 and 802.3 standards. Ethernet supports data bandwidths of

- 10 Mbps
- 100 Mbps
- 1,000 Mbps (1 Gbps)
- 10,000 Mbps (10 Gbps)
- 40,000 Mbps (40 Gbps)
- 100,000 Mbps (100 Gbps)

LLC and MAC Sublayers (10.1.1.1)

As shown in Figure 10-1, Ethernet standards define both the Layer 2 protocols and the Layer 1 technologies. For the Layer 2 protocols, as with all 802 IEEE standards, Ethernet relies on the two separate sublayers of the data link layer to operate: the LLC and MAC sublayers.

The *Ethernet LLC sublayer* handles the communication between the upper layers and the lower layers. This is typically between the networking software and the device hardware. The LLC sublayer takes the network protocol data, which is typically an IPv4 packet, and adds control information to help deliver the packet to the destination node. The LLC sublayer is used to communicate with the upper layers of the application and to transition the packet to the lower layers for delivery.

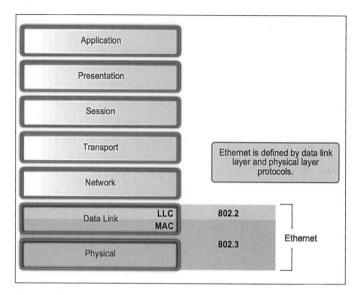

Figure 10-1 Ethernet Protocol

The LLC sublayer is implemented in software, and its implementation is independent of the hardware. In a computer, the LLC sublayer can be considered the driver software for the NIC. The NIC driver is a program that interacts directly with the hardware on the NIC to pass the data between the MAC sublayer and the physical media.

The *MAC sublayer* constitutes the lower sublayer of the data link layer. MAC is implemented by hardware, typically in the computer NIC. The specifics of the MAC sublayer are specified in the IEEE 802.3 standards. Figure 10-2 lists common IEEE Ethernet standards.

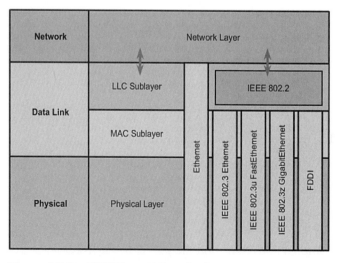

Figure 10-2 IEEE Ethernet Standards

MAC Sublayer (10.1.1.2)

As shown in Figure 10-3, the Ethernet MAC sublayer has two primary responsibilities:

- Data encapsulation

- Media access control

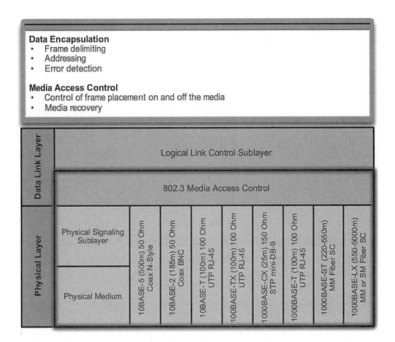

Figure 10-3   Ethernet MAC Sublayer

Data Encapsulation

The data encapsulation process includes frame assembly before transmission, and frame disassembly upon reception of a frame. In forming the frame, the MAC layer adds a header and trailer to the network layer PDU.

Data encapsulation provides three primary functions:

- **Frame delimiting:** The framing process provides important delimiters that are used to identify a group of bits that make up a frame. This process provides synchronization between the transmitting and receiving nodes.

- **Addressing:** The encapsulation process also provides for data link layer addressing. Each Ethernet header added in the frame contains the physical address (MAC address) that enables a frame to be delivered to a destination node.

- **Error detection:** Each Ethernet frame contains a trailer with a cyclic redundancy check (CRC) of the frame contents. After reception of a frame, the receiving node creates a CRC to compare to the one in the frame. If these two CRC calculations match, the frame can be trusted to have been received without error.

The use of frames aids in the transmission of bits as they are placed on the media and in the grouping of bits at the receiving node.

Media Access Control

The second responsibility of the MAC sublayer is media access control. Media access control is responsible for the placement of frames on the media and the removal of frames from the media. As its name implies, it controls access to the media. This sublayer communicates directly with the physical layer.

The underlying logical topology of Ethernet is a multi-access bus; therefore, all nodes (devices) on a single network segment share the medium. Ethernet is a contention-based method of networking. Recall that a contention-based method, or nondeterministic method, means that any device can try to transmit data across the shared medium whenever it has data to send. However, much like if two people try to talk simultaneously, if multiple devices on a single medium attempt to forward data simultaneously, the data collides, resulting in corrupted, unusable data. For this reason, Ethernet provides a method for controlling how the nodes share access through the use of a carrier sense multiple access (CSMA) technology.

Media Access Control (10.1.1.3)

The CSMA process is used to first detect if the media is carrying a signal. If a carrier signal on the media from another node is detected, it means that another device is transmitting. When the device attempting to transmit sees that the media is busy, it will wait and try again after a short time period. If no carrier signal is detected, the device transmits its data. It is possible that the CSMA process will fail and two devices will transmit at the same time. This is called a *data collision*. If this occurs, the data sent by both devices will be corrupted and will need to be re-sent.

Contention-based media access control methods do not require mechanisms for tracking whose turn it is to access the media; therefore, they do not have the overhead of controlled access methods. However, the contention-based systems do not scale well under heavy media use. As use and the number of nodes increase, the probability of successful media access without a collision decreases. Additionally, the recovery mechanisms required to correct errors due to these collisions further diminish the throughput.

As shown in Figure 10-4, CSMA is usually implemented in conjunction with a method for resolving media contention.

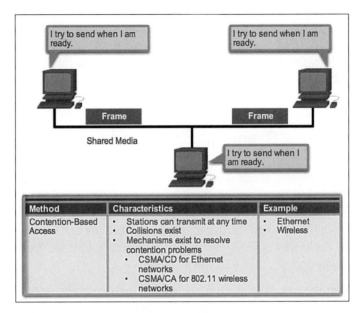

Figure 10-4   Contention-Based Access

The two commonly used methods are described next.

CSMA/Collision Detection

In carrier sense multiple access with collision detection (CSMA/CD), the device monitors the media for the presence of a data signal. If a data signal is absent, indicating that the media is free, the device transmits the data. If signals are then detected that show another device was transmitting at the same time, all devices stop sending and try again later. Traditional forms of Ethernet were developed to use this method.

The widespread incorporation of switched technologies in modern networks has largely displaced the original need for CSMA/CD in local-area networks. Almost all wired connections between devices in a LAN today are full-duplex connections—a device is able to send and receive simultaneously. This means that, although Ethernet networks are designed with CSMA/CD technology, with today's intermediate devices, collisions do not occur and the processes utilized by CSMA/CD are really unnecessary.

However, wireless connections in a LAN environment still have to take collisions into account. Wireless LAN devices utilize the carrier sense multiple access with collision avoidance (CSMA/CA) media access method.

CSMA/Collision Avoidance

In CSMA/CA, the device examines the media for the presence of a data signal. If the media is free, the device sends a notification across the media of its intent to use it. The device then sends the data. This method is used by 802.11 wireless networking technologies.

MAC Address: Ethernet Identity (10.1.1.4)

As previously stated, the underlying logical topology of Ethernet is a multi-access bus. Every network device is connected to the same, shared media, and all the nodes receive all frames transmitted. The issue is, if all devices are receiving every frame, how can each individual device identify if it is the intended receiver without the overhead of having to process and de-encapsulate the frame to get to the IP address? The issue becomes even more problematic in large, high-traffic-volume networks where lots of frames are forwarded.

To prevent the excessive overhead involved in the processing of every frame, a unique identifier called a MAC address was created to identify the actual source and destination nodes within an Ethernet network. Regardless of which variety of Ethernet is used, MAC addressing provides a method for device identification at the lower level of the OSI model. As you may recall, MAC addressing is added as part of a Layer 2 PDU. An Ethernet MAC address is a 48-bit binary value expressed as 12 hexadecimal digits (4 bits per hexadecimal digit).

MAC Address Structure

MAC addresses must be globally unique. The MAC address value is a direct result of IEEE-enforced rules for vendors to ensure globally unique addresses for each Ethernet device. The rules established by IEEE require any vendor that sells Ethernet devices to register with IEEE. The IEEE assigns the vendor a 3-byte (24-bit) code, called the Organizationally Unique Identifier (OUI).

IEEE requires a vendor to follow two simple rules, as shown in Figure 10-5:

- All MAC addresses assigned to a NIC or other Ethernet device must use that vendor's assigned OUI as the first 3 bytes.

- All MAC addresses with the same OUI must be assigned a unique value (vendor code or serial number) in the last 3 bytes.

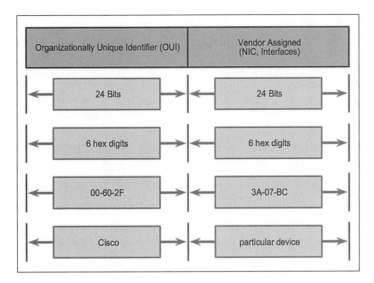

Figure 10-5   Ethernet MAC Address Structure

Frame Processing (10.1.1.5)

The MAC address is often referred to as a burned-in address (BIA) because, historically, this address is burned into read-only memory (ROM) on the NIC. This means that the address is encoded into the ROM chip permanently—it cannot be changed by software.

> **Note**
>
> On modern PC operating systems and NICs, it is possible to change the MAC address in software. This is useful when attempting to gain access to a network that filters based on BIA; consequently, filtering, or controlling, traffic based on the MAC address is no longer as secure.

MAC addresses are assigned to workstations, servers, printers, switches, and routers—any device that must originate and/or receive data on the network. All devices connected to an Ethernet LAN have MAC-addressed interfaces. Different hardware and software manufacturers might represent the MAC address in different hexadecimal formats. The address formats might be similar to

- 00-05-9A-3C-78-00

- 00:05:9A:3C:78:00

- 0005.9A3C.7800

When the computer starts up, the first thing the NIC does is copy the MAC address from ROM into RAM. When a device is forwarding a message to an Ethernet network, it attaches header information to the packet. The header information contains the source and destination MAC addresses. The source device sends the data through the network to the destination device.

Each NIC in the network views the information, at the MAC sublayer, to see if the destination MAC address in the frame matches the device's physical MAC address stored in RAM. If there is no match, the device discards the frame. When the frame reaches the destination where the MAC address of the NIC matches the destination MAC address of the frame, the NIC passes the frame up the OSI layers, where the de-encapsulation process takes place.

Video

Video 10.1.1.5

View the video in the online course for a demonstration of Ethernet frame forwarding.

Interactive Graphic

Activity 10.1.1.6: MAC and LLC Sublayer

Go to the online course and perform the MAC and LLC exercise.

Ethernet Frame Attributes (10.1.2)

This section explores the process of two aspects of Ethernet frames: encapsulation and frame size.

Ethernet Encapsulation (10.1.2.1)

Since the creation of Ethernet in 1973, standards have evolved for specifying faster and more flexible versions of the technology. This ability for Ethernet to improve over time is one of the main reasons that it has become so popular. Early versions of Ethernet were relatively slow, at 10 Mbps. The latest versions of Ethernet operate at 10 Gigabits per second and faster.

Video

Video 10.1.2.1

View the video in the online course for a demonstration of the Ethernet evolution timeline.

At the data link layer, the frame structure is nearly identical for all speeds of Ethernet. The Ethernet frame structure adds headers and trailers around the Layer 3 PDU to encapsulate the message being sent.

Both the Ethernet header and trailer have several sections of information that are used by the Ethernet protocol. Each section of the frame is called a field. As shown in Figure 10-6, there are two styles of Ethernet framing:

- IEEE 802.3 Ethernet standard, which has been updated several times to include new technologies

- Ethernet II standard, which is based on the DIX Ethernet standard

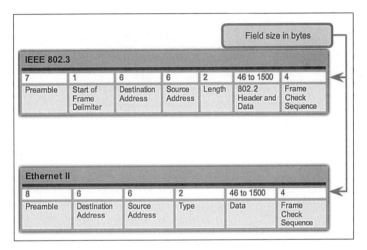

Figure 10-6   Comparison of 802.3 and Ethernet II Frame Structures and Field Size

The differences between framing styles are minimal. The most significant difference between the two standards is that IEEE 802.3 adds a Start of Frame Delimiter (SFD) field and changes the Type field to a Length field.

Ethernet II is the Ethernet frame format used in TCP/IP networks.

Ethernet Frame Size (10.1.2.2)

Both the Ethernet II and IEEE 802.3 standards define the minimum frame size as 64 bytes and the maximum as 1,518 bytes. This includes all bytes from the Destination Address field through the Frame Check Sequence (FCS) field. The Preamble and Start of Frame Delimiter fields are not included when describing the size of a frame.

Any frame less than 64 bytes in length is considered a "collision fragment" or "runt frame" and is automatically discarded by receiving stations.

The IEEE 802.3ac standard, released in 1998, extended the maximum allowable frame size to 1,522 bytes. The frame size was increased to accommodate a technology called virtual local-area network (VLAN). VLANs are created within a switched network and will be presented in a later course. Also, many quality of service (QoS) technologies leverage the User Priority field to implement various levels of service, such as priority service for voice traffic. Figure 10-7 displays the fields contained in the 802.1Q VLAN tag.

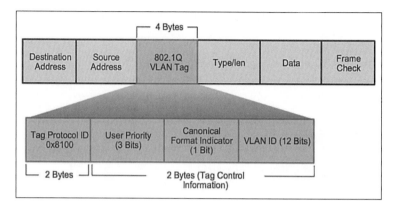

Figure 10-7   802.1Q VLAN Tag

If the size of a transmitted frame is less than the minimum or greater than the maximum, the receiving device drops the frame. Dropped frames are likely to be the result of collisions or other unwanted signals and are therefore considered invalid.

At the data link layer the frame structure is nearly identical. At the physical layer different versions of Ethernet vary in their method for detecting and placing data on the media.

Introduction to the Ethernet Frame (10.1.2.3)

The primary fields in the Ethernet frame are shown in Figure 10-8 and described here:

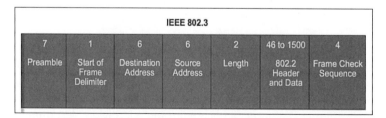

Figure 10-8   Ethernet Frame Fields

- *Preamble and Start of Frame Delimiter (SFD) fields*: The Preamble (7 bytes) and SFD, also called the Start of Frame (1 byte), fields are used for synchronization between the sending and receiving devices. These first 8 bytes of the frame are used to get the attention of the receiving nodes. Essentially, the first few bytes tell the receivers to get ready to receive a new frame.

- *Destination Address field*: This 6-byte field is the identifier for the intended recipient. As you will recall, this address is used by Layer 2 to assist devices in determining if a frame is addressed to them. The address in the frame is compared to the MAC address in the device. If there is a match, the device accepts the frame.

- *Source Address field*: This 6-byte field identifies the frame's originating NIC or interface.

- *Length field*: For any IEEE 802.3 standard earlier than 1997, the Length field defines the exact length of the frame's Data field. This is used later as part of the FCS to ensure that the message was received properly. Otherwise, the purpose of the field is to describe which higher-layer protocol is present. If the two-octet value is equal to or greater than 0x0600 hexadecimal or 1536 decimal, then the contents of the Data field are decoded according to the EtherType protocol indicated. If the two-octet value is equal to or less than 0x05DC hexadecimal or 1500 decimal, then the Length field is being used to indicate the use of the IEEE 802.3 frame format. This is how Ethernet II and 802.3 frames are differentiated.

- *Data field*: This field (46 to 1500 bytes) contains the encapsulated data from a higher layer, which is a generic Layer 3 PDU or, more commonly, an IPv4 packet. All frames must be at least 64 bytes long. If a small packet is encapsulated, additional bits, called a *pad*, are used to increase the size of the frame to this minimum size.

- *Frame Check Sequence (FCS) field*: The FCS field (4 bytes) is used to detect errors in a frame. It uses a cyclic redundancy check (CRC). The sending device includes the results of a CRC in the FCS field of the frame. The receiving device receives the frame and generates a CRC to look for errors. If the calculations match, no error occurred. Calculations that do not match are an indication that the data has changed; therefore, the frame is dropped. A change in the data could be the result of a disruption of the electrical signals that represent the bits.

Interactive Graphic

Activity 10.1.2.4: Ethernet Frame Fields

Go to the online course and perform the Ethernet frame fields exercise.

Ethernet MAC (10.1.3)

This section looks at the role of the MAC address in the Ethernet protocol.

MAC Addresses and Hexadecimal (10.1.3.1)

The use of the MAC address is one of the most important aspects of the Ethernet LAN technology. MAC addresses use hexadecimal numbering.

Hexadecimal is used both as a noun and as an adjective. When used by itself (as a noun), it means the hexadecimal number system. Hexadecimal provides a convenient way to represent binary values. Just as decimal is a base 10 numbering system and binary is a base 2 numbering system, hexadecimal is a base 16 numbering system.

The base 16 numbering system uses the numbers 0 to 9 and the letters A to F. Figure 10-9 shows the equivalent decimal and hexadecimal values for binary 0000 to 1111. It is easier for us to express a value as a single hexadecimal digit than as 4 binary bits.

Decimal and Binary equivalents of 0 to F Hexadecimal		
Decimal	Binary	Hexadecimal
0	0000	0
1	0001	1
2	0010	2
3	0011	3
4	0100	4
5	0101	5
6	0110	6
7	0111	7
8	1000	8
9	1001	9
10	1010	A
11	1011	B
12	1100	C
13	1101	D
14	1110	E
15	1111	F

Figure 10-9   Hexadecimal Numbering 1

Given that 8 bits (a byte) is a common binary grouping, binary 00000000 to 11111111 can be represented in hexadecimal as the range 00 to FF. Leading 0s are always displayed to complete the 8-bit representation. For example, the binary value 0000 1010 is shown in hexadecimal as 0A.

It is important to distinguish hexadecimal values from decimal values regarding the characters 0 to 9, as shown in Figure 10-10.

Selected Decimal, Binary, and Hexadecimal equivalents		
Decimal	Binary	Hexadecimal
0	0000 0000	00
1	0000 0001	01
2	0000 0010	02
3	0000 0011	03
4	0000 0100	04
5	0000 0101	05
6	0000 0110	06
7	0000 0111	07
8	0000 1000	08
10	0000 1010	0A
15	0000 1111	0F
16	0001 0000	10
32	0010 0000	20
64	0100 0000	40
128	1000 0000	80
192	1100 0000	C0
202	1100 1010	CA
240	1111 0000	F0
255	1111 1111	FF

Figure 10-10   Hexadecimal Numbering 2

Representing Hexadecimal Values

Hexadecimal is usually represented in text by the value preceded by 0x (for example, 0x73) or a subscript 16. Less commonly, it may be followed by an H (for example, 73H). However, because subscript text is not recognized in command-line or programming environments, the technical representation of hexadecimal is preceded with 0x. Therefore, the examples 0A and 73 would be shown as 0x0A and 0x73, respectively.

Hexadecimal is used to represent Ethernet MAC addresses and IPv6 addresses.

Hexadecimal Conversions

Number conversions between decimal and hexadecimal values are straightforward, but quickly dividing or multiplying by 16 is not always convenient. If such conversions are required, it is usually easier to convert the decimal or hexadecimal value to binary, and then to convert the binary value to either decimal or hexadecimal as appropriate.

With practice, it is possible to recognize the binary bit patterns that match the decimal and hexadecimal values. Figure 10-10 shows these patterns for selected 8-bit values.

MAC Address Representations (10.1.3.2)

On a Windows host, the **ipconfig /all** command can be used to identify the MAC address of an Ethernet adapter. In Figure 10-11, notice that the display indicates the Physical Address (MAC) of the computer is 00-18-DE-C7-F3-FB. If you have access to your Windows host, you may wish to try this on your own computer.

```
C:\>ipconfig/all

Ethernet adapter Local Area Connection:

    Connection-specific DNS Suffix  . : example.com
    Description . . . . . . . . . . . : Intel(R) Gigabit Network Connection
    Physical Address. . . . . . . . . : 00-18-DE-C7-F3-FB
    DHCP Enabled. . . . . . . . . . . : Yes
    Autoconfiguration Enabled . . . . : Yes
    IPv4 Address. . . . . . . . . . . : 192.168.1.67(Preferred)
    Subnet Mask . . . . . . . . . . . : 255.255.255.0
    Lease Obtained. . . . . . . . . . : Monday, November 26, 2012 12:14:48 PM
    Lease Expires . . . . . . . . . . : Saturday, December 01, 2012 12:15:02 AM
    Default Gateway . . . . . . . . . : 192.168.1.254
    DHCP Server . . . . . . . . . . . : 192.168.1.254
    DNS Servers . . . . . . . . . . . : 192.168.1.254
```

Figure 10-11   Physical Address of a Host

Depending on the device and the operating system, you will see various representations of MAC addresses, as displayed in Figure 10-12. Cisco routers and switches use the form XXXX.XXXX.XXXX, where X is a hexadecimal character.

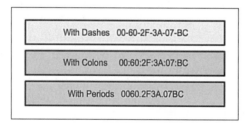

With Dashes	00-60-2F-3A-07-BC
With Colons	00:60:2F:3A:07:BC
With Periods	0060.2F3A.07BC

Figure 10-12   Different Representation of MAC Addresses

Unicast MAC Address (10.1.3.3)

In Ethernet, different MAC addresses are used for Layer 2 unicast, broadcast, and multicast communications.

A *unicast MAC address* is the unique address used when a frame is sent from a single transmitting device to a single destination device.

Video

Video 10.1.3.3

View the video in the online course for a demonstration of a unicast web page request.

Broadcast MAC Address (10.1.3.4)

A broadcast packet contains a destination IP address that has all 1s in the host portion. This numbering in the address means that all hosts on that local network (broadcast domain) will receive and process the packet. Many network protocols, such as DHCP and ARP, use broadcasts. How ARP uses broadcasts to map Layer 2 to Layer 3 addresses is discussed later in this chapter.

On Ethernet networks, the *broadcast MAC address* is 48 ones (1s) displayed as hexadecimal FF-FF-FF-FF-FF-FF.

Video 10.1.3.4

Video

View the video in the online course for a demonstration of broadcast packet transmission.

Multicast MAC Address (10.1.3.5)

Multicast addresses allow a source device to send a packet to a group of devices. Devices that belong to a multicast group are assigned a multicast group IP address. The range of IPv4 multicast addresses is 224.0.0.0 to 239.255.255.255. Because multicast addresses represent a group of addresses (sometimes called a host group), they can only be used as the destination of a packet. The source will always have a unicast address.

Multicast addresses would be used, for example, in remote gaming, where many players are connected remotely but playing the same game. Another use of multicast addresses is in distance learning through video conferencing, where many students are connected to the same class.

As with the unicast and broadcast addresses, the multicast IP address requires a corresponding multicast MAC address to actually deliver frames on a local network. The *multicast MAC address* is a special value that begins with 01-00-5E in hexadecimal. The remaining portion of the multicast MAC address is created by converting the lower 23 bits of the IP multicast group address into 6 hexadecimal characters.

Video 10.1.3.5

Video

View the video in the online course for a demonstration of a multicast transmission.

Lab 10.1.3.6: Viewing Network Device MAC Addresses

In this lab, you will complete the following objectives:

- Part 1: Set Up the Topology and Initialize Devices

- Part 2: Configure Devices and Verify Connectivity
- Part 3: Display, Describe, and Analyze Ethernet MAC Addresses

Mac and IP (10.1.4)

There are two primary addresses assigned to a host device:

- Physical address (MAC address)
- Logical address (IP address)

The MAC address and IP address work together to identify a device on the network.

MAC and IP (10.1.4.1)

The process of using the MAC address and IP address to find a computer is similar to the process of using the name and address of an individual to send a letter.

A person's name usually does not change. A person's address, on the other hand, relates to where they live, and thus can change. Similar to the name of a person, the MAC address on a host does not change; it is physically assigned to the host NIC and is known as the physical address. The physical address remains the same regardless of where the host is placed.

The IP address is similar to the address of a person. This address is based on where the host is actually located. Using this address, it is possible for a frame to determine the location of where a frame should be sent. The IP address, or network address, is known as a logical address because it is assigned logically. It is assigned to each host by a network administrator based on the local network that the host is connected to.

Interactive Graphic

Activity 10.1.4.1: Continental Boundaries

Go to the online course and perform the hierarchical nature exercise. The activity demonstrates the hierarchical nature of locating an individual based on a "logical" address. Click each grouping to view how the address filters down.

Both the physical MAC address and the logical IP address are required for a computer to communicate on a hierarchical network, just like both the name and address of a person are required to send a letter.

End-to-End Connectivity, MAC, and IP (10.1.4.2)

A source device will send a packet based on an IP address of the destination. One of the most common ways a source device determines the IP address of a destination device is through DNS, in which an IP address is associated to a domain name. For example, www.cisco.com is equal to 209.165.200.225. This IP address will get the packet to the network location of the destination device. It is this IP address that routers will use to determine the best path to reach a destination. So, in short, IP addressing determines the end-to-end behavior of an IP packet.

However, along each link in a path, an IP packet is encapsulated in a frame specific to the particular data link technology associated with that link, such as Ethernet. End devices on an Ethernet network do not accept and process frames based on IP addresses; rather, a frame is accepted and processed based on MAC addresses.

On Ethernet networks, MAC addresses are used to identify, at a lower level, the source and destination hosts. When a host on an Ethernet network communicates, it sends frames containing its own MAC address as the source and the MAC address of the intended recipient as the destination. All hosts that receive the frame will read the destination MAC address. If the destination MAC address matches the MAC address configured on the host NIC, only then will the host process the message.

Video

Video 10.1.4.2 1

View the video in the online course for a demonstration of an IP packet encapsulated in an Ethernet frame.

Video

Video 10.1.4.2 2

View the video in the online course for a demonstration of the data link layer.

How are the IP addresses of the IP packets in a data flow associated with the MAC addresses on each link along the path to the destination? This is done through a process called Address Resolution Protocol (ARP).

Lab 10.1.4.3: Using Wireshark to Examine Ethernet Frames

In this lab, you will complete the following objectives:

- Part 1: Examine the Header Fields in an Ethernet II Frame
- Part 2: Use Wireshark to Capture and Analyze Ethernet Frames

Packet Tracer Activity 10.1.4.4: Identify MAC and IP Addresses

This activity is optimized for viewing PDUs. The devices are already configured. You will gather PDU information in simulation mode and answer a series of questions about the data you collect.

Address Resolution Protocol (10.2)

This section looks at ARP and some of its issues.

Introduction to ARP (10.2.1.1)

Recall that each node on an IP network has both a MAC address and an IP address. In order to send data, the node must use both of these addresses. The node must use its own MAC and IP addresses in the source fields and must provide both a MAC address and an IP address for the destination. Although the IP address of the destination will be provided by a higher OSI layer, the sending node needs a way to find the MAC address of the destination for a given Ethernet link. This is the purpose of ARP.

ARP relies on certain types of Ethernet broadcast messages and Ethernet unicast messages, called ARP Requests and ARP Replies.

ARP Functions (10.2.1.2)

The ARP protocol provides two basic functions:

- Resolving IPv4 addresses to MAC addresses
- Maintaining a table of mappings

Resolving IPv4 Addresses to MAC Addresses

For a frame to be placed on the LAN media, it must have a destination MAC address. When a packet is sent to the data link layer to be encapsulated into a frame, the node refers to a table in its memory to find the data link layer address that is mapped to the destination IPv4 address. This table is called the ARP table or the ARP cache. The ARP table is stored in the RAM of the device.

Each entry, or row, of the ARP table binds an IP address with a MAC address. We call the relationship between the two values a *map*—it simply means that you can locate an IP address in the table and discover the corresponding MAC address. The ARP table temporarily saves (caches) the mapping for the devices on the local LAN.

To begin the process, a transmitting node attempts to locate the MAC address mapped to an IPv4 destination. If this map is found in the table, the node uses the MAC address as the destination MAC in the frame that encapsulates the IPv4 packet. The frame is then encoded onto the networking media.

Maintaining the ARP Table

The *ARP table* is maintained dynamically. There are two ways that a device can gather MAC addresses. One way is to monitor the traffic that occurs on the local network segment. As a node receives frames from the media, it can record the source IP address and MAC address as a mapping in the ARP table. As frames are transmitted on the network, the device populates the ARP table with address pairs.

An ARP request is a Layer 2 broadcast to all devices on the Ethernet LAN. The ARP request contains the IP address of the destination host and the broadcast MAC address, FFFF.FFFF.FFFF. Because this is a broadcast, all nodes on the Ethernet LAN will receive it and look at the contents. The node with the IP address that matches the IP address in the ARP request will reply. The reply will be a unicast frame that includes the MAC address that corresponds to the IP address in the request. This response is then used to make a new entry in the ARP table of the sending node.

Video 10.2.1.2

`Video`

View the video in the online course for a demonstration of the ARP process.

Entries in the ARP table are time-stamped in much the same way that MAC table entries are time-stamped in switches. If a device does not receive a frame from a particular device by the time the time stamp expires, the entry for this device is removed from the ARP table.

Additionally, static map entries can be entered in an ARP table, but this is rarely done. Static ARP table entries do not expire over time and must be manually removed.

ARP Operation (10.2.1.3)

Let's proceed to look at the way the ARP process operates.

Creating the Frame

What does a node do when it needs to create a frame and the ARP cache does not contain a map of an IP address to a destination MAC address? It generates an ARP request!

When ARP receives a request to map an IPv4 address to a MAC address, it looks for the cached map in its ARP table. If an entry is not found, the encapsulation of the IPv4 packet fails and the Layer 2 processes notify ARP that it needs a map. The ARP processes then send out an ARP request packet to discover the MAC address of the destination device on the local network. If a device receiving the request has the destination IP address, it responds with an ARP reply. A map is created in the ARP table. Packets for that IPv4 address can now be encapsulated in frames.

If no device responds to the ARP request, the packet is dropped because a frame cannot be created. This encapsulation failure is reported to the upper layers of the device. If the device is an intermediary device, like a router, the upper layers may choose to respond to the source host with an error in an ICMPv4 packet.

See Figures10-13 through 10-17 to view the process used to get the MAC address of the node on the local physical network.

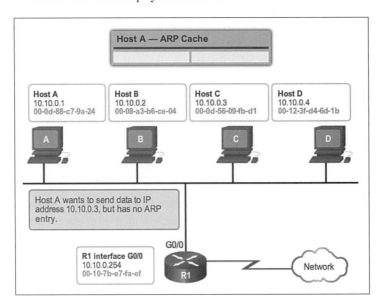

Figure 10-13   ARP Process: Communicating Remotely

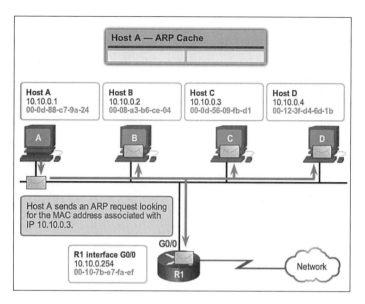

Figure 10-14   Broadcasting an ARP Request

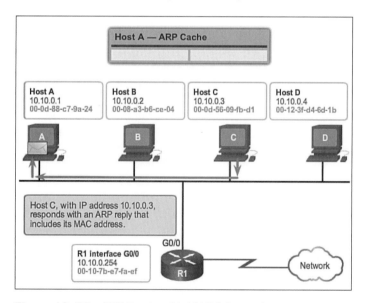

Figure 10-15   ARP Reply with MAC Information

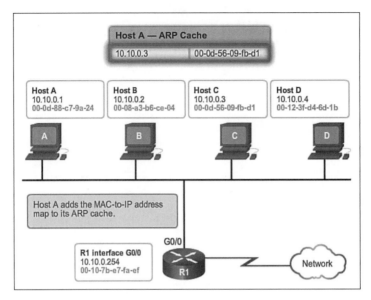

Figure 10-16   Adding MAC-to-IP Map in ARP Cache

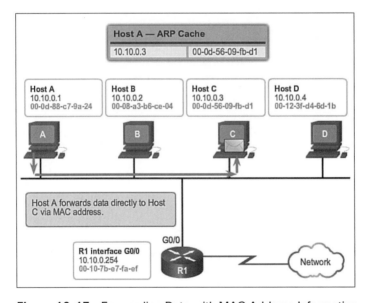

Figure 10-17   Forwarding Data with MAC Address Information

ARP Role in Remote Communication (10.2.1.4)

All frames must be delivered to a node on the local network segment. If the destination IPv4 host is on the local network, the frame will use the MAC address of this device as the destination MAC address.

If the destination IPv4 host is not on the local network, the source node needs to deliver the frame to the router interface that is the gateway or next hop used to reach that destination. The source node will use the MAC address of the gateway as the destination address for frames containing an IPv4 packet addressed to hosts on other networks.

The gateway address of the router interface is stored in the IPv4 configuration of the hosts. When a host creates a packet for a destination, it compares the destination IP address and its own IP address to determine if the two IP addresses are located on the same Layer 3 network. If the receiving host is not on the same network, the source uses the ARP process to determine a MAC address for the router interface serving as the gateway.

In the event that the gateway entry is not in the table, the normal ARP process will send an ARP request to retrieve the MAC address associated with the IP address of the router interface.

See Figures 10-18 through 10-22 to view the process used to get the MAC address of the gateway.

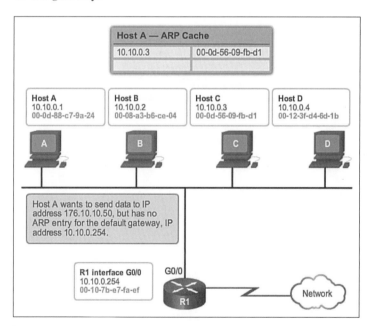

Figure 10-18 ARP Process: Communicating Remotely

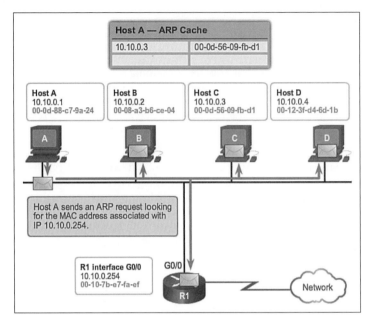

Figure 10-19   Broadcasting an ARP Request

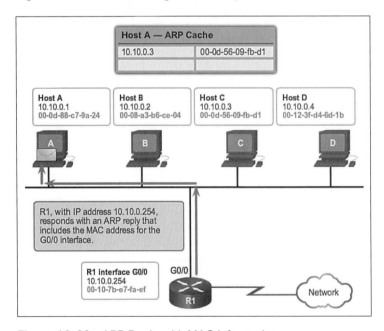

Figure 10-20   ARP Reply with MAC Information

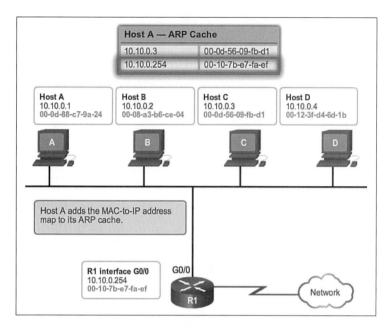

Figure 10-21   Adding MAC-to-IP Map in ARP Cache

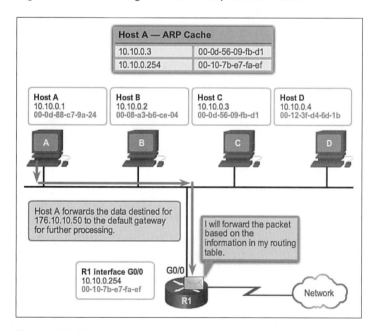

Figure 10-22   Forwarding Data with MAC Address Information

Removing Entries from an ARP Table (10.2.1.5)

For each device, an ARP cache timer removes ARP entries that have not been used for a specified period of time. The times differ depending on the device and its operating system. For example, some Windows operating systems store ARP cache entries for 2 minutes. If the entry is used again during that time, the ARP timer for that entry is extended to 10 minutes.

Commands may also be used to manually remove all or some of the entries in the ARP table. After an entry has been removed, the process for sending an ARP request and receiving an ARP reply must occur again to enter the map in the ARP table.

Each device has an operating system–specific command to delete the contents of the ARP cache. These commands do not invoke the execution of ARP in any way. They merely remove the entries of the ARP table. ARP service is integrated within the IPv4 protocol and implemented by the device. Its operation is transparent to both upper-layer applications and users. As shown in Figure 10-23, it is sometimes necessary to remove an ARP table entry.

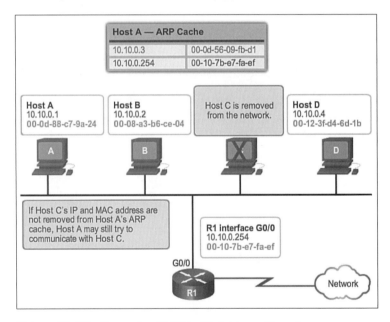

Figure 10-23   Removing MAC-to-IP Address Mappings

ARP Tables on Networking Devices (10.2.1.6)

On a Cisco router, the **show ip arp** command is used to display the ARP table, as shown in Figure 10-24.

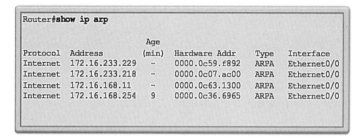

Figure 10-24 Router ARP Table

On a Windows 7 PC, the **arp –a** command is used to display the ARP table, as shown in Figure 10-25.

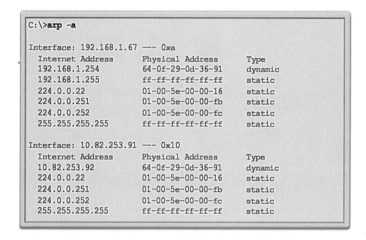

Figure 10-25 Host ARP Table

Packet Tracer Activity 10.2.1.7: Examine the ARP Table

This activity is optimized for viewing PDUs. The devices are already configured. You will gather PDU information in simulation mode and answer a series of questions about the data you collect.

Lab 10.2.1.8: Observing ARP with the Windows CLI, IOS CLI, and Wireshark

In this lab, you will complete the following objectives:

- Part 1: Build and Configure the Network

- Part 2: Use the Windows ARP Command

- Part 3: Use the IOS Show IP ARP Command

- Part 4: Use Wireshark to Examine ARP Exchanges

ARP Issues (10.2.2)

This section discusses how the ARP process can create problems and how to mitigate those problems.

How ARP Can Create Problems (10.2.2.1)

Figure 10-26 shows two potential issues with ARP.

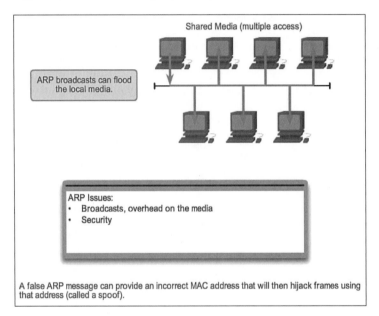

Figure 10-26   Potential Issues with ARP

Overhead on the Media

As a broadcast frame, an ARP request is received and processed by every device on the local network. On a typical business network, these broadcasts would probably have minimal effect on network performance. However, if a large number of devices were to be powered up and all start accessing network services at the same time, there could be some reduction in performance for a short period of time. For example, if all students in a lab logged into classroom computers and attempted to access the Internet at the same time, there could be delays. However, after the devices have sent out the initial ARP broadcasts and have learned the necessary MAC addresses, any effect on the network would be minimized.

Security

In some cases, the use of ARP can lead to a potential security risk. *ARP spoofing*, or *ARP poisoning*, is a technique used by an attacker to inject the wrong MAC address association into a network by issuing fake ARP requests. An attacker forges the MAC address of a device, and then frames can be sent to the wrong destination.

Manually configuring static ARP associations is one way to prevent ARP spoofing. Authorized MAC addresses can be configured on some network devices to restrict network access to only those devices listed.

Mitigating ARP Problems (10.2.2.2)

Broadcast and security issues related to ARP can be mitigated with modern switches. Cisco switches support several security technologies specifically designed to mitigate Ethernet issues related to broadcasts, in general, and ARP, in particular.

Switches provide segmentation of a LAN, dividing the LAN into independent collision domains, as shown in Figure 10-27. Each port on a switch represents a separate collision domain and provides the full media bandwidth to the node or nodes connected on that port. Although switches do not by default prevent broadcasts from propagating to connected devices, they do isolate unicast Ethernet communications so that they are only "heard" by the source and destination devices. So if there are a large number of ARP requests, each ARP reply will only be between two devices.

With regard to mitigating various types of broadcast attacks, to which Ethernet networks are prone, network engineers implement Cisco switch security technologies such as specialized access lists and port security.

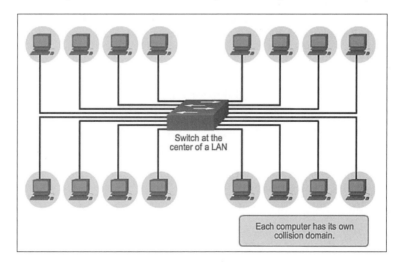

Figure 10-27 Segmentation

LAN Switches (10.3)

This section looks at LAN switching in general and discusses the fixed or modular switch option and Layer 3 switching. Switching technologies are crucial to network design, as they allow traffic to be sent only where it is needed in most cases, using fast, hardware-based methods.

Switching (10.3.1)

A switch is a telecommunication device that receives a message from any device connected to it, and then transmits the message only to the device for which the message was meant. This makes the switch a more intelligent device than a hub, which receives a message and then transmits it to all the other devices on its network. The network switch plays an integral part in most modern Ethernet LANs. This section further examines how switching works in a LAN.

Switch Port Fundamentals (10.3.1.1)

Recall that the logical topology of an Ethernet network is a multi-access bus in which devices share access to the same medium. This logical topology determines how hosts on the network view and process frames sent and received on the network. However, the physical topology of most Ethernet networks today is that of a star or extended star. This means that on most Ethernet networks, end devices are typically connected, in a point-to-point manner, to a Layer 2 LAN switch.

A Layer 2 LAN switch performs switching and filtering based only on the OSI data link layer (Layer 2) MAC address. A switch is completely transparent to network protocols and user applications. A Layer 2 switch builds a MAC address table that it uses to make forwarding decisions. Layer 2 switches depend on routers to pass data between independent IP subnetworks.

Interactive Graphic

Activity 10.3.1.1: Switch Operation

Go to the online course and perform the switch operation exercise.

Switch MAC Address Table (10.3.1.2)

Switches use MAC addresses to direct network communications through their switch fabric to the appropriate port toward the destination node. The switch fabric is the integrated circuits and the accompanying machine programming that allows the data paths through the switch to be controlled. For a switch to know which port to use to transmit a unicast frame, it must first learn which nodes exist on each of its ports.

A switch determines how to handle incoming data frames by using its MAC address table. A switch builds its MAC address table by recording the MAC addresses of the nodes connected to each of its ports. After a MAC address for a specific node on a specific port is recorded in the address table, the switch then knows to send traffic destined for that specific node out the port mapped to that node for subsequent transmissions.

When an incoming data frame is received by a switch and the destination MAC address is not in the table, the switch forwards the frame out all ports, except for the port on which it was received. When the destination node responds, the switch records the node's MAC address in the address table from the frame's Source Address field. In networks with multiple interconnected switches, the *MAC address tables* record multiple MAC addresses for the ports connecting the switches that reflect the node's beyond. Typically, switch ports used to interconnect two switches have multiple MAC addresses recorded in the MAC address table.

To see how this works, view each of the steps in Figures 10-28 through 10-33.

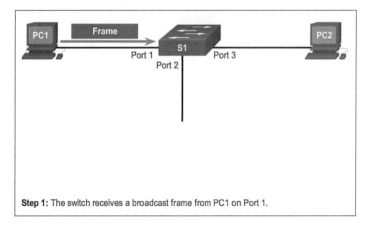

Step 1: The switch receives a broadcast frame from PC1 on Port 1.

Figure 10-28   MAC Addressing and Switch MAC Tables: Step 1

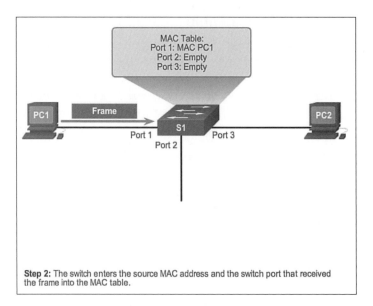

Figure 10-29 MAC Addressing and Switch MAC Tables: Step 2

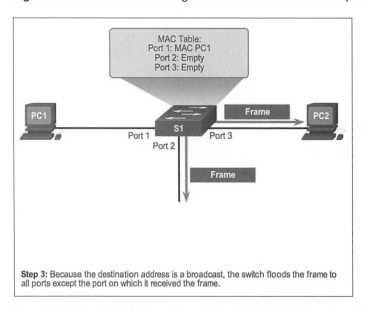

Figure 10-30 MAC Addressing and Switch MAC Tables: Step 3

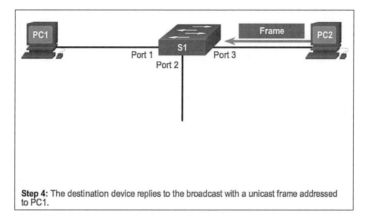

Step 4: The destination device replies to the broadcast with a unicast frame addressed to PC1.

Figure 10-31   MAC Addressing and Switch MAC Tables: Step 4

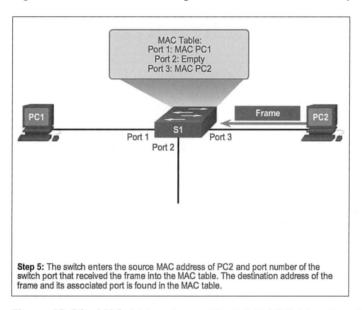

Step 5: The switch enters the source MAC address of PC2 and port number of the switch port that received the frame into the MAC table. The destination address of the frame and its associated port is found in the MAC table.

Figure 10-32   MAC Addressing and Switch MAC Tables: Step 5

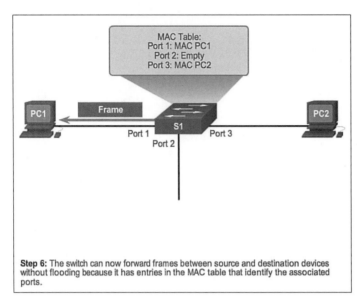

Figure 10-33   MAC Addressing and Switch MAC Tables: Step 6

The following describes this process:

Step 1.   The switch receives a broadcast frame from PC1 on Port 1.

Step 2.   The switch enters the source MAC address and the switch port that received the frame into the address table.

Step 3.   Because the destination address is a broadcast, the switch floods the frame to all ports except the port on which it received the frame.

Step 4.   The destination device replies to the broadcast with a unicast frame addressed to PC1.

Step 5.   The switch enters the source MAC address of PC2 and the port number of the switch port that received the frame into the address table. The destination address of the frame and its associated port is found in the MAC address table.

Step 6.   The switch can now forward frames between source and destination devices without flooding because it has entries in the address table that identify the associated ports.

Note

The MAC address table is sometimes referred to as a content addressable memory (CAM) table. Although the term CAM table is fairly common, for the purposes of this course, we will refer to it as a MAC address table.

Duplex Settings (10.3.1.3)

Though transparent to network protocols and user applications, switches can operate in different modes that can have both positive and negative effects when forwarding Ethernet frames on a network. One of the most basic settings of a switch is the duplex setting of each individual port connected to each host device. A port on a switch must be configured to match the duplex settings of the media type. There are two types of *duplex settings* used for communications on an Ethernet network: half duplex and full duplex.

Half Duplex

Half-duplex communication relies on unidirectional data flow, where sending and receiving data are not performed at the same time. This is similar to how walkie-talkies or two-way radios function in that only one person can talk at any one time. If someone talks while someone else is already speaking, a collision occurs. As a result, half-duplex communication implements CSMA/CD to help reduce the potential for collisions and detect them when they do happen. Half-duplex communications have performance issues due to the constant waiting, because data can only flow in one direction at a time. Half-duplex connections are typically seen in older hardware, such as hubs. Nodes that are attached to hubs that share their connection to a switch port must operate in half-duplex mode because the end computers must be able to detect collisions. Nodes can operate in a half-duplex mode if the NIC cannot be configured for full-duplex operations. In this case, the port on the switch defaults to a half-duplex mode as well. Because of these limitations, full-duplex communication has replaced half duplex in more current hardware.

Full Duplex

In full-duplex communication, data flow is bidirectional, so data can be sent and received at the same time. The bidirectional support enhances performance by reducing the wait time between transmissions. Most Ethernet, Fast Ethernet, and Gigabit Ethernet NICs sold today offer full-duplex capability. In full-duplex mode, the collision-detect circuit is disabled. Frames sent by the two connected end nodes cannot collide because the end nodes use two separate circuits in the network cable. Each full-duplex connection uses only one port. Full-duplex connections require a switch that supports full duplex or a direct connection between two nodes that each support full duplex. Nodes that are directly attached to a dedicated switch port with NICs that support full duplex should be connected to switch ports that are configured to operate in full-duplex mode.

Figure 10-34 shows the two duplex settings available on modern network equipment.

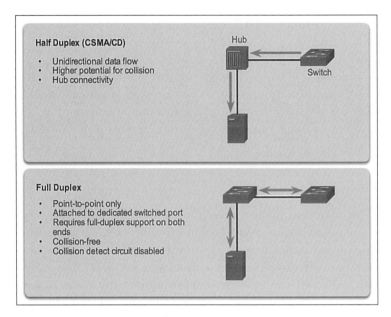

Figure 10-34   Duplex Settings

A Cisco Catalyst switch supports three duplex settings:

- The full option sets full-duplex mode.

- The half option sets half-duplex mode.

- The auto option sets autonegotiation of duplex mode. With autonegotiation enabled, the two ports communicate to decide the best mode of operation.

For Fast Ethernet and 10/100/1000 ports, the default is auto. For 100BASE-FX ports, the default is full. The 10/100/1000 ports operate in either half- or full-duplex mode when they are set to 10 or 100 Mbps, but when set to 1000 Mbps, they operate only in full-duplex mode.

Auto-MDIX (10.3.1.4)

In addition to having the correct duplex setting, it is also necessary to have the correct cable type defined for each port. Connections between specific devices, such as switch-to-switch, switch-to-router, switch-to-host, and router-to-host device, once required the use of a specific cable type (crossover or straight-through). Instead, most switch devices now support the **mdix auto** interface configuration command in the CLI to enable the *automatic medium-dependent interface crossover* (auto-MDIX) feature.

When the auto-MDIX feature is enabled, the switch detects the required cable type for copper Ethernet connections and configures the interfaces accordingly.

Therefore, you can use either a crossover cable or a straight-through cable for connections to a copper 10/100/1000 port on the switch, regardless of the type of device on the other end of the connection.

The auto-MDIX feature is enabled by default on switches running Cisco IOS Release 12.2(18)SE or later. For releases between Cisco IOS Release 12.1(14)EA1 and 12.2(18)SE, the auto-MDIX feature is disabled by default.

Frame Forwarding Methods on Cisco Switches (10.3.1.5)

In the past, switches used one of the following forwarding methods for switching data between network ports:

- Store-and-forward switching

- Cut-through switching

Figure 10-35 highlights differences between these two methods.

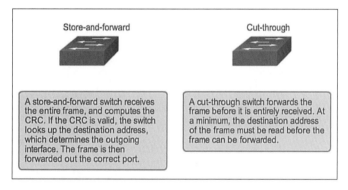

Figure 10-35 Switch Packet Forwarding Methods

In *store-and-forward switching*, when the switch receives the frame, it stores the data in buffers until the complete frame has been received. During the storage process, the switch analyzes the frame for information about its destination. In this process, the switch also performs an error check using the Cyclic Redundancy Check (CRC) trailer portion of the Ethernet frame.

CRC uses a mathematical formula, based on the number of bits (1s) in the frame, to determine whether the received frame has an error. After confirming the integrity of the frame, the frame is forwarded out the appropriate port toward its destination. When an error is detected in a frame, the switch discards the frame. Discarding frames with errors reduces the amount of bandwidth consumed by corrupt data. Store-and-forward switching is required for QoS analysis on converged networks where frame classification for traffic prioritization is necessary. For example, Voice over IP data streams need to have priority over web-browsing traffic.

Video

Video 10.3.1.5 Part 2

View the video in the online course for a demonstration of the store-and-forward process used on current models of Cisco Catalyst switches.

Cut-Through Switching (10.3.1.6)

In *cut-through switching*, the switch acts upon the data as soon as it is received, even if the transmission is not complete. The switch buffers just enough of the frame to read the destination MAC address so that it can determine to which port to forward the data. The destination MAC address is located in the first 6 bytes of the frame following the Preamble. The switch looks up the destination MAC address in its switching table, determines the outgoing interface port, and forwards the frame onto its destination through the designated switch port. The switch does not perform any error checking on the frame. Because the switch does not have to wait for the entire frame to be completely buffered, and because the switch does not perform any error checking, cut-through switching is faster than store-and-forward switching. However, because the switch does not perform any error checking, it forwards corrupt frames throughout the network. The corrupt frames consume bandwidth while they are being forwarded. The destination NIC eventually discards the corrupt frames.

There are two variants of cut-through switching:

- *Fast-forward switching*: Fast-forward switching offers the lowest level of latency. Fast-forward switching immediately forwards a packet after reading the destination address. Because fast-forward switching starts forwarding before the entire packet has been received, there may be times when packets are relayed with errors. This occurs infrequently, and the destination network adapter discards the faulty packet upon receipt. In fast-forward mode, latency is measured from the first bit received to the first bit transmitted. Fast-forward switching is the typical cut-through method of switching.

- *Fragment-free switching*: In fragment-free switching, the switch stores the first 64 bytes of the frame before forwarding. Fragment-free switching can be viewed as a compromise between store-and-forward switching and fast-forward switching. The reason fragment-free switching stores only the first 64 bytes of the frame is that most network errors and collisions occur during the first 64 bytes. Fragment-free switching tries to enhance fast-forward switching by performing a small error check on the first 64 bytes of the frame to ensure that a collision has not occurred before forwarding the frame. Fragment-free switching is a compromise between the high latency and high integrity of store-and-forward switching, and the low latency and reduced integrity of fast-forward switching.

Video

Video 10.3.1.6

View the video in the online course for a demonstration of the cut-through process.

Some switches are configured to perform cut-through switching on a per-port basis until a user-defined error threshold is reached and then they automatically change to store-and-forward. When the error rate falls below the threshold, the port automatically changes back to cut-through switching.

Interactive Graphic

Activity 10.3.1.7: Frame Forwarding

Go to the online course and perform the frame forwarding exercise.

Memory Buffering on Switches (10.3.1.8)

As discussed, a switch analyzes some or all of a packet before it forwards it to the destination host. An Ethernet switch may use a buffering technique to store frames before forwarding them. Buffering may also be used when the destination port is busy due to congestion and the switch stores the frame until it can be transmitted.

As shown in Table 10-1, there are two methods of memory buffering: *port-based memory buffering* and *shared memory buffering*.

Table 10-1   Port-Based and Shared Memory Buffering

Method	Description
Port-based memory	In port-based memory buffering, frames are stored in queues that are linked to specific incoming and outgoing ports.
Shared memory	Shared memory buffering deposits all frames into a common memory buffer that all the ports on the switch share.

Port-Based Memory Buffering

In port-based memory buffering, frames are stored in queues that are linked to specific incoming and outgoing ports. A frame is transmitted to the outgoing port only when all the frames ahead of it in the queue have been successfully transmitted. It is possible for a single frame to delay the transmission of all the frames in memory because of a busy destination port. This delay occurs even if the other frames could be transmitted to open destination ports.

Shared Memory Buffering

Shared memory buffering deposits all frames into a common memory buffer that all the ports on the switch share. The amount of buffer memory required by a port is dynamically allocated. The frames in the buffer are linked dynamically to the destination port. This allows the packet to be received on one port and then transmitted on another port, without moving it to a different queue.

The switch keeps a map of frame-to-port links showing where a packet needs to be transmitted. The map link is cleared after the frame has been successfully transmitted. The number of frames stored in the buffer is restricted by the size of the entire memory buffer and not limited to a single port buffer. This permits larger frames to be transmitted with fewer dropped frames. This is especially important to asymmetric switching, which allows for different data rates on different ports. This allows more bandwidth to be dedicated to certain ports, such as a port connected to a server.

Interactive Graphic

Activity 10.3.1.9: Switch It!

Go to the online course and perform the switch forwarding types exercise.

Lab10.3.1.10: Viewing the Switch MAC Address Table

In this lab, you will complete the following objectives:

- Part 1: Build and Configure the Network

- Part 2: Examine the Switch MAC Address Table

Fixed or Modular (10.3.2)

As we continue to look at switches, it is important we understand that we can purchase a modular switch, which enables us to build or modify the platform to suit our networking requirements. These switches, in general, are more expensive than the fixed switches, which do not offer the option of being able to be modified.

Fixed Versus Modular Configuration (10.3.2.1)

When selecting a switch, it is important to understand the key features of the switch options available. This means that it is necessary to decide on features such as whether Power over Ethernet (PoE) is necessary, and the preferred "forwarding rate."

As shown in Figure 10-36, PoE allows a switch to deliver power to a device, such as IP phones and some wireless access points, over the existing Ethernet cabling. This allows more flexibility for installation.

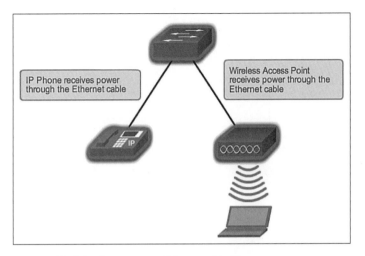

Figure 10-36 Power over Ethernet (PoE)

The forwarding rate defines the processing capabilities of a switch by rating how much data the switch can process per second. Switch product lines are classified by forwarding rates. Entry-layer switches have lower forwarding rates than enterprise-layer switches. Other considerations include whether the device is stackable or non-stackable, the thickness of the switch (expressed in number of rack units), and port density, or the number of ports available on a single switch. The port density of a device can vary depending on whether the device is a fixed configuration device or a modular device. These options are sometimes referred to as switch form factors, as shown in Figure 10-37.

Fixed Configuration Switches

Fixed configuration switches are just as you might expect, fixed in their configuration. What that means is that you cannot add features or options to the switch beyond those that originally came with the switch. The particular model you purchase determines the features and options available. For example, if you purchase a 24-port gigabit fixed switch, you cannot add additional ports when you need them. There are typically different configuration choices that vary in how many and what types of ports are included.

Modular Switches

Modular switches offer more flexibility in their configuration. Modular switches typically come with various chassis sizes that allow for the installation of different numbers of modular line cards. The line cards actually contain the ports. The line card fits into the switch chassis like expansion cards fit into a PC. The larger the chassis, the more modules it can support. As you can see in Figure 10-37, there can be many different chassis sizes to choose from. If you bought a modular switch with a 24-port line card, you could easily add an additional 24-port line card to bring the total number of ports up to 48.

Figure 10-37 displays examples of fixed configuration, modular, and stackable configuration switches.

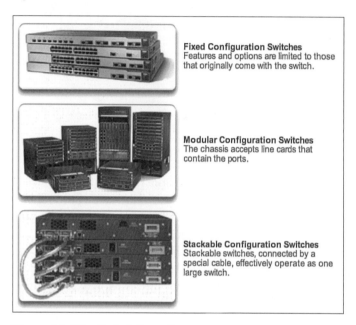

Fixed Configuration Switches
Features and options are limited to those that originally come with the switch.

Modular Configuration Switches
The chassis accepts line cards that contain the ports.

Stackable Configuration Switches
Stackable switches, connected by a special cable, effectively operate as one large switch.

Figure 10-37   Switch Form Factors

Fixed Configuration Cisco Switches (10.3.2.2)

The Cisco switch product lines described next and depicted in Figure 10-38 comprise the fixed configuration Cisco switches that are available.

Catalyst Express 500

The Catalyst Express 500 is Cisco's entry-layer switch. It offers the following:

- Forwarding rates from 8.8 Gbps to 24 Gbps
- Layer 2 port security
- Web-based management
- Converged data/IP communications support

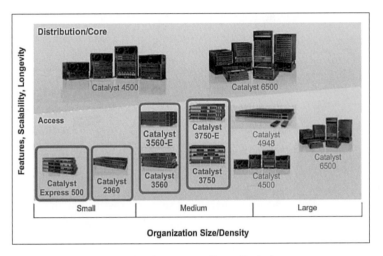

Figure 10-38   Fixed Configuration Cisco Switches

This switch series is appropriate for access layer implementations where high port density is not required. The Cisco Catalyst Express 500 series switches are scaled for small business environments ranging from 20 to 250 employees. The Catalyst Express 500 series switches are available in different fixed configurations:

- Fast Ethernet and Gigabit Ethernet connectivity

- Up to 24 10/100 ports with optional PoE or 12 10/100/1000 ports

Catalyst Express 500 series switches do not allow management through the Cisco IOS CLI. They are managed using a built-in web management interface, the Cisco Network Assistant, or the new Cisco Configuration Manager developed specifically for the Catalyst Express 500 series switches. The Catalyst Express does not support console access.

Catalyst 2960

The Catalyst 2960 series switches enable entry-layer enterprise, medium-sized, and branch-office networks to provide enhanced LAN services. The Catalyst 2960 series switches are appropriate for access layer implementations where access to power and space is limited.

The Catalyst 2960 series switches offer the following:

- Forwarding rates from 16 Gbps to 32 Gbps

- Multilayered switching

- QoS features to support IP communications

- Access control lists (ACLs)

- Fast Ethernet and Gigabit Ethernet connectivity

- Up to 48 10/100 ports or 10/100/1000 ports with additional, dual-purpose gigabit uplinks

The Catalyst 2960 series supports the Cisco IOS CLI, integrated web management interface, and Cisco Network Assistant. This switch series supports console and auxiliary access to the switch.

Catalyst 3560

The Cisco Catalyst 3560 series is a line of enterprise-class switches that includes support for PoE, QoS, and advanced security features such as ACLs. These switches are ideal access layer switches for small enterprise LAN access or branch-office converged network environments.

The Cisco Catalyst 3560 series supports forwarding rates of 32 Gbps to 128 Gbps (Catalyst 3560-E switch series).

The Catalyst 3560 series switches are available in different fixed configurations:

- Fast Ethernet and Gigabit Ethernet connectivity

- Up to 48 10/100/1000 ports, plus four small form-factor pluggable (SFP) ports

- Optional 10-Gigabit Ethernet connectivity in the Catalyst 3560-E models

- Optional Integrated PoE (Cisco pre-standard and IEEE 802.3af); up to 24 ports with 15.4 watts or 48 ports with 7.3 watts

Catalyst 3750

The Cisco Catalyst 3750 series switches are ideal for access layer switches in midsize organizations and enterprise branch offices. This series offers forwarding rates from 32 Gbps to 128 Gbps (Catalyst 3750-E switch series). The Catalyst 3750 series supports Cisco StackWise technology. StackWise technology enables you to interconnect up to nine physical Catalyst 3750 switches into one logical switch using a high-performance (32 Gbps), redundant, backplane connection.

Stackable switches can be interconnected using a special backplane cable that provides high-bandwidth throughput between the switches. StackWise enables you to interconnect up to nine switches using fully redundant backplane connections. As shown earlier in Figure 10-37, switches are stacked one atop the other, and cables connect the switches in daisy chain fashion. The stacked switches effectively operate as a single larger switch. Stackable switches are desirable where fault tolerance and bandwidth availability are critical and a modular switch is too costly to implement. Using cross-connected connections, the network can recover quickly if a single switch fails. Stackable switches use a special port for interconnections and do not use line ports for inter-switch connections. The speeds are also typically faster than using line ports for connection switches.

The Catalyst 3750 series switches are available in different stackable fixed configurations:

- Fast Ethernet and Gigabit Ethernet connectivity

- Up to 48 10/100/1000 ports, plus four SFP ports

- Optional 10-Gigabit Ethernet connectivity in the Catalyst 3750-E models

- Optional Integrated PoE (Cisco pre-standard and IEEE 802.3af); up to 24 ports with 15.4 watts or 48 ports with 7.3 watts

Modular Configuration Cisco Switches (10.3.2.3)

The Cisco switch product lines described next and depicted in Figure 10-39 comprise the modular configuration Cisco switches that are available.

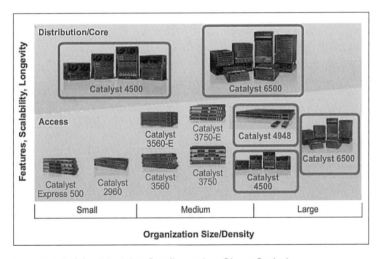

Figure 10-39 Modular Configuration Cisco Switches

Catalyst 4500

The Catalyst 4500 is the first midrange modular switching platform offering multilayer switching for enterprises, small- to medium-sized businesses, and service providers.

With forwarding rates up to 136 Gbps, the Catalyst 4500 series is capable of managing traffic at the distribution layer. The modular capability of the Catalyst 4500 series allows for very high port densities through the addition of switch port line cards to its modular chassis. The Catalyst 4500 series offers multilayer QoS and sophisticated routing functions.

The Catalyst 4500 series switches are available in different modular configurations:

- Modular 3-, 6-, 7-, and 10-slot chassis offering different layers of scalability
- High port density: up to 384 Fast Ethernet or Gigabit Ethernet ports available in copper or fiber with 10-Gigabit uplinks
- PoE (Cisco pre-standard and IEEE 802.3af)
- Dual, hot-swappable internal AC or DC power supplies
- Advanced hardware-assisted IP routing capabilities

Catalyst 4900

The Catalyst 4900 series switches are designed and optimized for server switching by allowing very high forwarding rates. The Cisco Catalyst 4900 is not a typical access layer switch. It is a specialty access layer switch designed for data center deployments where many servers may exist in close proximity. This switch series supports dual, redundant power supplies and fans that can be swapped out while the switch is still running. This allows the switches to achieve higher availability, which is critical in data center deployments.

The Catalyst 4900 series switches support advanced QoS features, making them ideal candidates for the back-end IP telephony hardware. Catalyst 4900 series switches do not support the StackWise feature of the Catalyst 3750 series, nor do they support PoE.

The Catalyst 4900 series modular switches are available in different fixed configurations with two half slots:

- Up to 48 10/100/1000 ports with four SFP ports or 48 10/100/1000 ports with two 10-Gigabit Ethernet ports
- Dual, hot-swappable internal AC or DC power supplies
- Hot-swappable fan trays

Catalyst 6500

The Catalyst 6500 series modular switch is optimized for secure, converged voice, video, and data networks. The Catalyst 6500 is capable of managing traffic at the distribution and core layers. The Catalyst 6500 series is the highest performing Cisco switch, supporting forwarding rates up to 720 Gbps. The Catalyst 6500 is ideal for very large network environments found in enterprises, medium-sized businesses, and service providers.

The Catalyst 6500 series switches are available in different modular configurations:

- Modular 3-, 4-, 6-, 9-, and 13-slot chassis
- LAN/WAN service modules
- PoE up to 420 IEEE 802.3af Class 3 (15.4W) PoE devices
- Up to 1152 10/100 ports, 577 10/100/1000 ports, 410 SFP Gigabit Ethernet ports, or 64 10-Gigabit Ethernet ports
- Dual, hot-swappable internal AC or DC power supplies
- Advanced hardware-assisted IP routing capabilities

Module Options for Cisco Switch Slots (10.3.2.4)

The Cisco switch product lines are widely deployed globally, in large part due to the flexibility they provide for add-on options. Not only does the Cisco IOS have the richest set of features available relative to any other network operating system, but the IOS is tailor-fit to each Cisco networking device, switches in particular.

To illustrate the options available, which are literally too voluminous to list here, we focus on the Catalyst 3560 switches. The Catalyst 3560 switches have *small form-factor pluggable (SFP) ports*, as shown in Figure 10-40, that support a number of SFP transceiver modules.

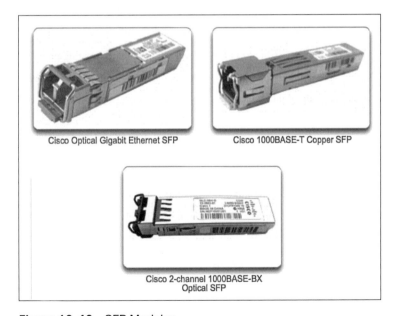

Cisco Optical Gigabit Ethernet SFP   Cisco 1000BASE-T Copper SFP

Cisco 2-channel 1000BASE-BX
Optical SFP

Figure 10-40   SFP Modules

Here is a list of the SFP modules supported on one or more types of 3560 switches:

Fast Ethernet SFP Modules

- 100BASE-FX (multimode fiber [MMF]) for 2 kilometers (km)
- 100BASE-LX10 (single-mode fiber [SMF]) for 2 km
- 100BASE-BX10 (SMF) for 10 km
- 100BASE-EX (SMF) for 40 km
- 100BASE-ZX (SMF) for 80 km

Gigabit Ethernet SFP Modules

- 1000BASE-SX 50/62.5 µm (MMF) up to 550/220 m
- 1000BASE-LX/LH (SMF/MMF) up to 10/0.550 km
- 1000BASE-ZX (SMF) up to 70 km
- 1000BASE-BX10-D &1000BASE-BX10-U (SMF) up to 10 km
- 1000BASE-T (copper wire transceiver)

10-Gigabit Ethernet SFP Modules

- 10G-SR (MMF) up 400 m
- 10G-SR-X (MMF) up to 400 m (supporting extended temperature range)
- 10G-LRM (MMF) up to 220 m
- FET-10G (MMF) up to 100 m (for Nexus fabric uplinks)
- 10G-LR (SMF) up to 10 km
- 10G-LR-X (SMF) up to 10 km (supporting extended temperature range)
- 10G-ER (SMF) up to 40 km
- 10G-ZR (SMF) up to 80 km
- Twinax (copper wire transceiver) up to 10 m
- Active Optical up to 10 m (for intra/inter-rack connections)

40-Gigabit Ethernet and 100-Gigabit Ethernet modules are supported on high-end Cisco devices, such as the Catalyst 6500, the CRS router, the ASR 9000 series router, and the Nexus 7000 series switch.

Layer 3 Switching (10.3.3)

Up to this point we have been discussing Layer 2 switching, switches that are unable to route packages between networks. This section looks at Layer 3 switches, which are switches that are capable of making decisions based on Layer 3 IP addresses.

Layer 2 Versus Layer 3 Switching (10.3.3.1)

In addition to determining the various switch form factors, it might also be necessary to choose between a *Layer 2 LAN switch* and a *Layer 3 switch*.

Recall that a Layer 2 LAN switch performs switching and filtering based only on the OSI data link layer (Layer 2) MAC address and depends on routers to pass data between independent IP subnetworks (see Figure 10-41).

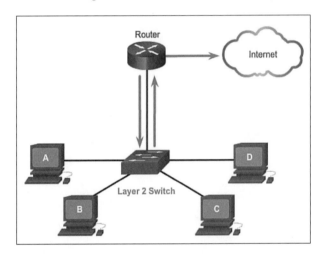

Figure 10-41   Layer 2 Switching

As shown in Figure 10-42, a Layer 3 switch, such as the Catalyst 3560, functions similarly to a Layer 2 switch, such as the Catalyst 2960, but instead of using only the Layer 2 MAC address information for forwarding decisions, a Layer 3 switch can also use IP address information. Instead of only learning which MAC addresses are associated with each of its ports, a Layer 3 switch can also learn which IP addresses are associated with its interfaces. This allows the Layer 3 switch to direct traffic throughout the network based on IP address information as well.

Layer 3 switches are also capable of performing Layer 3 routing functions, reducing the need for dedicated routers on a LAN. Because Layer 3 switches have specialized switching hardware, they can typically route data as quickly as they can switch.

Cisco Express Forwarding (10.3.3.2)

Cisco devices that support Layer 3 switching utilize Cisco Express Forwarding (CEF). Figure 10-43 shows the Layer 3 switching process. This forwarding method is quite complex, but fortunately, like any good technology, is carried out in large part "behind the scenes." Normally very little CEF configuration is required on a Cisco device.

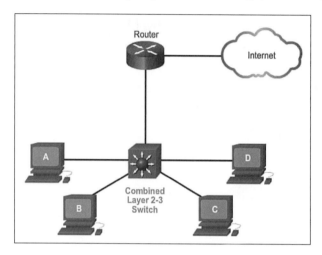

Figure 10-42   Layer 3 Switching

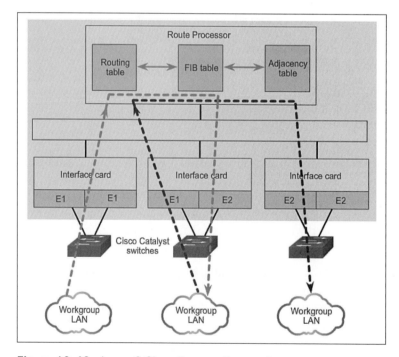

Figure 10-43   Layer 3 Cisco Express Forwarding

Basically, CEF decouples the usual strict interdependence between Layer 2 and Layer 3 decision making. What makes forwarding IP packets slow is the constant referencing back and forth between Layer 2 and Layer 3 constructs within a networking device. So, to the extent that Layer 2 and Layer 3 data structures can be decoupled, forwarding is accelerated.

The following are the two main components of CEF operation:

- Forwarding Information Base (FIB)

- Adjacency tables

The FIB is conceptually similar to a routing table. A router uses the routing table to determine the best path to a destination network based on the network portion of the destination IP address. With CEF, information previously stored in the route cache is, instead, stored in several data structures for CEF switching. The data structures provide optimized lookup for efficient packet forwarding. A networking device uses the FIB lookup table to make destination-based switching decisions without having to access the route cache.

The FIB is updated when changes occur in the network and contains all routes known at the time.

Adjacency tables maintain Layer 2 next-hop addresses for all FIB entries.

The separation of the reachability information (in the FIB table) and the forwarding information (in the adjacency table) provides a number of benefits:

- The adjacency table can be built separately from the FIB table, allowing both to be built without any packets being process switched.

- The MAC header rewrite used to forward a packet is not stored in cache entries, so changes in a MAC header rewrite string do not require invalidation of cache entries.

CEF is enabled by default on most Cisco devices that perform Layer 3 switching.

Types of Layer 3 Interfaces (10.3.3.3)

Cisco networking devices support a number of distinct types of Layer 3 interfaces. A Layer 3 interface is one that supports forwarding IP packets toward a final destination based on the IP address.

The major types of Layer 3 interfaces are

- **Switch virtual interface (SVI):** Logical interface on a switch associated with a VLAN, as shown in Figure 10-44.

- **Routed port:** Physical port on a Layer 3 switch configured to act as a router port.

- **Layer 3 EtherChannel:** Logical interface on a Cisco device associated with a bundle of routed ports.

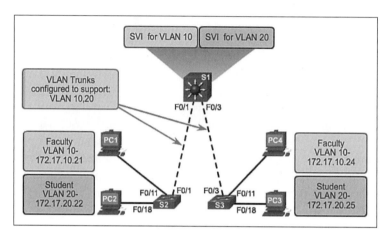

Figure 10-44   Layer 3 Switch Virtual Interface (SVI)

As shown previously, an SVI for the default VLAN (VLAN1) must be enabled to provide IP host connectivity to the switch and permit remote switch administration. SVIs must also be configured to allow routing between VLANs. As stated, SVIs are logical interfaces configured for specific VLANs; to route between two or more VLANs, each VLAN must have a separate SVI enabled.

Routed ports enable (Layer 3) Cisco switches to effectively serve as routers. Each port on such a switch can be configured as a port on an independent IP network.

Layer 3 EtherChannels are used to bundle Layer 3 Ethernet links between Cisco devices in order to aggregate bandwidth, typically on uplinks.

Note

In addition to SVIs and Layer 3 EtherChannels, other logical interfaces on Cisco devices include loopback interfaces and tunnel interfaces.

Configuring a Routed Port on a Layer 3 Switch (10.3.3.4)

A switch port can be configured to be a Layer 3 routed port and behave like a regular router interface. Specifically, a routed port

- Is not associated with a particular VLAN

- Can be configured with a Layer 3 routing protocol

■ Is a Layer 3 interface only and does not support Layer 2 protocol

Configure routed ports by putting the interface into Layer 3 mode with the **no switchport** interface configuration command. Then assign an IP address to the port.

Figure 10-45 shows an example of routed port configuration.

```
S1(config)#interface f0/6
S1(config-if)#no switchport
S1(config-if)#ip address 192.168.200.1 255.255.255.0
S1(config-if)#no shutdown
S1(config-if)#end
S1#
*Mar  1 00:15:40.115: %SYS-5-CONFIG_I: Configured from console by console
S1#show ip interface brief
Interface        IP-Address     OK? Method Status                Protocol
Vlan1            unassigned     YES unset  administratively down  down
FastEthernet0/1  unassigned     YES unset  down                   down
FastEthernet0/2  unassigned     YES unset  down                   down
FastEthernet0/3  unassigned     YES unset  down                   down
FastEthernet0/4  unassigned     YES unset  down                   down
FastEthernet0/5  unassigned     YES unset  down                   down
FastEthernet0/6  192.168.200.1  YES manual up                     up
FastEthernet0/7  unassigned     YES unset  up                     up
FastEthernet0/8  unassigned     YES unset  up                     up
<output omitted>
```

Figure 10-45   Routed Port Configuration

Packet Tracer Activity 10.3.3.5: Configure Layer 3 Switches

The Network Administrator is replacing the current router and switch with a new Layer 3 switch. As the Network Technician, it is your job to configure the switch and place it into service. You will be working after hours to minimize disruption to the business.

Summary (10.4)

Class Activity 10.4.1.1: MAC and Choose...

Note

This activity can be completed individually, in small groups, or in a full-classroom learning environment.

Please view the video located at the following link: http://www.netevents.tv/video/bob-metcalfe-the-history-of-ethernet.

Topics discussed include not only where we have come from in Ethernet development, but where we are going with Ethernet technology (a futuristic approach).

After viewing the video and applying the concepts learned in the video to what you learned in Chapter 10, go to the Web and search for information about Ethernet. Use a constructivist approach:

- What did Ethernet look like when it was first developed?

- How has Ethernet stayed the same over the past 25 years or so, and what changes are being made to make it more useful and applicable to today's data transmission methods?

Collect three pictures of old, current, and future Ethernet physical media and devices (focus on switches)—share these pictures with the class and discuss the following:

- How have Ethernet physical media and intermediary devices changed?

- How have Ethernet physical media and intermediary devices stayed the same?

- How will Ethernet change in the future?

Ethernet is the most widely used LAN technology in use today. It is a family of networking technologies defined in the IEEE 802.2 and 802.3 standards. Ethernet standards define both the Layer 2 protocols and the Layer 1 technologies. For the Layer 2 protocols, as with all 802 IEEE standards, Ethernet relies on the two separate sublayers of the data link layer to operate: the LLC and MAC sublayers.

At the data link layer, the frame structure is nearly identical for all speeds of Ethernet. The Ethernet frame structure adds headers and trailers around the Layer 3 PDU to encapsulate the message being sent. Both the Ethernet header and trailer have several sections of information that are used by the Ethernet protocol. Each section of the frame is called a field. There are two styles of Ethernet framing: the

IEEE 802.3 Ethernet standard and the DIX Ethernet standard (which is now referred to Ethernet II). The most significant difference between the two standards is that IEEE 802.3 adds an SFD field and changes the Type field to a Length field. Ethernet II is the Ethernet frame format used in TCP/IP networks.

As an implementation of the IEEE 802.2/3 standards, the Ethernet frame provides MAC addressing and error checking. Being a shared media technology, early Ethernet had to apply a CSMA/CD mechanism to manage the use of the media by multiple devices. Replacing hubs with switches in the local network has reduced the probability of frame collisions in half-duplex links. Current and future versions, however, inherently operate as full-duplex communications links and do not need to manage media contention to the same detail.

The Layer 2 addressing provided by Ethernet supports unicast, multicast, and broadcast communications. Ethernet uses ARP to determine the MAC addresses of destinations and map them against known network layer addresses.

Each node on an IP network has both a MAC address and an IP address. The node must use its own MAC and IP addresses in the source fields and must provide both a MAC address and an IP address for the destination. Although the IP address of the destination will be provided by a higher OSI layer, the sending node must find the MAC address of the destination for a given Ethernet link. This is the purpose of ARP.

ARP relies on certain types of Ethernet broadcast messages and Ethernet unicast messages, called ARP requests and ARP replies. The ARP protocol resolves IPv4 addresses to MAC addresses and maintains a table of mappings.

On most Ethernet networks, end devices are typically connected, in a point-to-point manner, to a Layer 2 LAN switch. A Layer 2 LAN switch performs switching and filtering based only on the OSI data link layer (Layer 2) MAC address. A Layer 2 switch builds a MAC address table that it uses to make forwarding decisions. Layer 2 switches depend on routers to pass data between independent IP subnetworks.

Layer 3 switches are also capable of performing Layer 3 routing functions, reducing the need for dedicated routers on a LAN. Because Layer 3 switches have specialized switching hardware, they can typically route data as quickly as they can switch.

Practice

The following activities provide practice with the topics introduced in this chapter. The Labs and Class Activities are available in the companion *Network Basics Lab Manual* (978-1-58713-313-8). The Packet Tracer Activities PKA files are found in the online course.

Class Activities

Class Activity 10.0.1.2: Join My Social Circle!

Class Activity 10.4.1.1: MAC and Choose...

Labs

Lab 10.1.3.6: Viewing Network Device MAC Addresses

Lab 10.1.4.3: Using Wireshark to Examine Ethernet Frames

Lab 10.2.1.8: Observing ARP with the Windows CLI, IOS CLI, and Wireshark

Lab 10.3.1.10: Viewing the Switch MAC Address Table

Packet Tracer Activities

Packet Tracer Activity 10.1.4.4: Identify MAC and IP Addresses

Packet Tracer Activity 10.2.1.7: Examine the ARP Table

Packet Tracer Activity 10.3.3.5: Configure Layer 3 Switches

Check Your Understanding

Complete all the review questions listed here to test your understanding of the topics and concepts in this chapter. The appendix, "Answers to the 'Check Your Understanding' Questions" lists the answers.

1. Which Ethernet sublayer is used to control network access using CSMA/CD?

    A. LLC

    B. MAC

    C. Data Link

    D. Physical

2. Which function or operation is performed by the LLC sublayer?

    A. It performs data encapsulation.

    B. It communicates with upper protocol layers.

    C. It is responsible for media access control.

    D. It adds a header and trailer to a packet to form an OSI Layer 2 PDU.

3. Which two functions or operations are performed by the MAC sublayer? (Choose two.)

   A. It is responsible for Media Access Control.

   B. It performs the function of NIC driver software.

   C. It adds a header and trailer to form an OSI Layer 2 PDU.

   D. It handles communication between upper and lower layers.

   E. It adds control information to network protocol layer data.

4. On Ethernet networks, the hexadecimal address FF-FF-FF-FF-FF-FF represents the _____ MAC address.

   A. Broadcast

   B. Unicast

   C. Multicast

   D. Independent

5. What type of address is 01-00-5E-0A-00-02?

   A. An address that reaches every host inside a local subnet

   B. An address that reaches one specific host

   C. An address that reaches every host in the network

   D. An address that reaches a specific group of hosts

6. Which destination address is used in an ARP request frame?

   A. 0.0.0.0

   B. 255.255.255.255

   C. FFFF.FFFF.FFFF

   D. AAAA.AAAA.AAAA

   E. The physical address of the destination host

7. What will a host do first when preparing a Layer 2 PDU for transmission to a host on the same Ethernet network?

   A. It will send the PDU to the router directly connected to the network.

   B. It will query the local DNS server for the name of the destination host.

   C. It will search the ARP table for the MAC address of the destination host.

   D. It will initiate an ARP request to find the MAC address of the destination host.

8. During an ARP spoofing attack, an intruder sends many inaccurate ARP replies in an attempt to associate incorrect IP addresses to a MAC address. How can a switch help to prevent this type of attack?

A. By not propagating ARP broadcast messages

B. By configuring static ARP associations

C. By verifying all ARP replies against its internal ARP table

D. By forwarding the ARP requests only to the correct destination node

9. What are two problems that can be caused by a large number of ARP request and reply messages? (Choose two.)

A. A large number of ARP request and reply messages may slow down the switching process, leading the switch to make many changes in its MAC table.

B. All ARP request messages must be processed by all nodes on the local network.

C. The ARP request is sent as a broadcast and will flood the entire subnet.

D. The network may become overloaded because ARP reply messages have a very large payload due to the 48-bit MAC address and 32-bit IP address that they contain.

E. Switches become overloaded because they concentrate all the traffic from the attached subnets.

10. What type of switch interface should be configured with an IP address so that the switch can be managed from any port on a specific VLAN?

A. Layer 2 EtherChannel

B. Layer 3 EtherChannel

C. Routed port

D. SVI

CHAPTER 11

It's a Network

Objectives

Upon completion of this chapter, you will be able to answer the following questions:

- What are the devices and protocols used in a small network?

- How does a small network serve as the basis of larger networks?

- Why are basic security measures needed on network devices?

- What are security vulnerabilities and general mitigation techniques?

- How do you configure network devices with device-hardening features to mitigate security threats?

- How do you use the output of the **ping** and **tracert** commands to establish relative network performance?

- How do you use the basic **show** commands to verify the configuration and status of a device interface?

- Which file systems are present on routers and switches?

- How do you apply the commands to back up and restore an IOS configuration file?

Key Terms

This chapter uses the following key terms. You can find the definitions in the Glossary.

expandability   page 550

operating system features and services   page 550

network applications   page 554

IMAP   page 555

infrastructure   page 556

Voice over IP (VoIP)   page 557

IP telephony   page 557

Real-Time Transport Protocol (RTP)   page 557

Real-Time Transport Control Protocol (RTCP)   page 557

information theft   page 560

identity theft   page 560

data loss/manipulation   page 560

disruption of service   page 560

reconnaissance attacks   page 565

access attacks   page 565

denial of service attacks   page 565

containment   page 567

inoculation   page 567

quarantine   page 567

Introduction (11.0.1.1)

Up to this point in the course, we have considered the services that a data network can provide to the human network, examined the features of each layer of the OSI model and the operations of TCP/IP protocols, and looked in detail at Ethernet, a universal LAN technology. The next step is to learn how to assemble these elements in a functioning network that can be maintained.

Class Activity 11.0.1.2: Did You Notice?

In this activity you will compare and contrast two different networks.

Note
Students can work singularly, in pairs, or in a full-classroom learning environment.

Go to the online course to perform the network compare and contrast practice activity.

Create and Grow (11.1)

This section takes a look at devices and protocols used in a small network, and what it takes to grow from a smaller to a larger network.

Devices in a Small Network (11.1.1)

Let's start by examining the different devices in a small network and how they are connected.

Small Network Topologies (11.1.1.1)

The majority of businesses are small businesses. It is not surprising then that the majority of networks are small networks.

With small networks, the design of the network is usually simple. The number and types of devices on the network are significantly reduced compared to that of a larger network, as shown in Figure 11-1. The network topologies for small networks typically involve a single router and one or more switches. Small networks may also have wireless access points (possibly built into the router) and IP phones. As for connection to the Internet, normally a small network has a single WAN connection provided by DSL, cable, or an Ethernet connection.

Managing a small network requires many of the same skills as those required for managing a larger one. The majority of work is focused on maintenance and trouble-shooting of existing equipment, as well as securing devices and information on the network. The management of a small network is done either by an employee of the company or by a person contracted by the company, depending on the size of the business and the type of business.

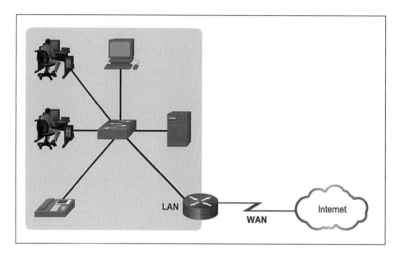

Figure 11-1   Typical Small Business Network

Device Selection for a Small Network (11.1.1.2)

In order to meet user requirements, even small networks require planning and design. Planning ensures that all requirements, cost factors, and deployment options are given due consideration.

One of the first design considerations when implementing a small network is the type of intermediate devices to use to support the network. When selecting the type of intermediate devices, there are a number of factors that need to be considered, as shown in Figure 11-2.

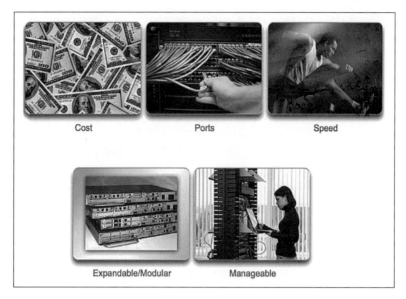

Figure 11-2   Factors to Consider in Choosing a Device

Cost

Cost is typically one of the most important factors when selecting equipment for a small business network. The cost of a switch or router is determined by its capacity and features. The device capacity includes the number and types of ports available and the backplane speed. Other factors that affect the cost are network management capabilities, embedded security technologies, and optional advanced switching technologies. The expense of cable runs required to connect every device on the network must also be considered. Another key element affecting cost consideration is how much redundancy to incorporate into the network—this includes devices, ports per device, and copper or fiber-optic cabling.

Speed and Types of Ports/Interfaces

Choosing the number and types of ports on a router or switch is a critical decision. Questions to be asked include

- Do we order just enough ports for today's needs, or do we consider growth requirements?

- Do we require a mixture of UTP speeds?

- Do we require both UTP and fiber ports?

Newer computers have built-in 1-Gbps NICs. 10-Gbps ports are already included with some workstations and servers. Although it is more expensive, choosing Layer 2 devices that can accommodate increased speeds makes it possible for the network to evolve without replacing central devices.

Expandability

Networking devices come in both fixed and modular physical configurations. Fixed configurations have a specific number and type of ports or interfaces, making them a poor choice for *expandability* of the network. Modular devices have expansion slots that provide the flexibility to add new modules as requirements evolve. Most modular devices come with a basic number of fixed ports and expansion slots. Switches are available with special additional ports for optional high-speed uplinks. Also, because routers can be used for connecting different numbers and types of networks, care must be taken to select the appropriate modules and interfaces for the specific media. Questions to be considered include

- Do we order devices with upgradable modules?
- What type of WAN interfaces, if any, are required on the router(s)?

Operating System Features and Services

Depending on the version of the operating system, a network device can support certain *operating system features and services*, such as

- Security
- Quality of service (QoS)
- Voice over IP (VoIP)
- Layer 3 switching
- Network address translation (NAT)
- Dynamic Host Control Protocol (DHCP)

Routers can be expensive, depending on the interfaces and features needed. Additional modules, such as fiber optics, increase the cost of the network devices.

IP Addressing for a Small Network (11.1.1.3)

When implementing a small network, it is necessary to plan the IP addressing space. All hosts within an internetwork must have a unique address. Even on a small network, address assignment within the network should not be random. Rather, the IP addressing scheme should be planned, documented, and maintained based on the type of device receiving the address.

Examples of different types of devices that will factor into the IP design are

- End devices for users
- Servers and peripherals
- Hosts that are accessible from the Internet
- Intermediary devices

Planning and documenting the IP addressing scheme helps the administrator to track device types. For example, if all servers are assigned a host address in the range 50 to 100, it is easy to identify server traffic by IP address. This can be very useful when troubleshooting network traffic issues using a protocol analyzer.

Additionally, administrators are better able to control access to resources on the network based on IP address when a deterministic IP addressing scheme is used. This can be especially important for hosts that provide resources both to the internal network and to the external network. Web servers or e-commerce servers play such a role. If the addresses for these resources are not planned and documented, the security and accessibility of the devices are not easily controlled. If a server has a random address assigned, blocking access to this address is difficult and clients may not be able to locate this resource.

Each of these different device types should be allocated to a logical block of addresses within the address range of the network.

Click the buttons in Activity 11.1.1.3 to see the method for assignment.

Interactive Graphic

Activity 11.1.1.3: IPv4 Address Planning and Assignment

Go to the online course and click through the buttons in the figure to see the method for IPv4 address planning and assignment.

Redundancy in a Small Network (11.1.1.4)

Another important part of network design is reliability. Even small businesses often rely on their network heavily for business operation. A failure of the network can be very costly. To maintain a high degree of reliability, redundancy is required in the network design. Redundancy helps to eliminate single points of failure. There are many ways to accomplish redundancy in a network. Redundancy can be accomplished by installing duplicate equipment, but it can also be accomplished by supplying duplicate network links for critical areas, as shown in Activity 11.1.1.4.

Activity 11.1.1.4: Redundancy to a Server Farm

Go to the online course and click the blue-highlighted devices and connections for additional information.

The smaller the network, the less the chance that redundancy of equipment will be affordable. Therefore, a common way to introduce redundancy is through the use of redundant switch connections between multiple switches on the network and between switches and routers.

Also, servers often have multiple NIC ports that enable redundant connections to one or more switches. In a small network, servers typically are deployed as web servers, file servers, or email servers.

Small networks typically provide a single exit point toward the Internet via one or more default gateways. With one router in the topology, the only redundancy in terms of Layer 3 paths is enabled by utilizing more than one inside Ethernet interface on the router. However, if the router fails, the entire network loses connectivity to the Internet. For this reason, it may be advisable for a small business to pay for a least-cost option account with a second service provider for backup.

Design Considerations for a Small Network (11.1.1.5)

Users expect immediate access to their emails and to the files that they are sharing or updating. To help ensure this availability, the network designer should take the following steps:

Step 1. Secure file and mail servers in a centralized location.

Step 2. Protect the location from unauthorized access by implementing physical and logical security measures.

Step 3. Create redundancy in the server farm that ensures if one device fails, files are not lost.

Step 4. Configure redundant paths to the servers.

In addition, modern networks often use some form of voice or video over IP for communication with customers and business partners. This type of converged network is implemented as an integrated solution or as an additional form of raw data overlaid onto the IP network. The network administrator should consider the various types of traffic and their treatment in the network design. The router(s) and switch(es) in a small network should be configured to support real-time traffic, such as voice and video, in a distinct manner relative to other data traffic. In fact, a good network design will classify traffic carefully according to priority, as shown in Figure 11-3. Traffic classes could be as specific as

- File transfer

- Email

- Voice

- Video

- Messaging

- Transactional

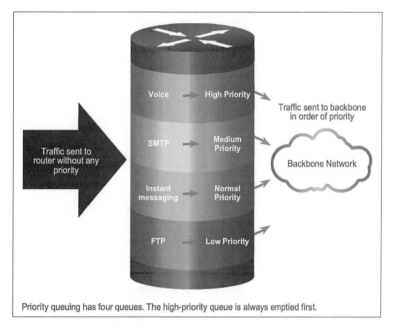

Figure 11-3   Prioritizing Traffic

In the end, the goal for a good network design, even for a small network, is to enhance productivity of the employees and minimize network downtime.

Interactive Graphic

Activity 11.1.1.6: Network Planning and Design

Go to the online course and perform the drag-and-drop exercise.

Protocols in a Small Network (11.1.2)

Several protocols are utilized in small networks, as described in this section.

Common Applications in a Small Network (11.1.2.1)

The network is only as useful as the applications that are on it. As shown in Figure 11-4, within the application layer, there are two forms of software programs or processes that provide access to the network: network applications and application layer services.

Figure 11-4   Windows Task Manager

Network Applications

Network applications are the software programs used to communicate over the network. Some end-user applications are network-aware, meaning that they implement application layer protocols and are able to communicate directly with the lower layers of the protocol stack. Email clients and web browsers are examples of this type of application.

Application Layer Services

Other programs may need the assistance of application layer services to use network resources, such as file transfer or network print spooling. Though transparent to an employee, these services are the programs that interface with the network and prepare the data for transfer. Different types of data, whether text, graphics, or video, require different network services to ensure that they are properly prepared for processing by the functions occurring at the lower layers of the OSI model.

Each application or network service uses protocols, which define the standards and data formats to be used. Without protocols, the data network would not have a common way to format and direct data. In order to understand the function of various network services, it is necessary to become familiar with the underlying protocols that govern their operation.

Common Protocols in a Small Network (11.1.2.2)

Most of a technician's work, in either a small network or a large network, will in some way be involved with network protocols. Network protocols support the applications and services used by employees in a small network. Common network protocols include

- DNS
- Telnet
- *IMAP*, SMTP, POP (email)
- DHCP
- HTTP
- FTP

Click the servers in the figure in Activity 11.1.2.2 for a brief description of the network services each provides.

Interactive Graphic

Activity 11.1.2.2: Network Services

Go to the online course and click each server for a brief description of network services provided.

These network protocols comprise the fundamental tool set of a network professional. Each of these network protocols defines

- Processes on either end of a communication session
- Types of messages
- Syntax of the messages
- Meaning of informational fields
- How messages are sent and the expected response
- Interaction with the next lower layer

Many companies have established a policy of using secure versions of HTTP, FTP, and Telnet protocols whenever possible. These protocols are HTTPS, SFTP, and SSH.

Real-Time Applications for a Small Network (11.1.2.3)

In addition to the common network protocols described previously, modern businesses, even small ones, typically utilize real-time applications for communicating with customers and business partners. Although a small company may not be able to justify the cost of an enterprise Cisco TelePresence solution, there are other real-time applications that are affordable and justifiable for small business organizations. Real-time applications require more planning and dedicated services (relative to other types of data) to ensure priority delivery of voice and video traffic. This means that the network administrator must ensure that the proper equipment is installed in the network and that the network devices are configured to ensure priority delivery. Figure 11-5 shows elements of a small network that support real-time applications.

Cable and switch   IP phones

Cisco Unified Communications 500 Series

Figure 11-5   Elements of a Small Network

Infrastructure

To support the existing and proposed real-time applications, the *infrastructure* must accommodate the characteristics of each type of traffic. The network designer must determine whether the existing switches and cabling can support the traffic that will be added to the network. Cabling that can support gigabit transmissions should be able to carry the traffic generated and not require any changes to the infrastructure. Older switches may not support Power over Ethernet (PoE). Obsolete cabling may not support the bandwidth requirements. The switches and cabling would need to be upgraded to support these applications.

VoIP

Voice over IP (VoIP) is implemented in organizations that still use traditional telephones. VoIP uses voice-enabled routers. These routers convert analog voice from traditional telephone signals into IP packets. After the signals are converted into IP packets, the router sends those packets between corresponding locations. VoIP is much less expensive than an integrated IP telephony solution, but the quality of communications does not meet the same standards. Voice and video over IP solutions for small businesses can be realized, for example, with Skype and non-enterprise versions of Cisco WebEx.

IP Telephony

In *IP telephony*, the IP phone itself performs voice-to-IP conversion. Voice-enabled routers are not required within a network with an integrated IP telephony solution. IP phones use a dedicated server for call control and signaling. There are now many vendors with dedicated IP telephony solutions for small networks.

Real-time Applications

To transport streaming media effectively, the network must be able to support applications that require delay-sensitive delivery. *Real-Time Transport Protocol (RTP)* and *Real-Time Transport Control Protocol (RTCP)* are two protocols that support this requirement. RTP and RTCP enable control and scalability of the network resources by allowing QoS mechanisms to be incorporated. These QoS mechanisms provide valuable tools for minimizing latency issues for real-time streaming applications.

Growing to Larger Networks (11.1.3)

Growth is a natural process for many small businesses, and their networks must grow accordingly. A network administrator for a small network will work either reactively or proactively, depending on the leaders of the company, which often include the network administrator. Ideally, the network administrator has enough lead time to make intelligent decisions about growing the network in line with the growth of the company.

Scaling a Small Network (11.1.3.1)

To scale a network, several elements are required:

- **Network documentation:** Physical and logical topology
- **Device inventory:** List of devices that use or comprise the network

- **Budget:** Itemized IT budget, including fiscal year equipment purchasing budget

- **Traffic analysis:** Documentation of protocols, applications, and services and their respective traffic requirements

These elements are used to inform the decision making that accompanies the scaling of a small network.

Protocol Analysis of a Small Network (11.1.3.2)

Supporting and growing a small network requires being familiar with the protocols and network applications running over the network. Although the network administrator will have more time in a small network environment to individually analyze network utilization for each network-enabled device, a more holistic approach with some type of software- or hardware-based protocol analyzer is recommended.

As shown in Figure 11-6, protocol analyzers enable a network professional to quickly compile statistical information about traffic flows on a network.

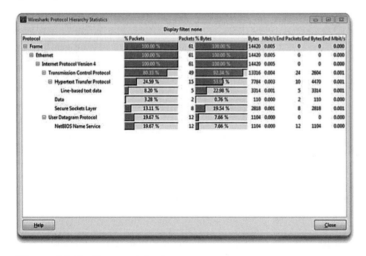

Figure 11-6　Protocol Analyzer

When trying to determine how to manage network traffic, especially as the network grows, it is important to understand the type of traffic that is crossing the network as well as the current traffic flow. If the types of traffic are unknown, the protocol analyzer will help identify the traffic and its source.

To determine traffic flow patterns, it is important to do the following:

- Capture traffic during peak utilization times to get a good representation of the different traffic types.

- Perform the capture on different network segments because some traffic will be local to a particular segment.

Information gathered by the protocol analyzer is analyzed based on the source and destination of the traffic as well as the type of traffic being sent. This analysis can be used to make decisions on how to manage the traffic more efficiently. This can be done by reducing unnecessary traffic flows or changing flow patterns altogether by moving a server, for example.

Sometimes, simply relocating a server or service to another network segment improves network performance and accommodates the growing traffic needs. At other times, optimizing the network performance requires major network redesign and intervention.

Evolving Protocol Requirements (11.1.3.3)

In addition to understanding changing traffic trends, a network administrator must also be aware of how network use is changing. As shown in Activity 11.1.3.3, a network administrator in a small network has the ability to obtain in-person IT "snapshots" of employee application utilization for a significant portion of the employee workforce over time.

Interactive Graphic

Activity 11.1.3.3: Software Processes

Go to the online course and click each process button for examples of processes running in the Windows operating system.

These snapshots typically include information such as

- OS and OS version
- Non-network applications
- Network applications
- CPU utilization
- Drive utilization
- RAM utilization

Documenting snapshots for employees in a small network over a period of time will go a long way toward informing the network administrator of evolving protocol requirements and associated traffic flows. For example, it may be that some employees are using offsite resources such as social media in order to better position a company with respect to marketing. When they began working for the company, these employees may have focused less on Internet-based advertising. This shift in resource utilization may require the network administrator to shift network resource allocations accordingly.

It is the responsibility of the network administrator to track network utilization and traffic flow requirements, and implement network modifications in order to optimize employee productivity as the network and business grow.

Keeping the Network Safe (11.2)

Keeping the network safe involves many aspects. This section looks at network device security measures; vulnerabilities and network attacks and how to mitigate them; and how to secure devices.

Network Device Security Measures (11.2.1)

This section looks at some of the categories of security threats as well as the concern of physical security and security vulnerabilities.

Categories of Threats to Network Security (11.2.1.1)

Whether wired or wireless, computer networks are essential to everyday activities. Individuals and organizations alike depend on their computers and networks. Intrusion by an unauthorized person can result in costly network outages and loss of work. Attacks to a network can be devastating and can result in a loss of time and money due to damage or theft of important information or assets.

Intruders can gain access to a network through software vulnerabilities, through hardware attacks, or by guessing someone's username and password. Intruders who gain access by modifying software or exploiting software vulnerabilities are often called hackers.

After the hacker gains access to the network, four types of threats may arise:

- *Information theft*: Breaking into a computer to obtain confidential information

- *Identity theft*: A form of information theft where personal information is stolen for the purpose of taking over someone's identity

- *Data loss/manipulation*: Breaking into a computer to destroy or alter data records

- *Disruption of service*: Preventing legitimate users from accessing services to which they should be entitled.

Click the images in Activity 11.2.1.1 to see more information.

Interactive Graphic

Activity 11.2.1.1: Categories of Threats

Go to the online course and click each blue-highlighted image for additional information.

Even in small networks, it is necessary to consider security threats and vulnerabilities when planning a network implementation.

Physical Security (11.2.1.2)

When you think of network security, or even computer security, you may imagine attackers exploiting software vulnerabilities. An equally important vulnerability is the physical security of devices, as shown in Figure 11-7. An attacker can deny the use of network resources if those resources can be physically compromised.

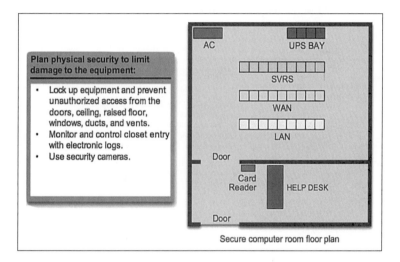

Figure 11-7   Physical Security Plan

The four classes of physical threats are

- **Hardware threats:** Physical damage to servers, routers, switches, cabling plant, and workstations

- **Environmental threats:** Temperature extremes (too hot or too cold) or humidity extremes (too wet or too dry)

- **Electrical threats:** Voltage spikes, insufficient supply voltage (brownouts), unconditioned power (noise), and total power loss

- **Maintenance threats:** Poor handling of key electrical components (electrostatic discharge), lack of critical spare parts, poor cabling, and poor labeling

Some of these issues must be dealt with in an organizational policy. Some of them are subject to good leadership and management in the organization.

Types of Security Vulnerabilities (11.2.1.3)

Three network security factors are vulnerability, threat, and attack.

Vulnerability is the degree of weakness which is inherent in every network and device. This includes routers, switches, desktops, servers, and even security devices.

Threats include the people interested and qualified in taking advantage of each security weakness. Such individuals can be expected to continually search for new exploits and weaknesses.

Threats are realized by a variety of tools, scripts, and programs to launch *attacks* against networks and network devices. Typically, the network devices under attack are the endpoints, such as servers and desktop computers.

There are three primary vulnerabilities or weaknesses:

- Technology, as shown in Figure 11-8

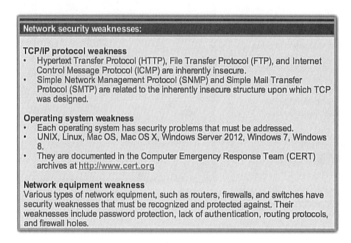

Figure 11-8 Vulnerabilities: Technology

- Configuration, as shown in Figure 11-9

Configuration Weakness	How the weakness is exploited
Unsecured user accounts	User account information may be transmitted insecurely across the network, exposing usernames and passwords to snoopers.
System accounts with easily guessed passwords	This common problem is the result of poorly selected and easily guessed user passwords.
Misconfigured Internet services	A common problem is to turn on JavaScript in web browsers, enabling attacks by way of hostile JavaScript when accessing untrusted sites. IIS, FTP, and Terminal Services also pose problems.
Unsecured default settings within products	Many products have default settings that enable security holes.
Misconfigured network equipment	Misconfigurations of the equipment itself can cause significant security problems. For example, misconfigured access lists, routing protocols, or SNMP community strings can open up large security holes.

Figure 11-9   Vulnerabilities: Configuration

■ Security policy, as shown in Figure 11-10

Policy Weakness	How the weakness is exploited
Lack of written security policy	An unwritten policy cannot be consistently applied or enforced.
Politics	Political battles and turf wars can make it difficult to implement a consistent security policy.
Lack of authentication continuity	Poorly chosen, easily cracked, or default passwords can allow unauthorized access to the network.
Logical access controls not applied	Inadequate monitoring and auditing allow attacks and unauthorized use to continue, wasting company resources. This could result in legal action or termination against IT technicians, IT management, or even company leadership that allows these unsafe conditions to persist.
Software and hardware installation and changes do not follow policy	Unauthorized changes to the network topology or installation of unapproved applications create security holes.
Disaster recovery plan is nonexistent	The lack of a disaster recovery plan allows chaos, panic, and confusion to occur when someone attacks the enterprise.

Figure 11-10   Vulnerabilities: Policy

All three of these vulnerabilities or weaknesses can lead to various attacks, including malicious code attacks and network attacks.

Interactive Graphic

Activity 11.2.1.4: Security Threats and Vulnerabilities (Part 1 and Part 2)

Go to the online course and read the security threats and vulnerabilities scenarios. Drag each scenario to its corresponding type of security threat.

Vulnerabilities and Network Attacks (11.2.2)

This section looks at several network vulnerabilities and attacks.

Viruses, Worms, and Trojan Horses (11.2.2.1)

Malicious code attacks include a number of types of computer programs that were created with the intention of causing data loss or damage. The three main types of malicious code attacks are viruses, Trojan horses, and worms.

A *virus* is malicious software that is attached to another program to execute a particular unwanted function on a workstation. An example is a program that is attached to command.com (the primary interpreter for Windows systems) and deletes certain files and infects any other versions of command.com that it can find.

A *Trojan horse* is different only in that the entire application was written to look like something else, when in fact it is an attack tool. An example of a Trojan horse is a software application that runs a simple game on a workstation. While the user is occupied with the game, the Trojan horse mails a copy of itself to every address in the user's address book. The other users receive the game and play it, thereby spreading the Trojan horse to the addresses in each address book.

Viruses normally require a delivery mechanism, a vector, such as a zip file or some other executable file attached to an email, to carry the virus code from one system to another. The key element that distinguishes a computer worm from a computer virus is that human interaction is required to facilitate the spread of a virus.

Worms are self-contained programs that attack a system and try to exploit a specific vulnerability in the target. Upon successful exploitation of the vulnerability, the worm copies its program from the attacking host to the newly exploited system to begin the cycle again. The anatomy of a worm attack is as follows:

- **The enabling vulnerability:** A worm installs itself by exploiting known vulnerabilities in systems, such as naive end users who open unverified executable attachments in emails.

- **Propagation mechanism:** After gaining access to a host, a worm copies itself to that host and then selects new targets.

- **Payload:** After a host is infected with a worm, the attacker has access to the host, often as a privileged user. Attackers could use a local exploit to escalate their privilege level to administrator.

Video 11.2.2.1: Malicious Code Attacks

This video demonstrates how malicious code attacks include a number of types of computer programs that were designed to attack the network. Go to the online course to view the animation.

Network Attacks (11.2.2.2)

In addition to malicious code attacks, it is also possible for networks to fall prey to various network attacks. Network attacks can be classified into three major categories:

- *Reconnaissance attacks*: The unauthorized discovery and mapping of systems, services, or vulnerabilities

- *Access attacks*: The unauthorized manipulation of data, system access, or user privileges

- *Denial of service (DoS) attacks*: The disabling or corruption of networks, systems, or services

Reconnaissance Attacks

External attackers can use Internet tools, such as the nslookup and whois utilities, to easily determine the IP address space assigned to a given corporation or entity. After the IP address space is determined, an attacker can then ping the publicly available IP addresses to identify the addresses that are active. To help automate this step, an attacker may use a ping sweep tool, such as fping or gping, which systematically pings all network addresses in a given range or subnet. This is similar to going through a section of a telephone book and calling each number to see who answers.

Activity 11.2.2.2: Reconnaissance Attacks

Go to the online course and click each type of reconnaissance attack tool to see an animation of the attack.

Access Attacks (11.2.2.3)

Access attacks exploit known vulnerabilities in authentication services, FTP services, and web services to gain entry to web accounts, confidential databases, and other sensitive information. An access attack allows an individual to gain unauthorized access to information that they have no right to view. Access attacks can be classified into four types. One of the most common types of access attack is the password attack. Password attacks can be implemented using a packet sniffer to yield user accounts and passwords that are transmitted as clear text. Password attacks can also refer to repeated attempts to log in to a shared resource, such as a server or router, to identify a user account, password, or both. These repeated attempts are called dictionary attacks or brute-force attacks. The other three access attacks are trust exploitation, port redirection and man in the middle.

Video

Video 11.2.2.3 (Section 2): Trust Exploitation

This video demonstrates how an attacker can access one system to then access another. Go to the online course to perform this practice activity.

DoS Attacks (11.2.2.4)

Denial of service (DoS) attacks are the most publicized form of attack and also among the most difficult to eliminate. Even within the attacker community, DoS attacks are regarded as trivial and considered bad form because they require so little effort to execute. But because of their ease of implementation and potentially significant damage, DoS attacks deserve special attention from security administrators.

DoS attacks take many forms. Ultimately, they prevent authorized people from using a service by consuming system resources.

Video

Video 11.2.2.4 (Section 2): Ping of Death

This video demonstrates how an attacker can launch DoS and distributed DoS (DDoS) attacks. Go to the online course to view the animation.

Interactive Graphic

Activity 11.2.2.5: Types of Attacks (Part 1, Part 2, and Part 3)

Go to the online course and read the type of security attack scenarios. Drag each attack type to its corresponding attack scenario.

Lab 11.2.2.6: Researching Network Security Threats

In this lab you will complete the following objectives:

- Part 1: Explore the SANS Website
- Part 2: Identify Recent Network Security Threats
- Part 3: Detail a Specific Network Security Threat

Mitigating Network Attacks (11.2.3)

This section examines how to respond to network attacks.

Backup, Upgrade, Update, and Patch (11.2.3.1)

Antivirus software can detect most viruses and many Trojan horse applications and prevent them from spreading in the network. Antivirus software can be deployed at the user level and at the network level.

Keeping up to date with the latest developments in these sorts of attacks can also lead to a more effective defense against these attacks. As new virus or Trojan applications are released, enterprises need to keep current with the latest versions of antivirus software as well.

Worm attack mitigation requires diligence on the part of system and network administration staff. The following are the recommended steps for worm attack mitigation:

- *Containment*: Contain the spread of the worm within the network. Compartmentalize uninfected parts of the network.

- *Inoculation*: Start patching all systems and, if possible, scanning for vulnerable systems.

- *Quarantine*: Track down each infected machine inside the network. Disconnect, remove, or block infected machines from the network.

- *Treatment*: Clean and patch each infected system. Some worms may require complete core system reinstallations to clean the system.

The most effective way to mitigate a worm attack is to download security updates from the operating system vendor and patch all vulnerable systems. This is difficult with uncontrolled user systems in the local network. Administering numerous systems involves the creation of a standard software image (operating system and accredited applications that are authorized for use on client systems) that is deployed on new or upgraded systems. However, security requirements change, so already-deployed systems may need to have updated security patches installed.

One solution to the management of critical security patches is to create a central patch server that all systems must communicate with after a set period of time, as shown in Figure 11-11. Any patches that are not applied to a host are automatically downloaded from the patch server and installed without user intervention.

Figure 11-11   OS Patches

Authentication, Authorization, and Accounting (11.2.3.2)

Authentication, authorization, and accounting (AAA, or "triple A") network security services provide the primary framework to set up access control on a network device. AAA is a way to control who is permitted to access a network (authenticate), control what they can do while they are there (authorize), and watch the actions they perform while accessing the network (accounting). AAA provides a higher degree of scalability than the console, aux, vty, and privileged EXEC authentication commands alone.

Authentication

Users and administrators must prove that they are who they say they are. Authentication can be established using username and password combinations, challenge and response questions, token cards, and other methods. For example: "I am user 'student.' I know the password to prove that I am user 'student.'"

In a small network, local authentication is often used. With local authentication, each device maintains its own database of username/password combinations. However, when there are more than a few user accounts in a local device database, managing those user accounts becomes complex. Additionally, as the network grows and more devices are added to the network, local authentication becomes difficult to maintain and does not scale. For example, if there are 100 network devices, all user accounts must be added to all 100 devices.

For larger networks, a more scalable solution is external authentication. External authentication allows all users to be authenticated through an external network server. The two most popular options for external authentication of users are RADIUS and TACACS+:

■ RADIUS is an open standard with low use of CPU resources and memory. It is used by a range of network devices, such as switches, routers, and wireless devices.

■ TACACS+ is a security mechanism that enables modular AAA services. It uses a TACACS+ daemon running on a security server.

Authorization

After the user is authenticated, authorization services determine which resources the user can access and which operations the user is allowed to perform. An example is, "User 'student' can access host serverXYZ using Telnet only."

Accounting

Accounting records what the user does, including what is accessed, the amount of time the resource is accessed, and any changes that were made. Accounting keeps track of how network resources are used. An example is, "User 'student' accessed host serverXYZ using Telnet for 15 minutes."

The concept of AAA is similar to the use of a credit card. The credit card identifies who can use it, identifies how much that user can spend, and keeps account of what items the user spent money on, as shown in Figure 11-12.

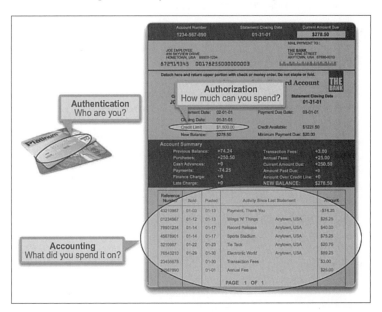

Figure 11-12 AAA Concept Is Similar to the Use of a Credit Card.

Firewalls (11.2.3.3)

In addition to protecting individual computers and servers attached to the network, it is important to control traffic traveling to and from the network.

A firewall is one of the most effective security tools available for protecting internal network users from external threats. A firewall resides between two or more networks and controls the traffic between them. It also helps to prevent unauthorized access. Firewall products use various techniques for determining what is permitted or denied access to a network. These techniques are

- **Packet filtering:** Prevents or allows access based on IP or MAC addresses.

- **Application filtering:** Prevents or allows access by specific application types based on port numbers.

- **URL filtering:** Prevents or allows access to websites based on specific URLs or keywords.

- **Stateful packet inspection (SPI):** Incoming packets must be legitimate responses to requests from internal hosts. Unsolicited packets are blocked unless permitted specifically. SPI can also include the capability to recognize and filter out specific types of attacks such as DoS attacks.

Firewall products may support one or more of these filtering capabilities. Additionally, firewalls often perform network address translation (NAT). NAT translates an internal IP address or group of IP addresses into an outside, public IP address that is sent across the network. This allows internal IP addresses to be concealed from outside users.

Firewall products come packaged in various forms, as shown in Figure 11-13 and described here:

- *Appliance-based firewalls*: An appliance-based firewall is a firewall that is built-in to a dedicated hardware device known as a security appliance.

- *Server-based firewalls*: A server-based firewall consists of a firewall application that runs on a network operating system (NOS) such as Linux or Windows.

- *Integrated firewalls*: An integrated firewall is implemented by adding firewall functionality to an existing device, such as a router.

- *Personal firewalls*: Personal firewalls reside on host computers and are not designed for LAN implementations. They may be available by default from the OS or may come from an outside vendor.

Figure 11-13 Cisco Security Appliances

Endpoint Security (11.2.3.4)

A secure network is only as strong as its weakest link. The high-profile threats most often discussed in the media are external threats, such as Internet worms and DoS attacks. But securing the internal network is just as important as securing the perimeter of a network. The internal network is made up of network endpoints, some of which are shown in Figure 11-14. An *endpoint*, or *host*, is an individual computer system or device that acts as a network client. Common endpoints are laptops, desktops, servers, smartphones, and tablets. If users are not practicing security with their endpoint devices, no amount of security precautions will guarantee a secure network.

Securing endpoint devices is one of the most challenging jobs of a network administrator because it involves human nature. A company must have well-documented policies in place, and employees must be aware of and follow those policies. Employees need to be trained on proper use of the network. Policies often include the use of antivirus software and host intrusion prevention. More comprehensive endpoint security solutions rely on network access control.

Figure 11-14   Network Endpoints

Endpoint security also requires securing Layer 2 devices in the network infrastructure to prevent against Layer 2 attacks such as MAC address spoofing, MAC address table overflow attacks, and LAN storm attacks. This is known as *attack mitigation*.

Securing Devices (11.2.4)

One method of mitigating security issues is to secure the different network devices. This section looks at several methods of doing that.

Introduction to Securing Devices (11.2.4.1)

Part of network security is securing actual devices, including end devices and intermediate devices such as network devices.

When a new operating system is installed on a device, the security settings are set to the default values. In most cases, this level of security is inadequate. For Cisco routers, the Cisco AutoSecure feature can be used to assist securing the system. Figure 11-15 shows a typical network with devices that need to be secured. There are some simple steps that should be taken that apply to most operating systems:

- Change default usernames and passwords immediately.

- Restrict access to system resources to only the individuals that are authorized to use those resources.

- Turn off and uninstall, when possible, any unnecessary services and applications.

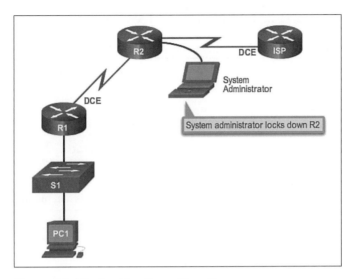

Figure 11-15   Locking Down Your Router

All devices should be updated with security patches as they become available. Often, devices shipped from the manufacturer have been sitting in a warehouse for a period of time and do not have the most up-to-date patches installed. It is important, prior to implementation, to update any software and install any security patches.

Passwords (11.2.4.2)

To protect network devices, it is important to use strong passwords. Here are standard guidelines to follow:

- Use a password length of at least 8 characters, preferably 10 or more characters. A longer password is a better password.

- Make passwords complex. Include a mix of uppercase and lowercase letters, numbers, symbols, and spaces, if allowed.

- Avoid passwords based on repetition, common dictionary words, letter or number sequences, usernames, relative or pet names, biographical information (such as birthdates, ID numbers, and ancestor names), or other easily identifiable pieces of information.

- Deliberately misspell a password. For example, Smith = Smyth = 5mYth or Security = 5ecur1ty.

- Change passwords often. If a password is unknowingly compromised, the window of opportunity for the attacker to use the password is limited.

- Do not write passwords down and leave them in obvious places such as on the desk or monitor.

Tables 11-1 and 11-2 provide examples of weak and strong passwords, respectively.

Table 11-1   Examples of Weak Passwords

Weak Password	Why It Is Weak
Secret	Simple dictionary password
Smith	Mother's maiden name
Toyota	Make of a car
Bob1967	Name and birthday of a user
Blueleaf23	Simple words and numbers

Table 11-2   Examples of Strong Passwords

Strong Password	Why It Is Strong
B67n42d39c	Combines alphanumeric characters
12^h u4@1p7	Combines alphanumeric characters and symbols, and also includes a space

On Cisco routers, leading spaces are ignored for passwords, but spaces after the first character are not ignored. Therefore, one method to create a strong password is to use a space in the password and create a phrase made of many words. This is called a *pass phrase*. A pass phrase is often easier to remember than a simple password. It is also longer and harder to guess.

Administrators should ensure that strong passwords are used across the network. One way to accomplish this is to use the same "brute force" attack tools that attackers use as a way to verify password strength.

Basic Security Practices (11.2.4.3)

When implementing devices, it is important to follow all security guidelines set by the organization. This includes naming devices in a fashion that allows for easy documentation and tracking but also maintains some form of security. It is not wise to provide too much information about the use of the device in the hostname. There are many other basic security measures that should be taken.

Additional Password Security

Strong passwords are only as useful as they are secret. There are several steps that can be taken to help ensure that passwords remain secret. Using the global configuration command **service password-encryption** prevents unauthorized individuals from viewing passwords in plaintext in the configuration file, as shown Figure 11-16. This command causes the encryption of all passwords that are unencrypted.

```
Router(config)#service password-encryption
Router(config)#security password min-length 8
Router(config)#login block-for 120 attempts 3 within 60
Router(config)#line vty 0 4
Router(config-vty)#exec-timeout 10
Router(config-vty)#end
Router#show running-config
-more-
!
line vty 0 4
  password 7 03095A0F034F38435B49150A1819
  exec-timeout 10
  login
```

Figure 11-16   Configuration File

Additionally, to ensure that all configured passwords are a minimum of a specified length, use the **security passwords min-length** command in global configuration mode.

Another way hackers learn passwords is simply by brute-force attacks, trying multiple passwords until one works. It is possible to prevent this type of attack by blocking login attempts to the device if a set number of failures occurs within a specific amount of time. The following command will block login attempts for 120 seconds if three failed login attempts occur within 60 seconds:

```
Router(config)# login block-for 120 attempts 3 within 60
```

Banners

A banner message is similar to a no-trespassing sign. *Banners* are important in order to be able to prosecute, in a court of law, anyone who accesses the system inappropriately. Banners serve as a means of letting intruders know that they are entering unauthorized areas of the network. Be sure banner messages comply with security policies for the organization. The following line of code shows how you would configure the message of the day banner.

```
Router(config)# banner motd #message#
```

Exec Timeout

Another recommendation is to set executive (exec) timeouts. By setting the *exec timeout*, you are telling the Cisco device to automatically disconnect users on a line after they have been idle for the duration of the exec timeout value. Exec timeouts can be configured on console, vty, and aux ports. The following command will disconnect users after 10 minutes of inactivity on a router:

```
Router(config)# line vty 0 4
Router(config-vty)# exec-timeout 10
```

Enable SSH (11.2.4.4)

This section looks at the function of SSH and explains how to enable SSH.

Remote Access via SSH

The legacy protocol to manage devices remotely is Telnet. Telnet is not secure. Data contained within a Telnet packet is transmitted unencrypted. Using a tool like Wireshark, it is possible for someone to "sniff" a Telnet session and obtain password information. For this reason, it is highly recommended to enable *Secure Shell (SSH)* on devices for secure remote access. It is possible to configure a Cisco device to support SSH using the following four steps, also shown in Figure 11-17:

Step 1. Ensure that the router has a unique hostname, and then configure the IP domain name of the network using the **ip domain-name** *domain-name* command in global configuration mode.

Step 2. Generate one-way secret keys for a router to encrypt SSH traffic. The key is what is actually used to encrypt and decrypt data. To create an encryption key, use the **crypto key generate rsa general-keys modulus** *modulus-size* command in global configuration mode, as shown next. The specific meaning of the various parts of this command are complex and out of scope for this course, but for now, just note that the modulus determines the size of the key and can be configured from 360 bits to 2,048 bits. The larger the modulus, the more secure the key, but the longer it takes to encrypt and decrypt information. The minimum recommended modulus length is 1,024 bits.

```
Router(config)# crypto key generate rsa general-keys modulus 1024
```

Step 3. Create a local database username entry using the **username** *name* **secret** *secret* global configuration command.

Step 4. Enable vty inbound SSH sessions using the line vty commands **login local** and **transport input ssh**.

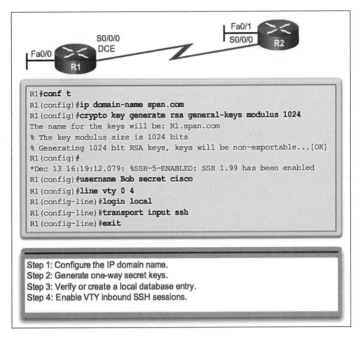

Figure 11-17   Configuring SSH

The router SSH service can now be accessed using SSH client software.

Lab 11.2.4.5: Accessing Network Devices with SSH

In this lab you will complete the following objectives:

- Part 1: Configure Basic Device Settings

- Part 2: Configure the Router for SSH Access

- Part 3: Examine a Telnet Session with Wireshark

- Part 4: Examine a SSH Session with Wireshark

- Part 5: Configure the Switch for SSH Access

- Part 6: SSH from the CLI on the Switch

Lab 11.2.4.6: Securing Network Devices

In this lab you will complete the following objectives:

- Part 1: Configure Basic Device Settings

- Part 2: Configure Basic Security Measures on the Router

- Part 3: Configure Basic Security Measures on the Switch

Basic Network Performance (11.3)

There are several ways of monitoring network performance; this section looks at several means of doing that.

Ping (11.3.1)

The ping protocol is often the first tool used to check network connectivity.

Interpreting Ping Results (11.3.1.1)

After the network has been implemented, a network administrator must be able to test the network connectivity to ensure that it is operating appropriately. Additionally, it is a good idea for the network administrator to document the network.

The ping Command

Using the **ping** command is an effective way to test connectivity. The test is often referred to as testing the protocol stack, because the **ping** command moves from Layer 3 of the OSI model to Layer 2 and then Layer 1. Ping uses the ICMP protocol to check for connectivity.

The **ping** command will not always pinpoint the nature of a problem, but it can help to identify the source of the problem, an important first step in troubleshooting a network failure.

The **ping** command provides a method for checking the protocol stack and IPv4 address configuration on a host as well as testing connectivity to local or remote destination hosts, as shown in Figure 11-18. There are additional tools that can provide more information than **ping**, such as telnet or trace, which will be discussed in more detail later.

IOS Ping Indicators

A ping issued from the IOS will yield one of several indications for each ICMP Echo Request message that was sent. The most common indicators are

- ! (exclamation mark) indicates receipt of an ICMP Echo Reply message. This indicates that the ping completed successfully and verifies Layer 3 connectivity.

- . (period) indicates a time expired while waiting for an ICMP Echo Reply message. This may indicate problems in the communication or that a connectivity problem occurred somewhere along the path. It may also indicate that a router along the path did not have a route to the destination and did not send an ICMP Destination Unreachable message. It also may indicate that ping was blocked by device security.

- **U** indicates an ICMP Destination Unreachable message was received. This indicates that a router along the path did not have a route to the destination address or that the ping request was blocked and responded with an ICMP Destination Unreachable message.

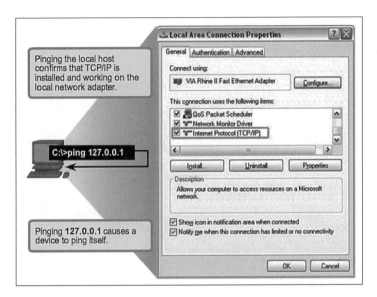

Figure 11-18   Testing Local TCP/IP Stack

Testing the Loopback

The **ping** command is used to verify the internal IP configuration on the local host. Recall that this test is accomplished by using the **ping** command on a reserved address called the loopback (127.0.0.1). This verifies the proper operation of the protocol stack from the network layer to the physical layer—and back—without actually putting a signal on the media.

You enter **ping** commands at a command line. Enter the **ping loopback** command with this syntax:

```
C:\> ping 127.0.0.1
```

The reply from this command would look something like this:

```
Reply from 127.0.0.1: bytes=32 time<1ms TTL=128
Reply from 127.0.0.1: bytes=32 time<1ms TTL=128
Reply from 127.0.0.1: bytes=32 time<1ms TTL=128
Reply from 127.0.0.1: bytes=32 time<1ms TTL=128
Ping statistics for 127.0.0.1:
Packets: Sent = 4, Received = 4, Lost = 0 (0% loss),
Approximate round trip times in milliseconds:
Minimum = 0ms, Maximum = 0ms, Average = 0ms
```

The result indicates that four 32-byte test packets were sent and were returned from host 127.0.0.1 in a time of less than 1 ms. TTL stands for Time-to-Live and defines the number of hops that the ping packet has remaining before it will be dropped.

Extended Ping (11.3.1.2)

The Cisco IOS offers an "extended" mode of the **ping** command. This mode is entered by typing **ping** in privileged EXEC mode, without a destination IP address. A series of prompts are then presented, as shown in the following example. Pressing Enter accepts the indicated default values. The example illustrates how to force the source address for a ping to be 10.1.1.1 (see R2 in Figure 11-19); the source address for a standard ping would be 209.165.200.226. By doing this, the network administrator can verify remotely (from R2) that R1 has the route 10.1.1.0/24 in its routing table.

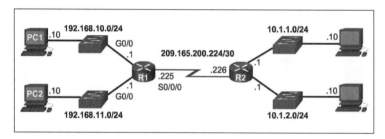

Figure 11-19   Extended Ping

```
R2# ping
Protocol [ip]:
Target IP address: 192.168.10.1
Repeat count [5]:
Datagram size [100]:
Timeout in seconds [2]:
Extended commands [n]: y
Source address or interface: 10.1.1.1
Type of service [0]:
Set DF bit in IP header? [no]:
Validate reply data? [no]:
Data pattern [0xABCD]:
Loose, Strict, Record, Timestamp, Verbose[none]:
Sweep range of sizes [n]:
Type escape sequence to abort.
Sending 5, 100-byte ICMP Echos to 192.168.10.1, timeout is 2 seconds:
!!!!!
Success rate is 100 percent (5/5), round-trip min/avg/max = 36/97/132 ms
```

Entering a longer timeout period than the default allows for possible latency issues to be detected. If the ping test is successful with a longer value, a connection exists between the hosts, but latency may be an issue on the network.

Note that entering "y" to the "Extended commands" prompt provides more options that are useful in troubleshooting.

Network Baseline (11.3.1.3)

One of the most effective tools for monitoring and troubleshooting network performance is to establish a network baseline. A baseline is a process for studying the network at regular intervals to ensure that the network is working as designed. A network baseline is more than a single report detailing the health of the network at a certain point in time. Creating an effective network performance baseline is accomplished over a period of time. Measuring performance at varying times (as shown in Figure 11-20 and Figure 11-21) and varying loads will assist in creating a better picture of overall network performance.

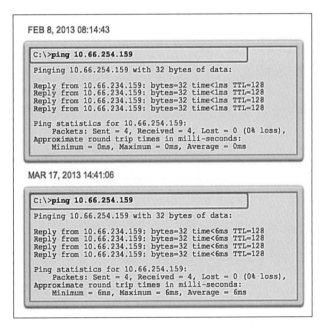

Figure 11-20   Run the Same Test...

```
FEB 8, 2013 08:14:43

C:\>ping 10.66.254.159

Pinging 10.66.254.159 with 32 bytes of data:

Reply from 10.66.234.159: bytes=32 time<1ms TTL=128
Reply from 10.66.234.159: bytes=32 time<1ms TTL=128
Reply from 10.66.234.159: bytes=32 time<1ms TTL=128
Reply from 10.66.234.159: bytes=32 time<1ms TTL=128

Ping statistics for 10.66.254.159:
    Packets: Sent = 4, Received = 4, Lost = 0 (0% loss),
Approximate round trip times in milli-seconds:
    Minimum = 0ms, Maximum = 0ms, Average = 0ms
```

```
MAR 17, 2013 14:41:06

C:\>ping 10.66.254.159

Pinging 10.66.254.159 with 32 bytes of data:

Reply from 10.66.234.159: bytes=32 time<6ms TTL=128
Reply from 10.66.234.159: bytes=32 time<6ms TTL=128
Reply from 10.66.234.159: bytes=32 time<6ms TTL=128
Reply from 10.66.234.159: bytes=32 time<6ms TTL=128

Ping statistics for 10.66.254.159:
    Packets: Sent = 4, Received = 4, Lost = 0 (0% loss),
Approximate round trip times in milli-seconds:
    Minimum = 0ms, Maximum = 0ms, Average = 0ms
```

Figure 11-21   ...at Different Times

The output derived from network commands can contribute data to the network baseline.

One method for starting a baseline is to copy and paste the results from an executed **ping, trace,** or other relevant command into a text file. These text files can be time stamped with the date and saved into an archive for later retrieval.

An effective use of the stored information is to compare the results over time (see Figure 11-22). Among items to consider are error messages and the response times from host to host. If there is a considerable increase in response times, there may be a latency issue to address.

The importance of creating documentation cannot be emphasized enough. Verification of host-to-host connectivity, latency issues, and resolutions of identified problems can assist a network administrator in keeping a network running as efficiently as possible.

Corporate networks should have extensive baselines...more extensive than we can describe in this course. Professional-grade software tools are available for storing and maintaining baseline information. In this course, we only cover some basic techniques and discuss the purpose of baselines.

You can find best practices for baseline processes here: http://www.cisco.com/en/US/tech/tk869/tk769/technologies_white_paper09186a008014fb3b.shtml.

Capturing **ping** command output can also be completed from the IOS prompt, as shown in Figure 11-23.

```
FEB 8, 2013 08:14:43

C:\>ping 10.66.254.159

Pinging 10.66.254.159 with 32 bytes of data:

Reply from 10.66.234.159: bytes=32 time<1ms TTL=128
Reply from 10.66.234.159: bytes=32 time<1ms TTL=128
Reply from 10.66.234.159: bytes=32 time<1ms TTL=128
Reply from 10.66.234.159: bytes=32 time<1ms TTL=128

Ping statistics for 10.66.254.159:
    Packets: Sent = 4, Received = 4, Lost = 0 (0% loss),
Approximate round trip times in milli-seconds:
    Minimum = 0ms, Maximum = 0ms, Average = 0ms
```

```
MAR 17, 2013 14:41:06

C:\>ping 10.66.254.159

Pinging 10.66.254.159 with 32 bytes of data:

Reply from 10.66.234.159: bytes=32 time<6ms TTL=128
Reply from 10.66.234.159: bytes=32 time<6ms TTL=128
Reply from 10.66.234.159: bytes=32 time<6ms TTL=128
Reply from 10.66.234.159: bytes=32 time<6ms TTL=128

Ping statistics for 10.66.254.159:
    Packets: Sent = 4, Received = 4, Lost = 0 (0% loss),
Approximate round trip times in milli-seconds:
    Minimum = 0ms, Maximum = 0ms, Average = 0ms
```

Figure 11-22   Compare Values

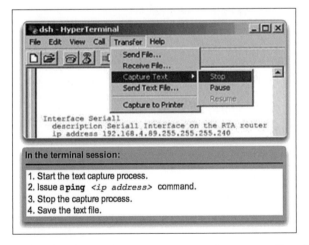

Figure 11-23   Router Ping Capture: Saving to a Text File

Tracert (11.3.2)

Another well-known tool is **tracert**. This section looks at how to use **tracert**.

Interpreting Tracert Messages (11.3.2.1)

A trace returns a list of hops as a packet is routed through a network. The form of the command depends on where the command is issued. When performing the trace from a Windows computer, use **tracert**, and when performing the trace from a router CLI, use **traceroute**, as shown in Figure 11-24.

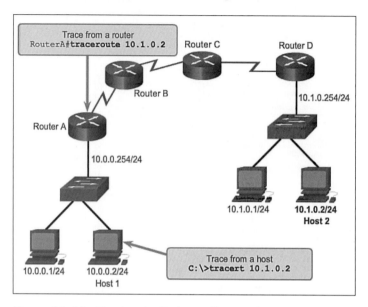

Figure 11-24   Testing the Path to a Remote Host

Like **ping** commands, **trace** commands are entered in the command line and take an IP address as the argument.

Assuming that the command will be issued from a Windows computer, we use the **tracert** form:

```
C:\> tracert 10.1.0.2

Tracing route to 10.1.0.2 over a maximum of 30 hops

1  2 ms  2 ms  2 ms  10.0.0.254

2  *  *  *  Request timed out.

3  *  *  *  Request timed out.

4  ^C
```

The only successful response was from the gateway on Router A. Trace requests to the next hop timed out, meaning that the next hop router did not respond. The trace results indicate that the failure is therefore in the internetwork beyond the LAN.

Capturing the **traceroute** output can also be done from the router prompt, as shown in Figure 11-25.

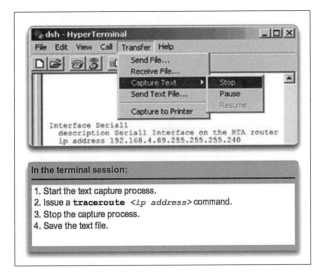

Figure 11-25   Router Traceroute Capture: Saving to a Text File

Packet Tracer Activity 11.3.2.2: Test Connectivity with Traceroute

This activity is designed to help you troubleshoot network connectivity issues using commands to trace the route from source to destination. You are required to examine the output of **tracert** (the Windows command) and **traceroute** (the IOS command) as packets traverse the network and determine the cause of a network issue. After the issue is corrected, use the **tracert** and **traceroute** commands to verify the completion.

Lab 11.3.2.3: Testing Network Latency with Ping and Traceroute

In this lab you will complete the following objectives:

- Part 1: Use Ping to Document Network Latency
- Part 2: Use Traceroute to Document Network Latency

show Commands (11.3.3)

There are numerous Cisco IOS **show** commands that can be used to test network connectivity; this section looks at some of those commands.

Common show Commands Revisited (11.3.3.1)

The Cisco IOS CLI **show** commands display relevant information about the configuration and operation of the device.

Network technicians use **show** commands extensively for viewing configuration files, checking the status of device interfaces and processes, and verifying the device operational status.

The status of nearly every process or function of the router can be displayed using a **show** command. The following are some of the more popular **show** commands:

- **show running-config** (see Figure 11-26)

```
R1#show running-config
<Output omitted>
Building configuration...
Current configuration : 1063 bytes
!
version 12.4
service timestamps debug datetime msec
service timestamps log datetime msec
no service password-encryption
hostname R1
enable secret 5 $1$i6w9$dvdpVM6zV10E6tSyLdkR5/
no ip domain lookup
!
interface FastEthernet0/0
 description LAN 192.168.1.0 default gateway
 ip address 192.168.1.1 255.255.255.0
 duplex auto
 speed auto
!
interface FastEthernet0/1
 no ip address
 shutdown
 duplex auto
 speed auto
```

Figure 11-26 Executing the **show running-config** Command

- **show interfaces** (see Figure 11-27)

```
R1#show interfaces
<Output omitted>
FastEthernet0/0 is up, line protocol is up
  Hardware is Gt96k FE, address is 001b.5325.256e
  (bia 001b.5325.256e)
  Internet address is 192.168.1.1/24
  MTU 1500 bytes, BW 100000 Kbit, DLY 100 usec,
     reliability 255/255, txload 1/255, rxload 1/255
  Encapsulation ARPA, loopback not set
  Keepalive set (10 sec)
  Full-duplex, 100Mb/s, 100BaseTX/FX
  ARP type: ARPA, ARP Timeout 04:00:00
  Last input 00:00:17, output 00:00:01, output hang never
  Last clearing of "show interface" counters never
  Input queue: 0/75/0/0 (size/max/drops/flushes);
  Total output drops: 0
  Queueing strategy: fifo
  Output queue: 0/40 (size/max)
  5 minute input rate 0 bits/sec, 0 packets/sec
  5 minute output rate 0 bits/sec, 0 packets/sec
     196 packets input, 31850 bytes
     Received 181 broadcasts, 0 runts, 0 giants, 0 throttles
     0 input errors, 0 CRC, 0 frame, 0 overrun, 0 ignored
     0 watchdog
```

Figure 11-27 Executing the **show interfaces** Command

■ show arp (see Figure 11-28)

```
R1#show arp
Protocol  Address             Age (min)  Hardware Addr   Type   Interface
Internet  172.17.0.1              -       001b.5325.256e  ARPA
FastEthernet0/0
Internet  172.17.0.2             12       000b.db04.a5cd  ARPA
FastEthernet0/0
```

Figure 11-28   Executing the **show arp** Command

■ show ip route (see Figure 11-29)

```
R1#show ip route
Codes: C - connected, S - static, R - RIP, M - mobile, B - BGP
       D - EIGRP, EX - EIGRP external, O - OSPF, IA - OSPF inter area
       N1 - OSPF NSSA external type 1, N2 - OSPF NSSA external type 2
       E1 - OSPF external type 1, E2 - OSPF external type 2
       i - IS-IS, su - IS-IS summary, L1 - IS-IS level-1, L2 - IS-IS level-2
       ia - IS-IS inter area, * - candidate default, U - per-user static route
       o - ODR, P - periodic downloaded static route

Gateway of last resort is not set
C    192.168.1.0/24 is directly connected, FastEthernet0/0
C    192.168.2.0/24 is directly connected, Serial0/0/0
R    192.168.3.0/24 [120/1] via 192.168.2.2, 00:00:24, Serial0/0/0
```

Figure 11-29   Executing the **show ip route** Command

- **show protocols** (see Figure 11-30)

```
R1#show protocols
Global values:
  Internet Protocol routing is enabled
FastEthernet0/0 is up, line protocol is up
  Internet address is 192.168.1.1/24
FastEthernet0/1 is administratively down, line protocol is down
FastEthernet0/1/0 is up, line protocol is down
FastEthernet0/1/1 is up, line protocol is down
FastEthernet0/1/2 is up, line protocol is down
FastEthernet0/1/3 is up, line protocol is down
Serial0/0/0 is up, line protocol is up
  Internet address is 192.168.2.1/24
Serial0/0/1 is administratively down, line protocol is down
Vlan1 is up, line protocol is down
```

Figure 11-30　Executing the **show protocols** Command

- **show version** (see Figure 11-31)

```
R1#show version
<Output omitted>
Cisco IOS Software, 1841 Software (C1841-ADVIPSERVICESK9-M),
Version 12.4(10b),
RELEASE SOFTWARE (fc3)
Technical Support: http://www.cisco.com/techsupport
Copyright (c) 1986-2007 by Cisco Systems, Inc.
Compiled Fri 19-Jan-07 15:15 by prod_rel_team

ROM: System Bootstrap, Version 12.4(13r)T, RELEASE SOFTWARE (fc1)
R1 uptime is 43 minutes
System returned to ROM by reload at 22:05:12 UTC Sat Jan 5 2008
System image file is "flash:c1841-advipservicesk9-mz.124-10b.bin"

Cisco 1841 (revision 6.0) with 174080K/22528K bytes of memory.
Processor board ID FTX1111W0QF
6 FastEthernet interfaces
2 Serial(sync/async) interfaces
1 Virtual Private Network (VPN) Module
DRAM configuration is 64 bits wide with parity disabled.
191K bytes of NVRAM.
62720K bytes of ATA CompactFlash (Read/Write)

Configuration register is 0x2102
```

Figure 11-31　Executing the **show version** Command

Viewing Router Settings with the show version Command (11.3.3.2)

After the startup configuration file is loaded and the router boots successfully, the **show version** command can be used to verify and troubleshoot some of the basic hardware and software components used during the bootup process. The output from the **show version** command includes

- The Cisco IOS Software version being used.

- The version of the system bootstrap software, stored in ROM memory, that was initially used to boot the router.

- The complete filename of the Cisco IOS image and where the bootstrap program located it.

- Type of CPU on the router and amount of RAM. It may be necessary to upgrade the amount of RAM when upgrading the Cisco IOS Software.

- The number and type of physical interfaces on the router.

- The amount of NVRAM. NVRAM is used to store the startup-config file.

- The amount of flash memory on the router. It may be necessary to upgrade the amount of flash when upgrading the Cisco IOS Software.

- The currently configured value of the software configuration register in hexadecimal.

Video

Video 11.3.3.2: show version Output

This video demonstrates how to identify the different features of the **show version** command output. Go to the online course to view this animation.

The configuration register tells the router how to boot up. For example, the factory default setting for the configuration register is 0x2102. This value indicates that the router attempts to load a Cisco IOS Software image from flash and loads the startup configuration file from NVRAM. It is possible to change the configuration register and, therefore, change where the router looks for the Cisco IOS image and the startup configuration file during the bootup process. If there is a second value in parentheses, it denotes the configuration register value to be used during the next reload of the router.

Click the Note icon at the bottom-right corner of the video 11.3.3.2 to obtain more information about the configuration register.

Viewing Switch Settings with the show version Command (11.3.3.3)

The **show version** command on a switch displays information about the currently loaded software version, along with hardware and device information. Some of the information displayed by this command includes

- **Software version:** IOS software version

- **Bootstrap version:** Bootstrap version

- **System up-time:** Time since last reboot

- **System restart info:** Method of restart (e.g., power cycle, crash)

- **Software image name:** IOS filename

- **Switch platform and processor type:** Model number and processor type

- **Memory type (shared/main):** Main processor RAM and shared packet I/O buffering

- **Hardware interfaces:** Interfaces available on the switch

- **Configuration register:** Sets bootup specifications, console speed setting, and related parameters

Packet Tracer Activity 11.3.3.4: Using show Commands

This activity is designed to reinforce the use of router **show** commands. You are not required to configure, but rather examine the output of several **show** commands.

Host and IOS Commands (11.3.4)

This section looks at several commands that you can use on the host to test connectivity.

ipconfig Command Options (11.3.4.1)

As shown in Figure 11-32, the IP address of the default gateway of a host can be viewed by issuing the *ipconfig* command at the command line of a Windows computer.

A tool to examine the MAC address of our computer is **ipconfig /all**. Note that in Figure 11-33, the MAC address of the computer is now displayed along with a number of details regarding the Layer 3 addressing of the device.

In addition, the manufacturer of the network interface in the computer can be identified through the OUI portion of the MAC address. This can be researched on the Internet.

The DNS Client service on Windows PCs optimizes the performance of DNS name resolution by storing previously resolved names in memory. The **ipconfig / displaydns** command displays all of the cached DNS entries on a Windows computer system.

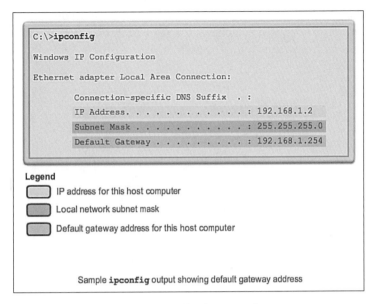

```
C:\>ipconfig

Windows IP Configuration

Ethernet adapter Local Area Connection:

        Connection-specific DNS Suffix  . :
        IP Address. . . . . . . . . . . : 192.168.1.2
        Subnet Mask . . . . . . . . . . : 255.255.255.0
        Default Gateway . . . . . . . . : 192.168.1.254
```

Legend

▭ IP address for this host computer

▭ Local network subnet mask

▭ Default gateway address for this host computer

Sample **ipconfig** output showing default gateway address

Figure 11-32 Using the **ipconfig** Command

```
C:\>ipconfig /all
Ethernet adapter Network Connection:
        Connection-specific DNS Suffix: example.com
        Description . . . . . . . . . . : Intel(R)
        PRO/Wireless 3945ABG Network Connection
        Physical Address. . . . . . . . : 00-18-DE-C7-F3-FB
        Dhcp Enabled. . . . . . . . . . : Yes
        Autoconfiguration Enabled . . . : Yes
        IP Address. . . . . . . . . . . : 10.2.3.4
        Subnet Mask . . . . . . . . . . : 255.255.255.0
        Default Gateway . . . . . . . . : 10.2.3.254
        DHCP Server . . . . . . . . . . : 10.2.3.69
        DNS Servers . . . . . . . . . . : 192.168.226.120
        Lease Obtained. . . . . . . . . : Thursday, May 03,
                                          2007 3:47:51 PM
        Lease Expires . . . . . . . . . : Friday, May 04,
                                          2007 6:57:11 AM
C:\>
```

Figure 11-33 Running the **ipconfig /all** Command

arp Command Options (11.3.4.2)

The *arp* command enables the creation, editing, and display of mappings of physical addresses to known IPv4 addresses. The **arp** command is executed from the Windows command prompt.

To execute an **arp** command, at the command prompt of a host, enter

```
C:\host1> arp -a
```

As shown in Figure 11-34, the **arp –a** command lists all devices currently in the ARP cache of the host, which includes the IPv4 address, physical address, and the type of addressing (static/dynamic), for each device.

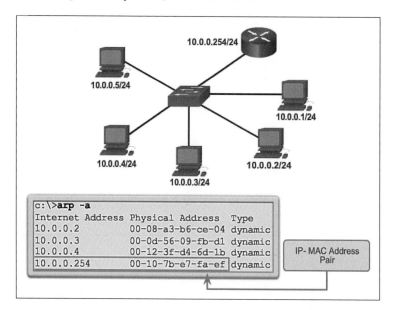

Figure 11-34 Learning About the Nodes on the Network

The cache can be cleared by using the **arp –d** command in the event the network administrator wants to repopulate the cache with updated information.

> **Note**
>
> The ARP cache only contains information from devices that have been recently accessed. To ensure that the ARP cache is populated, ping a device so that it will have an entry in the ARP table.

show cdp neighbors Command Options (11.3.4.3)

Examine the output from the *show cdp neighbors* (and **show cd neighbor details**) command in Figure 11-35, with the topology in Figure 11-36. Notice that R3 has gathered some detailed information about R2 and the switch connected to the Fast Ethernet interface on R3.

CDP is a Cisco-proprietary protocol that runs at the data link layer (Layer 2). Because CDP operates at the data link layer, two or more Cisco network devices, such as routers that support different network layer protocols, can learn about each other even if Layer 3 connectivity does not exist.

```
R3#show cdp neighbors
Capability Codes: R - Router, T - Trans Bridge,
                  B - Source Route Bridge
                  S - Switch, H - Host, I - IGMP,
                  r - Repeater, P - Phone

Device ID  Local Intrfce  Holdtme  Capability  Platform   Port ID
S3         Fas 0/0        151      S I         WS-C2950   Fas 0/6
R2         Ser 0/0/1      125      R           1841       Ser 0/0/1

R3#show cdp neighbors detail

Device ID: R2
Entry address(es):
  IP address : 192.168.1.2
Platform: Cisco 1841,  Capabilities: Router Switch IGMP
Interface: Serial0/0/1,  Port ID (outgoing port): Serial0/0/1
Holdtime : 161 sec

Version :
Cisco IOS Software, 1841 Software (C1841-ADVIPSERVICESK9-M),
Version 12.4(10b), RELEASE SOFTWARE (fc3)
Technical Support: http://www.cisco.com/techsupport
Copyright (c) 1986-2007 by Cisco Systems, Inc.
Compiled Fri 19-Jan-07 15:15 by prod_rel_team

advertisement version: 2
VTP Management Domain: ''

-----------------------------
Device ID: S3
Entry address(es):
Platform: cisco WS-C2950-24,  Capabilities: Switch IGMP
Interface: FastEthernet0/0,  Port ID (outgoing port):
FastEthernet0/11
Holdtime : 148 sec

Version :
Cisco Internetwork Operating System Software
IOS (tm) C2950 Software (C2950-I6Q4L2-M), Version 12.1(9)EA1,
RELEASE SOFTWARE (fc1)
Copyright (c) 1986-2002 by cisco Systems, Inc.
Compiled Wed 24-Apr-02 06:57 by antonino

advertisement version: 2
Protocol Hello:  OUI-0x00000C, Protocol ID-0x0112; payload
len-27, value-00000000FFFFFFFF0
10231FF000000000000000AB769F6C0FF0000
VTP Management Domain: 'CCNA3'
Duplex: full

R3#
```

Figure 11-35 Examining the CDP Neighbors

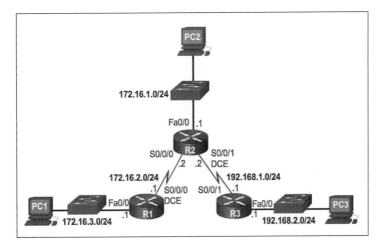

Figure 11-36 CDP Neighbor Topology

When a Cisco device boots up, CDP starts up by default. CDP automatically discovers neighboring Cisco devices running CDP, regardless of which Layer 3 protocol or suites are running. CDP exchanges hardware and software device information with its directly connected CDP neighbors.

CDP provides the following information about each CDP neighbor device:

- **Device identifiers:** For example, the configured hostname of a switch
- **Address list:** Up to one network layer address for each protocol supported
- **Port identifier:** The name of the local and remote port, in the form of an ASCII character string such as ethernet0
- **Capabilities list:** For example, whether this device is a router or a switch
- **Platform:** The hardware platform of the device; for example, a Cisco 1841 series router

The **show cdp neighbors detail** command reveals the IP address of a neighboring device. CDP will reveal the neighbor's IP address regardless of whether or not you can ping the neighbor. This command is very helpful when two Cisco routers cannot route across their shared data link. The **show cdp neighbors detail** command will help determine if one of the CDP neighbors has an IP configuration error.

For network discovery situations, knowing the IP address of the CDP neighbor is often all the information needed to telnet into that device. For obvious reasons, CDP can be a security risk. Because some IOS versions send out CDP advertisements by default, it is important to know how to disable CDP. To disable CDP globally, use the global configuration command **no cdp run**. To disable CDP on an interface, use the interface command **no cdp enable**.

Using the show ip interface brief Command (11.3.4.4)

In the same way that commands and utilities are used to verify a host configuration, commands can be used to verify the interfaces of intermediate devices. The Cisco IOS provides commands to verify the operation of router and switch interfaces.

Verifying Router Interfaces

One of the most frequently used commands is the **show ip interface brief** command. This command provides a more abbreviated output than the **show ip interface** command. It provides a summary of the key information for all the network interfaces on a router.

Figure 11-37 shows the topology that is being used in this example.

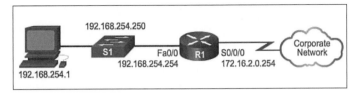

Figure 11-37   Interface Testing

In Activity 11.3.4.4 Part 2, click the **R1** button. The **show ip interface brief** output displays all interfaces on the router, the IP address assigned to each interface, if any, and the operational status of the interface.

Interactive Graphic

Activity 11.3.4.4 Part 2: Interface Testing

Go to the online course and click the **R1** button. The output of the **ip interface brief** command is displayed. Click the **S1** button. The output of the switch is displayed.

According to the output, the Fast Ethernet 0/0 interface has an IP address of 192.168.254.254. The last two columns in this line show the Layer 1 and Layer 2 status of this interface. The **up** in the Status column shows that this interface is operational at Layer 1. The **up** in the Protocol column indicates that the Layer 2 protocol is operational.

Also notice that the Serial 0/0/1 interface has not been enabled. This is indicated by **administratively down** in the Status column.

As with any end device, we can verify Layer 3 connectivity with the **ping** and **traceroute** commands. In this example, both the **ping** and **traceroute** commands show successful connectivity.

Verifying the Switch Interfaces

Continuing in Activity 11.3.4.4 Part 2, click the **S1** button. The **show ip interface brief** command can also be used to verify the status of the switch interfaces. The IP address for the switch is applied to a VLAN interface. In this case, the Vlan 1 interface is assigned an IP address of 192.168.254.250 and has been enabled and is operational.

The output also shows that the FastEthernet0/1 interface is down. This indicates either that no device is connected to the interface or that the device that is connected to this interface has a network interface that is not operational.

In contrast, the output shows that the FastEthernet0/2 and FastEthernet0/3 interfaces are operational. This is indicated by both the Status and Protocol being shown as **up**.

You can also test the Layer 3 connectivity of the switch with the **show ip interface brief** and **traceroute** commands. In this example, both the **ping** and **trace** commands show successful connectivity.

It is important to keep in mind that an IP address is not required for a switch to perform its job of frame forwarding at Layer 2. An IP address is only necessary if the switch will be managed over the network using Telnet or SSH. If the network administrator plans to remotely connect to the switch from a location outside of the local LAN, then a default gateway must also be configured.

Interactive Graphic

Activity 11.3.4.5: show Commands

Go to the online course and read each of the types of **show** command scenarios. Drag each **show** command to the correct **show** command scenario.

Lab 11.3.4.6: Using the CLI to Gather Network Device Information

In this lab you will complete the following objectives:

- Part 1: Set Up Topology and Initialize Devices
- Part 2: Configure Devices and Verify Connectivity
- Part 3: Gather Network Device Information

Managing IOS Configuration Files (11.4)

This section introduces both router and switch file systems and explains how to back them up and how to restore them.

Router and Switch File Systems (11.4.1)

Router and switch file systems are discussed in this section.

Router File Systems (11.4.1.1)

In addition to implementing and securing a small network, the job of the network administrator also includes managing configuration files. Managing the configuration files is important for purposes of backup and retrieval in the event of a device failure.

The Cisco IOS File System (IFS) provides a single interface to all the file systems a router uses, including

- Flash memory file systems

- Network file systems (TFTP and FTP)

- Any other endpoint for reading or writing data such as NVRAM, the running configuration, ROM, and others

With Cisco IFS, all files can be viewed and classified (image, text file, and so forth), including files on remote servers. For example, it is possible to view a configuration file on a remote server to verify that it is the correct configuration file before loading the file on the router.

Cisco IFS allows the administrator to move around to different directories, list the files in a directory, and create subdirectories in flash memory or on a disk. The directories available depend on the device.

The Figure 11-38 displays the output of the **show file systems** command, which lists all of the available file systems on a Cisco 1941 router, in this example. This command provides useful information such as the amount of available and free memory, the type of file system, and its permissions. Permissions include read only (ro), write only (wo), and read and write (rw), shown in the Flags column of the command output.

```
Router#show file systems
File Systems:

        Size(b)         Free(b)         Type    Flags   Prefixes
              -               -          opaque     rw    archive:
              -               -          opaque     rw    system:
              -               -          opaque     rw    tmpsys:
              -               -          opaque     rw    null:
              -               -          network    rw    tftp:
*      256487424       183234560         disk       rw    flash0: flash:#
              -               -          disk       rw    flash1:
         262136          254779         nvram      rw    nvram:
              -               -          opaque     wo    syslog:
              -               -          opaque     rw    xmodem:
              -               -          opaque     rw    ymodem:
              -               -          network    rw    rcp:
              -               -          network    rw    http:
              -               -          network    rw    ftp:
              -               -          network    rw    scp:
              -               -          opaque     ro    tar:
              -               -          network    rw    https:
              -               -          opaque     ro    cns:
```

Figure 11-38   File Systems

Although there are several file systems listed in Figure 11-38, of interest to us are the flash and NVRAM file systems.

Notice that the flash file system also has an asterisk preceding it. This indicates that flash is the current default file system. The bootable IOS is located in flash; therefore, the pound symbol (#) is appended to the flash listing, indicating that it is a bootable disk.

Flash File System

Figure 11-39 lists the content of the current default file system, which in this case is flash, as was indicated by the asterisk preceding its listing in Figure 11-38. There are several files located in flash, but of specific interest is the last listing. This is the name of the current Cisco IOS file image that is running in RAM.

```
Router#dir
Directory of flash0:/

 1 -rw-     2903 Sep  7 2012 06:58:26 +00:00  cpconfig-
                                              19xx.cfg
 2 -rw-  3000320 Sep  7 2012 06:58:40 +00:00  cpexpress.tar
 3 -rw-     1038 Sep  7 2012 06:58:52 +00:00  home.shtml
 4 -rw-   122880 Sep  7 2012 06:59:02 +00:00  home.tar
 5 -rw-  1697952 Sep  7 2012 06:59:20 +00:00  securedesktop-
                                              ios-3.1.1.45-k9.pkg
 6 -rw-   415956 Sep  7 2012 06:59:34 +00:00  sslclient-win-
                                              1.1.4.176.pkg
 7 -rw- 67998028 Sep 26 2012 17:32:14 +00:00 c1900-
                                              universalk9-
                                              mz.SPA.152-4.M1.bin

256487424 bytes total (183234560 bytes free)
```

Figure 11-39 Directory of Files on Flash

NVRAM File System

To view the contents of NVRAM, you must change the current default file system using the **cd** (change directory) command, as shown in Figure 11-40. The **pwd** (present working directory) command verifies that we are viewing the NVRAM directory. Finally, the **dir** (directory) command lists the contents of NVRAM. Although there are several configuration files listed, of specific interest is the startup-config file.

Switch File Systems (11.4.1.2)

With the Cisco 2960 switch flash file system, you can copy configuration files and archive (upload and download) software images.

The command to view the file systems on a Catalyst switch is the same as the command to view the file systems on a Cisco router: **show file systems** (as shown in Figure 11-41).

```
Router#cd nvram:
Router#pwd
nvram:/
Router#dir
Directory of nvram:/

  253  -rw-        1156       <no date>   startup-config
  254  ----           5       <no date>   private-config
  255  -rw-        1156       <no date>   underlying-config
    1  -rw-        2945       <no date>   cwmp_inventory
    4  ----          58       <no date>   persistent-data
    5  -rw-          17       <no date>   ecfm_ieee_mib
    6  -rw-         559       <no date>   IOS-Self-Sig#1.cer

262136 bytes total (254779 bytes free)
```

Figure 11-40   Directory of files in NVRAM

```
Switch#show file systems
File Systems:

       Size(b)      Free(b)      Type   Flags    Prefixes
*     32514048    20887552      flash      rw       flash:
            -            -      opaque     rw          vb:
            -            -      opaque     ro          bs:
            -            -      opaque     rw      system:
            -            -      opaque     rw      tmpsys:
        65536        48897       nvram     rw       nvram:
            -            -      opaque     ro      xmodem:
            -            -      opaque     ro      ymodem:
            -            -      opaque     rw        null:
            -            -      opaque     ro         tar:
            -            -     network     rw        tftp:
            -            -     network     rw         rcp:
            -            -     network     rw        http:
            -            -     network     rw         ftp:
            -            -     network     rw         scp:
            -            -     network     rw       https:
            -            -      opaque     ro         cns:
```

Figure 11-41   Cisco 2960 Switch File Systems

Many basic UNIX commands are supported on Cisco switches and routers: **cd** for changing to a file system or directory, **dir** to display directories on a file system, and **pwd** to display the working directory.

Back Up and Restore Configuration Files (11.4.2)

This section examines the several methods available to back up and restore IOS configuration files.

Backing Up and Restoring Using Text Files (11.4.2.1)

One of the methods of backing up and restoring IOS configuration files is to use text files.

Backing Up Configurations with Text Capture (Tera Term)

Configuration files can be saved/archived to a text file using Tera Term (see Figure 11-42).

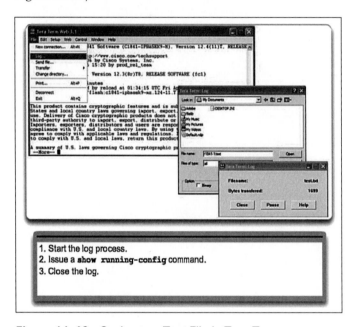

Figure 11-42   Saving to a Text File in Tera Term

As shown in Figure 11-42, the steps are as follows:

Step 1.   On the File menu, click **Log**.

Step 2.   Choose the location to save the file. Tera Term will begin capturing text.

Step 3.   After capture has been started, execute the **show running-config** or **show startup-config** command at the privileged EXEC prompt. Text displayed in the terminal window will be directed into the chosen file.

Step 4.   When the capture is complete, select **Close** in the Tera Term: Log window.

Step 5.   View the file to verify that it was not corrupted.

Restoring Text Configurations

A configuration can be copied from a file to a device. When copied from a text file and pasted into a terminal window, the IOS executes each line of the configuration text as a command. This means that the file will require editing to ensure that encrypted passwords are in plaintext and that non-command text such as "--More--" and IOS messages are removed.

Further, at the CLI, the device must be set at the global configuration mode to receive the commands from the text file being pasted into the terminal window.

> **Note**
>
> To facilitate the restore of the configuration, you also need to add a line such as "no shutdown" after each interface configured with an active IP address.

When using Tera Term, the steps are as follows:

Step 1. On the File menu, click **Send** file.

Step 2. Locate the file to be copied into the device and click **Open**.

Step 3. Tera Term will paste the file into the device.

The text in the file will be applied as commands in the CLI and become the running configuration on the device. This is a convenient method for manually configuring a router.

Backing Up and Restoring Using TFTP (11.4.2.2)

Another method of backing up and restoring IOS files is through the use of Trivial File Transfer Protocol (TFTP).

Backing Up Configurations with TFTP

Copies of configuration files should be stored as backup files in the event of a problem. Configuration files can be stored on a TFTP server or a USB drive. A configuration file should also be included in the network documentation.

To save the running configuration or the startup configuration to a TFTP server, use either the **copy running-config tftp** command, as shown in Figure 11-43, or the **copy startup-config tftp** command. Follow these steps to back up the running configuration to a TFTP server:

Step 1. Enter the **copy running-config tftp** command.

Step 2. Enter the IP address of the host where the configuration file will be stored.

Step 3. Enter the name to assign to the configuration file, or press the Enter key to continue.

Step 4. Press **Enter** to confirm each choice.

Note

You need to have a TFTP server running on the network for this part of the TFTP process to work.

```
Router#copy running-config tftp
Remote host []? 131.108.2.155
Name of configuration file to write[tokyo-config]?tokyo.2
Write file tokyo.2 to 131.108.2.155? [confirm]
Writing tokyo.2 !!!!!! [OK]
```

Figure 11-43 Using the **copy running-config tftp** Command

Restoring Configurations with TFTP

To restorethe running configuration or the startup configuration from a TFTP server, use either the **copy tftp running-config** command or the **copy tftp startup-config** command. Use these steps to restore the running configuration from a TFTP server:

Note

To facilitate the restore of the configuration, you also need to add a line such as "no shutdown" after each interface configured with an active IP address.

Step 1. Enter the **copy tftp running-config** command.

Step 2. Enter the IP address of the host where the configuration file is stored.

Step 3. Enter the name to assign to the configuration file.

Step 4. Press **Enter** to confirm each choice.

Using USB Ports on a Cisco Router (11.4.2.3)

The Universal Serial Bus (USB) storage feature enables certain models of Cisco routers to support USB flash drives. The USB flash feature provides an optional, secondary storage capability and an additional boot device. Images, configurations, and other files can be copied to or from the Cisco USB flash memory with the same reliability as storing and retrieving files using the CompactFlash card. In addition, modular Cisco Integrated Services Routers can boot any Cisco IOS Software image saved on USB flash memory.

Cisco USB flash modules are available in 64 MB, 128 MB, and 256 MB versions.

To be compatible with a Cisco router, a USB flash drive must be formatted in a FAT16 format. If that is not the case, the **show file systems** command will display an error indicating an incompatible file system.

Here is an example of the use of the **dir** command on a USB file system:

```
Router# dir usbflash0:
Directory of usbflash0:/
1 -rw- 30125020 Dec 22 2032 05:31:32 +00:00 c3825-entservicesk9-mz.123-14.T
63158272 bytes total (33033216 bytes free)
```

Ideally, USB flash can hold multiple copies of the Cisco IOS and multiple router configurations. The USB flash allows an administrator to easily move and copy those IOS files and configurations from router to router, and many times, the copying process can take place several times faster than it would over a LAN or WAN feature enables certain models of Cisco routers to support USB flash drives. Note that the IOS may not recognize the proper size of the USB flash, but that does not necessarily mean that the flash is unsupported. Additionally, the USB ports on a router are usually USB 2.0, as shown in Figure 11-44.

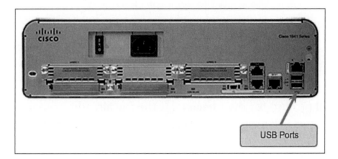

Figure 11-44   Cisco 1941 Router

Backing Up and Restoring Using a USB (11.4.2.4)

This section discusses backing up with a USB flash drive, as well as restoration from a USB flash drive.

Backing Up Configurations with a USB Flash Drive

When backing up to a USB port, it is a good idea to issue the **show file systems** command to verify that the USB drive is there and confirm its name, as shown in Figure 11-45.

```
R1#show file systems
File Systems:

        Size(b)        Free(b)      Type  Flags  Prefixes
              -              -     opaque    rw   archive:
              -              -     opaque    rw   system:
              -              -     opaque    rw   tmpsys:
              -              -     opaque    rw   null:
              -              -    network    rw   tftp:
*      256487424      184819712      disk    rw   flash0: flash:#
              -              -       disk    rw   flash1:
         262136         249270      nvram    rw   nvram:
              -              -     opaque    wo   syslog:
              -              -     opaque    rw   xmodem:
              -              -     opaque    rw   ymodem:
              -              -    network    rw   rcp:
              -              -    network    rw   http:
              -              -    network    rw   ftp:
              -              -    network    rw   scp:
              -              -     opaque    ro   tar:
              -              -    network    rw   https:
              -              -     opaque    ro   cns:
     4050042880     3774152704   usbflash    rw   usbflash0:
```

Shows the USB port and name: "usbflash0:"

Figure 11-45   Using the **show file systems** Command

Next, use the **copy** running-config **usbflash0:/** command to copy the configuration file to the USB flash drive. Be sure to use the name of the flash drive, as indicated in the file system. The slash is optional but indicates the root directory of the USB flash drive.

The IOS will prompt for the filename. If the file already exists on the USB flash drive, the router will prompt for overwrite, as shown in Figure 11-46.

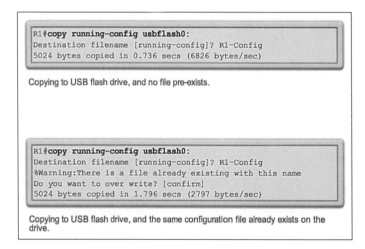

```
R1#copy running-config usbflash0:
Destination filename [running-config]? R1-Config
5024 bytes copied in 0.736 secs (6826 bytes/sec)
```

Copying to USB flash drive, and no file pre-exists.

```
R1#copy running-config usbflash0:
Destination filename [running-config]? R1-Config
%Warning:There is a file already existing with this name
Do you want to over write? [confirm]
5024 bytes copied in 1.796 secs (2797 bytes/sec)
```

Copying to USB flash drive, and the same configuration file already exists on the drive.

Figure 11-46   Using the **copy running-config usbflash0** Command

Use the **dir** command to see the file on the USB drive, and use the **more** command to see the contents, as shown in Figure 11-47.

```
R1#dir usbflash0:/
Directory of usbflash0:/
    1  drw-      0  Oct 15 2010 16:28:30 +00:00  Cisco
   16  -rw-   5024  Jan 7 2013 20:26:50 +00:00  R1-Config

4050042880 bytes total (3774144512 bytes free)
R1#more usbflash0:/R1-Config
!
! Last configuration change at 20:19:54 UTC Mon Jan 7 2013 by
admin version 15.2
service timestamps debug datetime msec
service timestamps log datetime msec
no service password-encryption
!
hostname R1
!
boot-start-marker
boot-end-marker
!
!
logging buffered 51200 warnings
!
no aaa new-model
!
no ipv6 cef
```

Figure 11-47 Using the **dir** and **more** Commands

Restoring Configurations with a USB Flash Drive

In order to copy the file back, it will be necessary to edit the USB R1-Config file with a text editor to make it a valid running-config file; otherwise, there are a lot of entries that are invalid commands and no interfaces will be brought up.

```
R1# copy usbflash0:/R1-Config running-config
Destination filename [running-config]?
```

Packet Tracer Activity 11.4.2.5: Backing Up Configuration Files

This activity is designed to show how to restore a configuration from a backup and then perform a new backup. Due to an equipment failure, a new router has been put in place. Fortunately, backup configuration files have been saved to a TFTP server. You are required to restore the files from the TFTP server to get the router back online with as little downtime as possible.

Lab 11.4.2.6: Managing Router Configuration Files with Tera Term

In this lab you will complete the following objectives:

- Part 1: Configure Basic Device Settings
- Part 2: Use Terminal Emulation Software to Create a Backup Configuration File
- Part 3: Use a Backup Configuration File to Restore a Router

Lab 11.4.2.7: Managing Device Configuration Files Using TFTP, Flash, and USB

In this lab you will complete the following objectives:

- Part 1: Build the Network and Configure Basic Device Settings
- Part 2: (Optional) Download TFTP Server Software
- Part 3: Use TFTP to Back Up and Restore the Switch Running Configuration
- Part 4: Use TFTP to Back Up and Restore the Router Running Configuration
- Part 5: Back Up and Restore Running Configurations Using Router Flash Memory
- Part 6: (Optional) Use a USB Drive to Back Up and Restore the Running Configuration

Lab 11.4.2.8: Researching Password Recovery Procedures

In this lab you will complete the following objectives:

- Part 1: Research the Configuration Register
- Part 2: Document the Password Recovery Procedure for a Specific Cisco Router

Summary (11.5)

Class Activity 11.5.1.1: Capstone Project - Design and Build a Small Business Network

Go to the online course to perform the Capstone Project. You will use Packet Tracer and a word processing application to complete the activity. This activity works best with two to three students per group. In this Capstone Project you will build a network from scratch.

Packet Tracer
☐ Activity

Packet Tracer Activity 11.5.1.2: Skills Integration Challenge

In this scenario the network administrator has asked you to prepare a router for deployment. Before it can be connected to the network, security measures must be enabled.

In order to meet user requirements, even small networks require planning and design. Planning ensures that all requirements, cost factors, and deployment options are given due consideration. An important part of network design is to ensure reliability, scalability, and availability.

Supporting and growing a small network requires being familiar with the protocols and network applications running over the network. Protocol analyzers enable a network professional to quickly compile statistical information about traffic flows on a network. Information gathered by the protocol analyzer is analyzed based on the source and destination of the traffic as well as the type of traffic being sent. This analysis can be used by a network technician to make decisions on how to manage the traffic more efficiently. Common network protocols include DNS, Telnet, SMTP, POP, DHCP, HTTP, and FTP.

It is a necessity to consider security threats and vulnerabilities when planning a network implementation. All network devices must be secured. This includes routers, switches, end-user devices, and even security devices. Networks need to be protected from malicious software, such as viruses, Trojan horses, and worms. Antivirus software can detect most viruses and many Trojan horse applications and prevent them from spreading in the network. The most effective way to mitigate a worm attack is to download security updates from the operating system vendor and patch all vulnerable systems.

Networks must also be protected from network attacks. Network attacks can be classified into three major categories: reconnaissance, access attacks, and denial of service. There are several ways to protect a network from network attacks:

- Authentication, authorization, and accounting (AAA, or "triple A") network security services provide the primary framework to set up access control on a network device. AAA is a way to control who is permitted to access a network (authenticate), to control what they can do while they are there (authorize), and watch the actions they perform while accessing the network (accounting).

- A firewall is one of the most effective security tools available for protecting internal network users from external threats. A firewall resides between two or more networks and controls the traffic between them. It also helps to prevent unauthorized access.

- To protect network devices, it is important to use strong passwords. Also, when accessing network devices remotely, it is highly recommended to enable SSH instead of the unsecured Telnet.

After the network has been implemented, a network administrator must be able to monitor and maintain network connectivity. There are several commands available toward this end. For testing network connectivity to local and remote destinations, commands such as **ping**, **telnet**, and **traceroute** are commonly used.

On Cisco IOS devices, the **show version** command can be used to verify and troubleshoot some of the basic hardware and software components used during the bootup process. To view information for all network interfaces on a router, the **show ip interface** command is used. The **show ip interface brief** command can also be used to view a more abbreviated output than is provided by the **show ip interface** command. CDP is a Cisco-proprietary protocol that runs at the data link layer. Because CDP operates at the data link layer, two or more Cisco network devices, such as routers that support different network layer protocols, can learn about each other even if Layer 3 connectivity does not exist.

Configuration files such as startup-config and running-config should be archived. These files can be saved to a text file or stored on a TFTP server. Some models of routers also have a USB port, in which case a file can be backed up to a USB drive. If needed, these files can be copied to the router and/or switch from the TFTP server or USB drive.

Practice

The following activities provide practice with the topics introduced in this chapter. The Labs and Class Activities are available in the companion *Network Basics Lab Manual* (978-1-58713-313-8). The Packet Tracer Activities PKA files are found in the online course.

Class Activities

Class Activity 11.0.1.2: Did You Notice?

Class Activity 11.5.1.1: Design and Build a Small Business Network

Labs

Lab 11.2.2.6: Researching Network Security Threats

Lab 11.2.4.5: Accessing Network Devices with SSH

Lab 11.2.4.6: Securing Network Devices

Lab 11.3.2.3: Testing Network Latency with Ping and Traceroute

Lab 11.3.4.6: Using the CLI to Gather Network Device Information

Lab 11.4.2.6: Managing Router Configuration Files with Tera Term

Lab 11.4.2.7: Managing Device Configuration Files Using TFTP, Flash, and USB

Lab 11.4.2.8: Researching Password Recovery Procedures

Packet Tracer
☐ Activity

Packet Tracer Activities

Packet Tracer Activity 11.3.2.2: Troubleshooting IPv4 and IPv6 Addressing

Packet Tracer Activity 11.3.3.4: Using **show** Commands

Packet Tracer Activity 11.4.2.5: Backing Up Configuration Files

Packet Tracer Activity 11.5.1.2: Skills Integration Challenge

Check Your Understanding

Complete all the review questions listed here to test your understanding of the topics and concepts in this chapter. The appendix, "Answers to the 'Check Your Understanding' Questions" lists the answers.

1. A small accounting firm consists of 20 workstations and 3 servers. The company is assigned a network of 209.165.200.224/27. What is a Cisco-recommended approach for managing the IP addressing scheme for the network?

   A. Assign static IP addresses for workstations and servers in a sequence of installation steps

   B. Divide the network into two subnets, one for workstations and the other for servers

   C. Add a DHCP server and assign dynamic IP addresses for workstations and servers via the DHCP server

   D. Assign static IP addresses for servers in the upper block of the address pool and allow dynamic IP addresses for workstations

2. A small advertising company has a web server that provides critical business service. The company connects to the Internet through a leased line service to an ISP. Which approach best provides cost-effective redundancy for the Internet connection?

   A. Add a second NIC to the web server

   B. Add another web server to prepare failover support

   C. Add another connection to the Internet via a DSL line to another ISP

   D. Add multiple connections between the switches and the edge router

3. What are two examples of maintenance threats to a network? (Choose two.)

   A. Poor labeling

   B. Unconditioned power

   C. Temperature extremes

   D. Physical damage to routers

   E. Lack of critical spare parts

4. Which statement is an example of a network security threat?

   A. A router is configured with a weak password.

   B. Telnet is used for all remote management of network devices.

   C. A switch is running an old version of IOS with known security bugs.

   D. A disgruntled employee has the administrator password to all of the network devices.

   E. The company security policy does not specify how many characters must be in a password.

5. Which malicious code attack is self-contained and tries to exploit a specific vulnerability in a system being attacked?

   A. Virus

   B. Worm

   C. Trojan horse

   D. Social engineering

6. Which AAA component assigns varying levels of rights to users of network resources?

   A. Auditing

   B. Accounting

   C. Authorization

   D. Access control

   E. Authentication

   F. Acknowledgement

7. When configuring a switch for SSH access, what other command that is associated with the **login local** command is required to be entered on the switch?

   A. **enable secret** *password*

   B. **password** *password*

   C. **username** *username* **secret** *secret*

   D. **login block-for** *seconds* **attempts** *number* **within** *seconds*

8. A user complains that the workstation cannot access the network. The network technician asks the user to issue the **ping 127.0.0.1** command. What is the purpose of using this command?

   A. To test the reachability of a remote network

   B. To verify that the NIC is configured with a static address

   C. To verify that the TCP/IP stack is operational

   D. To check that the workstation can reach a DHCP server

9. What conclusion can be drawn from the results of the following command issued by a user on the workstation?

```
C:\Users\user10> tracert www.cisco.com

Tracing route to e144.dscb.akamaiedge.net [184.50.224.170]
over a maximum of 30 hops:

 1    15 ms     2 ms     3 ms    192.168.10.254
 2     *         *         *      Request timed out.
 3    11 ms    12 ms    13 ms    173-219-253-70-link.sta.suddenlink.net [173.219.253.70]
 4    13 ms    15 ms    21 ms    173-219-253-224-link.sta.suddenlink.net [173.219.253.224]
 5    20 ms    19 ms    19 ms    173-219-253-234-link.sta.suddenlink.net [173.219.253.234]
 6    29 ms    22 ms    21 ms    xe-4-2-0.edge1.Washington1.Level3.net [4.79.20.57]
 7    21 ms    22 ms    21 ms    ae-4-90.edge2.Washington4.Level3.net [4.69.149.208]
 8    31 ms    21 ms    22 ms    xe-0-4-0-2.r04.asbnva02.us.bb.gin.ntt.net [129.250.9.153]
 9    41 ms    38 ms    38 ms    ae-7.r20.asbnva02.us.bb.gin.ntt.net [129.250.3.16]
10    98 ms    58 ms    60 ms    ae-3.r20.dllstx09.us.bb.gin.ntt.net [129.250.3.51]
11    61 ms    58 ms    65 ms    ae-2.r07.dllstx09.us.bb.gin.ntt.net [129.250.3.67]
12    65 ms    58 ms    66 ms    a184-50-224-170.deploy.akamaitechnologies.com
[184.50.224.170]

Trace complete.
```

A. One of the routers in the path is not operational.

B. A ping to the website takes about 63 milliseconds.

C. The IP address of the workstation is 192.168.10.254.

D. There are 12 hops between the workstation and the website.

10. While downloading an IOS image from a TFTP server, an administrator sees long strings of exclamation marks (!) output to the console. What does this mean?

A. The transfer is working.

B. The TFTP server is not responding.

C. The IOS file is corrupt and is failing the checksum verification.

D. There is not enough space in flash to hold the image.

Answers to the "Check Your Understanding" Questions

Chapter 1

1. C. Explanation: Differentiating and prioritizing types of traffic is an example of QoS.

2. Scalability, security, data integrity, and fault tolerance. Explanation: In order, the best terms are scalability, security, data integrity, and fault tolerance.

3. D. Explanation: Packet switching allows for messages to be sent along multiple paths. Circuit switching and leased lines use dedicated paths.

4. C. Explanation: Intranets connect LANs and WANs that should only be accessible by internal employees, whereas an extranet allows an organization to do business directly with other, external organizations by allowing them access to part of the internal network.

5. B. Explanation: In a BYOD environment, an organization can accommodate a variety of devices and access methods, including personal devices that are not under company control.

6. A. Explanation: Podcasting is an audio-based medium that enables people to record audio and use the Web to deliver their recordings to a wide audience.

7. D. Explanation: Collaboration tools give people the opportunity to work together on shared documents without the constraints of location or time.

8. C. Explanation: Message complexity might require special handling and delivery, whereas clear and concise messages are usually easier to understand. The other choices are external factors.

9. C. Explanation: Traditional networks used separate, dedicated networks for voice, video, and data. A converged network combines all three types of traffic on a single network.

10. B. Explanation: The Internet is a network composed of local networks connected by WANs.

11. A. Explanation: A router is a device that helps connect end devices. The other choices are end devices.

12. B. Explanation: A network infrastructure designed to support file servers and provide data storage is a SAN, or storage-area network.

13. A. Explanation: A WLAN is similar to a LAN but wirelessly interconnects users and end points in a small geographical area.

14. C. Explanation: The farther from the central office, the slower the connection. Cable companies provide cable modems, not DSL.

15. A, B, and D. Explanation: Availability is the assurance of timely and reliable access to data services. Network firewall devices, desktop and server antivirus software, and redundant network devices can ensure system reliability and mitigate threats.

Chapter 2

1. A, D, F. Explanation: With standard naming conventions, names should not begin with numbers, should not contain spaces, and should consist of only letters, digits, and dashes.

2. C. Explanation: The IOS is usually stored in flash and is copied to RAM when the device boots.

3. B. Explanation: The console port is the only out-of-band option offered here (an AUX port can work as well but it does not use a serial cable). The console port requires a console cable.

4. D. Explanation: The running configuration resides in RAM. If it is copied to NVRAM, it becomes the startup configuration. The startup configuration that is stored in NVRAM is copied to RAM and becomes the running configuration.

5. A. Explanation: User executive mode is the default access level. It does not require authentication until an access password is set. The debugging commands are not available at this level.

6. C. Explanation: Choice A is the command prompt for line configurations, B is not in configuration mode, and D is the prompt for interface configuration mode.

7. D. Explanation: Choices A and C require the device to already be in enable mode or configuration mode. Entering **enable** does not require a password if no password is set.

8. C. Explanation: The **exit** command moves the mode back one level. In this case, the router would return to global configuration mode from the more specific router configuration mode.

9. C. Explanation: The argument of a command is a variable; for example, following the word **show** in a **show** command there are many available variables (arguments) that can be entered.

10. B. Explanation: The help function assists the user in finding available valid syntax options or arguments when a space followed by a question mark is entered.

11. C. Explanation: Option C is the only option that will interrupt a process.

12. B and D. Explanation: The Up Arrow and Down Arrow keys are used to scroll through previous commands. The Left Arrow and Right Arrow keys move the cursor on a line.

13. B. Explanation: A and C are in configuration mode, and **show** commands need extra text to work on that level. The running configuration does not contain IOS information.

14. A and C. Explanation: Switches do not require configuration before being used on a LAN.

15. B. Explanation: The switch booted, so the IOS was present. With the default configuration present, the administrator was not locked out. The startup configuration is stored in NVRAM, not flash. B is the only likely answer.

16. C. Explanation: Dynamic Host Configuration Protocol (DHCP) allows end devices to have IP information automatically configured.

Chapter 3

1. C. Explanation: IPHD is not a protocol. All others are communications protocols.

2. A. Explanation: A group of interrelated protocols necessary to perform a communication function is called a protocol suite.

3. A, C, E. Explanation: Only A, C, and E are legitimate standards organizations.

4. B. Explanation: A protocol model closely matches the structure of a particular protocol suite. The hierarchical set of related protocols in a suite typically represents all the functionality required to communicate across a data network.

5. C. Explanation: The upper three layers of the OSI model are incorporated into the TCP/IP application layer.

6. A and C. Explanation: Standards do allow for proprietary protocols and encourage competition, so B and D are false.

7. D. Explanation: OSI Layer 7 is the application layer. Layer 1 is the physical layer, Layer 3 is the network layer, and Layer 4 is the transport layer.

8. B. Explanation: IP addressing and routing occur at the network layer, or Layer 3.

9. B. Explanation: Frame encapsulation occurs at the data link layer, which is OSI Layer 2.

10. A. Explanation: Physical media is described at the physical layer, or OSI Layer 1. If the NIC was the problem, then the issue would be at Layer 2.

11. D. Explanation: OSI Layers 1 (physical) and 2 (data link) combine to make the TCP/IP network access layer.

12. A. Explanation: Request for Comments, or RFCs, was the name of the initial documents describing protocols, and the name has remained in use.

13. A and C. Explanation: Bits are part of the TCP/IP network access layer and packets are part of the Internet layer.

14. D. Explanation: De-encapsulation occurs when the encapsulated frame arrives at its next-hop address.

15. A and D. Explanation: Packet PDUs have OSI Layer 3 source and destination IP addresses. MAC addresses are added in the framing process at OSI Layer 2.

16. B and E. Explanation: Ethernet frame PDUs have OSI Layer 2 source and destination MAC addresses.

Chapter 4

1. B. Explanation: The top three layers of the OSI model are combined in the TCP/IP model because they do not normally concern networking processes.

2. D. Explanation: All four are applications. Layer 7 is the application layer.

3. C. Explanation: The session layer, Layer 5, maintains dialogs between source and destination applications.

4. A. HTTP, SMTP, and POP, in that order, provide the services described.

5. B. Explanation: The protocol is indicated by http://, the server name is cisco.com, and the file is /index. DNS does convert cisco.com to an IP address, but DNS does not use tags.

6. C. Explanation: HTTPS is a secure form of HTTP, and the added security features require more processing power.

7. B and D. Explanation: HTTP does not use SSL, and HTTPS was developed after HTTP and uses more computing resources than HTTP.

8. C. Explanation: POP and POP3 are used to let the client retrieve mail from the server. SNMP is a network management protocol.

9. B. Explanation: POP is an email protocol, UDP is a transport protocol, and NDS is a Novell proprietary protocol.

10. D. Explanation: The DNS structure is like an inverted tree, and the root is the top level.

11. B. Explanation: nslookup provides information about the local network, including the default name server for the host on which the command is entered.

12. A. Explanation: DHCP provides IP addresses for devices to access a network.

13. A and C. Explanation: DHCP OFFER and DHCP ACK are issued by the DHCP server.

14. B. Explanation: FTP requires one connection for data transfer and another for commands to control the transfer.

15. A. Explanation: DNS resolves IP addresses. All others are functions of SMB, or Server Message Block.

Chapter 5

1. B and D. Explanation: Answers B and D are incorrect, respectively, because the session layer is responsible for establishing communication links, and port numbers are used to identify appropriate communication streams.

2. B and C. Explanation: B and C are transport layer functions. Frames are a data link layer function, and the presentation layer is not responsible for data delivery.

3. B. Explanation: TCP is the only transport layer protocol listed that reassembles data in a correct order.

4. A. Explanation: MAC addresses function at OSI Layer 2, and IP functions at OSI Layer 3. VLAN tags are a LAN process. Port numbers keep application conversations separate.

5. D and E. Explanation: Because of the ability of TCP to track actual conversations, TCP is considered a stateful protocol. A stateful protocol is a protocol that keeps track of the state of the communication session. UDP does not keep track, and is thus stateless. UDP does not establish a connection between the hosts before data can be sent and received, and is considered connectionless. TCP does establish the connection and is considered connection-oriented.

6. B. Explanation: IP, UDP, and IPX are connectionless, but FTP requires TCP's reliability to function successfully.

7. C. Explanation: TCP functions at OSI Layer 4, so C is not true.

8. B. Explanation: The transport layer does not perform any functions in the application layer.

9. D. Explanation: TCP provides methods of managing these segment losses, including retransmission of segments with unacknowledged data. It does not resend the entire message (B), and the user does not request missing data (A).

10. A. Explanation: UDP does not resend data (C, D), and it is commonly preferred to TCP when the needs of the application require the connectionless features.

11. B. Explanation: A, C, and D are false statements. UDP is better if an application can tolerate data loss, and TCP uses more processing overhead than UDP.

12. D. Explanation: A, B, and C are applications that require the connectionless nature of UDP. TCP's reliability processes would disrupt the flow of video, voice, and music.

13. B. Explanation: A, C, and D are all characteristics of UDP. TCP does provide ordered data reconstruction.

14. B. Explanation: A, C, and D are all characteristics of TCP. UDP provides best-effort delivery but does not know if data was successfully delivered.

15. C. Explanation: Each TCP segment has 20 bytes of overhead in the header encapsulating the application layer data. A UDP segment has 8 bytes of overhead.

16. C. Explanation: The combination of the source and destination IP addresses and the source and destination port numbers is known as a socket pair. The socket is used to identify the server and service being requested by the client. MAC addresses and SYN/ACK flags are not involved in the process.

17. D. Explanation: Port 80 is the well-known port for HTTP. Port 110 is POP3, port 21 is FTP control, and port 23 is Telnet.

18. B. Explanation: Port 110 is the well-known port for the Post Office Protocol (POP).

19. C. Explanation: The window size is measured in bytes and sends an acknowledgement indicating the next byte expected by the receiver.

20. D. Explanation: The first acknowledgement would be 2501. The second would add 2500 bytes.

21. B. Explanation: The SWQ and ACK messages indicate which data was successfully delivered. If data is sent and no ACK message is returned, data is re-sent. The three-way handshake establishes communication, and the window size controls how much data is sent at any given time.

22. C and D. Explanation: With a smaller window comes more overhead, thus more transmission time. The question is an example of dynamic, not static, window sizing. A smaller window would indicate there is more traffic and congestion on the network. The process is dynamic and the flow of data does not stop while windows are adjusted.

Chapter 6

1. B. Explanation: Routers are Layer 3 devices that perform path selection and then switch packets on the selected path to the destination.

2. B and D. Explanation: Layer 3 addresses are encapsulated at the network layer. IP addresses can be changed.

3. B. Explanation: Though some systems may still run IPX, AppleTalk, and DECNet, their use is relatively rare and unsupported.

4. A. Explanation: IP is the only connectionless technology and the only Layer 3 technology.

5. C and D. Explanation: Layer 3 does not involve reliability. Application data is at Layer 7.

6. B, E, and F. Explanation: Only B, E, and F relate to Layer 3.

7. B and E. Explanation: **route print** and **netstat** work on hosts. A, C, and D are router commands.

8. A, C, and D. Explanation: Only A, C, and D are in the routing table output.

9. A, B, and D. Explanation: A, B, and D are the only effects of broadcast storms.

10. C. Explanation: IP is media independent and not reliable, and gives packets IP addresses.

11. C and D. Explanation: Deliverability is a Layer 4 issue, and application data is a Layer 7 issue.

12. B and E. Explanation: B and E are the only possible choices.

13. C. Explanation: De-encapsulation removes Layer 2 data to expose Layer 3 data.

14. C. Explanation: Both routers and hosts need IP addresses to send and receive messages.

15. A and D. Explanation: Layer 2 data may change between the IP source and destinations; encapsulation happens in the sending host, and converts data into packets.

16. B and C. Explanation: B and C are the only true combinations.

17. B. Explanation: IP works on copper, fiber, and wireless technologies.

18. C. Explanation: TCP is OSI Layer 4.

19. C. Explanation: There are 32 bits, usually represented in four 8-bit numbers separated by a decimal.

20. D. Explanation: The local default route; that is, all packets with destinations that do not match other specified addresses in the routing table are forwarded to the gateway.

Chapter 7

1. 00000111. Explanation: 4 + 2 + 1 = 7.

2. C and D. Explanation: A unicast is sent to a specific host on a network. Directed broadcasts can be used to target both remote (distant) networks and local networks. Limited broadcasts are limited to the hosts that exist on the local network.

3. C. Explanation: The binary format for 255.255.255.224 is 11111111.11111111. 11111111.11100000. The prefix length is the number of consecutive 1s in the subnet mask. Therefore, the prefix length is /27.

4. B. Explanation: When comparing the entire range of numbers used by private and public addresses, most of the IPv4 addresses are in the public address range.

5. 2001:DB8:0:AB00::AB. Explanation: The double colon can be used only once to substitute for continuous hextets consisting of all 0s. Leading 0s can also be suppressed. Therefore, the correct representation is 2001:DB8:0:AB00::AB.

6. B. Explanation: Link-local addresses have relevance only on the local link. Routers will not forward packets that include a link-local address as either the source or destination address.

7. D. Explanation: The current practice is that ISPs assign a /48 global routing prefix to customers. This global routing prefix is the first 48 bits of a global unicast address. If /64 addresses are being used, then 16 bits are being used for Subnet IDs. $2^{16} = 65,536$, so 65,536 different subnets can be created.

8. Answer: A = Subnet ID, B = Global routing prefix, and C= Interface ID. Explanation: A global IPv6 unicast address contains three parts. The global routing prefix of an IPv6 address is the prefix, or network, portion of the address assigned by the provider, such as an ISP, to a customer or site. The Subnet ID field is used by an organization to identify a subnet within its site. The Interface ID field of the IPv6 Interface ID is equivalent to the host portion of an IPv4 address.

9. C and E. Explanation: ICMPv6 includes four new message types: Router Advertisement, Neighbor Advertisement, Router Solicitation, and Neighbor Solicitation.

10. B and D. Explanation: Answers B and D are the two options that depict network addresses. Answer B – 192.168.12.64/26 represents the .64 network. Answer D –18.18.12.16/28 represents the .16 network.

11. D. Explanation: The other choices are private, nonroutable IP addresses.

12. C. Explanation: Answer C represents two octets of eight ones or 16 ones, the third octet, 255, represent 6 ones, so if you add the first two octets number of ones, 16, plus the third octets 6 ones, you come up with the 22 ones or /22.

13. B. Explanation: This address block would give you 14 useful hosts plus a network address and a broadcast address. You could subnet these 16 IP addresses into four point-to-point link addresses. Sixteen addresses divided by four per network results in the answer of four WAN links.

14. C. Explanation: 255.255.255.224 would provide 30 hosts, enough for the 16 usable hosts you require. A 255.255.255.240 would only give you 14 usable hosts, enough for the computers but not for the two router interfaces.

15. B. Explanation: IPv4 goes from /2 to /30.

Chapter 8

1. C. Explanation: In order to create 32 subnets of equal size, 5 bits from the host portion of an IPv4 address must be borrowed ($2^5 = 32$).

2. E. Explanation: A /26 subnet has 6 bits for host addressing ($32 - 26 = 6$); 6 host bits gives 64 possible addresses ($2^6 = 64$). This means the range of addresses in the subnet is 192.168.1.0 through 192.168.1.63. However, the first address, 192.168.1.0, is the network address, and the last address, 192.168.1.63, is the broadcast address. Therefore, the first valid host address is 192.168.1.1 and the last valid host address is 192.168.1.62.

3. B. Explanation: A /29 mask means that 3 bits have been left for host bits. Using the formula $2^x - 2$, where x is the number of host bits, we know $2^3 - 2 = 6$; i.e., there are six valid host addresses on this network. Because one IP address (192.168.0.168) has already been assigned to a PC and there are six valid addresses, five more host addresses are left to be assigned on this network.

4. D. Explanation: The host 192.168.1.59 resides on network 192.168.1.48. The range of addresses on this network is 192.168.1.48 through 192.168.1.63. 192.168.1.48 is the network address, and 192.168.1.63 is the broadcast address for the network. The next subnet with a /28 network prefix will start at 192.168.1.64.

5. C. Explanation: Of the hosts listed, only host A: 192.168.1.59/26 and host B: 192.168.1.71/26 will require a router. This is because they are on two different subnets. Host A is on the 192.168.1.0/26 network and host B is on the 192.168.1.64/26 network. All other hosts in the other options reside on common subnets.

6. A. Explanation: The prefix notation is shown as /n, where n indicates the number of consecutive 1s in a subnet mask shown in binary form. /23 has 23 consecutive 1s in the subnet mask, where 16 of the 1s create the 255.255 part of the subnet mask. The next seven 1s in the mask represent the decimal values of

128, 64, 32, 16, 8, 4, and 2. 128 + 64 + 32 + 16 + 8 + 4 + 2 = 254 (the third number of the subnet mask of 255.255.254.0).

7. A. Explanation: A mask of 255.255.255.128 will result in 1 network bit and 7 host bits. This will satisfy the problem by yielding two subnets, each with 126 usable host addresses.

8. C and F. Explanation: To calculate the network number, write the host IP address in binary. Draw a line showing where the subnet mask 1s end. For example, with the IP address 192.31.7.200, the final octet (200) is 11001000. The line would be drawn between the 1100 and the 1000 because the subnet mask is /28. Change all the bits to the right of the line to 0s to determine the network number (11000000 or 192). Change all the bits to the right of the line to 1s to determine the broadcast address (11001111 or 207). Numbers that can be assigned to hosts on the same network are unassigned usable host addresses within the range of the network 192.31.7.192/28.

9. C. Explanation: When using VLSM, the network administrator can allocate host addresses more efficiently than with traditional subnetting. With traditional subnetting, every network has the same maximum number of hosts. With VLSM, the number of valid host addresses can vary according to the needs of each network.

10. B. Explanation: A nibble is 4 bits in length.

11. E. Explanation: The subnet mask is /20 or 255.255.240.0. This mask assigns 20 bits for the network portion of the IPv4 address. The host portion has 12 bits or 2^{12} addresses (including the broadcast and network addresses). So, there are 4096 – 2 = 4094 addresses available to be assigned to hosts.

12. A. Explanation: Note that sometimes VLSM stands for variable-length subnet masking, which refers to the process of using different masks in the same classful network, whereas variable length subnet mask refers to the subnet mask itself.

13. A. Explanation: Subnet 10.5.0.0 255.255.240.0 implies range 10.5.0.0 to 10.5.15.255, which does not overlap. Subnet 10.4.0.0 255.254.0.0 implies range 10.4.0.0 to 10.5.255.255, which does overlap. Subnet 10.5.32.0 255.255.224.0 implies range 10.5.32.0 to 10.5.63.255, which does overlap. Subnet 10.5.0.0 255.255.128.0 implies range 10.5.0.0 to 10.5.127.255, which does overlap.

14. D. Explanation: The four answers imply the following ranges: 172.16.0.0/21 = 172.16.0.0 to 172.16.7.255; 172.16.6.0/23 = 172.16.6.0 to 172.16.7.255; 172.16.16.0/20 =172.16.16.0 to 172.16.31.255; and 172.16.11.0/25 = 172.16.11.0 to 172.16.11.127. The subnet in the question, 172.16.8.0/22, implies a range of 172.16.8.0 to 172.16.11.255, which includes the range of numbers in subnet 172.16.11.0/25.

15. C. Explanation: The question lists three existing subnets, which together consume part of class C network 192.168.1.0. Just listing the last octet values, these subnets consume 0 to 63, 128 to 131, and 160 to 167. The new subnet, with a /28 mask, needs 16 consecutive numbers, and the subnet numbers will all be a multiple of 16 in the last octet (0, 16, 32, etc.). Looking at the consumed numbers again, the first opening starts at 64, and runs up through 127, so it has more than enough space for 16 addresses. So the numerically lowest subnet number is 192.168.1.64/28, with range 192.168.1.64 to 192.168.1.79.

Chapter 9

1. C and F. Explanation: The data link layer is divided into two sublayers, namely Logical Link Control (LLC) and Media Access Control (MAC). The LLC sublayer forms a frame from the network layer PDU into a format that conforms to the requirements of the network interface and media. A network layer PDU might be for IPv4 or IPv6. The MAC sublayer defines the media access processes performed by the hardware. It manages the frame access to the network media according to the physical signaling requirements (copper cable, fiber optic, wireless, etc.).

2.
A. Addressing	Physical addresses
B. Control	Flow control services
C. Data	Payload
D. Frame Check Sequence	Error detection
E. Frame Start	Beginning of the frame
F. Frame Stop	End of the frame
G. Type	Layer 3 protocol

Explanation: The Frame Start and Frame Stop fields are used to identify the beginning and the end of the frame. The Addressing field contains the physical addresses, also known as MAC addresses. The Type field identifies the Layer 3 protocol. The Control field identifies special flow control services, and the Error Detection field contains the frame check sequence(FCS). The FCS contains a checksum used to ensure that the data in the frame was received the same as how it was sent. The Data field contains the payload.

3. A and C. Explanation: The IANA is responsible for overseeing and managing IP address allocation, domain name management, and protocol identifiers. The EIA is an international standards and trade alliance for electronics organizations, and is best known for its standards related to electrical wiring, connectors, and the 19-inch racks used to mount networking equipment. The ISOC promotes the open development, evolution, and use of the Internet throughout the world.

4. C. Explanation: A point-to-point topology only connects two nodes. A bus is a legacy topology for LANs. Mesh and full mesh topologies have more connectivity than needed (all or most of the branches will be connected to each other). A hub and spoke design will connect the headquarters to all its branches, as desired.

5. B. Explanation: Both CSMA/CD and CSMA/CA are contention-based access control methods. With CSMA/CD, each end device monitors the media for the presence of a data signal. If the media is free, the device transmits data. With CSMA/CA, each end device also examines the media for the presence of a data signal. If the media is free, the device sends a notification across the media of its intent to use it. The device then sends data. With this method, CSMA/CA avoids possible collisions but does not completely stop them.

6. A, B, and C. Explanation: The Layer 2 address refers to the MAC address, a 48-bit address generally represented in hexadecimal format, and burned into the NIC.

7. B. Explanation: The physical layer is responsible for transmitting the actual signals across the physical media as bits. Exchanging frames, controlling media access, and performing error detection are all functions of the data link layer.

8. D. Explanation: DSSS and OFDM are encoding techniques used for wireless transmission. NRZ is the technique used for copper cable. Wavelength multiplexing is used to encode data for fiber-optic cable, resulting in different colors.

9. A. Explanation: The electromagnetic field allows information to pass from one cable pair to another.

10. D. Explanation: Wi-Fi is a trademark of the Wi-Fi Alliance and is used with certified products that belong to WLAN devices based on the IEEE 802.11 standards. It uses a contention system with CSMA/CA as the media access process. Bluetooth is a WPAN standard and is not considered to be Wi-Fi.

Chapter 10

1. B. Explanation: The two Ethernet sublayers are LLC and MAC. LLC manages communications with the upper layers. MAC is the lower sublayer and is responsible for encapsulating the data and getting it onto the network media. In order to get the data onto the media, a specific process must be used. Ethernet uses the CSMA/CD process.

2. B. Explanation: The Ethernet LLC sublayer has the responsibility to handle communication between the upper layers and the lower layers of the protocol stack. The LLC is implemented in software and communicates with the upper layers of the application to transition the packet to the lower layers for delivery.

3. A and C. Explanation: The MAC sublayer is the lower of the two data link sublayers and is closest to the physical layer. The two primary functions of the MAC sublayer are to encapsulate the data from the upper layer protocols and to control access to the media.

4. A. Explanation: On Ethernet networks, the broadcast MAC address is 48 binary 1s displayed as hexadecimal FF-FF-FF-FF-FF-FF.

5. D. Explanation: The multicast MAC address is a special value that begins with 01-00-5E in hexadecimal. It allows a source device to send a packet to a group of devices.

6. C. Explanation: The purpose of an ARP request is to find the MAC address of the destination host on an Ethernet LAN. The ARP process sends a Layer 2 broadcast to all devices on the Ethernet LAN. The frame contains the IP address of the destination and the broadcast MAC address, FFFF.FFFF.FFFF. The host with the IP address that matches the IP address in the ARP request will reply with a unicast frame that includes the MAC address of the host. Thus, the original sending host will obtain the destination IP and MAC address pair to continue the encapsulation process for data transmission.

7. C. Explanation: In order to encapsulate a Layer 3 PDU into a frame, the sending host needs to know the MAC address of the destination host. The sending host first checks the ARP table. If a match is found in the table, the host uses the MAC address as the destination MAC in the frame. Otherwise, it will initiate an ARP request to obtain the destination MAC.

8. B. Explanation: An ARP spoofing attack is based on an ARP reply (a unicast message). The intruder sends many ARP replies with its own MAC address and an IP address that is within the same network. The unsuspecting node receives this fake ARP reply and adds this entry to its ARP cache. Traffic from that unsuspecting node will be sent to the MAC address of the intruder. Authorized

MAC addresses can be configured on some network devices to restrict network access to only those devices listed.

9. B and C. Explanation: ARP requests are sent as broadcasts:
(1) All nodes will receive them, and they will be processed by software, interrupting the CPU.
(2) The switch forwards (floods) Layer 2 broadcasts to all ports.
A switch does not change its MAC table based on ARP request or reply messages. The switch populates the MAC table using the source MAC address of all frames. The ARP payload is very small and does not overload the switch.

10. D. Explanation: A switch virtual interface (SVI) is a logical interface associated with a specific VLAN. This logical interface can have an IP address assigned to it to allow for routing packets between VLANs or for remote management purposes. Routed ports are not associated with any specific VLANs and are configured on a single physical interface similar to an interface on a router. EtherChannel is used to combine multiple physical links into a single logical link in order to aggregate the bandwidth of the links.

Chapter 11

1. D. Explanation: A best practice and recommended approach for an IP addressing scheme is to assign static IP addresses to servers in a predetermined separate block, usually in the lower end or upper end of the host address range. With such an arrangement, the server traffic is easy to identify and security measures can be easily managed. For employee workstations, however, dynamic IP address assignment is recommended for the easy management of IP addresses.

2. C. Explanation: With a separate DSL connection to another ISP, the company will have a redundancy solution for the Internet connection, in case the leased line connection fails. The other options provide other aspects of redundancy, but not the Internet connection. The options of adding a second NIC and adding multiple connections between the switches and the edge router will provide redundancy in case one NIC fails or one connection between the switches and the edge router fails. The option of adding another web server provides redundancy if the main web server fails.

3. A and E. Explanation: Maintenance threats are types of physical threats to the network. They include routine maintenance tasks that, if ignored, could lead to disruptions in service. Examples include poor documentation, lack of spare parts, and using improper procedures when working with hardware. Unconditioned power is an example of an electrical threat, temperature extremes are an example of an environmental threat, and physical damage is an example of a hardware threat.

4. D. Explanation: A vulnerability is a weakness in the security of the network. Vulnerabilities include technology weaknesses such as the inherent insecurity of the Telnet protocol, configuration weaknesses such as a router configured with a weak password, and policy weaknesses such as a security policy that doesn't define a password policy. Threats involve people with the knowledge and motivation to take advantage of vulnerabilities in the network, such as a disgruntled employee with access to the network.

5. B. Explanation: A worm is a computer program that is self-replicated with the intention of attacking a system and trying to exploit a specific vulnerability in the target. Both viruses and Trojan horses rely on a delivery mechanism to carry them from one host to another. Social engineering is not a type of malicious code attack.

6. C. Explanation: Authorization is what assigns levels of right to users of a network resource.

7. C. Explanation: The **login local** command designates that the local username database is used to authenticate interfaces such as console or vty.

8. C. Explanation: The **ping 127.0.0.1** command is used to verify the proper operation of the TCP/IP protocol stack from the network layer to the physical layer and back. The operation of this command does not actually put a signal on the network media.

9. B. Explanation: The result shows a number of things. There are 11 hops between the workstation and the website (www.cisco. com). The first entry is the immediate router (default gateway) and the last entry is the website itself (see the IP address). Thus, the total number of hops is 11. The IP address of the next hop (router) is 192.168.10.254. The second router is not responding to the **ping** command, but is operational. A ping to the website takes 63 milliseconds. Tracert sends three pings, with the time 65/58/66.

10. A. Explanation: ! mark is the icon used to show transfer is in progress.

Numbers

802.11 Wireless   A series of specifications developed by IEEE for implementing wireless local area network (WLAN) computer communication.

A

Access attacks   A phrase used to describe an attack on a computer network that is designed to allow unauthorized access to computer resources.

ACK   A 1-bit flag in the TCP header that indicates the acknowledgement field is valid.

acknowledgement   A notification sent from one network device to another to confirm that some event (for example, receipt of a message) has occurred.

acknowledgement number   A 32-bit field in the TCP segment header that specifies the sequence number of the next byte this host expects to receive as a part of the TCP session. It is used to recognize lost packets and flow control.

Address Resolution Protocol (ARP)   The method for finding a host's hardware address from its IPv4 network layer address.

administrative distance   A rating of the trustworthiness of a routing information source. In Cisco routers, administrative distance is expressed as a numerical value between 0 and 255. The higher the value, the lower the trustworthiness rating.

American National Standards Institute (ANSI)   A voluntary organization comprised of corporate, government, and other members that coordinates standards-related activities, approves U.S. national standards, and develops positions for the United States in international standards.

American Standard Code for Information Interchange (ASCII)   A 8-bit code for character representation (7 bits plus parity).

amplitude modulation (AM)   Modulation technique whereby information is conveyed through the amplitude of the carrier signal. Compare with FM and PAM.

AND   One of three basic binary logic operations. ANDing yields the following results: 1 AND 1 = 1, 1 AND 0 = 0, 0 AND 1 = 0, 1 AND 0 = 0.

appliance-based firewalls   Hardware device designed to slow down or stop cyber-terrorists, hackers, DoS attackers, and malicious viruses from infiltrating a network or individual computer.

Application layer   Layer 7 of the OSI reference model. This layer provides services to application processes (such as electronic mail, file transfer, and terminal emulation) that are outside of the OSI model. The application layer identifies and establishes the availability of required communications resources.

argument   Additional data that is provided with a command to provide information used by the execution of the command. IOS command arguments are entered at the command-line interface (CLI) after the command.

ARP cache   A logical storage in a host's RAM to store ARP entries. *See also* ARP table.

ARP poisoning   A technique used to attack an Ethernet network by sending fake ARP messages to an Ethernet LAN. These frames contain false MAC addresses that "confuse" network devices, such as switches. As a result, frames intended for one node can be mistakenly sent to another node. *See also* ARP spoofing.

ARP spoofing   A technique used to attack an Ethernet network by sending fake ARP messages to an Ethernet LAN. These frames contain false MAC addresses that "confuse" network devices, such as switches. As a result, frames intended for one node can be mistakenly sent to another node. *See also* ARP poisoning.

ARP table   A logical storage in a host's RAM to store ARP entries. *See also* ARP cache.

asynchronous   Communication that does not use a common clock between the sender and receiver. To maintain timing, additional information is sent to synchronize the receive circuit to the incoming data. For Ethernet at 10 Mbps, the Ethernet devices do not send electrical signals for synchronization.

automatic medium-dependent interface crossover (AMDIX)   A version of the medium dependent interface (MDI) enabling a connection between corresponding devices. An MDI port or uplink port is a port on a switch, router, or network hub connecting to another switch or hub using a straight-through cable rather than an Ethernet crossover cable.

auxiliary (AUX) port   The purpose of the auxiliary port is for connecting to an external modem. Once configured, this modem can be used as a backup demand-dial connection to another location, or as a way to dial in to the router for troubleshooting purposes should regular connectivity fail.

B

backbone cabling   Cabling that provides interconnections between wiring closets, between wiring closets and the POP, and between buildings that are part of the same LAN. Backbone cabling is also known as vertical cabling.

banner motd   To configure the message-of-the-day (MOTD) banner that displays when the user logs in to a Cisco device, use the banner motd command. To revert to the default, use the no form of this command.

banners   Banners are informational messages that can be displayed to users. *See* banner motd for an example.

binary notation   A number system having a base of two, numbers being expressed by sequences of the digits 0 and 1: used in computing, as 0 and 1 can be represented electrically as *off* and *on*.

bits   Binary digits used in the binary numbering system. A bit can be 0 or 1.

branch routers   Branch routers come in two categories: general purpose and integrated services. General purpose routers typically focus on basic wide area network (WAN) routing, supporting a limited number of routing protocols and a variety of WAN interfaces. General purpose routers can be a good choice when one is interested in simple routing. A typical use case arises when customers need Layer 3 visibility with a full Internet routing table for a branch network with multiple WAN exit points, or when the service provider requires the customer to peer with their network. An integrated services router (ISR) allows the customer to take advantage of advanced technologies, enabling them to more effectively meet their strategic business challenges. It provides the option of telephony (VoIP) and streaming video, as well as WAN routing.

Bring Your Own Device (BOYD)   The policy of permitting employees or students to bring personally owned mobile devices (laptops, tablets, and smartphones) to their workplace or school, and use those devices to access privileged company/school information and applications.

broadcast   Data packet that will be sent to all nodes on a network. Broadcasts are identified by a broadcast address. Compare with multicast and unicast.

broadcast address   A logical address at which all devices connected to a multiple-access communications network are enabled to receive datagrams. A message sent to a broadcast address is typically received by all network-attached hosts, rather than by a specific host.

broadcast MAC address   Special address reserved for sending a message to all stations. Generally, a broadcast address is a MAC destination address of all ones.

broadcast transmission   *See* broadcast, unicast, and multicast.

bus   Common physical signal path composed of wires or other media across which signals can be sent from one part of a computer to another. Bus is also known as highway.

C

cable   A wire or bundle of wires that conducts electricity.

carrier sense multiple access with collision avoidance (CSMA/CA)   A mechanism used to regulate the transmission of data onto a network medium. CSMA/CA is similar to CSMA/CD except the devices first request the right to send, which hopefully avoids collisions. CSMA/CA is used in 802.11 WLANs.

carrier sense multiple access with collision detection (CSMA/CD)   The MAC algorithm used by Ethernet devices in a shared media. The protocol requires a node wishing to transmit to listen for a carrier signal before trying to send. If a carrier is sensed, the node waits for the transmission in progress to finish before initiating its own transmission. If a collision occurs and is detected, the sending node uses the backoff algorithm before retransmitting.

cellular   A radio network distributed over land areas called cells, each served by at least one fixed-location transceiver, known as a cell site or base station. In a cellular network, each cell uses a different set of frequencies from neighboring cells to avoid interference and provide guaranteed bandwidth within each cell.

central equipment room   Room where all networking equipment is located, normally in 19" equipment racks.

Cisco IOS (Internetwork Operating System)   Software used on most Cisco Systems routers and current Cisco network switches. (Earlier switches ran CatOS.) IOS is a package of routing, switching, internetworking and telecommunications functions integrated into a multitasking operating system.

class A   Network address class that contains all addresses in which the most significant bit is zero. The network number for this class is given by the next 7 bits, therefore accommodating 128 networks in total, including the zero network, and including the existing IP networks already allocated.

class B   Network address class in which all addresses have the two most-significant bits set to 1 and 0. For these networks, the network address is given by the next 14 bits of the address, thus leaving 16 bits for numbering host on the network for a total of 65,536 addresses per network.

class C   Network address class in which the 3 high-order bits are set to 1, 1, and 0, and designating the next 21 bits to number the networks, leaving each network with 256 local addresses.

classless addressing   An IPv4 addressing scheme that uses a subnet mask that does not follow classful addressing limitations. It provides increased flexibility when dividing ranges of IP addresses into separate networks. Classless addressing is considered the best in current network implementations.

CLI prompt   Cisco IOS have two basic command-line interface prompts: the user mode prompt (>) and the privileged mode prompt (#).

cloud computing   Computing provided as a service.

coaxial cable   Cable consisting of a hollow outer cylindrical conductor that surrounds a single inner wire conductor. The cable has three different layers of material surrounding the inner conducting material: the outer conductor, the insulator, and the protective outer jacket.

collaboration tools   Software that helps people collaborate. Anything that helps to solve a predefined task together as a group is an effective collaboration tool.

command   The statements you use to configure Cisco devices.

command reference   Document that contains Cisco IOS commands that are supported in many different software releases and on many different platforms.

connectionless   Term used to describe data transfer without the existence of a virtual circuit. Compare with connection-oriented.

connection-oriented   Term used to describe data transfer that requires the establishment of a virtual circuit.

console password   CLI command that allows you to password-protect the console port.

console port   DTE through which commands are entered into a host. It is an out-of-band management port. *See also* out-of-band access.

contention-based access   Access method in which network devices compete for permission to access the physical medium. Contrast with circuit switching and token passing.

context-sensitive help   The use of the question mark (?) while configuring Cisco Devices to receive help about the command syntax to be used.

controlled access   Selective restriction of access to a place or a resource.

converged network   The efficient coexistence of telephone, video, and data communications within a single network.

copper cable   The use of copper cable network connectivity versus wireless or fiber connectivity.

crosstalk   Interfering energy transferred from one circuit to another.

CSMA/Collision Avoidance   *See* carrier sense multiple access with collision avoidance (CSMA/CA).

CSMA/Collision Detection   *See* carrier sense multiple access with collision detection (CSMA/CD).

cut-through switching   Switches operating in cut-through switching mode start forwarding the frame as soon as the switch has read the destination details in the packet header. A switch in cut-through mode forwards the data before it has completed receiving the entire frame.

D

data   Application layer protocol data unit.

data encapsulation   The process by which a device adds networking headers and trailers to data from an application for the eventual transmission of the data onto a transmission medium.

data field   A specific place to store data, such as a column in a database or field in a data entry form.

data link address   The physical address that is burned into the network interface card (MAC address).

Data link layer   Layer 2 of the OSI reference model. This layer provides reliable transit of data across a physical link. The data link layer is concerned with physical addressing, network topology, line discipline, error notification, ordered delivery of frames, and flow.

datagrams   A basic transfer unit associated with a packet-switched network in which the delivery, arrival time, and order of arrival are not guaranteed by the network service.

dedicated leased line   Communications line that is indefinitely reserved for transmissions. A dedicated leased line is always activate, rather than switched as transmission is required.

de-encapsulation   A process by which an end device, after it receives data over some transmission medium, examines the headers and trailers at each successive higher layer, eventually handing the data to the correct application.

default gateway   A device on a network that serves as an access point to other networks. A default gateway is used by a host to forward IP packets that have destination addresses outside the local subnet. A router interface typically is used as the default gateway. When the computer needs to send a packet to another subnet, it sends the packet to its default gateway. Also known as default router.

denial of service (DoS)   A type of attack whose goal is to cause problems by preventing legitimate users from being able to access services, thereby preventing the normal operation of computers and networks.

destination IP address   The Layer 3 address to which the data is going.

destination IP address field   The field that houses the Layer 3 IP address to which the data is going.

destination MAC address field   The field that houses the Layer 2 MAC address to which the data is going.

DHCP (Dynamic Host Configuration Protocol)   A protocol used to dynamically assign IP configurations to hosts. The services defined by the protocol are used to request and assign an IP address, default gateway, and DNS server address to a network host.

dial-up   A form of Internet access that uses the facilities of the public switched telephone network (PSTN) to establish a dialed connection to an Internet service provider(ISP) via telephone lines. The user's computer or router uses an attached modem to encode and decode Internet Protocol packets and control information into and from analogue audio frequency signals, respectively.

differentiated services (DS field)   Differentiated services or DiffServ is a computer networking architecture that specifies a simple, scalable and coarse-grained mechanism for classifying and managing network traffic and providing quality of service (QoS) on modern IP networks. DiffServ can, for example, be used to provide low-latency to critical network traffic such as voice or streaming media while providing simple best-effort service to non-critical services such as web traffic or file transfers.

directly connected routes   A router can route packets to networks that are directly connected to it without running a routing protocol. Directly connected routes are loaded into the routing table by default.

disruption of service   Denial or disruption of service attacks affect the availability of data, services, and network elements. For the most part, service disruptions caused by computer intruders have been brought about by accidental actions. Unintentional disruptions caused by computer intruders are much more common than malicious disruptions.

DNS (Domain Name System)   An application layer protocol used throughout the Internet for translating host names into their associated IP addresses.

DNS server   An Internet-wide system by which a hierarchical set of DNS servers collectively hold all the name-IP address mappings, with DNS servers referring users to the correct DNS server to successfully resolve a DNS name.

DSL (digital subscriber line)   Public network technology that delivers high bandwidth over conventional telco local-loop copper wiring at limited distances. Typically used as an Internet access technology, connecting a user to an ISP.

Dual in-line memory module (DIMM)   A DIMM is a double SIMM (single in-line memory module). Like a SIMM, it's a module containing one or several random access memory (RAM) chips on a small circuit board with pins that connect it to the computer motherboard. A SIMM typically has a 32 data bit (36 bits counting parity bits) path to the computer that requires a 72-pin connector.

dual stack   Dual stack means that devices are able to run IPv4 and IPv6 in parallel. It allows hosts to simultaneously reach IPv4 and IPv6 content, so it offers a very flexible coexistence strategy.

duplex settings   Two types of settings used for communications on networks: half duplex and full duplex. A half duplex setting allows for communication in both directions, but only one direction at a time. A walkie-talkie is an example of a half duplex system. Full duplex would allow communication in both directions. The landline telephone is a good example of full duplex.

Dynamic Host Configuration Protocol for IPv6 (DHCPv6)   A protocol used to dynamically assign IPv6 configurations to hosts. The services defined by the protocol are used to request and assign an IP address, default gateway, and DNS server address to a network host.

dynamic random-access memory (DRAM)   A type of semiconductor memory in which the information is stored in capacitors on a Metal Oxide Semiconductor (MOS) integrated circuit. Typically each bit is stored as an amount of electrical charge in a storage cell consisting of a capacitor and a transistor. Due to leakage the capacitor discharges gradually and the memory cell loses the information. Therefore, to preserve the information, the memory has to be refreshed periodically.

dynamic window sizes   A new technique for TCP implementations to dynamically and automatically determine the best window size for optimum network performance. This technique results in greatly improved performance, a decrease in packet loss under bottleneck conditions, and greater control of buffer utilization by the end hosts.

E

EHWIC (Cisco Enhanced High Speed WAN Interface Card) slots   The EHWIC slot replaces the high-speed WAN interface card (HWIC) slot and can natively support HWICs, WAN interface cards (WICs), voice interface cards (VICs), and voice/WAN interface cards (VWICs). Two integrated EHWIC slots are available on the Cisco 1941 for flexible configurations for support of two modules: One double-wide HWIC-D or single-wide EHWIC/HWIC module and a second single-wide E-HIC/HWIC module are supported. Each HWIC Slot offers high data throughput capability.

electromagnetic interference (EMI)
Interference by magnetic signals caused by the flow of electricity. EMI can cause reduced data integrity and increased error rates on transmission channels. The physics of this process are that electrical current creates magnetic fields, which in turn cause other electrical currents in nearby wires. The induced electrical currents can interfere with proper operation of the other wire.

enable password   Unencrypted password used to allow access to privileged EXEC mode from IOS user EXEC mode.

Enable secret   Encrypted password used to limit access to privileged EXEC mode from IOS user EXEC mode.

end device   A device such as a desktop or mobile device that is used by an end user.

enterprise networks   An enterprise network is an enterprise's communications backbone that helps connect computers and related devices across departments and workgroup networks, facilitating insight and data accessibility. An enterprise network reduces communication protocols, facilitating system and device interoperability, as well as improved internal and external enterprise data management.

entrance facilities   Entrance facility refers to the entrance to a building for both public and private network service cables (including antenna transmission lines, where applicable), including the entrance point at the building wall or floor, and continuing to the entrance room or entrance space.

Ethernet   Baseband LAN specification invented by Xerox Corporation and developed jointly by Xerox, Intel, and Digital Equipment Corporation. Ethernet networks use CSMA/CD and run over a variety of cable types at 10 Mbps. Ethernet is similar to the IEEE 802.3 series.

Ethernet crossover   An Ethernet crossover cable is a type of Ethernet cable used to connect computing devices together directly. Normal *straight through* or *patch* cables were used to connect from a host network interface controller (a computer or similar device) to a network switch or hub. A cable with connections that "cross over" was used to connect two devices of the same type: two hosts or two switches to each other. Owing to the inclusion of Auto-MDIX capability, modern implementations of the Ethernet over twisted pair standards usually no longer require the use of crossover cables.

Ethernet LAN interfaces   Ethernet Networking Interface, or ENI, allows any computer on Ethernet network to access controllers allowing users to send production data, alarm messages, or status information to computers, cellular phones, or pagers capable of receiving email. The ENI module allows companies to leverage existing cable, hubs, switches, and routers already installed in facilities.

Ethernet LLC sublayer   In the seven-layer OSI model of computer networking, the logical link control (LLC) data communication protocol layer is the upper sublayer of the data link layer, which is itself layer 2. The LLC sublayer provides multiplexing mechanisms that make it possible for several network protocols (IP, IPX, Decnet and Appletalk) to coexist within a multipoint network and to be transported over the same network medium. It can also provide flow control and automatic repeat request (ARQ) error management mechanisms. The LLC sublayer acts as an interface between the media access control (MAC) sublayer and the network layer.

Ethernet Straight-through   A type of twisted pair copper wire cable for local area network (LAN) use for which the RJ-45 connectors at each end have the same pinout (i.e., arrangement of conductors). It is identical to crossover cable, except that in the latter the wires on the cable are crossed over so that the receive signal pins on the connector on one end are connected to the transmit signal pins on the connector on the other end. Straight-through cable is also commonly referred to as patch cable. However, this might be confusing in some situations because patch cable also has a broader definition that emphasizes the fact that there is a connector on each end rather than the equality (or lack thereof) of the pinouts. Straight-through cable is used to connect computers and other end-user devices (e.g., printers) to networking devices such as hubs and switches. It can also be used to directly connect like devices (e.g., two hubs or two switches) if the cable is plugged into an uplink port on one (but not both) of the devices. Crossover cable is used to connect two like devices without the use of an uplink port.

Exec Timeout   To configure the inactive session timeout on the console port or the virtual terminal, use the **exec-timeout** command. To revert to the default, use the **no** form of this command.

expandability   To increase the size, volume, quantity, or scope of.

expectational acknowledgement   Acknowledgement used by TCP where the ACK number sent back to the source to indicate the next byte that the receiver expects to receive.

experimental addresses   One major block of addresses reserved for special purposes is the IPv4 experimental address range 240.0.0.0 to 255.255.255.254. Currently, they cannot be used in IPv4 networks. However, these addresses could be used for research or experimentation.

extended star   A network topology characterized by a central location connected to multiple hubs. In an extended star, these interconnected hubs may be connected to more hubs. It is essentially a hierarchical topology but typically is drawn with the central site in the center, with the rest of the topology radiating outward in all directions. This is sometimes called a *hierarchical star*.

extranet   Part of a company's intranet that is extended to users outside the company (that is, normally over the Internet).

F

fast-forward switching   Fast-forward switching offers the lowest level of latency by immediately forwarding a packet after receiving the destination address. Because fast-forward switching does not check for errors, there may be times when frames are relayed with errors. Although this occurs infrequently and the destination network adapter discards the fault frame upon receipt. In networks with high collision rates, this can negatively affect available bandwidth.

fault tolerance   The design on networks that can continue to operate without interruption in the case of hardware, software, or communications failures.

fiber-optic cable   Physical medium that uses glass or plastic threads to transmit data. A fiber-optic cable consists of a bundle of these threads, each of which is capable of transmitting data into light waves.

FIN   A 1-bit field in the TCP header that is used by a device that wants to terminate its session with the other device. This is done by inserting the FIN flag in the flag field found in the TCP segment.

fixed configuration switches   A switch that is the opposite of a modular switch; you cannot add another module to a fixed configuration switch.

flash   A removable component that has memory space for storage. Used on the router or switch for storing the compressed operating system image.

flat network design   A flat network is a network in which all workstations are directly connected to each other, except for the presence of switches and can communicate without the need for intermediate devices such as routers. A flat network is one without subnets, as a result, its topology is not divided into layers or modules. Every station on a flat network receives a copy of every message sent. Security is poor and it is not possible to establish alternative paths to destinations.

flow control   The management of data flow between devices in a network. It is used to avoid too much data arriving before a device can handle it, causing data overflow.

Flow label field   Part of the IPv6 header, originally created for giving real-time applications special service. The flow label when set to a nonzero value now serves as a hint to routers and switches with multiple outbound paths that these packets should stay on the same path so that they will not be reordered. It has further been suggested that the flow label field be used to help detect spoofed packets

fragmentation   The dividing of IP datagrams to meet the MTU requirements of a Layer 2 and Layer 3 protocol.

fragment-free switching   One of three internal processing options on some Cisco LAN switches in which the first bits of the frame can be forwarded before the entire frame is received, but not until the first 64 bytes of the frame are received, in which case, in a well-designed LAN, collision fragments should not occur as a result of this forwarding logic.

frame The Layer 2 PDU that has been encoded by a data link layer protocol for digital transmission. Some different kinds of frames are Ethernet frames and PPP frames.

Frame Check Sequence A field in many data link trailers used as part of the error detection process.

frame encoding technique Refers to the many encoding techniques available to compress frames. MPEG coding is an example.

frequency modulation (FM) the encoding of information in a carrier wave by varying the instantaneous frequency of the wave. (Compare with amplitude modulation, in which the amplitude of the carrier wave varies, while the frequency remains constant.)

FTP (File Transfer Protocol) A standard network protocol used to transfer files from one host to another host over a TCP-based network, such as the Internet.

FTTH (fiber-to-the-home) and Access Networks Fiber reaches the boundary of the living space, such as a box on the outside wall of a home. Passive optical networks and point-to-point Ethernet are architectures that deliver triple-play services over FTTH networks directly from an operator's central office.

full duplex Communication that allows receipt and transmission simultaneously. A station can transmit and receive at the same time. There are no collisions with full-duplex Ethernet transmission.

G

GET message Programming command designed to retrieve information.

Gigabit Ethernet The common name for all the IEEE standards that send data at 1 gigabit per second.

Global configuration mode To configure a Cisco network device you must enter the Global Configuration operating mode. After passing thru the User EXEC and Privilege EXEC modes you enter the Global Configuration mode by entering the **configure** command.

global routing prefix An IPv6 prefix that defines an IPv6 address block made up of global unicast addresses, assigned to one organization, so that the organization has a block of globally unique IPv6 addresses to use in its network.

H

half-duplex Generically, any communication in which only one device at a time can send data. In Ethernet LANs, the normal result of the CSMA/CD algorithm that enforces the rule that only one device should send at any point in time.

header In computer networking, a set of bytes placed in front of some other data, encapsulating that data, as defined by a particular protocol.

Hexadecimal Numbering (Base 16) A number representation using the digits 0 through 9, with their usual meaning, plus the letters A through F to represent hexadecimal digits with values of 10 to 15. The right-most digit counts ones, the next counts multiples of 16, then $16^2=256$.

Hop limit field *See* Time-to-Live (TTL) field.

horizontal cabling   IW (inside wiring) or Plenum Cabling and connects telecommunications rooms to individual outlets or work areas on the floor, usually through the wireways, conduits or ceiling spaces of each floor.

host address   The IP address assigned to a computer.

host device   Any device on a network that has an IP address assigned to it.

host name   The alphanumeric name of an IP host.

HTTP (Hypertext Transfer Protocol)   The protocol used by web browsers and web servers to transfer files, such as text and graphic files.

HTTP Secure (HTTPS) protocol   A communications protocol for secure communication over a computer network, with especially wide deployment on the Internet. Technically, it is not a protocol in and of itself; rather, it is the result of simply layering the Hypertext Transfer Protocol (HTTP) on top of the SSL/TLS protocol, thus adding the security capabilities of SSL/TLS to standard HTTP communications.

hub and spoke   The hub-and-spoke distribution paradigm (or model or network) is a system of connections arranged like a chariot wheel, in which all traffic moves along spokes connected to the hub at the center. The model is commonly used in industry, in particular in transport, telecommunications, and freight, as well as in distributed computing.

I

identity theft   A form of stealing someone's identity in which someone pretends to be someone else by assuming that person's identity, typically in order to access resources or obtain credit and other benefits in that person's name. The victim of identity theft (here meaning the person whose identity has been assumed by the identity thief) can suffer adverse consequences if they are held accountable for the perpetrator's actions. Identity theft occurs when someone uses another's personally identifying information, such as their name, identifying number, or credit card number, without their permission, to commit fraud or other crimes.

IEEE 802.11   A set of medium access control (MAC) and physical layer (PHY) specifications for implementing wireless local area network (WLAN) computer communication in the 2.4, 3.6, 5 and 60 GHz frequency bands. They are created and maintained by the IEEE LAN/MAN Standards Committee (IEEE 802). The base version of the standard was released in 1997 and has had subsequent amendments. The standard and amendments provide the basis for wireless network products using the Wi-Fi brand. Although each amendment is officially revoked when it is incorporated in the latest version of the standard, the corporate world tends to market to the revisions because they concisely denote capabilities of their products. As a result, in the market place, each revision tends to become its own standard.

IEEE 802.15   A working group of the Institute of Electrical and Electronics Engineers (IEEE). IEEE 802 standards committee which specifies Wireless Personal Area Network (WPAN) standards. It includes seven task groups.

IEEE 802.16   A series of Wireless Broadband standards written by the Institute of Electrical and Electronics Engineers (IEEE). The IEEE Standards Board established a working group in 1999 to develop standards for broadband for Wireless Metropolitan Area Networks. The Workgroup is a unit of the IEEE 802 local area network and metropolitan area network standards committee.

IMAP, SMTP, POP (email) email protocols
IMAP (Internet Message Access Protocol) is a standard protocol for accessing email from your local server. IMAP is a client/server protocol in which e-mail is received and held for you by your Internet server. The SMTP (Simple Mail Transfer Protocol) protocol is used by the Mail Transfer Agent (MTA) to deliver your email to the recipient's mail server. The SMTP protocol can only be used to send emails, not to receive them. The POP (Post Office Protocol) protocol provides a simple, standardized way for users to access mailboxes and download messages to their computers.

inband router interfaces   The router interface you Telnet through. A way to connect to a Cisco router is in-band, through the program Telnet. Telnet is a terminal emulation program that acts as though it's a dumb terminal. You can use Telnet to connect to any active interface on a router, such as an Ethernet or serial port.

information theft   The process of obtaining data from a network you are not authorized to have access to.

infrastructure   In information technology and on the Internet, infrastructure is the physical hardware used to interconnect computers and users. Infrastructure includes the transmission media, including telephone lines, cable television lines, and satellites and antennas, and also the routers, aggregators, repeaters, and other devices that control transmission paths. Infrastructure also includes the software used to send, receive, and manage the signals that are transmitted.

initial sequence number (ISN)   Refers to the unique 32-bit sequence number assigned to each new connection on a Transmission Control Protocol (TCP)-based data communication. It helps with the allocation of a sequence number that does not conflict with other data bytes transmitted over a TCP connection. An ISN is unique to each connection and separated by each device.

inoculation   The action of inoculating or vaccinating your network against network threats.

instant messaging (IM)   Real-time communication between two or more people through text. The text is conveyed through computers connected over a network such as the Internet. Files can also be transferred through the IM program to share files. An example of an IM program is Microsoft Messenger.

Institute of Electrical and Electronics Engineers (IEEE)   An international, nonprofit organization for the advancement of technology related to electricity. IEEE maintains the standards defining many LAN protocols.

integrated firewalls   Firewalls that integrate the world's most proven firewall with a robust suite of highly integrated, security services for networks of all sizes: small and midsize business with one or a few locations, large enterprises, service providers, and mission-critical data centers.

intermediary devices   For communication to run smoothly across the network there are devices that place intermediary roles in networking. These intermediary devices provide connectivity and work behind the scenes to ensure that data flows across the network. These devices connect the individual hosts (end devices) to the network and can connect multiple individual networks to form an internetwork. Examples of intermediary devices are routers, switches, hubs, wireless access point, servers, modems, and security devices.

International Organization for Standardization (ISO)   An international standards body that defines many networking standards. Also, the standards body that created the OSI model.

International Telecommunication Union (ITU)   Organization responsible for issues that concern information and communication technologies. The ITU coordinates the shared global use of the radio spectrum, promotes international cooperation in assigning satellite orbits, works to improve telecommunication infrastructure in the developing world, and assists in the development and coordination of worldwide technical standards.

Internet   The network that combines enterprise networks, individual users, and ISPs into a single global IP network.

Internet Architecture Board (IAB)   The committee charged with oversight of the technical and engineering development of the Internet by the Internet Society (ISOC).

Internet Assigned Numbers Authority (IANA)   An organization that assigns the numbers important to the proper operation of the TCP/IP protocol and the Internet.

Internet Corporation for Assigned Names and Numbers (ICANN)   A nonprofit private organization headquartered in the Playa Vista section of Los Angeles, CA that was created on September 18, 1998, and incorporated on September 30, 1998 to oversee a number of Internet-related tasks previously performed directly on behalf of the U.S. government by other organizations, notably the IANA, which ICANN now operates. Major responsibility is coordination of the IP address spaces (IPv4 and IPv6) and assignment of address blocks to regional Internet registries, for maintaining registries of Internet protocol identifiers, and for the management of the top-level domain name space (DNS root zone), which includes the operation of root name servers.

Internet Engineering Task Force (IETF)   The standards body responsible for the development and approval of TCP/IP standards.

IP (Internet Protocol)   Network layer protocol in the TCP/IP stack offering a connectionless internetwork service. IP provides features for addressing, type-of-service specification, fragmentation and reassembly, and security. Documented in RFC 791.

Internet Protocol version 4 (IPv4)   In IP Version 4 (IPv4), a 32-bit address assigned to hosts using TCP/IP. Each address consists of a network number, an optional subnetwork number, and a host number. The network and subnetwork numbers together are used for routing, and the host number is used to address an individual host within the network or subnetwork.

Internet Protocol version 6 (IPv6)   In IP Version 6 (IPv6), a 128-bit address assigned to hosts using TCP/IP. Addresses use different formats, commonly using a routing prefix, subnet, and interface ID, corresponding to the IPv4 network, subnet, and host parts of an address.

Internet Research Task Force (IRTF)   Focuses on longer term research issues related to the Internet whereas the parallel organization, the IETF, focuses on the shorter term issues of engineering and standards making. The IRTF promotes research of importance to the evolution of the Internet by creating focused, long-term research groups working on topics related to Internet protocols, applications, architecture, and technology.

Internet Society (ISOC)   An international, non-profit organization founded in 1992 to provide leadership in Internet-related standards, education, and policy. It states that its mission is "to assure the open development, evolution and use of the Internet for the benefit of all people throughout the world." The Internet Society has offices near Washington, DC and in Geneva, Switzerland. It has a membership base comprising more than 130 organizational and more than 55,000 individual members. Members also form "chapters" based on either common geographical location or special interests. There are currently more than 90 chapters around the world.

Internetwork Operating System (IOS)   Cisco Internetwork Operating System software that provides the majority of a router's or switch's features, with the hardware providing the remaining features.

intranet   A corporate system such as a website that is explicitly used by internal employees. Can be accessed internally or remotely.

IPv4 address   A 32-bit number, written in dotted decimal notation, used by the IP to uniquely identify an interface connected to an IP network. It is also used as a destination address in an IP header to allow routing and as a source address to allow a computer to receive a packet and to know which IP address to send a response.

IP header   The header defined by the IP. Used to create IP packets by encapsulating data supplied by a higher-layer protocol (such as TCP) behind an IP header.

IP Telephony   IP telephony (Internet Protocol telephony) is a general term for the technologies that use the Internet Protocol's packet-switched connections to exchange voice, fax, and other forms of information that have traditionally been carried over the dedicated circuit-switched connections of the public switched telephone network (PSTN).

ipconfig   A console application in Microsoft Windows that displays all current TCP/IP network configuration values and can modify

Dynamic Host Configuration Protocol (DHCP) and Domain Name System (DNS) settings. In most cases, the **ipconfig** command is used with the command-line switch **/all**. This results in more detailed information than **ipconfig** alone.

IPv6 global unicast addresses   The global unicast address is globally unique in the Internet.

IPv6 link-local address   A link-local address is an IP address that is intended only for communications within the segment of a local network (a link) or a point-to-point connection that a host is connected to. Routers do not forward packets with link-local addresses.

L

LAN interface   A device designed to allow connectivity to a local area network.

Layer 2 LAN switch   Layer 2 switching uses the media access control address (MAC address) from the host's network interface cards (NICs) to decide where to forward frames. Layer 2 switching is hardware based, which means switches use application-specific integrated circuit (ASICs) to build and maintain filter tables (also known as MAC address tables or CAM tables). One way to think of a Layer 2 switch is as a multiport bridge.

Layer 3 switching   Layer 3 switching is all hardware-based packet forwarding, and all packet forwarding is handled by hardware ASICs. Layer 3 switches really are no different functionally than a traditional router and perform the same functions, making routing decisions based on Layer 3 addresses (IP addresses, or logical addresses).

length field   This 16-bit field, part of the IP header, defines the entire packet (fragment) size, including header and data, in bytes. The minimum-length packet is 20 bytes (20-byte header + 0 bytes data) and the maximum is 65,535 bytes—the maximum value of a 16-bit word. The largest datagram that any host is required to be able to reassemble is 576 bytes, but most modern hosts handle much larger packets. Sometimes subnetworks impose further restrictions on the packet size, in which case datagrams must be fragmented. Fragmentation is handled in either the host or router in IPv4.

link-local address   An IPv4 address in the range of 169.254.1.0 to 169.254.254.255. Communication using these addresses is used with a TTL of 1 and limited to the local network.

local-area network (LAN)   A network created for devices located in a limited geographic area, through which the company owning the LAN has the right to run cables.

local default route   A local default route of a computer that is participating in computer networking is the packet-forwarding rule (route) taking effect when no other route can be determined for a given IP destination address. All packets for destinations not established in the routing table are sent via the default route. This route generally points to another router, which treats the packet the same way: If a route matches, the packet is forwarded accordingly; otherwise the packet is forwarded to the default route of that router. The process repeats until a packet is delivered to the destination, or not finding the route (or default route) and packet is dropped by the router.

local host   Local host means this computer. It is a hostname that the computer's software and users may employ to access the computer's own network services via its loopback network interface. On most computer systems, local host

resolves to the address 127.0.0.1, which is the most-commonly used IPv4 loopback address, and to the IPv6 loopback address ::1. Using the loopback interface bypasses local network interface hardware. The local loopback mechanism is useful for programmers to test software during development independent of any networking configurations. If a computer has been configured to provide a website, directing its web browser to http://localhost may display its home page.

Logical Link Control (LLC)   The IEEE 802.2 standard that defines the upper sublayer of the Ethernet Layer 2 specifications (and other LAN standards).

logical ring topology   The Token Ring is the most common example of a network with different logical and physical topologies. Here, the physical topology is a star bus; that is, there is a length of cable from each computer that connects it to a central hub (called a Multi-Station Access Unit, or MSAU). Inside the hub, however, the ports are wired together sequentially in a ring, and they send data around the ring instead of sending it out to all ports simultaneously as it would if the network were a logical star.

logical topology   A map of the devices on a network representing how the devices communicate with each other.

loopback   A special reserved IPv4 address, 127.0.0.1, that can be used to test TCP/IP applications. Packets sent to 127.0.0.1 by a computer never leave the computer or even require a working NIC. Instead, the packet is processed by IP at the lowest layer and is then sent back up the TCP/IP stack to another application on that same computer.

M

MAC address   A standardized data link layer address that is required for every device that connects to a LAN. Ethernet MAC addresses are 6 bytes long and are controlled by the IEEE. Also known as a hardware address, a MAC layer address, and a physical address.

MAC address table   On a switch, a table that lists all known MAC addresses, and the bridge/ switch port out which the bridge/switch should forward frames sent to each MAC address.

MAC sublayer   The MAC sublayer provides addressing and channel access control mechanisms that make it possible for several terminals or network nodes to communicate within a multiple access network that incorporates a shared medium, e.g. Ethernet. The hardware that implements the MAC is referred to as a medium access controller.

Mail Delivery Agent (MDA)   A computer software component that is responsible for the delivery of email messages to a local recipient's mailbox. Also called an LDA, or local delivery agent. Within the Internet mail architecture, local message delivery is achieved through a process of handling messages from the message transfer agent, and storing mail into the recipient's environment (typically a mailbox).

Mail Transfer Agent (MTA)   Within Internet message handling services (MHS), software that transfers electronic mail messages from one computer to another using a client–server application architecture. An MTA implements both the client (sending) and server (receiving) portions of SMTP.

Management ports   The management ports on the switch allows multiple simultaneous Telnet or SNMP network management sessions. Because there is no separate management port on the Layer 3 switch routers, you can configure any Fast Ethernet or Gigabit Ethernet port as a management port.

Manchester encoding   Line code in which each bit of data is signified by at least one voltage level transition.

maximum transmission unit (MTU)   The largest IP packet size allowed to be sent out a particular interface. Ethernet interfaces default to an MTU of 1,500 because the data field of an Ethernet frame should be limited to , bytes, and the IP packet sits inside the Ethernet frame's data field.

Media Access Control (MAC)   The lower of the two sublayers of the IEEE standard for Ethernet. It is also the name of that sublayer (as defined by the IEEE 802.3 subcommittee).

media independent   The networking layers whose processes are not affected by the media being used. In Ethernet, these are all the layers from the LLC sublayer of data link upward.

media sharing   Media sharing sites allow you to upload your photos, videos, and audio to a website that can be accessed from anywhere in the world. You can then share that media with the world or just a select group of friends.

medium (media)   Storage and transmission channels or tools used to store and deliver information or data.

mesh networking   A type of networking in which each node must not only capture and disseminate its own data, but also serve as a relay for other nodes—that is, it must collaborate to propagate the data in the network.

metric   A unit of measure used by routing protocol algorithms to determine the best route for traffic to use to reach a particular destination.

metro Ethernet   A metropolitan area network (MAN) that is based on Ethernet standards. It is commonly used to connect subscribers to a larger service network or the Internet. Businesses can also use metro Ethernet to connect their own offices to each other.

modular switches   There are two types of switches available, modular and fixed configuration. Modular switches enable you to plug in different modules, allowing for scalable performance, configuration flexibility, and incremental expansion.

multicast   Sending a message to selected hosts that are part of a group. A single packet is copied by the network and sent to a specific subset of network addresses. These addresses are specified in the destination address field. Compare with broadcast and unicast.

multicast MAC address   The IANA owns the OUI MAC address 01:00:5e, therefore multicast packets are delivered by using the Ethernet MAC address range 01:00:5e:00:00:00 to 01:00:5e:7f:ff:ff.

multicast transmission   *See* multicast.

multiplexing   A process where multiple digital data streams are combined into one signal.

N

neighbor advertisement   A message defined by the IPv6 Neighbor Discovery Protocol (NDP), used to declare to other neighbors a host's MAC address. Sometimes sent in response to a previously received NDP Neighbor Solicitation (NS) message.

neighbor solicitation   A message defined by the IPv6 Neighbor Discovery Protocol (NDP), used to ask a neighbor to reply back with a neighbor advertisement, which lists the neighbor's MAC address.

network access protocols   All of the networking protocols operating over the data link and network layers of a computer network are categorized as network access protocols. These include ARP (address resolution protocol), NDP (neighbor discovery protocol), PPP (point to point protocol), tunneling protocol, and media access protocols of link layer.

network address   A dotted decimal number defined by the IPv4 protocol to represent a network or subnet. It represents the network that hosts reside in. Also called a network number or network ID.

network applications   Applications in which either the program you are using or the data you are working with or both reside on a network (often, but not always, the Internet). Network applications use a client-server architecture, where the client and server are two computers connected to the network. The server is programmed to provide some service to the client.

network media   Network media (sometimes referred to as networked media) refers to media mainly used in computer networks.

network service   A data storage, manipulation, presentation, communication, or other capability that is often implemented using a client-server or peer-to-peer architecture based on network protocols running at the application layer of a network.

network-aware applications   Network services that are always listening on the network for requests. Examples are DNS and DHCP.

next hop   The next gateway to which a Layer 3 packet is delivered. The next "hop" used to reach its destination.

nibble boundary   A nibble is 4 bits or one hexadecimal digit. A nibble boundary is using nibble aligned for subnet masks. By borrowing bits from the interface ID, the best practice is to subnet on a nibble boundary.

nonreturn to zero (NRZ)   Line code in which 1s are represented by one significant condition and 0s are represented by another.

nslookup   A service or a program to look up information in the DNS (Domain Name System).

nonvolatile RAM (NVRAM)   Random-access memory that does not lose its contents when the computer is shut down.

O

Open Systems Interconnection (OSI)   International standardization program created by ISO and ITU-T to develop standards for data networking that facilitate multivendor equipment interoperability.

operating system features and services   An operating system is the core software that allows a computer to run as an useful device, it manages the hardware, the user interface and all other software running on the computer. Each operating system available has its own set of features and services.

OSI model   Open System Interconnection reference model. A network architectural model developed by the ISO. The model consists of seven layers, each of which specifies particular network functions, such as addressing, flow control, error control, encapsulation, and reliable message transfer.

outgoing interface   In a routing table, part of a routing table entry that refers to the local interface out which the local router should forward packets that match the route.

out-of-band access   An important tool that enables you to gain access of equipment independent of the network connections. It essentially provides you with a backup path in case of network communication failure.

overhead   Resources used to manage or operate the network. Overhead consumes bandwidth and reduces the amount of application data that can be transported across the network.

P

packet   When used generically, this term refers to end-user data along with networking headers and trailers that are transmitted through a network. When used specifically, it is end-user data, along with the network or Internet layer headers and any higher-layer headers, but no lower-layer headers or trailers.

packet buffer   Memory space that is set aside specifically for either storing a packet that is awaiting transmission over a network or storing a packet that has been received over a network. The memory space is either located in the network interface card or in the computer that holds the card.

payload   The actual data that is encapsulated in a packet. The minimum payload is 42 octets when an 802.1Q tag is present and 46 octets when absent. The maximum payload is 1,500 octets. Nonstandard jumbo frames allow for larger maximum payload size.

peer-to-peer (P2P)   Calls for each network device to run both client and server portions of an application. Also describes a small local network where hosts can play the role of client and/ or server.

peer-to-peer (P2P) file sharing   The distribution and sharing of digital documents and computer files using the technology of peer-to-peer (P2P) networking.

peer-to-peer (P2P) networking   A type of decentralized and distributed network architecture in which individual nodes in the network (called "peers") act as both suppliers and consumers of resources, in contrast to the centralized client–server model where client nodes request access to resources provided by central servers.

personal firewalls   An application that controls network traffic to and from a computer, permitting or denying communications based on a security policy. Typically it works as an application layer firewall.

physical components   Refers to the physical components making up a modern organization. Components such as servers, computers, routers and switches, modems, storage devices and such.

Physical layer   The Physical layer consists of the basic networking hardware transmission technologies of a network. It is a fundamental layer underlying the logical data structures of the higher level functions in a network. Due to the plethora of available hardware technologies with widely varying characteristics, this is perhaps the most complex layer in the OSI architecture.

physical topology   The arrangement of the nodes in a network and the physical connections between them. This is the representation of how the media is used to connect the devices.

podcast   A digital media file or files that are distributed over the Internet using syndication feeds for playback on portable media players and personal computers.

Point-to-Point Protocol (PPP)   A protocol that provides router-to-router and host-to-network connections over synchronous point-to-point and asynchronous point-to-point circuits.

port number   A field in a TCP or UDP header that identifies the application that either sent (source port) or should receive (destination port) the data inside the data segment.

port-based and shared memory   In port-based memory buffering, frames are stored in queues that are linked to specific incoming and outgoing ports. In shared memory buffering all frames are stored into a common memory buffer that all the ports on the switch share.

POST message   Power-on self-test (POST) is a process performed by firmware or software routines immediately after many digital electronic devices are powered on. Perhaps the most widely known usage pertains to computing devices (personal computers, PDAs, networking devices such as routers, switches, intrusion detection systems and other monitoring devices). Other devices include kitchen appliances, avionics, medical equipment, laboratory test equipment—all embedded devices. The routines are part of a device's pre-boot sequence. When POST completes successfully, bootstrap loader code is invoked.

Post Office Protocol (POP)   A protocol that allows a computer to retrieve email from a server.

Power-on self-test (POST)   *See* POST message.

preamble and start frame delimiter fields   A data packet on an Ethernet link is called an Ethernet frame. A frame begins with preamble and start frame delimiter. A frame starts with a 7-octet preamble and 1-octet start frame delimiter (SFD).

prefix length In IP subnetting, this refers to the portion of a set of IP addresses whose value must be identical for the addresses to be in the same subnet.

Presentation layer In the seven-layer OSI model of computer networking, the presentation layer is layer 6 and serves as the data translator for the network. It is sometimes called the syntax layer. The presentation layer is responsible for the delivery and formatting of information to the application layer for further processing or display. It relieves the application layer of concern regarding syntactical differences in data representation within the end-user systems. An example of a presentation service would be the conversion of an EBCDIC-coded text computer file to an ASCII-coded file.

private address Defined in RFC 1918, an IP address that does not have to be globally unique because the address exists inside packets only when the packets are inside a single private IP internetwork. Private IP addresses are popularly used in most companies today, with NAT translating the private IP addresses into globally unique IP addresses, so the IP packet can be routed on the public Internet.

privileged executive (EXEC) mode An IOS administrative-level mode that supports access to configuration and management commands.

protocol data unit (PDUs) A generic term from OSI that refers to the data, headers, and trailers about which a particular networking layer is concerned.

protocol suite A delineation of networking protocols and standards into different categories.

protocols A written specifications that defines what tasks a service or device should perform. Each protocol defines messages.

public address An IP address that has been registered with IANA or one of its member agencies, which guarantees that the address is globally unique. Globally unique public IP addresses can be used for packets sent through the Internet.

pulse-coded modulation (PCM) A method used to digitally represent sampled analog signals. It is the standard form of digital audio in computers, CDs, digital telephony, and other digital audio applications. In a PCM stream, the amplitude of the analog signal is sampled regularly at uniform intervals, and each sample is quantized to the nearest value within a range of digital steps. PCM streams have two basic properties that determine their fidelity to the original analog signal: the sampling rate, the number of times per second that samples are taken; and the bit depth, which determines the number of possible digital values that each sample can take.

PUT message Adds a new message to the back of the message queue. A visibility timeout can also be specified to make the message invisible until the visibility timeout expires. A message must be in a format that can be included in an XML request with UTF-8 encoding.

Q

quality of service (QoS) A control mechanism that can provide different priorities to different users or data flows, or guarantee a certain level of performance to a data flow in accordance with requests from the application program.

Quarantine A method of taking questionable packets and "quarantine" them so the user has an opportunity to examine the packet and either process the packet or delete the packet.

R

random access memory (RAM)   Also known as read-write memory, RAM can have new data written to it and can have stored data read from it. RAM is the main working area, or temporary storage, used by the CPU for most processing and operations. A drawback of RAM is that it requires electrical power to maintain data storage. If the computer is turned off or loses power, all data stored in RAM is lost unless the data was previously saved to disk. Memory boards with RAM chips plug into the motherboard.

Real-Time Transport Control Protocol (RTCP)   RTP is used in conjunction with the RTCP. Although RTP carries the media streams (for example, audio and video), RTCP is used to monitor transmission statistics and quality of service (QoS) and aids synchronization of multiple streams. RTP is originated and received on even port numbers and the associated RTCP communication uses the next higher odd port number.

Real-Time Transport Protocol (RTP)   Defines a standardized packet format for delivering audio and video over IP networks. RTP is used extensively in communication and entertainment systems that involve streaming media, such as telephony, video teleconference applications, television services, and web-based push-to-talk features.

reconnaissance attacks   A kind of information gathering on network system and services. This enables the attacker to discover vulnerabilities or weaknesses on the network. It could be likened to a thief surveying through a car parking lot for vulnerable—unlocked—cars to break into and steal.

remote access via SSH   *See* Secure Shell (SSH).

remote host   A computer that resides in some distant location from which data are retrieved. It typically refers to a server in a private network

or the public Internet. However, it can also refer to a user's PC in another location that is accessed over the Internet for file transfer or remote control operation.

remote routes   Routes to networks that are not directly connected to a router.

Requests for Comments (RFC)   Series of documents and memoranda encompassing new research, innovations, and methodologies applicable to Internet technologies. RFCs are a reference for how technologies should work.

ring network   A network topology in which each node connects to exactly two other nodes, forming a single continuous pathway for signals through each node—a ring. Data travels from node to node, with each node along the way handling every packet.

Rollover cable   Also known as Cisco console cable or a Yost cable. A type of null-modem cable that is often used to connect a computer terminal to a router's console port. This cable is typically flat (and has a light blue color) to help distinguish it from other types of network cabling. It gets the name rollover because the pinouts on one end are reversed from the other, as if the wire had been rolled over and you were viewing it from the other side. This cabling system was invented to eliminate the differences in RS-232 wiring systems. Any two RS-232 systems can be directly connected by a standard rollover cable and a standard connector. For legacy equipment, an adapter is permanently attached to the legacy port.

ROM (read-only memory)   A class of storage medium used in computers and other electronic devices. Data stored in ROM cannot be modified, or can be modified only slowly or with difficulty, so it is mainly used to distribute firmware (software that is very closely tied to specific hardware, and unlikely to need frequent updates).

route timestamp   Timestamp is added to the routing table entry and is used to timeout routing entries.

router   A network device, typically connected to a range of LAN and WAN interfaces, that forwards packets based on their destination IP addresses.

Router Advertisement message (RA)   A message defined by the IPv6 Neighbor Discovery Protocol (NDP), used by routers to announce their willingness to act as an IPv6 router on a link. These may be sent in response to a previously received NDP Router Solicitation (RS) message.

Router Solicitation message (RS)   A message defined by the IPv6 Neighbor Discovery Protocol (NDP), used to ask any routers on the link to reply, identifying the router, plus other configuration settings (prefixes and prefix lengths).

routing   The process by which a router receives an incoming frame, discards the data-link header and trailer, makes a forwarding decision based on the destination IP address, adds a new data-link header and trailer based on the outgoing interface, and forwards the new frame out the outgoing interface.

Running-Config file   In Cisco IOS switches and routers, the name of the file that resides in RAM memory, holding the device's currently used configuration.

S

satellite   Artificial objects (as opposed to natural satellites, such as the Moon) placed in orbit around Earth. Used in communication applications to provide a path to pass data around the world.

scalability   The ability of a protocol, system, or component to be modified to fit a new need.

Secure Shell (SSH)   A protocol that provides a secure remote connection to a host through a TCP application.

security   Consists of the provisions and policies adopted by a network administrator to prevent and monitor unauthorized access, misuse, modification, or denial of a computer network and network-accessible resources. Network security involves the authorization of access to data in a network, which is controlled by the network administrator. Users choose or are assigned an ID and password or other authenticating information that allows them access to information and programs within their authority. Network security covers a variety of computer networks, both public and private, that are used in everyday jobs conducting transactions and communications among businesses, government agencies, and individuals. Networks can be private, such as within a company, and others which might be open to public access. Network security is involved in organizations, enterprises, and other types of institutions. It does as its title explains: It secures the network, as well as protecting and overseeing operations being done. The most common and simple way of protecting a network resource is by assigning it a unique name and a corresponding password.

segment   1. A collision domain that is a section of a LAN that is bound by bridges, routers, or switches. 2. In a LAN using a bus topology, a continuous electrical circuit that is often connected to other such segments with repeaters. 3. When used as a verb with TCP, refers to the work TCP does to accept a large piece of data from an application and break it into smaller pieces. When used as a noun with TCP, refers to one of those smaller pieces of data.

segmentation   In TCP, the process of taking a large chunk of data and breaking it into small-enough pieces to fit within a TCP segment without breaking any rules about the maximum amount of data allowed in a segment.

SEQ number (sequence number)   Number used to ensure correct sequencing of the arriving data.

serial WAN interfaces   A type of interface on a router, used to connect to some types of WAN links, particularly leased lines and Frame Relay access links.

Server Message Block (SMB)   An application-level network protocol mainly applied to shared access to files, printers, serial ports, and miscellaneous communications between nodes on a network.

server-based firewalls   A firewall that is hosted on a server, providing firewall services to hosts in its network.

service provider routers   Routers optimized for the use by service providers.

Session layer   In the seven-layer OSI model of computer networking, the session layer is Layer 5. The session layer provides the mechanism for opening, closing, and managing a session between end-user application processes—that is, a semi-permanent dialogue. Communication sessions consist of requests and responses that occur between applications. Session-layer services are commonly used in application environments that make use of remote procedure calls (RPCs).

shielded twisted-pair (STP) cable   A type of network cabling that includes twisted-pair wires, with shielding around each pair of wires, as well as another shield around all wires in the cable.

show cdp neighbors   A command that shows detailed information about the Cisco devices that are directly connected to your current device, including IP addresses. CDP is a Cisco proprietary protocol and will only detect Cisco products, although there are some vendors that do work with it. Additionally, LLDP was recently released, which is an industry standard of the Cisco Discovery Protocol and is supported on newer IOS.

Show command   The **show all** command displays most of the system configuration and status. The information displayed by this command is displayed by other **show** commands. Please refer to the referenced commands for specific information about the displayed information.

show ip interface brief command   Displays a brief summary of the interfaces on a device. It's useful for quickly checking the status of the device.

signaling method   Ways in which a signal can be physically created: as electrical impulses that travel over copper wire, as pulses of light that travel through strands of glass or plastic, as radio transmissions that travel over the airwaves, as laser or satellite transmissions, and as infrared pulses.

Simple Mail Transfer Protocol (SMTP)   An application protocol typically not used by end users. Instead, it is used by the network management software and networking devices to allow a network engineer to monitor and troubleshoot network problems.

social media   Refers to the means of interactions among people in which they create, share, and exchange information and ideas in virtual communities and networks.

socket   Software structure operating as a communications end point within a network device.

solicited-node multicast   An IPv6 multicast address valid within the local-link (for example, an Ethernet segment or a Frame Relay cloud). Every IPv6 host will have at least one such address per interface. Solicited-node multicast addresses are used in neighbor Discovery Protocol for obtaining the Layer 2 link-layer addresses of other nodes.

source IP address   The IP address of the originating host that is placed into the IP packet header.

source IP address field   The field that holds the source IP address.

source MAC Address field   The field that holds the source MAC address.

source routing   The capability whereby the sender can specify the route a packet should take.

standards organizations   Any organization whose primary activities are developing, coordinating, promulgating, revising, amending, reissuing, interpreting, or otherwise producing technical standards that are intended to address the needs of some relatively wide base of affected adopters.

star topology   A network topology in which endpoints on a network are connected to a common central device by point-to-point links.

startup-config file   In Cisco IOS switches and routers, the name of the file that resides in NVRAM memory, holding the device's configuration that will be loaded into RAM as the running-config file when the device is next reloaded or powered on.

stateful   A protocol, such as TCP, to track actual conversations and their state of the communication session.

Stateless Address Autoconfiguration (SLAAC)   Plug-and-play IPv6 feature that enables devices to connect themselves to the network without any configuration and without any servers (like DHCP servers).

stateless protocol   A communications protocol that treats each request as an independent transaction that is unrelated to any previous request so that the communication consists of independent pairs of requests and responses. A stateless protocol does not require the server to retain session information or status about each communications partner for the duration of multiple requests. In contrast, a protocol that requires keeping of the internal state on the server is known as a stateful protocol. Examples of stateless protocols include the Internet Protocol (IP), which is the foundation for the Internet, and the Hypertext Transfer Protocol (HTTP), which is the foundation of data communication for the World Wide Web.

static addressing   When network uses static addressing, each network interface has an assigned IP address that it uses all of the time or whenever it is online. When a network uses dynamic addressing, when a network interface asks to join the network, it is randomly allocated an IP address from a pool of available addresses within that network. Thus, under dynamic addressing, a computer may possess over time (for example, across reboots) a variety of different IP addresses, but under static addressing the computer has a well-defined IP address that it uses always and that no other computer ever uses. Dynamic addressing is most useful in applications such as dial-up networks, VPNs, and similar scenarios where end-user machines are intermittently connected to the network.

storage area network (SAN)   A dedicated network that provides access to consolidated, block-level data storage. SANs are primarily used to make storage devices, such as disk arrays, tape libraries, and optical jukeboxes, accessible to servers so that the devices appear like locally attached devices to the operating system. A SAN typically has its own network of storage devices that are generally not accessible through the LAN by other devices. The cost and complexity of SANs dropped in the early 2000s to levels allowing wider adoption across both enterprise and small to medium-sized business environments.

store-and-forward switching   A method of internal processing by LAN switches. The switch must receive the entire frame before it sends the first bit of the frame. Store-and-forward switching is the method used by Cisco switches.

subnet   A group of IP addresses that have the same value in the first part of the IP addresses, for the purpose of allowing routing to identify the group by that initial part of the addresses. IP addresses in the same subnet typically sit on the same network medium and are not separated from each other by any routers. IP addresses on different subnets are typically separated from one another by at least one router. Subnet is short for subnetwork.

subnet mask   A dotted decimal number that helps identify the structure of IP addresses. The mask represents the network and subnet parts of related IP addresses with binary 1s and the host part of related IP addresses with binary 0s.

Switch Form-Factor Pluggable (SFP)   Removal modules used in routers and switches to support a number of different network media.

SYN   A 1-bit flag in the TCP header used to indicate the initial value of the sequence number. The SYN flag is only set in the first two segments of the three-way TCP connection establishment sequence.

SYN segment   *See* three-way handshake.

synchronous   Communication that uses a common clocking signal. In most synchronous communication, one of the communicating devices generates a clock signal into the circuit. Additional timing information is not required in the header.

T

TCP/IP Application Layer   The application layer contains all protocols for specific data communications services on a process-to-process level. For example, HTTP specifies the web browser communication with a web server.

TCP/IP (Transmission Control Protocol/ Internet Protocol)   A network model defined by the IETF that has been implemented on most computers and network devices in the world.

telecommunication rooms   A room that consolidates all connectivity from the enterprise network and building control systems and distributes it to predetermined areas of the enterprise. It is the "horizontal" convergence point between the building's network backbone and workstations and conference rooms.

Telnet   Network service that supports CLI access to a remote host. It also can be used verify the application layer software between source and destination stations.

test-net address   The IPv4 address block 192.0.2.0 to 192.0.2.255 (192.0.2.0 /24) that is set aside for teaching and learning purposes. These addresses can be used in documentation and network examples.

Trivial File Transfer Protocol (TFTP)   Simplified version of FTP that allows files to be transferred from one computer to another over a network.

three-way handshake   To establish a connection, TCP uses a three-way handshake. Before a client attempts to connect with a server, the server must first bind to and listen at a port to open it up for connections—this is called a passive open. When the passive open is established, a client may initiate an active open. To establish a connection, the three-way (or 3-step) handshake occurs:

1. **SYN:** The active open is performed by the client sending a SYN to the server. The client sets the segment's sequence number to a random value A.

2. **SYN-ACK:** In response, the server replies with a SYN-ACK. The acknowledgment number is set to one more than the received sequence number—that is, A+1—and the sequence number that the server chooses for the packet is another random number, B.

3. **ACK:** Finally, the client sends an ACK back to the server. The sequence number is set to the received acknowledgement value—that is, A+1—and the acknowledgement number is set to one more than the received sequence number—that is, B+1.

At this point, both the client and server have received an acknowledgment of the connection. The steps 1, 2 establish the connection parameter (sequence number) for one direction and it is acknowledged. The steps 2, 3 establish the connection parameter (sequence number) for the other direction and it is acknowledged. With these, a full-duplex communication is established.

Time-to-Live (TTL) field   Time to live (TTL) or hop limit is a mechanism that limits the lifespan or lifetime of data in a computer or network. TTL may be implemented as a counter or timestamp attached to or embedded in the data. After the prescribed event count or time span has elapsed, data is discarded. In computer networking, TTL prevents a data packet from circulating indefinitely.

In computing applications, TTL is used to improve performance of caching or to improve privacy.

topology   The arrangement of networking components or nodes. Examples include star, extended star, ring, and mesh.

traffic class field   The bits of this field in the IPv6 packet hold two values. The 6 most-significant bits are used for differentiated services, which is used to classify packets. The remaining two bits are used for ECN; priority values subdivide into ranges: traffic where the source provides congestion control and noncongestion control traffic.

trailer   The trailer indicates the frame check sequence number. It is used for error control in a frame.

translation   In computer networking, Network Address Translation (NAT) is the process of modifying IP address information in IPv4 headers while in transit across a traffic routing device.

Transmission Control Protocol (TCP)   A Layer 4 protocol of the TCP/IP model, TCP lets applications guarantee delivery of data across a network.

Transmission Control Protocol/IP (TCP/IP)   TCP/IP (Transmission Control Protocol/Internet Protocol) is the basic communication language or protocol of the Internet. It can also be used as a communications protocol in a private network (either an intranet or an extranet). When you are set up with direct access to the Internet, your computer is provided with a copy of the TCP/IP program just as every other computer that you may send messages to or get information from also has a copy of TCP/IP.

tunneling   Computer networks use a tunneling protocol when one network protocol (the delivery protocol) encapsulates a different payload protocol. By using tunneling one can (for example) carry a payload over an incompatible delivery-network, or provide a secure path through an untrusted network. Tunneling typically contrasts with a layered protocol model such as those of OSI or TCP/IP. The delivery protocol usually (but not always) operates at a higher level in the model than does the payload protocol, or at the same level.

U

unicast   Message sent to a single network destination. Compare with broadcast and multicast.

Unicast MAC address   A MAC address in networking that represents a single device or interface, instead of a group of addresses (as would be represented by a multicast or broadcast address).

unshielded twisted-pair (UTP) cable   A general type of cable, with the cable holding twisted pairs of copper wires and the cable itself having little shielding.

User Datagram Protocol
(UDP)   Connectionless transport layer protocol in the TCP/IP protocol stack. UDP is a simple protocol that exchanges datagrams without acknowledgments or guaranteed delivery.

user executive (EXEC) mode   The limited CLI mode where the commands available to the user are a subset of those available at the privileged level. In general, use the user EXEC commands to temporarily change terminal settings, perform basic tests, and list system information.

V

variable length subnet masking (VLSM)   Ability to specify a different subnet mask for the same network number on different subnets. VLSM can help optimize available address space.

version field   The first header field in an IP packet is the four-bit version field. For IPv4, this has a value of 4 (hence the name IPv4).

virtual interface   A virtual interface or virtual network interface (VIF) is an abstract virtualized representation of a computer network interface that may or may not correspond directly to a physical network interface.

Voice over IP (VoIP)   Voice data encapsulated in an IP packet that allows it to traverse already implemented IP networks without needing its own network infrastructure.

VTY password   Abbreviated as VTY, virtual teletype is a command-line interface that enables users to connect to the daemon using the Telnet protocol. To connect to a VTY users must set up and use a VTY password.

W

WAN routers   A network device designed to forward packets to an external network such as the Internet. Routers are used to direct traffic to a network outside of the one they reside in. However, when routers are used within an enterprise to keep subnetworks divided, they would be called "routers" or possibly "core routers," but not WAN routers. The routers that make up the backbone of the Internet are known as "core routers."

weblogs (blogs)   A personal website or web page on which an individual records opinions, links to other sites, etc. on a regular basis.

Wide Area Network (WAN)   A part of a larger network that implements mostly OSI Layer 1 and 2 technology, connects sites that typically sit far apart, and use a business model in which a consumer (individual or business) must lease the WAN from a service provider (often a Telco).

wiki   A website that lets visitors add, edit, and delete content, typically without the need for registration. A good example of this is the site Wikipedia.com, where visitors can access the website and add their commentaries to already written articles or create a new article.

window size   As filed in the TCP header that is set in a sent segment, signifies the maximum amount of unacknowledged data the host is willing to receive before the other sending host must wait for an acknowledgment. Used for flow control.

wireless   *See* wireless technology.

wireless access point (WAP)   A network device that provides connectivity of wireless clients to connect to a data network.

Wireless LAN (WLAN)   A Local Area Network (LAN) that physically transmits bits using radio waves. The name "wireless" compares these LANs to more traditional "wired" LANs, which are LANs that use cables (which often have copper wires inside).

wireless technology   Technology that allows communication without needing physical connectivity. Examples of wireless technology include cellular telephones, personal digital assistants (PDA), wireless access points, and wireless NICs.

Index

F

H

L